S0-AVR-152

Guide To Modern English

For Grade Twelve

Richard K. Corbin

Chairman of the English Department,
Hunter College High School, New York City

Porter G. Perrin

Former Professor of English,
University of Washington, Seattle, Washington

Guide

To Modern

English

12

Scott, Foresman and Company

Chicago   Atlanta   Dallas   Palo Alto   Fair Lawn, N.J.

Designed by Donald Kriloff

Illustrated by Rainey Bennett

Copyright © 1963 by Scott, Foresman and Company
Printed in the United States of America

A Word of Introduction

The manifold objectives of GUIDE TO MODERN ENGLISH, Grade 12, can be summed up quite simply: to encourage in students a sincere desire to improve in language skills.

Experienced English teachers will not be deceived by the seeming modesty of this goal; they know—as we do—how ambitious it really is, how difficult of accomplishment. Our hope for a fair measure of success stems from the fact that we had no illusions about the difficulties of the job. We knew that to reach our goal, we would first have to help students to see *why* improvement in language skills is desirable and, more important, exactly *how* such improvement can be achieved. The best way to provide this help, we felt, was to guide the students through carefully devised experiences that would lead them beyond a mere verbal knowledge to a clear and deep understanding of the concepts. Only with such understanding can improvement become a reality.

Favorable reports from users of the other books in the series encourage us to feel sure that students will welcome—and profit from—the teaching approach used in this twelfth-grade GUIDE. It is an approach that relies primarily on a step-by-step clarification of the subject matter, whatever the topic under discussion (paragraph development, for example, or principles of semantics, fallacious reasoning, the sentence parts, the improvement of sentences, the doctrine of appropriateness in usage). As we worked on each section, we anticipated the difficulties a learner is likely to experience—and made it a point to resolve these difficulties, to answer the student's unasked questions. In doing so, we did not forget the importance of engaging the student's interest as well as his understanding: the explanations are written with a directness and simplicity that will attract and hold the twelfth-grader's attention; the illustrative material, always specific and concrete, which we used to make the concepts vividly clear and truly meaningful, will add to his pleasure.

The exercises, it should be noted, are as important as the text matter proper, for they are designed to reinforce the teaching, to ensure that students have grasped the points made in the explanations. The exercises are not easy; they cannot be—and still serve their intended purpose. But they are doable, never presenting problems that the text does not help the student to solve, to the extent of his ability at least. Because the exercises are thought-provoking and challenging, they will be conducive to growth; because they are doable, they will give students the feeling of accomplishment so essential to every learner.

As in the eleventh-grade book of the *Guide to Modern English Series,* the material is divided into two parts, to make both learning and teaching easier. Part One (the "teaching chapters") covers the basic material of the course, subject matter that can best be taught—and learned—by being presented in class for group study and discussion. Part Two, the INDEX, is an alphabetically arranged series of entries to which the individual student can refer, on his own, for answers to his specific language problems.

This two-part division of the book is of great practical value: it gives all students the benefit of the teacher's help while studying the basic material, yet it frees the teacher of the need for taking up time in class to discuss problems that only a few students need help with. Furthermore, the organization of the chapters in Part One is highly flexible, making it easy for the teacher (who best knows the abilities and needs of the students in *his* classes and the specific objectives of the courses *he* teaches) to determine the most desirable order in which to present the basic material.

It is our hope (1) that students will find this book deserving of its name—a *Guide* that will help lead them to an ever-increasing competence in speech, writing, and clear thinking; (2) that teachers will find it a truly useful ally in the classroom—a "silent partner" that will help with the work which must be done.

The Authors and Editors

Acknowledgments

Special thanks are due to the following for their gracious assistance with the photographs used in the two picture stories of the GUIDE: Mr. Robert W. Estin of the Illinois Institute of Technology, Chicago; Dr. Roger Shuy and Mrs. Elizabeth C. Lewis of Wheaton College, Wheaton, Illinois; and Mr. J. Keith Graham of the School of Speech, the staff of the Office of Information Services, and the members of the Zeta Tau Alpha and Theta Chi chapters—all of Northwestern University, Evanston, Illinois.

We are particularly grateful to Dr. Raven I. McDavid, Jr., of the Department of English and Linguistics of the University of Chicago, who, as critic reader of the picture story "American English Dialects," gave us invaluable advice on the regional dialects of the United States and on the work of the Atlas researchers.

Photographs and special artwork. Credit for the following original photographs, used in the picture stories, belongs to: Joseph Sterling, pages 181, 185, 186, and 300-309; Richard Hanley, pages 183, 184, and 187. The map on page 182 is the work of James Minnick. Credit for the cover photograph belongs to M. Halberstadt.

Contents

1   *Writing Your Compositions*

"The time has come," the Walrus said,
  "To talk of many things:
Of shoes—and ships—and sealing-wax—
  Of cabbages—and kings—
And why the sea is boiling hot—
  And whether pigs have wings."
          —Lewis Carroll, *Through the Looking-Glass.*

If you take a look at what you write, both in and out of school, you will see that you cover quite a range of subjects, whether or not you touch on any of those mentioned above. But whatever your subject may be, your *purpose* in writing is usually to explain something.

In letters to friends and relatives you may explain why you want to work after graduation or why you want to go to college, what your new after-school job is like, how you built a hi-fi set or made yourself a hat, why you did not like a certain movie or book.

In school tests or term papers you may explain how the Revolutionary War began, what *osmosis* means, what the difference is between an acid and a base, how you interpret Robert Frost's line "One could do worse than be a swinger of birches."

Soon you will be explaining on application forms why you think you should be hired for a given job or admitted to a certain college. Later will come still more explanations of any number of subjects, in the form of college examinations and term papers, and business letters and reports.

Therefore, in this chapter you will be concentrating mainly on writing that explains: expository writing, or exposition.

A well-known recipe for rabbit stew begins "First catch your rabbit." A recipe for writing might well begin "First get something to write about."

By now you have often been through the process of choosing and limiting a subject. You usually start with a more or less general subject in mind, preferably one in which you have a keen interest. This you limit and narrow down to fit the length of your paper (usually 300 to 500 words), keeping in mind as you do so the probable interests and knowledge of your readers.

The general subject "Getting along with others" you might limit to "Problems with brothers and sisters," and then narrow that down to "The hostility between my nine-year-old brother and me."

The general subject "Cars" you might limit to the less general one "Jeeps," and then narrow that down to "Why I drive a jeep." This subject would be suitable for an average audience, whereas another subject that might interest you—"How the jeep's four-wheel drive works"—would have to be discarded as too technical for most.

From the very broad subject "Forestry" you would move to one that is less broad, like "The work of the U.S. Forest Service." The latter you might limit to "The function of a Forest Service experiment station"; and this, which is still unsuitable for a short paper, you could narrow down to "Three current projects of our regional experiment station." This subject, too, is well chosen for an average group of readers. Whether interested in forestry or not, they will probably have some interest in a paper about their own region.

FOCUSING ON AN IDEA

Let's suppose you have hit on a subject which interests you, which is of a suitable size for your paper, and which you think will have some appeal for your readers. Now you are ready to consider exactly what idea you want to get across to your readers in writing about this subject. That is, you are ready to focus on a *central*, or *controlling*, idea for your composition.

For the theme about the jeep, you might work out this controlling idea:

> The ruggedness and dependability of the jeep, in all sorts of weather and on all sorts of terrain, make it ideal for me.

For the theme about a Forest Service experiment station, you might develop this one:

> Three current projects of the station are aimed at helping farmers in this area with the problem of soil conservation.

If your subject were "The hostility between my nine-year-old brother and me," you might focus on any one of these ideas:

> My relationship with my younger brother seems to have passed through three different stages, each a slight improvement on the one before it.
>
> I believe that my parents' constant comparisons of the two of us are responsible for our not getting along better.
>
> Over the years, I have worked out a surefire method for antagonizing a younger brother.

As you can see, the controlling idea of a composition need not be anything complex or profound. Sometimes it simply makes explicit the "angle" you wish to take in handling your subject. But if it is well thought out, it will serve a very important function. This is to guide or control your thinking as you write your paper—to help you select relevant material, arrange it logically, write effective opening and closing paragraphs, and so on.

A controlling idea that will keep you on the track in this way must have the following five characteristics:

1) It must be an *idea*, and not just a subject.

SUBJECT, NOT CONTROLLING IDEA: The book *Huckleberry Finn.*

GOOD CONTROLLING IDEA: Huck Finn leads a life that almost any boy would envy.

GOOD CONTROLLING IDEA: Huck starts out regarding Jim as a comic figure, but in the course of their adventures together, comes to feel a deep affection for him.

2) It must be an idea that you can state clearly and concisely in one sentence.

NEITHER CLEAR NOR CONCISE: *Huckleberry Finn* contains a number of the author's philosophical views, embodied in Huck's actions, but overlaid is a real adventure story, exciting to any boy; yet it, too, has its deeper notes.

A controlling idea as vague as this usually means that the writer needs to think longer and harder about what it is he wants to say in his paper. By giving further thought to the matter, he could come up with a clear, concise statement:

GOOD CONTROLLING IDEA: During a series of funny, exciting, and frightening adventures, Huck Finn makes some important discoveries about human nature.

3) Your controlling idea must be formulated in words that are exact enough to guide you as you write your paper.

TOO VAGUE: My family and I had some interesting experiences on our cross-country trip. [With only this to guide him, a writer could turn out a theme that was just a collection of unrelated experiences.]

GOOD CONTROLLING IDEA: On our cross-country trip we discovered a number of differences between people in various regions.

4) Your controlling idea must be capable of development. That is, you must be able to support or illustrate it by giving examples, reasons, arguments, causes, effects, etc.

INCAPABLE OF DEVELOPMENT: I got my Scotch terrier when he was a wobbly little pup and I was seven years old. [This is simply a statement of fact. It might make a good opening sentence for a theme, but it could not serve as a controlling idea.]

GOOD CONTROLLING IDEA: Getting a Scottie for a pet when I was seven made my life a lot happier.

GOOD CONTROLLING IDEA: Training a Scotch terrier is a process that calls for both patience and a sense of humor.

GOOD CONTROLLING IDEA: My Scottie is a frisky, clownish, contrary-minded creature, whom I could not do without.

A writer could illustrate or support the last three statements as he could not do the first.

5) Your controlling idea must give some indication of your feeling about, or attitude toward, your subject. Take this example:

The children next door, recent immigrants from Holland, have adapted to their new environment much more easily than have their parents.

If the writer has an objective attitude toward the adventures of his next-door neighbors—if he is interested in them, but has no particular feeling about them—then this controlling idea is satisfactory.

But suppose he is amused by the contrast between the children and the parents; suppose he finds it mildly comic that the seven-year-old has to guide her mother through the supermarket, and that the eight-year-old often has to explain American slang to his father. Then he should restate his controlling idea in some such way as this:

The family next door, recent immigrants from Holland, provide some amusing illustrations of how much more easily children can adjust to a new environment than adults can.

Or suppose he feels that the contrast between the two age groups has a rather sad aspect. Then this version would be better:

Because the Dutch children next door are adjusting to their new country much more easily than their parents, they seem, unfortunately, to be growing away from the parents.

Point 5 is an important one for this reason: when you have settled on what your attitude toward your subject is, you have also settled on how you want your readers to react—with the feeling that your dog is amusing and lovable, for example; with sympathy over your little-brother problem; with scientific interest in some technical material you are presenting; and so on. Then, because the reaction you want is clear in your own mind from the start, you are likely to write a composition that will call forth this reaction from your readers. You will be able to choose appropriate material and to write in an appropriate tone.

Often you will find that you can hit on a good controlling idea without much effort. At other times you will have to do a bit of thinking before you arrive at a controlling idea with the characteristics just described. Whatever the case, it is only when you do focus on such an idea that you truly have "something to write about."

Exercise 1 Read over the following pairs of controlling ideas. You will readily see that one of each pair is satisfactory and one is not. Be ready to tell which is which and to give reasons for your opinions.

1 a) Eustacia Vye in *The Return of the Native.*
   b) Eustacia Vye, in *The Return of the Native,* is a perverse character who seems to want whatever she doesn't have.
2 a) Education seemed to have two quite different meanings in the two elementary schools I attended.
   b) Education can mean many different things.
3 a) Benjamin Franklin's famous kite experiment was aimed at proving that lightning is electricity.
   b) Franklin conducted his famous kite experiment in June 1752.
4 a) Playing in the school band is a worth-while activity.
   b) Playing in the band has helped me to feel at home in a new school.
5 a) When I was a child, I spent a great deal of time with my Grandfather Martinson, who never seemed to criticize me (although he never encouraged me to behave badly, of course); in fact, he was often amused by behavior that got me into trouble with my other grandparents and relatives.
   b) All through my childhood, Grandfather Martinson was my favorite relative, because he considered my behavior natural and never tried to improve me.
6 a) By using the right technique, you can get through a gym class without exerting yourself at all.
   b) My purpose is to entertain my classmates by telling them some amusing facts about our gym classes.

Exercise 2 Be ready to tell in class what attitude you think is expressed toward the subject in each of these controlling ideas. (You may be able to describe the attitude in one word—*objective, approving, disapproving, loving, critical, amused, sad,* etc.—or you may find that to be accurate you need to describe it at greater length.)

1 The ruggedness and dependability of the jeep, in all sorts of weather and on all sorts of terrain, make it ideal for me.

2 If you play the trumpet and live in an apartment house, as I do, it is best to be extremely insensitive to criticism.

3 I feel that I have missed a lot by being an only child.

4 Each of the eleven men on a football team has a specific function to perform.

5 It takes brains, not just brawn, to play good football.

6 Education seemed to have two different meanings in the two elementary schools I attended.

7 Because my uncle's strong desire for a college education was never fulfilled, he is unfortunately determined that every one of his children shall go to college, regardless of their abilities and desires.

8 Over the years, I have worked out a surefire method for antagonizing a younger brother.

Exercise 3 For each of these very broad subjects, work out a limited subject suitable for a paper of 300 to 500 words, considering the interests and knowledge of your readers to whatever extent is possible. Write your five subjects on a sheet of paper, to be handed in.

1 A hobby, a favorite sport, or some other special interest
2 A favorite book
3 A family problem
4 A person you consider outstanding in some way
5 One of your school courses

Exercise 4 Choose three of the limited subjects you wrote for Exercise 3 and work out three controlling ideas, as follows:

1 A controlling idea for a composition in which you present factual information. For example:

A stamp collector inevitably picks up some knowledge of history and geography. [This comes from the broad subject area *a hobby*.]

With ten people in the family, we have a hectic time between 6:30 and 8:30 a.m. [*Family problem.*]

My father's old friend Tom Archer has many characteristics that people consider typically Texan. [*Outstanding person.*]

2 A controlling idea for a composition in which you explain a process, or method, or technique. For example:

In order to collect stamps for profit, you must follow a long-range plan. [*Hobby.*]

When I have overslept in the morning, I get to school on time anyway, by following my special emergency procedure. [*Family problem.*]

Preparing fresh fruit for freezing is quite a simple process. [*Homemaking course in school.*]

3 A controlling idea for a composition in which you present and support an opinion. For example:

I consider that the main disadvantage of being in a large family is the lack of privacy. [*Family problem.*]

In the first part of *David Copperfield* David's aunt is just an amusing stereotype, but I think that as the book continues she becomes more complex and more human. [*Favorite book.*]

The teen-age girl that _____ *Magazine* is written for seems to me to be an extraordinarily simple-minded creature, with few interests other than boys and clothes. [*Special interest.*]

Write your three ideas on a sheet of paper, to be handed in, and keep a copy for yourself.

GATHERING AND ORGANIZING YOUR MATERIAL

By the time you have a limited subject and a controlling idea for your paper, you have already made a start at gathering material for it, as well. Suppose you are planning a theme based on the following controlling idea:

Our ugly, run-down shopping district could be transformed by some cleaning and some good exterior decorating.

With this idea worked out, you can readily see that you need at least the following kinds of material in order to write about it: (1) criticisms of the shopping district, specific as well as general, and (2) suggestions for improving the appearance of the district, as specific as possible.

You already have in mind a number of facts and ideas, items that you thought of when cutting down your general subject, "Civic improvement," to the limited subject "Improving our downtown shopping district." Some of these are details you have observed on trips downtown (littered sidewalks, grimy buildings, blistered paint, signs with missing letters); some are remarks you have heard other people make ("The whole area looks so shabby"; "I do almost all my shopping in Nabortown now"); some are ideas you have simply thought of on your own ("With such a small shopping district we have an excellent setup for a mall").

The job of gathering your material, then, is well begun. You decide to continue it by strolling along the five-block shopping district with the express purpose of observing. In this way, you pick up some new facts and also check on the accuracy of your earlier observations.

Mulling over your material at this point, you judge that you have plenty of interesting things to say in criticizing the shopping district, but that you need more and better ideas on how to improve it. The few suggestions that you do have, if carried out, would hardly lead to the transformation you were thinking of when you worked out your controlling idea. Furthermore, you feel they are somewhat obvious—things that "everybody knows." You want to write a theme that will make your readers sit up and take notice; and to do this, you are convinced, you must have some less commonplace material.

For help in finding it, you turn to the library, where the *Readers' Guide to Periodical Literature* leads you to a number of relevant articles—reports on several cities that have beautified their downtown areas in various ways, and some general discussions like "Must Our Cities Be So Ugly?" by John E. Burchard of M.I.T. These articles provide you with just what you need, some ideas out of the ordinary. But you are now so wrapped up in your subject that you go further and request a brief interview with a Chamber of Commerce official, who is interested in discussing the matter.

After supplementing your own thoughts and observations in this way, through the articles and the interview, you are satisfied with your supply of facts and ideas. You have not only increased it, but enriched it.

You are well armed with material, then, but this is not to say that you are ready to write. For your material is just a hodgepodge. Criticisms of your town's shopping district, comparisons of it with Nabortown's, suggested improvements, comments on these by the Chamber of Commerce official—all are mixed together indiscriminately in your head, except for a few in the form of sketchy notes taken while reading and interviewing.

If (like many an inexperienced student) you plunged into the writing of your paper at this point, the result would also be a hodgepodge. Some ideas would be repeated; some would be lost. Illustrations might be given without a clear indication of what they were illustrating. Numerous revisions would probably be needed before the paper became even coherent. Therefore, it is necessary at this stage to organize your thinking and arrange your material accordingly.

This job is a simple one when you have a controlling idea like either of the following:

> Up to the moment of the shot, the events of Lincoln's last day were quite ordinary.
> In refinishing furniture, you must follow a set routine with the utmost patience.

Obviously, controlling ideas like these call for you to narrate incidents or to tell the steps in a process. You know from the start, then, that you will write a theme in which your material is arranged chronologically, in a 1-2-3 order, for that is the natural—or necessary—order for writing about such ideas. All the planning you are likely to do for such a theme is to get it straight in your mind what did happen first (or should be done first), what second, and so on.

Other controlling ideas also give you considerable guidance, of course, in organizing your ideas and planning your paper. This one calls for you to compare and contrast:

> Medicine and social work, two careers in which I am interested, offer some of the same satisfactions, but differ greatly in education needed and financial returns expected.

This one calls for you to present a cause and its effects:

> In large elementary-school classes, excellent results have been obtained by grouping children according to their ability in various subjects.

This one calls for you first to state a problem and then to suggest a solution or solutions:

> Our ugly, run-down shopping district could be transformed by some cleaning and some good exterior decorating.

These controlling ideas, in other words, give you the overall pattern, or the framework, of your composition. But they all leave you with the question of how best to arrange your items, or most of your items, *within* the framework of comparison and contrast, cause and effect, problem and solution. To determine the answer, you study your material.

A good way to start is to get your facts and thoughts down on paper in the form of a list—not worrying about their order, but just jotting them down as they occur to you. For the theme about the shopping district, the result would be something like this (except that in reality you would be unlikely to number your items or to write them out so fully):

1. A walk or bus ride along the five blocks shows a grimy, messy, completely uninviting area.
2. Great improvement would result from just cleaning it up.
3. Sidewalks slushy in winter, dirty and littered in other seasons.
4. Windows usually dirty; seldom sparkling clean.
5. Many signs with letters missing.
6. No trees or flowers.
7. Small things would help: attractive litter receptacles, flower baskets on lampposts, as in Nabortown.
8. Old, rusty streetcar tracks unsightly.
9. Tracks should be removed; no longer used.
10. Attractive pedestrian strip could replace them.
11. Buildings faded, dirt-colored.
12. On many of them, paint is peeling and blistered.
13. Occasional washing would greatly help their appearance.
14. Repainting would help even more, especially if bright colors were used.
15. Downtown Merchants' Association thinking of a clean-up, paint-up program at own expense, according to official.

16. He says Chamber of Commerce also interested in seeing area get beauty treatment.
17. Also says a real transformation would be so costly that tax-payers would have to help foot the bill—and a campaign of education would be necessary to win their approval.
18. Coördinated colors within a block would look good.
19. Bright awnings with large initials, as on one Nabortown building, also striking.
20. Removal of hot-dog and hamburger stands would help lessen the cheap and small-town look of the area.
21. Trees would add color and variety, also give coolness and shade in hot summer and take away from stark, bare look in winter.
22. With such a small area, we have good setup for a mall—the most beautiful kind of shopping district.
23. No cars in mall; benches and greenery instead.
24. Some malls even have fountains, pools, sculpture.
25. All very costly, but "Beautiful cities have never been the cheapest possible cities." (Burchard, "Must Our Cities Be So Ugly?")
26. Some improvements not too expensive—for example, repairing signs and sweeping sidewalks.

When you have set down all the facts and ideas you can think of, you are ready to sort them into groups of items, each clustering around some one topic. You decide that all except one of your items can be assigned to four groups, centering on four basic topics:

10

1. The unattractiveness of the area   (1, 3, 4, 5, 6, 8, 11, 12)
2. The possibility that improvements will some day be made   (15, 16, 17, 25)
3. Improvements through exterior decoration   (7, 10, 14, 18, 19, 21, 22, 23, 24)
4. Improvements through cleaning and tidying   (2, 9, 13, 26)

The item that does not fit into any of these is Number 20. Thinking it over, you realize that it is simply irrelevant to your controlling idea, and drop it from your planning.

Next you look over the groups of items and decide that you need more details for Group 2. Except for one good quotation concerning the costliness of civic improvement, you have only a few remarks by the Chamber of Commerce official on which to base your discussion of this topic. To fill in the gap, you return to the library and jot down some information that you skipped over on your first visit: the cost of setting up a mall, the difficulty or ease with which malls in various cities have been paid for, some comments on the value of downtown-improvement programs. This information helps you understand what problems are likely to arise in putting through an improvement program in your own town.

Now you are ready to consider the order in which to take up the four main topics. You have known from the start (see page 9) that you would begin by presenting the problem—the unattractiveness of the area. You now decide that the suggested improvements should come next, since they would lose much of their impact if separated from the description of the shopping district. You also decide that it is sensible to present first the simplest and most necessary improvements (those to be brought about by cleaning and tidying) and then go on to what you think of as the luxuries (the improvements to be brought about by exterior decoration). The last part of your composition, then, will deal with the possibility that these improvements will some day be made.

In the same way, you consider how best to arrange the items concerning each of these four main topics—the details you will use in discussing each. Under Topic 1 you decide to present your details as they would strike the eye of someone strolling along the area (an idea you got when jotting down your first item). Under Topics 2 and 3 you decide that the most sensible order is to go from the cheapest improvements to the most expensive.

You find that your items under Topic 4 cluster around two points: first, that there is considerable interest in beautifying the downtown area; second, that the costliness of most of the improvements you have suggested is likely to be a stumbling block in the way of their ever being carried out. You decide to discuss the costliness first, and then the interest, so that you can end your paper on an optimistic note—which you, personally, feel is justified.

Having made all these decisions, you record the results in the form of a written plan, an outline. Then you have before you your theme in skeleton form:

Title: Beauty Treatment

Controlling idea: Our ugly, run-down shopping district could be transformed by some cleaning and some good exterior decorating.

I. The ugliness of the district
   A. Its dirty, messy, run-down appearance
      1. Dirty buildings
      2. Peeling, blistered paint
      3. Grimy windows
      4. Messy sidewalks
      5. Signs with letters missing
      6. Rusty old streetcar tracks
   B. Its drab, colorless, generally unattractive appearance
      1. Muddy colors used on buildings and awnings
      2. Lack of trees, shrubbery
      3. Few benches, and those covered with advertising
      4. Large, nondescript metal litter cans
      5. General absence of bright color
II. How cleaning and tidying could improve it
   A. Regular cleaning jobs
      1. Keeping sidewalks shoveled and/or swept

2. Washing windows regularly
3. Keeping signs in good repair
4. Cleaning exterior walls occasionally
   B. Removing rusty old streetcar tracks
III. How some good exterior decoration could beautify it
   A. Adding color and beauty through small items
      1. Attractive litter receptacles
      2. Brightly painted benches at all bus stops, with no advertising on them
      3. Flower baskets on lampposts in summer
      4. Better-looking traffic lights and lampposts

   B. Repainting and redecorating buildings
      1. Using bright, cheerful awnings
      2. Painting doors in bright colors
      3. Using for buildings themselves some colors other than dark gray and dark brown
      4. Considering overall effect in any one block
   C. Adding greenery
      1. Shrubs on either side of entrances to stores
      2. Trees along Main Street
   D. Putting pedestrian strip in center of Main Street, where removal of tracks would leave good space
   E. Turning all or part of area into pedestrian mall in summer
      1. Barring area to cars
      2. Painting colorful designs on street, where people would be walking
      3. Putting benches, flowers, shrubs along street
      4. Letting a few restaurants set up tables in street
      5. Perhaps even bringing in fountains and sculpture, to turn it into real beauty spot
IV. Possibility that any of these improvements will be made
   A. Cost a stumbling block in way of extensive changes
      1. Reluctance of city to spend amount necessary to remove streetcar tracks
      2. Reluctance of store owners to spend amount necessary to repaint and redecorate
      3. Probable reluctance of city, merchants, and taxpayers to spend $60,000 or more for mall
   B. Growing interest a reason for optimism
      1. Public's complaints about present appearance of area
         a. Complaints in letters-to-editor columns
         b. Complaints heard in discussions
      2. Interest of Merchants' Association in clean-up, paint-up program
      3. Interest of Chamber of Commerce in extensive beauty treatment in which city and merchants would coöperate
   C. Likelihood that area will (very gradually) be transformed into "a thing of beauty"

This outline is a typical one in that it includes some information that was not in the original list, and excludes some details that were there. (Item 25, for example, was left out; it is likely to be useful in the written theme, but it is not needed in the plan. The same is true of the specific details given in items 17 and 21.)

Remember that the outline is, as we have said, only the skeleton of your theme. When you come to write the paper, you will put flesh on the bones by giving pertinent illustrations, examples, incidents, quotations—details like the ones mentioned in the preceding paragraph.

Remember, too, that you are not legally obliged to follow the arrangement of material in your outline. If when you come to write your first draft, you consider it desirable to take up topics or subtopics in a different order from the one in your plan, or to give some item a slightly different emphasis, go right ahead. In any case, the work you put into making a plan is unlikely to be wasted. For the thinking you do about your subject, the extent to which you analyze your facts and ideas as you lick your hodgepodge of material into usable shape, is of the greatest value to you in writing the paper. In fact, it may be of greater value to you than the completed, written outline itself.

Exercise 5 Be ready to tell in class what sources you personally would use to get material for a composition based on each of the following controlling ideas. The sources may be your own experience, talks with other people, reading, or a combination of these. Keep in mind that you would want as rich a collection of material as possible.

1 Up to the moment of the shot, the events of Lincoln's last day were quite ordinary.
2 In large elementary-school classes, excellent results have come from grouping children by their ability in various subjects.
3 A good many ways of treating the common cold have been worked out, but so far none seems to be completely effective.
4 High-school courses in driving have had a number of excellent results.
5 Documentary films are entertaining as well as educational.
6 For one who loves animals, a veterinarian's work could be extremely satisfying.
7 There are both advantages and disadvantages in attending a small college.
8 A selling job gives you training that stands you in good stead, whatever your future plans.
9 Earthquakes are brought about by a "fault" in the earth.
10 Diets are getting funnier all the time.

Exercise 6 Choose two of the controlling ideas in Exercise 5 and decide what *kind* of material would be needed for a paper based on each. Write your answers on a sheet of paper to be handed in.

[For example, suppose one of the controlling ideas you chose was as follows: "With two brothers and no sisters, I have had to learn to fight for my rights—sometimes in an unladylike fashion." Your answer might go something like this: "For a theme with this controlling idea, I think the writer would need two kinds of material: (1) Incidents in which the two boys united against the writer—to get a football game on TV rather than a play, for instance, or to get her to do some chores that they should have done. (2) Techniques that the writer has used to fight back—blackmailing them by threatening to "tell" about some misdemeanor, engaging in actual physical combat, etc."]

Exercise 7   Which of these controlling ideas would call for a paper in which the material is arranged in chronological order? What general pattern or framework is called for by the other controlling ideas (i.e., cause and effect, comparison and contrast, problem and solution, etc.)? Be ready to discuss your answers in class.

1   Despite obvious differences, the English game cricket and the American game baseball have much in common.
2   Preparing fresh fruits for freezing is quite a simple process.
3   My tendency to monopolize the phone is a great irritation to the other members of my family, who have tried to cope with it in various ingenious ways.
4   High-school courses in driving have had a number of excellent results.
5   By using the right technique, you can get through a gym class without exerting yourself at all.

WRITING THE FIRST DRAFT

When you settle down to write, one of your first considerations will be how and when to get across to your reader the controlling idea of your theme. You may decide you can do this most effectively with an explicit statement in the opening paragraph. For example:

"Boys will be boys" is a favorite saying of many adults. But when I was a child, I knew only one adult who really took it seriously, and didn't get angry when boys *were* boys. That was my grandfather. [Controlling idea in student's mind: "My grandfather was my favorite person all through my childhood, because he liked me the way I was and didn't try to improve me."]

Or you may decide to state the controlling idea in the second (or even the third) paragraph of your theme:

Would a big university or a small college be best for me? Should I try to go to a school in this area or one far from home

14

and family? Am I going to have trouble getting into one of the schools I think most highly of?

Many high-school seniors are discussing such questions with special interest these days. After doing a great deal of talking, and some listening, too, I have formed at least one opinion: Centertown College has much to offer. [Controlling idea in student's mind: "I think Centertown College, in our own city, offers several advantages to the prospective freshman."]

In some themes, you may consider it most effective not to state the controlling idea at all. Instead, you let the reader gradually understand it in the course of several paragraphs. This is a common device when the controlling idea is a very simple one, such as "My Scottie is a frisky, clownish, contrary-minded creature, whom I could not do without":

My Scotch terrier, Gavin, will sit up and beg for almost anything edible, from a hot dog (or someone's pointing finger, which he tends to mistake for a hot dog) to a cookie. If you make the error of giving him a cookie, though, or in fact anything but meat or cheddar cheese, he just pushes it around on the floor with his nose.

Nevertheless, I am pleased that he does sit up and beg for food, because that is really his only trick. He will not jump over obstacles—unless it is for his own pleasure, in the course of a game. He will not "speak" on command, though at other times he barks much too often and much too loudly to suit the neighbors.

He will not even sit up for his leash, instead showing his eagerness for a walk by seizing someone's sock, glove, overshoe, or slipper and shaking it violently. Next, if he is really pleased at the prospect of a walk, he will race around and around the house like a steam engine on a circular track, until I seize him and snap on his leash.

Nor is Gavin at all like those dogs who get their pictures taken playing companionably with cats. [Rest of paragraph consists of description of his hostile behavior when cats are around.]

One of his good qualities is his loyalty to me, but even that has its embarrassing side. [Rest of paragraph narrates such incidents as Gavin's attacking a friend of the writer while the two boys were roughhousing.]

By the end of the third paragraph, or at least the fourth, the reader knows exactly what idea the theme centers on.

The opening paragraph. Whichever approach you use in making clear your controlling idea, you will of course want to open your theme with a paragraph likely to get the reader interested in your subject. If you are stating the idea explicitly, do not be so straightforward about it as to be dull. For example:

15

I believe that science fiction, an increasingly popular form of writing, can be divided into three basic types. The first. . . .

On the other hand, be careful to avoid an overelaborate opening, one that starts too far away from your subject or controlling idea:

Why do people read? One answer is to get information, as when we read textbook assignments or news bulletins. A more common answer is for entertainment, or even escape. This is certainly the answer I must give in speaking of my own leisure-time reading. And of the various kinds of escape literature I like to read—murder mysteries, historical novels, science fiction—the last is my great favorite.

By now I have read enough of it to realize that certain basic patterns are often repeated. In fact, I have recognized three distinct types of science-fiction story. The first. . . .

For this theme about science fiction, an opening paragraph that avoids the two extremes might be as follows:

Hero A travels backward into time from the twenty-fifth century and almost gets himself killed in the nineteenth. Hero B is worrying about how he and his fellow earthmen can set up a colony on a planet infested with writhing, plantlike, but carnivorous creatures. Hero C is a robot who mysteriously finds himself developing human feelings.

These three characters and situations are typical of what I consider the three basic kinds of science-fiction story. . . .

This arouses interest, and does so through relevant material—material that helps clarify the writer's controlling idea.

The body of the paper. Try to proceed from your first paragraph to your last with as few pauses as possible. Do not worry until later about such details as grammar, spelling, and punctuation. Concentrate at this stage on saying what you have planned to say, as clearly as you can.

The number of paragraphs you write to cover the different sections of your outline will vary, depending on the amount of detail you use in developing each topic. For example, look at Section III of the outline on page 12. The items under III A you could cover in a paragraph; they are quite simple, and a detailed account would not really be possible.

To cover Section III B, on the other hand, you might need two or three paragraphs, because the items in this section call for a certain amount of descriptive detail. III C and III D again could be handled in one paragraph. But your coverage of III E would probably extend over two. This material would be new to many of your readers, and you would have to use considerable detail to make clear what a mall is and to show why you think a mall so desirable for your city.

Be sure to include in each paragraph enough detail to develop its topic adequately. Be careful, however, to include only relevant details, in order to keep the paragraph unified. Remember also to link each sentence smoothly with the next, to give the paragraph continuity. (Unity and continuity in paragraphs, as well as adequate development and methods of development, are discussed in detail in Chapter 2, "Writing Paragraphs.")

See that your paragraphs, like your sentences, are smoothly connected, so that the reader can move without effort from one topic to the next. In each paragraph, you should build on what has gone before. You can do this by repeating a key word or phrase from near the end of the preceding paragraph, by using a word like *this* or *that* which refers to a word or phrase near the end of the preceding paragraph, or by using (but not overusing) such words and phrases as *but, however, therefore, nevertheless, finally, in addition, a second reason, in the third place, on the next corner, when Grandpa arrived home.*

The final paragraph. Your closing paragraph should give a note of finality to your paper and should say something you want the reader to carry away with him. Sometimes you will find that when you have said all you want to say about the last item in your outline, you have such a closing paragraph.

Suppose, for example, a student wrote a theme with this controlling idea: "Bob Sawyer and Ben Allen, the young medical men in *Pickwick Papers,* are rowdy, unprofessional, and very funny." After discussing a number of incidents that develop this idea, he might end his paper with some such paragraph as this:

> The very last scene in which they appear shows them at their most typical. Staying at an inn with Mr. Pickwick, they learn that two of their fellow guests are bitter political foes. To enliven a dull evening, they purposely bring about a hot quarrel between the two. Then, hoping that a real fistfight will develop, Bob Sawyer and Ben Allen "dodge around" the two enemies, "each with a tortoise-shell lancet in his hand, ready to bleed the first man stunned."

The quotation makes a good stopping place. It comes from the last actual incident in the book in which the two men figure, an incident which neatly illustrates the controlling idea of the theme. There is no need for the writer to say anything more.

For some themes, however, you may find that you need a special ending paragraph that explicitly restates your controlling idea:

> Telling that story was typical of Grandpa. He wanted to help me out of a tight spot, and he also wanted Mom and Dad to realize that a boy can tell a few lies and still not grow up vicious. In other words, he wanted to teach them what he knew so well, that boys *will be* boys.

But do not concoct a special ending when you really have nothing more to say, out of fear that you will otherwise seem to stop too abruptly. Suppose a student wrote a theme with this controlling idea: "In refinishing furniture, you must follow a set routine with the utmost patience." For this theme, the following would surely strike most readers as a concocted, tacked-on ending:

> . . . Then, at last, your work is over.
>
> You may think the job sounds terribly difficult, messy, and unpleasant. But people who make a hobby or a business of refinishing furniture can really enjoy this kind of thing, believe it or not.

The writer would be well advised to delete the irrelevant paragraph about how enjoyable some people find it to refinish furniture and end his paper with the preceding sentence.

Avoid above all a final paragraph that apologizes or indicates in any way that you think poorly of your own work (for example, a paragraph with a sentence like "I hope that my definition of *democracy* is fairly clear, at least," or "Maybe I have let my enthusiasm for our local college run away with me"). If a reader feels inclined to criticize, this kind of remark will encourage him, rather than stop him.

It is a good idea to let a little time elapse before revising your first draft, for you can be much more objective about it after taking a slight rest from it. Since there are many points to check on at this stage, it is also a good idea to leave yourself enough time to go over the draft more than once. Asking yourself the following questions will help you to revise effectively.

Questions about content: Is the controlling idea clear? Is there any other material I should include to make the controlling idea clearer, more interesting, or more convincing to the reader?

Does every paragraph in the paper help illustrate or explain or develop my controlling idea, or have I included irrelevant material? In other words, does my theme have unity? (Remember that giving the reader irrelevant information can confuse him as much as omitting relevant material.)

Are all technical or specialized terms explained? Have I, anywhere in the paper, assumed knowledge on the part of the reader that he may not actually have?

Have I checked all my factual information so that I know it is accurate?

Questions about plan: Are my ideas arranged in a logical order? Have I told the reader first the things he should know first, and so on?

Have I given appropriate emphasis to the various topics, making it clear by their position and by the amount of space allotted to them which are more and which less important?

Questions about writing: Is my opening paragraph likely to catch the reader's interest? Does it start too far away from my first main topic?

Does my paper have continuity (coherence)? That is, are sentences and paragraphs smoothly linked so that the reader can move effortlessly from beginning to end without a break?

Are there any awkward sentences? Is the writing wordy? Are there words and phrases that can be deleted? Are there places where I can substitute one word for two or more?

Have I used specific, concrete, picture-making words wherever possible and appropriate?

Does my closing paragraph give a note of finality without seeming tacked on?

Questions about mechanics: Are there any mistakes in grammar, sentence structure, usage, spelling, punctuation, or capitalization?

Exercise 8 Gather material for, plan, and write a composition based on the first controlling idea you worked out for Exercise 4. If for some reason you do not wish to use this idea, work out another for a composition in which you present factual information.

Be sure to gather your material from all possible sources. Make use of the techniques described in the chapter for sorting and arranging material, writing effective opening and closing paragraphs, linking the paragraphs, and revising.

Exercise 9 Write a composition based on the second controlling idea you worked out for Exercise 4. If for some reason you do not want to use this idea, work out another for a composition in which you explain a process, method, or technique. (Remember that you will present the steps in the process in chronological order.)

Exercise 10 Write a composition based on the third controlling idea that you worked out for Exercise 4. If for some reason you do not wish to use that idea, work out another for a composition in which you express and support an opinion.

SPECIAL TYPES OF WRITING: ARGUMENT

In an argumentative paper you present and support a point of view on some controversial subject. Your purpose is not simply to explain your view and the reasons why you hold it, as it is in an exposition. Instead, as in a debate speech, it is to persuade the reader to see things your way, to convince him that he should share your view.

The steps in writing such a paper are the same as in writing exposition: you choose and limit a subject, develop a controlling idea (your point of view), gather material, make a plan, and so on. However, because your purpose is different, there are certain special considerations you will want to keep in mind. These considerations are dealt with here.

Your subject and point of view.   Make sure, to begin with, that the subject you choose *is* controversial, that it really has given rise to two or more opposing and widely held views. Putting the subject in the form of a question can help you determine whether or not it meets this requirement. For example:

Should students cheat on exams?
Should dog haters be allowed to poison others' pet dogs?

It can readily be seen that these subjects are not truly controversial, for these questions would be answered *No* by the vast majority of people. If you wrote a paper in which you argued that students should not cheat on examinations or that dog haters should not go around poisoning dogs, you would just be setting up a straw man for the purpose of knocking it down.

Make sure, also, that your subject is suitable for the length of paper you plan to write. If it is too broad, your limited space will make it impossible for you to write a persuasive argument. For you will have to summarize in general statements the material supporting your view, instead of presenting it in convincing detail.

These subjects are appropriate in size for student arguments:

Is our Student Council doing a useful job?
Do we have an adequate guidance service in our school?
Is physical punishment an effective means of disciplining children?

Different students would naturally have different views on these controversial subjects. For example:

What our Student Council has been doing is useful enough, but it should have more areas of responsibility in which to act.
Our guidance service is, in my opinion, inadequate both in quantity and in quality.
I think physical punishment, though sometimes a great relief to an angry parent, is completely ineffective in improving a child's behavior.
Physical punishment can be extremely effective in child discipline, but only if adults take great care not to overuse it.

Remember that your view need not, and often cannot, be based on the idea that something is good or bad, right or wrong—*black or white.* Instead (as in the first and last examples just given) it will often be that something is good or bad, right or wrong, *to a certain extent.*

Note: In the discussion that follows, a number of points are illustrated by reference to the example theme "Stoplights Wanted," which is printed on pages 22-24. The discussion will be much more meaningful to you if you read the theme now—and then read it again, after going through the rest of this section.

Your material. In preparing to write an argumentative composition, you gather and study material concerning all possible views on your subject—material hostile, as well as favorable, to your view. One reason for this is to ensure that your view is a sound one. If as a result of your study you decide that it is not, you can modify it in good time.

The main reason, however, is that to write an intelligent and persuasive argument you must not only know the case for your view, but you must also be aware (and in your argument show that you are aware) of the case for the opposition.

You need, then, the following three kinds of material for your argumentative paper:

1) *Material that supports your view.* This will consist of accurate factual statements, sound opinions, and logical reasoning about these facts and opinions. In the example theme this kind of material is presented in paragraphs 3 to 7.

2) *Flaws in the case for the opposition,* including flaws in the criticisms of your view. These will consist of inaccurate factual statements, unsound opinions, and fallacious (crooked) reasoning.

In the example paper the opposition's criticisms are presented and answered in paragraphs 8 to 11. An argument based on a more complex subject than "Stoplights Wanted" would probably deal at greater length with opposing views.

3) *Points that you and the opposition agree on.* The reason why you concern yourself with this sort of material is that when you come to write your argument, it helps you to cope with the hostile reader. For the best way to disarm such a reader is to admit that there is something to be said for his view.

In "Stoplights Wanted," the writer makes use of such material in paragraph 1, where he casually mentions that drivers, too, have problems to face on Center Street, and in paragraphs 11 and 12, where he expresses emphatic agreement that to install conventional traffic signals at Center and Fifth would be unfair to drivers. As a result the hostile reader is quite likely to decide that this writer is a reasonable fellow—and that his argument should be considered with a mind at least part way open.

In gathering the first and second kinds of material, you will, of course, have to know how to distinguish between statements-of-fact and statements of opinion, how to test them for accuracy and soundness, and how to recognize logical and fallacious reasoning. Chapter 3, "Language and Thinking," and Chapter 4, "On Thinking Logically," discuss these matters in great detail.

Your outline. Do a painstaking job of sorting and outlining your material. Then read over your outline slowly and critically, looking for facts and opinions you have not checked thoroughly, gaps in your supporting material, and fallacies in your reasoning. Such flaws—which can be fatal in this kind of writing—are easier to spot and to remedy when your argument is in skeleton form than when it is completely written.

Your writing. "Stoplights Wanted" illustrates a number of techniques that will help you write a clear and persuasive argument.

Paragraphs 1 and 2 give very briefly all the introductory material needed by the reader: the question, a brief "history" of the controversy, and the writer's view. The final paragraph summarizes everything the reader should carry away with him: the writer's view, again, and the main reasons why he holds it.

Smooth transitions from one paragraph to another and from one part of the argument to another are provided by the words, phrases, and sentences printed in italics. The reader has no trouble realizing when the writer is moving from one supporting point to another, when he is beginning an account of objections to his view, etc.

A calm, friendly, reasonable tone is maintained throughout the paper. The writer does not sound as though he is quarreling with the reader; nor does he sound as though his sole purpose in writing the composition is to reduce some opponent to a pulp. In presenting his own views he is never dogmatic, but uses such phrases as "in my opinion," "there seems to me," and "I suggest." In dealing with what the opposition says, he is respectful, not condescending or belittling (see especially paragraph 11). This kind of tone disposes a reader to give thoughtful attention to an argument, whereas a wrangling tone may anger him, causing him to close his mind.

Paragraphs 4 to 6, describing the writer's experiences and observations at the intersection, illustrate the fact that vivid writing can be every bit as important in argument as in other kinds of composition. Since those experiences and observations make up the bulk of the writer's supporting material, it is essential for him to impress them on the reader's mind. He does so by writing them up in abundant detail, using specific, concrete, picture-making words. The resulting description enables the reader to visualize the plight of the students, and so is likely to arouse his sympathy for them.

AN ARGUMENTATIVE COMPOSITION

Title:	Stoplights Wanted
Subject:	Are traffic signals needed at the intersection of Center and Fifth Streets?
Writer's view:	Traffic signals of the push-button type should be installed at this intersection.

[1] Are traffic signals needed at the intersection of Center and Fifth Streets? This question has been argued off and on in our city

for several years. A number of Northeast High School students, who have to cross at this busy intersection to get to school, answer *Yes*. A number of men and women who drive to work in the morning, and who already cope with heavy traffic and numerous stoplights as they go along Center Street, answer *No*.

[2] As one of the Northeast High students involved, *I believe* that traffic signals of the push-button type should be installed here. (The type of signals I mean would enable the pedestrian crossing Center to get a green light for a brief time by pressing a button. The rest of the time the light would remain green for the drivers going along Center.)

[3] *Why do I think signals are needed?* Here are some figures that will help answer the question. Teams of student observers, stationed at this intersection for five school mornings, found that in the peak period between 8:30 and 8:55 an average of 260 students crossed at this intersection and an average of 325 cars drove through it. This, I think, is a heavy concentration of cars and pedestrians.

[4] *Now let us look* at the kind of problem created by *this concentration*. Having attended Northeast High for over three years now, I have had ample experience and can testify that any morning will serve as a good example. Yesterday, for instance, I stood and waited with a group of eight or nine others. We looked to the right and looked to the left. There was no hope: the cars kept streaming past. A girl stepped out timidly and got about two feet from the curb, but finding that the drivers ignored her pleading glances, lost her nerve and scurried back to the sidewalk.

[5] Two boys strode out boldly and managed to outbluff a driver here and a driver there, and little by little got across. After every few steps, though, they had to stand for a moment, with cars whizzing past a few inches in front of them and a few inches behind. For this reason not many of us on the curb were willing to follow their example.

[6] For a moment it looked as though our whole group would be able to start across—but no, some cars were turning onto Center from Fifth. Finally there was an honest-to-goodness gap in the line of cars, and we all surged out together. By the time we made it across, the cars were streaming past again and another waiting group had taken our place.

[7] *This situation,* which occurs every weekday morning at Center and Fifth, seems to me ample reason for installing push-button traffic signals there.

[8] *The people who disagree* make two objections to the idea of installing signals. The first is usually expressed as follows: Since the problem is acute only in the mornings, for no more than an hour at most, and since there are traffic lights at First and at Ninth Streets on Center, it is ridiculous to suggest that another set of lights is needed. Northeast High students who find Fifth such a

difficult place to cross can surely go a little out of their way and cross with the lights at one of those streets.

[9] *In reply* to this point of view, I say that any student who lives fairly close to First or Ninth is likely to be using that street already to get to school; the rest of us cross at Fifth because we live much closer to it than to the streets mentioned. As far as inconvenience is concerned, there seems to me little to choose between crossing there, with all the trouble it involves, and walking out of one's way to cross with existing lights.

[10] *The second objection* is made by people who admit that the present situation is inconvenient for pedestrians, and perhaps unfair to them. But, they ask, would the installation of signals not be just as inconvenient and unfair for the drivers? They would then encounter three lights in a row, each only four blocks from the last. Furthermore, those who drive on Center at other times of day than the morning rush hour would have to do a great deal of stop-and-go driving for the benefit of only a small number of pedestrians.

[11] *My answer* is that this objection would be completely valid if conventional traffic lights were the only kind in existence. The installation of such signals would indeed inconvenience the drivers. In fact, as the objection implies, they would reverse the present situation and put the whole burden of inconvenience on the drivers. But this is precisely why I say that push-button lights are called for. They would enable the students to get across without interminable waiting and nervous strain. Then, when students were out of the way, they would enable drivers to carry on without interruption.

24

[12] *To summarize* my argument, I believe there is a need for traffic signals at Center and Fifth, where the present situation is extremely inconvenient for Northeast High students in the mornings. But I readily admit that the installation of conventional traffic lights would be unfair, because it would simply shift the whole burden of inconvenience to the drivers. Therefore, I suggest the use of push-button signals as a fair solution to the problems of both groups.

Exercise **11** Find a piece of argumentative writing in a recent newspaper, and clip it out. Good sources are the editorials, columns in which the writer editorializes, and letters to the editor. (If you have several days' newspapers handy, you may be able to get a whole series of letters on some one controversy.)

Read over the argument, considering these questions: Is the writer's view clearly stated? Is the material supporting that view adequate? Do the facts and opinions seem to be sound? Are there any logical fallacies in the argument? Does the writer seem aware of other views that exist? Is he able to show flaws in these views? Is his tone reasonable? Is the writing effective? How persuasive do you think the argument is?

Be ready to discuss your evaluation of the argument in class.

Exercise **12**   Following are a number of views on controversial subjects. You may choose one of these, or work out one of your own, as the controlling idea for an argumentative composition.

Do a thorough job of gathering and evaluating material on both, or all, sides of the controversy. Remember to use all possible sources of material. Write your argument, keeping in mind all the points made in the preceding discussion.

1   An average TV week in this city gives us a good many programs that are well worth seeing. [Or: gives us almost nothing worth seeing.]
2   Bicycle riding on city streets has become so dangerous that it should be prohibited.
3   The high-school course should be extended to five years. [Or: should be compressed into three years.]
4   Drivers who violate traffic laws should be punished by having their licenses revoked, rather than by fines.
5   Mathematics should be a required subject for all students in every year of high school.

SPECIAL TYPES OF WRITING:

PERSONAL NARRATIVE

By now you have written a great many personal narratives (probably starting way back in grade school with themes on "How I Spent My Summer Vacation," and "My Hobby"). In this kind of writing, as you know, your purpose is to entertain your reader by sharing your experiences with him. You may choose to write about a one-incident experience like an embarrassing moment, or you may write about an experience made up of a series of incidents, like your first week in a new school. In either case, of course, you tell about the things that happened in the order that they happened.

One characteristic of good narratives is that they contain an abundance of detail. If a writer says in general terms that he once got a bad case of stage fright and could hardly move or speak his lines, he is unlikely to arouse more than a mild interest in his reader. But if he uses specific details (telling how the shaking of his legs made it impossible for him to saunter onto the stage as he was supposed to, giving the lines he should have replied to but couldn't, quoting the angry commands hissed at him by his fellow actors as he stood there in silence), he has a good chance of bringing the experience to life for the reader.

Another characteristic of good narratives that may not have been called to your attention before is that they make a point. For a brief personal narrative this point is likely to be a simple one—for example, "High-school students can be quite chilly to a newcomer" or "Years ago, I painfully learned that honesty is the best policy."

Suppose a writer does not have such a point in mind, but sets out simply to write about "My first week in a new school" or "My experience as a thief." Then he is telling a story just for the sake of telling, and will be tempted to ramble, introducing any interesting details that occur to him. This could result in a disjointed story and a bored reader. Having in mind the point the narrative is to make (however simple the point may be) prevents this, for like the controlling idea of an exposition, it helps a writer to keep on the track.

Once you have decided on a point to make in writing your personal narrative, you need do only two more things by way of preparation. First, make sure you have recalled in as much detail as possible the experience you want to write about. Second, make a mental plan to follow in writing—that is, get it straight what happened first, what happened second, and so on. Suppose you are planning a narrative with this point:

> On my first day as a camp counselor, the eight boys in my charge provided me with a steady stream of problems.

You might have in mind the following chronology:

1. Dealing with Bobby, the "Weeper," who was already homesick.
2. Trying to get them to make their beds decently, and stopping fistfight between two of them who wanted same top bunk.
3. Squelching complaints about food at lunch.
4. Trouble keeping them quiet and in bunks during rest hour.
5. Peaceful period away from them, while teaching the beginners' swimming class, followed by unpleasantness at supper table: "cliques" already forming, creating problem of one boy who was left out.
6. Hysterical silliness at bedtime.
7. Boy falling out of bunk.

You would also, of course, have in mind a host of details to use in writing up each of these incidents.

When you write your narrative, do not begin with a paragraph that "leads up" to your experience. Instead, plunge right into it:

> I looked at the eight little boys who were to be in my charge during their two weeks at Camp Manatoola. One was crying quietly. Two hefty ones, wearing camp caps, camp kerchiefs, and camp sweaters, were punching each other. Two others were whispering and giggling, obviously, I thought, about me —their counselor. The other three seemed to be hopefully waiting for some fun to start.

This is a much more effective opening than would be a paragraph explaining how you had prepared for this job by working for two seasons as an assistant counselor, or telling how worried you had been for the past month about taking on the responsibilities of a full-fledged counselor.

As you write, keep in mind the point of your narrative; it will help you identify and reject any irrelevant details that may suggest themselves. For the camp theme these might be such details as that Bobby, the "Weeper," eventually came to love camp life, or that a boy in the next cabin got an attack of asthma on that very first day. Since these facts have nothing to do with the point of the story, and would only get in the reader's way, you would not include them.

Conversation or dialogue should be used—but not overused—in your narratives. A good rule to follow is to use it chiefly where you have occasion to recall exact wording. (For the camp theme an effective bit might be this easily remembered criticism of the lunch menu by one little boy: "2, 4, 6, 8! What don't we appreciate? Hash! Hash! Booooooooooo!") When you decide to use dialogue, you will find the Index item **Conversation** helpful.

There is no need to write an elaborate ending, an ending in which you try to sum up or round off your narrative, like this:

> ... Then I crawled wearily into my own bed and fell asleep.
>
> The same sort of incidents happened every day, for two weeks. But as I became more experienced, they became just routine. I could handle them with half my mind on something else. That is why I can look back now and laugh at my nightmarish first day as a counselor.

Instead, simply tell the reader what happened last and then stop:

> I helped Joey, now half asleep again, into his bunk. I tucked his blankets in firmly and shoved him right over against the wall. I made sure that no sound but breathing could be heard from the other seven bunks. Then I fell into my own cot, and sleep blotted out all the troubles of that nerve-wracking day.

Exercise 13   Choose an experience in your life that you would like to tell about in a brief narrative composition. Work out the point that you want to make in telling your story. Write the narrative, keeping in mind the suggestions given in the preceding discussion.

The following list of general statements may suggest a subject for your narrative.

1   Judging people by appearances may lead to bad mistakes.
2   Girls aren't the only ones who can't keep secrets.
3   Pride often goes before a fall.
4   Sometimes it isn't good to mind your own business.
5   It is a shock to learn that you can hate (or be disloyal, etc.).
6   Children can be extraordinarily cruel.
7   Revenge is not always sweet.
8   Prejudice is usually based on ignorance.
9   Most people would like to relive the past in order to change their behavior on at least one occasion.

You will rarely see or be called on to write a composition that is pure description. Descriptive writing generally occurs in more or less brief passages within other types of writing.

It is used most extensively in narratives, where descriptions of persons, places, and things help the reader to share your experience. But expository and argumentative writing sometimes call for description, too. A process theme explaining how to build a hi-fi cabinet might contain a description of the finished product. A composition about the advantages of jeeps might call for a description of a rough route that the writer's jeep traveled successfully. And an example of description in an argument may be seen in paragraphs 4 to 6 on page 23.

The following five points will help you in writing descriptive passages of various types:

1) It is important to observe keenly what you want to describe, and to remember well what you have observed. Whatever your purpose in writing a description (see points 2 and 3), you must have plenty of accurate details to draw on. The colors of the sky, the sea, the sand, the bathing suits, the beach balls and umbrellas; the sounds made by the waves, the children, and the lifeguards with their megaphones; the smell of the water, the hot dogs, the popcorn; the feel of the cool breeze and the hot sand—an abundance of details like these would help you write a really vivid description of a beach scene.

2) Sometimes your purpose in describing is to give the reader a rather complete, factual picture of some person, place, or thing. Then you will include all the important details that you yourself observed—in the description of a person, for example, details about his features, coloring, height, build, clothing, and mannerisms.

3) More often the primary purpose of your description is to give a certain impression. Having decided how you feel about the person, place, or thing you are describing, you choose from your stock of details those that will help the reader to feel the same way. Often this can be done best with only a few details, as in this passage:

> Leaving the theatre one evening not long ago, I caught sight of a mounted policeman riding down the street, his bay horse picking its way delicately among the taxis and limousines, guided by only the faintest motion of the reins in the officer's left hand. It was drizzling, and the horse and the black waterproof coat and hat of the policeman were glistening. . . .—Edith Iglauer, "A Reporter at Large: The Mounted Men," *The New Yorker,* November 24, 1962.

These few details give the reader an impression of grace and beauty, even before the writer adds that to her "this was a beautiful sight."

4) After you have decided what details to use, you must decide in what order to present them. If you are trying to give an objective, true-to-life picture, you will find it best to follow some such spatial order as near to far, left to right, top to bottom, etc., so that the reader will not get lost. But suppose you are trying to give the reader your impression of a person, place, or thing. Then you will find it most effective to present the details in the order in which they first attracted your attention. You will probably start with the most striking detail—the blazing fire, for instance, in a room whose welcoming appearance you want the reader to visualize.

5) To turn out a vivid description, you need not only the well-observed details mentioned in point 1, but well-chosen words, too—concrete words that appeal to the senses. Notice how many such words are used in the following descriptive passage from Pierre Berton's history of the Klondike gold rush:

> All that fall [after it was learned that no supplies could arrive until spring, and a winter of famine was inevitable] the exodus from Dawson continued. . . .
>
> Scores attempted to return up the frozen river to the passes, rending their clothes, shredding their moccasins, and shattering their sleighs on the sharp blocks of ice that were sometimes heaped as high as twenty feet. As they stumbled on, they jettisoned their sleds, their food, their clothes, even their shoes, keeping only a single blanket apiece and a meager amount of provisions, with no shelter but a campfire to keep them from death by freezing.
>
> All of this time the temperature hung at fifty below zero, so cold that any man moving faster than a tortoise pace felt the chill air sear his lungs. On November 29 the temperature dipped again to sixty-seven below, so that the trees cracked like pistol shots with the freezing and expanding sap, and cooked beans turned hard as pebbles, and the touch of metal tore the skin from naked fingers.—Pierre Berton, *Klondike*. Copyright 1958 by McClelland & Stewart Limited, Toronto.

Exercise 14   Find and copy three descriptive passages. (A passage may be a single paragraph, several paragraphs, or a part of a long paragraph.) At least one should describe a person and at least one should describe a place. Bring your passages to class and be prepared to discuss what each is primarily designed to do (give a factual picture or an impression?) and how well it succeeds.

Exercise 15   Write two brief descriptions—one of a person, one of a place or scene or object. Remember that in describing a place or scene, you can often appeal to more than one sense. (You can see the possibilities, for example, in a description of a bakery, of a subway or bus on a rainy day, of a children's birthday party, of a study hall just before dismissal time, of a machine shop.)

Writing

2 *Paragraphs*

A well-written expository paper is composed of a series of related paragraphs. Each paragraph is a group of sentences in which the writer discusses one topic—one small phase of his subject. By presenting the different phases, one at a time, in an effective order, the writer leads his readers step by step to an understanding of the subject as he sees it.

THE IMPORTANCE OF PLANNING

A writer who recognizes that it is his responsibility to lead his readers "step by step" does not have to be persuaded of the value of *planning* before he begins the actual writing of a paper. He realizes that before he can effectively lead others, he must first know himself what "steps" have to be taken and in what order.

Before he starts writing, therefore, he figures out a plan—a "map" showing the ground he will cover and the path he will follow in covering it. From this map will come the answers to such questions as "How many paragraphs should there be in this paper?" and "What should be included in each paragraph?"

To see an example of how this works, let's suppose that you are to write a paper on the rise and fall of the Stanley Steamer, an ancestor of today's prestige cars. After carefully thinking over your material, you decide that to give a clear picture of your subject you must cover four main topics:

I. The early days of the Stanley Steamer business
II. The qualities that made the Steamer a success
III. Factors that damaged the Steamer business
IV. The last days of the Stanley Steamer

Under each of these main topics, you group—as subtopics—various items to be discussed. Under the third main topic, for example, you might list the following items:

III. Factors that damaged the Steamer business
    A. The Stanley brothers' insistence on selecting their customers
    B. Their stand against credit buying
    C. The prohibitively high price of the Steamer
    D. The Stanleys' refusal to advertise
    E. Their unwillingness to make changes

With a plan as carefully worked out as this to guide you, writing the paragraphs will be relatively easy: you simply take up the points in the outline one at a time.

The number of paragraphs you actually write will depend not only on the number of main headings in your outline but also on the amount of material you have to give about each. If, for example, you have only a few details to give about the first main heading (The early days of the Stanley Steamer business), you could easily cover them in a single paragraph. But for the third main topic (Factors that damaged the Steamer business), under which you listed five subtopics, you would very probably need more than one paragraph. In fact, you might well have enough interesting details on each of the subtopics to warrant using a separate paragraph for each, as this writer did:

And the Stanleys were "cussed" indeed. A customer simply couldn't walk in and buy a Stanley Steamer. He had to be "screened," like a candidate for an exclusive club. If the Stanleys decided he didn't have the right personality for their car, they wouldn't even take his order. Even when a customer's order was accepted, this didn't necessarily mean he would get a Steamer. If he did or said anything to displease the Stanleys between the time of placing the order and the actual production of the car, he would be refused delivery. This happened to a customer who asked for a written guarantee. The Stanleys, who figured their word was guarantee enough, showed the gentleman to the door.

This was hardly the way to build a business, let alone sell cars, and a modern automobile salesman would blanch at such treatment of a customer. It is a measure of the Stanley Steamer's worth that it continued to sell as well and as long as it did, especially since one never left the factory until it had been paid for in hard cash. The Stanleys just didn't believe in credit or installment buying, which they regarded as somewhat immoral.

The price of a Steamer was high for its day—in 1917, about $2500—and there weren't many people around that had that kind of cash. Sales were steady but never spectacular. The Stanley was a prestige car, and although many people would have liked one, they simply couldn't afford it. If the car had been sold on credit, and more people had gotten to own one and know its wonderful qualities, it is possible the Steamer would never have been allowed to pass away.

However, there were other matters that contributed to its death. The Stanleys didn't believe in advertising. They figured that it was a waste of money that should go into the improvement of their product. In later years, when the Stanley Steamer was suffering from all sorts of rumors, some judicious advertising might have saved the firm. Instead, the Stanleys stubbornly stuck by their policy of letting the Steamer "advertise itself."

Nor would they give in to the demands of style and mass production, which would have increased the popularity of the car and brought its price down. Except for a few streamlined racers and an early rakish model known as the Gentlemen's Speedy Roadster, the lofty, solid, individually-created Stanleys bore a resemblance to a prairie schooner. Almost always painted black, they had long, rounded hoods, which added to their funereal aspect. They looked like coffins.—John Carlova, "The Stanleys and Their Steamer," *American Heritage*, February 1959.

Notice how the sentences in each of these paragraphs work together to make clear one subtopic, one phase of the main topic. By focusing attention on one small phase at a time, the writer effectively leads his readers to a clear understanding of the subject as a whole.

ADEQUATE DEVELOPMENT IN PARAGRAPHS

Your success in getting your readers to see your subject as you see it depends in great part on how well you "develop" each phase, or topic. To develop a topic adequately, you must provide enough details about it—specific details—to make it meaningful. Unless you do, your readers will come away from the paragraph with only a hazy idea of what you had in mind.

Let's suppose that in a paper on Sinclair Lewis, one of the topics you plan to include is Lewis's zeal for orderliness. Your reading has led you to picture Lewis as overly concerned, almost fanatical, about orderliness—a view of him you want your readers to share. You can hardly expect to succeed, however, if you develop the topic like this:

Sinclair Lewis carried orderliness to excess. He was always methodical and orderly in his work. Neatness and order were very important to him in his home life, too. In fact, his insistence on order at home was often quite annoying to others.

The vague, general statements used in this paragraph do little to make the topic idea clear. They do not tell enough about Lewis to distinguish him from hundreds of other men who might be described as neat and orderly. And since they give no concrete instances of orderliness carried "to excess," how is the reader to know what the writer was thinking of when he wrote the first sentence? All the reader gets from the paragraph is a blurred picture.

To give a clear, sharply focused picture, you must supply specific details, details of the sort Dorothy Thompson has used in these paragraphs:

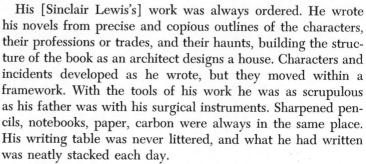

> His [Sinclair Lewis's] work was always ordered. He wrote his novels from precise and copious outlines of the characters, their professions or trades, and their haunts, building the structure of the book as an architect designs a house. Characters and incidents developed as he wrote, but they moved within a framework. With the tools of his work he was as scrupulous as his father was with his surgical instruments. Sharpened pencils, notebooks, paper, carbon were always in the same place. His writing table was never littered, and what he had written was neatly stacked each day.
>
> In his home he demanded an orderliness that sometimes drove me to exasperation. He smoked continuously but could not endure a half-filled ash tray. But he also could not endure an ash tray, or anything else, that was not exactly where it should be, nor a meal that was not served punctually to a second. He always hung his clothes on exactly the proper hangers, and his bureau drawers might have been kept by the best-trained valet.—Dorothy Thompson, "The Boy and Man from Sauk Centre," *The Atlantic*, November 1960.

Kinds of Details

Various kinds of details can be used to develop topics. The purpose of a particular paragraph generally suggests the best kind to use.

Details giving examples. Suppose that the purpose of one of your paragraphs is to show the influence advertising has had on the public. By using details giving specific examples, as the writer of the following paragraph has done, you can make sure your readers will get a clear idea of this influence:

> It is quite obvious that advertising has been very effective in swaying popular opinion as to the qualities of consumers' goods and in influencing the choice of those goods. It was primarily the advertising man who lifted the product of the cigarette manufacturers from its status of lowly "coffin nail" to that of a national necessity. Folkways with regard to gum

chewing were created by publicity. The citizen's preoccupation with the cleanliness of his teeth and skin surfaces was developed largely from the information provided in the advertisements he read. The hunt for germs in the various orifices and on the surfaces of the body was stimulated by the manufacturers of germicides. Information and misinformation about food values have led to fashions in foods. Cereals used for the American breakfast have been pounded, exploded, inflated, sieved, and woven, as the "scientific" facts propounded by the advertising man have convinced consumers that their foods should be so treated. And so on. Opinions and behavior have been rapidly changed as the advertiser has presented his phantasmagoria of changing information.—William Albig, *Modern Public Opinion*. Copyright © 1956 by McGraw-Hill Book Company, Inc., New York.

Details telling an incident. Sometimes, giving the details of an incident that illustrates the point you want to make is the best way to clarify a topic. For example:

Before the child has learned that the main use of language is to conceal either thought or the absence of thought, he speaks with a force, a conciseness, and a cleanliness of diction worthy of Ernest Hemingway. When our son Kim was less than three, he had already begun to look with a somewhat jaundiced eye on the competitive charms of his baby sister, Anne. It was at that time that we moved to the country and were compelled to leave behind us our Japanese cook. We asked Kim what he thought would be a nice good-by present for Kami. He reflected for no more than a few seconds. Then his face cleared. "Give him Anne," he said. I have read novels that conveyed no more than these three words.—Clifton Fadiman, *Any Number Can Play*. Published by The World Publishing Company, Cleveland. Copyright © 1957 by Clifton Fadiman.

Details giving reasons. A good way to persuade your readers to share your opinion about a topic is to provide details giving reasons in support of your view. The specific reasons given in the following paragraph, for example, make quite clear why the writers hold the opinion expressed in the first sentence:

The American building-trades craftsman is in many ways in an enviable position. A beginner can be paid while he learns. His services are in demand, as the market for skilled craft labor is almost indefinitely expanding. His wages are good in spite of his unavoidable idle time. He has a great deal of freedom of choice and can usually work for whom he chooses or—in the true American fashion—go into business for himself. More than in most fields, he can be either employee or employer as it benefits him most. Give him his tools and he can go where he pleases!—Pauline Arnold and Percival White, *Homes: America's Building Business*. Published by Holiday House, New York. Copyright 1960 by White and Arnold.

Details giving similarities and/or differences. Details pointing out similarities or differences, or both, are most effective in making clear the central idea of some paragraphs. Notice how well the *similarities* detailed in the following paragraph clarify and support the topic idea stated in the first sentence:

> There is less difference than the intelligentsia would have us believe between the daily grind of the "serious" novelist or biographer in his cloister and the reporter filing his daily dispatch with the wind of the world in his face. They are both writing "pieces." The monkish pro has a scene to finish or a chapter to defeat; the secular pro has an event to trap, a flavor to identify. They are, whatever the theoretical conditions of their freedom to pause and polish, both working in spurts and against a measured mile. The disparity between the quality of their stuff is still no more or less than that between two men of different talent; it has very little to do with the accidental binding of one man's pieces into a book and the scattering of the other man's pieces into a hundred issues of his paper.— Alistair Cooke, "Journalists Who Make History," *The Atlantic,* November 1959.

In the next paragraph, the use of details pointing up *differences* between two men helps to make a vivid characterization:

> Frederick ("Fritz") Loewe is Viennese, emotional, a flamboyant gambler who thinks the second biggest thrill on earth is to drop $30,000 in a single night at the casino tables, then tell about it for weeks. Alan Jay Lerner is cool, self-controlled, and self-censored, a planner who will not even put money in his own shows because, as he firmly explains, "I don't bet." Loewe likes to recall that he "starved" for 20 years; Lerner has always been wealthy. Short, lean, with the sallow skin of the heart patient, Loewe is 59 and looks it; about the same height (5 ft. 6½ in.), with small bones and an unweathered complexion, Lerner is 42 and could pass for a graduate student. Both men are intensely ambitious for the critical success of their work, but Lerner clothes his self-esteem in mannered diffidence while Loewe shrugs: "I'm too old to be modest. I'm a genius and I know it."—"Two Parfit Broadway Knyghts," *Time,* November 14, 1960.

Details enumerating steps. If the purpose of a paragraph is to explain how something works or how to do something, the main details will be the steps in the process. In some paragraphs, it might also be helpful to include steps to be avoided. In fact, a reader who used the following explanation would probably find such details vitally important.

A solitary traveler who stumbles into quicksand is in a more awkward situation, but even his case is not desperate if he knows what to do. Attempts to force a way to shore will prove worse than useless; standing still and yelling will be fatal unless help arrives soon. The trapped man's first move must be to drop his pole behind him, if he is foresighted enough to have one, and fall back upon it, meanwhile stretching his arms out at right angles to his body. In this position he could float in water and he will certainly float on sand if he gets rid of any heavy object he may be carrying. He may now call out for help. If there is no prospect of help, the victim may begin to rescue himself. The first step in this operation is to get the pole at right angles to the body beneath the shoulders and then work it down until it is supporting the hips. It is difficult work, but once done, the individual is in a position to pull his legs out of the mire, one at a time. He should do this slowly and with frequent rests. Once his feet are out, he looks about and selects the shortest route to solid ground. He then begins rolling toward his goal. Rolling is the easiest—and indeed the only—way of getting off the soft area. It can be done in short stages, but rests must be taken on the back with arms outstretched or he will begin to sink again. The pole is pulled along and used for support.—Gerard H. Matthes, "Quicksand," *Scientific American*, June 1953.

Details giving causes and effects. To give a clear picture of the topic, you may sometimes need details telling the *causes* that led to a particular event or the *effects* that followed as the result of a particular event. See how vividly the writer of the following paragraph details effects resulting from the Civil War:

The demands of war did other things, such as hastening transformation of the North from a country of farmers and small manufacturers to a highly organized industrial region. The voracious waste of war showed its infinite power to stimulate all the productive forces of the people. A great boot and shoe industry grew up in New England during the last two years of fighting, specifically to supply the needs of soldiers. The necessity of feeding the same men created the new packing plants in Chicago. McCormick's reaper, patented long before war began, had to await that tragedy before it and other agricultural machinery made much headway. The making of guns in frantic haste caused expansion of what had been a doddering iron and steel industry. It was much the same with nearly all manufacture. And even before the war ended, a great migration had started as both natives and foreigners set out to see what lay beyond the Mississippi.—Stewart H. Holbrook, *The Age of the Moguls.* Published by Doubleday & Company, Inc., New York. Copyright 1953 by Stewart H. Holbrook.

Many paragraph topics are developed by a combination of different kinds of details. The writers of the following paragraph, for example, develop it mainly by giving *reasons* for the reluctance of many qualified men to run for office. But they also include details giving a specific *example* of the sort of vote-getting tactics these men resent.

It also goes without saying that many qualified men are reluctant to run for mayor or for any other elective office. They realize that the term of a mayor is short-lived, and even if they make good records in office, the best of them are soon retired from public life. Then too the able man is often compelled to run against an opponent whose code of ethics permits him to use sound trucks, jazz bands, and other forms of exhibitionism to win. In one of his campaigns for mayor of Chicago, "Big Bill" Thompson appeared on a platform with two caged rats. He characterized these animals as his two opponents. He carried on a conversation in which he belittled them, being careful, however, to exhibit himself in a favorable light. His audience howled approval, his exhibitions made the headlines of the papers, and the people elected him to office. Such opponents know mass psychology and they are able vote-getters. But instead of debating issues, they indulge in personalities. Capable men resent such tactics, nor will they stoop to practice them. Their services can command higher salaries in the business world, where they will also have more peace of mind. They are reluctant to give up security for political uncertainty. The result is that mediocrity too frequently reigns at the city hall.— Theodore P. Blaich and Joseph C. Baumgartner, *The Challenge of Democracy.* Copyright 1956 by McGraw-Hill Book Company, Inc., New York.

Exercise 1   Read the following paragraphs carefully. Then write on a sheet of paper (1) the topic idea of each paragraph and (2) the method of development used in each (that is, tell whether the details enumerate steps, point out similarities and/or differences, tell an incident, give examples, reasons, or causes and effects). You may decide that more than one method is used in a single paragraph.

A   As the war progressed, the jeep's versatility seemed endless. Fitted out with stretchers, it became a front-line ambulance. A jeep plus a radio was a mobile command post. Jeeps hauled planes to dispersal bunkers. Soldiers raced them uphill, as in a famous cartoon by Bill Mauldin, to get hot radiator water for shaving. In the Philippines a jeep equipped with flanged wheels pulled a fifty-two-ton railroad supply train for nineteen miles at twenty miles an hour. When Patton's armored divisions raced across France, the lead vehicle, out in front of the foremost tanks, was often as not a jeep.—Dickson Hartwell, "The Mighty Jeep," *American Heritage,* December 1960.

B   Upon reflection, one feels more and more the hollowness of some of the pieces of advice grown people are fond of giving beginners, such as "Know your subject," "Write out of a full mind," and "Write just as you think." It is often just because the mind is full of one's subject that the first easy composition needs the later laborious correction. For the full mind is always running off at tangents, lugging in nonessential stuff, expatiating, and suggesting extraneous footnotes and addenda. Nor is it any safer to write just as you think *and stop with that,* for the mind is like a spirited horse, which will take the bit at any moment and go racing off cross-lots, to the detriment of both logic and restraint.—Robert M. Gay, *Reading and Writing.* Published by Little, Brown and Company, Boston. Copyright 1935 by Robert M. Gay.

C   The Bostonian group of Motley, Prescott, and Parkman was homogeneous in many ways. All three men were educated at Harvard, all were wealthy, and all kept themselves aloof from the changing industrial society of a contemporary America with its rising tide of democratic politics. As gentlemen, as amateurs, they devoted their lives to the writing of narrative history. Motley went to Europe for his subject matter; Prescott followed the Spaniards to the New World; Parkman found his destiny in the American forest. Wealth combined with hard work to unearth the documents, and writing could then begin. Each of them followed the contemporary European method of writing history. Their themes had a unity, at once dramatic and romantic, that centered on leading personages. The arrangement of the facts was intentionally dramatized to capture the imagination and sympathy of the reader. For them, as for Carlyle, history was "heroic."....—"Rival Approaches to History: Gentlemen versus Players," *American Writing Today,* edited by Allan Angoff. Copyright 1957 by New York University Press.

D   Rivers may be regarded as the destroyers of lakes. Those rivers that discharge their waters into lakes commonly carry a burden of sediment, mostly silt. The still waters of a lake check the flow of the incoming streams, and the major load of sediment is dropped near the inlet, but some of the silt is more widely distributed over the lake bottom. Gradually the lake becomes shallower, until it is finally filled. In just this way many lakes that existed during and after the last glacial epoch

have been silted up and have now completely disappeared.—
George T. Renner and Associates, *Global Geography.* Copyright 1944 by Thomas Y. Crowell Company, New York.

E   Today, only murder and a few other serious offenses are punishable by death; in medieval times many crimes were capital crimes. Courts might order death by burning at the stake. For a lesser punishment than death, courts might order a condemned person's legs, nose, or hands cut off, or his scalp removed. Imprisonment was less common than it is in modern times. Condemned men were often sent to a lifetime of service as galley slaves. Humanitarian justice as we know it today was unheard of.—William Habberton and Lawrence V. Roth, *Man's Achievements Through the Ages.* Copyright 1956 by Laidlaw Brothers, Inc., River Forest, Illinois.

Exercise **2**   In a current nonfiction book or article (from such a magazine as *Holiday, Natural History, The Saturday Evening Post, Fortune, Scientific American, Harper's,* or *The Atlantic*), find two paragraphs that use details in different ways to develop the topics. Copy (or, if the magazine is yours, clip and mount) each of the paragraphs on a sheet of paper. At the end of each paragraph, give the source. [For a book: the author, the title, and the page. For a magazine: the author, the title of the article, the name and date of the magazine, and the page.] Then write, in sentences, answers to the following questions. You may be asked to read one of your paragraphs to the class and to discuss your answers to the questions with your classmates.

1 What is the topic idea of the paragraph?
2 What method of development is used in the paragraph?
3 How effectively is the topic developed? For example, are the details in the paragraph specific enough to make the writer's ideas about the topic meaningful? Has the writer provided enough details to give the reader who knows little or nothing about the topic an adequately clear picture of it?

Exercise **3**   Be ready to discuss in class the method of development you think would be most effective in writing a paragraph on each of the following topics. (Would you supply details that give examples, tell an incident, state reasons, point out similarities and/or differences, enumerate steps or parts, or give causes and effects? Or would you use a combination of any of these?) Be ready also to suggest specific details that might be used in each paragraph.

1 Yes, I've seen the movie, but I still prefer the book.
2 The heroes of many Westerns have much in common with Robin Hood.
3 Don't tell me that the truth "never hurts anyone."
4 If frankness is a virtue, it's a dangerous one.

5   Home isn't home any more, now that Mother is on a diet.
6   Preparing for a final examination takes a whole semester.
7   Heaven, too, must be "paved with good intentions."
8   An income tax is more equitable than a property tax.
9   It takes know-how to pack groceries for supermarket customers.
10 Our mailman has a new motto: "Caveat Rover."

Exercise 4   Choose one of the topics listed in Exercise 3 and develop it into a paragraph of from 150 to 200 words. (If none of the topics interests you, use one of your own, perhaps one suggested by those in the list.)

Exercise 5   Prepare (for class discussion) a list of specific details that might be used in developing each of the following topics. (One is a quotation.) During the discussion, take notes on the various details suggested. After all the topics have been discussed, choose one to develop into a paragraph of 150 to 200 words. In your paragraph, you may want to restate the topic in your own words. Feel free to use details suggested by others as well as your own.

1   Our school has its own set of status symbols.
2   Hobbies do not have to make money to be profitable.
3   I would like to join the Peace Corps.
4   Mrs. Malaprop has a host of modern counterparts.
5   There are no distant points in the world any longer.—Wendell L. Willkie, *One World*.

Exercise 6   Follow the directions given for Exercise 5.

1   Cheating may pay, but is it worth the price?
2   What a wealth of meaning can be packed into a few words by making use of literary allusions. [For example: "tilting at windmills," "Achilles' heel."]
3   Should scholarships be awarded to students who do not need financial help to go to college?
4   A house is infinitely communicative and tells many things besides the figure of its master's income.—Robert William Chapman, *The Portrait of a Scholar*.
5   Words may varnish facts; they cannot alter them.—H. J. Smith, *Mrs. Bumpstead-Leigh*.

UNITY IN PARAGRAPHS

A certain TV comedian used to introduce a topic and then tell a string of jokes, each taking him farther and farther away from the idea he started with. Finally, when he did want to get back to the original topic, he would say, "But I digress," and then wait for the laugh that inevitably followed. One reason this remark struck people as funny, of course, was that no one really cared whether the comedian stuck to the topic or not. All his audience expected or wanted was to be amused.

Unlike the comedian's audience, a writer's audience does expect him to stick to the topic he introduces. If, for example, the topic of the third paragraph of a paper on hurricanes is the havoc they create, readers will expect the whole paragraph to develop this one central idea—the terrible destructiveness of these tropical storms. Then, if the paragraph suddenly veers away from hurricanes and goes off into details about another topic—the enormous waste caused by forest fires, for instance—readers will be justifiably annoyed and perhaps confused. The writer, by introducing this irrelevant topic, has destroyed the **unity** of the paragraph and lessened its effectiveness.

The first step to take in achieving unity in the paragraphs you write is to plan your paper carefully before the actual writing. Once you have decided on the topics you will present and have firmly in mind the various details to use in developing each topic, you will be less likely to get sidetracked, as you write, by an associated, but irrelevant, idea.

Topic Sentences

The second step in achieving unity in your paragraphs is to make frequent use of topic sentences. A **topic sentence** is a statement, in general terms, of the central idea of a paragraph. Expressing this central idea in words will clarify your own understanding of the idea and so will help you make it clear to your reader. Besides, with a topic sentence to use as a guide, you will find it easier to recognize and discard any irrelevant details that may come to mind as you are writing the paragraph.

Topic sentences are helpful guides for the reader also, since they indicate, clearly and concisely, the various topics discussed in a paper. A topic sentence at the beginning of a paragraph is especially useful, for it immediately focuses the reader's attention on the central idea to be developed:

> *Most of our knowledge, acquired from parents, friends, schools, newspapers, books, conversation, speeches, and radio, is received verbally.* All our knowledge of history, for example, comes to us only in words. The only proof we have that the Battle of Waterloo ever took place is that we have had reports to that effect. These reports are not given us by people who saw it happen, but are based on other reports: reports of reports of reports, which go back ultimately to the first-hand reports given by people who did see it happening. It is through reports, then, and through reports of reports, that we receive most knowledge: about government, about what is happen-

ing in China, about what picture is showing at the downtown theater—in fact, about anything which we do not know through direct experience.—S. I. Hayakawa, *Language in Thought and Action.* Copyright 1939, 1940 by S. I. Hayakawa. Copyright 1941, 1949 by Harcourt, Brace & World, Inc., New York.

Sometimes, instead of one sentence, two or more sentences are used to state the central idea of a paragraph:

I have left to the last what is the sharpest difference of all between our two systems [of education]. *This is our system of specialization, in which England is, I think, unique in the world.* A student will take the examination for the Ordinary Level of the General Certificate of Education at the age of fifteen or sixteen in a wide range of subjects drawn both from the humanities and from the natural sciences. But once he has passed that examination, he will specialize. That is to say, he will devote two thirds, or perhaps even more, of his time in school to a narrow range of subjects. In one boy's case it may be physics, chemistry, and mathematics; in another's it may be chemistry and biology, or it may be history or modern languages and literature, or classical languages and philosophy. But, whatever the choice, the greater part of the pupil's attention, in the classroom and in his private study time, is given to his specialty, and he will take the advanced level examination at eighteen in his special subjects only. When he gets to the university, the specialization is even more intense. The range of subjects does not usually get any narrower, but the student gives 100 per cent of his time to it.—Sir Geoffrey Crowther, "English and American Education; Depth versus Breadth," *The Atlantic,* April 1960.

43

Not all topic sentences come at or near the beginnings of paragraphs. You may sometimes decide that a general statement of the topic will be most helpful to readers at the end, where it can summarize the idea developed in the preceding sentences, as in the following paragraph:

The manufacture of the automobile, without which we could not carry on our present economic and social life, requires materials from eighteen different countries. The operation of our beauty shops depends upon securing products from seventeen countries. Clothing manufacturers require materials from twenty-one different countries. The radio, which holds a very important place in American industry and in the American home, is dependent upon eighteen items from countries outside the United States. The industry that provides us with our stationery supplies draws upon twenty-four different countries. Fifteen different outside resources are used in the manufacture of our telephones. *Obviously then, for some of our most basic supplies, we are dependent on others.*—Nelson L. Bossing and Robert R. Martin, *Solving Our Problems in a Democracy.* Copyright 1956 by Laidlaw Brothers, Inc., River Forest, Illinois.

Occasionally, you will find it effective to begin a paragraph with a general statement of the topic and then restate it in a final ("clincher") sentence that drives home the main point. For example:

> *One really surprising fact in the story of the cowboy is that he existed for so short a time.* He was a product of a day when the grazing range of the West was open and free for the use of all, a day when the cattle of many outfits ran together over the hilly miles of sweet grass. The cattle industry did not begin to develop until well after the Civil War, when the steel fingers of the railroads probed the lonely stretches of the Middle West, making Eastern markets accessible. And by the turn of the century the free range had been fenced and controlled. *Thus the cowboy of legend—the "American Cavalier"—strutted the dusty stage of Western history for only about three decades, roughly from 1870 to 1900.*—"The Cowboy Nobody Knows," *Aramco World,* January 1960.

In a paper in which each phase of the subject is discussed at length, a writer often uses a single sentence to state a topic that he then develops in two (or more) paragraphs. This topic sentence is usually placed at or near the beginning of the first paragraph:

> *The ultimate objectives of scientific research are twofold.* There is, first, the cultural need of extending the boundaries of all knowledge. Science is an intellectual adventure which is just as important to modern life as literature or art. "The scientist," wrote Henri Poincaré, the eminent French mathematician, "does not study nature simply because it is useful. He studies it because he delights in it, and he delights in it because it is beautiful."
>
> Secondly, scientific knowledge is useful. It can be used to build a better world. Scientific discoveries and inventions have already greatly increased the life expectancy of our people. Three hundred and fifty years ago, the life expectancy of a newborn babe was only twenty years. One hundred years ago it was thirty-five. At the turn of the present century it had reached forty-nine, and today when a baby girl is born in the United States she has a good chance of enjoying almost seventy-four years of life (67.3 years for a baby boy). Medical advance has made possible the wiping out of such earlier scourges as smallpox, yellow fever, polio, malaria, and tuberculosis.—Bernard Jaffe, *Men of Science in America.* Published by Simon and Schuster, Inc., New York. Copyright © 1944, 1958 by Bernard Jaffe.

Since these paragraphs develop a single topic—the two ultimate objectives of scientific research—they could, of course, have been written as one. But a careful reading suggests reasons for the writer's using two paragraphs. First, a single paragraph would have been rather long. And a very long paragraph, besides looking a bit forbidding, tends to be somewhat difficult to read and digest. Second, and more important, by presenting the two objectives in separate paragraphs, the writer can more effectively emphasize the distinction between them. (A convenient term for two or more paragraphs that develop a single topic is **super-paragraph**.)

Many paragraphs do not need a topic sentence; the central idea is unmistakable without its being expressed in words. For example:

> Of those who drop out of college, some leave for financial reasons, and this is often tragic because these people in many cases do well in college before they have to leave. Some leave because of poor health. A few are drafted. Many leave for "personal" reasons—marriage, family mixups, or just the realization that college is not the place for them.—Robert U. Jameson, "How to Stay in College," *The Saturday Evening Post*, October 2, 1954.

Since every sentence in this paragraph helps convey one central idea (various reasons why students leave college), a topic sentence would have been superfluous.

A final word: Useful as topic sentences are to both writers and readers, remember that merely having a topic sentence in a paragraph does not in itself guarantee unity. Unity means *oneness*. You will have a unified paragraph only if all the sentences stick to *one* topic, if all help to develop *one* central idea.

Exercise 7   Each of the following paragraphs contains an irrelevant sentence that was not part of the original. Read each paragraph carefully and then copy on a sheet of paper (1) the topic sentence that tells what the paragraph is about and (2) the sentence that does not belong in the paragraph because it is not related to the topic.

A   The type of person attracted to lawn sports varies from game to game. A man making his way up the executive ladder will perforce be a golfer, while a junior clerk is satisfied with volleyball. A farmer is at home throwing horseshoes, but he may be ill at ease on a golf course. Movie stars swim; and curates, writers, and editors play croquet. Lewis Carroll must have been familiar with this game, for one of the funniest episodes in *Alice's Adventures in Wonderland* is Alice's weird croquet match with the Red Queen. Among kings, Gustav of Sweden was better known for his backhand than for his royal decrees.—David Dempsey, "Your Private Playground," *Holiday*, September 1959. Reprinted by special permission from *Holiday*. © 1959 by The Curtis Publishing Company, Philadelphia.

B   Delivery of supplies for the DEW [Distant Early Warning] Line has been a major problem ever since these multiple radars were established in the 1950's to warn the North American continent of aerial attack. The stations spread from the low arctic coast of Alaska to Greenland at intervals of about 100 miles, with small relay points between; and every plank, electronic device, gallon of fuel, and can opener must be brought to them. Planes, tractor trains, and ships were used in building the DEW Line, the work proceeding in winter at sixty below, and in summer among swarms of mosquitoes. Many people think there are few of these insects in Alaska because of the extremely cold winters, but anyone who has spent a summer in the marshy arctic lands can testify to the existence of large and voracious swarms of the pests. In winter the shallow, frozen sea pushes 100-foot ridges of pressure ice against the shore; in summer the swampy tundra is impassable. Makeshift airfields permit delivery of fresh food and mail most of the year, but the small planes able to use them cannot carry significant weights of steel or oil. Tractor trains inching over the frozen tundra are slow and expensive. Thus, for resupply, the Air Force personnel, Canadians, and United States civilians who occupy the five-to-fifty-man posts must depend on sealifts in summer.—William L. Worden, "The Ice Is Their Enemy," *The Saturday Evening Post*, January 28, 1961. © by The Curtis Publishing Company, Philadelphia.

C   The feat [Lindbergh's planned nonstop flight from New York to Paris in a one-engine plane] was impossible, many said. Perhaps someday it would be done, but not in 1927, when the aerodynamics of long-distance flying were yet in a primitive state. They pointed to the one, pitifully small engine, the difficulties of aerial navigation over the trackless ocean, the fact that Lindbergh was alone and would get no rest. They pointed to the four men already dead, and three injured, in similar attempts, and to the fact that less than two weeks before, two Frenchmen had been lost without a trace while trying to accomplish the flight in reverse, from Paris to New York. Even Lloyd's of London refused to quote odds on the chances for success. Actually, the first nonstop transatlantic flight had been made eight years earlier, but by two men flying only about half the distance that Lindbergh planned to fly alone. The newspapers called the young pilot a "daring youth," and a "flyin' fool."—"The Long, Lonely Flight," *Aramco World*, May 1960.

D   Because man had so good a brain, he evolved in the way he did. Other creatures had been able to kill only animals smaller or weaker than themselves. But, as he evolved over thousands of years, man's brain helped him to make tools and weapons with which he could kill even those animals that were larger and stronger than he was. Although prehistoric man probably killed only to get food or to defend himself, men today go hunting and fishing mainly for sport. By using his brain he slowly learned to plant crops to increase his food supply, and to make clothes and shelters that protected him from weather that might otherwise have caused his death. Of course his brain also enabled him eventually to construct a language, and to put it into written, or permanent, form. When he could write down the things he knew and descriptions of the world about him, he was able to preserve what he had learned for those who came after him. In this way each generation could know more than did the one before, and man could develop more rapidly than other creatures, which were able to learn only from their own experience.—Sam and Beryl Epstein, *Prehistoric Animals.* Copyright © 1956 by Franklin Watts, Inc., New York.

E   What oceanographers are finding out today promises much more, in terms of human welfare, than the exploration of outer space. The oceans may, indeed, hold the keys to the survival of mankind. They can yield food aplenty for a world population that threatens to triple within the next century. They may provide a safe dumping ground for the deadly wastes of the atomic age. Disposal of this radioactive garbage is a major problem; the U.S. has spent many millions to build huge, concrete-encased underground steel tanks to hold high-energy waste material from nuclear reactors at Oak Ridge, Los Alamos, and Richland. It may even be possible for man to manipulate the climate by triggering subtle changes in the circulation of the water.—George A. W. Boehm, "The Exploration of 'Inner Space,'" *Fortune,* November 1959.

Exercise 8   The lettered items in each of the following groups are specific details about a single topic. Read the details in each group carefully. Then decide which of the three sentences following the details would be the best to use as the topic sentence of a paragraph developed by the details. Write the sentences on a sheet of paper, numbering each with the number of its group. Be ready to explain your choices in class.

1 a) Colonial schools operated only two or three months a year.
   b) Only boys attended colonial schools.
   c) Schools had few books and little other equipment.
   d) Teachers sometimes poorly educated.
   The sentence that best expresses the topic is:
   Education has improved a great deal since the eighteenth century.
   American colonists neglected their children's education.
   By modern standards, colonial schools were poor.

2 a) Licorice extract is added to tobacco in cigars and cigarettes to retain moisture and to give a mild taste.

b) Also used in treatment of some physical disorders, such as stomach ulcers and certain kinds of anemia.

c) By-products of licorice used in making fire-fighting foam.

d) Licorice-root fibers used in manufacture of boxboard and insulation board.

The sentence that best expresses the topic is:

Scientists have found many new uses for licorice and other plants.

Although licorice is probably best known as a candy flavoring, it has other important uses.

Herbs like licorice are very useful in industry.

3 a) Green country boys joined whaling crews to find adventure.

b) For some men, whaling provided the only available jobs.

c) Chance of slightly higher pay attracted poor Portuguese fishermen.

d) Officers, especially the captain, could make a great deal of money from one successful voyage.

e) Despite hard work and generally low pay, some seamen liked whaling.

The sentence that best expresses the topic is:

Men might become whalers for one of several reasons.

Except for the officers, the crews of most whaling ships were composed of inexperienced men.

Many different kinds of seamen signed up for whaling voyages.

4 a) Veins carry blood from all parts of body except lungs to right side of heart.

b) Other veins carry blood from lungs to left side of heart.

c) Blood next moves from auricles (receiving chambers) to ventricles (pumping chambers).

d) Heart muscles contract.

e) Blood in right ventricle thereby forced into pulmonary artery and carried to lungs.

f) Blood in left ventricle forced into aorta, a large artery, and carried to other parts of body.

g) Heart muscles relax.

The sentence that best expresses the topic is:

The heart pumps blood at an amazing rate of speed.

The human heart is a remarkable organ.

The pumping action of the heart helps circulate blood through the body.

5 a) Some workers must handle poisonous materials, such as the white lead used in paint manufacturing.

b) Others are exposed to noxious gases or fumes, as in the production of chemicals.

c) Health of foundry workers and others imperiled by sudden and great changes in temperature.

d) Miners, underwater construction workers, and others run risk of injury or death from sudden changes in air pressure.

The sentence that best expresses the topic is:

Workers in dangerous occupations should be better protected.

The workers in some occupations face great dangers to their health and safety.

Safety rules and devices are important to the well-being of workers.

6 a) Some family names describe a physical characteristic of the original bearer: Stout, Long, Whitehead, Bellini (pretty), Malenkov (little), Borodin (bearded), Poincaré (square fist).

b) Other names describe a character trait of the first bearer: Gutmann (good man), Lesage (wise), Gorky (bitter), Cortés (polite), Baruch (blessed), Blunt, Moody, Proud.

c) Still others suggest a similarity between the original bearer and some animal: Lyon, Beaver, Wolfe, Fox, Crabbe, Baer (bear), Pecora (sheep).

The sentence that best expresses the topic is:

Many family names are derived from the personal characteristics of the original bearers.

A man's last name tells what kind of people his ancestors were.

Names reveal a great deal about the people who own them.

CONTINUITY IN PARAGRAPHS

As any successful cook will agree, producing a good cake depends not only on using the right ingredients, but also on putting those ingredients together properly. So too with paragraphs. Concrete details are the basic ingredients of most effective paragraphs. But just listing a number of specific, relevant details will not necessarily lead a reader to view a topic as you want him to. You have to present the details in such a way that the reader will see the same relationships between them that you do.

In other words, in addition to adequate development and unity, an effective paragraph has **continuity**, or coherence: the relationship between details is clear. The thought moves smoothly from sentence to sentence, leading the reader straight to the point intended.

Continuity Through Order

Continuity is achieved primarily by arranging details in a sensible, reasonable order. The topic and the kind of development used in a particular paragraph generally suggest the best order for the details.

Chronological order.   The most sensible order for the details in a paragraph explaining how to make or do something (how to make artificial ice, for example, or how to paint a car) is obvious. The reader will find the steps in a process clearest and easiest to follow if they are given in the order in which they are to be done— in a chronological, or time, order.

A chronological order is also the best for narrative details. By giving the details in the order in which they took place, telling first what happened first, second what happened second, what third, what next, and so on, you help the reader see an event almost as clearly as he would have seen it had he been present.

Spatial order.   Details presenting a rather factual description are usually clearest in a spatial order. For instance, you might give descriptive details about a building or a historical monument in an order moving from far to near; that is, in the order they would strike a viewer's eye as he approached the site and came closer. Details meant to give the reader an idea of the appearance of a movie set might be presented as they would be seen looking from left to right, or right to left. For descriptive details about a person, one arrangement might be a rather general movement from head to foot, as here:

> He was a tall, thin old man with a bald head, which shone pinkishly dirty, and a grizzled beard so long he could tuck it in his belt. He was over sixty, to judge by his hard, seamed face, but there was no sag of age to his body. He was lank and ungainly, but, even with his wooden peg, he moved as swiftly as a snake.—Margaret Mitchell, *Gone With the Wind.* Copyright 1936 by The Macmillan Company, New York.

Usually more than one arrangement is possible. Choose the order you think will be most effective in helping the reader form the picture you would like him to form of a particular person, place, or thing.

Logical order.   The details in many expository paragraphs, of course, have neither a chronological nor a spatial relationship. Yet to be sure that the thought in a paragraph will be clear and move in a straight line, a good writer arranges the details in some sort of "logical" order. It is not by chance that he puts detail *c* before detail *d* but after detail *b*; he always has a specific reason for ordering his details as he does.

For example, in arranging details for a paragraph on four hazards faced by deep-sea divers, you might decide that, since the squeeze and ballooning are hazards only for suit-and-helmet divers, you will give details about these hazards first. Then you could end with details about nitrogen narcosis and the bends, which are hazards for all divers, whatever their equipment. In a paragraph developed by details giving reasons, you might start with what you think is your least convincing and end with your most convincing reason. Similarly, details giving specific examples might be arranged in an order of interest or of drama, moving from the least interesting or dramatic to the most interesting or dramatic. In still other paragraphs, the order of the details might be one of increasing difficulty; detail *a* would be presented first because it helps to clarify detail *b*, which, with detail *a*, contributes to a more ready understanding of detail *c*, and so on.

Continuity Through Sentence Links

Essential though it is, the arrangement of details in an orderly progression does not, by itself, ensure coherence in a paragraph. The sentences in the paragraph must also be so closely knit that the reader can easily follow the line of thought from one sentence to the next. By tying sentences together with sentence links, a good writer prevents his readers from encountering any sudden or distracting gaps in the thought.

Direct links. Read the following sentences twice, the second time omitting the italicized word:

> John really enjoyed the life of a merchant seaman. *Nevertheless,* all during the trip to Murmansk and back he complained constantly and vowed he was never going to sea again.

Notice what a difference the italicized word makes. Without it, a reader would certainly be puzzled, at least momentarily, by the connection between John's enjoying the life of a merchant seaman and his complaining and vowing never to go to sea again. But when the word *Nevertheless* is inserted, it is immediately clear that the writer intends the idea expressed in the second sentence to contrast with the one expressed in the first. As you can see, one good way to show the relationship between two sentences and to bridge any gap in thought between them is to tie them together with a direct linking word like *Nevertheless.*

Other direct linking words and expressions can be used to tie sentences presenting contrasting ideas. For example:

But ...	On the other hand ...
Yet ...	However ...
Still ...	In spite of ...

Sometimes pairs of links are useful to emphasize a contrast between two sentence ideas:

At first ... Later ...
In spring ... In fall ...
As a child ... As an adult ...

When one sentence states a cause and the next states its result or effect, the relationship can best be shown by beginning the second sentence with a linking word or expression like:

Therefore . . .	So . . .
Consequently . . .	As a result . . .
For this reason . . .	Because of this . . .

And in paragraphs that include details giving reasons or examples, direct links like the following can be used:

For example . . .	In addition . . .
Another time . . .	For one thing . . .
To begin with . . .	In the second place . . .
Furthermore . . .	Finally . . .

In a narrative or an explanation of a process, in which it is extremely important for the time relationship of the details to be clear and easy to follow, sentences generally need to be linked with adverbial expressions like these:

First . . .	Before the bell rang . . .
The second step . . .	At noon . . .
Afterward . . .	After a while . . .
Meanwhile . . .	In the next act . . .

Similarly, in descriptive paragraphs, the most necessary links are those showing spatial relationships. For example:

Below . . .	To the right of the barn . . .
Outside . . .	Around the corner . . .
Directly ahead . . .	Near the foot of the cliff . . .

Indirect links. In addition to direct links, there are other effective ways of tying sentences together: using pronouns that refer to nouns in preceding sentences, repeating key words or phrases, and using synonyms that "echo" important words in previous sentences. In the following paragraph, for example, Arnold Bennett uses only two direct linking words—*And* and *Nevertheless*. Yet notice how the italicized "indirect" links help hold the ideas together:

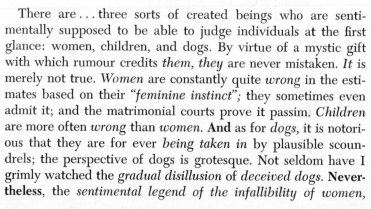

There are . . . three sorts of created beings who are sentimentally supposed to be able to judge individuals at the first glance: women, children, and dogs. By virtue of a mystic gift with which rumour credits *them, they* are never mistaken. *It* is merely not true. *Women* are constantly quite *wrong* in the estimates based on their *"feminine instinct"*; they sometimes even admit it; and the matrimonial courts prove it passim. *Children* are more often *wrong* than *women*. **And** as for *dogs*, it is notorious that they are for ever *being taken in* by plausible scoundrels; the perspective of dogs is grotesque. Not seldom have I grimly watched the *gradual disillusion* of *deceived dogs*. **Nevertheless**, the *sentimental legend of the infallibility of women,*

children, and dogs will persist in Anglo-Saxon countries.— Arnold Bennett, *The Author's Craft*. Copyright 1914 by Double-day & Company, Inc., New York.

By the use of such pronouns as *them, they,* and *It;* such "echo" words as *feminine instinct, wrong, being taken in, gradual disillusion, sentimental legend,* and *infallibility;* and the repetition of the key words *women, children,* and *dogs,* Bennett leads the reader smoothly, sentence by sentence, to a clear understanding of the point he is making.

In the following paragraph, the writer uses *no* direct links. Yet by her skillful use of indirect links (key words and echo words, especially), she makes the relationship between sentences and the movement of thought from one sentence to the next unmistakably clear.

> One of the most extraordinarily widespread sounds of the undersea is the crackling, sizzling sound, like dry twigs burning or fat frying, heard near beds of the snapping shrimp. *This* is a small, round *shrimp,* about half an inch in diameter, with one very large claw which it uses to stun its prey. *The shrimp* are forever clicking the two joints of *this claw* together, and it is the thousands of *clicks* that collectively produce the *noise* known as *shrimp crackle.* No one had any idea *the little snapping shrimps* were so abundant or so widely distributed until *their signals* began to be picked up on hydrophones. *They have been heard* all over a broad band that extends around the world, between latitudes 35°N and 35°S, (for example, from Cape Hatteras to Buenos Aires) in *ocean waters* less than 30 fathoms deep.—Rachel L. Carson, *The Sea Around Us.* Published by Oxford University Press, New York. Copyright 1950, 1951 by Rachel L. Carson.

Wherever direct links are needed to bridge the gap in thought between two statements, be sure to use them. But guard against the overuse of such links; used unnecessarily, they will merely get in your reader's way. Take a cue from the last illustrative paragraph: by providing indirect links, you can tie sentences together simply and naturally.

Exercise 9   The sentences in the following paragraphs are in a scrambled order. By studying the relationships between sentence ideas and noting direct and indirect links, you should be able to arrive at the original order of the sentences. Copy each paragraph, putting the sentences in this order. Then circle in pencil the direct and indirect links that helped you determine the right order.

A   (1) A Lyceum was a voluntary organization supported by small membership fees and designed to promote "the improvement of its members in useful knowledge." (2) To their lecture platforms came the most eminent men of the day. (3) They provided libraries, small scientific museums, discussion groups, and lectures. (4) The various Lyceums formed a loose federation. (5) This was the Lyceum movement which began in Massachusetts. (6) The Jacksonian period saw the first large-scale effort to provide adult education.—Henry W. Bragdon and Samuel P. McCutchen, *History of a Free People*. Copyright © 1960 by The Macmillan Company, New York.

B   (1) Charities are worthy—some of them—but are they worth such abasement? (2) At the close of the banquet our guest arose and delivered himself of as monumental a series of banalities as it has ever been my ill fortune to hear. (3) I was never so pleased in my life as when he kicked us all downstairs, and never gave a penny. (4) Backslapping may not always be for business reasons, but it is usually for pecuniary reasons. (5) Finally we gave our guest a rousing vote of thanks for a most instructive evening. (6) In some dim way it restored my self-respect. (7) The basic idea of the dinner was to obtain money from him in order that a certain charity might make up its deficit. (8) When he seated himself, amid vast applause, we, the hosts, arose one by one, and respectfully asked questions and were grateful for answers that we knew to be absurd. (9) I recall participating in a dinner to a man who was as stupid as he was rich. (10) Later, because his publicity man had used my name, I wrote him a letter—a slimy, unctuous letter—recalling his brilliant address and the needs of the charity in question.—Stuart Chase, "The Luxury of Integrity," in *The Nemesis of American Business*. Published by The Macmillan Company, New York. Copyright by Stuart Chase.

C   (1) Only a few children filled the blank with "leg" and most of them were scored low in intelligence. (2) A limited vocabulary, it is true, restricts the range of our thinking. (3) But later it was learned that the expression "is to" was unfamiliar to these children. (4) And this may lead us, mistakenly, to think of people as being unintelligent merely because certain words are unfamiliar to them. (5) They would have said "goes with"; that is, a hand "goes with" an arm. (6) Language is ...indispensable to human thinking, but this does not mean that mental ability is the same as having a large vocabulary. (7) The children in an underprivileged neighborhood, for example, did very poorly in an intelligence test which contained questions such as this: "A hand is to an arm as a foot is to a _____." (8) And when "goes with" was substituted for "is to" in the same test, they did very well, and scored high in "intelligence."—Lionel Ruby, *The Art of Making Sense*. Published by J. B. Lippincott Company, Philadelphia. Copyright 1954 by Lionel Ruby.

D   (1) Wood is composed of long, springy fibers of cellulose banded together and stiffened by a durable and highly stable natural plastic called lignin. (2) Lignin is another story. (3) More than a century ago chemists conceived the ambition of separating [the] cellulose and lignin from each other and exploiting the virtues inherent in each. (4) Its great promise remains locked up in the natural structure of wood; it is a chemical enigma and a major industrial waste. (5) These desirable properties it owes in great measure to the two main substances that make up its peculiar structure. (6) With cellulose, chemists have had some success: in the form of paper, rayon, plastics, and explosives it is one of the most important commodities we owe to industrial organic chemistry. (7) Wood is a structural material unmatched in its strength, elasticity, lightness, and beauty.—F. F. Nord and Walter J. Schubert, "Lignin," *Scientific American*, October 1958.

E   (1) The replacement of skin, feathers, antlers, or fingernails is a kind of regeneration. (2) Salamanders also can regenerate a missing leg or tail. (3) The hasty sacrifice is repaired at leisure, for these animals can replace the lost parts by the process of regeneration. (4) While other animals, including man, cannot grow limbs at any stage, they exhibit the faculty of regeneration in less dramatic ways. (5) Indeed, the ability to regenerate is a fundamental property of living matter. (6) Trying to capture a lizard by the tail or a crab by its claw can be a frustrating experience. (7) The tail or the claw snaps off in the hand of the would-be captor, and the prey escapes. (8) Some animals, such as frogs, enjoy this advantage only in their younger days, and as adults must make one set of limbs last a lifetime.—Marcus Singer, "The Regeneration of Body Parts," *Scientific American*, October 1958.

Exercise 10   In a current nonfiction book or magazine, find a paragraph in which linking devices do an especially good job of tying sentences together. Copy (or clip and mount) the paragraph on a sheet of paper. At the end of the paragraph, give the source (following the instructions given in brackets in Exercise 2 on page 40). Then circle in pencil all direct and indirect links used in the paragraph. You may be asked to put your paragraph on the board so that the class can consider and discuss the linking devices used. If references are made in the paragraph to ideas presented in the preceding paragraph or paragraphs in the chapter or article, explain these references to the class before the discussion begins.

Exercise 11 Write a narrative paragraph, using as the opening or closing sentence one of the following (or a similar sentence of your own). Plan the paragraph before you write, deciding what specific details are needed to make the topic clear, and arranging them in a chronological order. Before handing the paragraph in, circle in pencil all direct and indirect linking devices used to tie the sentences.

1 Until last Saturday morning, I thought that bagging groceries in a supermarket was the dullest job in the world.
2 I am convinced that my father can read minds.
3 The magazine writer who claimed that a handmade gift would be inexpensive was not writing about mine.
4 To err is human; to correct someone too often is dangerous.
5 Never, never brag about anything to a younger brother.
6 My career as a basketball referee began and ended last night.
7 I still insist it wasn't my fault that I had to take my driver's test a second time.
8 Hearing only what you want to hear can lead to trouble.
9 Evidently no one told our neighbor's dog that he was man's best friend.
10 Only the brave should play the tuba.

Exercise **12** Write a descriptive paragraph, using as the topic sentence one of the following (or a similar sentence of your own). Be sure to use enough specific details and to arrange them in an order that will give the reader a clear picture of the person, place, or thing described.

Exchange paragraphs with a classmate. After reading his paragraph carefully, circle in pencil all direct links he has used to tie sentences together. If you find any spot where the movement of thought is interrupted or unclear, make a note of it at the bottom of the paragraph and, if you can, suggest a way the sentences might be rearranged or tied together. When your paragraph is returned, check the links circled and note any lack of continuity pointed out by your classmate.

1 The change was so great that I could hardly believe that I was in the Kerrys' basement.
2 The president of the bank might have stepped straight out of a newspaper cartoon.
3 Mother is ashamed to let guests see my little sister's favorite stuffed toy.
4 Bobby took one look at the motel room and said, "Home was never like this."
5 Grandmother has aged a great deal in the last year.
6 Nothing looks more desolate than an abandoned building.
7 The view from the top row in the stadium leaves much to be desired.
8 I could see immediately why my father never forgot the one-room school he had attended.
9 As the plane banked, we got a bird's-eye view of the city below.
10 The street, a short block between two busy thoroughfares, was dark and uninviting.

Exercise **13** A. Choose one of the following topics (or substitute one of your own) as the topic of a paragraph of from 150 to 250 words. As you plan and write the paragraph, keep in mind the questions listed in Part B of this exercise.

1   The consequences of procrastinating
2   How to enjoy a symphony
3   Problems involved in cross-continental moving
4   The numerous everyday words derived from American Indian tongues
5   Uses of public-opinion polls
6   Balancing idealism with practicality
7   How dust can help produce an explosion
8   The difference between a bull market and a bear market
9   Responsibilities of the small community newspaper
10   How the invention of the phonograph affected musical taste
11   What makes a baseball game exciting
12   Seven-digit telephone numbers—progress or confusion?
13   Difficulties of communication between scientist and layman
14   Annoying mannerisms of speech
15   The importance of privacy
16   The validity of first impressions

B. Exchange paragraphs with a classmate. Read his paragraph carefully. Then, on a separate sheet of paper, write in complete sentences the answers to the following questions. Return the paragraph, with your answers, to the owner.

Consider thoughtfully your classmate's answers to the questions about your paragraph. Discuss with him any criticisms you do not understand or that you disagree with. Hand in his answers with your paragraph.

1   Is the central idea of the paragraph stated in a topic sentence? If it is, what is the sentence? If it is not, what is the central idea of the paragraph? Would the paragraph be clearer if a topic sentence were provided?
2   Has the writer used enough details to make the topic clear? If you think the paragraph could be improved by the inclusion of additional details, tell what kind, and why.
3   Do all the sentences in the paragraph stick to the topic? Which, if any, do not? Reconsider any irrelevant sentence you have noted. In your opinion, is the thought in the sentence really irrelevant or has the way the writer stated it made it seem irrelevant?
4   Is the movement of thought in the paragraph clear and easy to follow? Do the sentences hold together? If not, point out any gaps in thought that need to be bridged. What direct and indirect links has the writer used to tie sentences together?
5   What other specific criticisms or suggestions for improvement can you make about the paragraph?

3   *Language and Thinking*

Every newspaper reader and television viewer today must know something of the outstanding powers of the electronic computer, or electronic brain, as it is popularly called. The last two Presidential elections probably brought computers to the screen in their most important TV role, predicting the election results; but the machines have also played a part in many other television shows. In newspapers and news magazines, headlines like the ones on the facing page are constantly catching your eye (even if you lack the interest to read the articles) to notify you of the latest achievements of these eccentrically named computers.

As you are probably aware, then, ENIAC, UNIVAC, LARC, OARAC, SCANDEX, ALWAC, MIDAC, STRETCH, and their cousins have in the last few years taken over a great number of man's jobs. (And as you can see from the headlines, they have had success in some of his games as well.) Not only are the machines famous for their lightning calculations, but that they have also handled such assignments as translating, devising names for new chemical products, composing music (both classical and tin-pan alley), and rating a person's ability to do a certain kind of work.

Nevertheless, experts agree that the human brain is superior to the electronic. Even regarded simply as a computing machine, the human brain is evidently far more efficient. It has been said that if it were possible to build a machine which could perform exactly like the human brain, that machine would have to be the size of a skyscraper and would need all the power of Niagara Falls to run it. Furthermore, the electronic brains cannot do what we call *creative* thinking. They can only follow exact, detailed instructions carefully prepared and translated into a special code by mathematical experts.

It seems unlikely, therefore, that the machines will ever get the upper hand of us, as they are shown doing in some science-fiction stories. But this is no reason to rest on our laurels. If we take an objective look at ourselves, we can all see room for improvement in our powers of thought. A study of some of the principles of semantics (the branch of linguistics that deals with such matters as the meanings of words and the relationship between language and thinking) will help us in making the improvement.

Language and thinking. "I know what I mean, but I just can't express it" is a common remark that indicates a confused picture of the relationship between language and thinking. No one knows exactly what that relationship is, but we do know enough to say that a truer picture of it is given by the semihumorous comment "How can I know what I think until I hear myself say it?" For our thinking is done primarily with words; it is doubtful whether we really "have" a thought until we can put it into words. Obviously, then, the better we understand how language works—what uses it serves, what effects words have on our attitudes and actions, in what ways words may cause misunderstanding—the better will be our ability to think.

THE USES OF LANGUAGE

Some of the knowledge each of us has acquired has come to us through first-hand experience. Anyone who has spent his summer vacations at a lakeside cottage, for example, has probably discovered for himself that, pleasant as it is to lie on the beach all day, a too-long exposure to the sun causes a painful burn. And anyone fortunate enough to have had a dog has probably learned, on his own, a great deal about the proper care and training of dogs.

Most of our knowledge, however, we have acquired at second hand, through the spoken or written words of people who have had the first-hand experiences and have reported their findings and observations. It is through these reports (and reports of reports) that we have come to know the greater part of what we do know about people, places, and events of the past and the present. It is through these reports that we get most of the information we make use of in our everyday living.

Interestingly enough, the very fact that language plays such a vitally important role in our acquiring knowledge may be at the bottom of a mistaken notion which many of us have: that the only function of language is to convey information and that everything we read and hear is intended only to provide us with more facts to add to our store of knowledge. The truth is that the informative function is only one of several that language has, and the giving of information is only one of the purposes for which people speak and write. Let's consider briefly the major uses and purposes of language.

To communicate information. A primary use of language is, of course, to give factual information about people and things:

> Al Barnes keeps his service station open until midnight.
> The Blue Line buses run every half hour on Sunday.
> Park Street is blocked off for repairs.
> Smallpox is a highly contagious disease.
> The bridge just north of town has been washed out.

The value of informative language needs little discussion; we can all readily think of dozens of situations in which statements like those shown above, for example, would be useful—perhaps even vital—to us. Indeed, the importance of the informative use of language can hardly be exaggerated: without it, scientific, social, and intellectual progress would be impossible. By using language that informs, human beings can pool their knowledge; one generation can learn from and build on the work of other generations. Because men can, and do, exchange information, they have been able to build homes, towns, cities; to organize churches, schools, governments, industries; to make new scientific discoveries; in short, to help one another live civilized lives.

To express feelings. If language could be used only to communicate factual information, this would probably be a very efficient world—but a dull and unhuman one. For we are more than "thinking machines," interested only in facts. We have feelings and attitudes about people and things—and a need to express these feelings, to share them with others. Part of the miracle of language is that it provides us the means to do so:

61

> Isn't it a beautiful day!
> Spinach? Ugh, that slimy old stuff!
> His roommate is dreamy—positively dreamy.

To affect the feelings of others. In using "expressive" language, we sometimes have a double purpose—not only to reveal our own feelings and attitudes but to affect those of our listeners, so that they will feel as we do about some person or thing:

> I just know that I would hate to have to deal with anyone as downright sneaky and mean as he.
> In fact, if I were a millionaire, I'd live in San Francisco—the most beautiful, friendly, and exciting city I've ever seen.

To influence the actions of others. A fourth major use of language is to influence the behavior of others, to get them to do what we want them to do. Sometimes we use words that make this "directive" purpose obvious:

> Turn off that TV, Sam, and get to work on your history report.
> Vote for Zernke, and put an end to Mayor Hilker's wasteful spending.

At other times, we use a less direct approach to get the action we want:

> I know you like Red Skelton, Sam, but isn't your history report due tomorrow?
> All intelligent voters fully realize the dangers of the fiscal irresponsibility shown by our present mayor.

Language does several jobs at one time.   Language, in actual use, is much more complex than the preceding classification makes it seem. Discussing separately the major uses of language suggests that each always exists in a pure, clearly distinct form—that every time a person speaks (or writes), he has only one purpose in mind and his words do only one thing: they inform, express feelings, arouse feelings, or influence the actions of others. But this is rarely the case. A speaker often has more than one purpose, though one may be uppermost in his mind; and his words usually do more than one job at the same time.

Consider, for example, this statement made by a student-council member at a meeting of the council:

> "As for that silly contest we sponsor every fall to choose a homecoming queen: it not only leads to jealousy, backbiting, and resentment; but, more important, it takes time away from what should be our main concern—our studies."

The speaker's words are intended to do several jobs. First, they are meant to inform her listeners of various drawbacks of the yearly contest. They clearly reveal her feeling of disapproval and are intended to arouse a similar feeling in her listeners. They are also intended to influence the actions of her listeners, to get them to vote against continuing the contest.

Sometimes (and this adds to the complexity of language) the words a speaker uses may have an effect that is not intended. A number of the student-council members, for example, might interpret the statement of the speaker as an attempt to impress them with a pretended interest in scholarship. Still other members might interpret her words as a symptom of sour grapes. And so, even though she was not actually trying to impress and was not prompted by sour grapes, her words would not influence these members to vote as she wanted them to.

Often the tone of voice of the speaker or the tone of his writing (friendly, amused, coaxing, sarcastic, pompous, patronizing, angry, etc.) is an important part of the communication, a clue to the real significance of his words. Take, for example, this statement:

> "*Gangsters at Large?* This is really a fine program for youngsters to watch."

If one considers only the literal meaning of the words, the statement would seem to be a fine recommendation. But the sneering, sarcastic tone that accompanied the words would indicate the real meaning—a condemnation of the program.

Since words can be doing several jobs at the same time, the main purpose for which they are used may not always be apparent. Yet unless we are aware of the main purpose behind particular statements, we may not grasp their full significance. As a result, we may find ourselves doing what a speaker or writer wants us to—without really understanding how it happened. The experience of Tom Sawyer's friends on the day that Aunt Polly ordered Tom to whitewash the fence is an excellent case in point. Tom, who disliked work, was quite ingenious, and soon hit on a way to get his friends to take over the job. Had they realized Tom's main purpose in telling them what fun it was to whitewash, what skill was needed to do the job right, and what a privilege it was, they would have run off in a hurry. But they gave no thought to Tom's real purpose in saying all these things—and so his "propaganda" worked; it got them to do what he wanted. His friends not only put three coats of whitewash on the fence, but paid Tom for the "privilege."

A Program for Self-Defense

It is not only in fiction, of course, that people are taken in by words; Tom Sawyer's friends have numberless counterparts in real life. All of us, in fact, can draw a moral from the fence-whitewashing story: unless we understand how language works, we (like Tom's friends) will unwittingly let words influence us in ways that do not serve our own best interests.

Before further discussion of this matter, one point must be clearly understood. All of the uses of language are important; all have a rightful place in our lives. There is nothing wrong with any of them, *in itself*. It is just as essential to us to use language to express our feelings and to influence the feelings and actions of others as it is to use language to convey information.

However, if we are to deal intelligently with language, we must be able to distinguish these uses. For our own protection, we must know, when we listen to others or read what they say, just what their words are doing *for us* and *to us*. To begin with, we must learn to recognize words that affect our feelings; for once our feelings are aroused, they may block our thinking at a time when clear thinking is necessary. Second, if we are to make intelligent decisions and reach sound conclusions to problems, we must learn how to assess the value and reliability of statements that we read and hear; for clear thinking is impossible without reliable data. Finally, we must learn to take into account the speaker's purpose, for the purpose has an important bearing on the significance of his words and the effects they have on us. The rest of this chapter will elaborate on these points.

Exercise 1 Read the following statements and be ready to discuss in class the purpose or purposes the statements serve and the effect or effects they would have (or might have) on listeners or readers. Which of the statements might have an effect or effects that the speaker or writer probably did not intend? Explain.

1 [Said by a police chief in an interview] "In fact, arrests for speeding have doubled here in the last six months."

2 [Overheard on a school bus] "No, that conceited show-off Dave Brougher was elected captain, worse luck."

3 [Said by a student to a disappointed friend on report-card day] "After all, good grades aren't everything! I just read an article which said that Winston Churchill used to get poor grades—and he certainly turned out OK."

4 [Said by a mother to her son at Saturday breakfast] "Tom, that front lawn of ours is getting to be an eyesore—or have you been too busy with your social life to notice the dandelions and other weeds?"

5 [In an advertisement] "Nine out of ten of the fashion models interviewed said they prefer *Marquise,* the face cream for lovely ladies."

6 [Said by the president of a service club to a member] "Our past experience has shown that the success of the charity project depends largely on the ability and drive of the chairman in charge. Frankly, Jim, I know of no one as well qualified as you to take over the job."

7 [From a newspaper article] "At present our colleges are not turning out nearly enough engineers, mathematicians, and physicists to meet the needs of industry and government."

8 [Overheard at an art gallery] "That mess is a great work of *art*? They must be joking. My kid brother could do better blindfolded!"

BE WARY OF LOADED WORDS

Why do perfume manufacturers so often give their products French names? Why do people who would scorn *third-class* accommodations on a ship gladly buy the same traveling space when it is labeled "tourist class"? What is there about words like "Salisbury steak" and "pâté de foie gras" that makes the foods they name seem so much more desirable than *ground-beef patty* and *goose-liver paste*? The answer to all these questions lies in the connotations of the words.

What connotations are. The basic meaning of a word, the person or thing it actually refers to, is its **denotation**. But in addition to this basic meaning, a word may have **connotations**—special shades of meaning suggested by or associated with the word. The noun *executive,* for example, denotes simply "a person whose function is to manage business affairs"; but to most people the word connotes overtones of importance, business acumen, and enviable social status.

The connotation is an important part of the "complete meaning" of many words—so important a part, in fact, that two words having the same denotation may communicate quite different ideas. For instance, although *youthful* and *puerile* have the same basic meaning, their differing connotations make *youthful* a term of approval and *puerile* a term of disapproval. The French *amour* means simply "love"; but for many English-speaking people, French words have a connotation of glamor that makes *L'Amour* a much more effective name for a perfume than its English equivalent.

Words get their connotations from our experiences with the words and with the persons or things they refer to. The word *quack,* for example, has unfavorable connotations for most of us, because nearly every time we have heard it, it has been used to refer to a doctor the speaker considers incompetent or fraudulent. The word *physician,* on the other hand, has favorable connotations for most of us, since we associate it with a person we can count on for help, comfort, and advice.

Since the connotations of words come from people's experiences, the connotations of a particular word may differ from one person to another. The word *snake,* for example, would probably have unpleasant connotations for a girl whose brother used to scare her by dangling a snake before her or hiding it in her empty lunch box. To her brother, a would-be biologist who had spent many interesting hours studying snakes, the word would recall pleasant experiences and therefore would have favorable connotations. To their parents, *snake* might be a "neutral" word, one that arouses in them no feelings one way or the other.

Loaded words. Our special concern here is words that have strong connotations for almost all people—words commonly referred to as **loaded.** Outstanding among loaded words are the names of certain minority groups (not the nicknames alone, but even the regular names). Through long use by people prejudiced against these groups, the names have acquired extremely strong connotations. In fact, people who are free from this prejudice often hesitate to use these names, for fear of appearing to insult the groups referred to.

The word *bureaucrat* is another good example. Its denotation is simply "an official of a government department." But to most people the word suggests an official overly ambitious for personal power, indifferent to the public's welfare and opinion, lacking in initiative, and tending to delay action with endless red tape. These unfavorable connotations are so strong that they take over, making it almost impossible for us to use the word for its denotative meaning alone.

Equally strong are the connotations of such loaded words as *radical, politician, shyster, reactionary, totalitarian, fascist,* and *leftist.*

Many words, of course, are loaded with favorable connotations: *patriot, liberty, peace, justice, science, democracy, underdog, loyalty.* Consider the word *American.* In its most common use, it denotes simply "a citizen of the United States." But how much more than that it connotes! And its connotations for us are so integral a part of the word as we use it that no reader of this book is likely to need a description of them.

Loaded words can be dangerous words; their danger lies in the fact that they are emotion-arousing words—and emotions are usually obstacles to clear thinking. Here is what often happens: When people hear such a word as *politician* or *un-American, patriot* or *American,* they tend to be affected emotionally by its connotations and to forget that it is only a word, a label. If someone speaks of an organization as "un-American," many of his listeners automatically react as though it is a subversive group, composed of scoundrels. And they react this way with no evidence whatsoever, simply as a result of the word's being used. If someone says that the organization or political party he represents is "100 per cent American," many of his listeners react automatically as though they know it is 100 per cent worthy of their support. And so, eager to foster a "worthy" group, they unthinkingly give it their support—which is exactly what the speaker had counted on their doing. Because their emotions have blocked their thinking, they do not even realize that they have let loaded words influence their actions and make their decisions for them.

Loaded words are extremely useful; effective speakers and writers, both scrupulous and unscrupulous, know that by using such words they can usually further their cause, whatever it may be. Because these words (for all their danger) are so useful, we cannot reasonably expect people to stop using them. But for our own protection, we must know how to handle them, how to keep them from tricking us into unwise actions and decisions.

In dealing with these words, we will find it helpful to keep in mind that words are *merely* symbols, symbols that stand for persons and things. If we keep this in mind, we will not be so likely to let an emotion-arousing word determine our reactions to the person or thing the word stands for. After all, a speaker's use of the word *politician* to refer to the opposition's candidate does not magically cause the candidate to be a person of questionable ethics; a speaker's use of the word *American* to describe his organization does not magically cause the organization to be worthy. *Politician* and *American* are simply words, words the speaker has very likely chosen because their connotations suit his purposes: to defeat the candidate, to gain support for his own organization.

Whether the candidate really deserves the disapproval implied by the connotations of *politician,* whether the organization actually merits the approval suggested by the connotations of *American*—these are matters that must be decided on other grounds. A thinking person arrives at such conclusions on the basis of adequate and accurate information. He does not let the feelings aroused by the connotations of words blind him to the need for evidence.

A word of warning is in order here lest the discussion above be interpreted as a wholesale condemnation of connotative words. An awareness of the power of loaded words is necessary for protecting ourselves against confusing labels with reality, against accepting connotations for evidence—*on occasions when evidence is needed.* But this does not mean that connotative words should be outlawed from our speech and writing.

Without connotative words, we could not easily express our feelings and attitudes toward the subjects we discuss. Many of our communications, therefore, would not only be coldly impersonal but *incomplete,* since our feelings and attitudes are an important part of the meaning we want to convey. Through a judicious use of connotative words, we can let others "see" things as we see them, we can so affect the emotions and imagination of others that they will fully share our experiences. Of course, in justice to our subjects and to ourselves, we should make sure that our feelings and attitudes are based (insofar as possible) on an unprejudiced observation of people and things as they actually are.

Exercise 2   A.   Each of the following statements contains a word or words whose connotations are strong enough to reveal—and arouse—a feeling of disapproval. Imagine a situation in which each of the statements might be used. Then rewrite the statement so that it could still be used in the same situation—but would be "neutral." [Example: "The Davidsons are highbrows and very stand-offish people" might be rewritten "The Davidsons, whose main interests are books and music, keep pretty much to themselves."]

1   Oh, don't expect Dave Spence to buy a ticket to that concert; he's a longhair, as you ought to know.
2   We asked the congressman for his views on the proposed sales tax, but he pussyfooted, as we had expected he would.
3   Those two shysters spent all morning haggling over the terms of the contract.
4   Why vote for Adams? He's in his dotage and ought to retire.
5   If your dad takes that job, you'll be moving to a jerkwater town and enrolling in a hick school.
6   Whenever I think of her, I think of junk jewelry, flashy shoes, and gaudy clothes.
7   Some slicker from a bush league out on the Coast high-pressured Sam into signing up with them.

B.   Be ready to discuss this question: What value is there in "translating" these connotative statements to neutral statements?

(To get your thinking started: Imagine yourself the person referred to in statement 4 or 6. Would you have a fair chance of being judged objectively by a stranger who had nothing but statement 4 or 6 to judge you by?)

Exercise 3   A.   Imagine that you are writing a story to submit for publication in a magazine for general readers. One of your main concerns is to describe the characters in a way that will lead the reader to share your feelings about them. Which of the terms in the following groups would be most effective to use in referring to characters you want readers to dislike? (List your answers on a sheet of paper.)

1   reserved, close-lipped, reticent
2   always observant, always kibitzing, always noticing
3   she mollycoddled her sons, she was an indulgent mother
4   a hard worker, a diligent worker, an eager beaver
5   his suave manner, his unctuous manner, his urbane manner
6   always agreeable, a yes-man, a prize toady
7   one of Latimer's henchmen, one of Latimer's staunch supporters
8   her sarcastic comments, her incisive remarks, her crisp epigrams

B.   Which of the terms in the following groups would be most effective to use in referring to characters that you want the reader to approve of?

1   a zealot, an enthusiast, a fanatic
2   masterful, domineering, arrogant
3   determined, obstinate, mulish
4   his prosy explanations, his humdrum explanations, his down-to-earth explanations
5   scholarly, schoolmarmish, pedantic
6   parsimonious, economical, stingy
7   hidebound, conservative, narrow-minded
8   these hooligans, these high-spirited youths, these vandals

Exercise 4   Divide the following words into three groups: (1) those that have favorable connotations for you, (2) those that have unfavorable connotations, and (3) those that are neutral. Compare lists in class to see how the majority classified the words. In instances where your lists differ from those of the majority, see if you can explain the probable reasons. (Clue: What experiences have you had that gave a particular word certain connotations that it does not have for most of your classmates?)

1 rebel (noun)	7 fireworks	13 New Orleans
2 Hawaii	8 research	14 old-fashioned
3 safari	9 factory	15 physics lab
4 Labor Day	10 conformist	16 mountain climbing
5 sorority	11 a VIP	17 income taxes
6 landlord	12 popularity	18 country school

Exercise 5 Be ready to discuss the following questions in class.

1 Why do some hotels and office buildings have a "twelfth" floor and a "fourteenth" floor but not a "thirteenth" floor? Does calling the thirteenth floor the "fourteenth" make that floor other than the thirteenth in the building? If you were to be manager of a new hotel or office building, what would you call the floor above the twelfth—the "thirteenth" or the "fourteenth"? Why? If you were to be a guest at a hotel, would you stay in Room 1313 on Floor 13? If not, why not?

2 As a child, you were probably taught to respond to the taunts of a playmate by retorting with this verse: "Sticks and stones will break my bones, / But names will never hurt me." Was the verse effective: did it silence the taunts? Did you, as a child, believe what you said—that names did not "hurt"? Do you *now* think that names cannot hurt one? Can you describe an incident (from your own experience or that of others) in which "names" did hurt? Was the hurt actually caused by the names—or by people's unthinking reaction to the names?

3 In Shakespeare's *Romeo and Juliet,* Juliet (who is lamenting the fact that Romeo bears a name that is bitterly hated by her family) says: "What's in a name? that which we call a rose / By any other name would smell as sweet." Do you agree with Juliet that names don't matter? Do you agree, for example, that an American Beauty would be as fragrant if it were called a "thornbloom" or a "pricklebloom"? Will all people agree? If so, can you explain why it is that so many people (in particular, stars of the stage, opera, screen, and ballet) have changed their names? What *is* in a name that Juliet's statement does not take into account?

4 Why is it important for speakers and writers to understand the power of connotations? Why is it important for listeners and readers?

Exercise 6 For the next day or two, be on the lookout for statements containing loaded words—in advertisements, in newspaper columns, in political speeches or debates, in discussions in history or social-science classes, in conversations with friends, in TV interview shows. Be ready to give a two-minute oral report on your findings. In your report you might touch on such points as these: Did the speaker or writer who used the loaded words seem to be using them *intentionally* to affect the feelings of his audience—or did he seem unaware of the fact that he was using loaded words? Did the speaker or writer present any evidence to justify his use of the loaded words —or did he seem to expect his audience to accept the loaded words and their connotations as "evidence"? In speech situations, how did the listeners react? Did they accept without question the loaded words; did they challenge the speaker to produce evidence; or did they retort with loaded words of their own? Did you catch yourself using loaded words? (Remember to make your report "concrete" by giving specific examples of the loaded words you found.)

DISTINGUISH BETWEEN FACTS AND OPINIONS

As mathematicians are well aware, the electronic brain cannot be expected to answer questions and solve problems if the material that is fed into it is incorrect or inadequate. The same is true of the human brain. It is important, therefore, that we know how to get the "right" material to use in our thinking. Though some of the material we might use will come from our own observation, most of it will come from our reading and listening. How can we determine whether the material we find is reliable, valid, and adequate? As a first step in answering this question, let's consider two kinds of statements.

Facts and opinions. "Let's get down to facts," we say, or "Stick to the facts," or "What are the facts of the case?" Our words suggest that we fully realize the importance of facts in reaching a decision or solving a problem. Yet despite this apparent respect for facts, many of us do not know how to recognize when we have a "fact." Sometimes when we appear to have one in our grasp, we have instead a judgment, a personal opinion.

Suppose that in gathering material for a paper on your local schools, you hear or read the following statements:

Lemont Junior High, designed for 500 students, now has an enrollment of 765.

Lemont students are getting an inferior education.

Though both of these statements provide "information," they are of quite different types. The first is what we will call a **statement-of-fact**; the second is a **statement of opinion**. Since the *type* of statement determines what tests to apply in evaluating the information, we must know the distinction between the two types.

Statements-of-Fact

Each of the following, like the sentence about Lemont Junior High's enrollment, is a *statement-of-fact*:

The staircases at Burton School are made of wood.
The staircases at Burton School are made of steel and concrete.

Carbon tetrachloride removes paint stains.
Carbon tetrachloride does not remove paint stains.

The telegraph was invented by an American, Samuel Morse.
An Italian, Guglielmo Marconi, invented the telegraph.

As you can see by comparing the examples in each pair, a statement-of-fact is not necessarily a true statement. It is, however, a statement whose truth or falsity can be proved. Because such statements deal only with "facts"—that is, with persons, places, objects, occurrences, or processes that actually exist or did exist—their truth or falsity can be established by objective means.

Checking facts.   Many statements-of-fact can be proved true or false by *personal observation* or by *experimentation*. Going directly to the Burton School, for instance, and examining its staircases would show which of the two statements about their construction is true—if, indeed, either is. And experimenting with carbon tetrachloride to see what effect it actually has on paint stains would determine which of the conflicting statements is an accurate report. We seldom do such experimenting ourselves (unless we are particularly interested in some matter or are "from Missouri"). There is no need to, for in most instances reliable reports of experiments done by others are readily available. A chemist in the neighborhood, for example, or a local dry cleaner could attest to the effectiveness of carbon tetrachloride as a paint-stain remover. Science books and encyclopedias are storehouses of such information.

To check the truth of statements-of-fact dealing with the past, we must, of course, *refer to the records,* to the reports of others. If the facts in question have to do with an event of the recent past, there are available—through newspapers, magazines, TV, and radio— many reports from trained, on-the-spot observers. If the facts are not recent, there are such sources as diaries, letters, newspaper files, biographies, histories, dictionaries, world almanacs, and encyclopedias to refer to. Documentary evidence that Morse, not Marconi, invented the telegraph could readily be found in many of these sources.

The two preceding paragraphs are not to suggest that you must personally check every statement-of-fact you read. This would not only be impossible but unnecessary. Most writers can be trusted to give information that checks with the facts. Writers who deliberately—or carelessly—present inaccurate information are few, and their inaccuracies do not go unnoticed for long. Whether to accept without question the statements-of-fact which you *hear* is another matter. Much depends on the person who makes the statements: Is he a competent observer? Is his memory reliable? Can you safely assume that he knows the facts?

Unnecessary as it is to verify *all* statements-of-fact, you should keep in mind that mistakes are possible, even from generally reliable sources. When you are gathering data to use in solving an important problem or in arriving at an important decision, then, it would be wise to check the "facts" before accepting them. Without accurate data, you are unlikely to get correct answers or reach valid conclusions.

Statements of Opinion

Here are four more statements that you might read or hear in gathering material for a paper on your local schools:

The classes at Fairfax Academy are limited to twenty students.

Fairfax Academy is the best high school in the state.
Every school ought to limit its classes to twenty students.
A diploma from Fairfax will ensure any student's acceptance at any Ivy League college.

All of these sentences, too, provide "information"; but again notice the difference in the *kind* of information they give. The person who made the first statement is simply presenting a report on the size of the Fairfax classes. His statement says nothing about what he thinks of the limited classes; it indicates neither his approval nor his disapproval. Because the statement is purely factual (a statement-of-fact), it can easily be proved either true or false.

The other statements, in contrast, are not purely factual. Whoever made the second statement is expressing his personal view of the academy's quality. Whoever made the third statement is telling what *in his opinion* every school should do. And the person who made the last statement is clearly revealing—through his rosy prediction—his judgment that Fairfax is a first-rate school.

Statements like these, all expressions of opinion, *cannot* be proved true or false. Not everyone will agree that Fairfax is the "best" in the state or that its diploma is an open sesame to any college. Nor will everyone agree that twenty students per class should be the limit. (Why not fifteen? Why not twenty-five?) Complete agreement on these points cannot be reached, because there are no universally accepted standards by which to measure the quality of schools or to determine the ideal class size for all schools, all teachers, all students. Such things are matters of opinion; and while opinions can be vigorously defended (or attacked), they cannot be proved (or disproved), as factual statements can generally be.

Evaluating opinions. To say that opinions cannot be proved true or false is not to say that they are worthless. Some are worthless, of course; but opinions that are sound are highly valuable to us, especially in reaching decisions about matters for which we do not have (and cannot get) all the facts. In determining the soundness of a particular opinion, we should consider several points.

First, how authoritative is the source? Is the person who expressed the opinion an expert on the subject? Does he have enough training and experience in this particular area to indicate that his opinion stems from knowledge of the facts? If, for example, a person seldom reads anything but detective novels, his judgment about the literary merits of a Jane Austen novel, a Shaw play, or an E. B. White essay is hardly likely to be sound.

72

Second, is the opinion supported by facts? Does the speaker or writer explain why he thinks as he does? Are his reasons convincing —that is, are they based on adequate and relevant facts? If not, it would be wise to get more information before accepting his views, no matter how impressive they sound or how much you would like to believe them.

Last, consider the possibility that self-interest may have motivated the opinion. A selfish purpose—a chance to profit financially, politically, socially, or professionally—often leads people to express views that are not warranted by the facts. Though self-interest alone is not a sure sign that a particular opinion is unsound, its presence should put you on your guard against accepting the opinion without inquiring into the facts.

Exercise 7   Study the following statements carefully. Then on a sheet of paper, indicate whether each is a statement-of-fact ("S.F.") or a statement of opinion ("S.O.") or a combination ("Both"). Be ready to explain how you arrived at your classifications.

1   Only five students in my French class of thirty-seven got an A in the course.
2   Four of these five students had had two years of Latin.
3   The best preparation for prospective students of French is a two-year course in Latin.
4   The senior dance was the most successful social event of the year.
5   The dance was held in the grand ballroom of the Clayton Hotel, and Marty Mimick and his band—the "Inimitables"— played until midnight.
6   "You'll never find a better buy than that 1961 white convertible out there on the lot, sir."
7   "It's a one-owner car that has been driven only thirty thousand miles, and four new tires are included in the price."
8   It is obvious to anyone but a child that for the past year Mayor Sprekke has had secret ambitions to become governor.
9   At his press conference this afternoon Mayor Sprekke announced that, though he appreciated the honor, he had refused to be his party's candidate for governor.
10   All tickets for the first week's performances of Utah Williamson's new Broadway drama were sold out a month before the opening night.
11   Williamson's new play is the finest that this greatest of American playwrights has ever written.
12   The dean of the Broadway critics referred to Williamson's latest drama as "a four-hour bore."
13   The best way—in fact, the only way—to encourage a real interest in scholarship is to give scholastic achievements the same sort of recognition that is given to outstanding performances in athletics.

14 Miss Crainforde gave me a C on my last theme, yet it was an exact copy of a theme I got an A on two years ago from Mr. Paul.

15 Miss Crainforde is not a competent judge of good writing.

16 We ought to keep our schools open twelve months of the year.

17 It is ridiculous to close schools for three months each year; long summer vacations are no longer necessary in our country—as they were in the days when students had to help out on the family farms.

18 It is a waste of time to vote: this town is being run by a powerful clique of politicians and their puppets in city hall.

19 The turnout in yesterday's election was even larger than it was in the primary; 94 per cent of the voters went to the polls.

20 We can count on the fact that our newly elected aldermen will do a much better job than their unlamented predecessors.

21 *The Furies Unleashed* is a surefire cinch to win an Academy Award; it cost twenty million dollars to produce and has fifteen stars in the cast.

Exercise 8   Be ready to discuss in class this statement: "An awareness of the difference between statement of fact and judgment is basic to straight thinking." Make the discussion as "concrete" as possible—for example, by describing situations in which mistakenly accepting an opinion statement as a "fact" would lead a person to make an unwise decision or reach an unsound conclusion. (The statements in Exercise 7 may suggest situations for you to discuss. You are to feel free to take examples from the exercise, but the discussion will be livelier if you think up your own situations and statements.)

Exercise 9   A.   Write twelve statements—nine to be statements-of-fact and three, statements of opinion—about one of these subjects: traditions at your school, local politics, a school course you are now taking or one you have completed, the teen-age recreation center in your town, a book that has influenced your life, a book or a movie that you heartily disliked.

B.   Be ready to discuss the following questions: Which did you find easier to write—the statements-of-fact or the statements of opinion? Why do you think this was so? Do the statements-of-fact you wrote indicate the reasons for your holding the opinions you do? If a person unfamiliar with your subject asked you for information about it, which of your statements would he find more useful in making a sound decision—the facts or the opinions? Why? Which do you think he would find more interesting? Why? If you wanted information about an unfamiliar subject, which would you prefer—facts from which to draw your own conclusions, ready-made opinions to accept, or a combination of the two? [From the answers to these questions, a student writer should be able to draw a valuable hint for making his writing more effective. Can you tell what it is?]

As the preceding section indicates, the reliability of the data we gather to use in our thinking will depend in great part on the accuracy of the factual statements and the soundness of the opinions. It will also depend on how well we steer clear of **slanting**. Slanting enters our lives in two ways: (1) what we read and hear may be slanted, (2) we ourselves may take a slanted view when observing things and people.

As an obvious example of the first sort, any sales talk you read or hear is likely to be slanted. The door-to-door salesman of the Quikandeezy opener tells you about the speed and ease with which his product opens cans. He does not point out that it makes a dangerously jagged cut; nor does he mention that another popular opener, the Zippee, stays sharp longer. The department-store advertisement of a new line of tweed coats concentrates on the up-to-date styling and the variety of colors. It does not mention that the fabric is sleazy or that coats of similar quality can be bought elsewhere for several dollars less.

Slanting in a sales talk or advertisement is, of course, hardly a surprise. You expect it. You are well aware that there is an ulterior motive involved—that someone is going to profit by your doing as the salesman or the advertisement suggests. It is up to you to keep your head and look for any disadvantages in doing as suggested. "*Caveat emptor*"—"Let the buyer beware"—is well-known advice that most people follow.

Slanted reports. Worthy of more study is slanting in material that is supposed to present accurate, impartial information—a news report of a current event, for instance; an article on the issues involved in a local, state, or national controversy; or a chapter on living conditions in a certain area. Slant in these (if there is any) may not be easy to recognize: there may be no loaded words or personal judgments that would warn one of bias on the writer's part. Every sentence in a report—in the account of a battle, let's say—may be factual and true. But if all the facts the writer included make one army look courageous and the other cowardly, whereas some of the facts he omitted would show the armies in a different light, the report is *slanted* and basically false.

Reports that are slanted by the writer's selecting details which favor a particular bias are not hard to find. For example, newspapers and news magazines (reflecting the allegiance of their publishers) may bear down heavily on the excellent reasons workers in some industry have for striking *or* on the unreasonableness they show and the damage they cause in doing so. In a town considering the building of a new school on a certain site, interested citizens will write letters to the editor in which they either point out only the desirable features of the site *or* dwell only on its drawbacks. Each of these reports, as you can see, would give the reader an incomplete picture, a distorted view. Therefore none of them, *by it-self,* would provide adequate data on which to base a valid opinion or reach a sound decision.

Important as it is to be on guard against slanted reports, it is just as important not to jump to the conclusion that everything you read or hear is slanted. There are many responsible writers and speakers who can be counted on to give accurate, impartial information. Although it is not infallible, here is a good test to use in evaluating reports. If the account seems to include all pertinent details—and for most subjects this will mean that both favorable and unfavorable aspects are touched on—the writer has done his best to present a "fair" picture. But if all the details point in one direction, either exclusively *for* or *against* the subject, it is quite likely that the writer has intentionally or inadvertently "stacked the cards." It would hardly be wise, then, to accept his information without first searching for more data to fill in the possible gaps in his report.

Slanted observations. Having material presented to us in a biased manner is just one side of the coin; the other is that we ourselves often take a slanted view of things. An obvious example is the view we take when we are very fond of someone. "Love is blind" is a familiar saying. A more accurate, though less catchy, version would be "Love is biased." When in love, we can see nothing but good looks, humor, kindness, charm. Signs of selfishness or meanness or bad temper are invisible. Most of us are in favor of this kind of slanting, of course. But when we turn away from personal relationships, the situation is different.

Let's suppose you are to write a report on juvenile delinquency, a report to be based on material you get through reading and observation. If before you begin your search for data, you have already made up your mind that delinquency is due entirely to parental neglect, chances are that you will be blind to other causes from which delinquency stems. You have developed, unconsciously, a slanted view of the subject that will keep you from seeing it as it actually is. Or suppose that your parents have imbued you with their own strong feelings about their political party. You are likely, especially if their training started when you were very young, to have a slanted view of that party—to see all of its virtues and none of its defects. Nothing is more likely to keep you from finding adequate, correct data to use in your thinking than unconscious slanting.

Where you fear you may be biased, it is a good idea to try to force yourself to slant in another direction from your natural one. As a result of this mental exercise, you may find yourself eventually revising some of your less tenable opinions. At any rate, it will help you spot your biases and train you to make allowances for them. For example, suppose you hear an idea that originated in the North (or South) and you know yourself to be strongly biased against all things Northern (or Southern). Make a special effort to give this one idea a fair hearing on its own particular merits—just as when you feel a strong wind pushing you forward, you make a special allowance for it by leaning backward. And who knows? This one idea may turn out to be exactly the material you need in solving a problem or reaching a sound decision.

Exercise **10** A.　Choose one of the following numbered items to use as the subject of a report. Prepare and bring to class (1) a list of statements-of-fact that are *favorable* to the subject and (2) a list of statements-of-fact that are *unfavorable* to the subject.

1　A character in a novel or movie (preferably a novel or movie most of the class is familiar with)
2　A city in which you once lived or one which you know well from frequent visits there
3　A notable figure in history or one now in the news
4　A job (summer or part-time) that you have had
5　An item that the owner might offer for sale—a house in your neighborhood, for example; a used car or boat; etc.

B.　Several students will be called on to read their lists aloud or to write them on the board. The class is to consider each statement, making sure that it is *factual* (and not a statement of opinion or a statement containing a connotative word which reveals a personal bias). Then, for each pair of lists, the class is to discuss these questions: What would be the effect on the reader if he were presented with a report containing only the favorable statements? a report containing only the unfavorable statements? Would this be true of all readers—the clear thinkers as well as the lazy thinkers? Even though such reports do not give the reader ready-made opinions for him to swallow, do they make certain opinions inescapable?

C.　Write a one-paragraph report on the subject you chose for part A of this exercise. The report is to be factual and "balanced," containing both favorable and unfavorable details to give readers an accurate, objective picture of the subject. [Note: It is not always possible—or necessary—to present one favorable detail for every single unfavorable one that is presented. An objective view of many subjects will reveal that the favorable facts actually outnumber or outweigh the unfavorable ones (or vice versa). The important consideration in presenting factual reports is to be as accurate and impartial as possible.]

Exercise **11**　Many of the statements we make in conversations reveal that we have—somehow—acquired slanted views which keep us from seeing certain subjects as they actually are. The following numbered items are all statements of this type; you may recognize several as statements you have made or have heard your friends make. Choose one of the statements, carefully think over the subject it deals with, and prepare to explain to the class the dangers of a blind acceptance of this slanted view. In your explanation, you are to present evidence (from your own observation or found through reading about or discussing the matter) showing that the view expressed is actually indefensible and that holding the view would block straight thinking and lead to unintelligent decisions.

1 "It's social suicide for a teen-ager not to go along with the crowd."
2 "Why should I bother to read, when I can go to the movies? The movie version of any book is better than the written version."
3 "The only students who get to be 'big wheels' at our school are athletes or those from wealthy homes."
4 "If you want to get ahead in a business organization, it isn't what you know but who you know."
5 "Students of extremely high intelligence are generally unhappy, overly shy people who never have any fun."

***Exercise* 12**   Find in a newspaper or magazine an editorial (or a column in which the writer editorializes) that you think is interesting enough to share with the class. In preparing to discuss the editorial, consider such questions as these: Which of the sentences are statements-of-fact and which are statements of opinion? Are the opinions supported adequately by facts? Does the writer make use of strongly connotative words that reveal his personal attitudes? Has the writer "stacked the cards" in his selection of facts? If the editorial could be assumed typical, would you consider the writer a valuable source for readers to consult regularly? Why?

BE WARY OF EITHER-OR

Good or *bad, rich* or *poor, brave* or *cowardly, interesting* or *boring, smart* or *stupid, right* or *wrong.* From our earliest years we are led to think of persons and things in terms of opposites or extremes, in terms of **either-or.** Wherever we go, we can find people taking the view that anyone who is not a highly vocal patriot must be a traitor; that any idea which is not "modern" is too antiquated to consider; that a school subject must have a practical, dollars-and-cents value, or it is completely worthless; that *their* opinion is absolutely right, and any other opinion is entirely wrong.

Salesclerks suggest to parents that they must either buy a color TV or cause maladjustment in their children. High-school students tell newcomers that they must either join a closed club or be considered social failures. Campaigners warn voters that they must either elect a certain candidate or see their country ruined within the next four years.

It is easy to see what is wrong with these either-or statements. Each presents us with just two extremes to choose from, when in reality more than two possibilities exist. It is only in fiction that all

men fit neatly into one of two groups, the "bad guys" or the "good guys"; in real life, there are many shades of gray between these black and white extremes. It is only in children's stories that problems have just two solutions—one wholly desirable, the other wholly undesirable. In real life, most problems have several possible solutions, the best one usually a compromise found somewhere between the extremes.

Each of the either-or statements in the first two paragraphs ignores the middle ground that actually exists between the two extremes. Each implies that the two choices exhaust the possibilities when, as a matter of fact, they do not. It is hardly true, for example, that a person must either loudly proclaim his patriotism or be a traitor. It is possible to love and support one's country without a lot of fanfare, just as it is possible to speak patriotically yet act traitorously—to mention only two other possibilities.

Watch out for either-or thinking in what you read and hear. The writer or speaker who presents you with just two choices, who states firmly that "it has to be this or that," is quite likely oversimplifying the case (often because he wants you not to think for yourself, but to think as he wants you to). Be careful not to let the two choices he presents blind you to the need of considering other possibilities. Remember that sound answers and solutions can generally be found only by considering all the data, not just the extremes.

Exercise **13** The following statements are based on either-or thinking. Study each item carefully to get a clear idea of the trap it presents to the unwary listener. For each statement, write (1) the two alternatives that are presented as the only choices available and (2) at least two other possibilities which the speaker has excluded from consideration. Be ready to discuss in class an ulterior motive which might have prompted each statement.

1 "If the referendum calling for the building of a junior high school in the Allerton subdivision is rejected, the students at Mercer and Wilson will be on a double shift within two years."

2 "Why should you—or anyone—want to work for a big firm in a big city? I used to work for one and I know the score. The only way you can get promoted to a really good job in the top ranks is to keep shining up to the bosses and stabbing your co-workers in the back."

3 "Recreation is just as important in life as work is. But nowadays a teen-ager has to have a car and a decent allowance, or he might as well forget about recreation."

4 "Mr. Zutler argues that his shack was built long before the area was declared a residential zone and the new, expensive houses were put up. But that shack of his, with its cluttered-up yard, is not only an eyesore; it's a threat to us property owners. Unless we can get the city council to order Zutler to tear down the shack, real-estate values in this area will dwindle to zero."

4 *On Thinking Logically*

Among the many famous quotations extolling the value of experience are these:

Experience is the best of schoolmasters.—Carlyle
Experience is our only teacher, both in war and peace.—W. S.
　　Landor
Experience joined with common sense,
To mortals is a providence.—Matthew Green

The last of these adages probably presents the most accurate picture. It is true that man can and does learn a great deal from experience, not only his own but that of others. But the fact that man has "common sense"—that is, the ability to reason—makes it possible for him to make use of what he learns from experience to learn something more, to add immeasurably to his store of knowledge.

All of us have this ability to reason—the ability, in other words, to draw valid conclusions or inferences from facts that we know or assume. What is more, we seem to have this ability from our earliest years; it is not something we have to be taught. For example, all of us probably had childhood experiences from which we learned some such facts as these: (1) touching the lit end of a cigarette hurt, (2) tossing a lighted match into a wastebasket made the paper burst into flames, and (3) poking a finger into the glowing ring of a gas stove raised a painful blister. But because we could reason, we went beyond these three facts to further knowledge: we drew from the facts the valuable inference that any and all fire burns.

Some time later we may have been tempted to jump over an inviting pile of flaming leaves in a neighbor's yard. We didn't need *experience* to teach us that the jump was dangerous. Flaming leaves mean fire, and we "knew" that fire burns, so we wisely refrained from jumping.

Homely as this example is, it does serve to illustrate the important point that all of us (not just scientists, great scholars, philosophers, and logicians) make use of the principles of logic. Every day of our lives, we think in accordance with these principles. But some-times—perhaps often—our reasoning is not as correct as it might be; we do not think straight and so end with unsound conclusions. By studying some of the principles of reasoning, we can learn ways of checking our thinking to make sure it is clear and logical. In our study we will consider two opposite kinds of reasoning: inductive and deductive.

INDUCTIVE REASONING

To get a close-up view of *inductive reasoning* in action, let's watch a biologist at work. The biologist, we will suppose, has become interested in studying a newly discovered disease of cattle. He begins his studies by examining the blood of some forty-seven cows that have the disease. In each case, he finds a certain germ, which we will call germ X. At this point in his studies he says to himself, "Since I have found no exceptions in these forty-seven cases, it's a pretty safe bet that germ X is *always* present in the blood of cows with this disease." In his notes, he phrases this conclusion more formally: All cows with this disease will have germ X in their blood. After further research, the biologist reaches other important conclusions; but let's interrupt his work for a moment to take a closer look at what he has done so far.

First of all, he has examined only a limited number of cows. Forty-seven might seem a large number to us, but the biologist realizes that it represents merely a "sample" of all the cows that have, have had, or will have the disease. Nevertheless, on the basis of the evidence provided by this sample, he arrives at a conclusion that applies to *all* cows with the disease—those he has not examined as well as those he has. Reasoning that what is true of the forty-seven individual cases he observed will probably be true of all cases, he makes the "inductive leap" from the evidence provided by *some* to a general conclusion about *all*. This process of reasoning from individual cases or particular instances to a generalization is called **induction**.

The biologist continues his studies. He examines forty-two more cows, half of them healthy and half of them sick, though they do not have the disease he is investigating. In each of these forty-two cases, he finds that germ X is not present in the blood. So he makes a second generalization: Germ X is *never* present in the blood of cows that do not have the disease. Finally, on the basis of

82

all the facts he has learned (that forty-seven cows with germ X have the disease, and forty-two cows without germ X do not have the disease), he reasons inductively to a third generalization: All cows whose blood contains germ X have this disease. Then he publishes a paper in which he presents his three generalizations—three *potentially valuable* additions to knowledge.

Our referring to these generalizations as only "potentially" valuable would not surprise the biologist. For he knows, as all scientists know, that any conclusion about *all* which is based on the evidence of *some* is a probability, not a certainty. He knows it is possible that further investigation might turn up instances which would disprove the truth of his findings. However, since the evidence on which he based his reasoning was sound, chances are that his generalizations have a high degree of probability, high enough to make them valuable guides for others to use.

All of us, like our imaginary biologist, make generalizations. But too many of us, unlike the biologist, often generalize too hastily— and on the basis of too little evidence. On the first day of school, for example, we see a sophomore student rudely bump into a classmate in a corridor. A week later we see two other sophomores elbow their way to the front of a cafeteria line—and immediately we generalize: "Sophomores! None of them have any manners."

Or we hear the neighborhood gossip telling about a family that is dishonestly accepting relief from the city, and we vaguely remember a similar instance in a TV soap opera we saw. From this molehill of evidence, we build a mountainous generalization: "All people on relief rolls nowadays are cheaters." Or at a party we meet an exchange student from England who reveals an amazing knowledge of literature, science, mathematics, history, and art. After an evening with him we write a three-page composition whose controlling idea is "British students are better educated than American students." (And to "prove" it, we describe in detail the many accomplishments of the exchange student!)

It does not take a logician to point out that these three generalizations are **fallacies**—errors in reasoning. None of them is based on enough evidence to lead to a valid inference. Three sophomores, however rude, are only a tiny part of a class of four hundred, not a big enough sample to warrant charging the whole class with discourtesy. Three pencils pulled at random from a shipment of four hundred would quite likely be a fair sample on which to generalize about the quality of the whole group of pencils; one would usually be safe in assuming that the three were representative of the lot. But sophomore students, unlike products made to specifications, differ greatly; we cannot safely assume that the behavior of three is characteristic of all.

Basing a generalization about all relief families on two instances —one reported by a neighbor, one from a TV melodrama—is sloppy reasoning indeed. In the first place, second-hand "evidence" drawn from such sources is hardly likely to be reliable. In the second place, the very fact that the families were of special interest to a gossip and a playwright would suggest the possibility (at least) that dishonest relief clients are not typical of the group. The evidence is far from complete enough; further investigation would quickly uncover many instances of families legitimately on relief rolls. The generalization, therefore, is worthless.

Making the inductive leap from a few facts about a British student to a generalization about the education of all students in two countries is more an acrobatic feat than sound reasoning. The biologist, you will remember, observed not only cows with the disease but cows without it, to make his evidence as complete and foolproof as possible. Here we observed only one student with obviously high intelligence. But what about British students of only average intelligence? What about American students—bright and average? Unless we have an adequate sample of both groups, we cannot arrive at a generalization that a thinking person would accept as reasonable.

Tests for generalizations. As you have learned, any generalization about *all* that is based on the evidence of *some* can be only a probability, not a demonstrable certainty. However, you can give your generalizations a high degree of probability by observing three common-sense rules.

First, use a big enough sample; investigate a reasonable number of instances. Second, make sure the sample is fair—that is, representative of the whole. Third, do not slant your evidence by ignoring instances that contradict your first observations. If there are many of these "negative" instances, you should qualify your generalization: *not* "Every student in this school disapproves of having a double shift," *but* "Eighty per cent of the students in this school disapprove of a double shift" or "A majority of the students. . . ." If you find only very few negative instances and you can honestly dismiss them as unimportant or untypical, you will probably not qualify the generalization. On hearing the evidence you present to support it, most people will accept it as a statement that is *generally* true and, therefore, sound.

From the fact that hasty generalizing is an all too common human failing plus the fact that generalizations, however sound, are not certainties, we might jump to the conclusion that generalizations are useless. On the contrary; they are indispensable to us as guides in making countless decisions. "The burnt child dreads the fire," as the proverb says, because fortunately he was able to generalize that all fire burns. The successful comedian owes much of his success to his having generalized, on the basis of past experiences, that a certain type of joke is always good for a laugh. And the success of many a teacher stems from his having generalized, on the basis of past observations, that all students respond well to a particular method of teaching. Using the generalizations as a start-ing point, the child, the comedian, and the teacher can draw con-clusions on which they base frequent decisions like these: "I won't play with these matches"; "I must be sure to include several varia-tions of this joke on my program tomorrow"; "I'd better use this teaching method in my classes today, even though it takes much time and effort."

Exercise 1 Read each of the numbered items carefully, and be ready to discuss in class the answers to the questions (in brackets) that fol-low each.

1 To collect data for an article on college life, a student reporter spends a day on the campus of a nearby university. Among his many activities, he visits one class—a graduate seminar in lin-guistics. He is deeply impressed by the seriousness of the stu-dents, their obvious intelligence, their background knowledge, their articulate arguments in discussing a controversial matter. As the introductory sentence for his article, the student reporter writes: "College students of today, unlike their pre-Sputnik counterparts, are grimly serious, intellectually mature, extremely well informed, and highly articulate." [Do you think the re-porter reached a valid generalization? Why or why not? If you were the editor of the school paper, what revisions, if any, would you suggest the writer should make? If the writer com-plained that your suggested revisions would make his opening sentence sound less impressive, what answer would you give him?]

2 "We are told that five years ago the literary magazine had to be discontinued for lack of student support. But times have changed. A poll taken at the last meeting of the Writers Club discloses that 96 of its 123 members want, and promise to sub-scribe to, a monthly literary magazine. So the faculty can rest assured on this point: 75 per cent of the student body, at the very least, will back the project by buying subscriptions." [The writer here has wisely qualified his generalization (75 per cent reflects the proportion disclosed in the sample), so that at first glance it seems valid. But what important factor has he neg-lected to take into account?]

3 "It isn't the teen-agers—it's the elderly drivers who are the real menace on our streets and highways. Why, last week alone the *Evening News* reported four accidents that involved drivers from sixty-six to seventy years of age. We need a new state law: no man or woman over sixty-five should be given a driver's license." [What two generalizations does the speaker make? Is the evidence on which he bases the generalizations ade-quate? What evidence would be needed to justify the second generalization?]

4 *Panel speaker A:* "I carefully checked the records and discovered this interesting bit of information: No student taking the honors course in English at our school has had a course in advanced math, physics, or chemistry."

Panel speaker B: "On the basis of my rather extensive research, one observation seems to me inescapable: American high schools are not giving their students the intensive training in science they need to meet the challenges of the space age." [Which of the two quoted passages contains an inductive generalization? Why is the statement of the other speaker *not* an inductive generalization? On the basis of speaker A's statement, would the audience be justified in inferring that his school was neglecting its responsibility to help train scientists for our country's future needs?]

Exercise 2 For the next day or two, be on the lookout for generalizations made by others—in newspaper or magazine articles, in advertisements, in class discussions, in radio or TV interview programs, in conversations outside of school. Be ready to present in class a brief report on two of the generalizations you find—one that you consider sound, one that you consider unsound. In your report you are to demonstrate, by applying the three rules for testing generalizations, why you are justified in labeling one generalization "unsound" and the other "sound."

Exercise 3 Write a composition (no more than 500 words) in which you present a number of examples or instances to serve as evidence that a certain generalization is reliably sound. You may state the generalization in the first part of your paper and follow it with the evidence you have marshaled to support it; or you may reverse this order, using the evidence to lead into the generalization. The generalization may be one you have arrived at through your own past observations, or it may be one that you have heard or read and have been impressed by.

The following list may suggest a generalization to use in your paper. (If you choose one from the list, feel free to change it—by qualifying it, for example, or by making it affirmative rather than negative, etc.)

1 Men, unlike women, are not slaves to fashion.
2 Intelligent people learn from the mistakes *of others*.
3 You can't make a silk purse out of a sow's ear.
4 As George Stoddard once said, "We can often make a silk purse out of what we thought was a sow's ear."
5 No one can get a good job nowadays without a college diploma.
6 "Today's teen-agers," says the author of this article, "lack the pioneer spirit. They are not fired with ambition to achieve great goals; they will gladly settle for 'a job with security.'"

7 Television programs will be as good as you, the viewers, want them to be.
8 English spelling is badly in need of reform.

Your teacher may call on several students to read their compositions to the class. The rest of the class may be asked to comment on the adequacy of the evidence each writer presents in support of his generalization.

DEDUCTIVE REASONING

To begin our study of this second kind of reasoning, let's go back to the biologist's paper, which (we will suppose) has been printed in a scientific journal. A veterinarian reads the paper with interest. He has been puzzled for some time by an unfamiliar disease that has been affecting the cattle in his area. The symptoms could be those of several different diseases, but he has not been able to determine just which. After reading the biologist's paper, he examines the blood of his sick cattle, and in every instance he finds germ X. Reasoning from this evidence, he concludes that it is this particular disease and not some other which is making his cattle sick. Having reached this conclusion, he can successfully treat his cases. (The biologist's generalization, as you see, has already paid off.)

Now let's examine the reasoning used by the veterinarian to reach his conclusion—the kind of reasoning called **deductive**.

The veterinarian has two important bits of "knowledge" to work with. First, he has the biologist's generalization about a whole class, which he uses as a starting point in his reasoning:

> All cows whose blood contains germ X are cows that have this disease.

Second, he has his own evidence showing that his sick cows are included in the class:

> My cows are cows whose blood contains germ X.

Applying the generalization to his particular case (his sick cows) leads to a logical conclusion:

> Therefore my cows are cows that have this disease.

The Syllogism

The form of deductive reasoning used by the veterinarian is known as a **syllogism**—a **categorical syllogism**, to be exact (there are other types which we will not cover). In this type of syllogism there are three parts: a *major premise* (the general statement),

87

a *minor premise* (the particular case), and a *conclusion* (the deductive inference that logically follows from the two premises). For example:

MAJOR PREMISE: All graduates of Fuller Business College are experts in typing and shorthand.
MINOR PREMISE: Mary Ellis is a graduate of Fuller.
CONCLUSION: Therefore Mary Ellis is an expert in typing and shorthand.

[Notice that each statement in the syllogism contains a "subject term" and a "predicate term" connected by a linking verb:

IN THE MAJOR PREMISE: *graduates of Fuller* are *experts in typing and shorthand*
IN THE MINOR PREMISE: *Mary Ellis* is *graduate of Fuller*
IN THE CONCLUSION: *Mary Ellis* is *expert in typing and shorthand*

Notice also that the entire syllogism contains only three different terms, each used twice: *graduate(s)* and *expert(s)* and *Mary Ellis*. Each of the three terms names a different class of things. All categorical syllogisms are based on this pattern of three terms, each used twice.]

If one accepts the truth of the major premise in this syllogism, and if the minor premise is true, the conclusion is inevitable, as can be demonstrated in the following diagrams. Suppose we had a huge arena in which we could put all experts in typing and shorthand:

Since the major premise tells us that all Fuller graduates are among these experts, we know that they will be in the arena:

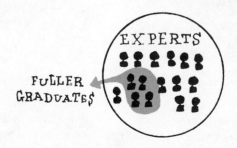

The minor premise tells us that Mary Ellis is a Fuller graduate, so we put her in the Fuller circle:

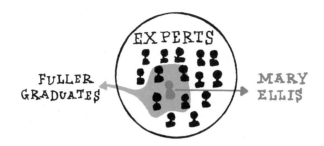

Placing Mary in the Fuller circle, as this third diagram shows, *necessarily* places her in the large class of experts also—thus demonstrating the truth of the conclusion: "Mary Ellis is an expert in typing and shorthand."

When we reason inductively, the best we can do is to reach conclusions that are highly probable. But when we reason deductively, by means of syllogisms, we can reach conclusions that are necessarily true. We can, that is, with two ifs: *if* the premises we use are true (or can be assumed true) and *if* our reasoning is correct.

Checking on these ifs is a bit harder than one might think, because though we constantly use deductive reasoning in our everyday speech and writing, we seldom express a deductive train of thought in the form of a fully stated syllogism. None of us, for example, ever presents an argument that sounds like this:

89

All mushrooms picked in Bond's Woods are edible mushrooms.
These mushrooms are mushrooms picked in Bond's Woods.
Therefore these mushrooms are edible mushrooms.

Instead we usually compress our train of reasoning into this sort of statement: "Don't worry; these mushrooms are perfectly safe to eat —they came from Bond's Woods." Notice that here we begin with the conclusion ("These mushrooms are safe") and simply omit the major premise, feeling that it is unnecessary to state a point which is clearly implied.

Sometimes we omit a minor premise, assuming that it is too obvious to mention: "We can count on Fleming's vote and Dobson's; aldermen from the West Side wards always vote for all school bills." If this incomplete syllogism (called an *enthymeme*) were expressed as a full syllogism, it would go like this:

All West Side aldermen are aldermen who always vote for school bills.
Fleming and Dobson are West Side aldermen.
Therefore Fleming and Dobson are aldermen who will vote for the proposed school bill.

Testing deductive reasoning. Why should we bother to study the syllogism when we do not actually speak or write in full syllogisms? Surely we are not going to be urged to use these artificial-sounding, three-part syllogisms when, as we have just seen, we can make our meaning clear without them? No one, least of all a logician, would recommend our using full syllogisms in our daily speech and writing. But a logician would point out that a good way to determine the soundness of our reasoning (and that of others) is to mentally "translate" incomplete syllogisms into full syllogisms by filling in the omitted major or minor premises. Then we can more readily check the truth of the premises and the correctness of the reasoning. Let's see how this works.

1) Here is a statement of the sort that might be heard at a committee meeting: "I know John Loren will make an excellent editor in chief for the school paper because he has an A-plus average in English." Since skill in English is obviously a must for an editor in chief, this argument seems quite convincing—at first. But let's examine it closely. The conclusion we are asked to accept is that John "will make an excellent editor in chief." The speaker gives only one premise (the fact that John has an A-plus average in English), which we know is the *minor* premise because it states a particular case. What is missing, then, is the *major* premise—the generalization that serves as a starting point in the deductive reasoning:

> All students who have an A-plus average in English are persons who will make excellent editors in chief.
> John Loren is a person who has an A-plus average in English.
> Therefore John is a person who will make an excellent editor in chief.

Once the implied major premise is put into words, we recognize immediately that it is not true. We know many such students who do not have the administrative ability, say, to handle an editor in chief's work. Since the major premise is not true, the conclusion is hardly reliable. A clear thinker would not decide on John for the editor's job on the basis of the quoted statement alone.

2) Arguments like the following one crop up constantly in speech and writing: "No responsible citizen would vote for Mr. Frazer. The man must be a Communist, as anyone would know, because he keeps criticizing our government's foreign policy, just as all Communists do." Is the conclusion here justified? To find out, let's translate the argument into a full syllogism, supplying the major premise:

> All Communists are persons who criticize American foreign policy.
> Mr. Frazer is a person who criticizes American foreign policy.
> Therefore Mr. Frazer is a Communist.

We can accept both premises as true. But when we check the reasoning, we find that the conclusion does not *necessarily* follow from the evidence given in the premises. The major premise tells us only that all Communists are critical of our policy; it does not say that all critics of our policy are Communists. People other than Communists may be critical of our policy, so the conclusion is not justified. The reasoning is fallacious. As the following diagram shows, Mr. Frazer can be in the group of critics without necessarily being a member of the Communist group:

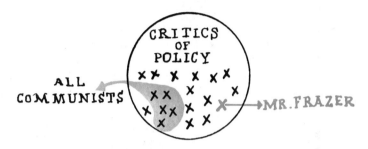

3) "You agree, don't you, that people who go to the opera are true devotees of music? Well, then, since you do agree on this, you'll have to admit that Mrs. Kurtzell is not the devotee she claims to be. In the three years we have known her she has never attended the opera." Here again we have fallacious reasoning:

91

> All opera goers are true devotees of music.
> Mrs. Kurtzell is not an opera goer.
> Therefore Mrs. Kurtzell is not a true devotee.

The conclusion does not necessarily follow from the premises. The major premise tells us only that all opera goers *are included* in the large class of devotees; it does not tell us that the opera goers make up the *whole* class. Other people, even people who hate opera, may very well be in the devotee class. So the fact that Mrs. Kurtzell never attends the opera does not, by itself, justify the conclusion.

4) As a final example, let's examine an argument which might have appeared in a letter to the editor of your local paper: "Why

is 'Mr. Justice-For-All' so alarmed? I say it is inconceivable that our school-board members, who have time and again proved to be fair-minded, will be so unjust as to fire Principal Weelor—or any other employee—without giving him a hearing." Filling in the implied major premise, we get this syllogism:

> No fair-minded persons are persons who treat employees unjustly.
> Our board members are fair-minded persons.
> Therefore our board members are not persons who will treat Mr. Weelor unjustly.

Here the reasoning is correct. Anyone who accepts the truth of the premises (and most people would) will have to accept the conclusion as true, for it *necessarily* follows from the premises. A diagram will show the correctness of the reasoning:

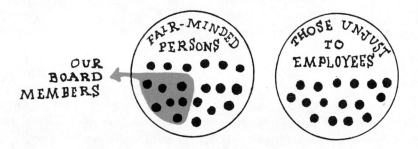

We have two completely separated circles because the major premise tells us that *no* fair-minded persons are included in the class of the unjust. And when we put the school-board members in the class of the fair-minded, as the minor premise states, we see that the conclusion is inescapable: the board members are *not* included in the class of the unjust.

Note: Those of you who will take a full course in logic at college or study logic on your own will quickly discover that in the preceding section we have presented a very simplified treatment of the logician's techniques for testing the validity of deductive reasoning. But our treatment, simple as it is, has two worth-while purposes: (1) to familiarize you with certain terms (*syllogism, deduction, fallacy, major premise,* etc.) which you will be meeting often in your reading and (2) to give you help in detecting some of the most common flaws in everyday deductive reasoning. An awareness of ways in which the reasoning process can go astray will not only protect you from being taken in by the unsound thinking of others, but will also help you improve your own thinking.

Exercise 4 Be ready to discuss in class each of the following arguments. The members of the class, working together, are to analyze the arguments to determine which they would accept as valid and which they would not accept—and why. In analyzing each item, the class is to follow the pattern used in the preceding section: (1) translate the argument into a full syllogism, making sure that the syllogism is so worded that it contains only three different terms, each used twice; (2) check the truth of the premises; (3) check the correctness of the reasoning. For each syllogism whose premises can be accepted as true, a diagram is to be drawn (on the board) showing that the conclusion does or does not *necessarily* follow from the premises.

1 [From a sports page] All members of this sports-page staff agree that this year's team is a surefire cinch to win both the regional and the state trophies, because these men have what all championship teams have—a fighting spirit and great teamwork.

2 [Overheard on a bus] "I say that Perkins is *not* a great writer, and I can prove it. Not one of the many books he has written has become a best seller. You don't have to take my word for it; I can show you the best-seller lists from *Publishers' Weekly* for the last five years."

3 [From a book review] In his preface to *The Liberal Takes the Stand* the author states explicitly that he is a liberal. But his book makes it quite clear that, by his own definition, he is not a true liberal. "All liberals," he says, "are open-minded to ideas which challenge tradition." Yet in three spots that I can point out, he shows himself to be extremely narrow-minded in his sarcastic condemnation and savage rejection of certain suggested reforms.

4 [Said at a board meeting] "Gentlemen, I can explain what's wrong. A study of these reports shows clearly that all TV shows which emphasize the sensational get high ratings—impressively high. As long as this executive board persists in its policy of producing only programs of intellectual appeal—programs that do not emphasize the sensational—our shows will *never* achieve high ratings. It's as simple as that, gentlemen."

5 [Overheard in an office cafeteria] "How did I know that applicant lied about his having worked at the Parker Company in Boston these past three years? It's elementary, my dear Miss Watson. In the course of our interview I discovered that he just didn't know what all proper Bostonians know—that *tonic* is their word for *soda pop*."

6 [From an argumentative composition] Instead of merely complaining about the cheating that goes on in our school, let's do something constructive. Let's get the faculty to introduce the honor system here. The system works at Grayson College, and it works at Croydon Military Academy; so we can rest assured that it will work here.

7 [Said by a young wife] "Professor Markle, I was delighted to hear you say that all geniuses have an infinite capacity for taking pains. I have always *suspected* that that perfectionist husband of mine was a genius, but now I *know* that he is."

8 [Said by a visitor from a Communist nation, in answer to the question "Won't you be criticized at home for visiting a capitalist nation?"] "No; no one will criticize me at home, because we are a free country." [Several news commentators who reported the interview found the visitor's answer quite amusing. Do you? Why?]

9 [Said by a mother to her son, who has turned down a movie invitation to work on his mathematics assignment] "Jerry, I just can't understand why you should be the slightest bit worried about flunking trigonometry. After all, you got an A in both algebra and geometry."

10 [Overheard at a restaurant in a Midwest town] "You just can't believe what that Milly Frettner says. She tells everyone that she is only twenty years old. But she must be at least twenty-four. She has to be. Three years ago, when I was an election clerk in our precinct, she was a registered voter."

FALLACIES IN ARGUMENTATION

In the preceding section the word *argument* was used several times; and with the help of context clues, you probably arrived at a fairly clear idea of its intended meaning. In logic, *argument* does not mean a dispute of the "yes, it is—no, it isn't" type. It means a piece of writing or speech in which we present (1) our point of view on a subject about which there can be differences of opinion and (2) reasons that support our point of view. Since the purpose of argumentative speech or writing is to persuade others to agree with us, the supporting reasons must provide convincing evidence that our opinions—our conclusions—are sound.

If the arguments you advance are to be acceptable to straight thinkers, you must first of all avoid the errors in reasoning discussed in the preceding sections. But you must also learn to recognize and to avoid other fallacies common in argumentation: begging the question, *post hoc* reasoning, and ignoring the question.

Begging the Question

Here is an argument that may remind you of your grade-school days: "Why do I think Jim Greinertz is a cheater? Because he cheats; that's why."

To anyone but a child, this is a most unsatisfactory argument. The speaker gives no real evidence to prove the truth of his con-

clusion about Jim. Instead, he merely makes a statement that assumes *as already proved* the very point he is supposed to be proving. The speaker, to use the logician's term, is **begging the question**—he is evading the issue by simply assuming as true a conclusion whose truth needs to be proved. In begging the question, he is actually reasoning in a circle; his reasoning amounts to nothing more than "My conclusion is true because it is true."

Begging the question seldom occurs in as obvious a form as the example above, in which "Because he *cheats*" so openly echoes "Jim is a *cheater*." The fallacy is usually hidden in a maze of fine-sounding words, as in this: "Every American student should be required to learn a foreign language because in our modern world it is absolutely essential to know more than one language." This seems all right at first glance, but a second look would reveal its absurdity: "Knowledge of a foreign language is essential because it is essential."

A more subtle form of begging the question is common in argumentation. A writer for a school paper, for example, may begin his editorial like this: "Let's face the issue squarely. Why should we, the student body, accept without protest the unfair decision of the faculty that all social clubs are to be disbanded? If *we* do not fight for our rights, how can we . . . ?"

Whether the editorial writer realizes it or not, he has begged the question; he has evaded the very point at issue—the fairness or unfairness of the faculty's decision. His use of the word *unfair* to characterize the decision shows that he has assumed, and expects others to assume, that the decision *is* unfair. But the acceptability of his conclusion (that students should protest) depends on his proving the unfairness of the decision. Merely asserting that it is "unfair" does not prove that it is.

The "Post Hoc" Fallacy

It is somehow easier to detect other people's fallacies than our own—especially when we are the victims of the fallacious reasoning. Suppose, for example, that you have dropped in next door to wait for your friend George, who has promised you a ride to the movies. George arrives a few minutes later with his report card, which shows that his chemistry grade has dropped fifteen points. After one quick glance at the card his father says, "Well, I should have known better last month than to let you buy that jalopy. The very day you got it your school work started to suffer. We'll just have to lock the car in the garage, since it's obvious that getting that thing cost you your place on the honor roll. I really should have known. . . ."

This would hardly be the time to discuss logic with George's father, yet you realize that he has jumped to an unfair conclusion in decreeing that the car be locked up. You are George's laboratory partner and know that several other factors—not the car—contributed to his low chemistry grade: he had missed three days of class discussion because of illness; he had botched an important experiment and was therefore late in handing in a report; having crammed all of the night before, he had done less well than usual on the six weeks' test; and so on. His father had mistakenly assumed that, since George's poor grade *followed* his acquiring the car, the poor grade was *caused* by his getting the car. This mistake in reasoning is called the **"post hoc" fallacy,** from the Latin *post hoc, ergo propter hoc*—"after this, therefore because of this."

The *post hoc* fallacy is easy to fall into. Before we can figure out a solution to many of the problems that concern us, we must know what caused the problems. But in our understandable hurry to reach the solution, we often tend to oversimplify matters, to act as if a given event has just a single cause—a preceding event. The truth is that there are generally many causes, many preceding events, which contribute to any given result. Moreover, the mere fact that event A precedes event B in time does not mean that there is necessarily a causal connection between the two. There may be; there may not be.

Unless we keep these points in mind, we will (like the imaginary father above) present arguments that are as fallacious as the following one:

> Our city made a bad mistake in voting to go back to having a mayor, after ten years of a city-manager form of government. Not two months after the mayor was sworn in, three of our major industries moved out of town, the school-expansion program bogged down, and property taxes were increased 20 per cent. How can we expect to prosper as a city if we keep the mayoral form of government?

Such reasoning is no more valid (though it pretends to be) than that of a superstitious actor who insists on wearing a frayed green tie in one scene of every play. "This tie," he explains, "brings good luck; I was wearing it the day I got my first good part, ten years ago." Even the most inept mayor could not *alone* have caused all the city's problems in two months; getting rid of the mayor will not, in itself, bring about a solution. Only the unthinking or the prejudiced would accept the argument.

To convince a thinking audience that you have a reasonable solution to a particular problem, you must present arguments that will stand up under scrutiny. Before presenting an argument based on a cause-effect relationship, test its soundness by asking yourself questions like these: Is event A, which I am assuming to be the cause of event B, sufficient to produce event B? Would event B always necessarily occur as a result of event A? Could event B occur without event A? (If so, event A and event B may have no causal connection; at any rate, event A cannot be considered the sole cause of B.) What other events occurred which may have contributed to produce event B?

Ignoring the Question

Early in the preceding chapter, we pointed out that computing machines cannot do what we call creative thinking; they simply follow instructions. In fairness to the machines, it also has to be pointed out that an asset accompanies their defect—they cannot be distracted from their tasks. Once instructions have been fed into the electronic brain, it carries on automatically, straight down the line. The only thing that can keep it from coming out with the right answer, short of a mechanical breakdown of some sort, is a mistake or omission in the material that has been fed into it, or a mistake in the coding of that material.

We, on the other hand, have a defect that accompanies our chief asset. Being human, we can do creative thinking; but being human, we can be distracted from the task in hand—our minds can easily be diverted away from the straight and narrow path between question and logical answer, between problem and reasonable solution.

How easily we can be distracted from the question at issue is shown by how frequently off-the-point arguments win acceptance. Day after day, for example, we hear arguments that go like this: "I don't care what Mr. Payne says; I think Oscar Fogelson should have won the state essay contest, and I can prove it. Oscar is our best writer; two of his stories were published in *Student Showcase* last year. I know for a fact that he worked harder than a galley slave, doing research for his essay and revising his drafts over and over again. Besides, it's high time someone from our school won; the last three years the prize has gone to contestants from Purvis Academy. What's more, those Purvis fellows don't need the money, while someone like Oscar—without a father to support the family— needs it badly."

The question actually at issue here is "Why should Oscar's essay have been awarded the prize?" Yet, as you can see, not one of the statements the speaker makes (true as they may be) is relevant to the point at issue: the merits of the *essay*.

Why does an argument as weak as this seem convincing to many listeners? Perhaps the main reason is this. Because the speaker's statements appeal to his listeners' emotions (pride in a fellow student's accomplishments, admiration for hard work, rivalry between schools, sympathy for the underdog, etc.), they distract attention away from the fact that the speaker has **ignored the question.** He has not given any evidence to prove his conclusion; he has merely made his listeners want to believe it. Unfortunately, wanting to believe a conclusion does not make the conclusion valid.

Though there are many ways of ignoring the question, perhaps the most common is to use the **argumentum ad hominem** ("an argument directed to the man"). The following example will illustrate the form this fallacy takes. Suppose Mr. Ecks, an advertising executive, is asked to reply to a magazine article in which the author, Professor Johndoe, severely criticizes the advertising business. Mr. Ecks writes a very brief reply: "Johndoe's criticisms are absolutely unwarranted. But what else could one expect from the professor? It is a matter of record that he is—and always has been—opposed to free enterprise."

Notice that instead of sticking to the matter under discussion (the alleged shortcomings of the advertising business), Mr. Ecks launches into an attack on the professor. Now the discreditable fact that the professor opposes free enterprise does cast suspicion on his motives, but it is quite irrelevant to the question at issue at the moment (are his criticisms unjustified or not?). But by calling attention to the fact, Mr. Ecks causes a distraction that will keep many people from realizing how completely he has ignored the question. Although he has presented no evidence to prove his conclusion, these people will accept it as valid. The regrettable consequence is that neither Mr. Ecks nor those who are persuaded by his fallacious argument will take a close, thoughtful look at the professor's criticisms to see what merit they may have. Yet getting an objective view of a problem is a necessary step in finding a sensible solution for it.

Exercise 5   Study each of the following arguments. On a sheet of paper, identify the fallacy involved in each (begging the question, *post hoc,* ignoring the question, *argumentum ad hominem*). Be ready to discuss what sort of evidence would be needed to make each argument logically acceptable.

1   Unfortunately, too many people, blinded by partisan loyalties, refuse to admit how disastrous the policies of the Demopublicans are. Yet history itself makes this only too clear. Every time a Demopublican administration has taken over, this state has suffered a severe recession.

2   I have but one comment to make—no novelist should ever take to heart an unfavorable book review. If literary critics really knew anything about writing, they would write books themselves.

3   Anyone who truly believes in the glorious principles on which our great democracy was founded will vote against continuing this undemocratic system of giving merit raises to only a select few.

4   Mr. Cleary's charge that the graduates of this high school cannot spell can easily be disproved. Mr. Cleary conveniently ignores the fact that three of the last five state spelling-bee win-

ners have come from this school. And he needs to be reminded that spelling isn't so easy as it used to be in his generation, what with all the new scientific terms that have been added to our language.

5   We, the undersigned, have a question to ask of the "Mr. Cautious" whose letter was printed in last night's paper. Why should the taxpayers' good money be spent for an investigation? We don't need an investigating committee to tell us that corrupt city officials should be thrown out of office.

6   Floyd Klingbeil, my candidate for Student Council president, has without doubt the best qualifications for this important post. Everyone likes Floyd. Why? Because he is not the reformer type that is always finding fault with our student-government setup and suggesting changes—like another candidate whose name I need not mention.

7   Plagiarizing is dishonest because it is basically not honest to take another writer's words and pass them off as one's own.

8   Of course I stick up for the Hillyer twins; it isn't their fault that they keep getting into trouble with the police. Until that mother of theirs got herself a job at the shoe factory, they were as fine a pair of youngsters as we've ever had in this neighborhood.

9   Fellow citizens, since any audience as intelligent as this one wants fact—and not campaign oratory—I will rely on facts alone to *prove* that our candidate, Protheroe Quillaunt, is the thinking man's choice for mayor. In three of the last four elections, the people of this fair city have wisely chosen the candidates of *our* great party to serve as mayor. That the voters' trust in the ability and integrity of our party's candidates was justified is clearly shown by the fact that two of these three former mayors have gone on to further triumphs: one is now the governor of this magnificent state; the other, our junior senator. My friends, since I'm sure you will all agree with me that only a man of this same high caliber deserves to be elected, I know you will cast your ballots for our truly deserving candidate—Pro Quillaunt.

Exercise 6   During the next week, look for examples of fallacious arguments in magazine articles, editorials, letters to the editor, advertisements, radio and TV discussion programs, class discussions, and out-of-school conversations. Bring to class, for discussion, any examples you can spot. [See also Exercise 7.]

Exercise 7   As you search for examples of fallacious arguments for Exercise 6, you will come across examples of effective, logically valid arguments. Bring to class, for discussion, one or two examples of these effective arguments.

The cure for unintelligent reading consists in the re-stating in one's own words of what one has read.

— Robert M. Gay

Paraphrasing

5

and Précis Writing

According to a recent magazine article, one of the main reasons why students fail in college is that they do not know how to study. In another article, the director of a university orientation program estimated that 95 per cent of those entering college lack adequate study skills. High-school and college students themselves often complain that they have not learned how to get as much as they should from their studying. In fact, teen-agers in one survey listed the need for effective study habits as their fourth most important problem.

Chances are that you, too, would like to improve your study techniques. As a starter, this chapter will show you how to make effective use of two of the most valuable study aids—paraphrasing and précis writing.

PARAPHRASING

Often you can read a story or article or poem and at once grasp the writer's meaning. But not all writing is so readily understandable. When a writer uses rather involved or figurative or technical language or packs a great many ideas into a few concise sentences, even the best of readers need to weigh his words carefully to find all the meaning intended. A good way to deal with such writing is to **paraphrase** it—to "translate" the writer's thoughts into your own words.

As you compare the following paraphrase with the original, notice that both convey the same meaning. Only their wording differs. In the paraphrase the language is simpler, more familiar, easier to understand in a first reading:

<table>
<tr><td>ORIGINAL</td><td>PARAPHRASE</td></tr>
<tr><td>

The disposition of mankind, whether as rulers or as fellow-citizens, to impose their own opinions and inclinations as a rule of conduct on others, is so energetically supported by some of the best and by some of the worst feelings incident to human nature, that it is hardly ever kept under restraint by anything but want of power.
—John Stuart Mill, *On Liberty*.

</td><td>

Every man, whether in a position of authority or not, has a tendency to try to make others act as he thinks they should or as he would like them to. And this tendency is so strongly supported by his emotions, both noble and base, that about the only thing which keeps it in check is not having the power to enforce it.

</td></tr>
</table>

The chief advantage to be gained from paraphrasing is that it will help make you a thoughtful, critical reader. If you simply skim through a difficult passage, you will get little or nothing from it. But if you take the time and effort needed to figure out the author's meaning and to restate it in your own words, you not only will understand what the author is driving at, but you will also be better able to judge his skill with words and the value of his ideas.

How to Paraphrase

Paraphrasing prose. The first step in paraphrasing is to read the selection enough times to get a thorough understanding of the writer's thoughts. It is important to look up any word whose meaning you do not know. Having only a vague idea of whom or what a particular word refers to, or guessing at the definition of a word and guessing wrong, may cause you to misinterpret a sentence or even a paragraph.

In some passages you may find not only archaic or obsolete words (words no longer used, like *maugre* and *wight*) but also words whose present meaning is quite different from the meaning they had for the writer. These words of changed meaning are more likely to cause trouble than an archaic or obsolete word, since at first glance you might mistakenly assume that you know what they mean. You would notice several words of this type if you were reading Sir Walter Raleigh's "The Last Fight of the *Revenge*." In one place, for example, Raleigh says that the enemy, after many hours of violent combat, would have preferred to "hearken to a composition" rather than continue the attack. Could Raleigh have meant that the enemy would rather listen to a theme than fight? This is hardly likely—as the context would indicate. If you looked up *composition* in an unabridged dictionary, you would discover that it is used here with its old meaning of "truce." That the enemy was willing to consider a *truce* makes sense. Whenever you come across statements that do not make sense to you in spite of seeming to contain no unfamiliar words, it is a good idea to look up the key words to see whether they, like *composition,* may not be words of changed meaning.

Sometimes it may be technical terms (*atonality, polyester,* or *natural selection,* for example) that cause you difficulty. Many of these a dictionary will help you translate into simpler, more meaningful terms. And even when there is no simple substitute for a technical expression, a dictionary or another reference book will usually make its meaning clear enough so that you can understand the writer's thought.

When the writer has expressed an idea in figurative language, you must go beyond the literal meaning of his words and search out the intended meaning. Let's assume, for instance, that in a passage you were reading, the writer had quoted this proverb: "If the beard were all, a goat might preach." The intent of the proverb, as the context and a bit of thought would show, is not to make an interesting observation about goats, but about men. You would miss the writer's point unless you could interpret the proverb in some such way as "Age alone does not bring a man wisdom" or "Time makes a young man old but not necessarily wise."

Once you are sure that you thoroughly understand the passage, the next step is to write out the paraphrase, sentence by sentence— using words that are *clear and meaningful to you.* Some of the words, naturally, will be the same as those in the original passage: there is no point in substituting synonyms for words whose meanings are familiar to you.

When you finish the paraphrase, check it against the original to make sure that it restates every idea expressed there. Make sure, too, that it does not contain any ideas or connotations the author did not clearly intend.

Finally, spend a few minutes going over your paraphrase to check the spelling and punctuation and—more important—to revise sentences to make them as smooth and effective as possible. This last step will give you valuable practice in writing clearly and precisely.

Paraphrasing poetry. Mark Van Doren once said: "A poem exists only when its writer and its reader meet inside of it and conspire to ignore everything save what it says."[1] In essence, he was describing what happens when you paraphrase a poem successfully—when you sift through the words till the basic thought emerges, when you take the long, close look that a good poem deserves, when you meet the challenge of a poem with your intellect as well as your feelings.

103

---

[1]From *Enjoying Poetry.*

In paraphrasing poetry, you follow the same general procedure as in paraphrasing prose. Below, for example, are eight lines from Alexander Pope's "An Essay on Man." First read the lines, as many times as necessary, to determine what central thought they convey. Then go through the lines once again, restating in your own words the thought developed by the poet.

> Behold the child, by nature's kindly law,
> Pleased with a rattle, tickled with a straw:
> Some livelier plaything gives his youth delight,
> A little louder, but as empty quite:
> Scarfs, garters, gold amuse his riper stage,
> And beads and prayer books are the toys of age:
> Pleased with this bauble still as that before,
> Till tired he sleeps, and life's poor play is o'er.

Now compare your restatement of Pope's verse with the following paraphrase of it:

> It takes little to capture the interest of a child; he is easily entertained by playing with a rattle or by being tickled with a straw. As a youth, he no longer enjoys such simple pleasures; but what does interest him has no more value. In middle age, his main concerns are wearing fine clothes and making money. In his old age, rosaries and books of prayer occupy his time—and bring him as much satisfaction as did his previous interests. This is the sad pattern of man's life—to the very end.

Paraphrasing poetry, as this example shows, involves interpretation. In order to bring out the intended meaning, you often have to put into words ideas that are only hinted at by the poet. Be sure, however, that when you expand a thought, there is something specific in the poem to support your interpretation.

Because poetic language is figurative and highly connotative, because good poetry is meant to suggest much more than it actually says, no paraphrase can possibly reproduce the effect of a good poem, nor can it always convey all the meaning suggested by the poem. But unless you can give in your own words the central thought of a poem, it is unlikely that you can go on to fully experience its effect or appreciate the wealth of meaning it holds. Perceiving the ideas and images that a poet's words are meant to arouse depends in great part on understanding what main thought they are intended to develop.

Your first paraphrases will probably go slowly. But as your experience and skill grow, you will be able to work faster. In fact, once you master the skill, you will find yourself mentally paraphrasing whenever you read (or hear) a difficult passage worthy of thought and study. By doing this, you will get the difficult material into a form that you can assimilate, relate to your own knowledge, and thus be more likely to remember. The rewards, as you will discover, far exceed the time and effort required.

Exercise 1 Study the following passage until you are sure you thoroughly understand it. Be ready to explain in class the meaning of all difficult or unfamiliar words, and to discuss ways in which the passage might be paraphrased. After the discussion, each member of the class is to write a paraphrase of the passage. Your teacher may ask you to read your version to the class or to write it on the chalkboard for comparison with others.

Whatever you think your own excellencies may be, do not affectedly display them in company; nor labour, as many people do, to give that turn to the conversation which may supply you with an opportunity of exhibiting them. If they are real, they will infallibly be discovered, without your pointing them out yourself, and with much more advantage.—Philip Dormer Stanhope, Earl of Chesterfield, *Letters to His Son.*

Exercise 2 Choose four quotations, two from group A and two from group B, and study them until you are sure you understand their underlying thought. Then write a paraphrase of each, making clear the point the writer was driving at. (Your paraphrases will probably be somewhat longer than the quotations.)

Your teacher may call on several students to write their paraphrases on the chalkboard so that the class may compare various versions of the same quotations.

Group A
1 Ask not that events should happen as you will, but let your will be that events should happen as they do, and you shall have peace.—Epictetus
2 It is hard for an empty sack to stand upright.—Benjamin Franklin
3 An institution is the lengthened shadow of one man.—Ralph Waldo Emerson
4 We are not to expect to be translated from despotism to liberty in a feather bed.—Thomas Jefferson
5 Nothing so needs reforming as other people's habits.—Mark Twain
6 In the final choice a soldier's pack is not so heavy as a prisoner's chains.—Dwight D. Eisenhower
7 You might as well fall flat on your face as lean over too far backward.—James Thurber, *Fables for Our Time.*
8 Even a snail can fly through space if it attaches itself to a dragon's tail.—Ernest Bramah
9 The covetous man is ever in want.—Horace
10 Ennui, felt on the proper occasions, is a sign of intelligence.—Clifton Fadiman, *Reading I've Liked.*

Group B
1 You must cut off the fountain, if you would dry up the stream.
—Timothy Shay Arthur
2 Until the donkey tried to clear
The fence, he thought himself a deer.
—Arthur Guiterman, *A Poet's Proverbs.*
3 He that governs well leads the blind; but he that teaches gives him eyes.—Robert South
4 Prejudice and precedent are the two watchdogs at the door of progress.—Charles F. Kettering
5 Bees are not as busy as we think they are. They just can't buzz any slower.—Kin Hubbard
6 To be a leader of men one must turn one's back on men.—Havelock Ellis
7 Cut thy coat according to thy cloth.—Robert Burton
8 Half the failures in life arise from pulling in one's horse as he is leaping.—Julius and Augustus Hare
9 What is not good for the swarm is not good for the bee.—Marcus Aurelius Antoninus
10 He who has little silver in his pouch must have the more silk on his tongue.—Edward Bulwer-Lytton

Exercise 3 Write a paraphrase of one or more of the following selections, as assigned by your teacher. Be ready to read your paraphrase to the class.

1   I have known several very genteel idiots whose whole vocabulary had deliquesced into some half-dozen expressions. All things fell into one of two great categories—*fast* or *slow.* Man's chief end was to be a *brick.* When the great calamities of life overtook their friends, these last were spoken of as being *a good deal cut up.* Nine tenths of human existence were summed up in the single word, *bore.* These expressions come to be the algebraic symbols of minds which have grown too weak or indolent to discriminate. They are the blank checks of intellectual bankruptcy....—Oliver Wendell Holmes, *The Autocrat of the Breakfast Table.*

2   If you would particularly gain the affection and friendship of particular people, whether men or women, endeavour to find out their predominant excellency, if they have one, and their prevailing weakness, which everybody has; and do justice to the one, and something more than justice to the other. Men have various objects in which they may excel, or at least would be thought to excel; and, though they love to hear justice done to them where they know that they excel, yet they are most and best flattered upon those points where they wish to excel, and yet are doubtful whether they do or not.—Philip Dormer Stanhope, Earl of Chesterfield, *Letters to His Son.*

3   When, in disgrace with fortune and men's eyes,
I all alone beweep my outcast state
And trouble deaf heaven with my bootless cries
And look upon myself and curse my fate,
Wishing me like to one more rich in hope,
Featured like him, like him with friends possessed,
Desiring this man's art and that man's scope,
With what I most enjoy contented least;
Yet in these thoughts myself almost despising,
Haply I think on thee, and then my state,
Like to the lark at break of day arising
From sullen earth, sings hymns at heaven's gate;
For thy sweet love remembered such wealth brings
That then I scorn to change my state with kings.
                  —William Shakespeare, Sonnet 29.

4   ... Men are grossly unequal—and, what is more, can never
be made equal—in all qualities of mind, body, and spirit.

The good society rests solidly on this great truth. The social
order is organized in such a way as to take advantage of ineradicable natural distinctions among men. It exhibits a class
structure in which there are several quite distinct levels; most
men find their level early and stay in it without rancor, and
equality of opportunity keeps the way at least partially open
to ascent and decline. At the same time, the social order aims
to temper those distinctions that are not natural. It recognizes   **107**
the inevitability and indeed the necessity of orders and classes,
but it insists that all privileges, ranks, and other visible signs of
inequality be as natural and functional as possible. The Conservative, of course—and this point is of decisive importance—
is much more inclined than other men to consider artificial distinctions as natural. Equity rather than equality is the mark of
his society; the reconciliation rather than the abolition of classes
is his constant aim. When he is forced to choose between liberty and equality, he throws his support unhesitatingly to
liberty. Indeed, the preference for liberty over equality lies at
the root of the Conservative tradition.—Clinton Rossiter, *Con-
servatism in America*. Published by Alfred A. Knopf, Inc., New
York. Copyright © 1955 by Clinton Rossiter.

5   My wealth is health and perfect ease;
     My conscience clear my chief defense;
I neither seek by bribes to please,
     Nor by deceit to breed offense:
Thus do I live; thus will I die;
Would all did so well as I!
          —Sir Edward Dyer, "My Mind to Me a Kingdom Is."

6   I remember the players have often mentioned it as an honor
to Shakespeare, that in his writing (whatsoever he penned) he

never blotted out a line. My answer hath been, "Would he hath blotted a thousand." Which they thought a malevolent speech. I had not told posterity this, but for their ignorance, who chose that circumstance to commend their friend by, wherein he most faulted; and to justify mine own candor: for I loved the man, and do honor his memory, on this side idolatry, as much as any.—Ben Jonson, *Timber, or Discoveries Made Upon Men and Matter.*

7   Nor need we be surprised that men so often embrace almost any doctrines, if they are proclaimed with a voice of absolute assurance. In a universe that we do not understand, but with which we must in one way or another somehow manage to deal, and aware of the conflicting desires that clamorously beset us, between which we must choose and which we must therefore manage to weigh, we turn in our bewilderment to those who tell us that they have found a path out of the thickets and possess the scales by which to appraise our needs.

Over and over again such prophets succeed in converting us to unquestioning acceptance; there is scarcely a monstrous belief that has not had its day and its passionate adherents, so eager are we for safe footholds in our dubious course. How certain is any one of us that he, too, might not be content to follow any fantastic creed, if he was satisfied that nothing would ever wake him from the dream? And, indeed, if there were nothing to wake him, how should he distinguish its articles from the authentic dictates of verity?—Learned Hand, "A Plea for the Freedom of Dissent," *The New York Times Magazine,* February 6, 1955.

8   This life a theatre we well may call,
    Where every actor must perform with art;
Or laugh it thro' and make a farce of all,
    Or learn to bear with grace his tragic part.
                  —Palladas (Translated by Robert Bland)

9   It was my misfortune, perhaps, to be bred up among Dissenters, who look with too jaundiced an eye at others, and set too high a value on their own peculiar pretensions. From being proscribed themselves, they learn to proscribe others; and come in the end to reduce all integrity of principle and soundness of opinion within the pale of their own little communion. Those who were out of it, and did not belong to the class of Rational Dissenters, I was led erroneously to look upon as hardly deserving the name of rational beings. Being thus satisfied as to the select few who are "the salt of the earth," it is easy to persuade ourselves that we are at the head of them, and to fancy ourselves of more importance in the scale of true desert than all the rest of the world put together, who do not interpret a certain text of Scripture in the manner that we have

been taught to do. You will (from the difference of education) be free from this bigotry, and will, I hope, avoid everything akin to the same exclusive and narrow-minded spirit.—William Hazlitt, "On the Conduct of Life; or, Advice to a School-Boy," *Table Talk.*

10 Though naturally pensive, yet I am fond of gay company, and take every opportunity of thus dismissing the mind from duty. From this motive I am often found in the center of a crowd; and wherever pleasure is to be sold am always a purchaser. In those places, without being remarked by any, I join in whatever goes forward, work my passions into a similitude of frivolous earnestness, shout as they shout, and condemn as they happen to disapprove. A mind thus sunk for a while below its natural standard is qualified for stronger flights, as those first retire who would spring forward with greater vigor.— Oliver Goldsmith, *The Citizen of the World.*

11 Silence in love bewrays more woe
   Than words though ne'er so witty;
A beggar that is dumb, you know,
   Deserveth double pity.
Then misconceive not, dearest heart,
   My true, though secret passion;
He smarteth most that hides his smart,
   And sues for no compassion.
            —Sir Walter Raleigh, "The Silent Lover."

12 No man is an island, entire of itself; every man is a piece of the continent, a part of the main. If a clod be washed away by the sea, Europe is the less, as well as if a promontory were, as well as if a manor of thy friend's or of thine own were: any man's death diminishes me, because I am involved in mankind; and therefore never send to know for whom the bell tolls; it tolls for thee.—John Donne, *Devotions upon Emergent Occasions.*

Exercise 4 From your reading or from a reading assignment for another class, select one paragraph or one stanza of verse that you think worthy of paraphrasing. Copy the passage on a sheet of paper and, below it, write your paraphrase. Be prepared to read both the original and the paraphrase in class and to invite comment on the clearness, completeness, and accuracy of your version.

PRÉCIS WRITING

A French critic and writer, Charles Augustin Sainte-Beuve, once said that without the habit of making notes people read as they eat cherries. What he meant was that people who gulp down paragraph after paragraph, never pausing to think over an author's ideas, get very little out of their reading.

Some material, of course, should be gulped. A mystery story that you read to pass the time on a train ride will probably contain few ideas worth pondering over. And you should certainly skim through an encyclopedia article if you want only to find the date of a battle or the name of a national dance. But when it comes to reading assigned for your courses, you can be sure of finding a number of ideas worthy of careful consideration, ideas that cannot be understood well (much less remembered) in a quick reading. To cope effectively with such material, you need to take notes.

There are several different ways to take notes, each of them useful in certain circumstances. Taking notes right in the book itself—by underlining the important ideas, circling key words, putting checks or brief notations in the margins—is perhaps the most convenient way, but a way to be used only if you own the book. In some assigned readings there will be little of importance to remember, perhaps only some statistics, a formula or two, or the chief exports and imports of a country. In such instances, you would simply jot down the essential points in as brief a form as possible, since more elaborate notes would hardly be necessary.

You will find that the best way to handle some reading assignments, say a chronological account of the events leading up to a war or a detailed explanation of the functions of various government agencies, is to make an outline. But other assigned readings—such as an essay on political theory, a report of a scientific experiment, or an article on the culture of a primitive tribe—may not lend themselves so well to outlining. An excellent way to deal with such material is to write a **précis**—a brief but careful summary of the writer's essential thought.[1]

The Steps in Précis Writing

Let's consider the procedure you would follow if you were to make a précis of the following short selection from a book by Harold A. Larrabee.

The first step is to read the selection—at least twice. Skim through it once to get a general idea of the content, what one writer calls "an aerial view of the topography of the thought." In the second reading, take a close-up look at the ideas the writer expresses. This time, read slowly and thoughtfully, stopping to look up unfamiliar words and to mull over difficult passages. It is also a good idea to pause now and then to test your understanding by restating the author's meaning in your own words.

---

[1] *Précis* is usually pronounced prā′sē, sometimes prā sē′; the plural is spelled the same but is pronounced with a final z sound: prā′sēz or prā sēz′.

Here is the selection:

"Facts," as Smollett and many other writers have remarked, "are stubborn things"; or, as the poet Burns put it, "they downa be disputed." The brute facts, as they are sometimes called, are what, in a thorough inquiry at any given time, or especially over a period of time, we cannot seem to get rid of; they are more or less blunt indications of states of affairs to which we are ultimately obliged to adjust ourselves in order to get along in the world. They can, of course, be temporarily obscured or glossed over with fictions, romances, and all manner of pretenses by the tender-minded, or even in some instances completely ignored. Men have deliberately refrained from inquiry; they have been deceived by illusions; and they have deceived themselves times without number ever since there have been human beings on earth. There are some matters concerning which it does seem as if the old saying *Mundus vult decipi* ("The world wishes to be deceived") were still true. Witness the comment of President Barnard of Columbia, himself a scientist, in 1873: "Much as I love truth in the abstract I love my sense of immortality still more, and if the final outcome of all the boasted discoveries of modern science is to disclose to men that they are more evanescent than the shadow of the swallow's wing upon the lake ... give me then, I pray, no more science. I will live on in my simple ignorance, as my fathers did before me; and when I shall at length be sent to my final repose, let me ... lie down to pleasant, even though they may be deceitful, dreams."

But the will to believe what is pleasing, whether or not it is contrary to fact, must always battle with the counter-will to find out what is so; and there is abundant evidence that, in the long run, even apparently "vital lies" display poor staying powers. The facts, as we say, have a way of catching up with their most determined ignorers. Men, in other words, are forced to inquire objectively into some matters if they wish to survive and to satisfy their dearest desires. It may, of course, literally take centuries to dispel a universal acceptance of the existence of witches, sea serpents, and vampires as facts of physical Nature instead of as illusions, or facts of abnormal psychology. Certainly we should expect that many of our present opinions concerning matters of fact will look just as silly to the wiser men of a few centuries hence.—Harold A. Larrabee, *Reliable Knowledge*. Published by Houghton Mifflin Company, Boston. Copyright 1945 by Harold A. Larrabee. [423 words]

Probably the most you can gather from a first, quick reading is that the selection has to do with the importance of facing facts. But by the time you finish the second, more careful reading, you should have a fairly clear understanding of the various points the author presents. Then you are ready to determine which of these points you will include in the précis and which of them you will leave out.

For instance, Larrabee gives quite a bit of space to a surprising statement made by a former president of Columbia University—that if science were to disclose that men are not immortal, he preferred to remain ignorant of the fact. Will you include this quotation? No. A précis should contain only the author's main ideas. Interesting and revealing as it is, the quotation does not express an essential idea; it is merely a detail intended to support and clarify a main point—that men sometimes willfully ignore facts. Supporting details (quotations, examples, figures of speech, and so on), no matter how interesting, are generally not included in a précis.

As you sort out the main points, it is a good idea to jot them down, especially if there are several. For the Larrabee selection, the main points are these:

> Facts cannot be disputed.
> Facts can be and have been purposely overlooked or hidden, for a time.
> Facts may be deliberately ignored.
> Man's will to know what really *is* wins out eventually.
> Facts are needed for survival and for attainment of desired goals.
> The struggle between what men want to believe and what they must believe may take centuries.

(If the selection were in a book or a magazine of your own, you could underline or put a check in the margin next to the main ideas instead of listing them.)

The next step is to write out the précis, giving the gist of the selection as concisely as you can. Although you will need to use some key words and phrases from the original, you should express the ideas in your own words in so far as possible.

As you write, keep in mind that summing up an author's thoughts means not only stating his main points, but also showing what they add up to. By comparing these two versions of Larrabee's last three main points, you can see why simply stating them is unsatisfactory:

... Man's will to know what really *is* will win out eventually. Facts are needed for survival and for the attainment of desired goals. The struggle between what men want to believe and what they must believe may take centuries.	... Ultimately, because facts are necessary for survival and for the attainment of desired goals, man's will to know what really *is* will win out over the acceptance of what is more pleasant to believe, although the struggle may take centuries.

In the version on the left, the main points are given accurately. But because the connection between them is not clear, the author's intended meaning is somewhat obscure. The second version, on the other hand, shows both what points the author has expressed and how they are related. It clearly reflects the author's thoughts.

When you finish writing the précis, check it against the original to see that you have not omitted any essential ideas and that you have expressed the writer's intended meaning accurately. Make sure also that you have not allowed any opinions of your own to slip in. You might not always agree with an author, but the précis should be restricted to reporting *his* ideas from *his* point of view.

Then, since your aim is to express ideas as concisely as possible, go over the précis one more time, to eliminate any unnecessary words and to combine related sentences wherever you can. But be careful not to distort the meaning.

Your finished précis might read something like this:

> Facts cannot be disputed. It is true that they can be and have been purposely overlooked, hidden, or even ignored—for a time. But ultimately, because facts are necessary for survival and for the attainment of desired goals, man's will to know what really *is* will win out over the acceptance of what is more pleasant to believe, although the struggle may take centuries. [64 words]

This précis gives the gist of the Larrabee selection in sixty-four words, about one seventh the length of the original.

One question most beginning précis writers ask is how long a précis should be. Now that you have gone through the steps, you can probably give the answer: Until it is written, there is really no telling how long a particular précis will be or should be. The précis of a paragraph in which an author has presented several main points, with few illustrative details, might well be half the length of the passage. The précis of a magazine article with few main ideas and a great many examples and quotations might turn out to be only one tenth the length of the original, or even less. Although you should strive to make your summary as brief as you possibly can, you should not be unduly concerned about the length. The important thing is not how long or how short a précis is, but how accurately and clearly it sums up the main ideas.

At first you will need to take the steps slowly. But as with any other skill, the more you practice, the more adept you will become. In time you may find yourself telescoping some steps, or omitting one or two, especially in dealing with simple material.

After you have mastered the technique, you will find it useful in many ways—in taking notes on lectures and discussions, for example, in gathering material for papers and talks, in preparing committee reports, laboratory reports, and so on. It will also prove helpful in writing examinations, for an essay question is often really a request for a précis of what you have learned about a specific topic.

You might not always have time or need to *write out* a précis. After reading a newspaper editorial or listening to a political speech, you would probably just sum up the writer's or speaker's main points in your mind. But whether your précis is written or mental, taking the time and effort to put the gist of someone else's ideas into your own words is sure to make those ideas more meaningful to you and help you remember them. In addition, précis making provides valuable practice in expressing ideas clearly and concisely—an ability you can put to good use in all your speaking and writing.

Exercise 5 Be prepared to tell in class what main ideas are presented in the following selection. As members of the class point out main ideas, one student is to list them on the board. After all the main points have been listed, each class member is to write a précis of the selection, using the list as a guide.

Consider the activities of the ghost writer. According to the rules of this flourishing new profession, he writes the speech for somebody else to deliver or the article or book for somebody else to sign. In certain cases he endeavors to put into words the somebody else's general thoughts, but in other cases the somebody else has no general thoughts, and it is his function to supply them. Thus he foists on the public an entirely false picture of his client; he puts brains— his brains—into a man of straw; and far worse, he abuses the craft of letters which the Lord has given him by writing words in which he places no credence while neatly dodging responsibility by placing his client's name above them. As a writer I have frequently been invited to "ghost" under such circumstances and once or twice have been sorely tempted by the size of the fee. Fortunately my economic circumstances at the time were such that I could afford to refuse. Heaven knows when, unfortunately, they will be such that I cannot afford to refuse. But when I fall, I shall know that my position as a responsible professional man—voicing his own thoughts and signing his own stuff—has come to an end.—Stuart Chase, "The Luxury of Integrity," in *The Nemesis of American Business*. Published by The Macmillan Company, New York. Copyright by Stuart Chase. [211 words]

Exercise 6 Write a précis of one or more of the following selections, as assigned by your teacher. Be ready to read your précis to the class.

1   The rocket-bomb follows penicillin as the night the day. A new technique for dealing with dreadful wounds is followed by new ways of inflicting them. Having found means to prolong his pitiable span of life, Man proceeds to cut himself down in the high-noon of his youth. He creates the ideals of justice and

mercy only to treat his fellow-man with an inhumanity that would puzzle a normal tiger. In his domestic life he builds Better Homes, equipped with every sort of labor-saving device (though in reality labor is the only occupation that gives him any real satisfaction, and his so-called pleasures more often than not goad him to drink), and promptly lays them flat with high explosives, driving himself into the wilderness to perish with quite unnecessary discomfort. New methods of communication are followed up by customs, censorships, tariffs, frontiers, travel restrictions, and, if necessary, wars so that countries now literally within speaking distance of each other, are more isolated than in the days of sail and coach. Generalizing roughly, the Martian, on his return, would have to report that Man, having found ways to make his life longer and better, at once, as though goaded by invisible Furies, sets about making it shorter and worse. And this, the Martian would decide, is just plain stupid.—I. A. R. Wylie, "The Little Woman," *Harper's*, November 1945. [217 words]

2   Another popular misconception is the notion that great talent is usually highly specific. We tend to assume that the man of extremely high talent is narrowly gifted. But the research evidence indicates that gifted individuals generally have many talents rather than a single talent. If the individual is promising in one line, the best guess is that he will be promising in a number of lines.

115

He probably will not develop his gifts along all the lines open to him, so in later life he may seem less broadly talented than he actually is. Some narrowing is inevitable. There are limitations of time and energy. And there is a "tyranny of talent" which tends to force the narrowing of anyone with extraordinarily high ability in a specific line. Once the talent is discovered it is often so highly rewarded that the individual is apt to neglect (or not to discover) his other talents; and society abets him in this neglect. With all those clavichord recitals at age seven, Mozart could not have had much time for exploration of his other gifts. Such one-sided development may be essential to the highest reaches of performance, and it might be foolish to try to prevent it in people of great talent. But anyone responsible for very gifted young people would do well to assist them in exploring the full range of their talents where possible, and to postpone at least for a time the tyrannical narrowing down.—John W. Gardner, *Excellence*. Published by Harper & Row, New York. Copyright © 1961 by John W. Gardner. [244 words]

3   The average American of today bristles with indignation when he is told that this country was built, largely, by hordes of undesirables from Europe. Yet, far from being derogatory,

this statement, if true, should be a cause for rejoicing, should fortify our pride in the stock from which we have sprung.

This vast continent with its towns, farms, factories, dams, aqueducts, docks, railroads, highways, powerhouses, schools, and parks is the handiwork of common folk from the Old World, where for centuries men of their kind had been as beasts of burden, the property of their masters—kings, nobles, and priests —and with no will and no aspirations of their own. When on rare occasions one of the lowly had reached the top in Europe he had kept the pattern intact and, if anything, tightened the screws. The stuffy little corporal from Corsica harnessed the lusty forces released by the French Revolution to a gilded state coach, and could think of nothing grander than mixing his blood with that of the Hapsburg masters and establishing a new dynasty. In our day a bricklayer in Italy, a house painter in Germany, and a shoemaker's son in Russia have made themselves masters of their nations; and what they did was to re-establish and reinforce the old pattern.

Only here, in America, were the common folk of the Old World given a chance to show what they could do on their own, without a master to push and order them about. History contrived an earth-shaking joke when it lifted by the nape of the neck lowly peasants, shopkeepers, laborers, paupers, jailbirds, and drunks from the midst of Europe, dumped them on a vast, virgin continent and said: "Go to it; it is yours!"—Eric Hoffer, "The Role of the Undesirables," *Harper's,* December 1952. [289 words]

4   It will be found that the fundamental fault of the female character is that it has *no sense of justice.* This is mainly due to the fact . . . that women are defective in the powers of reasoning and deliberation; but it is also traceable to the position which Nature has assigned to them as the weaker sex. They are dependent, not upon strength, but upon craft; and hence their instinctive capacity for cunning, and their ineradicable tendency to say what is not true. For as lions are provided with claws and teeth, and elephants and boars with tusks, bulls with horns, and the cuttlefish with its cloud of inky fluid, so Nature has equipped woman, for her defense and protection, with the arts of dissimulation; and all the power which Nature has conferred upon man in the shape of physical strength and reason has been bestowed upon woman in this form. Hence dissimulation is innate in women, and almost as much a quality of the stupid as of the clever. It is as natural for them to make use of it on every occasion as it is for those animals to employ their means of defense when they are attacked; they have a feeling that in doing so they are only within their rights.—Arthur Schopenhauer, "On Women." [213 words]

5   ...If you try to escape from death, you lose life. That is the moral—and the danger—of our obsessive fear today.

At the beginning of the recent depression, a man I knew suddenly became rich. He bought a large estate in a remote but fertile farming country and set out to make it self-sufficient. It was to provide everything necessary for life, flour from his own wheat, meat from his own herds, fish from his own ponds, electricity from his own power plant. All this was because the revolution (the paralyzing but never specifically defined terror of those days) might break out any moment. His plan was entirely unworkable. His power plant would stop operating as soon as the gasoline trucks stopped making deliveries. The mobs he envisioned would overrun his place like locusts. And so on. It was a panic dream, a nightmare. But I wondered, even if his dream of safety could be realized, what his life would be worth to him. Just beyond his high fences his fellow countrymen would be meeting their destiny, warring horribly perhaps, and dying by the thousands—but grappling with the problems of the real world and working out some way of going on. They would be alive. My friend, digesting his dinner in safety, would have no part in their experience. He would be withdrawn from human destiny, and so, while he walked his peaceful fields, he would be dead.—Bernard DeVoto, "Homily for a Troubled Time," *Woman's Day*, January 1951. Reprinted by permission of Mrs. Bernard DeVoto. [240 words]

6   Man is an animal, but a queer one. He possesses the herd instinct, so that he readily forms tribes, gangs, nations. But, unlike other gregarious animals, he has the instinct for solitude as well. Consequently he is always contradicting himself in his conduct and getting into muddles—one of which we are examining now. He wants to be alone even when he is feeling fit. That is one of the differences between a man and a chicken. A chicken wants to be alone only when it is feeling poorly. When a hen withdraws herself from her female companions and even from her gentleman friend and walks about in solitude with a glassy eye, making sad little noises, you know she is probably ill. The other hens think so too, and give her a peck in passing, to show how different they are feeling themselves.

But a man who goes about alone is probably not ill, but trying to enter his Ivory Tower. He needs the Ivory Tower just as much as he needs the human chicken-run, the city. Both are part of his heritage—solitude and multitude. He is the gregarious animal who wants to be alone even when he feels well, and his glassy eye and sad little noises are often symptoms of something important. He may be getting a clearer view of the world, or thinking out a social problem, or developing his spirit, or creating a poem. He may be bored with the life around him, which is regrettable, and, worse still, he may be afraid of it. But, whatever his motive, he has an incurable desire to be alone. The instinct may not be as old as his gregarious instinct, but it goes back to the beginning of civilization, and has a particular bearing on the development of literature, philosophy, and art. As far back as history stretches, we can see men trying to retire into their Ivory Towers and there to resist or to modify the instincts which they possess as members of the herd.—E. M. Forster, "The Ivory Tower," *The Atlantic*, January 1939. [340 words]

7   *Name-calling.* It is a common unfairness in controversy to place what the writer dislikes or opposes in a generally odious category. The humanist dismisses what he dislikes by calling it *romantic;* the liberal, by calling it *fascist;* the conservative, by calling it *communistic.* These terms tell the reader nothing. What is *piety* to some will be *bigotry* to others. *Non-Catholics* would rather be called *Protestants* than *heretics.* What is *right-thinking* except a designation for those who agree with the writer? Social security measures become *creeping socialism;* industrial organizations, *forces of reaction;* investigation into communism, *witch hunts;* prison reform, *coddling;* progressive education, *fads and frills.* Such terms are intended to block thought by an appeal to prejudice and associative habits. Three steps are necessary before such epithets have real meaning. First, they must be defined; second, it must be shown that the object to which they are applied actually possesses these qualities; third, it must be shown that the possession of such qualities in this particular situation is necessarily undesirable. Unless a person is alert and critical both in choosing and in interpreting words, he may be alienated from ideas with which he would be in sympathy if he had not been frightened by a mere name.— Robert Gorham Davis, *A Handbook of English.* Published by Harvard University Press, Cambridge.   [206 words]

8   The uneasiness, the malaise of our time, is due to this root fact: in our politics and economy, in family life and religion— in practically every sphere of our existence—the certainties of the eighteenth and nineteenth centuries have disintegrated or been destroyed and, at the same time, no new sanctions or justifications for the new routines we live, and must live, have taken hold. So there is no acceptance and there is no rejection, no sweeping hope and no sweeping rebellion. There is no plan of life. Among white-collar people, the malaise is deep-rooted; for the absence of any order of belief has left them morally defenseless as individuals and politically impotent as a group. Newly created in a harsh time of creation, white-collar man has no culture to lean upon except the contents of a mass society that has shaped him and seeks to manipulate him to its alien ends.

For security's sake, he must strain to attach himself somewhere, but no communities or organizations seem to be thoroughly his. This isolated position makes him excellent material for synthetic molding at the hands of popular culture—print, film, radio, and television. As a metropolitan dweller, he is especially open to the focused onslaught of all the manufactured loyalties and distractions that are contrived and urgently pressed upon those who live in worlds they never made.—C. Wright Mills, *White Collar*. Copyright 1951 by Oxford University Press, New York. [227 words]

Exercise 7 From a magazine or book of nonfiction, copy an interesting, well-written paragraph that contains ideas worth studying. Then write a précis of the paragraph. You may be called on to read both the original and the précis in class and to ask your classmates to comment on the clearness, conciseness, and accuracy of your summary.

Exercise 8 Your teacher, or someone appointed by your teacher, will read the following selection (or one of his choice) to the class—twice. The first time the selection is read, listen to get a general idea of its content. During the second reading, jot down the main points covered in the selection. Then, using your notes, write a précis. Several members of the class may be asked to read their précis, or to write them on the chalkboard, for comparison and discussion by the class.

After a good many years of observing human nature in action, I have firmly concluded that two qualities make the difference between leaders and men of average performance. They are curiosity and discontent. These deep human urges work together, I believe, to motivate all human discovery and achievement.

I have never known an outstanding man who lacked either curiosity or discontent. And I have never known a man of small achievement who had both. The two belong together. Without discontent, curiosity is merely idle. Without curiosity, discontent is only useless hand-wringing.

Together, curiosity and discontent count for much more than mere ambition. Galileo was not ambitious when he dropped objects of varying weights from the Leaning Tower at Pisa and timed their fall to the ground. Nor was Jean Henri Fabre when he sat day after day beside ant hills, studying the difference between instinct and reason. These men, and all men whose names are large in history, were curious and asked "Why? Why? Why?" And they were discontented because there were no acceptable answers.— Charles H. Brower, "Keys to Achievement." Copyright 1956 by The Reader's Digest Association, Inc., Pleasantville, New York, from *Town Journal*.

HAMLET

6 *The Research Paper*

To most people the word *research* suggests scientists and scholars at work, systematically investigating a subject in order to discover new facts about it or to arrive at new conclusions. The research may be done in a chemistry or physics laboratory, in a jungle or a desert, at the site of an archaeological excavation or among dusty boxes of manuscript unearthed in an attic—in fact, wherever the researcher has access to original sources of information.

To write the paper assigned in this chapter, you too will have to do research. But unlike the professional researcher, you will do most of your work in the school or city library. And instead of using original sources of information, you will be using secondary sources—information that has been gathered and reported by others. It will be your job to (1) choose a subject for study, (2) make a systematic investigation of it, primarily in books and magazines, and (3) write a report incorporating your findings.

This kind of research most of you will be doing at some time after you leave high school. If you go on to college or a technical school, you will be writing a number of term papers. When you go to work in any of a wide range of jobs, you will be called on to make reports of various kinds, long and short, simple and complicated.

As an accountant, for instance, you might find yourself preparing a report on some company's financial records. As a staff member in an advertising agency, you might be asked to compile reports on the advertising done by your clients' competitors. As a forester, you might have to write a series of reports on experiments in reducing soil erosion. You can probably think of many other examples in such fields as medicine, sales work, teaching, personnel work, law. Both in school and on the job, then, you are likely to need the training you will get by writing a research paper this term.

This paper may be the longest you have ever written (usually 1000 to 2000 words), but it need not be the most difficult. Thousands of people before you have done the same kind of writing job, and there has gradually developed a pattern, or procedure, for handling it efficiently. That procedure is laid out step by step in this chapter, for you to follow.

STEP ONE: FOCUSING ON A SUBJECT

It could be argued that choosing a subject is the most important step in the writing of a research paper. If you choose the "wrong" subject—one that you are not truly interested in, one that is so large it overwhelms you with material, one that turns out to be too difficult for you to handle—you may be bored and unhappy for the duration of the project. And the chances are that the paper you write under these circumstances will not be very successful. But if you choose your subject with care, you are likely to turn out a good piece of work and to enjoy doing it.

How do you go about making a careful choice? Let's look at three members of a twelfth-grade class to see how they deal with this matter.

Their teacher has told them that a common way to start is to pick a field—a general subject area—that they are really interested in and would like to know more about. (He suggests that to get ideas they think about their hobbies, the work they hope to do in the future, the courses they are taking in school, and any interests they may have developed through newspaper and magazine articles, and radio and TV programs.) After making this first choice, they can get the subject narrowed down to a size suitable for their 1000 to 2000 word papers.

Carol does not take long to decide on her general field; it is American history—to her the most interesting subject in school. She decides to limit that to recent history, and tentatively chooses as her subject the role of the United States in the Korean War of 1950-53. In discussing this tentative subject in class, the teacher points out that it is much too large and that Carol should narrow it down still further. Carol remarks in some surprise that she had read an encyclopedia article that covered the whole subject of the Korean War in little more than 2000 words. In fact, she readily admits, she had expected to get a good deal of her material from the article.

The teacher explains that, first of all, the research paper should be the exact opposite of the encyclopedia article. The article gives a brief account of all the most important incidents and people and ideas connected with the war; the research paper should cover in considerable detail one limited aspect of the war. In other words, he says, an encyclopedia article tells a little about a lot; a research paper tells a lot about a little. He ends by stating emphatically that a research paper must never simply rehash an encyclopedia article. The article should provide nothing more than a jumping-off place, by giving the student a general picture of the subject area he is investigating.

Carol thinks it all over, reviews the material in the encyclopedia article and in her American-history textbook, and decides on a subject that her teacher readily approves—the dismissal of General Douglas MacArthur from his Far Eastern commands during the Korean War. (When Carol starts to gather material, she is surprised to learn that there is far more than she can use, even for this small-sounding topic.)

Alan wants a scientific subject. Leafing through copies of *Science News Letter, Science Digest,* and other favorite magazines, he finds an article on peaceful uses of atomic energy. He thinks this a promising general subject; but when he tries to limit it to atomic energy as a source of electricity, or the use of atomic energy in treating cancer, he finds that the available material is much too technical for him. He asks, therefore, whether it would not be best to write a paper covering several peaceful uses of atomic energy— so that he can steer clear of technical sources. As he rather expected, his teacher says this would produce too encyclopedic a paper. He says, too, that he is afraid Alan would find himself basing such a paper almost entirely on the original article. His work in that case, as Alan agrees, would be more like a book report than a research paper.

Looking for another subject, Alan finds an article on electronic computers that leads him to his final choice—automation and un-employment. This seems an ideal subject for him, since it has to do with a scientific or technological development, and yet is a subject that he should be able to handle easily, with perhaps occasional help from his science teacher.

Hal, who played the part of Hamlet when his English-literature class performed scenes from Shakespeare's plays, starts out with the idea of writing about famous Hamlets—actors through the ages who have been outstanding in the role. But after hearing in class a number of discussions like the two described, he decides to look at some of the available library material before he makes this topic his final choice. Browsing through two books about famous actors makes it clear to him that the topic is much too big. Even a drastically pruned list of outstanding Hamlets from Shakespeare's time to our own would have to include the names of at least eight actors. And on most of their performances, Hal finds, there is an abundance of material. He is forced to conclude that if he chose this topic, he would still be at the reading stage when the deadline for submitting the paper arrived.

Next he thinks of comparing the performances of the first Hamlet, Richard Burbage (a leading actor in the group that Shakespeare wrote for), and Laurence Olivier, who starred in the 1947 movie *Hamlet*. He drops this idea when he finds that there is almost no material on the sixteenth-century actor.

Hal finally lights on the subject "Three Famous Hamlets of the Twentieth Century: John Barrymore, John Gielgud, and Laurence Olivier." He then works out for his paper a "controlling idea" (an explicit statement of the central idea he intends to develop): "These three skillful actors brought to their audiences three interpretations of the difficult role of Hamlet, equally interesting and equally outstanding, but each quite different from the others." When he assures his teacher that he intends to include very little, if any, biographical material, and will deal primarily with the way the three men played Hamlet, this subject is approved.

These examples should give you an idea of some of the pitfalls to avoid in choosing a subject. In making your own choice, keep in mind the following four questions:

1) What general subject am I most interested in? (A sincere interest is essential if you are to enjoy the project and turn out a good piece of work.)

2) What particular aspect of this subject would I like to go into more deeply? Should this aspect be narrowed down still further, considering the approximate length of the paper and the length of time I have to complete the project?

3) On thinking over my limited subject, can I formulate a clear and concise controlling idea that I can effectively develop?

4) Can I get plenty of material—material understandable to me?

***Exercise* 1** Bring to class a list of three or four subjects that you would find interesting to investigate and write a research paper on. Each of the subjects is to be limited enough to be treated adequately in a paper of from 1000 to 2000 words. The following list of subjects —all too broad—may suggest areas of special interest in which you will find suitable subjects.

Abstract Art	Espionage
Age of Chivalry	European Education
Air Traffic Control	Famous Bridges
American Folklore	Famous Jewels
Archaeology	Farming
Atomic Submarines	Fictional Detectives
Ballet	Great Disasters
Chain Stores	Imagist Poetry
Crime Detection	International Languages
Dialects	Journalism
Education in America	Man-made Satellites
Elizabethan Theater	Merchant Marine

Migratory Birds	Skin Diving
New Nations	Soap Operas
Olympics	Sports Cars
Peace Corps	Stage Design
Political Parties	Stereophonic Sound
Propaganda	Student-Exchange Programs
Radar	Teaching the Handicapped
Renaissance	Transportation
Rocks and Minerals	Twentieth-Century Novel

Exercise 2 After a class discussion of the lists prepared for Exercise 1, choose a subject for your research paper. (Although it is likely that you will prefer one from your own list, you are to feel free to use any subject suggested by a classmate which he does not intend to use.) Then work out a controlling idea for your paper. To make sure that the controlling idea you work out will be truly useful to you, review the five characteristics of a good controlling idea on pages 3-5.

STEP TWO: GATHERING INFORMATION

As you have seen, you actually start to gather information at the time you are deciding on your subject. You may read an encyclopedia article or glance at a book or two in order to narrow your subject down to the right size. And you have to look over the available material to some extent to make sure you will be able to get plenty of information about any subject you are considering. But at this second stage in the preparation of your paper, you gather information in a more organized fashion, using your controlling idea as a guide in selecting material that is relevant.

Where will you get the information? Depending on your subject, you may get some of it from your own observation. (Hal, for instance, will use in his paper some of the observations he made when he saw a revival of the movie *Hamlet.*) Depending on your subject again, you might get some information from other people. (If Alan can arrange an interview with the personnel manager of an automobile assembly plant in his town, he may learn some things about automation and unemployment that he could not learn anywhere else.) But most of the information in your paper will come from printed material—books, magazine articles, pamphlets, newspapers. This means that you will be making extensive use of your library.

Your first job in the library is to make a **working bibliography**, a list of just about all the books, articles, and pamphlets you can find that deal with your subject.

Start with the *card catalogue,* and look under all subject headings you can think of that relate to your subject. (Hal checks not only under BARRYMORE, JOHN; GIELGUD, JOHN; and OLIVIER, LAURENCE; but also under ACTING; ACTORS; HAMLET; SHAKESPEARE; and THEATER.) When you decide that a book sounds useful, add it to your list, jotting down not only the author and the title (underlined), but the publisher's name, the place and date of publication, and the library call number.

Next look for magazine articles on your subject. As you may know, the *Readers' Guide to Periodical Literature* serves the same purpose here that the card catalogue does for books. Hal checks the issues of the *Guide* for the years in which each of his three actors appeared as Hamlet—for Barrymore 1922, for Gielgud 1936, and for Olivier 1948, the year the movie *Hamlet* was first shown. As a result he adds to his working bibliography some fifteen or twenty magazine articles. Alan, on the other hand, uses only the two most recent volumes of the *Guide* to search for articles on automation, but he too ends with a long list.

Whatever your subject, add to your list any and all articles you think will be useful, noting down the author (if given), title (in quotes), name of magazine (underlined), volume and page number, and date.

Newspapers too can be a rich source of material. If your library carries *The New York Times Index,* you can look under the appropriate subject headings in this reference work. Although the *Index* refers only to material in the *Times,* you can usually be sure that other newspapers carried articles on the same subjects at about the same time.

Remember that most libraries keep a file of newspaper clippings. If your subject is a current one, ask your librarian (the reference librarian, if your library has one) to help you find any pertinent material in the file.

Pamphlets can also be a mine of information, especially on current topics. Ask the librarian for the *Vertical File Index,* published monthly, which does for pamphlets the same thing that the *Readers' Guide* does for magazine articles. Many of the pamphlets listed there your library will have in its *vertical,* or *pamphlet, file.* If you want a pamphlet that is not in the file, the *Index* will tell where you can send for it and whether or not there is a charge. (Many pamphlets are free; others are sold for a nominal fee.)

Depending on your subject, it could also be worth your while to check the *Monthly Catalogue of United States Government Publications* in your library. It may give you the titles of additional pamphlets on your subject published by the United States Government Printing Office.

At this point you may have a working bibliography so long that it would be impossible to read all the listed material in the time available. Your next step is to prune the list, leaving yourself with a bibliography of a reasonable size, made up of the best material on your original list.

On the question of size, your teacher will probably be able to give you a rough idea of how much reading it would be appropriate to do. For most high-school research papers, from five to fifteen sources would be reasonable; but the length of your bibliography naturally depends on your subject and the type of material you have found. Hal ends with a long list of twenty-four sources, because many of them are brief drama reviews and others are books from which he can use only one chapter. Alan has a list almost as long for his paper on automation, because most of his sources are magazine articles. Carol, on the other hand, has a bibliography containing only eight sources—but four of these are books on General MacArthur and Korea which she is planning to read from cover to cover.

At any rate, do not make the mistake of keeping in your bibliography everything you could possibly get through in the allotted time, regardless of the fact that some sources cover the same ground. The idea that a bibliography a yard long will create a good impression is nonsense. The amount of thought you give to your material and the way you write about it are the factors that will determine the impression your paper makes.

Choosing the best material on your list is not always easy. How are you to decide what is best? No one rule will fit all circumstances, but the following suggestions will help. Generally speaking—unless you have a topic like Hal's—you will want to begin with the most recent material you can find. For Alan this means choosing most of his magazine articles on automation from those written in the last two or three years, though articles on the subject can be found from as far back as 1955. For Carol it means being sure to include a book on General MacArthur that she finds was published in 1960. True, the General's recall by President Truman occurred in 1951, but additional facts may have been brought to light and new interpretations made of the facts in the years since then.

The second suggestion is to find out who are recognized authorities in your field (your librarian and teacher can help you) and to be sure you include some of their writing in your bibliography. Sometimes material written by people who are not experts may be easier to read and digest, and therefore useful to give you a start on your subject. But before you get through, you will want to consult the experts.

Finally, if your topic is one on which you know there is disagreement, make sure that your reading includes the two or more different opinions held. This is important for Carol, who must consider the judgments of both those who thought President Truman was right to dismiss General MacArthur, and those who thought the President made a mistake. It is important also for Hal: to get a clear and accurate picture of the three Hamlets, he must read the few negative reviews they received as well as the mass of praise.

Exercise 3   Before going to the library to begin your search for material, read the Index articles ***Card catalogue*** and ***Readers' Guide*** to refresh your knowledge of how to use these reference tools.

Compile a working bibliography for your paper. Bring it to class to be checked by your teacher, who may be able to suggest other possible sources of useful material, if your list is dangerously short.

STEP THREE: READING AND TAKING NOTES

The most practical way to take notes for a research paper is not on sheets of paper, but on note cards (or on slips of paper of note-card size). You can get cards either 3 x 5 inches or 4 x 6 inches; if your handwriting is large, you will like the 4 x 6 size better. Take your notes in ink, using only one side of the card. Put on each card only one point—one fact or quotation or idea, or a few closely related facts that you are sure you will use in one spot in your paper. The reason for this method is that it will make organizing the material so much easier. For example, look at Hal's material.

Hal is reading one book and six magazine articles about Laurence Olivier's Hamlet. Suppose he took a sheet or two of notes on each of these seven sources. In his paper he is most unlikely to follow any one of these sources for long. He may, in fact, be combining points from three or four of them in one paragraph. Therefore, when organizing his paper he would have to copy and recopy notes on fresh sheets to get his information arranged as he wants it. And in doing this, he might very well lose track permanently of some points. But with cards, each containing information on one point, he can simply shuffle his notes—arrange and rearrange them with ease—until he sees how they will best fit together. (The fact that the cards get so much handling is the reason for using ink; penciled notes would smudge.)

Before you actually start taking notes on a particular source, make a bibliography card for it. For books and magazine articles, follow the form shown in these examples from Hal's cards:

Source number

Author	Webster, Margaret ①
Title	Shakespeare Without Tears
Publisher	The World Publishing Company
Place and date	New York, 1942
Call number	822.3 DW5

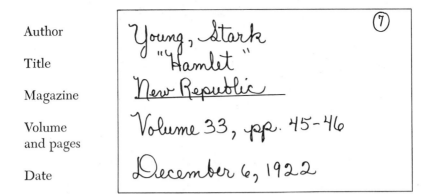

Author	Young, Stark
Title	"Hamlet"
Magazine	New Republic
Volume and pages	Volume 33, pp. 45-46
Date	December 6, 1922

(card numbered 7 in upper right-hand corner)

For encyclopedia articles and pamphlets, follow the form shown in these examples from Alan's cards:

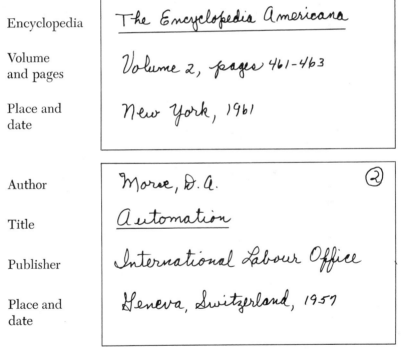

Title	"Automation"
Encyclopedia	The Encyclopedia Americana
Volume and pages	Volume 2, pages 461-463
Place and date	New York, 1961

(card numbered 1 in upper right-hand corner)

Author	Morse, D. A.
Title	Automation
Publisher	International Labour Office
Place and date	Geneva, Switzerland, 1957

(card numbered 2 in upper right-hand corner)

Each bibliography card, you will notice, has been given a number—in the upper right-hand corner. When the students are taking notes, they will use these numbers on their note cards, to identify the source from which the information comes. Using the source numbers eliminates the need for writing authors and titles innumerable times.

With the bibliography card made out, you are ready to begin reading. At this point you will find that it pays to know how to skim. A chapter in a book, or a magazine article, may contain only one or two pages of material that you can use. If you read the whole chapter or article rapidly, skimming over it to get a general idea of what it offers, you can spot these pertinent pages. Then you can return to them and read them carefully, taking notes on what you read. If you start out reading everything with concentration, you will waste a lot of time, at least as far as your research paper is concerned.

Be just as selective in taking notes. Do not waste your time writing down everything you read; take notes only on what you think is quite likely to be useful. When you do find something that you want in your notes, jot it down briefly and *in your own words*. Here, for example, is a note Hal took after reading a statement made by John Gielgud (quoted in Rosamond Gilder's *John Gielgud's Hamlet*):

Original sentence:

> "I do not believe that in this realistic age we are likely to see many more Hamlets played by men of forty or fifty years of age; at least I devoutly hope that I shall not be one of these."

Hal's note:

Source number

Slug	*Gielgud: age of Hamlet* ⑨
Page reference and note	p. 72: G. didn't think 40-50 yr. olds would or should play H. + hoped _he_ wouldn't, when that old.

Notice that in addition to the note itself, the card contains (1) the source number in the upper right-hand corner, (2) the page reference, just before the note itself, and (3) a heading, called the *slug*, that indicates what phase of his subject the note deals with. The first two items are necessary because Hal may need to check the source again or may need this information for a footnote. The slug will be a great help later, in sorting the cards and organizing the paper.

Occasionally you will want to quote some source verbatim. Do this only (1) when an author has expressed himself outstandingly well, so that no paraphrase can give the same effect or (2) when you consider it important to include in your paper the exact statement of a particular authority. If you take too many notes in the form of direct quotation, you will have a hard time writing the paper in your own words. When you do quote directly, be sure to

copy every word and every punctuation mark exactly, and enclose the words in quotation marks to remind yourself that you must do so in the paper.

Sometimes you will want to make a summary of the important points in a whole passage. Shown here is a long passage from a book about Laurence Olivier, followed by Hal's summary:

Original passage:

> They decided that the film should last two and a half hours, and this meant that a full two hours of the play had to be sacrificed. It meant, in fact, not Shakespeare's *Hamlet,* but a simplified essay in Hamlet, a new pattern to be made out of the larger pattern of the play. If it was to be a good *film,* it was necessary to be quite ruthless, and to simplify a highly complex and diffuse psychological study into a straightforward, logically-told story. It must be easy to follow, which meant that they would have to discard irrelevancies of plot, transpose scenes, even move phrases in certain speeches, and modernize a few of the more incomprehensible Elizabethan words. Olivier knew, as every artist knows when he tries to reduce something complex into brief, simple, and popular terms, that he'd be disliked by the purists and the scholars, and by those critics who demand absolute integrity. But he believed that was compensated by bringing part of Shakespeare to a far greater audience than had ever seen or heard him before. There would only be time to present one main facet of Hamlet's personality, and this must be kept constantly to the front; so he decided they would concentrate on "that particular fault" of Hamlet—irresolution.—Felix Barker, *The Oliviers.* Published by J. B. Lippincott Company, Philadelphia. Copyright 1953 by Felix Barker.

Hal's note:

Olivier: simplified Hamlet (16)

p. 301: Bec. of decision to make movie 2 hrs. shorter than play, drastic cuts had to be made. Meant simplifying plot & presenting only 1 facet of H's personality — irresolution. O. felt that bringing Sh. to new, larger audience would compensate for inevitable criticism.

Notice that in his notes Hal has used as few words as possible and has abbreviated freely. Do the same in your notes (making sure that the abbreviations will be clear to you when you reread them).

Whatever form your notes take, be sure to distinguish between the author's facts and his opinions. In Hal's material it is usually simple to tell the difference, without specially labeling opinions. Alan, however, has to be careful to make the distinction. For example, here is a note on his fifth source, "Three Myths of Automation" (an article by Charles C. Killingsworth in the December 17, 1960, issue of *The Nation*). Notice the words Alan has underlined to indicate that the statement is one of opinion rather than of fact:

Alan's note:

Employers' efforts to help

p. 469: Companies almost always find new job for worker replaced by machine. But, author says, this doesn't solve unemployment problem — just shifts it to men now looking for jobs & not finding them.

At the time you take your notes, make sure that they are accurate—that facts and figures are exactly right, and that you have not twisted an author's meaning. This will save rechecking later.

Exercise 4 Plan a systematic program of reading for your paper. Make a bibliography card for each book, article, or pamphlet you use as a source. Take careful notes on your reading, remembering to head each of your note cards with a slug and to keep to a single topic on each card.

Exercise 5 On a day or days specified by your teacher, bring to class the note cards you have made. You may be called on to display to the class examples of cards in which you have (1) paraphrased a short passage, (2) noted an opinion expressed by an authority on your subject, (3) summarized a long passage, (4) copied a direct quotation. (Be ready to explain why you thought it important to quote the author's exact words.)

Hal begins this next part of the project as you will, by sorting notes according to their slugs. In taking notes, he has used the slug *The role of Hamlet* for analyses of the part and for opinions on how Hamlet should and should not be acted. After picking out all note cards with that slug and putting them together with a rubber band, he turns to the numerous notes on the three actors (usually referred to on his cards by their initials). These notes are headed with slugs like *JB: in ghost scene, JB: praise from critics, JG: "To be or not to be," LO: with Ophelia, LO: adverse criticism.* Hal sorts them into packs, one for each actor. Now, with four groups of cards—each group dealing with a major phase of his subject—he is ready to begin outlining.

The Index article **Outline form** will explain to you (if you have not already become familiar with them) the different types of outlines writers use. Hal and his classmates are required to turn in with their papers a formal outline—either a topic outline or a sentence outline. But their teacher has encouraged them to jot down ideas in any form in the early stages of outlining, and to work out the proper phrasing of the headings only when the ideas are arranged to their satisfaction.

Hal takes out four clean sheets of paper and writes one of his major headings at the top of each:

133

    I.   The role of Hamlet
   II.   Barrymore's Hamlet
  III.   Gielgud's Hamlet
  IV.   Olivier's Hamlet

As he begins to look through his cards for possible subheads, he realizes that he seems to have two kinds of notes for each actor—some dealing with the general approach to the role and some describing what the actor did in specific scenes. He will have a much more interesting paper, he decides, if instead of simply writing about the actors in chronological order, he adds a section and sets his paper up like this:

    I.   The role of Hamlet
   II.   General description of Barrymore's Hamlet
  III.   General description of Gielgud's Hamlet
  IV.   General description of Olivier's Hamlet
   V.   Comparison of the way the three men handled six important scenes
       A. Hamlet's first scene
       B. Ghost scene
       C. Scene with Ophelia

D. "To be or not to be" soliloquy
E. Scene with mother
F. Play within the play

He juggles his cards accordingly, writes his new heading on a fifth sheet of paper, and then sets to work to fill in the details, the subheads. In his first pack of cards, those dealing with the role of Hamlet, Hal has considerable detail about costuming and staging that he finds very interesting. But after some hard thought he decides that it is irrelevant to his paper and sets it aside. He keeps for Section I only material that he thinks gives necessary background for Sections II-V. On the basis of the remaining notes in the pack, he is able to jot down three subheads under Roman numeral I:

I. The role of Hamlet: a difficult and challenging role
  A. Inconsistencies in Hamlet's behavior
  B. Question of his madness—real or pretended?
  C. Two extremes for actor to avoid—being too "intellectual" and being too "hammy"

Turning to his other packs of cards, he finds that here, too, he must eliminate a number of notes. For the most part they contain interesting biographical information—the fact that Gielgud was related to the famous actress Ellen Terry, that Olivier was knighted during the filming of *Hamlet*, that John Barrymore surprised one audience by doing a tap dance between Acts III and IV of *Hamlet*, and so on. He keeps only material having to do with how the three men played Hamlet, and uses that to work out subheads and sub-subheads.

If you have done a good job of reading and taking notes, you, too, will end up with more material than you can or should use in your paper. Don't try to keep it all, relevant or not, simply because it represents so much work on your part. The idea that you must not waste anything you have on hand is a good one for the housewife, but a bad one for the writer.

After much writing, scratching out, and rewriting, Hal has a topic outline. It is a rough blueprint of his paper—so rough that it would not mean much to anyone else. Section IV, for instance, looks like this:

IV. Olivier—director and star of 1947 movie
  A. Simplification of Hamlet's character
    1. Why simplification was necessary
      a. To fit 4½ hour play into 2½ hours
      b. To appeal to mass audience
    2. How simplification was achieved
  B. Advantages in movie version
    1. Close-ups
    2. Handling of soliloquies

134

C. Adverse criticism of Olivier's Hamlet
   1. Made Hamlet seem shallow
   2. Brought no originality to part
   3. Revealed no motivation for Hamlet's actions
D. Praise
   1. For avoiding extremes of overacting and underacting
   2. For skillfully suggesting Hamlet's satire and bitterness
   3. For being a "strong" and "princely" Hamlet

Preparing a sentence outline (if one is required) would take more effort than working out a topic outline. The chief advantage of a sentence outline, Hal would find, is that it forces him to think out the relationships between the various parts of his paper and thus helps him make sure that all parts will fit together in a neat whole. Even though working out the sentences for the outline would take time, it would make the actual writing of his paper a fairly easy job. You can see why by studying Section IV of his subject as it might appear in a sentence outline:

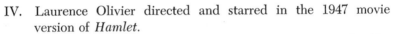

IV. Laurence Olivier directed and starred in the 1947 movie version of *Hamlet*.
   A. The outstanding feature of the movie version was that the character of Hamlet was simplified: the movie concentrated on just one of Hamlet's traits—irresolution, the inability to make up his mind.
      1. This was not done because Olivier felt it was the best way to act Hamlet; it was necessary because this was a movie instead of a stage play. **135**
         a. Since the play runs 4½ hours and the movie was to be 2½ hours, many cuts had to be made.
         b. And since, as a movie, it was aimed at a mass audience (including people who knew absolutely nothing about Hamlet *or* Shakespeare), it seemed necessary to simplify the complicated character to make the play understandable.
      2. A look at three of the big cuts that were made will show how the cutting tended to simplify the character of Hamlet:
         a. The speech that starts "How all occasions do inform against me" was cut; it shows Hamlet feeling confident and resolute, determined to avenge his father.
         b. The parts of Rosencrantz and Guildenstern were cut; this meant leaving out scenes that show Hamlet being fierce, shrewd, and able to handle any plotting against him.
         c. The speech that starts "O, what a rogue and peasant slave am I" was cut; it shows what a complicated person Hamlet is: he knows he's irresolute, he's unhappy about it, but he can't do anything about it.

B. Although playing Hamlet in a movie had some disadvantages, it also had some advantages.
  1. By using close-ups, Olivier was often able to get across strong emotions through facial expressions, while he was speaking lines in a quiet, restrained way.
  2. He also was able to make the soliloquies much more believable by doing them as Hamlet's thoughts, instead of talking to himself like a stage Hamlet; his voice spoke the words softly on the sound track, but he remained still as if thinking, without moving his lips.
C. Three main criticisms were leveled at Olivier's portrayal.
  1. Because of the simplification, some critics felt he made Hamlet a shallow person.
  2. He brought nothing new to the part (as both Barrymore and Gielgud had).
  3. He did not bring out any motivation—any underlying reason why Hamlet acted as he did.
D. But most critics, except for disliking the simplification, felt that Olivier's performance was outstanding.
  1. He was not hammy; but he was not too "intellectual" and restrained, as some felt Gielgud had been.
  2. Though he made the audience very sympathetic to Hamlet, he did not soft-pedal Hamlet's satirical and bitter humor, as some have done.
  3. He was a very strong Hamlet, and—although forty years old—was graceful and princely.

Though you do not want to spend as much time in outlining your paper as in writing it, it is only sensible to try to turn out a good, detailed outline. It will pay dividends when you come to the next step.

Exercise 6   After sorting your notes into the categories that will provide the principal divisions of your paper, ·work out an outline—either a topic or a sentence outline, as directed by your teacher. Your teacher may schedule a conference to go over your outline with you and (if necessary) to discuss with you ways in which you might improve the organization of your material.

STEP FIVE: WRITING

THE FIRST DRAFT

When Hal sits down to write, he wonders for whom he should seem to be writing—his teacher alone? his classmates? an imaginary group of readers interested in drama (as though the paper were going to be published in *Theatre Arts* magazine)?

He is also uncertain about the general style to use. He does not want to sound unnaturally formal, but he knows that his customary style, used for short papers on "What's Right with Teen-agers" and "How My Dog Trained Me," is inappropriate for a research paper.

Many students find that they bog down at this point; you may be one of them. If so, here is a good device for getting over the first hurdle: Imagine that you are writing for an intelligent reader who is interested in the subject but knows little about it. You, who by now are something of an expert on the subject, are sitting down to explain it to him. You want to make it as clear as possible, and you also want to keep alive his interest. With this in mind, you should find it easier to write a clear, concise, and readable account of what you have learned.

As for style, one of the main differences between this paper and others you have written is that here your style should be impersonal. This means that you do not refer to yourself at all unless absolutely necessary, and then you make the reference as brief as possible. Hal, for instance, may need to use a phrase or two like "in my opinion" when he is discussing the performance of *Hamlet* that he himself has seen. But he should not scatter *I*'s all over the paper nor give the impression that his having seen the film is of major importance.

Perhaps the main point for you to remember at this stage is that your paper should be written *in your own words*. After all, one of the aims of this project was for you to learn something new by extensive reading, and then to write a paper that tells what *you* have learned. Don't just reproduce what you have read, then, in a paper studded with quotation marks. Get your material away from the form in which you found it.

This will be hard to do, you will find, unless you are thoroughly familiar with the material, unless you have thought over the ideas long enough to make them your own. Before you start writing, therefore, read through both your notes and your outline once or twice more to make sure that you have an accurate and clear-cut picture of the subject in mind. Then pick up your pencil and start writing.

Write the first draft as rapidly as you can and with as few interruptions as possible. You will probably want to pause to look over each major section of your outline as you come to it, to remind yourself of the ground to cover. But while writing each section, do not refer to your note cards unless necessary—to find figures or dates, for example, or to get the exact words of a quotation. At this stage don't stop to worry about errors in grammar, spelling, and punctuation. You can correct those later. Right now concentrate on getting your ideas down on paper. Use only one side of the sheet, double-space your writing, and number the pages. All this will make it easier when you come to revise.

Wherever you use facts or opinions borrowed from one of your sources, insert in parentheses (or in the margin) a check mark or the source number and page from which the material comes. Then you will know where footnotes are needed in your final version.

On this subject, remember that although it is important to give credit in a footnote whenever you borrow anything *specific* from a source, it is also important not to overfootnote. After all, your paper will include a bibliography. This alone would make it clear that you got your material from various sources, and would protect you from the charge of **plagiarism**. (See Index article **Plagiarism**.)

Some of your sentences will contain information that is repeated in all of your sources and that could be found in many others—for example, a statement in Hal's paper that John Barrymore won great acclaim, both in New York and in London, for his portrayal of Hamlet. Such sentences as these should not be footnoted. Other sentences may contain information generally known or opinions generally held—like a statement of Hal's that every well-known tragic actor has tried the role of Hamlet. Such sentences as these do not need footnotes, either.

Footnotes are needed for sentences like the following:

> Gielgud tried walking around the stage while reciting the "To be or not to be" soliloquy, but eventually decided that this was too distracting.[1] [A specific fact borrowed from one source and not to be found in any other so far as Hal knows.]

> George Jean Nathan said that most critics look for a certain amount of ham acting in this role.[2] [An opinion expressed by one writer.]

> As Margaret Webster has commented, "There is not one 'right' Hamlet, with all the others wrong."[3] [A direct quotation.]

The footnotes themselves are placed at the bottom of the page on which the footnoted sentences appear, separated from the text by a short line:

---

[1]Rosamond Gilder, *John Gielgud's Hamlet*, p. 55.
[2]George Jean Nathan, *The Morning After the First Night*, p. 93.
[3]Margaret Webster, *Shakespeare Without Tears*, p. 110.

Sometimes information taken from a single source is presented in several consecutive sentences, rather than just one. In such instances, the number calling attention to the footnote is usually placed after the last of the sentences. (For further information, see the Index article **Footnotes**.)

Exercise 7 Write the first draft of your paper, following the suggestions given in the preceding section. Remember that your outline is a guide—not a strait jacket. If, while you are writing, you think of a better order in which to present certain ideas or details, do not hesitate to depart from the order shown in your outline.

STEP SIX: REVISING

THE FIRST DRAFT

Try to schedule the various stages of your writing so that you can set aside your first draft for a day or two before revising it. This will enable you to be more critical—to see more clearly the weaknesses that are an inevitable part of a rapidly written first version. Make sure you allow yourself enough time for a careful and unhurried revision. Many writers find that they must spend almost as much time in revising the first draft as in writing it.

Consider the content. Revision can best be done in two stages. First consider the content. Throughout the paper, have you given enough specific details to make your points clear to your reader (who, remember, has intelligence and interest, but who knows less about the subject than you)? Have you progressed smoothly from point to point, so that your reader will grasp the connection between one part of the paper and the next? Are your facts accurate, and have you reproduced accurately the opinions of other writers whom you are citing? Have you cluttered the paper with unnecessary repetition or irrelevant material?

How about those difficult spots, the beginning and the end? Will your first paragraph make the reader want to keep on reading? Will it give him a good idea of what to expect from the paper? Does your conclusion sound too abrupt, as if you had been suddenly interrupted? Does it sound tacked on? Or does it round off the paper neatly? Questions like these will suggest possible changes for the better.

Consider the style and mechanics. When you think that you have done your best with content, you can go on to consider style and mechanics. Try reading the paper aloud to see how it sounds. Combine sentences that sound too choppy; split up sentences that are too long and complicated for easy reading. Replace vague words with words that are more lively and specific. Cut out unnecessary words and phrases. Cut out unnecessary references to yourself, and any phrases that detract from the impersonal style of the paper. Check for errors in grammar, spelling, and punctuation. Do a thorough job. Now that you are so near the end, you will want to make your writing do justice to the material you have so carefully gathered.

Whenever possible, make your corrections right on the first draft, between the lines or in the margins. When you need to make longer alterations, put them on separate sheets, labeling them so that you will know exactly where they belong.

Exercise 8   Revise the first draft of your paper. Keep working at your revisions until you can honestly say to yourself that you have done your best.

STEP SEVEN: PREPARING THE FINAL COPY

For your final copy, use a good grade of paper, leave wide margins at the sides, and double-space the lines, except for footnotes. If you can, type the paper (and be sure to leave time for proofreading and for correcting typographical errors). If you do not type, see that your handwriting is neat and legible. Number in the upper right-hand corner all the pages except the first.

In this copy, you will add the footnotes that your first draft has shown to be necessary. First make a final check for other spots that may need footnotes—and for spots where you have called for footnotes but do not need them. Next work out the footnotes completely and legibly on scratch paper, referring to the Index article **Footnotes** to make sure you use the right forms. Then copy the footnotes carefully at the bottom of the right pages.

With the footnotes out of the way, you have only a few other details to take care of. Your paper, when submitted, must include the following:

1) A **title page**, giving the title of your paper, your name, the name of the course, and the date the paper is submitted (plus anything else your teacher may ask you to include). All this information is centered neatly on the page or arranged according to your teacher's directions.

2) A copy of your **final outline**, to serve readers as a table of contents. At the right of each main heading, insert the number of the page on which that topic begins. If your paper in its final form differs from the outline in any way, be sure to change the outline accordingly.

3) A **final bibliography**—a list of all the books, magazine articles, and other published materials that you actually used in preparing your paper. The bibliography, by identifying the sources from which your information was drawn, gives due credit to these sources and adds a note of authority to your work. It also serves the purpose, an important one in published material, of suggesting further reading for anyone who may be especially interested in the subject.

In putting together your bibliography, leave out sources that you have read but not found useful. Include all sources that helped you, whether or not you have referred to them in footnotes. Refresh your memory about the proper forms and the punctuation of your bibliography items by reading through the article *Bibliography* in the Index.

Two additional sections seldom required—or needed—in a high-school research paper are (1) a **preface**, or **foreword**, and (2) an **appendix**. A few students in Hal's class, however, decide that there are some things they would like to say that they could most conveniently put in a preface. Alan, for instance, wants to acknowledge the help that he received in writing his paper on automation from the personnel staff of the local automobile assembly plant. After working it out on scratch paper, he writes his acknowledgment on a separate sheet with the centered heading *Preface.*

If you have any information you think interesting enough to give the reader, but not suitable for inclusion in the actual paper, you may put it in an appendix. Carol, for instance, has copied a number of newspaper headlines giving immediate reactions to the news of General MacArthur's dismissal in April 1951. She has summarized the reactions of the press in the body of the paper; but thinking that the direct quotations would make an interesting addition, she types them up on a separate sheet headed *Appendix.*

When Hal submits his paper, he assembles the parts in this order:

1 Title page
2 Outline (serving as a table of contents)
3 The paper (all pages numbered but the first)
4 Bibliography

141

Alan's preface goes between the title page and the outline. Carol puts the appendix she has prepared at the very end, after the bibliography.

After all the parts of your own paper are assembled in order, fasten them together with paper clips or bind them in a manila folder. If you use a folder, write or type on it the same information that is given on your title page. Then, at last, your job is done.

When you have handed in your paper—confident that you have read widely, thought your material through, reported accurately, and checked and rechecked for possible errors and flaws—you will have a rare feeling of pride and achievement. This is your immediate reward. But you will find as the years go by that the experience you have gained continues to produce dividends—in college, in business, and in community affairs.

Exercise 9   Make a final copy of your research paper, complete with footnotes. Carefully proofread your work and make needed corrections neatly and legibly.

Exercise 10   Prepare for your paper a title page, a final copy of your outline, a final bibliography (and a preface and appendix, if you have planned to include these). Assemble the various parts of your paper and submit it on the day assigned.

7 *How Words Work*

This chapter—"How Words Work"—will review the terms you will need in order to analyze and solve the grammatical problems that may come up in your speech and writing. Many of these problems will be taken up in Chapter 9, "Standard Word Forms." The grammar you review and master here will come in handy in Chapters 10 and 11 also, when you work on avoiding sentence errors and on writing more effective sentences.

THE FOUR FUNCTIONS OF WORDS

As you learned long ago, there are seven parts of speech, which work together to communicate meaning.[1] Actually, these seven kinds of words work in just four different ways: they name, assert, modify, or connect.

Words That Name

The largest group of words in the language are **nouns**—words used to name persons, places, things, qualities, actions, or ideas:

The *stranger* gave *David* fifty *cents* and thanked him for his *kindness.*

Her *uncle* devoted ten *years* to the *collection* of these *specimens.*

---

[1] An eighth part, the interjection, which expresses strong feeling, has little or no grammatical relation to other words in a sentence (for example: Ouch! Oh!). Since it causes no difficulty, it is not considered here.

For convenience we often use **pronouns** instead of nouns. Pronouns are words that represent (or "mean") persons, places, or things without naming them. Pronouns help us make our speech less awkward, since by using them we can avoid the unpleasant repetition of nouns. Compare, for instance, these two versions of the same statement:

> When Clifford saw Sally, Clifford told Sally that if Sally would meet Clifford at the south entrance after school Clifford and Sally could ride home together with Mr. Keane.
>
> When Clifford saw Sally, *he* told *her* that if *she* would meet *him* at the south entrance after school *they* could ride home together with Mr. Keane.

There are several different kinds of pronouns:

PERSONAL: I, me; you; he, him; she, her; it; we, us; they, them
POSSESSIVE: mine, yours, his, hers, its, ours, theirs
DEMONSTRATIVE: this, that, these, those
INTERROGATIVE: who, whose, whom, which, what
INDEFINITE: all, another, any, both, each, either, everyone, neither, few, many, none, one, other, several, some, somebody, etc.
RELATIVE: who, whom, whose, which, that
REFLEXIVE: myself, yourself, himself, herself, itself, ourselves, yourselves, themselves
INTENSIVE: same forms as reflexives

144

Words That Assert

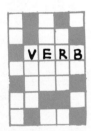

The words we use to "assert" or express action, condition, or being are **verbs**:

> The cow *jumped* over the moon.   [Physical action.]
> We *believed* his story at first.   [Mental action.]
> The milk *smells* sour, but he *is* sure it *is* fresh.   [Condition, being.]

The verb may express a command:

> *Move* to the rear of the bus.

The verb often consists of two, three, or four words—a main verb plus one or more auxiliary, or helping, verbs that express various shades of meaning:

> Jerry *is watching* a television program.
> *Have* you ever *been stung* by a wasp?
> The members *should have been notified* sooner.

Verbs of more than one word are sometimes called *verb phrases* or *phrasal verbs*.

Words That Modify

Words that are used to make the meaning of other words more exact are modifiers. **Adjectives**, which modify nouns or pronouns, answer such questions as what kind? which? whose? how many?

> Put *that small leather* chair in *his* room.
> Have you *any* linen *wider* than *this* piece?
> *The first four* questions were *the hardest* ones.

Adverbs, which modify verbs, adjectives, other adverbs, or whole sentences, answer such questions as how? when? where? to what extent?

> She grabbed the telegram and *quickly* ran *upstairs*. [Modify the verb *ran*.]
> Martha was *unusually* tall. [Modifies the adjective *tall*.]
> Dad *very* rarely complains about the noise. [Modifies the adverb *rarely*.]
> *Unfortunately*, there was nothing else to do. [Modifies the whole sentence.]

Words That Connect

Prepositions, conjunctions, and some pronouns are used as connecting words. **Prepositions** are words placed before nouns or pronouns (called the objects of the preposition) to show their relationship to some other word in the sentence:

> The magazines *on* the top shelf should be returned *to* the library. [*On* shows the relationship between *magazines* and the object of the preposition, *shelf; to* shows the relationship between *should be returned* and the object *library.*]

Prepositions may consist of more than one word:

> We left early *because of* the rain.
> He kept working *in spite of* the noise.

Conjunctions join words, phrases, or clauses:

> Helen *and* I can bring rolls *or* salad, *but* we can't bring both. [Coördinating conjunctions, joining parts of equal value.]
> *Neither* the doctor *nor* the nurse was in. [Correlative conjunctions, used in pairs.]
> The auditorium was cold and damp; *however*, no one left. [Conjunctive adverb, used both as an adverb and as a conjunction.]
> Call me *if* she comes. [Subordinating conjunction, joining parts not equal in value.]

The **relative pronouns**—*who, which,* and *that*—are used to join adjective clauses to the words they modify:

The man *who* answered the phone was quite abrupt.
Did you see the dress *that* she bought?

As you know, a word may have several different meanings, and what a word means at any one time depends on the way it is used (John designed the *set* for the play. She gave us another *set* of dishes). Not only the meaning, but the part of speech of a word, is determined by its use. You cannot tell, for example, what part of speech *back* is until you see how it is used in a sentence:

Back the car out of the garage. [Verb.]
Tim sat in the *back* seat with Phil. [Adjective.]
Please step *back* and give him room. [Adverb.]
I hung my coat on the *back* of my chair. [Noun.]

Exercise 1 On a sheet of paper, list the thirty-five italicized words (or verb phrases) in the following paragraph. After each word, tell what function it has in its sentence and what part of speech it is. [Example: *You* is a naming word, a pronoun.]

You are, in the *first* place, in a *rather awkward* position *physically* [in a diving suit]. Your body *is encased* in a canvas suit, *and* between you and the suit is a *cushion* of air. Each of your *feet* is weighed down with twenty pounds *of* metal, fifteen of which you *can detach* in emergency, *if* necessary. *Around* your shoulders is a breastplate of *bronze,* weighing *forty* pounds. The breastplate hangs *about* your neck and upper chest like a medieval piece of armor. Your head is in a *metal* helmet screwed to the breastplate. In this helmet there *is* a *glass* plate, three inches in *diameter,* directly in front of your face. Through this you *can see,* and you had better rub its *inside* with tobacco so that your *breath* will not cloud *it. Your* hands are *free, because* the suit *ends* with *elastic* bands at your wrists, *but* you cannot scratch your face with *these* hands. *Count* the number of times you *touch* your nose, cheeks, eyes, and chin *in* two hours, and you know what this means. Undersea you can't scratch. You *just* itch and bear it.—John D. Craig, *Danger Is My Business.* Published by Simon and Schuster, Inc., New York. Copyright 1938 by John D. Craig.

Exercise 2 After reading each of the following sentences, write a sentence of your own in which the italicized word has a different function. [Example: He *set* the table for dinner. (*Set* functions as an asserting word.) They played a *set* of tennis. (*Set* functions as a naming word.)]

1 They were asked to read a best-selling *novel* by Monday.
2 The two oldest girls *iron* the clothes after school.
3 To her dismay, Pat found herself on an *express* train.

4   The whole *cast* was there for dress rehearsal—and on time!
5   We had to borrow *ice* cubes for the lemonade.
6   What *excuse* did Seth give for not showing up last night?
7   Once again I heard the *whistle.*
8   Did you hear the school program over the *radio* last night?
9   Sue laid her book *down* and helped me do the dishes.
10 After a pep talk by the coach, the team always plays *better.*
11 Sam and I took a *long* time deciding what to order.
12 Didn't the old library stand *opposite* the police station?

THE SENTENCE PARTS

More important than knowing the parts of speech is knowing how words work together to communicate meaning. We express a thought not through isolated words but by grouping words together in a sentence in such a way that the relationship between them is clear. As you review the various parts of a sentence, notice the great part *word order* plays in showing the relationship between them.

Subjects and Verbs

The basic parts of the standard sentence are the subject and the verb. The *subject* is the word or group of words that names the person or thing about which the *verb* makes a statement or asks a question. The subject—usually a noun or pronoun—is the starting point of the statement and in the typical sentence precedes the verb, as in the next three examples:

Another **telegram** *arrived* early the next morning.
As a result **we** quickly *changed* our plans.
What *happened* then? **Who** *notified* the family?

In some sentences the order is "inverted," and the subject follows or comes between parts of the verb:

IN SOME QUESTIONS: Where *is* my **pen?** *Did* **anyone** here *see* it?
AFTER EMPHATIC MODIFIERS: Down *came* the **elm** with a crashing and splintering of branches. Never before *had* **we** *seen* such a sight.
AFTER AN INTRODUCTORY "THERE":   There *is* a bad **leak** in the roof.

The subject does not necessarily name the "doer" of the action expressed by the verb; it may (as the subject of a "passive verb") name the receiver of the action:

DOER: Our **team** *defeated* Elmwood a month ago.
RECEIVER: Our **team** *was defeated* by Elmwood yesterday.

Compound subjects and verbs. Two (or more) words, joined by a conjunction, may be the subject of one verb:

Jim and *I* plan to hitchhike across the country next summer.
Either *math* or *science* is a good major for a pre-engineering student.
Of all the sports *baseball, hockey,* and *tennis* are my favorites.

The verb, also, may be compound:

Two boys *walked* in and *looked* around.
I *listened* to his story, but *did* not *believe* it.
Tom often *takes* tickets or *hands* out programs.

Complete subjects and predicates. While the actual name of the person or thing the verb tells about is commonly referred to as the *subject,* it is more accurately called the *simple subject,* to distinguish it from the *complete subject,* which is the naming word plus all of its modifiers. Similarly, the verb is often called the *simple predicate;* the verb and the words used with it to tell about the subject are called the *complete predicate.*

The spy Enoch Cosby, who posed as a British agent working out of New York, narrowly escaped being hanged by his own countrymen.

Here the simple subject is *spy;* the complete subject is *The spy Enoch Cosby, who posed as a British agent working out of New York.* The simple predicate is *escaped;* the complete predicate is *narrowly escaped being hanged by his own countrymen.*

Direct Objects

S·V·O

In a sentence like "Everyone there grinned" or "The whistle blew" the meaning of the verb is clear and complete. But in many sentences the meaning of the verb is not complete without a *direct object*—a word that names the person or thing that receives the action. In the standard sentence the direct object follows the verb:

Brown *hit* the **champ** hard with a right to the jaw.
Why *didn't* you *call* **Sue** and **me**? [Compound direct object.]

Occasionally, for emphasis, the object comes first, followed by the subject and then the verb:

The hardest **problems** *I* always *leave* till last.

Indirect Objects

S·V·IO·O

With some verbs (*give, bring, show, ask, buy, tell* ...) a second object is often used to name the person or thing to or for whom the action is done. This *indirect object* almost always comes before the direct object:

> Mike bought his **brother** a *tricycle.*
> Give **Larry** a *quarter.*
> Who told **Bob** and **you** the *news?* [Compound indirect object.]

Predicate Complements

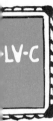

The meaning of a *linking verb* (one that expresses condition or state of being rather than action—*be, seem, grow, feel, become...*) is completed by a *predicate complement.* The complement, which generally follows the verb, may be either an adjective modifying the subject, or a noun or pronoun meaning, or referring to, the same person or thing as the subject:

> Nancy *grew* more and more **beautiful.** [Predicate adjective.]
> Hal *was* the only good **pitcher** on the team. [Predicate noun.]
> My favorites *are* **those.** [Predicate pronoun.]

Predicate complements are also used to complete the meaning of passive verbs in sentences like these:

> David was elected *chairman.* [Predicate noun.]
> The walls had been painted *green.* [Predicate adjective.] 149

Objective Complements

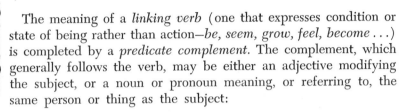

When such action verbs as *call, name, elect, appoint, make, dye, paint, think,* and *consider* are used, our sentences are likely to have four basic parts—a subject, a verb, a direct object, and an *objective complement.* The objective complement, usually a noun or an adjective, generally follows the direct object:

> Professor Cooper called *Myron* a **genius.**
> They elected *him* **president.**
> Alice dyed the *dress* **blue.**
> The committee thought our *plan* **unworkable.**

As these examples show, the objective complement (whether noun or adjective) tells what the direct object is named, or elected, or made to become, or thought to be.

Appositives

The meaning of subjects, objects, or complements is often made clearer by a word or group of words directly following them, renaming or explaining. These words, "in apposition with" the nouns or pronouns they follow, are called *appositives*:

> All minor injuries—*cuts, bruises,* and pulled *muscles*—are treated by the nurse in the school infirmary. [In apposition with the subject *injuries.*]
> Mr. Byrd described two planets—*Mars* and *Saturn.* [In apposition with the direct object *planets.*]
> The first one in line was Mary, the class *president.* [In apposition with the predicate complement *Mary.*]

An appositive may sum up the meaning of a whole group of words:

> Nancy chews gum noisily and constantly—a *habit* that drives her friends to distraction.

Sometimes an appositive, instead of directly following the word it explains, precedes it:

> A rootin', tootin' *cowboy* in the old days, Two-Gun Pete finds retirement dull today.

For emphasis an appositive may be placed last, even when the word it refers to is in the first part of the sentence:

> Just two of the books on that shelf are his—*The Spy* and *Main Street.*

Exercise 3   Divide a sheet of paper into two columns. In the first column, write the simple subject of each of the following sentences; in the second, write the verb. Some of the subjects and verbs are compound; be sure to list all parts of these. Number your answers with the numbers of the sentences.

1   Did everything in the warehouse burn?
2   The band, with mascots in tow and the director walking alongside, approached the reviewing stand.
3   With a little more study, Lucy could have passed the test.
4   During the first six weeks each student is assigned three novels.
5   Aren't all these details confusing you?
6   Some of the most inspiring scenery in the world awaits you right here in America.
7   Dee and the three other girls were finally found at Lola's.
8   But the music should have been sent to Phyllis.
9   Each of the students must take a driving test.
10   Joe is setting up apparatus for his chemistry experiment.
11   There are probably a number of people adventurous enough to risk a rocket flight to the moon.
12   Bea, why don't you go to camp with us this summer?
13   Mr. Stewart, the principal, and Mr. Green are both planning to go to the Philippines.

14 Out onto the field came the team, resplendent in their bright new uniforms.

15 Your report should have been written and then given to the secretary.

16 Down into the shaft went the rescue party, solemn, grim, and determined.

17 Though not in the mood to concentrate on anything as technical as physics, Bill sat down and opened his book.

18 Tina threw her paper down and flounced out of the room.

19 Down the street screamed the fire engine, frantically trying to reach the fire.

20 Annoyed by his sarcasm, Beth suddenly banged the piano keys, rose from the bench, and fled from the room.

Exercise 4   Divide a sheet of paper into five columns. In the first column, write the subject of each of the following sentences. In the second, write the verb. In the third, write the indirect object. In the fourth, write the direct object. In the fifth, write the predicate complement. No sentence will contain all these parts. Number your answers with the numbers of the sentences.

1 Joe was without question the best athlete in our gang.

2 Reluctantly he handed Ed the long-overdue money.

3 How can I possibly face all those people?

4 Food cooked over a campfire always tastes good.

5 After the great fire only two buildings remained on the north side of the river—the water tower and the pumping station.

6 I told them only the truth.

7 At a party he is a complete and unadulterated bore!

8 The guards turned back a truck and two cars at the iron bridge.

9 All of us—Kim, Frank, and I—want him for biology.

10 Even after careful washing, the spinach seems sandy.

11 She became panic-stricken at the thought of speaking before the class.

12 Will you bring Isabel and me a Coke?

13 Ever since the accident Cynthia has been feeling bad.

14 Mr. Hill, the man with the jolly disposition, is our mayor.

15 Uncle Phil always does his own repair work.

16 Our graduating class gave the school a television set.

17 Isn't the tall man standing near the desk Mr. Burns?

18 Wayne, has Kathy given you the new schedule?

19 Bill and I collected the books and returned them to her.

20 Many great men have been considered foolish by their contemporaries.

Exercise 5   Divide a sheet of paper into three columns. In the first column, write the subject of each of the following sentences; in the second, write the verb. In the third column, copy the italicized word (or words) in each sentence and, after it, tell how it is used (as direct object, indirect object, predicate complement, objective complement, or appositive). Number your answers with the numbers of the sentences.

1 Why hadn't either of them told *Mr. Luce* the truth?
2 Of course, Laura considered it a *compliment.*
3 Shouldn't Brigid have paid *any* of the bills?
4 The glares of the passers-by made Al more and more *nervous.*
5 Occasionally Mrs. Foxx or her daughter would make *him* a cup of tea or some lemonade.
6 The last witness for the prosecution was Max Turgenev, an unemployed *steam fitter* from Hasbrouck Heights.
7 But how many *calls* does the average telephone salesman make in two hours?
8 How *improbable* Don's story must have sounded to the judge.
9 Mrs. Carter's *pearls* he had hidden in a box of oatmeal.
10 Almost all of her stories, rambling *tales* of her girlhood in Indiana, were published first in small literary magazines.
11 Could the shadow on the porch have been Roger Emery, the neighborhood *joker?*
12 Weren't some of the senator's answers purposely *ambiguous?*
13 On the other hand, none of the boys found the work *easy.*
14 By noon three items remained on the sale counter—two dented sprinkling *cans* and a rusty *pair* of pruning shears.
15 Never once during that time did Tom offer *anyone* a ride.
16 Right now Ken's car payments are the *least* of his worries.

WORD GROUPS

We often use groups of closely related words in sentences to do the same work that single words do. These groups, called *phrases* and *clauses,* may serve as nouns, as adjective modifiers, or as adverb modifiers.

Phrases

Prepositional phrases. A *prepositional phrase,* made up of a preposition plus a noun or pronoun called its object, functions as a modifier—either adjective or adverb:

The man *with the white flag* is the official starter. [Adjective phrase modifying the noun *man.*]
Ernie stumbled *over the skates.* [Adverb phrase modifying the verb *stumbled.*]
Aren't you curious *about them?* [Adverb phrase modifying the adjective *curious.*]

Participial phrases.   A *participle* is a verb form used as an adjective:

ACTIVE PARTICIPLES: the *howling* dog   [A dog that is howling.]
the *screaming* child   [A child that is screaming.]
the *retreating* troops   [The troops that are retreating.]
PASSIVE PARTICIPLES: *broken* toys   [Toys that have been broken.]
rotted timbers   [Timbers that have been rotted.]
the *bent* twig   [A twig that has been bent.]

Though they do the work of modifiers, not of verbs, participles are like verbs in that they can have objects, complements, and modifiers of their own. Together with these words, they form *participial phrases* that are used to modify nouns and pronouns:

> *Grabbing a sandwich from the tray,* Tom hurried to the door. [The whole participial phrase modifies *Tom.* Inside the phrase, *sandwich* is the object of *Grabbing; from the tray* is an adverb phrase modifying *Grabbing.*]
> *Having been warned about his temper,* Laura wasn't surprised at this outburst.   [The whole phrase modifies *Laura. About his temper* is an adverb phrase modifying *Having been warned.* Notice that a participle, like a verb, may be more than one word—*Having been warned.*]

A participle may modify a word right in the phrase itself:

> *His voice trembling with anger,* he ordered us to leave.   [The participle *trembling* modifies *voice.*]
> Dan was slouched in a corner of the seat, *his head covered with a newspaper.*   [The participle *covered* modifies *head.*]

153

A phrase of this kind, containing a participle and the word it modifies, is called an *absolute phrase. Absolute* here means "independent"; the phrase, in other words, has no *grammatical* connection with the rest of the sentence. But it is related in meaning, since it adds descriptive details to the statement.

Gerund phrases.   The *-ing* form of the verb—when used as a noun—is called a *gerund:*

> *Complaining* won't help.   [Compare this with "A complaint won't help."]
> Why not try *coöperating*?   [Compare this with "Why not try coöperation?"]

Gerunds, like all nouns, may be modified by adjectives. Like verbs, gerunds may have objects, complements, and adverb modifiers. These modifiers and complements, together with the gerunds, form *gerund phrases* that may have any of the noun uses:

SUBJECT: *Any whispering in class* made her angry.
PREDICATE NOUN: Her only interest was *feeding the goldfish.*

OBJECT OF VERB: I don't like *being scolded in front of people.*
[Notice that the gerund may be more than one word—*being scolded.*]

OBJECT OF PREPOSITION: He won't have to worry about *saving for a rainy day.*

APPOSITIVE: Our first job, *painting the fence,* took all morning.

Infinitive phrases. A third "verbal" is the *infinitive,* the simple form of the verb, usually preceded by *to: to sing, to run, to think.* Infinitives, like the other verbals (participles and gerunds), may have objects, complements, and modifiers, which together form phrases that are used in sentences as single words might be used. They may be used as nouns, adjectives, or adverbs:

AS A NOUN: *To turn back now* would be foolish. [Subject of *would be.*]
Ronald offered *to pay for the book.* [Object of *offered.*]

AS AN ADJECTIVE: Larry always has plenty of money *to spend on movies.* [Modifies the noun *money.*]

AS AN ADVERB: She went home *to get her skates.* [Modifies the verb *went;* tells why she went.]
I wasn't eager *to help with the dishes.* [Modifies the adjective *eager.*]

After certain verbs (*dare, help, need*) the *to* is sometimes not used:

No one in the room dared *contradict* him.
Did you help *iron* the clothes?

An infinitive phrase used as a subject may follow the verb:

It would be foolish *to turn back now.*
Wouldn't it be foolish *to turn back now?*

The *it* in these sentences is called an *expletive* or an *anticipatory subject.* It is not the real subject of the sentences; it is just a "dummy" subject. It has no particular meaning in these sentences; it serves merely as an introductory word. It is like the word *there* in the sentence "There are only three cookies left."

Exercise 6 On a sheet of paper, list all the prepositional phrases in each of the following sentences. Underline the objects of the prepositions. After each phrase, write the word it modifies and tell whether the phrase is used as an adjective or adverb. Number your answers with the numbers of the sentences.

1 We scrambled over the fence and ran through the orchard at breakneck speed.
2 The girl with the lisp is Jerry's cousin from Baltimore.
3 By Friday the girls in the first tent were no longer speaking to each other.

4 Martha piled Tommy's toys behind Dad's chair, flicked a dust cloth over the tables, and smoothed the cushions on the sofa.

5 He propped the frames for the sketches Dan had brought us against the wall.

6 The new tennis ball rolled off the table and bounced down the porch stairs into a puddle of water.

7 He quickly pulled up alongside the platform, and within an hour the crates were safely stored inside the warehouse.

8 In spite of his sarcasm I knew he was happy about his job.

9 Ken was sitting between Alice and Sue in the booth near the window.

10 Because of her encouraging remarks, he has been working like a steam engine.

Exercise 7 Each of the following sentences contains one or more participles. Divide a sheet of paper into two columns. In the first column, list each participle. In the second, write the word that each participle modifies. Number your answers with the numbers of the sentences.

1 All broken test tubes must be replaced by the chemistry students.

2 Bill appeared on the stage, his face painted beyond recognition.

3 I saw him leaning out the window, shouting and waving at the passers-by.

4 Otto, busily mixing the formula, didn't notice the water in the beaker boiling dry.

5 Running to catch a bus, Doris tripped and sprained her ankle.

6 Perched in a corner of the loft, his head propped against a sack of feed, George fell asleep.

7 Alex, looking very unhappy, was leaning against the fence, watching the game.

8 Marching up to the counter, the woman began rummaging through the stack of freshly folded shirts.

9 Forest fires are often caused by smoldering embers left by careless campers or picnickers.

10 Blinded by the dazzling snow, almost frozen after the long journey, the explorer had great difficulty in finding and striking his matches.

Exercise 8 Each of the following sentences contains one or more gerunds. Divide a sheet of paper into two columns. In the first column, list each gerund. In the second, tell how the gerund is used. Number your answers with the numbers of the sentences.

1 Joining clubs is a good way of meeting new people.

2 Harold doesn't like making speeches in front of the class.

3 Standing next to Ed made Joan appear taller than she is.

4   All Bill's friends have been worrying about his quitting school in June.
5   We ended by going downtown and watching the parade.
6   Without a doubt dancing helps in developing grace, poise, and confidence.
7   After looking all over the house for the missing copy of *Seventeen,* Helen stopped searching and bought a new one.
8   Without having stirred from his chair, Nero Wolfe had succeeded in solving the mystery.
9   The reporter's constant worry is meeting a deadline.
10   Larry's first job, interviewing Mickey Mantle, made him the envy of the staff.

Exercise 9   Each of the following sentences contains one or more infinitives. Divide a sheet of paper into two columns. In the first column, list each infinitive. In the second, tell how the infinitive is used. Number your answers with the numbers of the sentences.

1   Diantha's only ambition is to become a great actress.
2   Young people should learn to think for themselves.
3   Bert's summer job, clerking in a store, helped pay his college expenses.
4   We weren't particularly eager to appear in the stunt show.
5   Ann went to Canada to visit relatives for a week, and then decided to work there.
6   Don is sure to forget the key if you don't remind him.
7   To be successful doesn't necessarily mean to be wealthy.
8   Does Mr. Theodore intend to come on Saturday to play for the auditions?
9   Sometimes it is hard to understand Dad's moods.
10   She wants to know if anyone has an umbrella to lend her.

156

Clauses

Subordinate clauses, like phrases, are groups of closely related words that are used as single words in a sentence. A subordinate clause differs from a phrase in one important respect—a clause has a subject and verb of its own:

PHRASE: I like teachers *with a sense of humor.*
CLAUSE: I like teachers *who have a sense of humor.* [*Who* is the subject, and *have* is the verb of the clause.]

PHRASE: He gave me the money *before leaving the office.*
CLAUSE: He gave me the money *before he left the office.* [*He* is the subject, and *left* is the verb of the clause.]

Adjective clauses.   *Adjective clauses,* which do the work of adjectives, are usually joined to the nouns or pronouns they modify (called *antecedents*) by relative pronouns—*who, which, that*—or by relative adverbs—*when, where, why, after:*

Any boy *who likes walking* can make good money as a caddy.

Here is the magazine *that I borrowed from Helen.*

Will you ever forget the day *when Mr. Keeler caught Bob skipping school*?

The month *after we moved* Dad was transferred to Boston.

Often the adjective clause has no introductory word:

He kept the dime *he found in the chair.* [Instead of *that he found in the chair.*]

Noun clauses. Noun clauses are introduced by subordinating conjunctions (*that, if, whether*), by adverbs (*when, where, why, how*), by adjectives (*which, whatever*), or by pronouns (*who, whoever, which, what*). They may have any of the noun uses in a sentence:

SUBJECT: *What he says* doesn't affect me.

PREDICATE COMPLEMENT: The question is *which excuse would sound best.*

OBJECT: Loren told us *that he had bought the tickets.*

OBJECT: Mary said *she sold the piano.* [The introductory word *that* is sometimes not used.]

INDIRECT OBJECT: Give *whoever answers the phone* Dad's message.

OBJECT OF PREPOSITION: We argued for hours about *when we should start.*

APPOSITIVE: I like Ed's idea *that we hitchhike to save money.*

Adverb clauses. Adverb clauses, like single-word adverbs, modify verbs (He always does *as he pleases*), adjectives (It's later *than you think*), adverbs (She worked harder *than we did*), or whole statements (*As he explained,* he was held up by traffic).

Adverb clauses are introduced by subordinating conjunctions (*while, when, after, where, because, if, since, although, unless, so that, whether, no matter how, as if, than, wherever, in order that, as . . .*) that show how the clauses are related to the rest of the sentence. Many different relationships can be shown:

TIME: *After the smoke cleared,* everyone rushed back into the chemistry room. [Tells when everyone rushed.]

PLACE: Sit *wherever you like.* [Tells where you should sit.]

REASON: He realized that she was annoyed *because he had danced with Martha.* [Tells why she was annoyed.]

MANNER: Everything went off *as we had planned.* [Tells how everything went off.]

PURPOSE: Joe helped me rake the lawn *so that we could get to the show on time.* [Tells Joe's purpose in helping.]

CONDITION: I will ask for a refund *if you will.* [Tells under what condition I will ask.]

DEGREE: Uncle Will was *so* angry *that Fred didn't dare ask for the car.* [Tells how angry Uncle Will was.]

CONCESSION: Laura is never crabby, *no matter how tired she is.* [Tells that the main statement is true, in spite of the opposing circumstance.]

Exercise 10   On a sheet of paper, list all the adjective clauses in the following sentences. After each clause, write its antecedent—the word it modifies.

1   Eleanor's sister, who lives in La Grange, is planning a trip that might include Eleanor.
2   Anyone whose last name begins with S or T is to report today.
3   Alford Park, which is two miles from here, is the only place where we can play baseball without disturbing someone.
4   There are many reasons why Ed is not going out for football.
5   The day after I arrived I met a pen pal to whom I had been writing for three years.
6   The ten-dollar bill that Uncle Fred had given me was not in the drawer where I had left it.
7   On the morning that the accident happened I was riding to work with Bill, whose car is a battered 1953 sedan.
8   Her new book, which was published last year, is about the men who blundered in the charge of the Light Brigade.

Exercise 11   On a sheet of paper, list all the noun clauses in the following sentences. After each clause, tell how it is used.

1   Miss Meyer's only comment on my paper was that it was two weeks late.
2   Usually whatever I say is wrong.
3   Actors and actresses often quarrel over who should get top billing.
4   The fact that I gave my report first meant that I could relax during the rest of the meeting.
5   Did Frank tell you he would be thirty minutes late?
6   The policeman asked the boy what his name was and why he wanted to run away from home.
7   Who the real thief was will never be known.
8   That he disapproves of our plan is obvious; the question is whether or not he will interfere.

Exercise 12   On a sheet of paper, list all the adverb clauses in the following sentences. Tell what relationship is shown by each clause (time, place, manner, and so on).

1   I washed and polished the car so that Dad would be in a good mood at dinner.

2 Wherever Dave went, Jerry was sure to follow.
3 Donna talked on the telephone so long that the other party on her line had to ask her to hang up.
4 Although Jim hadn't done anything to be proud of, he acted as though he had conquered the world.
5 Miss Sullivan is annoyed if we come in after the bell has rung.
6 In Rome, do as the Romans do.
7 Whenever Mr. Russell asks for volunteers, Chuck raises his hand.
8 Since Tim was the oldest, he was given first choice.

Exercise **13**   Pick out the subordinate clauses in the following sentences and be ready to tell what kind of clause each is. Be ready also to tell what words the adjective clauses modify, what relationships the adverb clauses show, and how the noun clauses are used.

1 All things are difficult before they are easy.
2 The size of a man can be measured by the size of the thing that makes him angry.—J. K. Morley
3 Man lives by habit indeed, but what he lives for is thrills and excitements.—William James
4 Tolerance of differing opinion is the only attitude that makes possible a free press.—William L. Chenery
5 An error doesn't become a mistake until you refuse to correct it.—O. A. Battista
6 Humanity is not so adult that it can do without hero-worship. —Roger Lloyd
7 Whoever has an idea has a bargaining tool.—Aimee Buchanan
8 Sometimes one pays most for the things one gets for nothing. —Albert Einstein
9 When we have not what we like, we must like what we have.
10 Opinions cannot survive if one has no chance to fight for them. —Thomas Mann
11 Very frequently a fight for what is right degenerates into a quarrel for what is left.—*Wit and Wisdom*
12 One learns to itch where one can scratch.—Ernest Bramah
13 Results! Why, man, I have gotten a lot of results. I know several thousand things that won't work.—Thomas A. Edison
14 I wish he would explain his explanation.—Byron
15 Facts do not cease to exist because they are ignored.
16 All I know is what I read in the papers.—Will Rogers
17 There are two kinds of people in one's life—people whom one keeps waiting—and the people for whom one waits.—S. N. Behrman
18 The word "prejudice" means "pre-judgment." Learning facts after judgment has been passed does astonishingly little to change the judgment.—Mildred H. McAfee
19 The only people who never fail are those who never try.—Ilka Chase

159

20   The problem, what man will do with the enormous power which science has put into his hands, is probably the most vital and alarming problem of modern times.—Julian Huxley

KINDS OF SENTENCES

A common way of classifying sentences is by their structure—that is, by the number and kind of subject-verb units they contain. This sort of classifying divides sentences into four groups: simple, compound, complex, and compound-complex.

Simple Sentences

A *simple* sentence is one that has only one subject and verb, either or both of which may be compound:

Uncle Bill smiled.
Norma and Sue looked at each other.
Without saying another word, Jerry opened the desk drawer,
    pulled out the letter, and handed it to his sister to read.
Pots and pans came tumbling down from the top shelf and
    landed at her feet in a prolonged series of crashes.

A sentence may be long or short, may or may not have objects, complements, or modifiers—but if it has only one subject and one verb, it is a simple sentence.

Compound Sentences

A *compound* sentence is one made up of two (or more) simple sentences. The simple sentences—called "coördinate clauses" since they are of equal importance grammatically—may be joined by a coördinating conjunction (*and, but, for, yet, or, nor, so*):

Bob nominated Dave Brooks, and Ken Hilton nominated me.
    [Notice the comma before the *and*.]
My brother still had a dollar, but he didn't want to spend it.
Give him something to do, or he'll pester us all afternoon.

Or the coördinate clauses may be joined simply by putting a semi-colon between them:

Norma went right home; she was expecting a phone call from
    Ed.
I waited until after supper; then I told Mother the news.
Most of the article is a rehash of Professor Hill's ideas; still it
    is worth reading.

Complex Sentences

A *complex* sentence is one that contains one or more subordinate clauses:

> Aunt Helen couldn't hear a word *that he said.*
> They wondered later *why Frank had been so sarcastic.*
> *If Jerry comes,* should we show him the snapshots *you brought?*

Compound-Complex Sentences

A *compound-complex* sentence is one that contains two or more main clauses and one or more subordinate clauses:

> Call Jack before he leaves the house, or he'll forget to lock the doors. [Two main clauses: *Call Jack* and *he'll forget to lock the doors.* One subordinate clause: *before he leaves the house.*]

Exercise 14 On a sheet of paper, classify each sentence in the following passage as simple, compound, complex, or compound-complex. Be ready to explain how you arrived at your answers.

(1) A stocky, broad-shouldered man walked at the head of the caravan. (2) He seemed shorter than he really was, because of the tall grass around him and the broad-brimmed hat of coarse straw which he wore. (3) A few steps behind him followed a boy of about nine years of age. (4) The boy's blond hair was clearly marked against his brown, sunburnt neck; but the man's hair and neck were of exactly the same shade of brown. (5) From the looks of these two, and still more from their gait, it was easy to guess that here walked father and son.

(6) Behind them a team of oxen jogged along; the oxen were drawing a vehicle which once upon a time might have been a wagon, but which now, on account of its many and grave infirmities, ought long since to have been consigned to the scrap heap— exactly the place, in point of fact, where the man had picked it up. (7) Over the wagon box long willow saplings had been bent, in the form of arches in a church chancel—six of them in all. (8) On these arches, and tied down to the body on each side, were spread first of all two hand-woven blankets, that might well have adorned the walls of some manor house in the olden times; on top of the blankets were thrown two sheepskin robes, with the wool side down, which were used for bed-coverings at night. (9) The rear of the wagon was stowed full of numberless articles, all the way up to the top. (10) A large immigrant chest at the bottom of the pile, very long and high, devoured a big share of the space; around and above it were piled household utensils, tools, implements, and all their clothing.—O. E. Rölvaag, *Giants in the Earth.* Copyright 1927 by Harper & Brothers, New York.

161

8 *The Levels of Usage*

If a foreign exchange student—say a boy from France—were staying in your home for a year while he attended your high school, the two of you would have many lively discussions about American and French customs and attitudes and about language. His observations on our language would be not only interesting but instructive, for he would probably direct your attention to certain features which you, as a native speaker of English, had never before been *consciously* aware of.

Back home, the French boy had studied English for six years; and he speaks it well, with only a slight trace of accent. Yet before the end of the first week of school, he ruefully reports that the English he learned in Paris seems to be different from much of the English he now hears around him each day. And that is not all: he has noticed that his fellow students keep switching from one kind of English to another. They use one kind in debate class and another in the halls after school. They speak one kind of English at a student-council meeting—and quite another at the student-council mixer. Your guest is frankly puzzled. "Which kind of English should I use?" he asks. "Which kind is best?"

Your first reaction is to deny that there are different kinds of English. But after thinking over what he has said, you realize that he has a point. Certainly the English in *The Adventures of Huckleberry Finn* and that in the Gettysburg Address are of different kinds —and neither is like the kind you ordinarily use. Come to think of it, you yourself use more than one kind of English. What is more, you realize that you often shift, without conscious thought, from one to another. You use a rather dignified kind of English when you write a business letter, but change easily to a carefree, casual kind when you dash off a note to your best friend. When you introduced the French student to the superintendent, you said, "Mr. Sullivan, may I present Jean Martin, our exchange student from Paris." Yet five minutes later at your cafeteria table you automatically shifted your introduction to "Hey fellows, this is Jean Martin, the Frenchman I was telling you about."

Why did you shift from one kind of English to another? You shifted because you somehow sensed that different kinds of English were appropriate in these different situations. And you were right: the "Hey fellows" kind of English, so appropriate in talking with your close friends, would have been noticeably out of place in speaking to the superintendent.

Appropriateness is obviously an important factor in language. The English you use must, first of all, be **clear**. But to be truly effective, it must also be **appropriate**—to the audience, to the subject, and to the occasion. Improving your skill in speech and writing is not a simple matter of memorizing and then applying a set of rules; the effective use of language is far too vast and complex a subject to be reduced to rules. Judgment, not rules, is the key to improving your English—judgment that comes through observant reading, thoughtful listening, and considerable practice in speech and writing of your own. Learning more about the different kinds of English and their uses will help make such practice both meaningful and efficient.

The levels of usage. For convenience, the different kinds of English can be sorted out into three major categories: *informal English, formal English,* and *nonstandard English.* Two of these kinds, the informal and the formal, belong to the **standard level** of English—that is, to the level used by educated people. The **nonstandard level**, on the other hand, is used by people who have not had much education or whose education has had little effect on their speech and writing.

Contrary to what many people believe, our standards in language are not set by a handful of experts—by the dictionary makers and the professional grammarians. They are set, instead, by thousands of people, people skilled in the use of language. They are the people who teach in our schools, write our books, produce our newspapers and magazines. They are the people who run our government and handle our diplomatic relations. They are the people who preach our religions and treat our sick, who plead and judge our legal cases, who manage our businesses and our industries. And they are people in less prominent positions too; for they may be housewives or retired policemen, as well as newsboys or baby-sitters. In fact, anyone who cares about language and uses it well helps to set language standards.

To understand the differences between standard and nonstandard English and between formal and informal English, let's examine each one closely.

NONSTANDARD ENGLISH

Next morning half the bunch mostly vetrans went to the ball park which isn't no better than the one we got at home. Most of them was vetrans as I say but I was in the bunch. That makes things look pretty good for me don't it Al? We tossed the ball round and hit fungos and run round and then Callahan asks Scott and Russell and I to warm up easy and pitch a few to the batters. It was warm and I felt pretty good so I warmed up pretty good. . . . So I went in and after I lobbed a few over I cut loose my fast one. Lord was to bat and he ducked out of the way and then throwed his bat to the bench. Callahan says What's the matter Harry? Lord says I forgot to pay up my life insurance. He says I ain't ready for Walter Johnson's July stuff.—Ring W. Lardner, *You Know Me Al*. New York: Charles Scribner's Sons, 1960, pp. 27-28.

165

This passage is from a book that has become a baseball classic, Ring Lardner's *You Know Me Al*. The book, subtitled "A Busher's Letters," consists of letters from a rookie pitcher, Jack Keefe, to his friend Al. Jack's overconfidence and lack of sophistication have kept generations of readers chuckling, even while they rooted inwardly for him to help the White Sox win the "serious"—as Jack calls any baseball series.

You have probably *heard* language like Jack's on more than one occasion: nonstandard English is primarily a spoken language. But studying a sample in print makes it easier to identify the specific trademarks, or characteristics, of this kind of English. You will find, for example, that all speakers of nonstandard English use verb forms like the "throwed," "don't it," and "most of them *was*" that Jack Keefe uses in his letter. They also tend to use the present tense in relating past events, as Jack does when he writes "then Callahan asks," "Lord says," and "He says I ain't ready." And speakers of nonstandard English use many double negatives, like the "isn't no better" which Jack uses in the passage quoted.

In "then Callahan asks Scott and Russell and I to warm up," Jack uses the pronoun *I* in a way quite usual in nonstandard English, though *me* would be used at the standard level. (He also writes, in other letters, "the game between *we* and the Venice Club," "*him* and I have got to be pretty good pals," and "a big man like *I* needs good food.") His use of the adjective *good* in "I warmed up pretty good" and his use of *ain't* are also typical of nonstandard speech.

Another trademark of nonstandard English, although it is not especially noticeable in the quotation from *You Know Me Al,* is the overuse of slang. In fact, a user of nonstandard English is likely to have in his vocabulary only two or three slang expressions of approval or disapproval, which he uses over and over again. Everything he likes is "swell" and everything he dislikes, "lousy"—or whatever the current equivalents may be. In the spoken language, pronunciation may also distinguish the nonstandard level from the standard; you have probably heard such nonstandard pronunciations as "dese," "dem," "southmore," "attack-ted," "ath-a-letics," and "genu-wine."

Nonstandard English, then, is the kind of English that is consistently marked by many or most of these characteristics. This kind of English (as the sample from *You Know Me Al* indicates) may be both colorful and economical, and it usually conveys the intended meaning very well. But for educated people it is neither appropriate nor adequate to express all their ideas; they need to use the standard varieties in order to get along well in their communities and in their work. As an educated person, you will want to avoid nonstandard English in all your speech and writing.

INFORMAL ENGLISH

How would you like to have a dog that walks quietly by your side in the street, sits when you tell him to, and comes when called? And, for good measure, he won't bite the mailman, chase children on bicycles, or chew up chair legs.

Well, he's yours for the asking because that is the picture of any garden variety dog that has been given basic training in canine etiquette. Furthermore, you can give him that training yourself—you do not have to be a professional dog handler. But you will have to take a little time to learn what to do and how to do it. Otherwise, you might end up with an animal that's more monster than saint.—"What Every Good Dog Should Know," *Changing Times,* January 1962.

These paragraphs are written in the kind of English educated people use most—standard informal English. The use of contractions is one trademark by which you can recognize this passage as informal English. An even better sign is its direct, conversational tone; the writer seems almost to be chatting with his readers face to face. His use of *you* and *yours* contributes to this tone of informality and directness; so does his simple vocabulary, including such everyday expressions as *for good measure, chew up chair legs, yours for the asking, garden variety dog, end up with,* and the introductory *Well.*

Most books and articles intended for the general public are written in informal English. A writer who wants to reach a great number of readers knows that he will best succeed by presenting his subject simply and directly, in a style that will put his readers at ease. The following paragraphs are taken from a magazine article on Greek history, a subject which many writers would discuss in scholarly, formal English. But the author of this article uses informal English, so that general readers, as well as students of history, will find the article interesting and rewarding.

> Modern historians now begin their account as far back as 1600 B.C. This was a time when Greek-speaking tribes, after drifting into Greece from the north for several centuries, carved up the country into feudal kingdoms and founded the Mycenaean civilization.
>
> In sprawling fortresses rising menacingly above plain and seacoast, Mycenaean rulers surrounded themselves with barbaric splendor and grew wealthy on war booty, piracy and trade. Mycenaean life, as Homer pictured it, was a romantic round of battles and banquets. But the ancient kings were also hardheaded businessmen who administered their tightly organized economies with the help of professional bureaucrats. Men like Agamemnon and Menelaus and Odysseus would scarcely have launched a thousand ships for the sake of a woman's face, however beautiful. More probably, Agamemnon led his confederates to war because Troy was meddling with commerce through the nearby Hellespont.—"From Agamemnon to Alexander," *Life,* January 18, 1963.

The readability of these paragraphs is due in great part to the writer's skillful use of informal English (a carefully edited informal English, to be sure). His sentences, as in all good informal English, are so neatly and simply constructed that the reader moves easily from one point to the next. The writer's word choice, which gives the paragraphs a colloquial flavor, deserves special notice —particularly his *carved up the country, hardheaded businessmen,* and *meddling with commerce.* By using such words—words close to the reader's everyday experience—he makes the reader forget the centuries that separate him from the people of Ancient Greece. By using such words, he makes the ancient past seem vividly present.

Informal English is the most generally useful of the three kinds of English. It is appropriate for almost any subject, from dog training to ancient history, from sports events to the latest discoveries in medical science, from a personal narrative to a serious discussion on the causes of war. It is a flexible kind of English, appropriate in situations of widely varying degrees of "informality"—ranging from a bowling banquet to a meeting of a board of directors, from a friendly get-together in the neighborhood to a round-table discussion to be telecast to the nation. Informal English is, in fact, so flexible that a speaker or writer can use it to achieve whatever tone he thinks best suited to his audience. The tone may be friendly, impersonal, sarcastic, sincere, ironic, or humorous. Or, if circumstances warrant, the tone may be serious, as in the following paragraphs from a speech given by Astronaut John Glenn shortly after his three-orbit space flight of February 20, 1962.

> Today, I know that I seem to be standing alone on this great platform—just as I seemed to be alone in the cockpit of the *Friendship 7* spacecraft. But I am not. There were with me then—and are with me now—thousands of Americans and many hundreds of citizens of many countries around the world who contributed to this truly international undertaking voluntarily and in a spirit of coöperation and understanding. . . .
>
> We are proud to have been privileged to be part of this effort, to represent our country as we have. As our knowledge of the universe in which we live increases, may God grant us the wisdom and guidance to use it wisely.—Lieutenant Colonel John H. Glenn, Jr., to the Joint Session of Congress, February 26, 1962.

Colonel Glenn's speech was delivered in Congress, a place where many people would feel compelled to use the most scholarly language they could manage. But Colonel Glenn chose to use, instead, an informal kind of English—at no point so informal that it could be considered inappropriate to the dignified setting and occasion, but at every point informal enough to sound natural, conversational, direct.

Informal English, then, is the kind of English appropriate to most subjects, most audiences, and most occasions. Since it is the most generally useful of the three kinds of English, your main goal as a student of language should be to learn to use it with skill.

FORMAL ENGLISH

> . . . With the return of happiness a gentle benignity flowed from the aged Queen. Her smile, once so rare a visitant to those saddened features, flitted over them with an easy alacrity; the blue eyes beamed; the whole face, starting suddenly from its pendulous expressionlessness, brightened and softened and cast over those who watched it an unforgettable charm. For in her last years there was a fascination in Victoria's amiability which had been lacking even from the vivid impulse of her youth. Over all who approached her—or very nearly all—she threw a peculiar spell. Her grandchildren adored her; her ladies waited upon her with a reverential love. The honour of serving her

obliterated a thousand inconveniences—the monotony of a court existence, the fatigue of standing, the necessity for a superhuman attentiveness to the minutiae of time and space. As one did one's wonderful duty one could forget that one's legs were aching from the infinitude of the passages at Windsor, or that one's bare arms were turning blue in the Balmoral cold.—Lytton Strachey, *Queen Victoria.* Copyright 1921 by Harcourt, Brace & World, Inc., New York.

Probably the most prominent characteristic of formal English is its extensive vocabulary. As you can see in the above passage from Lytton Strachey's biography of Queen Victoria, the writer uses many words and phrases not ordinarily found in everyday speech, such as *benignity, so rare a visitant, easy alacrity, pendulous expressionlessness, amiability, reverential, obliterated, minutiae,* and *infinitude.* Much formal English is marked by the presence of literary vocabulary of this kind, which must be used with care. The mere sprinkling of difficult or bookish words through writing does not make that writing either formal or effective. But where such words are appropriate, their skillful use can do much to add exactness and richness of meaning to an author's expression.

Consider the most unordinary word *infinitude* in "one could forget that one's legs were aching from the infinitude of the passages at Windsor." Such a word is decidedly not informal, and it might be jarringly out of place in an informal description of something large or long or seemingly endless. But used appropriately, as Mr. Strachey has used it in his paragraph, *infinitude* is both forceful and vivid.

169

Another important trademark of formal English is rather long and involved sentences. A piece of writing composed entirely of such sentences, far from being good formal English, would probably be both monotonous and extremely difficult to read. But subject matter suitable for expression in formal English will often involve ideas that are abstract and complex. To express such ideas effectively, a writer will need some sentences that are longer and more involved than he would ordinarily use in good informal English. Such sentences may require careful reading, occasional slowing down to be sure you are following the whole thought; but they reward the care demanded of the reader by tying together a number of related ideas into a more effective total impression.

Both the vocabulary and the sentence structure of formal English help to give it a tone different from that of even the most carefully written informal English. Informal English, as you have seen, can range from casual speech to expression that is serious and exact —but still direct and conversational. Formal English, on the other hand, is almost always rather impersonal. The writer does not usually involve the reader directly: he does not often use the second-person pronoun *you.* He avoids slang, contractions, regional-

Standard

Formal
(Mostly written)

Legal documents

Reference works; some textbooks

Impersonal reports

Books and articles for professional audiences

Literature for a limited audience: essays, much poetry, some fiction and biography

Some newspaper editorials and features

Addresses and lectures to restricted audiences

Informal
(Spoken and written)

Most novels and short stories; some poetry

Magazine articles and books on subjects of general interest

Business letters; advertising copy

Newspaper writing

General conversation of educated people

Letters to intimate friends or family

Conversation with family or close friends

Nonstandard
(Mostly spoken)

Conversation of many people in their work and personal affairs

Dialogue of some characters in plays, stories, and comic strips

isms, and colloquialisms. He keeps a distance, in a sense, between himself and his subject, and between himself and his reader.

This is not to suggest that coldness is a requirement or even a characteristic of formal English. Quite the contrary. At another point in his biography of Queen Victoria, in discussing her relationships with her large family during her old age, the author writes this:

> She took a particular delight in her grandchildren, to whom she showed an indulgence which their parents had not always enjoyed, though, even to her grandchildren, she could be, when the occasion demanded it, severe. The eldest of them, the little Prince Wilhelm of Prussia, was a remarkably headstrong child; he dared to be impertinent even to his grandmother; and once, when she told him to bow to a visitor at Osborne, he disobeyed her outright. This would not do: the order was sternly repeated, and the naughty boy, noticing that his kind grandmama had suddenly turned into a most terrifying lady, submitted his will to hers, and bowed very low indeed.

The formal vocabulary and sentence structure in no way interfere with the warmth and humor of the anecdote, nor with the "realness" of the Queen and her grandson.

Formal English is not limited to such literary types as fiction and biography. Serious writing about various fields of learning— about the arts, philosophy, economics, mathematics, linguistics, and so on—also lends itself to this kind of English. So in addition to involved sentence structure and scholarly vocabulary, formal English is often marked by the use of the specialized vocabulary of a technical subject. This is especially likely to be true if a writer intends his work for an audience with some knowledge of his subject. In writing about conducting an orchestra, for instance, an author might use such terms as *tempo, repertoire, polyphony, reading, virtuosi,* and *maestro.* In the following paragraph, from a forestry expert's explanation of why pine trees are fragrant, you will notice such terms as *volatile oils, resin, terpenes, aldehydes,* and *heptane.*

> In the Sierra Nevada of California there grow two pines: Digger pine of the dry, hot foothills, and Jeffrey pine of the cool, high altitudes. Volatile oils of their resin have not a drop of piny-smelling terpenes; their fragrance comes from several aldehydes much diluted with a gasolinelike substance called heptane. Heptane alone possesses no more fragrance than cigarette lighter fluid. With the addition of the aldehydes it becomes pleasantly fragrant, filling the whole forest with a mellow odor which is described by some as vanilla and by others as pineapple.—Nicholas T. Mirov, "The Fragrance of Pines," *The Atlantic,* September 1959.

The effective use of figurative language and of allusions to literature, to history, to the Bible—or to any source educated readers may be expected to know—is also common in much formal writing. Of course figures of speech are not found only in formal English. But the figurative language used in this kind of English tends to be more scholarly and elaborate than that used in informal writing and speech. Consider the following paragraph from a short story by Stephen Crane:

> At six-o'clock supper, the Swede fizzed like a fire-wheel. He sometimes seemed on the point of bursting into riotous song, and in all his madness he was encouraged by old Scully. The Easterner was encased in reserve; the cowboy sat in wide-mouthed amazement, forgetting to eat, while Johnnie wrathily demolished great plates of food. The daughters of the house, when they were obliged to replenish the biscuits, approached as warily as Indians, and, having succeeded in their purpose, fled with ill-concealed trepidation. The Swede domineered the whole feast, and he gave it the appearance of a cruel bacchanal. He seemed to have grown suddenly taller; he gazed, brutally disdainful, into every face. His voice rang through the room. Once when he jabbed out harpoon-fashion with his fork to pinion a biscuit, the weapon nearly impaled the hand of the Easterner, which had been stretched quietly out for the same biscuit.—Stephen Crane, "The Blue Hotel," *Twenty Stories.* Copyright 1940 by Alfred A. Knopf, Inc., New York.

This passage is made more vivid and colorful by the mythological allusion, *bacchanal,* and such telling figures as *fizzed like a fire-wheel, encased in reserve, demolished great plates of food,* and *approached as warily as Indians.*

Throughout this section, there has been frequent reference to the "writer" or "author" of formal English; but there has been no mention of the speaker, or of formal speech. As a matter of fact, this kind of English is most often written English. You will probably meet it in spoken form only in the serious addresses of public speakers on significant occasions. And such speeches are also written English in the sense that they ordinarily are carefully planned and rehearsed beforehand—usually written out, often memorized before delivery or read from manuscript (or from a teleprompting device). The major address that will be given at your graduation exercises may be a speech of this kind, as may be that of your class valedictorian on the same occasion.

Formal English is used for the most part, then, by educated people who have reason to do serious writing. It is the language of some fiction and biography, some essays and criticism. It is the language of legal documents; of many textbooks, especially those written for use at the college level; of most technical books and articles; and of many encyclopedias and other reference books. It is the language of important reports, such as many organizations and businesses require of their members or staffs.

As a high-school student, it is true, you do not ordinarily do these kinds of writing. But it does not follow that you never use formal English. You use it for some of the research papers you write in school. If you should enter an essay contest or a science competition requiring a formal report on your experiments and findings, you would need facility in this kind of English. You will use it if you are on your school's debate squad or take part in classroom debates. And your awareness of the traits of this admittedly more difficult kind of English will make your reading of it both more profitable and more enjoyable.

Exercise 1   Find and bring to class two paragraphs that are examples of good informal English. They should be from two different sources. (You may find that magazines are a good place to look.) Be ready to read your paragraphs to the class and to explain why you classify them as informal English.

Exercise 2   Find and bring to class two paragraphs that are examples of good formal English. The paragraphs should be from two different sources. Be ready to read your paragraphs to the class and to point out the trademarks that characterize them as formal English.

SPECIAL KINDS OF LANGUAGE

Slang.   The secret of using slang is really no secret at all: use it only when it is appropriate. Slang is not appropriate in formal English. Its appropriateness in informal English depends on the subject matter and on circumstances of time, place, and audience.

When slang is appropriate, it can add vitality to your language. New slang is usually quite expressive and is fun to use besides, since it makes you feel part of an "in-group." Unfortunately, new slang does not stay new for long. In fact, the more widely a slang word or phrase is used, the more quickly it becomes stale. Much slang passes out of fashion and is replaced by newer expressions quite soon. Would you refer to someone you admire as a "peach" or something you approve as "peachy"? Would you call someone you dislike a "goon"? Yet these words were once considered clever and up to date. Some of the terms you use now will soon seem just as dated—or just as pointless.

Other slang terms may stay around for a long time but gradually cease to have any meaning beyond a vague indication of approval or disapproval. Using such words adds no more to your speech or writing than does calling everything you like "fine" and everything you dislike "awful." Words like *neat* and *punk,* or *dreamy* and *dopey,* are slang of this kind and add little to style or meaning.

Occasionally a slang term becomes an accepted part of the language, instead of fading into meaninglessness or oblivion. *Bonus*, for instance, was once stockbrokers' slang. *Carpetbagger* originally was a slang term of disapproval, but today anyone referring to the days in American history when carpetbaggers were active would use that name, even in the most formal context. *To turn down* (meaning "refuse") and *scamper* are other terms that once were considered slang.

Slang is usually more appropriate in speech than in writing. It may add vividness and humor to relaxed conversation, but it should be used sparingly in written work. No matter how effective the slang you use seems at the time of writing, chances are that it will be less so in the future. A slang expression, remember, may become meaningless or dated. It may also strike some readers as a little too casual, even flippant.

Does this mean you should limit your use of slang to conversation with close friends? Not at all. If you are writing fiction, and using slang would be natural for the characters in your story, you would have to use that slang to make their speech seem real and believable. If you are writing a sports column for your school paper, or some other feature you want to be up to date and informal, you would use the slang appropriate to your subject today, even though it might date your material in the future. In any informal writing that you intend to sound chatty and light, you might use some slang that expresses particularly well your meaning and your mood. But slang should always be used sparingly and with caution, and certainly in serious writing you should carefully consider the advisability of *any* slang expression that you are tempted to use.

If you read a great deal and listen with interest to the speech of people who use language well, you will gradually develop reliable judgment about the appropriateness of slang. Then, when you feel sure a slang expression is effective, you will probably be right. Or, to put it the other way around, if there is any rule of thumb to follow in using slang, it is this: when in doubt, don't.

Shoptalk. People in any occupation use quite naturally the shoptalk connected with their work. Stagehands, for instance, use terms like *flat, proscenium, keystone, dutchman, rachet, to size, prop,* and *cyc.* Among electricians *cathode, resistance, circuit,* and *amp* are heard. Some shoptalk terms (*proscenium, keystone, rachet, cathode, size*) are the technical names for parts, tools, or processes; others are convenient nicknames or abbreviations for these names. (A *dutchman* is a strip of cloth used to cover the crack between two *flats*—canvas-covered frames used as scenery. *Prop* is short for *property* and *cyc* for *cyclorama.* In electricians' shoptalk, *ampere* becomes *amp* for short.) Sometimes a common word is used as a nickname in the shoptalk of many different kinds of work. *Dog,* for example, is used in many mechanical fields as a nickname for instruments that grip or hook.

Shoptalk, then, is the special vocabulary of technical terms, abbreviations, and nicknames used by people interested in a particular field. It is not limited to occupations. Students have a kind of shoptalk dealing with school affairs. Hobbies and other special interests of any kind involve shoptalk too. Ham radio operators use terms like *rig, transceiver,* and *patch* and such expressions as 73 (meaning "regards"), *QSG* ("Have you a doctor nearby?"), and *Calling CQ* ("Does anybody anywhere feel like talking—about anything?"). Scuba divers and skiers, collectors of rocks and of stamps, jazz enthusiasts and opera buffs all know and use shoptalk in discussing their special interests. Whether or not you have had any kind of job, you probably already use one or more varieties of shoptalk.

Sometimes shoptalk words move into the general vocabulary. You have seen this happen recently in the field of space exploration. Because interest in this exciting frontier runs high, people have been quick to take over some of the shoptalk of the astronauts and space technicians, such as *AOK, go* (in phrases like "All systems are go"), *to splash down,* and *to scrub.* Familiar even earlier were *countdown, blastoff,* and *launching pad.* As space travel advances, undoubtedly even more shoptalk terms, now unknown to most of us, will become a part of our vocabularies.

Like other kinds of language, shoptalk is effective only when it is appropriate. Some shoptalk expressions, especially some of the convenient abbreviations and nicknames, are quite slangy and do not belong in formal contexts—in written reports, for instance. And no shoptalk is appropriate when you are talking to people who will not understand it. When you use shoptalk, keep your audience in mind—as, of course, you should do at all times. If you want to explain something about your work or your hobby, and the shoptalk that comes so easily to your tongue will mean nothing to your hearers, either stick to words they do know or be careful to explain the special terms you are using.

175

Exercise 3   Compile a list of ten to fifteen slang terms that you consider particularly expressive and colorful. (Include only those terms that no one will mind discussing in class.) Write a definition of each term. In class, discuss which of the terms are the most effective and why. Consider, too, whether you agree with your classmates' definitions.

Your teacher may wish to appoint a committee to compile an alphabetical list of the most effective slang contributed, together with as accurate definitions as they can arrive at.

Exercise 4   Compile a list of eight or more shoptalk terms used in some field you know well from your own experience (for example, sew-

ing, woodworking, skiing, sailing, printing, dancing, photography).
Arrange your list in alphabetical order, and write your own definitions for the words and expressions you include. Your teacher may want to appoint a committee to make a bulletin-board display of the most interesting lists.

GENERAL USAGE

In the preceding discussion of the three main kinds of English, the chief emphasis was on the differences between them—on the trademarks that set each kind off from the others. Yet, as you can see by going back over the example passages, there are actually more similarities than differences between the three kinds of English. In each example there are only a few words and constructions that mark the passage as nonstandard or informal or formal. The rest of the words and constructions (the major part of each passage) are in **general usage**. Everyone uses such words and constructions, no matter what kind of English he is speaking or writing. They are always appropriate.

Words like *expatiate* and *assemblage*, which have a decidedly formal flavor, must be used with care, since they are appropriate only in formal contexts. Words like *gab* and *gang*, with their colloquial overtones, also need careful handling, since they would seem inappropriate except in very informal situations. But words like *discuss* and *group*, words that are in general usage, can be freely used in any situation. They are appropriate at any time, in any place.

Like *discuss* and *group*, most of the words and constructions in our language are in general usage. This is a decided advantage, for it means that we can concentrate our attention on getting our ideas across—without having to worry about the appropriateness of every word that we use.

Exercise 5   The words in each of the following groups vary; one is found chiefly in formal usage, one in informal usage, one in general usage. Be ready to tell how you would classify the words.

1   apparel, clothes, duds
2   pilfer, steal, swipe
3   irascible, irritable, techy
4   buttinsky, interloper, intruder
5   discomfit, disturb, rattle
6   appellation, moniker, name
7   dull, dumb, fatuous
8   common sense, gumption, sagacity
9   bossy, imperious, overbearing
10   adulation, flattery, soft soap

11 failure, fiasco, flop
12 fastidious, picky, particular

USING THE INDEX

Questions of usage, like the proverbial bad penny, keep turning up. You rarely go through a week without running into several interesting problems that involve usage choices. For example:

L
—A friend invites you to criticize his final draft of an essay for a state contest and then balks when you point out that in one of his sentences he should have used *as*—and not *like*—as a conjunction. He insists on keeping *like*, reminding you of the slogan "Winstons taste good *like* a cigarette should." You disagree, despite the slogan. Which of you is right in this instance?

B
—In the first paragraph of an editorial in the Sunday paper you see this sentence: "These critics, we fear, do not understand the basic differences between communism, fascism, and socialism." You are puzzled. Shouldn't the writer have used *among*, instead of *between*, since he is referring to more than two things?

H
—While going over the answer to an essay question in a history test, you decide to change the verb in the sentence "They hanged the two captives the following morning" from *hanged* to *hung*—telling yourself that *hung* must be right since it "sounds right." But you no sooner hand in your paper than you start wondering. Should you have kept the form *hanged*?

177

In Part Two of this book—the Index—you can find answers to questions like these. The Index consists of a series of entries, most of which deal with usage matters. The entries are listed in alphabetical order (as in any index), to make it easy for you to find the particular item you want.

If, for example, you are really interested in the problem of *like* vs. *as*, you have only to turn to the *L*'s in the Index and find the entry **like, as**; it will give you the information you need. If you are really curious about the editorial writer's use of *between*, you can quickly satisfy your curiosity: it would take only a minute to check the entry **between, among** and discover why *between* was the right choice for his sentence. And the answer to your question about the appropriate form of *hang* for your sentence is just as readily available: it could be had for the slight effort it takes to find and read the **hanged, hung** entry in the *H*'s.

Along with the entries on matters of appropriate usage, the Index contains articles that will refresh your memory on specific points of grammar (**Predicate complement, Gerund, Clause**, and **Appositives**, for example). Other entries explain the conventions of punctuation (**Abbreviations, Comma, Dash, Colon, Quotation** *marks*, etc.). And the Index also takes up a number of general subjects of value and interest to students of language: for example, **American and British usage**, **Borrowed words**, **Dialect**, **Imagery**, **Propaganda**, and **Gobbledygook**.

The Index was designed to meet your special needs. It includes those items of usage—and grammar and punctuation—that are most likely to cause problems for high-school students. Though you will sometimes need to refer to it when doing certain of the exercises in this book, the Index is primarily intended as a do-it-yourself reference book. Get into the habit of going to it with your specific questions. Browse through it now and then and read the items that catch your interest. As you become increasingly familiar with the Index, many of the matters of usage and grammar and punctuation that trouble you will be cleared up. And once the bothersome details of the language are under control, your speech and writing will gain noticeably in effectiveness and in ease.

***Exercise* 6** This exercise has a two-fold purpose: to give you practice in using the Index and to acquaint you with the various kinds of information it contains. The words in boldface type in the following questions indicate the entries in which you will find the answers. Write out your answers on a sheet of paper.

1 What form of the word **alumnus** should be used in "Both my parents are _____ of Carleton College"?
2 Suppose that you are asked, on a literature test: "**Compare** Bret Harte's short stories *with* those of Sarah Orne Jewett." Should you limit your discussion to the similarities between the two writers' stories, or should you point out the differences as well?
3 How is the **noun clause** used in "Dave's suggestion, that we hold a Book Fair, was voted down"?
4 By adding one word, change the following sentence from informal to formal usage: "He is **very** impressed with everything European."
5 In which of these items should a **hyphen** be used: *a well timed entrance, it was well timed, three fourths of the students, a two thirds majority*?
6 In what ways do **American and British usage** differ? What are the American equivalents of the expressions *games mistress, bonnet,* and *queue up*? What are these expressions called? What do the English call words like *windshield, movies,* and *lifeguard*?
7 The words *noticeable* and *outrageous* are exceptions to the **spelling** rule that requires dropping a final silent *e* before suffixes beginning with a vowel. Why is the *e* kept in these words?
8 Is *at* or *by* the idiomatic **preposition** in this sentence: "Everyone was disconcerted _____ Jack's malicious comment"?

9 **Malapropisms** make interesting conversation pieces. What are they? Give two examples of your own.

10 Which would be more appropriate in a formal book report: "*A Tale of Two Cities* is quite **different** *from* Dickens's other novels" or "*A Tale of Two Cities* is quite different *than* Dickens's other novels"?

11 Would a careful speaker use **disinterested** or **uninterested** in the following sentence: "Mr. Pine seemed rather _____ in our problems"?

12 In formal English, would **likely, liable,** or **apt** be used in this sentence: "His explanation is _____ to be clearer than the one in the book"?

Exercise 7 Look up the following items in the Index. Take enough notes so that you will be ready to discuss in class the appropriate and inappropriate use of each item.

1	angle	12	less, fewer
2	boughten	13	locate
3	bunch	14	lot of, lots of
4	center around	15	mad
5	considerable	16	math
6	couple of	17	no-account
7	due to	18	no place
8	funny	19	pair
9	have got	20	plenty
10	had better	21	raise, rear
11	inside of	22	try and, try to

Exercise 8 When the Index labels words and expressions as "formal," "informal," "nonstandard," "colloquial," or "written," it is simply reporting the language practices of speakers and writers throughout the nation. You will find it interesting and instructive to make a similar report, based on the usage in your own community.

Each member of the class is to choose one usage item (or more) to keep track of during the next few weeks. (For example, you might choose to observe the use of *It's me—It is I, can—may, hanged —hung, reason is because—reason is that, good—well, job—position, lie—lay,* or *bad—badly.*)

When you have chosen the item you intend to observe, see what the Index has to say about it. Then, each time you come across the item, make notes on how it is used. Your notes should include such information as this: Which form was used? Who used it (friend, teacher, professional sportswriter...)? What were the circumstances (written or spoken English, formal or informal situation)?

At a date set by your teacher, you are to report your findings to the class. Did you find that the usage in your community tallies with the usage described in the Index? In what ways (if any) does it differ?

American

English

Dialects

University of Michigan News Service

This is Dr. Hans Kurath. He is directing editor of the Linguistic Atlas of the United States and Canada, a record of the way people talk in different towns and cities and larger areas of our country—a record of the vocabulary, pronunciations, and grammatical forms peculiar to each region. Dr. Kurath and his associates began collecting data for the Atlas before you were born; and when their work is finished, it will fill many huge volumes. So far, although only the material dealing with New England speech has appeared in Atlas form, an increasing number of articles and books based on Atlas research are being published. These deal predominantly with dialect differences along the Atlantic coast. Because the eastern part of our country was settled earliest, dialect patterns became more firmly established there than elsewhere, and to this day they remain more pronounced there than in other sections.

Dr. Kurath and the scholars working with him began by devising a questionnaire to help them get information on regional speech. Armed with this questionnaire, they travel through much of our country, interviewing in each community selected, two or more native inhabitants, people whose families have lived there for several generations. Usually at least one of those interviewed (called **informants**) is an elderly person who has spent his life in the area and who has had little schooling. And at least one is a person of high-school education, a little younger, usually with some travel experience. By talking to these informants, the Atlas researchers learn the local words for everyday objects and actions. They also record, in a technical phonetic script, the pronunciations used by their informants. When, through many such interviews, they have gathered enough data, they can define a dialect region and point out its special features.

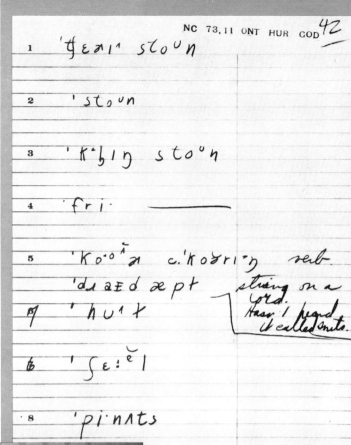

1. ˈʤɛɹɪⁿ stoʊn

2. ˈstoʊn

3. ˈkʰˑʰɪŋ stoʊn

4. ˈfriˑ ——————

5. ˈkoˑoⁿ ɹ cˑˈkoɹˑiˑŋ verb
   ˈdɹ æɛd æpt | string on a cord.
6. ˈhuˑɪt | Have I heard it called smita.

7. ˈʃɛˑᵊl

8. ˈpiˑnʌts

This Atlas researcher makes a tape recording against which to check his phonetic transcription (shown above) of the informant's speech.

A **dialect** is speech that is characteristic of a fairly definite area or social class. It is speech that does not attract attention to itself within the region or social context where it is normally used. Every dialect is marked by a combination of words, meanings, pronunciations, and grammatical forms that set it off from the speech of other groups. Linguistic scholars now believe that there are three main dialect regions in the continental United States: the Northern, the Midland, and the Southern.

Adapted from W. Nelson Francis, *The Structure of American English.* Copyright 1958 by The Ronald Press Company.

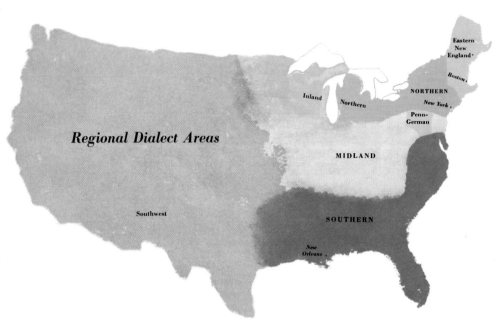

Regional Dialect Areas

Eastern New England is a distinct dialect region within the Northern area. In this section most speakers pronounce words like *half, glass,* and *path* with the "ah" sound of *father*. They often intrude an *r* between vowel sounds, so that *idea of* becomes "idear of," and *law of* turns into something like "lore of"; but they usually slight the *r* in such words as *eastern* ("eastuhn") and *disappear* ("disappeah").

In the Inland region of the Northern speech area, a traveler from the East or South would be aware of hearing every *r* pronounced firmly and would notice a sound like the "ah" of *father* in such words as *on, fog,* and *frog*. Some pronunciation differences found in the South are the dropped *r* similar to that of the New England region; an "ah" sound for long *i* in such words as *I, my,* and *fine;* and the one-syllable pronunciation "miz" for *Mrs.* Characteristics of both Northern and Southern speech are heard in the Midland area, but there are distinctive features too; among these is an *r* sound heard in *wash* ("warsh") and *Washington*.

Across the street from historic Faneuil Hall in Boston are many wholesale markets like this one. A speaker of the Eastern New England dialect would call it a "mahket."

The most commonly used names for many familiar objects differ from locality to locality; and these vocabulary differences, like differences of pronunciation, help to distinguish dialects. Which of the following terms are usual where you live?

doughnut, fried cake, cruller, fat cake, nut cake, olicook, fossnock, riz doughnut, sinker

dragon fly, darning needle, devil's darning needle, schneider, snake feeder, snake eater, mosquito hawk

seesaw, teeter board, dandle, tippity bounce, teetertotter, cocky horse, ridy horse, up'n down, tinter board, tilting board

Ewing Galloway

A public park in
a New England town is often
called a *common* or *green*.
This is the Boston Common.

In the New England area, *tonic* is sometimes used to mean soda or pop, a milk shake made with ice cream is called a *frappe* (pronounced "frap"), and the living room of a house may be the *best room*.

184

In Rhode Island, you might hear a deep-dish apple pie called *apple Jonathan* or *apple slump;* and on nearby Cape Cod, a boy caught skipping school to go fishing would quite likely admit to having *hooked Jack.*

In the Inland Northern dialect area, a drinking fountain may be called a *bubbler*. In this area, too, a small-town business building like this one is sometimes called a *block*.

U.S.D.A. Photograph

In this field, peanuts—*goobers* to a Southern dialect speaker—are being harvested.

To most people in the Southern dialect region, a faucet is a *spigot* or a *spicket*. A Southerner is likely to use *tote* when people in other areas would say "carry," and *carry* when he means to escort or take with him another person. A Southerner also may be heard to *reckon*, rather than to think or to guess.

In vocabulary, as in pronunciation, the Midland area dialect shows characteristics of both the Northern and the Southern variety. A pail is called a *bucket*, as it is in the South; and a wishbone may be known by that general term, as it is in the North, or referred to by the Southern term *pully bone* (or *pull bone*). In this area window shades are often called *blinds*.

Creek (or *crick*), *brook*, *kill*, *branch*, *fork*, *rio*, and *arroyo* are all regional words for a small stream, though several of these terms are used in some areas to designate streams of different sizes. In the Midland area, especially the North Midland, the term *run* is often used.

H. Armstrong Roberts

186

With travel widespread and rapid communication commonplace, vocabulary differences are tending to diminish. The commercial term *cottage cheese*, for example, is rapidly replacing such regional names as *Dutch cheese, smearcase, sour-milk cheese, pot cheese, curds,* and *clabber cheese.* But new regional variations can still arise today. A case in point is found on the superhighways that are rapidly spanning our country; on these roads the places where travelers obtain food and car service are variously named, as are the highways themselves. On the Ohio *Turnpike*, such an area is a *Service Plaza;* on the Indiana *Toll Road* it is a *Service Area.*

A station along the more recently opened Illinois *Tollway* is called an *Oasis.* As you can see, the restaurant part spans the highway.

Within the major dialect regions are found many interesting speech "islands." One of these is the area where Pennsylvania German, a dialect distinctive because of its many idioms, is spoken. Some examples are "It wonders me" (meaning "It amazes me"); "got awake" for awoke or woke up; and the use of "all" to mean ended or all gone, as in "The bread was all yesterday" or "The rain is all."

In the area where a traveler would hear the colorful Pennsylvania-German dialect spoken, he would also see colorfully painted buildings like this barn.

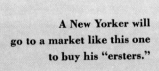

Armstrong Roberts

A New Yorker will go to a market like this one to buy his "ersters."

The regional dialect that is called Brooklynese (although it is heard throughout the New York City area) is familiar to almost everyone through radio, television, and films. Among the notable features of this colorful dialect is the use of the same vowel sound in words like *oil* and *earl*, *oyster* and *turtle*. Hence, to a visitor from another part of the country, *olive oil*, in this dialect, sounds like "olive earl."

Magnum Photos, Inc.

In New Orleans a merry-go-round at a carnival or amusement park is called *flying horses.*

Another speech island is the New Orleans area. Here a sidewalk is called a *banquette,* and a county is referred to as a *parish* (as it is in all of Louisiana).

Besides idiomatic expressions and varying names for common objects, a regional dialect may include special words for local landscape features, for occupations and tools that are more or less local, and for foods that are regional specialties.

Ewing Galloway

The picturesque French Quarter of New Orleans is renowned for its special foods. A restaurant there may feature *jambalaya*; and a candy store, *pralines*.

H. Armstrong R

The dialect used in the Southwestern and Western parts of our country contains many special local words, such as *peyote, coulee, sierra, mesquite, piñon, vaquero,* and *vara* (a surveyor's measure in the Southwest).

Dialect words, phrases, and pronunciations are sometimes called **localisms** or **provincialisms.** In speaking to or with people of your own area, it is appropriate for you to use localisms, avoiding, of course, those not in good standing among the educated people of your community. But in speaking to people unfamiliar with the dialect of your region, you will want to avoid words, phrases, or pronunciations that might seem overly conspicuous or might be confusing or distracting to your hearers.

In informal writing, localisms are often appropriate—in stories or personal narratives especially, where they help make the setting seem real and the conversation of the people seem natural.

Jesse Stuart is one of the many American authors who make effective use of regional dialects in their writing. You have probably read some of his stories, such as "The Split Cherry Tree" and "This Farm for Sale." Mr. Stuart uses the dialect of the area about which he writes, the Kentucky mountain country.

9   *Standard Word Forms*

Of all the major languages, English would seem to have the best chance of becoming the universal language. Next to Chinese (which has many completely different dialects, so that communication between the Chinese is difficult), English is spoken by the greatest number of native speakers. The geographic spread of the English language is quite impressive: English is spoken and is used as an official language on at least four continents. It is also used as a second language by many people in Europe, Latin America, the Middle East, and the Far East.

One of the advantages English has as a potential world language is its relative freedom from *inflections* (changes in the forms of words to show tense, number, case, gender, person, and so on). Most English verbs, for instance, have only four distinctive forms (*walk, walks, walking, walked*). Most nouns form their plurals regularly (by adding *s* or *es*) and their possessives with the same forms spelled with an apostrophe (*'s* or *s'*); and only a few change their form to show gender (for example, *waiter, waitress; hero, heroine*). The only pronouns that have separate case forms are the personal pronouns (*I, me, mine*, etc.) and the relative and interrogative *who* (*who, whom, whose*). With the exception of *this* and *that*, which have the plurals *these* and *those*, our adjectives do not change in form to show number. Those of you who are studying foreign languages—Latin, Spanish, French, German, or Russian—can attest to the fact that these languages are much more highly inflected than English, and therefore much more difficult to master.

Yet although there are comparatively few inflections in English, these few are responsible for a disproportionate number of errors. This chapter, which presents a review of word forms, stresses the usages that most frequently cause trouble. Special attention is paid to differences between formal and informal usage as well as to differences between standard and nonstandard forms.

VERBS

Tense Forms

Our verbs have six tenses, six groups of forms that we use to show actions occurring at different times:

PRESENT: He *plays* baseball. He *is playing* now. *Does* he *play* well?

PAST: He *played* yesterday. *Did* he *play* yesterday? He *was playing* then. He *used to play* left field.

FUTURE: He *will play* tomorrow. He *is going to play* again next week.

PRESENT PERFECT: He *has played* for six years. He *has been playing* for six years.

PAST PERFECT: He *had played* for years before he entered high school.

FUTURE PERFECT: By the end of this year he *will have played* in forty high-school games.

Though the tense forms vary, notice that all of them are derived from what are called the three principal parts of the verb: the **present infinitive** (*play*), the **past tense** (*played*), and the **past participle** (*played*). Only two tense forms—the simple present (*play*) and the simple past (*played*)—are single words. The other forms are phrases in which auxiliary, or helping, verbs are used with the main verb.

Regular verbs. The past tense and the past participle of most verbs are formed by adding -*ed* to the infinitive:

INFINITIVE	PAST TENSE	PAST PARTICIPLE
depend	depended	(have) depended
imply	implied	(have) implied
refer	referred	(have) referred
stop	stopped	(have) stopped
save	saved	(have) saved

Irregular verbs. Verbs whose principal parts are formed in other ways than by adding -*ed* to the infinitive are called *irregular*. A few irregular verbs have the same form for all three principal parts. For example:

burst	burst	burst		hit	hit	hit
cast	cast	cast		let	let	let
cost	cost	cost		shut	shut	shut

Some have the same form for the past tense and the past participle:

bend .	bent	bent		hold	held	held
bleed	bled	bled		seek	sought	sought
buy	bought	bought		sleep	slept	slept
dig	dug	dug		sling	slung	slung
feed	fed	fed		teach	taught	taught
grind	ground	ground		tell	told	told
hear	heard	heard		win	won	won

Others have different forms for the past tense and the past participle:

come	came	come		know	knew	known
do	did	done		ride	rode	ridden
drink	drank	drunk		ring	rang	rung
drive	drove	driven		run	ran	run
fall	fell	fallen		see	saw	seen
fly	flew	flown		shake	shook	shaken
give	gave	given		throw	threw	thrown
go	went	gone		wear	wore	worn

(For a more complete list of irregular verbs, turn to the Index article **Principal parts of verbs.**)

In standard English, the forms in the second column (not the third) are used alone, as the simple past tense:

> Ken *saw* them first. [Not: Ken *seen*.]
> Irene *did* the dishes last night. [Not: Irene *done*.]
> Then he *began* to complain. [Not: he *begun*.]

The forms in the third column (not the second) are used with auxiliary, or helping, verbs:

> They *have rung* the wrong bell. [Not: They *have rang*.]
> Paul *had* already *drunk* the ginger ale. [Not: Paul *had drank*.]
> She *was worn* out from the exertion. [Not: She *was wore* out.]

Exercise 1 Be ready to read each of the following sentences aloud, using the appropriate standard form of the verb in parentheses. (If you need help, refer to the Index article **Principal parts of verbs.**)

1 I could have (*swear*) that Nora hadn't (*write*) to me all year.
2 Before we had (*eat*) lunch, a neighbor (*come*) in to chat.
3 The lining of Sue's coat was (*tear*).
4 Pat had (*swim*) to the island twice during the summer.
5 Mr. Price had (*bring*) two of his best salesmen to the meeting.
6 The pond was (*freeze*) solid.
7 Eileen's car (*run*) out of gas again yesterday.
8 In his hurry to open the letter, Bob had (*tear*) the check in two.
9 An hour later they (*begin*) to realize their mistake.
10 Almost everyone who has (*take*) the course has (*speak*) well of it.

11 The suède-lined shoes have (*wear*) holes in her socks.
12 Any one of us could have (*break*) that ash tray!
13 Did you hear what (*become*) of Frank?
14 Yes, we (*see*) Bill yesterday.
15 Where could Marilyn have (*go*)?

Exercise 2   Be ready to read aloud each of the following sentences, changing the verb phrase in italics to the simple past.

1 Nobody *had seen* any rattlesnakes near the camp.
2 Joe *had swum* to shore.
3 Marge *has done* me a real favor, one I'll never forget.
4 He *had begun* to suspect the cook, but could prove nothing.
5 What *has become* of your coin collection?
6 Finally even Sally *had run* out of breath!
7 Pat *had swung* the lazy Susan around once more.
8 The Fabers *had come* a day early.
9 Larry *has drunk* all the iced tea in the pitcher.
10 Kathy *had seen* the Baltimore oriole first.
11 Bill *had run* to catch the bus but missed it.
12 Betty *has* never *done* any upholstering before.
13 Irwin *had seen* the satellite in orbit.
14 Betty *had brought* a friend with her.
15 He *had done* his best to meet the deadline.

194
Exercise 3   Before doing this exercise, read the article **lie, lay** in the Index.
  Be ready to read the following sentences aloud, substituting for each blank the appropriate standard form of *lie* (lie, lay, lain, lying) or *lay* (lay, laid, laid, laying).

1 The hit-and-run victim was _____ in the street.
2 Interns lifted him carefully and _____ him on a stretcher.
3 The dog often _____ near the fence and growls.
4 The papers have been _____ there since yesterday.
5 No, Hawkins Swamp _____ just beyond those hills, sir.
6 Oscar was _____ in the hammock, fast asleep.
7 The album has _____ there for over a year, accumulating dust.
8 This time policemen _____ in wait for the thief and caught him.
9 I must have _____ awake half the night, worrying.
10 The wet hockey gloves were _____ on the radiator, just where Hank had _____ them.
11 Yesterday the cornerstone of the new school was _____.
12 Anyone who _____ on that cot very long will get a stiff back.
13 The note was still _____ there, in plain sight.
14 Once again Marilyn had _____ in the sun too long.
15 Although I complained loudly, Joel _____ at his ease on the sofa while I _____ the tile.

16 When Mom came, Ken _____ very still, pretending to be asleep.

17 I noticed that a cat was _____ in the middle of the road.

18 The fog _____ over the valley for an hour and then lifted.

19 She _____ down for an hour every afternoon but seldom sleeps.

20 She was _____ down when we left.

Exercise 4 Before doing this exercise, read these articles in the Index: **learn, teach; leave, let; rise, raise; sit, set.**

Be ready to read each of the following sentences aloud, using the appropriate verb to express the intended meaning.

1 Sue enjoys just (*setting, sitting*) there, watching people pass by.

2 Dad has been (*leaving, letting*) me drive the car.

3 Rob (*learned, taught*) me all I know about sailing.

4 Will the watchman (*leave, let*) us in after work hours?

5 The twins can't (*sit, set*) still even for five minutes!

6 The bus driver (*let, left*) us off at the wrong stop.

7 An old man was (*sitting, setting*) on the park bench.

8 The dog wouldn't (*leave, let*) go of the bone.

9 No one should (*sit, set*) in the antique chair.

10 (*Leave, Let*) the light bulb cool first.

11 The river will probably (*rise, raise*) another three inches by midnight.

12 She wouldn't (*leave, let*) me pay for the flowers. 195

13 They had (*let, left*) us just enough room to park our Volkswagen.

14 Prices have (*raised, risen*) steadily during the past year.

15 Marge's mother won't (*leave, let*) her wear eye shadow.

16 (*Leave, Let*) the dough (*rise, raise*) another fifteen minutes.

17 Harry wouldn't (*leave, let*) anyone push him around.

18 Andy usually (*sits, sets*) in the front seat with Dad.

19 Don't (*leave, let*) him pick the apples before they are ripe.

20 Dad wouldn't (*leave, let*) her drive in city traffic.

Special Problems in Sequence

Using the past perfect. In telling about two past actions, one of which was completed quite some time before the other, do not use the simple-past form for both verbs. Instead, use the past-perfect tense for the earlier of the two actions.

POOR: Later the townspeople *built* a museum where the original fort *stood*. [Using the simple-past form for both verbs makes it seem as if the museum was built on top of the fort.]

IMPROVED: Later the townspeople *built* a museum where the original fort **had stood.**

Tenses of verbals.   Participles and infinitives have two tenses, the present (*doing, being done; to do, to be done*) and the perfect (*having done, having been done; to have done, to have been done*).

The perfect tense of the verbal is used to show action that took place before the action of the main verb:

> *Having done* his share of the work, he felt free to leave.
> We are sorry *to have inconvenienced* you yesterday.

Otherwise the present tense is used:

> *Feeling* that he had been insulted, he sulked the whole evening.
> She had intended *to bring* her camera.   [Not: *to have brought.* The intention—which she had in the past—was *to bring* the camera, not *to have brought* it.]

Exercise 5   Be ready to read the following sentences aloud, using the verb forms appropriate in standard English.

1   We had wanted (*to see, to have seen*) Niagara Falls last summer.
2   (*Driving, Having driven*) for three hours, Dad was tired and stopped for a cup of coffee.
3   Ralph found Spanish easy because he (*spent, had spent*) several summers in Mexico.
4   (*Running, Having run*) to catch the bus, Mr. Owens lost his hat.
5   (*Running, Having run*) to catch the bus, he was out of breath.
6   Norma insisted that she (*took, had taken*) her polio shots already.
7   Don would have liked (*to stay, to have stayed*) at camp a week longer.
8   After the house (*was, had been*) vacant for five months, Dad finally sold it.
9   (*Missing, Having missed*) the target twice, Jerry took careful aim.
10   Rob certainly did not expect (*to be treated, to have been treated*) like a child.
11   Larry (*almost finished, had almost finished*) varnishing the floor when the doorbell rang.
12   (*Sitting, Having sat*) at the switchboard all day, Ann did not want to sit at a movie all evening.
13   The Cramers had fully intended (*to buy, to have bought*) a Renault last summer.
14   Where the oak (*stood, had stood*), there was now a gaping hole.
15   Mr. Elton examined the statue carefully. He (*saw, had seen*) one like it several years before, in Samoa.
16   Would Elsie have liked (*to bring, to have brought*) a friend along?

17 Pete couldn't cut the grass, because our neighbors (*borrowed, had borrowed*) our lawn mower the week before and (*didn't return, hadn't returned*) it.

18 I am sorry (*to miss, to have missed*) you last week.

19 Hadn't he planned (*to catch, to have caught*) the late train?

20 Ken rowed directly to the spot where he (*caught, had caught*) the pike last summer.

21 Sue telephoned to find out if we (*left, had left*).

22 Mr. Timm was hoping (*to receive, to have received*) the shipment from Port Arthur by the end of the week.

Subjunctives

Wishes and if-clauses. Subjunctive forms, though far less common than they once were, are still generally used in formal English in wishes and in *if*-clauses that are contrary to fact or highly doubtful:

> Barbara wishes she *were* eighteen again.
> He acts as if he *were* the expert, not she.
> If Ted *were* one year older, he could vote.

Note, however, that when no strong doubt is suggested, the indicative is used:

> If Ted *was* at the meeting, he must have seen her.

197

In informal English the indicative is often used in wishes and in *if*-clauses:

> Barbara wishes she *was* eighteen again.
> He acts as if he *was* the expert, not she.

Had, not *would have,* is used to show that a wish or condition refers to the past:

> I wish Maureen *had invited* me. [Not: *would have invited.*]
> If he *had been notified,* the calamity might have been averted.

That-clauses. The subjunctive is also used in *that*-clauses after verbs of insisting, requesting, suggesting, and recommending, and after expressions like *it is necessary, it is important,* and *it was urged:*

> Mrs. Forbes insisted that Paul *apologize.*
> He requests that all heirs *be* present at the reading of the will.

In sentences like these, both in formal and in informal English, people often avoid the subjunctive by rephrasing the idea:

> Mrs. Forbes insisted that Paul *should apologize.*
> He requests all heirs *to be* present at the reading of the will.

Exercise 6   Be ready to read aloud the following sentences, using the form of the verb (in parentheses) that would be appropriate in formal English.

1   Al wished he (*was, were*) relaxing at the beach instead of struggling with a legal brief.
2   If you (*had, would have*) found a lion cub in your tent, what would you have done?
3   He recommends that Ed (*take, takes*) a vitamin pill each day.
4   If only Irene (*was, were*) not so far away!
5   Paul suggests that Dave (*pay, pays*) part of the bill.
6   If I (*was, were*) in your place, I would tell him.
7   If they (*would have, had*) arrived yesterday, they would surely have attended the board meeting today.
8   I wish it (*was, were*) possible to see you now.
9   If John (*would not have, had not*) been a weak king, there might have been no Magna Charta.
10   George acts as if the rule (*was, were*) made to be broken.
11   The committee recommends that the treasurer (*is, be*) relieved of his duties.
12   If he (*break, breaks*) his parole once more, he goes back to prison.
13   How I wish Erik (*was, were*) with us now!
14   Is it necessary that the applicant (*be, is*) eighteen years old?
15   If they (*would have, had*) read the newspaper, they would have known about the election returns.
16   It is necessary that he (*comes, come*) at the time assigned.
17   She acts as if she (*was, were*) the only one in the apartment.
18   Mark would have voted against the bill if he (*would have, had*) been there.
19   If Socrates (*was, were*) alive today, what would he think of our high school?
20   Later Marie wished she (*would have, had*) bought the album.

Agreement with the Subject

Since errors in subject-verb agreement are common, some of the special problems are reviewed here.

Modifiers between subject and verb.   Phrases or clauses coming between the subject and the verb do not affect the subject-verb agreement. A singular subject followed by a phrase or clause containing a plural noun is still singular:

> A **quart** of strawberries *seems* more than enough for four servings. [Not: *seem.*]
> The **batch** made with raisins and black walnuts *was* the best. [Not: *were.*]

His **interest** in sports, especially boxing matches and polo
  games, *is* not surprising.   [Not: *are.*]
The **story** of the terrible experiences the refugees suffered
  through during these days *is* very moving. [Not: *are.*]

Similarly, a plural subject followed by a phrase or clause containing a singular noun is still plural:

The **estimates** submitted by one contractor interested in the
  project *appall* us. [Not: *appalls.*]
The **opportunities** for growth that this job offers to the beginner *are* highly important. [Not: *is.*]

When a parenthetical phrase beginning with a preposition like
as well as, together with, with, in addition to, and *along with* comes
between the subject and the verb, the phrase does not affect the
subject-verb agreement:

Mrs. Marks, as well as her sister, *goes* to ridiculous lengths to
  save money. [Not: *go.*]
The **guard,** along with the teller and the head bookkeeper,
  was under suspicion. [Not: *were.*]

If a singular verb after such a phrase sounds "wrong" to you, it
may be because the meaning seems obviously plural, as here:

My father, together with my two uncles, *was working* hard to
  get the hay into the barn before the storm broke.   **199**

Changing the *together with* to *and* and then using a plural verb will
emphasize the plural meaning—and improve the sound of the
sentence:

My father *and* my two uncles *were working* hard to get the hay
  into the barn before the storm broke.

Subject and complement of different number.   In some sentences the subject and the predicate complement may be of a different number. In such sentences the verb agrees with the subject,
not with the predicate complement:

His greatest delight *was* his children.
His children *were* his greatest delight.

Titles.   The subject of a sentence may be the title of a book,
article, painting, song, or sculpture, or the name of a country, organization, or business firm. Even though the title or name may be
plural in form, a singular verb is used with it, since it is considered
the name of one thing:

"Three Bags Full" *is* an appropriate title for a Christmas story.
The Netherlands *has* a long and fascinating history.
The Knights of Pythias *was founded* in 1864.
Charles Wingate's Sons *manufactures* ink.

Indefinites. Singular verbs are used with the indefinite pronouns and adjectives *each, every, either, neither, anyone, anybody, one, everyone, everybody, someone, somebody, nobody, no one:*

> Each of the men *works* in the Loop.
> Everybody in the tents *was awakened* by the crash.
> Every one of the elms and maples *has been sprayed.*
> Neither of the clocks *keeps* accurate time.

Words of measure. Each of the following subjects, although plural in form, names a single unit of time or measure (length, distance, amount, weight). Such subjects are usually followed by singular verbs:

> Six weeks *seems* a long time to wait.
> Four and a half acres *does* not *provide* enough space.
> Ten dollars *was* too much to pay.

A singular verb is used with words like *some, all, more,* and *most* and nouns like *half, third,* and *part* when they tell **how much** of something is meant. A plural verb is used when the words tell **how many** are meant.

> Some of the material *has faded.* [Tells how much.]
> Some of the cookies *are* stale. [Tells how many.]
> Two thirds of the stock *remains* unsold. [Tells how much.]
> One third of the students *live* on campus. [Tells how many.]

A singular verb is used with *the number,* meaning "the quantity"; a plural verb with *a number,* meaning "several" or "many":

> The number of errors *was* unbelievable. ["The quantity" of.]
> A number of people *were* already *picnicking.* [Meaning "several" or "many."]

Collective nouns. Either a singular or a plural verb may be used with a collective noun (one that names a group of persons or things, like *band, choir, jury, herd, family*). If the group is thought of as a single unit acting together, a singular verb is used. If the individual members of the group are thought of as acting individually, a plural verb is used.

> The band *is going* to the Rose Bowl this year.
> The band, as usual, *were straggling* into the auditorium in groups of two or three.

Plural form—singular meaning. A singular verb is used with subjects like *physics, economics, measles, mumps,* and *checkers,* which are plural in form but singular in meaning:

> Physics *is required* of all engineering students.
> Isn't measles catching?
> After chess, checkers *seems* monotonous.

Compound subjects. A plural form of the verb is generally used with a compound subject connected by *and:*

> The owner and the editor *determine* the policy of the paper.

But if the parts of a compound subject refer to the same person or thing or are thought of as a unit, a singular form of the verb is used:

> The owner and editor, Mr. Carson, *writes* the editorials. [One person.]
> The stress and strain *was beginning* to undermine his health.
> The apple pie and cheese *appeals* to me. [Thought of as a combination and hence as one item of food.]

When a whole compound subject is modified by the indefinite adjective *each* or *every,* a singular verb is used:

> Each name, address, and telephone number *has been verified.*
> Every man, woman, and child *needs* a balanced diet.

When the parts of a compound subject are connected by *or, nor, either . . . or,* or *neither . . . nor,* the verb usually agrees with the nearer part:

> Charles or Fred *is* the man to see.
> Neither criticism nor ridicule *disturbs* him.
> Either the twins or George *is going* to take charge.
> Either George or the twins *are going* to take charge.

But if the subject is plural in idea, a plural verb is often used in informal English, especially in questions and in negative sentences. For example:

> *Have* Jim or Tom *arrived?* [Formal: *Has* Jim or Tom *arrived?*]
> Neither the president nor the vice-president *have signed.* [Formal: *has signed.*]

When the subjects are of different persons, in formal usage the verb agrees with the nearer part:

> He or you *are* to drive.   You or he *is* to drive.

People often avoid the necessity of such a choice of verb form by rewording the sentences:

> You will drive, or he will.   He will drive, or you will.

In sentences like the following, the verb agrees with the affirmative part, not the negative:

> You, not I, *are invited.*   I, not you, *am invited.*

People often avoid the problem by rewording the sentences:

> You are invited, not I.   I am invited, not you.

201

Verb before subject. Sometimes the verb (or part of it) comes before the subject. Regardless of its position, the verb generally agrees with the subject:

> When **were** *you* in Cleveland?
> Last of all **comes** *Amahl* on his crutches.
> **Doesn't** *one* of those clocks **work**?
> **Are** there any *messages* for me?
> There **are** several *letters* and one *magazine* in today's mail.
>   [Compound subject.]

In informal usage the expletive *there* is sometimes followed by a singular verb when the first part of the compound subject is singular:

> There *is* one magazine and several letters in today's mail.

Relative pronouns. Used as a subject, the relative pronoun *who, which,* or *that* is followed by a singular verb when its antecedent is singular and by a plural verb when its antecedent is plural:

> Sylvia is the only **one** of those girls who *has held* a job.   [The antecedent of *who* is *one.* The meaning is "Of those girls, Sylvia is the only one who has held a job."]
> He is one of those **people** who *irritate* her.   [The antecedent of *who* is *people,* not *one.* The meaning is "Of those people who irritate her, he is one."]

In informal speech a singular verb is sometimes used in sentences like the second of those just given: "He is one of those people who *irritates* her."

Exercise 7   Be ready to read each of the following sentences aloud, using the verb form (in parentheses) that would be appropriate in formal English.

1   Anyone who must work with those big files (*has, have*) my sympathy.
2   Twenty minutes (*was, were*) all Dad could take of the deafening power drill.
3   Only one of the members (*plan, plans*) to attend the conference.
4   The unsung heroes in yesterday's airplane accident (*was, were*) the ground crew.
5   Each of the delegates (*has, have*) to sign the document.
6   (*Was, Were*) there many people at the concert?
7   Price, Clark and Company (*import, imports*) giftware.
8   Macaroni and cheese (*taste, tastes*) good after a long hike.
9   She is the only one of the girls who consistently (*type, types*) more than sixty words a minute.

202

10 One attraction of the apartments (*is, are*) the new appliances.
11 Dr. Burton or his receptionist usually (*answers, answer*) the phone.
12 The assembly hall, as well as some of the classrooms, (*need, needs*) to be repainted.
13 (*Is, Are*) *All the King's Men* based on the life of Huey Long?
14 The author and illustrator (*has, have*) promised to show some of her sketches.
15 Neither rain nor snow (*prevent, prevents*) Mrs. Clark from attending church on Sundays.
16 Some of the debaters, together with their coach, (*has, have*) left for Denver.
17 Elsie is one of those people who (*don't, doesn't*) know when to stop talking.
18 Neither of the plants (*seem, seems*) to be thriving.
19 Measles sometimes (*has, have*) unfortunate aftereffects.
20 The number of languages offered (*amazes, amaze*) me.
21 Among the items displayed by the Dobson sisters (*was, were*) a water color of the New York City skyline.
22 Everybody on the seventh, eighth, and ninth floors (*is, are*) complaining about the elevator service.
23 (*Do, Does*) he and his brothers still practice law?
24 Every report in those drawers (*contain, contains*) classified information.
25 Horseshoes (*is, are*) always a popular game at the park.   **203**

Exercise 8   Rewrite each of these sentences, following the directions given in parentheses and making any other changes that are necessary. Be ready to give reasons for all the changes you make.

1 Where was his billfold found? (After *billfold* insert *and keys.*)
2 Some of the contractor's bids were accepted. (Change *Some* to *One.*)
3 One fourth of the herd is sick. (Change *herd* to *animals.*)
4 The new nations face grave problems. (Change *new nations* to *United Nations.*)
5 Ellen or the twins usually bring a radio. (Begin with *The twins.*)
6 Some of his ideas sound worth while. (Change *Some* to *Neither.*)
7 Her voice irritates many people. (After *voice* add *as well as her mannerisms.*)
8 The emergency sessions were successful. (Begin with *Only one of.*)
9 Refusing the invitation seems sensible to me. (Begin with *Your reasons for.*)
10 The commissioner was trapped in the smoldering building. (After *commissioner* add *along with the three firemen.*)

11 The pewter candleholders were Tom and Alice's gift. (Begin with *Tom and Alice's gift.*)

12 Paul is the only one who has applied. (Change *the only one* to *one of the many.*)

13 The graduating class is meeting in the library. (Change *meeting in the library* to *trying on their caps and gowns.*)

14 Where is the ancient temple? (Before *the ancient temple* add *the ruins of.*)

15 Those equations seem correct. (Begin with *Her explanation of.*)

16 Do Pete's sisters ever come with him to the club? (Insert *brother or his* after *Pete's.*)

17 According to Harriet, most of the fruit was inedible. (Change *fruit* to *oranges.*)

NOUN FORMS

Plurals and Possessives

Although most nouns form their plurals and possessives regularly, some few nouns do present problems. For instance, should you write "There are two *Larrys* in class" or "two *Larries*"? Which is correct, "her brothers-in-law's cars" or "her brothers-in-laws' cars"? When is the plural form *indexes* preferred? When *indices*? The Index articles **Plurals of nouns** and **Possessive case** will help you with these and similar questions.

***Exercise* 9**   Before doing this exercise, read the article **Plurals of nouns** in the Index.

On a sheet of paper, write the plurals of the following words, using your dictionary when you are uncertain. The words followed by an asterisk have two acceptable plurals; give both of them. Be ready to write the plurals from dictation of the singulars.

1	ranch	14	shelf	27	stadium*
2	city	15	silo	28	clubwoman
3	box	16	half	29	index*
4	zero*	17	oasis	30	grandchild
5	Dorothy	18	Jenkins	31	diagnosis
6	arch	19	go-between	32	Swiss
7	chintz	20	baby	33	cactus*
8	Eskimo*	21	*and* [the word]	34	radius*
9	business	22	beau*	35	mother-in-law
10	fresco*	23	cupful	36	*t* [the letter]
11	tomato	24	stop watch	37	antenna*
12	motto*	25	kindergarten	38	phenomenon*
13	lady	26	fiasco*	39	analysis

40	alley	44	wisdom tooth	48	ratio
41	ally	45	novelty	49	maid of honor
42	Burmese	46	heir apparent	50	monarch
43	hippopotamus*	47	two-by-four	51	chief of staff

Exercise 10   Before doing Exercise 10, read the article **Possessive case** in the Index.

The italicized item in each of the following groups tells what is owned. The second item names the owner or owners. On a sheet of paper, write the number of each group. After it, write the possessive form of the owner followed by the name of the thing owned.

Example: *mustache*   the villain
               the villain's mustache

1	*diagnosis* the doctor		21	*strike* the longshoremen
2	*tracks* the field mice		22	*commission* the broker
3	*luncheon* the clubwomen		23	*sequins* Mrs. Jones
4	*encore* the soprano		24	*itinerary* the Ameses
5	*flowers* our neighbor		25	*medals* the heroes
6	*leases* the tenants		26	*chessboard* Paul and Ed
7	*suit* the plaintiff		27	*cottage* my aunt and uncle
8	*gloves* ladies		28	*moccasins* the Indians
9	*lassos* cowboys		29	*profit* the car dealer
10	*convertible* Charles		30	*eyes* Betty and Ruth
11	*brew* the witches		31	*routines* the tap-dancers
12	*patio* the Harrises		32	*talk* the consul general
13	*orders* their wives		33	*fee* the notary public
14	*hoofs* the horses		34	*teacup* her mother-in-law
15	*stew* the hobo		35	*marks* the proofreaders
16	*igloo* the Eskimos		36	*diary* the ten-year-old
17	*catch* the fishermen		37	*food* the puppies
18	*jokes* the alumni		38	*fees* the surgeons
19	*ukulele* the twin		39	*records* the registrar
20	*ukulele* the twins		40	*jack* the mechanic

205

PRONOUNS

Nominative and Objective Forms

The nominative-case forms of the personal pronouns (*I, you, he, she, it, we, you, they*) are used when the pronoun is the subject of the verb:

Ellen and *she* discovered the leak.   [Not: Ellen and *her*.]
We men must stick together.   [Not: *Us* men.]
"Who will ask Mr. Lemon?" "Not *I*."   [In casual conversation "Not *me*" is common.]

The objective-case forms (*me, you, him, her, it, us, you, them*) are used when the pronoun is a direct object, indirect object, or object of a preposition:

> We saw Mary and *him* last week.   [Not: Mary and *he.*]
> They intended to ask Bob or *him.*   [Not: Bob or *he.*]
> "Did he notify anyone?" "Yes, Glen and *me.*"   [Not: Glen and *I.*]
> Mr. Elton gave Tom and *them* the tickets.   [Not: Tom and *they.*]
> Mr. Owens promised *us* girls summer jobs.   [Not: *we* girls.]
> Everyone was ready except Nancy and *her.*   [Not: Nancy and *she.*]

Predicate complements.   In standard English the nominative-case forms are used as predicate complements:

> ["I'd like to speak with Susan."]   "This is *she.*"
> It was *we* who made all the noise.
> It might have been *he* that you heard.

People who feel that the nominative-case form sounds too formal usually find ways of avoiding the problem:

> ["I'd like to speak with Susan."]   "This is Susan."
> We were the ones who made all the noise.
> He might have been the one you heard.

206

(For a discussion of *It's me,* see the Index.)

Appositives.   An appositive pronoun agrees in case with its headword (the word it explains):

> Two speakers—Pat and *she*—had the flu.   [Not *her;* the pronoun is in apposition with the subject *speakers.*]
> Dad gave the boys—Terry and *him*—permission to drive the car.   [Not *he;* the pronoun is in apposition with the indirect object *boys.*]

Pronouns in comparisons.   When a personal pronoun is the subject of the omitted verb in an elliptical clause of comparison, the nominative-case form is used:

> Don is a better tennis partner than *he* [is].   [In the full clause *than he is, he* is the subject of *is.*]

When the pronoun is the object of the omitted verb, the objective-case form is used:

> Since Erik seldom gets upset, the traffic bothered me more than [it bothered] *him.*   [In the full clause *than it bothered him, him* is the object of *bothered.*]

In casual conversation the objective-case pronouns are often heard in sentences like "He's shorter than *her*" and "You're just as poky as *me*"—probably because the pronoun comes at the end of the sentence, where the objective-case form normally comes. But in more careful speech, as well as in writing, the nominative-case forms are used.

Sometimes either a nominative-case pronoun or an objective-case pronoun may be used, depending on the meaning intended. For example:

> They misjudged Paul as much as *I* [misjudged him].
> They misjudged Paul as much as [they misjudged] *me*.

In sentences like these it is especially important to use the case form of the pronoun that will make the intended meaning clear to others.

Who *and* whom.　The nominative-case form *who* (and its compound *whoever*) is used as subject of a sentence or clause and as predicate complement:

> *Who* was allowed inside the vault?　[Subject of *was allowed*.]
> Do you know the man *who* was nominated?　[Subject of *was nominated* in the adjective clause *who was nominated*.]
> Give *whoever* comes to the door a sample.　[Subject of *comes* in the noun clause *whoever comes to the door*.]
> I don't know *who* she is.　[Predicate complement in the noun clause *who she is*.]

207

The objective-case form *whom* (and its compound *whomever*) is used as direct object and as object of a preposition:

> *Whom* did the superintendent recommend?　[Object of *did recommend*.]
> None of us could guess *whom* he was imitating.　[Object of *was imitating* in the noun clause *whom he was imitating*.]
> Give the free tickets to *whomever* you like.　[Object of *like* in the noun clause *whomever you like*.]
> *Whom* did you vote for, and why?　[Object of *for*.]
> The people *whom* they turned to for help responded generously. [Object of *to* in the adjective clause *whom they turned to for help*.]

In informal English, *who* is commonly used at the beginning of a sentence, even when the pronoun is used as the object of a verb or a preposition:

> *Who* did the superintendent recommend?
> *Who* did you vote for, and why?

But when a preposition comes immediately before the pronoun, both informal and formal English use *whom*:

> To *whom* did you give the formula?
> For *whom* was the message intended?

Interrupting expressions like *I thought, you remember,* and *did you say* do not affect the use of *who* in its own clause:

Do you know *who* I thought would be nominated? [Not *whom; who* is the subject of *would be nominated.*]

Harry Jackson, *whom* you remember nobody liked at first, is now quite popular. [Not *who; whom* is the object of *liked.*]

There was no doubt about *who* Dad thought would win. [Not *whom; who* is the subject of *would win.*]

Exercise 11 Be ready to read the following sentences aloud, using the pronoun forms (in parentheses) that are appropriate in standard written English.

1 It is strange that he was so curious about you and (*they, them*).
2 I'm sure Sandra and (*she, her*) would contribute if they could.
3 Finally he told Kay and (*I, me*) what was troubling him.
4 Bruce and (*he, him*) constructed a plaster model of the ship-yard.
5 The bad news bothered Georgia and (*she, her*) all afternoon.
6 Lash drives too fast to suit Mary and (*I, me*).
7 Prescott is a more likely candidate than (*she, her*).
8 The two boys in the horse costume were Andy and (*he, him*).
9 Between you and (*I, me*), I would rather not go until later.
10 You and (*he, him*) will be ushers, won't you?
11 Give the memo to the sports editors, Donna and (*he, him*).
12 Even three of (*we, us*) boys could not manage to pay that bill!
13 The only ones who refused were Betty and (*she, her*).
.14 Just two boys, Brad and (*I, me*), remembered the directions.
15 It might have been (*they, them*) who spilled the paint.
16 We do not know anyone who is better liked than (*she, her*).
17 We both shoveled the snow, but Mrs. Russo paid Tom more than (*I, me*).
18 I'm going to tell Helen and (*she, her*) what I really think.
19 It must be (*they, them*) in the hall now.
20 I haven't mentioned the matter to Ken or (*he, him*).
21 It took three of (*we, us*) nurses to calm the patient in Room 204.
22 Did they ask you and (*she, her*) for lunch?
23 The powdered wigs looked strange on Jake and (*he, him*).
24 Mother says that my brother is grouchier than (*I, me*).
25 The hat suits you much better than (*she, her*).
26 We were both to blame, so why punish me more than (*he, him*)?
27 The co-captains, Jack and (*he, him*), will receive awards.
28 Leo ignored both Rob and (*she, her*) at the dance.
29 (*We, Us*) fellows helped push the car.
30 Mr. Cousins gave George and (*we, us*) some pointers on golf.

Exercise 12   Be ready to read aloud each of the following sentences, choosing the form of the pronoun (in parentheses) that is appropriate to use in formal English. Be ready to give the reasons for your answers.

1 The pharmacist (*who, whom*) was asked to fill the prescription could not read it.
2 The other pharmacist to (*who, whom*) he showed it was also puzzled.
3 Mr. Burke hired Tom Petry, (*who, whom*) he considered was best qualified for the position.
4 A reward will be given to (*whoever, whomever*) returns the dog.
5 Even Mr. Adams did not know (*who, whom*) they were.
6 The chief engineer, (*who, whom*) we heard he had quarreled with, was fired soon afterward.
7 (*Who, Whom*) do you think will be promoted to the vice-presidency?
8 Listen carefully, (*whoever, whomever*) you are!
9 (*Who, Whom*) was asked to take over the business, and by (*who, whom*) was he asked?
10 Velvet Pants, (*who, whom*) they had jeered at, was the only one brave enough to face the bull.
11 Give (*whoever, whomever*) changes the tire a generous tip.
12 (*Who, Whom*) do you suppose Ted saw today!
13 Miss Coe, (*who, whom*) he said he had recommended, was not hired.
14 Invite (*whoever, whomever*) you want, of course.
15 (*Who, Whom*) stood up for (*who, whom*) during the argument?
16 My choice for governor will be (*whoever, whomever*) I feel is most honest and capable.
17 Rex Burns, (*who, whom*) I first heard last year, is my favorite.
18 Mrs. Fales, (*who, whom*) she had wanted to meet, was not there.
19 (*Who, Whom*) shall I say will be responsible for the group?
20 The dentist (*who, whom*) I usually go to is on vacation now.
21 Why should you care about (*who, whom*) came first?

209

Using Pronouns and Nouns with Gerunds

A pronoun or a proper noun (*Ruth, Gerald*) directly before a gerund is usually in the possessive form:

His countermanding Mr. Daly's orders added to the confusion.
They were surprised at *my* agreeing with them.
She did not like *his* repeating the same old jokes.
They did not mention *Edwin's* losing his temper.

Usage is divided when a common noun directly precedes a gerund. In formal English the possessive form is usual; in informal English, the ordinary form is often used:

FORMAL: He objected to his *wife's* taking the job.
INFORMAL: He objected to his *wife* taking the job.

The ordinary form is generally used for plural nouns:

Do you approve of *students* keeping such late hours?

When emphasis is wanted for the noun or pronoun rather than for the gerund that names the action, the ordinary form of the noun and the objective form of the pronoun are used:

Frankly, we were amazed at *Edwin* losing his temper, since he is usually so placid.
Imagine *me* agreeing to such a division of the property!

Exercise **13** Be ready to read each of the following sentences aloud, using the appropriate form of the pronoun or noun (in parentheses).

1 (*Him, His*) complaining about a headache is certainly unusual.
2 Have you heard about (*Jean, Jean's*) winning the first prize?
3 We are looking forward to (*you, your*) visiting us next year.
4 There is no excuse for (*Ellen, Ellen's*) arriving late.
5 I know the reason for (*them, their*) withdrawing their support.
6 I object to (*Joe, Joe's*) getting all the credit when he did so little work.
7 (*You, Your*) joining us would just complicate matters.
8 He was surprised at (*us, our*) remembering his name.
9 Don't you recall (*me, my*) telling you about the accident?
10 Uncle Ken appreciated (*you, your*) loading the car for him.
11 It was (*us, our*) calling his bluff that really upset him.
12 Have I written you about (*Dad, Dad's*) promising me a car?

Agreement with Indefinites

Singular pronouns are generally used to refer to the indefinite pronouns *one, anybody, anyone, each, either, neither, everybody, everyone, somebody, someone, nobody,* and *no one:*

Neither of the men felt that *he* was responsible.
Somebody had caught *her* heel in the escalator.
Before anyone signs the contract, *he* should read the fine print.
    [The masculine form *he* is used even if the "anyone" turns out to be feminine.]

In informal conversation, plural pronouns are often used in such sentences, but such plurals are inappropriate in writing and in more formal speech.

Sometimes the indefinite pronouns are so obviously plural in meaning that using singular pronouns to refer to them would sound ridiculous. For example:

> When *everybody* had arrived, Mr. Bates told **him** the good news.

In informal English a plural pronoun would be used in sentences like this. In formal English the sentence would be rephrased so as not to violate the grammatical agreement.

INFORMAL: When *everybody* had arrived, Mr. Bates told **them** the good news.

FORMAL: When *all the members* had arrived, Mr. Bates told **them** the good news.

Exercise 14 Be ready to read the following sentences aloud, using the forms of the pronouns (in parentheses) appropriate in standard written English.

1 I think that when somebody has made a mistake (*he, they*) should be willing to admit it.
2 Each of the delegates knows that (*he, they*) must pay (*his, their*) own expenses.
3 If anybody asks you, tell (*him, them*) that I sent you.
4 Everyone at the meeting said (*he, they*) could come.
5 Either of the girls can show (*her, their*) slides today.
6 No one knows how (*he, they*) will act in an emergency.
7 Anybody could open that safe if (*he, they*) really wanted to.
8 Unless someone will let us use (*his, their*) car, we cannot go tomorrow night.
9 Tell each of them to remember (*his, their*) part of the bargain.
10 If anyone wants (*his, their*) money back, (*he, they*) must have (*his, their*) receipt with (*him, them*).
11 Nobody is to wipe (*his, their*) boots on the new carpet!
12 It seemed that everyone who entered the contest expected (*her, their*) cake to win the prize.
13 Neither of the witnesses hesitated to tell (*his, their*) story.
14 Everybody on the south side must provide (*his, their*) own transportation.
15 Even if anyone shouts, (*he, they*) can't be heard there.

211

Exercise 15 Before doing this exercise, read these entries in the Index: **Intensive pronouns; myself; Reflexive pronouns; them; theirself, theirselves.**

Each of the following sentences contains one or more forms not appropriate in formal English. Be ready to read the sentences aloud, substituting the appropriate forms.

1 Them are exactly the colors Sally and myself picked out.
2 There is an uneasy truce between Ken and ourselves.

3 They decided the time had come to make theirselves scarce.
4 My friend Ardys and myself went backstage after the play to meet Miss Cornell.
5 George drove the Ellises and ourselves home after the party.
6 Mr. Peters himself promised the jobs to your cousin and yourself.
7 Mrs. Oakdale and myself thank you for your hospitality.
8 Them are the ones we ourself painted.
9 Either your brother or yourself must have drawn that cartoon.
10 The next day a reporter from Baltimore interviewed Pete, Randy, and myself.
11 Even experts like your friend and yourself will have to admit that them are well done.
12 Bob Vanderstern and myself were the only ones who filled out one of them applications.

MODIFIERS

Adjective or Adverb

Whether to use the adjective or the adverb form of a modifier depends on what work the word does in the sentence. If the word modifies the meaning of a noun or a pronoun, it is an adjective. If it modifies the meaning of a verb, an adjective, or another adverb, it is an adverb.

ADJECTIVE: Lois is always *neat*.   [Modifies the noun *Lois*.]
ADVERB: Lois always dresses *neatly*.   [Modifies the verb *dresses*.]

ADJECTIVE: They thought him *strange*.   [Modifies the pronoun *him*.]
ADVERB: They thought him *strangely* unresponsive.   [Modifies the adjective *unresponsive*.]

The nonstandard use of the adjective form instead of the adverb form should be avoided:

NONSTANDARD: He walked very *awkward*, as if he had a stiff knee.
STANDARD: He walked very *awkwardly*, as if he had a stiff knee.

Adjective After Linking Verb

Verbs like *look, feel, sound, taste, grow,* and *smell* are used sometimes as action verbs and sometimes as linking verbs. When used as action verbs, they are often followed by adverbs:

Before crossing the street, she looked *carefully* in all directions.
Keith felt his way *nervously* down the tunnel.
She tasted the mixture *cautiously*.

But when used as linking verbs, they are followed by predicate adjectives modifying the subject:

The pirate looked *ferocious.* [Not *ferociously;* it modifies *pirate*, not the verb *looked.*]

Don't your eyes feel *tired* after such close work? [Not *tiredly;* it modifies *eyes*, not the verb *Do feel.*]

The mixture tasted *bitter.* [Not *bitterly;* it modifies *mixture*, not the verb *tasted.*]

Exercise 16   Before doing this exercise, read these entries in the Index: **bad, badly; good, well.**

Be ready to read aloud each of the following sentences, choosing the adjective or the adverb (in parentheses) that should be used in standard written English. Be prepared to explain your choices.

1   Frank drives very (*cautious, cautiously*), as a rule.
2   Laura felt (*bad, badly*) about keeping them waiting.
3   How (*sudden, suddenly*) the room became quiet.
4   Hal talked (*sarcastic, sarcastically*) to the bus driver.
5   Why does he sound his *r*'s so (*strange, strangely*)?
6   No matter how (*good, well*) he plays, I just don't like the song.
7   The sauce on the egg rolls tastes (*strange, strangely*).
8   If you dress (*warm, warmly*), you will be all right.
9   How can he sound so (*cheerful, cheerfully*) on such a gloomy day!
10   The car runs (*good, well*) even though it is old.
11   He shouldn't feel (*bad, badly*); it was an accident.
12   Why does she always dress so (*conspicuous, conspicuously*)?
13   How (*sickening, sickeningly*) Aunt Polly's home remedy sounded!
14   Bill said he could get out of the job (*easy, easily*).
15   The cheese may smell (*horrible, horribly*) but it tastes (*delicious, deliciously*).
16   Our Great Dane eats (*hearty, heartily*).
17   When Nora asked if the jalopy would make it, Buck looked (*doubtful, doubtfully*).
18   After being closed all winter, the cottage smelled (*musty, mustily*).
19   Please pack each box (*separate, separately*).
20   We'll never forget how (*peculiar, peculiarly*) they looked.
21   In Swiss villages no more than fifteen miles apart the same vowel may be sounded (*different, differently*).
22   Kathleen danced so (*graceful, gracefully*) that it was a joy to watch her.
23   The man in the hall did look rather (*suspicious, suspiciously*).
24   Marguerite sounded (*excited, excitedly*), as always.
25   Why would Marvin, of all people, leave so (*sudden, suddenly*)?

213

Adjectives and adverbs have three forms to indicate degrees of the quality they name:

POSITIVE	COMPARATIVE	SUPERLATIVE
sharp	sharper	sharpest
careless	more careless	most careless
soon	sooner	soonest
quickly	more quickly	most quickly

The comparative and superlative degrees are formed in two ways: by adding *-er* and *-est* to the simple (positive) form or by putting *more* and *most* before it. The *-er* and *-est* forms are usual for short adjectives; the *more* and *most* forms, for longer ones and for all adverbs ending in *-ly*.

Either of the two forms may be used for a number of adjectives and adverbs: *oftener, more often; happiest, most happy.* The emphasis wanted in a particular sentence, as well as the sound, will then determine which form is used:

Our cat is even *lazier* than our dog. [Emphasis is on the laziness.]

Our cat is even *more lazy* than our dog. [Emphasis is on the degree of laziness.]

But both forms should not be used together, as in *more softer* and *most softest*. This "double comparison" was usual in Shakespeare's time but is nonstandard today.

A few adjectives and adverbs have irregular comparisons:

	POSITIVE	COMPARATIVE	SUPERLATIVE
ADJECTIVES:	bad	worse	worst
	far	farther, further	farthest, furthest
	good, well	better	best
	little	less, lesser	least
	much, many	more	most
ADVERBS:	well	better	best
	little	less	least
	much	more	most

The comparative forms are ordinarily used in comparing two persons or things, and the superlative forms in comparing more than two:

Ruth is *taller* than Marilyn.

Isn't Annette the *tallest* of the girls in the cast?

Who works *more efficiently*, Pete or Andy?

Of all the employees, Larry works *most efficiently*.

But in informal speech the superlative is often used in a comparison of two items:

> This is the *most interesting* of the two volumes. [Formal: *more interesting*.]
>
> Which story do you like *best*—"The Gold Bug" or "The Purloined Letter"? [Formal: *better*.]

Exercise 17   Be ready to read each of the following sentences aloud, supplying the form (in parentheses) that would be appropriate to use in standard written English.

1 Of the two cats, the lilac-point Siamese is (*more, most*) likely to take the prize.
2 Who dresses (*dowdier, more dowdily*), Mrs. Smith or her daughter?
3 We felt (*safer, more safely*) with the door locked.
4 Please answer (*prompter, more promptly*) than you did last time.
5 The (*larger, largest*) of these two desks is the (*better, best*) buy.
6 Tom danced even (*clumsier, more clumsily*) than his brother.
7 Both men know their trade, but Jim works (*steadier, more steadily*) than Ed.
8 Larry looks (*neater, more neatly*) than he did a year ago.
9 Who would you say had the (*more, most*) trying day at the office, Mr. Curtis or his secretary?
10 She spoke much (*crosser, more crossly*) to me yesterday.
11 Their dog barks much (*fiercer, more fiercely*) than ours.
12 Although Emily was the (*more, most*) talented of the three Brontë sisters, Charlotte enjoyed the (*greater, greatest*) renown.
13 Which is (*worse, worst*), to go to the dentist now or to risk losing the tooth?
14 He sounds (*politer, more politely*) than his brother.
15 The second clown was dressed even (*odder, more oddly*) than the first one.

Exercise 18   Before doing this exercise, read these entries in the Index: *a, an; Double negative; kind, sort; kind of, sort of; kind of a, sort of a; most, almost; them; this here, that there.*

Each of the following sentences contains one or more forms that are not appropriate in standard written English. Be ready to read the sentences aloud, substituting the appropriate forms.

1 There wasn't scarcely enough space left for the trombone.
2 Most all the members came late because of the storm.
3 After the physical-fitness test Jerry's muscles felt kind of sore.
4 Obviously he hadn't learned nothing about Irish history.
5 This here TV was so loud I couldn't scarcely hear the phone.

6 Most anyone could have solved that there puzzle.
7 I just don't like them kind of songs.
8 Joe felt so badly that he couldn't hardly speak.
9 Those sort of grapes are often sour.
10 On Friday night Dave most always goes dancing.
11 They didn't hear nobody come in.
12 That is a honor they don't scarcely deserve.
13 Allan sort of expected to find Mr. Dale in the garden.
14 That kind of a fur does not hold up good.
15 He looked kind of cheerful for a change.
16 Babe Ruth autographed this here ball for me.
17 Those kind of commercials annoy me.
18 That there is a unusual kind of a stamp.
19 What sort of a person should you choose for a friend?
20 That there cake won first prize at the county fair.

IDIOMATIC PREPOSITIONS

Foreign students learning English as a second language have much the same experience as we do in studying a foreign language. They find that learning isolated vocabulary items (nouns, verbs, adjectives, etc.) is relatively easy, but mastering the *idioms*—the expressions and constructions peculiar to the language—is quite difficult. To the foreign student, such English idioms as *to be beside oneself, hard of hearing, to give one's mind to it, to be taken in by his lies,* and *easy does it* seem strange and puzzling—understandably so, since their actual meaning is quite different from the literal meaning of the words themselves. To us, the idioms seem perfectly natural and clear; having heard them from childhood, we learned them effortlessly and use them automatically.

Particularly difficult for a foreign student are our idioms involving prepositions, most of which pose no problems to us. Because we have grown up with our language, we can—without conscious thought—use the idiomatic prepositions in contexts like these:

> feared **for** his life, *but* his fear **of** the dark
> proud **of** her work, *but* takes pride **in** her work
> tampering **with** the lock, *but* meddling **in** his affairs
> **in** deference **to** him, *but* **out of** respect **for** him

Only occasionally do we have doubts about which preposition is idiomatic in a particular expression. This usually happens when we are using words that are rather new to us or words that are followed by different prepositions in different contexts. Then we may wonder whether to say *afflicted by* or *afflicted with*. Should we say *acquiesce in, acquiesce with,* or *acquiesce to*? When should we use *accompanied by* and when *accompanied with*? *angry at* and *angry with*? *compared to* and *compared with*?

In the Index you will find answers to questions like these. Separate entries are given for many troublesome words—for instance, **agree** (*with, to, on*), **conclude** (*by, with, from*). In section 3 of the Index article **Preposition** you will find a list of prepositional idioms. For words not in this list or not covered in separate Index items, consult a dictionary.

In using prepositions, bear in mind that when two words requiring different prepositions are used with a single object, both prepositions should be given:

> Nora showed real appreciation *for* and interest *in* music. [Not: Nora showed real appreciation and interest in music.]

But when the two words require the same preposition, it need not be repeated:

> We appreciate her *interest* and *belief in* us.

Exercise **19**   Before doing this exercise, read in the Index the article **Preposition,** section 3. For help with other idiomatic prepositions, refer to separate Index items.

Be ready to read the following sentences aloud, using the prepositions (in parentheses) appropriate in standard written English.

1   Acrophobia is a great fear (*for, of, toward*) high places.
2   The traveler was encumbered (*with, by*) much luggage.   **217**
3   Marie has become quite proficient (*at, in, with*) French.
4   He had borrowed the kodak (*off, off of, from*) a friend.
5   Jerry has a partiality (*to, for, toward*) blondes.
6   The defendant was accompanied (*by, with*) his lawyers.
7   Carolyn parted (*with, from*) the necklace reluctantly.
8   Two of the explorers died (*of, by, with*) pneumonia.
9   We were annoyed (*by, with, at*) the slow service.
10   The minister concluded the sermon (*by, with*) a poem.
11   We agreed (*with, to*) Ted's plan.
12   Mr. Ott is an authority (*on, about, for*) the Incas.
13   In some respects Mr. Olson's plan is similar (*to, with*) yours.
14   Sonia has an abhorrence (*toward, of, for*) snakes.
15   He is intolerant (*toward, to, of*) opposition, however justified it may be.
16   When we parted (*with, from*) them, they were still angry (*with, toward*) us.
17   She hankered (*for, after, to*) her old home in Norway.
18   In Mexico, Brent's familiarity (*in, with, of, for*) the local customs was a distinct asset.
19   Disconcerted (*by, with, for*) his lapse of memory, the chairman began to stutter.
20   Applicants are hired on merit, irrespective (*of, to, for*) their religious or political affiliations.

ON REVISION:
OFTEN MUST YOU
TURN YOUR STYLUS
TO ERASE, IF YOU
HOPE TO WRITE
SOMETHING WORTH
A SECOND READING.
—HORACE

HORACE
65-8 B.C.

10 *Improving Sentence Structure*

Writing, says Jacques Barzun in *Teacher in America,* "is designed to be read; it is not supposed to be a challenge to clairvoyance." Certainly no writer ever intends his work to be obscure or confusing. Then why is it that so much writing reads as though it were meant to test the patience and ingenuity of the reader?

One reason is that writers do not always take time to think through their ideas. They have a vague notion of what they want to say, and put down the first words that come to mind. But unless a writer has considered his ideas carefully and thoroughly understands them himself, how can he hope to express his meaning clearly and accurately to someone else?

Another reason is that writers do not always take time to revise their work. In his first draft, a writer—intent upon his subject matter and absorbed in getting his thoughts down on paper—is quite likely to turn out faulty sentences. These faulty sentences, if left uncorrected, are a handicap to the reader; they divert his attention and slacken his reading pace. Most readers resent having to pause, even momentarily, to unsnarl a tangled sentence or to figure out the intended meaning of an ambiguous construction. And their resentment is justifiable: it is, after all, the writer's responsibility to revise his work. Revision is an important *part* of writing.

As a first step in revising your papers, experiment with the practice (followed by many experienced writers) of reading your first draft aloud, sentence by sentence. In listening to what you have written, try to put yourself in the reader's place—to hear your own words as though you were the reader and were approaching the subject for the first time. In this way, you can more easily get an objective view of your work and discover the spots that might not seem clear to others.

This sentence-by-sentence examination of a paper will be much more efficient if you first learn the kinds of errors to look for. Fortunately, there are only a few, and they can be mastered with only a little study.

This chapter will show you how to recognize and correct the most common faults in sentence structure. The next chapter will discuss ways of making really "good" sentences out of grammatically correct—but ineffective—ones. The two chapters together should help you learn to write so that a reader will be able to read your sentences not only with ease, but also with the kind of pleasure that comes from having a thought put to him with skill and consideration.

IMPROVING AWKWARD SENTENCES

Some sentences are troublesome or puzzling to the reader because the writer's intended meaning is obscured by faulty, or **awkward**, constructions. Awkward sentences result when a writer (1) phrases his ideas clumsily, (2) arranges his words or groups of words in an unnatural or confusing order, or (3) puts his words together so that they mean something he does not intend them to mean. To make your sentences read smoothly, you should learn to avoid such awkward constructions as misplaced, squinting, and dangling modifiers; interrupted or shifted constructions; faulty pronoun references; and faulty comparisons.

Misplaced Modifiers

Modifiers should be placed in such a way that they do not seem to attach themselves to words they are not intended to modify. Especially likely to cause momentary confusion or unintentional amusement are modifiers that are added at the ends of sentences:

MISPLACED: Full instructions are given for growing the chrysanthemums *in the seed catalogue.*

IMPROVED: *In the seed catalogue* full instructions are given for growing the chrysanthemums.

MISPLACED: The Brewsters complimented George on the fine performance he had given *as they were leaving the auditorium.*

IMPROVED: *As they were leaving the auditorium,* the Brewsters complimented George on the fine performance he had given.

MISPLACED: A literary agent sold the manuscript *to a publisher* that Jay had worked on for four years.

IMPROVED: A literary agent sold *to a publisher* the manuscript that Jay had worked on for four years.

MISPLACED: The ex-soldier found it difficult to drive a car *handicapped by an old war wound.*

IMPROVED: *Handicapped by an old war wound,* the ex-soldier found it difficult to drive a car.

Watch out for a participial phrase at the beginning of a sentence to make sure that it is not intended to modify a word at the end:

MISPLACED: *Living behind the Iron Curtain,* Radio Free Europe proved a great blessing to many news-hungry and truth-loving people.

IMPROVED: Radio Free Europe proved a great blessing to many news-hungry and truth-loving people *living behind the Iron Curtain.*

[For a discussion of the placement of such words as *only, almost, even, hardly, nearly, just,* and *scarcely,* see the entry **only** in the Index.]

Exercise 1   Revise each of the following sentences so that the misplaced modifier clearly modifies the word it is intended to modify. Be ready to read your revised sentences aloud.

1   He lost the fortune that he had spent his life accumulating in one day.
2   The inscription on the tablet was translated by an expert that had been found in the ancient ruins.
3   Mr. Gump did not notice that he had been shortchanged by the ticket agent hurrying to catch the North Shore train.
4   Ambrose agreed to take the children to the department store that was staging a puppet show to humor his mother-in-law.
5   The principal said he hoped all the students would give to the Community Fund when the student body met yesterday.
6   The king left all his personal records and papers to the state archives after he abdicated for the benefit of future historians.
7   The movie was produced by a Frenchman who later had a nervous breakdown at a cost of three million dollars.
8   Yesterday there was a debate on the bill to provide financial aid to displaced persons in the Senate.
9   The queen conferred a title on the prime minister that dated far back into history.
10   At last, battered and torn but still readable, she found the book.

Squinting Modifiers

A modifier placed so that it may reasonably modify either a word preceding it or a word following it is called a **squinting modifier.** Squinting modifiers are not usually a hazard in speech, because the speaker's tone or inflection tells which meaning he intends. But in writing, confusion is possible unless the modifier is placed so that it refers unmistakably to whichever construction it is meant to modify.

CONFUSING: Henry will be asked *as soon as possible* to resign from the club.

CLEAR: *As soon as possible* Henry will be asked to resign from the club.   [Or: Henry will be asked to resign from the club *as soon as possible.*]

Frequently, inserting *that* in the proper place will prevent any possible misunderstanding of the intended meaning:

CONFUSING: Mr. Rains discovered *after the accident* his automobile insurance had been canceled.

CLEAR: Mr. Rains discovered *that* after the accident his automobile insurance had been canceled.   [Or: Mr. Rains discovered after the accident *that* his automobile insurance had been canceled.]

Dangling Modifiers

A modifier is said to **dangle** if there is in the sentence no word that it can sensibly modify:

Searching through the contents of the old sea chest, his grandfather's missing sextant was found.

Most readers expect a verbal phrase at the beginning of a sentence to modify or relate to the subject of the sentence. But the subject of the example sentence is *sextant,* and obviously a sextant cannot do any *searching.* To make the intended meaning clear, the writer will have to provide another subject, one that can sensibly be modified by the verbal phrase:

Searching through the contents of the old sea chest, *Marty* found his grandfather's missing sextant.

In supplying the right subject, the writer will sometimes have to rephrase other parts of the sentence too:

DANGLING INFINITIVE PHRASE: *To become a member of the President's cabinet,* confirmation by the Senate is required.

CORRECTED: To become a member of the President's cabinet, *an appointee must be confirmed* by the Senate.

DANGLING GERUND PHRASE: *After working at my mathematics assignment all morning,* a walk through the park was refreshing.

CORRECTED: After working at my mathematics assignment all morning, *I found* a walk through the park refreshing.

Many dangling modifiers, particularly prepositional phrases or elliptical clauses, are more easily corrected if the modifier is changed to a full subordinate clause:

DANGLING PREPOSITIONAL PHRASE: *At the age of three,* Miriam's father quit his job and went back to college.
CORRECTED: *When Miriam was three,* her father quit his job and went back to college.

DANGLING ELLIPTICAL CLAUSE: *While barbecuing the chickens in the rotisserie,* the electricity went off all over the house.
CORRECTED: *While Dad was barbecuing the chickens in the rotisserie,* the electricity went off all over the house.

DANGLING PARTICIPIAL PHRASE: *Having radioed that my boat was foundering on the shoal,* the Coast Guard came to my rescue.
CORRECTED: *After I had radioed that my boat was foundering on the shoal,* the Coast Guard came to my rescue.

Watch out for dangling modifiers at the end of sentences:

DANGLING: Laura's French accent was perfect, *having spent ten years in Paris.*
CORRECTED: Having spent ten years in Paris, *Laura had* a perfect French accent.

DANGLING: One of the priceless figurines fell out of the case *while dusting the top shelf.*
CORRECTED: One of the priceless figurines fell out of the case *while I was dusting the top shelf.*

223

Exercise 2   All but one of the following sentences contain either a squinting modifier or a dangling modifier. Rewrite the sentences containing dangling modifiers, correcting them in one of the two ways you have learned. Rewrite in two ways each sentence containing a squinting modifier, being careful to show both of the possible meanings. Number your answers with the numbers of the sentences.

1   Browsing in the library, a book on mastodons caught my eye.
2   As a freshman in high school, there was no basketball team in the city that could beat ours.
3   If boiled, peeled, and served with a piquant sauce, the guests will enjoy the lobsters.
4   After playing bridge for two hours, the Scrabble board was brought out.
5   When recommending larger appropriations for the Navy, the expression "Speak softly and carry a big stick" was used by President Theodore Roosevelt.
6   And then, to get Ann's attention, didn't that crazy fool drop the tray!
7   Accustomed to reading articles that were badly written, the manuscript in front of him was an unexpected delight.

8 Mr. Fogl advised Jones at the beginning of the year to take out a patent on his new invention.

9 To acquire the Panama Canal Zone, a payment to the Republic of Panama of $10,000,000 down and $250,000 annually was agreed upon by the United States.

10 My employer promised me after a year I would get a raise.

11 Regional differences in speech offer no serious communication difficulties when traveling in the United States.

12 Anyone who could produce an alibi immediately became a suspect in his eyes.

Interrupted Constructions

Readers have come to expect sentences to follow a certain order: Subject—Verb—Object or Subject—Verb—Complement. If the usual order is interrupted by long modifiers that could better be placed elsewhere, the sentences may sound awkward or be hard to read:

AWKWARD: A tornado, *while we were at a movie with some friends of my father's,* ripped the back porch off our house.

IMPROVED: *While we were at a movie with some friends of my father's,* a tornado ripped the back porch off our house.

AWKWARD: Frank read, *because he wanted to become a great surgeon,* many books on anatomy.

IMPROVED: Frank read many books on anatomy *because he wanted to become a great surgeon.* [Or, for special emphasis on the modifier: Frank, *because he wanted to become a great surgeon,* read many books on anatomy.]

Phrases that form a natural word-unit, also, should not be needlessly interrupted by long modifiers:

AWKWARD: She typed at, *according to her employer,* an unbelievable speed.

IMPROVED: *According to her employer,* she typed at an unbelievable speed.

Exercise 3 In each of the following sentences a long modifier interrupts the natural word order. In one sentence the interruption is justified. Revise each of the awkward sentences by moving the modifier to some other position in the sentence.

1 Janice was considered, in spite of her quick temper and her sharp tongue, one of the most attractive girls in school.

2 He tried to, for the sake of pleasing his father, make an especially good record during the first semester.

3 Vernon knew that, in order to remain on the team, he would have to follow the training rules conscientiously.

4 The presiding officer of the Senate cast, because there was a tie on Senator Robinson's resolution, the deciding vote.
5 The class elected me, in spite of the fact that I did not want the office, to the student senate.
6 Harley thought, after he had considered the problem for a while, of several subjects for his research paper.

Shifted Constructions

An important principle in many sports is that of *following through*. Following through means that a motion, such as the stroke or swing of a golf club, a baseball bat, or a tennis racket, once started, should be continued through to the end of its arc. To shift or change the direction of the motion before it is completed will interfere with the smooth, even movement of the ball. A play that is not followed through is ineffective and awkward.

To follow through is an important principle in writing too. Shifting unnecessarily from one grammatical construction to another lessens the effectiveness of a sentence and makes it unpleasant to read. But using **parallel constructions**, that is, using the same grammatical forms to express details that serve a like purpose in the sentence, helps to hold the sentence together and give it emphasis. Compare these two examples:

225

The playwright was *brilliant, versatile,* and a *wit.*
The playwright was *brilliant, versatile,* and *witty.*

Three details about the playwright, all of them descriptive, are mentioned, but in the first sentence they are not expressed in parallel form. The writer started off with two adjectives and then shifted unnecessarily to a noun. In the second sentence, the three parallel adjectives show immediately the equality of the three details. Even when a sentence is as easy to understand as the first one is, parallel constructions will make it sound smoother.

The plainest indication of a need for parallelism is the presence of either a coördinating conjunction or a pair of correlative conjunctions: *and, but, or, either ... or, neither ... nor, both ... and, whether ... or,* or *not only ... but (also).* In revising the sentences in first drafts of your papers, therefore, check all items joined by one of these, to make sure that, wherever possible, you have expressed them in parallel forms. Watch out for such shifted constructions as these:

NOUN—CLAUSE SHIFT: Albert Schweitzer is a distinguished *musician,* a noted *philosopher,* and *his work as a great humanitarian is acclaimed by all mankind.*

PARALLEL NOUNS: Albert Schweitzer is a distinguished *musician,* a noted *philosopher,* and a great *humanitarian* whose work is acclaimed by all mankind.

INFINITIVE PHRASE—GERUND PHRASE SHIFT: The United States and other governments collaborate in maintaining a patrol *to destroy* icebergs and *for warning* merchant ships of their presence.

PARALLEL INFINITIVE PHRASES: The United States and other governments collaborate in maintaining a patrol *to destroy* icebergs and *to warn* merchant ships of their presence.

PARALLEL GERUND PHRASES: The United States and other governments collaborate in maintaining a patrol *for destroying* icebergs and [*for*] *warning* merchant ships of their presence.

GERUND PHRASE—CLAUSE SHIFT: Dr. Raymond told me that I could cure my cold *by drinking* orange juice and *if I would get plenty of rest.*

PARALLEL GERUND PHRASES: Dr. Raymond told me that I could cure my cold *by drinking* orange juice and [*by*] *getting* plenty of rest.

INFINITIVE PHRASE—CLAUSE SHIFT: Paul did not know whether *to go* on to college or *if he should start working* after finishing high school.

PARALLEL INFINITIVE PHRASES: Paul did not know whether *to go* on to college or *to start* working after finishing high school.

When shifted constructions with a coördinating conjunction cannot easily be made parallel, you will probably find that the ideas themselves are not really parallel. Try to rephrase the sentence so that a parallel construction is not called for:

SHIFTED: Jack told me *to come* over to his house and *that he would help me with my French.*

IMPROVED: Jack told me that if I came over to his house he would help me with my French.

When using correlative conjunctions, be sure they are placed just before the constructions that are parallel:

MISPLACED: The comments he made at this press conference **not only** *aroused* controversy at home **but also** *in Asia.*

PARALLEL: The comments he made at this press conference aroused controversy **not only** *at home* **but also** *in Asia.*

MISPLACED: I **neither** *found* his bongo playing **nor** *his glockenspiel practice* objectionable.

PARALLEL: I found **neither** *his bongo playing* **nor** *his glockenspiel practice* objectionable.

Shifts in compared or contrasted ideas.   Parallel constructions are often needed when you are comparing or contrasting ideas:

SHIFTED: *Using a seam ripper* is a safer way to take out stitches than *if you use an old razor blade.*

PARALLEL: *Using a seam ripper* is a safer way to take out stitches than *using an old razor blade.*

SHIFTED: In his book *The New American Practical Navigator*, Nathaniel Bowditch showed mariners how to navigate *by mathematics and celestial observation* instead of *using dead reckoning and luck*.

PARALLEL: In his book *The New American Practical Navigator*, Nathaniel Bowditch showed mariners how to navigate *by mathematics and celestial observation* instead of *by dead reckoning and luck*.

Other shifted constructions.   Unnecessary shifts in tense, voice, number, and person should also be avoided:

SHIFT IN TENSE: Then Dr. Roop, the bacteriologist at the hospital, *looked* into his microscope and *identifies* the microbe instantly.

CONSISTENT: Then Dr. Roop, the bacteriologist at the hospital, *looked* into his microscope and *identified* the microbe instantly.

SHIFT IN VOICE: At the meat market Bob *tried* to get a prime cut of tenderloin, but only choice cuts *were to be found*.

CONSISTENT: At the meat market Bob *tried* to get a prime cut of tenderloin but *could find* only choice cuts.

SHIFT IN NUMBER: In the folklore of the supernatural, the *poltergeist is* a noisy ghost; *they* are usually blamed for rappings and other unexplained sounds.

CONSISTENT: In the folklore of the supernatural, *poltergeists are* noisy ghosts; *they* are usually blamed for rappings and other unexplained sounds.

SHIFT IN PERSON: A *person* can always ask directions at a filling station if *you* think *you* are on the wrong road.

CONSISTENT: *You* can always ask directions at a filling station if *you* think *you* are on the wrong road. [Or: A *person* can always ask directions at a filling station if *he* thinks *he* is on the wrong road.]

Exercise 4 Rewrite the following sentences, correcting the shifted constructions by changing them to parallel forms and placing any misplaced correlatives immediately before the parallel items.

1   The captain told the sergeant to decode the message and that he should give it to the general.

2   Hal not only had become interested in studying mushrooms and toadstools but also lichens and mosses.

3   Whenever a famous actor came to town, we would ask them to demonstrate make-up techniques for our Little Theater.

4   He thought Mt. Fuji was more beautiful than when he saw the Matterhorn.

5   Training horses and to round up cattle were his main jobs on the ranch last summer.

6   Neal was good-natured but a rather stupid person.

227

7 The book was written in India, translated in Germany, and a company in London published it.

8 Tony angrily ran up to the bully and defies him to carry out the threat.

9 My piano teacher had endless patience, great understanding, and her musical taste was excellent.

10 To build the pyramids, the Egyptians not only had to understand geometry but also the principle of the inclined plane.

11 The old man was hated by his tenants, shunned by his neighbors, but the children at the Leonard School idolized him.

12 He decided that walking the three miles would be better than not to go at all.

13 My father advised me to budget my time, that I should date only on weekends, and I ought to cut down the number of my outside activities.

14 Anyone can learn to aquaplane well if you practice a little.

15 Censuring other people's actions is often much easier than to try to be tolerant and sympathetic.

16 A person should prepare for old age long before the time they plan to retire.

Careless Use of Pronouns

In speech and writing, pronouns are indispensable as words used in place of nouns to refer to people, places, or things without specifying them by name. Usually the word that a pronoun refers to—its **antecedent**—is made clear in its context. For instance, in a sentence like "Tammy bought the gloves because *they* were marked down," the pronoun *they* so clearly refers to its antecedent *gloves* that no reader could possibly misunderstand the intended meaning. But if the writer omits the antecedent, or if he so phrases a sentence that it is not clear which antecedent the pronoun refers to, the reader is likely to be puzzled.

Vague reference. When the antecedent of a pronoun is not definitely stated, the reference is said to be **vague.** You can correct a vague pronoun reference by replacing the pronoun with a noun:

NO ANTECEDENT: James liked to read about farming, although he had never been on *one.*

CLEAR: James liked to read about farming, although he had never been on a *farm.*

NO ANTECEDENT: Pauperism was once considered a serious criminal offense. *They* were often thrown into prison, deprived of the right to vote, and otherwise humiliated for being poor.

CLEAR: Pauperism was once considered a serious criminal offense. *Debtors* (or *Paupers*) were often thrown into prison, deprived of the right to vote, and otherwise humiliated for being poor.

If the antecedent is "hidden" in a subordinate construction—that is, if it is a noun used as a modifier or as a possessive—the reference will also be vague and perhaps confusing:

CONFUSING: As a home economist, Agnes had specialized in fish cookery, although she seldom ate *them* at home.

CLEAR: As a home economist, Agnes had specialized in fish cookery, although she seldom ate *fish* at home.

CONFUSING: Kid Gallagher then sent a fast knockout blow to the young boxer's jaw, who had gamely stayed in the ring for eleven rounds.

CLEAR: Kid Gallagher then sent a fast knockout blow to the jaw of the young boxer, who had gamely stayed in the ring for eleven rounds.

Pronouns such as *which, this,* and *that* are sometimes used to refer to a group of words or a whole idea rather than to a single noun antecedent:

Mrs. Atkins was always sympathetic, *which* made her popular with members of the senior class.

But if there is in the sentence any single noun to which the pronoun might seem to refer, the sentence should be revised to make the intended meaning clear.

CONFUSING: I always turned to Larry for advice, *which* my family disapproved of.

CLEAR: My family disapproved of my always turning to Larry for advice.   [Or: I always turned to Larry for advice—a practice my family disapproved of.]

Indefinite reference.   The use of *it* and *they* without a definite antecedent is common in everyday speech. But in writing, the **indefinite** use of these pronouns should be avoided.

FAULTY: In Allen Drury's *Advise and Consent it* tells about political life in Washington.

BETTER: Allen Drury's *Advise and Consent* tells about political life in Washington.

FAULTY: Since science has become so important in the space age, *they* need mathematicians more than ever.

BETTER: Since science has become so important in the space age, mathematicians are needed more than ever.   [Or: Since science has become so important in the space age, industry and the government need mathematicians more than ever.]

Ambiguous reference.   Sometimes a pronoun is placed so that it might refer to either of two antecedents; in other words, its reference is **ambiguous.** You can correct ambiguous pronoun references (1) by replacing the pronoun with a noun, (2) by moving the pronoun closer to the intended antecedent, or (3) by rephrasing the sentence:

CONFUSING: The association of Sigmund Freud and Carl Gustav Jung ended in 1912, when *he* set forth new and conflicting psychoanalytic theories.

CLEAR: The association of Sigmund Freud and Carl Gustav Jung ended in 1912, when *Jung* set forth new and conflicting psychoanalytic theories.

CONFUSING: Mr. Esco forgot to call Mr. Robbins when *he* was in St. Louis.

CLEAR: When *he* was in St. Louis, Mr. Esco forgot to call Mr. Robbins. [Or: When Mr. Robbins was in St. Louis, Mr. Esco forgot to call *him*.]

CONFUSING: Oliver decided not to compete against Chuck in the relay, because *he* had a weak knee.

CLEAR: Oliver, *who* had a weak knee, decided not to compete against Chuck in the relay.

A sentence that contains two or more pronouns referring to different antecedents may also be ambiguous. Often the only way the ambiguity can be removed is by rewriting the sentence:

CONFUSING: Mr. Egan heartily disliked Mr. Dixon even though *he* always treated *him* fairly.

CLEAR: Although Mr. Dixon always treated him fairly, Mr. Egan heartily disliked him. [Or, if the other meaning is intended: Mr. Egan heartily disliked Mr. Dixon but always treated him fairly.]

Exercise 5 Rewrite the following sentences, correcting the vague, indefinite, and ambiguous pronoun references.

1 I like to dance, but I don't get invited to them very often.
2 The plane crashed into the aircraft carrier's side that was leading the convoy.
3 I know Aunt Kay would rather have lunch at Pierre's than at the motel because it is much swankier and more expensive.
4 The producers decided to leave the song in the musical comedy despite the fact that it was too long.
5 Dad decided to invest his share of the money in Aunt Mabel's play, which Mother told him was stupid.
6 Then Nora asked Mr. Theisen what he thought of nursing as a career for her. He disapproved, saying that they had to work too hard and earned too little.
7 Jenny criticized Mrs. Gregory rather sharply because she had a sarcastic nature.
8 On the sign in the oculist's shop it said, "Eyes examined while you wait"!

9   Hetty and Zelna had dinner together last night, but she didn't tell her about having been to the movie with Ben on Saturday.

10 Although we passed many furniture factories during our tour of Georgia, we didn't stop to look at any for our new house.

11 Voting is such a serious responsibility that I want to know both sides of every issue before I cast my first one.

12 In Ed's letter it tells how his friend Byron, who is a first-rate pistol shot, taught the King of Nepal to shoot from the hip.

Faulty Comparisons

When making comparisons (showing how or to what degree two or more things are alike or unlike), writers sometimes fail to express their intended meaning accurately. Comparisons should be phrased so that the reader can see at first glance what two things are being compared:

FAULTY: The marble in the vestibule is different from the rotunda.   [Marble is being compared with a part of the building.]
CORRECTED: The marble in the vestibule is different from *that* in the rotunda.

FAULTY: His ability to produce new varieties of plants was almost as remarkable as Luther Burbank.   [Ability is being compared with a man.]
CORRECTED: His ability to produce new varieties of plants was almost as remarkable as *Luther Burbank's.*

If comparisons are made between persons or things of the same class, be sure to use such phrases as "than any other," "than anyone else," or "than the other" with adjectives or adverbs in the comparative degree:

FAULTY: Probably O. Henry uses surprise endings in his stories more often *than any* fiction writer.   ["Any fiction writer" includes O. Henry too.]
CORRECTED: Probably O. Henry uses surprise endings in his stories more often *than any other* fiction writer.

FAULTY: My mother was friendlier to the bad-tempered postman *than anyone* in our neighborhood.   ["Anyone in our neighborhood" also includes the mother.]
CORRECTED: My mother was friendlier to the bad-tempered postman *than anyone else* in our neighborhood.

Phrases with "any" and "other" should not be used after adjectives and adverbs in the superlative degree:

FAULTY: Mr. Walker is the most learned *of any other judge* on the state Supreme Court.   [Or: the most learned *of all the other judges.*]

CORRECTED: Mr. Walker is the *most learned judge* on the state Supreme Court.   [Or: the most learned *of the judges;* the most learned *of all the judges.*]

Exercise 6   Rewrite these sentences, correcting the faulty comparisons.

1   The thunder lizard, a seventy-one-foot dinosaur, was larger than any animal that ever lived on land.
2   Is it true that Chicago's crime rate is higher than New York?
3   The new treasurer's fiscal policies are the same as his predecessor.
4   The Congressional Medal of Honor is the highest of all the other military decorations a person can win.
5   A man's brain weighs three tenths as much as an elephant.
6   Madame Perrino has the best-trained voice of all the other sopranos in the opera company.
7   The fables of La Fontaine are just as entertaining as Aesop.
8   I like *The Brothers Karamazov* better than any novel by Dostoevski.
9   The peeling on this lemon is almost as thick as a grapefruit.
10   The vegetables at the farmers' market are fresher than the grocery store.
11   Sisyphus, who even tried to outwit the gods, was one of the craftiest of all the other personages of ancient Greek legend.
12   The calendar developed by the Mayas was more accurate than the early Egyptians.

CORRECTING SENTENCE ERRORS

Throughout your years of reading, you have learned that a sentence begins with a capital letter and ends with a period. But, as this section of the chapter makes clear, it is not the capital letter and the period that make a sentence; it is the words in between. To avoid sentence errors—fragments and run-togethers—you must be careful not to punctuate your sentences either too soon or not soon enough.

Revising Sentence Fragments

Sentence fragments are groups of words that have been inadvertently detached from the sentences to which they belong:

Mr. McLean traveled extensively through the Ozark Mountains. *Collecting folk tales and songs from farmers, storekeepers, and itinerant peddlers.*

The italicized word group, though it has been punctuated as a separate sentence, is not a sentence. If you read it over carefully,

you will notice that (1) the group has no subject and no verb, and (2) taken by itself, it does not make complete sense. It does not tell the reader who is doing the collecting. The word group actually is a participial phrase intended to modify *Mr. McLean,* and should have been written as part of the sentence containing the word it modifies:

> Mr. McLean traveled extensively through the Ozark Mountains, collecting folk tales and songs from farmers, storekeepers, and itinerant peddlers.

Most sentence fragments, like the participial phrase you have just seen, are subordinate constructions of one sort or another. For example:

> A knight in full armor could not really fight well. *Because he was carrying as much as his own weight in metal and padding.*

Though the italicized group of words in this example has a subject and a verb, the conjunction *Because* shows that the group is intended as an adverb clause telling the reason why a knight could not fight well. The clause should be attached to the sentence containing the verb it modifies:

> A knight in full armor could not really fight well, because he was carrying as much as his own weight in metal and padding.

Common kinds of sentence fragments. In proofreading your papers, look for sentence fragments that may have crept in. Any that you find will probably be of one of the following types:

PREPOSITIONAL PHRASE: Randy took the teasing as well as he could. *In spite of the chip on his shoulder.*
CORRECTED: Randy took the teasing as well as he could, in spite of the chip on his shoulder.

PARTICIPIAL PHRASE: In the Arakan Pagoda in Mandalay there is a twelve-foot image of Buddha. *Covered with gold leaf four inches thick.*
CORRECTED: In the Arakan Pagoda in Mandalay there is a twelve-foot image of Buddha, covered with gold leaf four inches thick.

ABSOLUTE PHRASE: The actor strutted across the stage. *His egotism showing with every step.*
CORRECTED: The actor strutted across the stage, his egotism showing with every step.

INFINITIVE PHRASE: In the middle of the rehearsal Heifetz stopped the orchestra. *To replace the broken string on his violin.*
CORRECTED: In the middle of the rehearsal Heifetz stopped the orchestra to replace the broken string on his violin.

GERUND PHRASE: Arthur showed proof that he was meant to be. king of England. *By pulling the magic sword Excalibur from the enchanted stone.*

CORRECTED: Arthur showed proof that he was meant to be king of England by pulling the magic sword Excalibur from the enchanted stone.

APPOSITIVE: His aunt believed in curing a cold by using home remedies. *Such as cambric tea and mustard plasters.*

CORRECTED: His aunt believed in curing a cold by using home remedies, such as cambric tea and mustard plasters.

PART OF COMPOUND OBJECT: I saw that his shoelace had come untied. *Also that he was having a hard time keeping up with us.*

CORRECTED: I saw that his shoelace had come untied and that he was having a hard time keeping up with us.

ADVERBIAL CLAUSE: Whooping cranes may soon become extinct. *Unless our present conservation policies prove to be adequate.*

CORRECTED: Whooping cranes may soon become extinct, unless our present conservation policies prove to be adequate.

ADJECTIVE CLAUSE: Date growing is a leading industry of the Southwest. *Where the soil is too alkaline for ordinary crops.*

CORRECTED: Date growing is a leading industry of the Southwest, where the soil is too alkaline for ordinary crops.

234

PART OF COMPOUND VERB: The carvings were made in the Philippines. *And shipped to San Francisco by air.*

CORRECTED: The carvings were made in the Philippines and shipped to San Francisco by air.

Occasionally you will find a fragment that is cut off from the beginning of a sentence:

FRAGMENT: *If my grandfather had had the training and opportunities that are available today.* He would have become a well-known philologist.

CORRECTED: If my grandfather had had the training and opportunities that are available today, he would have become a well-known philologist.

Most sentence fragments are unintentional. Professional writers, however, will sometimes use a sentence fragment purposely, to create a special effect or to call attention to especially important words:

If it was privilege that caused what we call evil, it was privilege that had to be dealt with, not men. *Not big men, not bad men, not crooks, and not capitalists—not even the capitalist class!*—Lincoln Steffens, *Autobiography.* Copyright 1931 by Harcourt, Brace & World, Inc., New York.

The occasional use of such a fragment in your writing is not objectionable. Many teachers, however, will ask that you indicate by a footnote or a note in the margin of your paper that the fragment has been used intentionally.

Recognizing minor sentences. Most English sentences are of what is sometimes called the "major" type. They have a subject and a verb, and, as you have seen, they make sense by themselves. But there are also sentences of a "minor" type that do not follow the usual patterns. Such sentences, used mainly in conversation, lack subjects or verbs, or both, yet are perfectly good sentences. Here are some common examples:

1) Exclamations and interjections:

Eek! Hm! Good morning. What a silly excuse! The nerve of some people! Good old Murphy!

2) Commands and requests:

Ted! Quiet! Down in front! Encore! A diving suit and a pair of swim fins, please.

3) Specific answers to questions:

["Did Mr. Everett call?"] "Not yet." ["Which car do you like best?"] "That one. The red sedan." ["How did you get here?"] "On the 4:45 from Abilene."

4) Questions:

"Everything okay?" "Any messages for me?" ["He has read all of Dickens's novels."] "Really?" ["I saw Mr. Sampson yesterday."] "Who?"

5) "Equational" sentences:

The less said, the better. Once a thief, always a thief. So far, so good.

6) "Appositional" sentences (in which a predicate complement is set beside the subject without a linking verb):

Mr. Sayres a genius? An intolerable situation, this! Impractical suggestions, all of these.

7) Transitional sentences (by which one part of a speech or composition is linked to another):

So much for the advantages of an air-pollution control program. Now for the obstacles to expect in setting one up.

Notice that even though these minor sentences lack subjects and verbs, they are, in their contexts, *independent units*, capable of standing alone to express the intended meaning. In this important respect, they differ from sentence fragments, as the following examples show:

> Why do so many tourists buy their French francs in Switzerland? *To get a better exchange rate for their dollars.* [Minor sentence.]
>
> Most of the tour group bought their French francs in Switzerland. *To get a better exchange rate for their dollars.* [Sentence fragment.]

In the first example the italicized words are a minor sentence that forms the direct answer to a question posed by the writer. In the second example, however, the same words are a fragment—a detached modifier of the verb *bought.*

Careful writers learn to distinguish between minor sentences and sentence fragments. The minor sentence in an appropriate context is an acceptable form of expression. The fragment, however, is rarely acceptable in any form of writing.

***Exercise* 7** Two of the following numbered items contain two complete sentences. Each of the other fourteen consists of one or more complete sentences and one or more sentence fragments. Decide which items contain fragments. Then, on a sheet of paper, rewrite these items, correcting the fragments. Be prepared to explain what kind of fragment each of the corrected items was.

1 Dr. Finch was an Egyptologist. A scientist who studies the monuments, history, and language of ancient Egypt.
2 Seen in the red glare of the sunset. The mountain reminded her of a Japanese print she had once seen.
3 For eighteen months Geronimo held off five thousand United States troops and five hundred Indian auxiliaries. With a force of only thirty-five men, eight boys, and one hundred women.
4 Mr. Ford wrote to the Oriental Institute in Chicago. To get help in translating the scroll his Arabian friend had sent him.
5 The belief that opals are unlucky seems to have been originated by Sir Walter Scott in his novel *Anne of Geierstein.* In the Middle Ages opals had symbolized good fortune.
6 Gene turned on his heel and stormed out of the room. Without realizing that Ted's remark had been meant as a joke.
7 Dr. Parker deplored the conformity of today's youth. Also the tastelessness with which they dress.
8 Three hundred ninety light years away from the solar system is Antares. The brightest star in the constellation Scorpio.
9 Obsidian, a natural glass, is formed when lava flows onto the surface of the ground. And cools so suddenly that separate minerals do not have time to form.
10 In telling the class about his hobby, Eric referred to himself as a "coin collector." Although secretly he preferred the more elegant term "numismatist."

11 Professor Minter hurried across the campus. His gown flying in the wind and his white hair blowing down over his eyes.

12 Aztec jewelers used gold more often than silver. Because silver rarely occurs pure in nature, it was harder for them to get.

13 While the principal congratulated him, Rudy stood there nervously. Shifting his weight from one foot to the other.

14 The common field daisy is a species of chrysanthemum. Its seeds were brought to the New World in a load of hay. Which was sent to feed the horses of Burgoyne's army.

15 Although we had carefully smoked some glass, we did not see the eclipse. Because the clouds moved in front of the sun. And blocked our view.

16 Frank Jeffries, our star wrestler, could not move without groaning in pain. After his first jujitsu lesson with Jiro Ohara.

Exercise 8 Decide which of the numbered groups of words in the following story are major sentences, minor sentences, and sentence fragments. Then copy the story on a sheet of paper, correcting the sentence fragments and underlining the minor sentences. Number each of the sentences in your copy with the number or numbers of the word groups. [Your first sentence, for example, should be numbered (1-3).]

(1) Although Christopher, a little Greek boy who lived on a farm outside Athens, was only ten years old. (2) He was already helping to support his family. (3) By tending sheep for Mr. Stavros, the owner of considerable acreage thereabouts. (4) Whenever he had time to be alone, however, Christopher loved to wander off by himself. (5) Especially to those parts of Mr. Stavros's farm that were dotted with the remains of the golden civilization of ancient Greece. (6) There he used to roam amid the debris of his country's past. (7) Looking for bits of marble and potsherds. (8) Or other treasures that a boy of ten likes to collect. (9) One day while sifting through some rubble, Christopher came across a small statue of great beauty. (10) "Hey! What a find! (11) A valuable statue, this, I'll bet." (12) His voice attracted the attention of Mr. Stavros. (13) Who was walking close by. (14) Mr. Stavros approached the boy and began speaking to him gruffly. (15) "The statue, please. (16) The quicker the better for you, my boy." (17) Christopher trembled. (18) He was frightened, but he did not want to give up his treasure. (19) "Where did you find it?" Mr. Stavros asked. (20) Christopher hesitated before answering him. (21) "Under the rocks and chips from that fallen column." (22) Mr. Stavros grabbed the statue from Christopher's hand and walked off. (23) Leaving the child disconsolate at the loss of his prize. (24) But Christopher did not remain unhappy long. (25) In the day-to-day need for helping his family to live, he all but forgot his lost statue. (26) And why not? (27) After all, out of sight, out of mind. (28) So much for this part of the story. (29) Now for the sequel. (30) Years

237

later, when Christopher was grown, he saw the statue in a run-down antique shop. (31) And remembered the incident of his childhood. (32) Imagine his surprise! (33) His very own statue! (34) He quickly entered the shop. (35) And bought the statue at a fraction of its real worth. (36) The treasure of his childhood was his at last!

Revising Run-together Sentences

In many of the paragraphs you write there are likely to be two sentences which are so closely related in meaning that they seem to form a single thought unit. Because of this close relationship, student writers often run the two sentences together as one, using only a comma (or sometimes no punctuation at all) between them:

> From the mine at Ballarat came the largest gold nugget ever found, it weighed 2280 ounces.
> First the microphone went dead then the guest speaker tripped over a floodlight on his way out to the rostrum.

A careful writer avoids **run-together sentences** like these. He does not leave it to his readers to figure out for themselves that what *seems* to be a single sentence is really two separate statements; he makes it clear where the first statement ends and the second one begins.

Correcting run-together sentences. The easiest way to correct run-together sentences is to use a period or a semicolon to show a definite break between the two statements:

> From the mine at Ballarat came the largest gold nugget ever found. It weighed 2280 ounces. [Two sentences.]
> First the microphone went dead; then the guest speaker tripped over a floodlight on his way out to the rostrum. [Now a compound sentence.]

Sometimes a run-together sentence can be corrected by inserting a coördinating conjunction (preceded by a comma) that expresses the relationship between the two sentences:

RUN-TOGETHER: We tried all the suggestions made by the farm agent, we still couldn't get the artichokes to grow.

CORRECTED: We tried all the suggestions made by the farm agent, **but** we still couldn't get the artichokes to grow. [Now a compound sentence.]

RUN-TOGETHER: Don't miss Tennessee Williams's new play, you will miss seeing one of the hits of the season.

CORRECTED: Don't miss Tennessee Williams's new play, **or** you will miss seeing one of the hits of the season. [Now a compound sentence.]

Frequently, however, the best way to correct a run-together sentence is not by punctuating it differently or by adding a coördinating conjunction, but by rephrasing it:

RUN-TOGETHER: On his return from China, Marco Polo brought noodles back to Italy, there they became the national food.

REVISED: On his return from China, Marco Polo brought noodles back to Italy, *where they became the national food.* [Adjective clause.]

RUN-TOGETHER: Probably the noisiest intersection in the world is New York's Times Square, it registers an ear-damaging 92 decibels on a sound-level meter.

REVISED: Probably the noisiest intersection in the world is New York's Times Square, *which registers an ear-damaging 92 decibels on a sound-level meter.* [Adjective clause.]

RUN-TOGETHER: The masonry on the new school building had not been completed, the bricklayers were still out on strike.

REVISED: The masonry on the new school building had not been completed, *because the bricklayers were still out on strike.* [Adverb clause.]

RUN-TOGETHER: Bach's music was almost forgotten, then Mendelssohn revived it and gave it back to the world.

REVISED: Bach's music was almost forgotten *until Mendelssohn revived it and gave it back to the world.* [Adverb clause.] **239**

RUN-TOGETHER: Just beyond the visitors' gallery was a spiral staircase, this led down to the floor of the stock exchange.

REVISED: Just beyond the visitors' gallery was a spiral staircase *leading down to the floor of the stock exchange.* [Participial phrase.]

RUN-TOGETHER: Jeremy ruined the first panful of taffy, he pulled the whole batch with dirty hands.

REVISED: Jeremy ruined the first panful of taffy *by pulling the whole batch with dirty hands.* [Gerund phrase.]

RUN-TOGETHER: Hokusai was a prolific creator of Japanese wood-block prints, he produced about thirty thousand pictures.

REVISED: Hokusai, *a prolific creator of Japanese wood-block prints,* produced about thirty thousand pictures. [Appositive.]

Exercise 9 Decide which of the following sentences are run-togethers. Then on a sheet of paper, copy all the run-together sentences, correcting them either by replacing the comma with a semicolon or by using a period and starting a new sentence. Number your answers with the numbers of the sentences.

1 Diane was frightened at the speed of the car, it was going ninety-five miles an hour.

2 In his own time Wyatt Earp was better known as a gambler than as the marshal of Dodge City and Tombstone, in fact, he was never a regularly commissioned U.S. marshal in any city.

3 The earliest medieval castles were built of timber, stone castles did not appear until late in the eleventh century.

4 In 1844 the Liberty Party polled enough votes in New York to throw that state's electoral vote to James K. Polk, consequently, Henry Clay, the Whig candidate, lost the presidency.

5 The United States is governed by representatives rather than by the direct rule of the people and is, therefore, a republic, not a pure democracy.

6 The English horn is not a true horn, it is a woodwind instrument of the oboe family.

7 Philosophers of India like to speculate on the mysteries of life and the universe, Chinese philosophers tend to emphasize moral and ethical solutions to man's earthly problems.

8 Dr. Pangloss was an incurable optimist, he insisted that "all is for the best in this best of all possible worlds."

9 Unlike many Western heroes, Buffalo Bill Cody was not a fraud, nevertheless, his fame was considerably enhanced by his own extravagant storytelling.

10 Although James I of England was very learned, he lacked political tact and was thus known as "the wisest fool in Christendom."

11 The cynic, who thrives on sour grapes, is a great bore, the Pollyanna, who fares on sweet lemons, is equally tiring.

12 One day, on hearing someone run up behind him after a gun battle, Wild Bill Hickok turned around and fired, then he discovered that he had plugged his own deputy.

Exercise **10** Decide which of the following numbered items are run-together sentences. Then on a sheet of paper, correct each run-together sentence by inserting a comma and an appropriate coördinating conjunction (*and, or, for,* or *but*) to make a compound sentence. If a sentence is correct, write "Correct" after its number.

1 At first we didn't worry about the Coopers, then the news of the uprising in Stanleyville began to get more ominous.

2 While working with radioactive materials, you must be heavily shielded, the radiation will cause severe burns or even death.

3 The trial was only three weeks off, still there was no trace of the missing witness.

4 As we were leaving the Grand Canyon, the filling-station attendant advised us to stop first at the Wupatki National Monument, then at Sunset Crater.

5 Go to the art gallery during the Corot exhibit, you will see why the critics wrote such glowing reviews.

6 Mrs. Meadows said she always tried to keep her words soft and sweet, she never knew when she might have to eat them.

7   Stop the engine of the motorboat before attempting to rescue a drowning swimmer, the spinning propeller may injure the victim.

8   The frogman waited until the octopus was directly overhead, then he sent the harpoon flying to its target.

9   Rob always stood up for himself, his twin brother gave up easily under any kind of pressure.

10 After Beethoven had finished conducting his Ninth Symphony, one of the soloists had to turn him around to face the audience, he was too deaf to hear the applause.

11 Even though we had sold most of the farm animals, there were two horses and a henhouse full of chickens to be disposed of.

12 The professional gambler in the Wild West often sought to become a sheriff or marshal, then he could wear a gun, a "useful" piece of equipment in a game for high stakes.

Exercise **11** Correct the following run-together sentences by changing one of the sentences in each to a subordinate clause, a verbal phrase, or an appositive. Be ready to read your sentences aloud.

1   When the flight became rougher, the stewardess brought us Dramamine, it kept us from becoming airsick.

2   Along the top of the aqueduct lay a flume, this carried the water across the valley from one mountain to the other.

3   According to legend, Zeus instigated the Trojan War, he wanted to rid the earth of excess population.

4   The computer even played tic-tac-toe successfully, it beat everyone who played against it.

5   Bat Masterson was a shrewd and crafty confidence man, he once stole forty ponies from some Indians and sold them for $1200.

6   Many of our ancestors refused to eat tomatoes, they believed that tomatoes were poisonous.

7   Just before he died, Beethoven expressed his rage against the world, he shook his fist defiantly at a thunderstorm outside.

8   The world's first long-range artillery was created by the Chinese, they used small rockets to increase the range of their arrows and lances.

9   We couldn't proceed with our farm-improvement plans, we didn't have enough security for a bank loan.

10 At the end of the garden was a trellis, this supported an array of honeysuckle and morning-glories.

11 Dime novelist Ned Buntline was an all-around rascal, he was jailed several times for rioting and once barely escaped being lynched.

12 The noise from the battle was so great that Beethoven secluded himself in the cellar, there he put a pillow over his head and continued writing his "Emperor" Concerto.

241

11 *Writing Effective Sentences*

Every reader of detective fiction is familiar with the usual pattern: In the first pages of a mystery novel, a murder is committed. Then in chapter after chapter the clues pile up. Yet though every page discloses new evidence, no clear picture of the crime emerges. At last, however, just before the book ends, the famous detective steps forward and, after a shrewd interrogation of the suspects, presents a brilliant analysis of the crime and solves the case.

How does he succeed, when everyone else (including the reader, usually) fails? The clues—the evidence found by the police, the motives of the suspects, their alibis—are known by all. But everyone except the detective thinks of these clues as separate, isolated items—instead of as parts of a puzzle that must somehow be fitted together to produce a clear picture. Of all the characters in the book, the detective alone seems to have mastered the trick of solving crime puzzles. He carefully assesses each detail to determine whether it is of major importance or of minor importance in the picture. He just as carefully figures out how the various details are related, so that he can fit them together properly. When he finishes, his picture of the crime is clear-cut and accurate because (1) he has not let unimportant details obscure the important ones and (2) he has shown the relationship that actually exists between the details.

In this brief, oversimplified account of the methods of the fictional detective lies a valuable clue for anyone interested in improving his writing. The effectiveness of the sentences you write will depend in great part on how well you put together the details you have to tell. Like the detective, you must take into account both the comparative importance of the details and the relationship between them. Once you have done so, you will find it fairly easy to construct effective and accurate word pictures of your subjects—as the following section will show.

PRESENTING EFFECTIVE WORD PICTURES

Showing the Comparative Importance of Details

The editor of your school paper, coming across sentences like these in a news report on a local Science Fair, would very likely sharpen his blue pencil:

> Tom Johnson won first prize for his seven-foot robot. It was made from scrap metal and discarded machine parts. Tom is a senior at West High.

It is not hard to figure out what is wrong with these sentences, what makes them sound so childish. The reporter has provided all the necessary details, yes. But he has presented the details as three separate items—instead of fitting them together to produce a clear, pleasing word picture. Moreover, he has expressed each of the details in the same grammatical form (a sentence), as if all were equally important. But only the first detail (Tom's winning the prize) is of major importance. The other two, though necessary in the picture, are of less importance: one merely describes the robot; the other simply identifies Tom. To make these minor details fit neatly into the picture, the writer must cut them down to size. He can easily do this by expressing one as an *appositive* and the other as a *participial phrase*:

> Tom Johnson, *a senior at West High,* won first prize for his seven-foot robot, *made from scrap metal and discarded machine parts.*

Combining the three details into one sentence brings the three related parts of the picture together. And subordinating the minor details makes the important detail stand out clearly, as it should.

In looking over first drafts of your compositions, watch for closely related details that you have put in separate sentences. By expressing the descriptive and identifying details in grammatically subordinate constructions, you can combine the related sentences into a single, adult-sounding sentence that presents an effective word picture in one piece. See how easily it can be done:

FIRST-DRAFT SENTENCES	IMPROVED
Our first job was to scrape off the old wallpaper. It took us three days. It left us with aching backs.	Our first job, *scraping off the old wallpaper, took* us three days and *left* us with aching backs. [Gerund-phrase appositive and compound verb.]

Fireman Jack Claxton was the first to go up the ladder and through the window. He was wearing a filter mask. Suffocating gases were escaping from the window.

Fireman Jack Claxton, *wearing a filter mask,* was the first to go up the ladder and through the window, *from which suffocating gases were escaping.* [Participial phrase and adjective clause.]

Five minutes later Paula staggered off the roller coaster. Her heart was pounding furiously. Her head was still swimming from the wild ride.

Five minutes later Paula staggered off the roller coaster, *her heart pounding furiously and her head still swimming from the wild ride.* [Absolute phrases.]

In the examples you have seen so far, the less important details have been fairly easy to spot. But suppose your first-draft sentences were like these:

> The disastrous Russian campaign marked the beginning of the end for Napoleon. Over 250,000 men were lost in the campaign.

Either of these sentences might be "reduced" to an adjective clause. The choice will depend on which detail you want to have major prominence in the picture. Simply place that detail in the main clause, and subordinate the other:

> *The disastrous Russian campaign,* in which over 250,000 men were lost, *marked the beginning of the end for Napoleon.* [Attention is focused on the effect on Napoleon's career.]
> *In the disastrous Russian campaign,* which marked the beginning of the end for Napoleon, *over 250,000 men were lost.* [Attention focused on awesome number of casualties.]

If, on the other hand, you want the two details to have equal prominence, leave them in separate sentences.

Exercise 1 Combine the details in the following groups of sentences into "one-piece" word pictures in which the minor details do not overshadow the major details. In writing your revisions, be sure to set off any *nonrestrictive* elements (appositives, verbal phrases, absolute phrases, adjective clauses) you use in combining details. In two of the sentences you will need a compound verb.

1 The Annual Jumping Frog Jubilee attracts contestants from all over the world. It is held in Angels Camp, California.
2 Even Senator Welles was shocked at the drastic reform bills proposed by the new legislature. He is a nationally known liberal.
3 The grinning two-year-old stood in the doorway. Her face and arms were smeared with lipstick.

4 Only one thing angers Dr. Thompson. That is to have to wait for tardy patients.

5 Roy Jennings was the ship's navigator. He stepped aboard the schooner last. He was glowering moodily, as usual.

6 Near the river we discovered a three-mile footpath. The Indians had used this path years ago.

7 Noah Webster's blue-backed *Speller* was originally published in 1783. It came into widespread use during the nineteenth century. It was still in use as late as the 1900's.

8 Mrs. Spencer's raucous voice and nasal twang appalled Mr. Benedict. He was a soft-spoken Bostonian with a Harvard accent.

9 The big plane took off from the improvised landing strip. Its wheels cleared the power lines by less than a foot.

10 Frances Perkins was the first woman Cabinet member in the United States. She served as Secretary of Labor under President Franklin D. Roosevelt.

11 A minute later the crooner pushed the two reporters aside. He made a dash toward the stage door. The band of autograph hunters was trailing close behind him.

12 The kiwi is the only bird in the world that uses a sense of smell to locate food. Its sensitive nostrils are in the tip of its beak.

Pointing Up Relationships

Between Details

By skillfully combining details, you can do more than show their comparative importance; you can also point up the relationship that actually exists between them. To see how, let's consider these sentences, which are like those you might find in the first draft of a narrative:

> My cousin Sally would not go near the corral. She had once been frightened by an angry bull.

Both of these sentences have to do with one main idea—Sally's misgivings about the corral. The first sentence tells *what* Sally did that indicated her misgivings: she refused to go near the corral. The second sentence explains *why* she refused to do so. By using a participial phrase to give the reason, you can combine the two parts of the idea (the what and the why) in a way that makes the relationship between them clear at a glance:

> *Having once been frightened by an angry bull,* my cousin Sally would not go near the corral.

Gerund phrases, infinitive phrases, and adjective clauses are also useful in combining sentences. Notice how sharply the relationships between details can be highlighted when these constructions are used to bring together the various parts of a word picture:

247

SEPARATE SENTENCES	COMBINED
The skin diver took short breaths. He spaced them at fairly long intervals. In this way he managed to conserve the air left in his tanks.	**By** *taking short breaths and spacing them at fairly long intervals,* the skin diver managed to conserve the air left in his tanks. [Gerund phrases with *By.*]
Tom won the potato-sack race. Then he ran in the relay. He did not stop to rest in between.	**After** *winning the potato-sack race,* Tom ran in the relay, **without** *stopping to rest in between.* [Gerund phrases with *After* and *without.*]
My brother was in an ugly mood. He had stayed up all night. He was studying for a history test.	My brother, *who had stayed up all night to study for a history test,* was in an ugly mood. [Adjective clause and infinitive phrase.]
Nora Larkin volunteered to supply the latest records for the dance. Her father owns a music store.	Nora Larkin, *whose father owns a music store,* volunteered to supply the latest records for the dance. [Adjective clause.]

You will find that adverb clauses are especially effective in combining related details, for in using an adverb clause, you must begin with a conjunction that tells *specifically* what the relationship is. Notice how clearly the subordinating conjunctions in the combined sentences point up the relationships between the details:

Vincent sneered at his sister's fear of cats. He was very superstitious himself, however. He would go out into the street rather than walk under a ladder.	**Although** *Vincent sneered at his sister's fear of cats,* he was **so** superstitious himself **that** *he would go out into the street rather than walk under a ladder.*
Timmy darted across the driveway. His father was just backing the car out of the garage.	**Just as** (or **when**) *his father was backing the car out of the garage,* Timmy darted across the driveway.
The Foreign Legion did not make its records public. Criminals in the organization were safe during their term of service.	**Because** (or **Since**) *the Foreign Legion did not make its records public,* criminals in the organization were safe during their term of service.

At the end of the day's journey	At the end of the day's journey
the wagons would be drawn up	the wagons would be drawn up
in a circle. The pioneers could	in a circle **so that** *the pioneers*
then defend themselves from	*could defend themselves from*
attack on all sides.	*attack on all sides.*

Exercise 2 Decide how the sentences in each of the following groups are related. Then, by using a participial phrase, a gerund phrase, or an adjective clause, combine them into one sentence in which the relationship between the details is clearly indicated.

1 Carl was disgusted by the silly initiation pranks. He decided to resign from the club.
2 Mike had locked his ignition key inside his car. He was standing on the curb. He was hoping to hitch a ride.
3 The physicians analyzed a few strands of Napoleon's hair. By doing so, they found evidence that arsenic may have been partly responsible for his death.
4 Terry offered to pay for the broken headlight. He realized how angry I was at this point.
5 Debby had to drink water all evening to quench her thirst. She had eaten two helpings of the hot curried chicken.
6 Galileo perfected the newly invented telescope. Then he was able to expand his studies of the stars.
7 William Johnson dealt fairly with the Indians while Superintendent of Indian Affairs. For this he was made a war chief by grateful Mohawks.
8 The man next to me started fidgeting before the end of the first act. His view of the stage was blocked by a pillar.
9 Bert had been told about Mrs. Duff's lack of tact. He was not surprised at her seemingly rude questions.
10 Phil sold me his telescope to pay for the two prom tickets. Then he learned that his girl had the measles.
11 Dad was depressed at the thought of losing his job. He could not eat any of the food on his plate.
12 Domenic's parents would not let him go out for boxing. They disapproved, on principle, of all fighting.
13 Mr. Harper, the assistant principal, made himself almost as popular as the basketball team. He dismissed classes in time for the first game.
14 The judges were still laughing as they presented the Funniest Skit trophy to Boyd. His version of *Hamlet* would have done credit to Jerry Lewis.

Exercise 3 Each of the numbered items consists of two or more details expressed in separate sentences. Figure out which of the following subordinating conjunctions should be used to show the relationship between the details: *since, because, although, though, when, while, after, so that, as soon as, so . . . that.* Then (by making use of one or more adverb clauses) combine the details into one sentence.

Punctuation note: In writing your revised sentences, be sure to set off with commas all introductory adverb clauses and all nonrestrictive adverb clauses you use.

1 Darcy was in a clump of sagebrush more than fifty feet away. He was able to film the fight between the coyote and the rattler. His camera was equipped with a telephoto lens.

2 Natural gas can be used both as a fuel and as a raw material. Louisiana's huge reserves of natural gas have a double attraction for industry.

3 The demand for the first postal cards placed on sale in Great Britain in 1870 was extremely great. Police had to be called to control the crowds at the post office.

4 Bert saw the telltale scratches on the fender of the sedan. He immediately recognized it as the hit-and-run car.

5 Eskimos in the arctic must work hard to survive. But they learn to avoid the kind of exertion that causes sweat. The constant subzero cold makes any moisture on the body dangerous.

6 The unsuspecting cavalrymen were preparing for a frontal attack at the mouth of the canyon. At the same time, hundreds of Apaches on the cliffs above them were quietly drawing their bows.

7 For weeks he studied the ancient ornaments in the museum. He could then make copies to sell to the unsuspecting tourists.

8 The Indians had seemed genuinely civilized and content during their two-year stay in England. Then they were returned to Tierra del Fuego. They reverted almost immediately to their natural savagery.

Exercise 4 Decide how the sentences in each of the following groups are related. Then combine them into one good sentence, using any of the ways you have learned. (Your combined sentences should accurately reflect both the comparative importance of the details and the relationship that actually exists between them.) Be ready to read your revised sentences aloud.

1 *The Moon and Sixpence* was written by Somerset Maugham. It is based on the life of the painter Paul Gauguin. Gauguin gave up his job, his home, and his family. He went to the South Seas to paint.

2 Holgrave pressed the hidden spring. The picture then fell off the wall. This revealed a hole. Inside the hole lay the parchment. It was covered with a century's dust.

3 Orson Welles's broadcast of *The War of the Worlds* on Halloween of 1937 was extremely realistic. Thousands of people ran out into the streets panic-stricken. They thought that Martians had invaded the earth.

4 According to some archaeologists, the Biblical Tower of Babel was one of a number of massive, terraced pyramids. These pyramids are called "ziggurats." They were used as temples in ancient Mesopotamia.

5 Jody wrapped the calf in a blanket. He also gave it plenty of food. And so he managed to keep it alive.

6 Thad was determined to win the debate. So he spent every spare minute in the library. He was searching for statistics to strengthen his argument.

7 Navaho and Zuni jewelry is among the most beautiful in the world. It is generally made of silver and turquoise. These are the materials most readily available to the Indian craftsmen.

8 Melville had been a sailor for many years. So he was able to make his sea novels unusually exciting and realistic. He based them in part on his own experiences of mutiny and capture by cannibals.

9 The weather station had to be self-sufficient in winter. It was surrounded by miles of treacherous ice floes. These floes completely isolated the station.

10 Many people find Henry James's novels dull. But his story "The Turn of the Screw" has been read and enjoyed by millions. It was recently adapted for the movies.

Avoiding Faulty Coördination

When the details in a group of related sentences *are not* of equal importance, they are most effectively combined by subordinating· the minor details, as you have seen. But when the details in a group of related sentences *are* of equal importance, they deserve equal prominence in the word picture. You can easily give them this equal prominence: simply put the related sentences together, joining them with a coördinating conjunction (*and, but, yet, for*...):

RELATED AND EQUALLY IMPORTANT: My coat was two sizes too large for him. Dave's was much too small.
COMBINED: My coat was two sizes too large for him, *and* Dave's was much too small. [Now a compound sentence.]

RELATED AND EQUALLY IMPORTANT: Peter did most of the work. Jim got all the credit.
COMBINED: Peter did most of the work, *but* Jim got all the credit.

Combining two sentences by coördinating them ("giving them equal rank") is perhaps the easiest way to bring related details together. It is also an effective way—if it is used with discrimination.

The chief sources of trouble are the conjunctions *and* and *so.* These words are such handy connectives for joining one sentence to another that beginning writers tend to use them indiscriminately, as "all-purpose" connectives, good for any occasion. Unfortunately, they are not so versatile as this. Their overuse in compound sentences makes writing dull and monotonous; their inappropriate use may obscure the intended meaning.

Too many and's.   Check your first drafts carefully. If you find that nearly all the sentences are compound sentences with *and,* you can be sure that you are not expressing your ideas as well as you might. A closer examination may show, for example, that you have used an *and* to join ideas that are too far apart in meaning to be combined in a compound sentence. Such ideas are better separated:

UNRELATED: People in the Foreign Service serve two years in each country, and my brother hopes to be assigned to Bolivia.
IMPROVED: People in the Foreign Service serve two years in each country. My brother hopes to be assigned to Bolivia.

Or you may have used *and* when the relationship that actually exists between the items is not one that *and* can show. *And* cannot clearly show the real connection between contrasting ideas, for instance. In the following example, the coördinating conjunction *but* (or *yet*) would indicate the relationship more accurately:

MISRELATED: The new burner was supposed to cut our heating bills in half, and they are now higher than ever.
IMPROVED: The new burner was supposed to cut our heating bills in half, *but* (or *yet*) they are now higher than ever.

Sometimes, to make clear the relationship, you will have to rephrase the sentence, changing a main clause to a subordinate clause:

251

UNRELATED	IMPROVED
Uncle Jim decided to move back to the old homestead, and he could live comfortably on his small pension.	Uncle Jim decided to move back to the old homestead, *where he could live comfortably on his small pension.*
A tempered glass tube looks and feels like ordinary glass, and it is extremely strong, and it can be used to pound a nail into a block of wood.	*Although a tempered glass tube looks and feels like ordinary glass,* it is *so* strong *that it can be used to pound a nail into a block of wood.*

A compound sentence in which items of unequal importance are joined by *and* is almost sure to present a lopsided picture. By subordinating the minor details, you can easily improve such sentences:

UNEVEN	IMPROVED
The leading role was played by a tall, handsome woman, and her voice was as deep as Tallulah Bankhead's.	The leading role was played by a tall, handsome woman *with a voice as deep as Tallulah Bankhead's.* [Or: *whose voice was as deep as....*]

The Hope diamond is a pale-blue stone, and it weighs 44.5 carats, and it is commonly believed to bring misfortune to its owners.	The Hope diamond, *a pale-blue stone weighing 44.5 carats,* is commonly believed to bring misfortune to its owners.

Your paragraphs may still contain too many *and*-sentences even after you have revised the poor ones. If so, you may get a little variety by turning a perfectly "good" compound sentence into a simple sentence with a compound verb. (This can be done whenever the subject of each clause refers to the same person or thing.)

COMPOUND SENTENCE: Charlotte saw the truck coming toward the old man, and she screamed at him to get out of its way.

COMPOUND VERB: Charlotte *saw* the truck coming toward the old man and *screamed* at him to get out of its way.

And often, with just a bit of thought, you can rephrase an *and*-sentence so that it effectively says the same thing in a different way. For example:

WITH "AND":   Albert had studied algebra the year before, and he was able to give me a great deal of help.

REPHRASED: Albert, *who had studied algebra the year before,* was able to give me a great deal of help.   [Adjective clause.]

REPHRASED: *Having studied algebra the year before,* Albert was able to give me a great deal of help.   [Participial phrase.]

REPHRASED: *Since Albert had studied algebra the year before,* he was able to give me a great deal of help.   [Adverb clause.]

Too many so's.   The compound sentence with *so*—"Something happened, **so** something else happened"—is a familiar pattern. It is also a good and useful pattern—if used sparingly. But many students tend to become enslaved to it, grinding out one *so*-sentence after another with monotonous regularity. As a result, their writing has a dreary, humdrum quality that makes it tiresome to read:

> My parents strongly believe in bringing up children to be "useful citizens," **so** last summer they suggested that I sign up as a volunteer worker at the hospital. I had been looking forward to three lazy months at the beach, **so** I protested. But I found it impossible to talk them out of the idea, **so** I finally agreed to call Miss Klein, the director of the volunteers, to discuss the matter. I learned that I would be needed only one afternoon a week, **so** I breathed a sigh of relief and promised to be there every Tuesday at noon.
>
> I had had some experience with operating a movie projector, **so** Miss Klein promptly assigned me the job of showing movies to the convalescent patients. Unfortunately, the first film I showed was a very old one, **so** it kept breaking in the most exciting spots. **So** I . . . .

No one needs to rely so heavily on this one pattern, when there are a number of other, more effective, ways to express the ideas. The two paragraphs might be rephrased like this, for example:

> Last summer my parents, *who strongly believe in bringing up children to be "useful citizens,"* suggested that I sign up as a volunteer worker at the hospital. *Since I had been looking forward to three lazy months at the beach,* I protested. But *finding it impossible to talk them out of the idea,* I finally agreed to call Miss Klein, the director of the volunteers, to discuss the matter. *On learning that I would be needed only one afternoon a week,* I breathed a sigh of relief and promised to be there every Tuesday at noon.
>
> *Because I had had some experience with operating a movie projector,* Miss Klein promptly assigned me the job of showing movies to the convalescent patients. Unfortunately, the first film I showed was *such* an old one *that it kept breaking in the most exciting spots.* I . . . .

When looking over your own first drafts, keep these substitute patterns in mind. They will help you get rid of the excess *so's* in your writing.

Exercise 5 Rewrite each of the following sentences, expressing the same details without using the conjunction *and* or *so* to join main clauses.

253

1 "Audrey" was the first hurricane of 1957, and it caused the death of 390 people in the United States alone.
2 The world's population is increasing at a tremendous rate, so scientists must constantly be searching for new sources of food.
3 Washington Irving and Nathaniel Hawthorne served the United States as diplomats in various countries, and they are usually thought of as writers.
4 Henry Ford introduced mass-production methods into his automobile plant, and then he could sell his cars at a very low price, and the average man could afford to buy one.
5 The ragged old derelict found the mission door locked, so he wandered back to the park.
6 Mr. Mallen complained incessantly about his job, and he never found the courage to look for another.
7 Grant had a naïve trust in all his appointees, and many of them were dishonest, so he was blind to the graft and corruption that marred his administration.
8 The fire engines came screaming down the street past the cafeteria, so we all dashed to the windows so we could see where the trucks were going.
9 The capybara is the largest rodent in the world, and it measures four feet in length and weighs up to one hundred thirty pounds, and it looks rather like an oversized guinea pig.

10 The crofters had been unsuccessful in gaining the reforms they needed, so they organized their own political party, and this organization became the first independent Labour Party in the history of Parliament.

AVOIDING WORDINESS

Artists frequently use the term "busy" to refer to sketches or designs that are cluttery—loaded with unnecessary, distracting elements. The same term could be applied to many word pictures, for writers often clutter up their sentences with unnecessary words, words that contribute nothing to the meaning, words that merely distract and weary the reader. The first step in making sure that your sentences will not strike your readers as "busy" is to learn to recognize the various forms that wordiness may take.

Deadwood

Though a certain amount of deadwood crops up in almost everyone's first drafts, it is easy to get rid of in revision. If you have written "Browning's *poems* are hard *poems* for me to understand," simply cross out the second *poems*. If you have carelessly said the same thing in two different ways ("a paralyzed man *who couldn't move*"), or if you have belabored the obvious ("tall *in stature*, dark *in coloring*, and handsome *in appearance*"), simply delete the superfluous words. With the deadwood pruned away, your sentences will be more forceful. Notice the improvement in the following sentences when the unnecessary words (in brackets) are removed:

> At a previous meeting [before this] Mrs. Oaks had been honored as one of the [original] founders of the club.
> Since the crate was so heavy [in weight], Marty knelt down [on his knees in order] to get a firm grip on it.
> Jerome's photograph [showing a view] of Brooklyn Bridge [one morning] at dawn [just when the sun was rising in the east] won first prize in the state contest.

Words like *very, much, highly, certainly, quite, extremely,* and *tremendously* need watching. Used sparingly, these words can intensify meaning, as the writer or speaker intends. But overused, they produce an opposite effect: they become mere deadwood that lessens, rather than intensifies, the force of the modified words:

> Harvey's answer was [very] clumsy and tactless.
> Mrs. Burns is [extremely] strong-minded and [very] talkative.
> For several weeks after the accident, Eve [certainly] felt [tremendously] nervous and tense.

Roundabout Expressions

Another kind of wordiness comes from expressing ideas in an inflated, roundabout way instead of going directly to the point. Notice how much more pleasing the revised sentences are than their indirect, long-winded counterparts:

WORDY	DIRECT
It is rarely the case that John takes a book home except during exam week.	John rarely takes a book home except during exam week.
It is during the time of day when the sun goes down that traffic accidents most frequently occur.	Traffic accidents most frequently occur at dusk.
Owing to the fact that industrial fumes are injurious from the health point of view, many cities pass ordinances for the explicit purpose of regulating the amount of smoke in the air.	Because industrial fumes are injurious to health, many cities pass ordinances to regulate the amount of smoke in the air.

Excessive Predication

A writer who puts almost every little detail into a separate clause—who uses more subject-verb units than he needs to—is sure to sound wordy. This kind of wordiness, known as "excessive predication," can easily be corrected by reducing some of the clauses to phrases or single words:

TOO MANY PREDICATIONS	MORE ECONOMICAL
While Joe was driving along the old road that goes by the mill, he saw a car that had been in a wreck and that the owner had abandoned, and he decided that he would report what he saw to the police.	While driving along the old mill road, Joe saw a wrecked and abandoned car and decided to report it to the police.
The first short story that he wrote was about a battle that was fought with machine guns in the mountains which are in the part of Spain which is not far from the French border.	His first short story was about a machine-gun battle fought in the mountains of Spain, not far from the French border.

Excessive Details

Packing an excessive number of details into a single sentence produces the same effect that wordiness does. By saying too much, and saying it all at once, a writer may obscure his main points and tax his reader's endurance. Notice how hard it is to focus your attention on the main points in the following sentence (from a report on the conquest of Mexico):

> Then one day the Indians, among them slaves, magicians, and *caciques* (local chieftains), arrived in camp bearing two huge ornamented disks, one of silver and one of gold; a head-dress made from the feathers of the quetzal, a bird with long tail feathers; a Spaniard's helmet filled with gold dust worth $3000; and a number of gold ornaments—gifts that the Indians innocently hoped would satisfy the Spaniards' appetite for gold and would induce them to return home.

Though all of these details might well be brought up—and discussed rather fully—in a book-length treatment of the subject, many of them are out of place in a short report. Because they are irrelevant here, they seem trivial, even puzzling, to a reader.

In revising an overloaded sentence of your own, keep your reader in mind: eliminate all details except those that shed light on your main points. Then write up the pertinent information in a readable sentence. Or if one sentence will not conveniently do the job, use two:

> Then one day the Indians arrived in camp bearing rich gifts—including two huge ornamented disks (one of silver and one of gold) and a helmet filled with gold dust. In their innocence the Indians hoped that these gifts would satisfy the Spaniards' appetite for gold and induce them to return home.

Exercise 6   Read the following sentences carefully and decide how to revise them to avoid deadwood, roundabout expressions, and excessive predication. Then rewrite each sentence, expressing the ideas simply and directly.

1   It is always the case that in the fall of every year I get homesick for the state of Connecticut.
2   Her brother, who is a student at law school, loves to bring up controversial subjects that everyone has a different opinion about.
3   The Clayton Company contributed a $2500 donation as their gift to the new hospital.
4   Before she makes a right-hand turn, she always switches on the turn signal that indicates to other drivers that she intends to turn; but then—to the dismay of the drivers behind her—she swerves far over into the lane that is on the left-hand side.

5 The suit of armor that was sold at the auction that was held in the old barn that belongs to the Johnsons supposedly dates back to the time when King Alfred the Great was ruling.

6 Even though we spent all of the whole morning calking the boat for the purpose of making it watertight, we could not get rid of the leak which was near the keel.

7 The first assignment that was given to the new reporter was that he was supposed to go out and interview the men who were out on strike and find out just what it was that they were complaining about.

8 It was just three days before the concert was to take place that I discovered that my flute solo that I was going to play was supposed to go twice as fast as the tempo at which I had been practicing it.

9 Terry designed and built a sailing dinghy that was twelve feet long, and the paint that he used to paint it with was a bright red in color.

10 After we had hiked a total distance of five miles toward our destination, which meant that we had only two more miles to go on our seven-mile hike, we stopped so that we could explore an abandoned farmhouse that no one was living in any more.

GAINING EMPHASIS

If you combine related details effectively and if you avoid wordiness, your sentences are almost sure to be good. But by making use of various devices for achieving *emphasis,* you can often make good sentences even better.

Emphasis Through Word Order

The principle is simple: To gain emphasis for the words or ideas that you want stressed, put them where they will be most noticed. Let's see how this works.

Varying the sentence order. The parts of an English sentence usually fall into a particular order. Subjects usually precede verbs; verbs usually precede objects or complements; and so on. By departing from this usual order, you can draw attention to a part of the sentence that you want to stand out as most important:

USUAL ORDER

We have heard that argument before.

The warfare in the provinces was even more savage.

EMPHATIC

That *argument* we have heard before. [Object first.]

Even more *savage* was the warfare in the provinces. [Complement first.]

| They had never before been faced with such a challenge. | *Never before* had they been faced with such a challenge. [Adverb modifiers first.] |

| I can get along without a power lawn mower. | A power *lawn mower* I can get along without. [Object of preposition first.] |

| Mary is shy and submissive at school; she rules the roost at home. | *At school* Mary is shy and submissive; *at home* she rules the roost. [Adverb phrases first.] |

| The black, silent night seemed for a while to cut him off from the rest of the world. | The night, *black and silent,* seemed for a while to cut him off from the rest of the world. [Adjectives shifted.] |

The end of a sentence, like the beginning, is an emphatic position. Why waste it on relatively minor details that might better be placed somewhere else? By arranging a sentence so that important details fall at the end, you can gain prominence for the details—and strengthen the entire sentence.

WEAK	MORE FORCEFUL
Tommy could think of nothing but home and his pet rat Alice during his first few days at Camp Wabaningo.	During his first few days at Camp Wabaningo, Tommy could think of nothing but home and his pet rat Alice.
There are thirteen stoplights, none of them synchronized, in the two and one-half mile drive between my house and school.	In the two and one-half mile drive between my house and school, there are thirteen stoplights, none of them synchronized.
Mr. Hanish could tell that Central High had lost another game, just by watching Joe slouch into the living room.	Mr. Hanish could tell, just by watching Joe slouch into the living room, that Central High had lost another game.

Using the order of climax. Whenever it is possible, arrange the items of a series in the order of climax, moving from the least important item to the most important. By following this order, you gain emphasis, especially for the item that comes last.

WEAK	MORE FORCEFUL
The windstorm scattered the laundry all over the yard, knocked down the old elm tree, and rattled the windowpanes.	The windstorm rattled the windowpanes, scattered the laundry all over the yard, and knocked down the old elm tree.

After Ron's third speeding offense, the judge revoked his
license for a year, fined him
twenty dollars, and made him
attend two sessions of traffic
school.

After Ron's third speeding offense, the judge made him
attend two sessions of traffic
school, fined him twenty dollars, and revoked his license
for a year.

Emphasis Through Balanced Sentences

Occasionally you may want to direct your reader's attention to
a particularly important thought or to point up a contrast or comparison. A striking way to do this is to use a "balanced" sentence—
one in which the constructions are conspicuously parallel:

USUAL

Though Jim gave a good
speech, it wasn't as good as
Harry's was.

BALANCED FOR EMPHASIS

Jim's speech was good; Harry's
was even better.

He kept on trying to make an
impression on us, but he didn't
succeed.

The more he tried to impress
us, the less we were impressed.

He felt lonelier than he had
ever felt before, even though
he had never been less alone
than he was now.

Never had he been less alone;
never had he been more lonely.

259

Emphasis Through Forceful Verbs

If the subject of a transitive verb names the doer of the action,
the verb is called *active*; if the subject names the receiver of the
action, the verb is called *passive*:

ACTIVE: The dog *bit* the man.
PASSIVE: The man *was bitten* by the dog.

Though both active and passive verbs are useful, they are not
equally effective in all situations. In many contexts, for example,
a sentence like "The cyclone *flattened* every building on the block"
would convey your intended meaning clearly and forcefully. But
suppose the context is one in which you want to emphasize the receiver of the action rather than the doer. You can easily get this
emphasis by using a passive verb:

Every building on the block *was flattened* by the cyclone.

Or suppose that the doer of the action is unknown or is too unimportant or too obvious to need mention in the context. Here

again, the passive verb is preferable, for it permits you to express your meaning clearly and efficiently, without useless words to detract from the force of your sentences:

> *Beowulf* was written during the seventh or eighth century. [No one knows for sure who wrote it.]
> The flag should be lowered at sunset. [The doer is unimportant.]
> All local stores will be closed on Labor Day. [It is obvious that the owners or managers will close them.]

Except for situations like these, however, active verbs are preferable. They ordinarily make a sentence simpler, more direct, and more emphatic than passive verbs do:

AWKWARD PASSIVE VERBS	FORCEFUL ACTIVE VERBS
Moby Dick, War and Peace, and *The Agony and the Ecstasy* were read last year by Tom and me from cover to cover.	Last year Tom and I read *Moby Dick, War and Peace,* and *The Agony and the Ecstasy* from cover to cover.
As soon as it was discovered by the Jacobsons that their house had been broken into by a burglar, the police were called by them.	As soon as the Jacobsons discovered that a burglar had broken into their house, they called the police.

Emphasis Through Repetition

The shortest way of putting across an idea is not always the most effective way. The literal meaning of "Do you swear to tell the truth?" is about the same as "Do you swear to tell the truth, the whole truth, and nothing but the truth?" Yet everyone would agree that the longer statement is more forceful than the short one.

Intentional repetition, used wisely, can be an effective means of gaining emphasis. Repeating prepositions, possessive adjectives, or articles before the various nouns in a series, for example, emphasizes their distinctness:

WITHOUT REPETITION	EFFECTIVE REPETITION
In every restaurant, club, and home, people gathered to hear the President's message.	In every restaurant, in every club, in every home, people gathered to hear the President's message.
Anxiously he scanned the crowd for those he most wanted to see—his mother, children, and wife.	Anxiously he scanned the crowd for those he most wanted to see—his mother, his children, his wife.

Similarly, the intentional repetition of key words or of important ideas expressed in different words can help to suggest emotion or strong feeling:

During that year there was a scarcity of jobs, food, and hope.	It was a year of scarcity: a scarcity of jobs, a scarcity of food, a scarcity of hope.
All I remember of that camping trip is ants—on the ground, on the table, and in my sleeping bag.	All I remember of that camping trip is ants—ants on the ground, ants on the table, ants in my sleeping bag.

Exercise 7 Read the following sentences carefully. Then rephrase them, improving their emphasis. In some sentences the order of the ideas should be changed. In others, a passive verb should be changed to an active verb. Be ready to read your revised sentences aloud.

1 He no longer cared whether he won or lost, by the end of the campaign.
2 London was enjoyed so much by Samuel Johnson that he could hardly be persuaded by Boswell to go on a tour of the Hebrides.
3 The hailstorm completely destroyed our five hundred acres of corn, injured one of the calves, and damaged Mother's herb garden.
4 The woman in front of me began to nod and then fell sound asleep as the speaker droned on in his plodding, repetitive way. **261**
5 Before the games began, the arena was entered by the gladiators, and their greeting was shouted to the emperor: "We who are about to die salute you."
6 We left that apartment two months before the lease expired: it was infested with large black roaches, though it was inexpensive and roomy.
7 Like any dictator, he gained power through intimidation, out-and-out force, and persuasion.
8 The characters line themselves up into two distinct groups—the "good guys" and the "bad guys"—as Act I progresses.
9 No special honors were ever received by Thoreau from the colleges and learned societies of the Boston area—perhaps because his sharp tongue and antisocial behavior were feared by them.
10 On the forty-ninth day they found Helen, her feet so badly frostbitten that she could not walk, her broken arm healed but still in a splint for protection, and her face smudged with dirt and tearstains.

Exercise 8 Find, copy, and clearly label one or more examples of these emphasis-gaining devices: (1) unusual sentence order, (2) the order of climax, (3) balanced construction, and (4) effective repetition. Some particularly good sources are proverbs, famous speeches, and well-written articles like those in *The Atlantic* and *Harper's.*

Increasing

and Using

12   *Your Vocabulary*

The words in your vocabulary often serve as clues to experiences you have had. If, for example, you have gone out for archery, you are almost sure to know words like *quiver, fletch, stele,* and *nock.* If you have spent a summer working in a logging camp, you are probably at home with such terms as *swamper, peavey, undercut,* and *spar tree.* Most, if not all, the baseball terms in your vocabulary you learned on a baseball diamond. And any hours you may have spent in a physics or chemistry laboratory would be reflected in your familiarity with dozens of scientific terms.

The most natural and easiest way to increase your store of words, then, is to add to your store of experiences, to do new things. Every new experience—every new job, hobby, club, sport, trip— will introduce you to new words. If you take up chess, you will become familiar with chess terms as you move *rooks, pawns, knights, bishops* around the board trying to *checkmate* your opponent's *king.* Learning to fence will teach you such terms as *foil, parry, épée, riposte,* and *cutover.* Attending a series of concerts can acquaint you with words like *concerto, sonata, coda, reprise,* and *fugue.* And if, as is likely, you make use of these words in talking and writing about your new activities, they will become a permanent part of your vocabulary.

But having first-hand experience with the thing or action a word stands for is not the only way to learn new words. There are in your vocabulary many words whose meanings you learned through a different, less direct kind of experience—through seeing or hearing them used by others. And you can learn many more words in the same way. For example, suppose that in reading a short story you come upon the word *parsimonious* for the first time, in the following sentence:

> A **parsimonious** man, Philip Mason spent no more than was absolutely necessary on his only daughter's wedding.

The wording of the sentence suggests that Mason's being a "parsimonious man" explains why, unlike so many fathers, he spent as little as possible on the wedding. So you can surmise that *parsimonious* has something to do with wealth or spending. It probably means either "having little wealth; poor" (he couldn't afford to spend more), or "careful with money; frugal" (he was unwilling to spend more). With only this sentence to go on, you can't be sure which. But knowing the exact meaning is not essential here; for even without knowing it, you can still understand the writer's main point and follow the story.

However, you are likely to recall this sentence about Mason the next time the word *parsimonious* comes to your attention. This time, let's say, you hear a panelist in a TV discussion on public housing state:

> Much of the blame for poor housing conditions can be laid at the door of **parsimonious** landlords, who spend not a penny more than the law requires, and often not even that, to keep their property in repair.

After hearing this statement, you can be pretty sure that *parsimonious* has little or nothing to do with a lack of means. After all, if these "parsimonious" landlords couldn't afford to make repairs, the panelist would hardly place so much blame on their shoulders. The reason the landlords spend so little must be that they are "stingy" or "frugal."

Soon after, a remark made by a neighbor would indicate that the meaning you had arrived at was the right one:

> But there's a lot of difference between being economical and being **parsimonious**, as Mrs. MacMasters is. She's the sort of person that would wash paper plates and use them over again.

Since the neighbor uses the word to describe a practice most people would agree was carrying economy to extremes, *parsimonious* surely means "extremely frugal; stingy; miserly."

Each time you met the unfamiliar word *parsimonious,* the **context** (the passage in which it appeared) provided clues to help you figure out its meaning. And each encounter after the first provided a check on the sense you had previously worked out. So by the time you had observed the word in use three times, you had an accurate idea of its meaning. By getting into the habit of watching for context clues and taking advantage of them, you can easily add many new words to your vocabulary.

Context Clues to Watch For

Direct clues. Occasionally, knowing that a word he uses will be unfamiliar to most of his readers, a writer gives an outright explanation of its meaning. Very often he puts this direct clue in the same sentence, immediately after the word, as here:

> At its **apogee**, *the point in its orbit most distant from the earth*, Explorer I was 1800 miles in space.

But sometimes the explanation is given in a preceding or following sentence. For example, notice how the first of these sentences provides a clear-cut clue to the meaning of *nefarious* in the second:

> For years only his victims knew how wicked and unethical Mr. Barlow was in his dealings. When his **nefarious** practices were exposed, most of his acquaintances were shocked.

Examples as clues. Frequently a writer or speaker gives examples that reveal the meaning of an unfamiliar word:

> The *Evening News* reporter was not the only one who noticed the **solecisms** in the mayor's inauguration speech. I winced every time he said "him and I," "they was," and "I can't hardly believe."

The three quoted illustrations make it obvious that here *solecism* means "a violation of accepted grammatical usage." 265

Contrasts as clues. Somewhat less obvious than a direct explanation or examples is the clue provided by a contrast between two parts of a sentence (or between two sentences). For example:

> Although Roy dislikes company and parties, his wife Helen is quite **gregarious**.

In this sentence (as signaled by the word *Although*) Roy's and Helen's attitudes are contrasted. And since Roy's attitude is one of dislike, you could safely assume that Helen's is just the opposite and that *gregarious* means "fond of company; sociable."

Comparisons as clues. Still another kind of clue that can help you determine the meaning of a new word is a comparison like the one in the following sentence:

> Simon Ward's penetrating criticism of the play was as **trenchant** as a surgeon's scalpel.

The comparison of Ward's criticism to a surgeon's scalpel (a small, straight, very sharp knife) suggests that *trenchant* means "sharp; cutting; keen." Sharp, cutting criticism would very likely be "penetrating."

Clues from similar words. Occasionally, the clues to the meaning of an unfamiliar word come partly from the context and partly from the similarity between the new word and a word you already know. For example:

> Prince Rupert was an ambitious man, who, after ruling the empire during the fifteen years of Olga's minority, bitterly resented the **diminution** of his power that followed upon her coronation.

Since the word *diminution* resembles two other words you know —*diminish*, meaning "to become smaller; lessen; reduce," and *diminutive*, meaning "small; little; tiny"—you might guess its meaning to be related, to have something to do with smallness or reduction in size or amount. A careful consideration of the context would supply evidence to support this guess. If Prince Rupert no longer ruled after Olga became queen, his power would certainly be less than it had been. And, being ambitious, he would naturally resent that lessening. By putting two and two together (the similarity and the context), you could infer that *diminution* means "a lessening; a reduction; a decrease."

A familiarity with prefixes, suffixes, and roots often provides the needed clues. *Malevolent,* for example, may be a new word to you. But knowing the meaning of such common words as *maltreat, maladjusted,* and *malediction* (in which the prefix *mal-* or *male-* means "badly; wrong; ill") and *benevolent* (which means "doing or inclined to do good" and has the same root as *malevolent*), you could figure out that *malevolent* means "doing or inclined to do evil." Or suppose the verb *rejuvenate* is new to you. First break it into its parts: re + juven + ate. From words like *reheat* and *reread,* you know that its prefix *re-* probably means "again." You know from verbs like *liquidate* and *domesticate* that the suffix *-ate* often means "make or cause to be." And since *rejuvenate* has the same root as the familiar *juvenile* ("young; youthful"), you can guess that they are related in meaning. Combining the three clues, then, suggests that *rejuvenate* means "to make or cause to be youthful again."

Be sure, however, to check against the context every meaning you arrive at in this manner, or you may go astray. For example, figuring out the meaning of the word *redoubtable* from the meanings of its parts (re doubt able) might lead you to conclude that the word means "to be doubted again." But this meaning would make little sense in the following context:

> George found it hard to believe that this clumsy, rather foolish little man was the **redoubtable** Dean Willis he had heard so much about.

If you checked with a dictionary, you would find that the meaning of *redoubtable* is "formidable; fearsome; causing alarm." The word is derived from the Old French verb *redouter,* meaning "to fear; to dread."

Exercise 1   Using context clues, figure out the meaning of the italicized word in each of the following pairs of sentences. (If you are uncertain about any meaning you work out, check it with a dictionary.) Then, on a sheet of paper, write your definition of each word and a sentence using the word. Be ready to point out in class the clues that helped you determine the meanings of the words.

1 a) Mr. Noonan's furrowed brow and tightened lips *presaged* trouble for someone in the office.
   b) According to Captain Kovotny, the natives believe that a falling star *presages* death and disaster.

2 a) Whenever Professor Roth mentioned how *invaluable* Mr. Rinky's help had been, the old gentleman beamed.
   b) Lunt said that the logs of merchant sailing ships had proved *invaluable*. Only in them could he find some of the information he needed for his chapter on early American shipping.

3 a) Al was friendly and good-natured with everyone but Mrs. Beck. The reason for his *animosity* toward her was a mystery to us.
   b) As the herds of sheep became more numerous and reduced the amount of free range available, the cattlemen's *animosity* toward the sheepmen increased.

4 a) The withdrawal of all troops from the city will *obviate* any fighting among them.
   b) His resignation *obviated* the necessity of firing him.

5 a) Dr. Heiser explained that all too often a new drug seems good in its first trials but proves, on further testing, to have *deleterious* aftereffects.
   b) Some authorities claim that the rising juvenile crime rate proves that TV programs about crime and violence are *deleterious* to children.

6 a) Too late he realized that murder is an *irrevocable* deed.
   b) John's lawyer pointed out that the judge's decision was not *irrevocable*; it could be reversed by a higher court.

7 a) There is no greater *anomaly* in nature than a bird that cannot fly.—Charles Darwin
   b) The men in Hardy's mill worked a nine-hour day, an *anomaly* in an age when most laborers toiled from sunrise to sunset.

8 a) As John Fiske says, probably the most tedious bore on earth is the man who feels it incumbent upon him always to be *facetious,* to turn everything into a joke.
   b) Her *facetious* remarks seemed to pain Uncle George rather than amuse him.

9 a) As time dragged on, and no word came from the courtroom, the crowd behind the police cordon became more and more *restive*.

267

b) Although the boys grew *restive* under the new teacher's strict discipline, the girls seemed unperturbed by it.

10 a) The new president's first move was to put an end to the *intramural* warfare being waged by lesser company executives.

b) The members of the debate team that represents Preston High in interscholastic competition are chosen on the basis of their performances in a series of *intramural* debates.

Exercise 2   Bring to class an example of a word used in a context that reveals its meaning, preferably a word you think will be unfamiliar to most of your classmates. The example may be from a book (textbooks provide many good examples), a newspaper, or a magazine; you may have heard it while listening to a speaker at a meeting, in a movie, on radio, or on TV. Write the example on a sheet of paper, and after it give the source: the writer or speaker; the name of the publication, movie, or program; the date (if a newspaper or magazine or program); and the page number (if a publication). Be sure you quote accurately the passage containing the word.

You may be asked to write your example on the board or to read it to the class, and then discuss with your classmates the context clues that make clear the meaning of the word.

Exercise 3   Think of a word that is likely to be unfamiliar to most of your classmates, but one you think they would find useful in their speech and writing. Use this word (underline it) in three or four sentences whose contexts provide clues to its meaning. Vary the kinds of clues you use.

Several students may be asked to write their sentences on the board and then call on members of the class to point out the context clues that reveal the meaning of the underlined word.

MAKING FULL USE OF YOUR VOCABULARY

Although so far we have been discussing your vocabulary (singular), you really have not one vocabulary but two. By far the larger is your **recognition** vocabulary, which includes all those words you understand when you see or hear them used. The other—your **active** vocabulary—consists of those words that you actually use in speaking or writing.

Transferring Words to Active Vocabulary

You, like many other students, may occasionally complain that your vocabulary is too small, a complaint that may not be strictly accurate. What is more likely true is that your *active* vocabulary is inadequate, that you are trying to trade ideas with a handful of coins, while leaving most of your treasure locked up in your recognition vocabulary. But why leave useful words lying dormant when, with a bit of effort, you can transfer them to your active vocabulary, where they can help you communicate ideas more clearly and vividly?

The dictionary and your vocabulary. In transferring words to your active vocabulary, you will find the dictionary invaluable. If you are to use the words effectively, you must know more about them than just their meaning in context. If, for example, you were not sure of the pronunciation of *incongruous* (is it "in con gru'ous" or "in con'gru ous"?), you would hesitate, and rightly so, to use it in a conversation—even though you thought it exactly the right word to express your intended meaning. And in your writing you could not safely use such words as *effervescent* and *surreptitious,* apt as they might be, unless you knew their correct spelling.

Make it a habit, therefore, to check in a dictionary the pronunciation and the spelling of words that you find yourself wanting to use in a conversation or in your writing. Then the next time you have occasion to use the words, you can do so without the risk of mispronouncing or misspelling them.

The main reason for checking with a dictionary in transferring words to your active vocabulary is to ensure your using the words accurately. It is true that through context clues you can arrive at the meaning of many words. But unless you see some words several times in different contexts, you may not be able to use them correctly in sentences of your own. For example, suppose you had seen the word *abjure* in only one context, in the sentence "The duke was forced to *abjure* his claim to the throne." Using context clues, you could determine that here *abjure* means "give up." With only this much to go on, you might then use the word in such a sentence as this:

> Captain Magruder took up chess when his gout caused him to *abjure* more strenuous games like golf and tennis.

But if you checked in a dictionary, as it is wise to do when using new words for the first time in your own writing, you would not leave *abjure* in this sentence. The dictionary would show you that *abjure* has a more specific meaning than you had realized from seeing it in only one context; it means "give up on oath; renounce solemnly"—certainly not the meaning you intended. It is highly improbable that the captain took a solemn oath to give up golf and tennis.

Errors are especially likely to occur in transferring to your active vocabulary words that are similar in sound or appearance but differ in meaning, words like *eminent—imminent, ingenious—ingenuous, temerity—timidity*. Though you understand the meaning of these words when you read or hear them used by others, you may easily confuse them the first time or two that you use them.

Sometimes your intended meaning will be clear in spite of your use of the wrong word. For example, if in a report you wrote, "At the meeting we were introduced to Dr. Ribera, the director of the Pearson Observatory, and several other *imminent* astronomers," most readers would know immediately that you meant *eminent*, not *imminent*. In this particular context, *imminent* doesn't make sense. [See Index entry **Malapropism**.]

More often, however, the confusion of two words may mislead your audience. For instance, suppose you reach into your recognition vocabulary for a word that means "clever; original and inventive." But instead of *ingenious*, the word you want, the similar-sounding word *ingenuous* ("frank; naïve; artless") comes to mind, and you use it in this sentence of a story:

> Frank's answers to these questions showed how truly *ingenuous* he was.

Since *ingenuous* makes sense in this context, a reader would assume that the meaning expressed was the meaning intended. As a result, he will come away from the story with a mistaken idea of Frank.

Communicating ideas accurately also involves choosing words that best express the precise shade of meaning you intend. Sometimes the right word comes to mind immediately. But just as often, it does not; and you have to spend a little time thinking out exactly what meaning you want to convey and then finding or recalling the word that will best convey it.

Suppose that in a paper describing the main characters in a novel, you write the following sentence:

> Why the author included a character like Mrs. Payne is a puzzle to me; she delays the action time and time again with her sentimental reminiscences.

In reading over your first draft, you realize that the word *sentimental* will not give the reader the impression you want him to get. To arrive at a more exact word, you think over your impression of Mrs. Payne's reminiscences. They are sentimental, you decide; but it is a rather weak, sticky sentimentality. And in telling her recollections, Mrs. Payne so exaggerates her feelings that she seems to be putting on an act. What you need to replace *sentimental* is a word whose meaning is similar but which also implies insincerity and excessive emotion. But you can recall no such word.

At this point, the thing to do is turn to a dictionary to see if it gives a synonym of *sentimental* that conveys the meaning you want. Many dictionaries group synonymous words and show distinctions in their meanings and examples of their uses. A synonym study, or synonymy, is usually entered after the word in the group conveying the most general meaning. Cross references are entered under the other words. In *Webster's New World Dictionary*, this synonym study is at the end of the entry *sentimental:*

SYN.—**sentimental** suggests emotion of a kind that is felt in a nostalgic or tender mood (*sentimental* music) or emotion that is exaggerated, affected, foolish, etc. (a trashy, *sentimental* novel); **romantic** suggests emotion aroused by that which appeals to the imagination as it is influenced by the idealization of life in literature, art, etc. (a *romantic* girl waiting for her Prince Charming); that is **mawkish** which is sentimental in a disgustingly weak, insincere, or exaggerated way (a *mawkish* soap opera); that is **maudlin** which is tearfully or weakly sentimental in a foolish way (an intoxicated, *maudlin* guest); **gushy,** an informal word, implies an effusive display of sentiment or enthusiasm (*gushy* congratulations).

From *Webster's New World Dictionary*, College Edition, copyright © 1962 by The World Publishing Company.

After carefully reading the distinctions in the meanings of the five synonyms in the group, you would probably decide that *mawkish* most precisely conveys the meaning you intend in the sentence about Mrs. Payne. Neither *romantic* nor *gushy* is accurate; and *maudlin*, though closer in meaning, does not suggest insincerity or affectation.

Synonyms can add variety as well as exactness to your work. If you find you are using a certain word rather frequently, try substituting a synonym now and then. But be careful. Although their meanings are similar, synonyms can rarely be used interchangeably. Because of subtle differences in meaning or connotation, one word is generally more accurate or appropriate than another in a certain context. Test the synonym in the context before using it. **271**

Exercise 4   Most of the phonetically spelled words in the following list are probably in your recognition vocabulary. With the help of the pronunciation key at the end of the exercise, identify each word. Next, look up the word in a dictionary, to check its correct spelling and any irregular forms it may have. Then rewrite the sentences that follow the word list, substituting for the italicized phrase in each sentence the listed word (correctly spelled) that carries the same meaning. Be ready to read your sentences aloud in class.

biv′ü ak *or* biv′wak	fach′ü əs
kōz sā leb′rə	gül′ish
dil′ə tan′ti *or* dil′ə tänt′	hol′ə kôst
dis trôt′	in trēg′ *or* in′trēg
i bul′yənt	mem′wär *or* mem′wôr
eks pā′shi āt	rän′də vü

1   After listening to Vedder's *fiendish and loathsome* tales, most of the boys had nightmares.

2 He was convinced that Sexton would never have taken part in any *secret, underhand plot* against the prime minister.
3 The men followed the river to the foot of Stoney Mountain, where they *camped in tents* for the night.
4 I could hear Major Ott in the other room, *talking at great length* on the Revolutionary War, as usual.
5 When Gregor did not keep either of his *appointments to meet at a certain time and place* with Magda, we felt sure he had been captured.
6 Weeping and *in a state of mental conflict and confusion,* the mother of the kidnaped boy pushed the doctor aside and ran out.
7 Even though they contain some inaccuracies, the *autobiographical records of facts and events based on personal observations* of great men have proved exceedingly valuable to historians.
8 According to Asher, few of his students were serious painters; most were *dabblers with a superficial interest in the arts.*
9 The *very enthusiastic* cheers of the crowd brought tears of gratification to the queen's eyes.
10 After the *great destruction of human lives and property by fire* in 1666, laws were passed in London forbidding the erection of wooden buildings.
11 The controversy over the Sacco-Vanzetti case, a *famous case of the 1920's,* has never entirely died out.
12 Gorse's toadying relatives pretended to be amused and instructed by his *stupidly silly but smug* comments.

Key:
hat, āge, cãre, fär; let, ēqual, tėrm; it, īce; hot, ōpen, ôrder; oil, out; cup, pùt, rüle, ūse; ch, child; ng, long; th, thin; ᴛʜ, then; zh, measure; ə represents *a* in about, *e* in taken, *i* in pencil, *o* in lemon, *u* in circus.

Exercise 5 Quite likely you have met all the italicized words in the following sentences in your reading, but you may not have heard all of them used in speech. Look up the meaning and pronunciation of any word you are uncertain about. Then write a sentence using each italicized word in the same meaning in which it is used in the exercise. Be prepared to read the exercise sentences and your own sentences in class, pronouncing the italicized words correctly.

1 In the Martins' ultramodern home, Victorian furniture would look *incongruous.*
2 The heckling of the crowd *disconcerted* the speaker.
3 Had the *machinations* of the two stockholders been successful, they would have gained control of the company.
4 Ward's *succinct* report left no doubt about who had started the riot.

5 While they waited, they carried on a *desultory* conversation.
6 A practical-minded man, Adams had little patience with *quixotic* reformers.
7 The members of the Conway *cabal* sought to depose Washington.
8 The leaders of the alliance were apparently not *en rapport*.
9 A man of Fred's *acumen* should have detected so obvious a fraud.
10 Despite Stern's *blatant* objections, the council voted to accept the committee report.
11 The defense attorney's *casuistry* failed to sway the jury.
12 Unless stopped, Mrs. Gaul would discuss doctors, hospitals, and operations *ad nauseam*.

Exercise 6 In brackets after each sentence are two words that are frequently confused by writers and speakers. Look up the meaning of each word in a dictionary. Then, on a sheet of paper, write the word in each pair that is correct to substitute for the blank in the sentence. After it, write a sentence using the other word.

1 Gold, silver, and bronze medals were awarded to the first-, second-, and third-place winners, _____. [respectfully, respectively]
2 Although he displayed a godlike indifference, Lewis was _____ enough to be hurt by the vicious attacks of his enemies. [human, humane]
3 Myra had no choice but to _____ to Mrs. Garvey's wishes. [accede, cede]
4 Dividing the property between the two nephews seemed the most _____ way to dispose of it. [equable, equitable]
5 Compared to Jan's vague ramblings, Hubert's explanation was a model of _____. [perspicacity, perspicuity]
6 Mirrors are often used in small rooms to create an _____ of space. [allusion, illusion]
7 Dewey's vigorous and successful _____ of racketeers in New York City undoubtedly helped him win the election for District Attorney of New York County. [persecution, prosecution]
8 I thought Sylvia would never stop talking; she seemed _____ by the sound of her own voice. [enhanced, entranced]
9 The Battle of Bannockburn was a _____ victory for the Scots, since it reëstablished their independence from England. [decided, decisive]
10 Barry was scrupulous in his _____ of local customs, even those he thought rather ridiculous. [observance, observation]
11 Finding that the circuit-court decision left several questions concerning the new law unanswered, the company decided to appeal to the Supreme Court for a _____ interpretation. [definite, definitive]

12　Jonah's first novel excited few _____ comments; most reviewers thought it dull and amateurish.　[laudable, laudatory]

Exercise 7　Read the following problems carefully and look up the italicized words in your dictionary, an unabridged dictionary, or a dictionary of synonyms. [See Index entry **Synonym**.] Be ready to tell in class which word you would use in each situation, and why. You may also be asked to suggest situations in which you would use the other words.

1　Would you use the word *bathos* or *pathos* to indicate that you thought the attempt by a newspaper columnist to wring sympathy from readers was so overdone it was absurd?

2　Which word—*fluent, glib,* or *garrulous*—would be best to use in referring to a classmate who speaks so continuously, mostly about trivialities, that it is hard to get a word in edgeways when she is around?

3　To refer to a person who has authoritative knowledge and discrimination in matters of art, would you use the word *aesthete, connoisseur,* or *dilettante*?

4　Is *legend* or *myth* the more accurate word to describe an unverifiable story about a Western hero like Wyatt Earp or Buffalo Bill?

5　Suppose you are writing a paper about things and activities that were extremely popular for a short time, like hula hoops. Which would be the better word to use—*fad* or *vogue*?

6　Would the word *barbaric* or *barbarous* be more appropriate to describe the conduct of an army that killed the entire population of a town after it had surrendered?

7　Suppose that you want to stress that in a TV series on the Revolutionary War the events portrayed actually happened as shown. Should you use the word *authentic* or *genuine*?

8　Both *extort* and *extract* mean "to draw out with force." Which is the more accurate to use in telling how a melodrama villain, by threatening to foreclose the mortgage on her parents' home, obtained the heroine's consent to marry him?

9　To describe a man who is an expert in judging and choosing fine food and drink, would you use *gourmand* or *gourmet*?

10　Is *reticent* or *taciturn* the word to use in writing about a person who avoids conversation, even about so ordinary a topic as the weather or a recent baseball game?

Exercise 8　Since the eight words in the following list are words of the sort you will often come across in your reading, most of them are probably in your recognition vocabulary. All the words would prove valuable additions to your active vocabulary. Learning the etymology of each of the words will sharpen your understanding of its meaning, thereby making it easier for you to transfer the word to your active vocabulary.

Look up each word, noting its spelling, its pronunciation, and its various meanings. Then on a sheet of paper, list the words and, after each, write a brief account of its etymology.

1 jeremiad   5 to shilly-shally
2 shibboleth   6 buncombe
3 iconoclast   7 stentorian
4 chauvinism (*or* chauvinist)   8 shambles

***Exercise* 9** Be ready to describe a situation in which each of the eight words listed in Exercise 8 would be a particularly apt word to use. Then use the word in a sentence that you might use in telling or writing about the situation. [For example: Suppose you have a friend who has been monopolizing every conversation to complain mournfully about the many troubles he has. The word *jeremiad* would be an excellent one to use in referring to his prolonged tales of woe: "I knew from past experience that unless he was stopped, Paul would stretch his complaint into an endless jeremiad."]

Using Words Effectively

Sometimes the words you use may be accurate enough but still are weak and ineffective. To avoid dulling the point of your ideas, choose words carefully, with an eye to the impact they will have on others.

Avoid "big words." One of the ways a playwright or novelist makes a character seem pompous or ridiculous is by having him use **"big words"**—words that are more formal or more difficult than they need to be for the meaning they convey. To show the officious self-importance of a really rather insignificant man, for example, an author might have him say to his neighbor, "I undertook to communicate our condolences to Mrs. Epworth." Now *undertook, communicate,* and *condolences* are not particularly long or unusual words, but they are much too heavy and formal for the situation. A less pompous man would have said, more appropriately, "I told Mrs. Epworth how sorry we all were."

It is not likely that you are guilty of using "big words" in your speech, but they may occasionally creep into your writing if you are not alert. Wanting an idea to seem important or elegant, you might use words like *conflagration* (for *fire*), *incarcerated* (for *jailed*), *indigent* (for *poor*), and *veracious* (for *honest*). But the effect you intend is not likely to come off, for "big words" tend to shift the reader's attention from what you say to how you say it. As a result, your meaning is obscured, or the reader is annoyed because he thinks you are showing off, or both.

For some kinds of writing, of course, rather long or less common words are necessary and should be used without hesitation. In a botany report, for instance, technical words like *ancipital, serration, bifarious, sporophyll* would be not only necessary to make certain ideas clear but also appropriate both to the subject matter and to the reader. And words such as *ubiquitous, ephemeral,* and *debacle* are frequently needed to carry the right tone and meaning in a piece of formal writing.

But in most of the writing you do, which is neither very technical nor very formal, beware of "big words." A good way to test for them is to read aloud what you have written. If you find that you have used words you would not naturally or unselfconsciously use in *speaking* about the same subject, you should consider substituting simpler, more direct words. The more naturally you express an idea, the more understandable and interesting it is likely to be to readers.

Avoid euphemisms. A **euphemism** is a mild, indirect word or phrase used in place of one that is more explicit or harsh or that may have disagreeable connotations. In general, euphemisms are appropriate only when a more direct word would be unkind or unnecessarily distressing to someone. For example, in speaking or writing to someone about a recent death in his family, the use of such words as *loss* instead of *death, passed away* instead of *died,* and *laid to rest* instead of *buried* is considered a thoughtful expression of sympathy. But in most other, less personal situations many people find euphemisms humorous, old-fashioned, affected, or down-right annoying.

Although there will probably always be some words judged inappropriate for general use, "polite society" no longer calls a *leg* a *limb.* Most people today are impatient with what they consider false gentility and evasion of reality. They prefer direct expression and are rather scornful of such substitutions as *memorial park* for *cemetery* or *graveyard, expectorate* for *spit, sanitary engineer* for *garbage collector, company representative* for *salesman, terminate his services* for *fire him.*

Be alert for euphemisms in your speech and writing. Of course, if you have heard a particular word or phrase used often at home or in your community, you may not recognize it immediately as a euphemism. But once you do, avoid it, especially in writing. Because euphemisms frequently distract the reader or listener and create an unfavorable or false impression, they are seldom effective in getting meaning across.

Avoid trite words. A **trite expression** (or *hackneyed phrase* or *cliché* or *bromide*) is a phrase worn out by overuse. It is usually a quotation or figure of speech that was fresh and striking when new, but through repeated use has become flavorless and dull. To put it tritely, since *familiarity breeds contempt,* it *goes without saying* that a *goodly number* of people *take a dim view* of expressions that are somewhat *the worse for wear.*

In speech, which moves rapidly and leaves the listener little time to consider the speaker's expression, an occasional cliché may go unnoticed. In fact, because trite expressions come easily to mind and help a speaker voice his ideas without hesitating or groping for words, almost everyone uses some clichés in conversation.

But avoid trite expressions in your writing. To a reader, particularly a well-read, discriminating reader, trite expressions are signs of inexperience or indifference. He assumes either that you don't recognize a cliché when you see one or that you don't care enough about what you say to make an effort to say it freshly. What is worse, he is likely to conclude that your ideas are as unoriginal as your expression.

In revision be on the lookout for three kinds of trite expressions. The first is the worn-out figure of speech: *Mother Earth, the Grim Reaper, an undercurrent of excitement, have an ace up one's sleeve, slow as molasses, clear as crystal, a blanket of snow,* and so on. Once in a while an outworn figure will suggest the pattern for a new one. But unless you can produce a good *original* figure, it is better to state your meaning directly.

A second kind of trite expression to avoid is the threadbare quotation or proverb, such as *music hath charms, where ignorance is bliss, love's young dream, all work and no play,* and *better late than never.* Because they have been used so often, such expressions have little impact. If you use a quotation, make it a fresh, pertinent one from your own reading.

277

Also avoid such overworked phrases as *a sigh of relief, ripe old age, fast and furious, each and every, slow but sure, few and far between, with bated breath, in this day and age.* If a phrase is so familiar that a reader could probably supply a missing word (if you left a blank instead), you should, as a rule, omit the phrase.

Until you have acquired wide reading experience, you may occasionally use an expression that seems fresh to you but is thought trite by a more experienced reader. However, if you are careful to sift out all the worn-out phrases you recognize in your work, the one or two you are unaware of are not likely to damage the effectiveness of your ideas.

Use specific words. Consider the difference in the exactness of meaning conveyed in the first sentence below and the two that follow it:

> As soon as Jerry finished putting up the sign, a man walked over to look at it.
>
> As soon as Jerry finished tacking the eviction notice on the door, an old news vendor shuffled over to peer at it.
>
> As soon as Jerry finished pasting the menu on the cafeteria window, a traffic policeman strode over to study it.

What makes the difference is the kind of words used in the sentences. Because the **general** words used in the first sentence—

putting, sign, man, walked, look—can refer to any one of a number of persons, things, or actions, the meaning conveyed is rather vague. In fact, the picture the reader comes away with may be somewhat different from the one the writer had in mind.

On the other hand, the more **specific** words used in the second and third sentences—*tacking, pasting, eviction notice, menu, news vendor, traffic policeman, shuffled, strode, peer,* and *study*—convey definite, clear-cut persons, things, and actions. As a result, these sentences give the reader a sharply focused, exact picture, one probably very similar to the writer's.

Which kind of words you should use in a particular situation depends on your purpose. If you are summarizing, outlining an idea, or presenting a broad, overall picture, general words will do. But to make clear a particular idea or draw a close-up picture, specific words are needed.

Use allusions. An especially effective way of getting meaning across is through an **allusion**—a brief reference to a person, place, thing, or event that is familiar to most people. For example, suppose that in a magazine article a writer (who either had incontestable evidence or enjoyed libel suits) alluded to a government employee, a Mr. Roe, as "a Benedict Arnold." Because almost everyone knows who Benedict Arnold was and why he is so well remembered, the writer's intended meaning would be immediately clear to readers. They would know the writer was suggesting that, like General Arnold, Mr. Roe was a traitor, a man willing to betray his country to its enemies, a man who deserved the contempt of his fellow citizens. Notice that, by using this allusion, the writer not only suggests what kind of man Mr. Roe is but also how he feels about Mr. Roe.

History is not the only source of allusions; literature and current events also provide many. For example, by alluding to your older brother Mike as "another Peter Pan" (the boy in Barrie's play who wanted never to grow up), you could show you disapprove of Mike's refusal to accept responsibilities proper to a person of his age. Referring to a friend's car as "a second cousin of Jack Benny's Maxwell" would convey an idea of the age and general appearance of the car perhaps far better, for most people, than a detailed description would. And an allusion to a local baseball play-off as "Centerville's World Series" would make clear that the play-off was a big event in the life of Centerville, that it drew many spectators, and that it was a hard-fought contest. The context in which you make the allusion would reveal whether you meant it to be humorous, derogatory, or simply informative.

As you listen to others or read what others have written, take special notice of how the allusions they use help to make their meaning vivid and memorable. But don't stop there. Use allusions to give clarity and effectiveness to your own speech and writing.

Exercise **10**   Rewrite each of the following sentences, substituting clear, simple, informal words for big words, euphemisms, and trite words. Be prepared to read your revised sentences in class and to explain why you made the changes you did.

1 I first saw the light of day in Pendle, Ohio, on May 20, 1947.
2 Arthur, who had narrowly escaped a watery grave, lay on the beach more dead than alive.
3 It had been three years since the famous thespian last trod the boards.
4 After partaking of a sumptuous repast at a restaurant down the road, the boys wended their way back to the motel.
5 Jake admitted that he had joined the ranks of the unemployed.
6 The sanitary engineer chided his confreres for their indolence.
7 All eyes were focused on Mrs. Reed, who for the second time that day was at a loss for words.
8 It was Mr. Caron's wont to consume a bowl of cereal before retiring.
9 When her husband went to his reward, Mrs. Patz was left without a penny to her name.
10 Mr. Kent procured a table for us near the dance floor by bestowing a generous gratuity on the headwaiter.

Exercise **11**   During the next few days note any euphemisms, big words, or trite expressions you read or hear. Jot down the sentences in which they are used. Bring your examples to class and be ready (1) to read one or two to your classmates and (2) to suggest for each a fresher and more effective way of expressing the same meaning.

Observing ineffective and overworked expressions used by others may serve to make you aware of your use of a similar word or phrase in your own speech or writing. If so, as one of your examples, name the word or expression and suggest an appropriate expression that you might substitute for it.

Exercise **12**   Because the italicized words and phrases in the following sentences are so general in meaning, the sentences give only vague, hazy word-pictures. Choose one of the sentences to use as the opening sentence of a paragraph. Then write the paragraph, using specific words that will give a clear, close-up picture of the topic.

1 My hotel room contained the most *unprepossessing assortment of old furniture* I've ever seen. *[favorable]*
2 The Smiths all had *unusual occupations*.
3 After seeing *a few of the automobiles on exhibit*, we understood why Dad and Tony had been so fascinated by them.
4 Next, *several pieces of exquisite jewelry* were auctioned off.
5 Harry had some very definite, although rather peculiar, *ideas about food*.

6 Even Aunt Susan, a compulsive tidy-upper, was daunted by *the clutter on Chad's workbench.*

7 The last passenger to come aboard was a man so loaded down with *photographic equipment* that he could hardly walk.

8 *A variety of shabby articles* leaned dejectedly against each other in the tiny display window of the pawnshop.

9 The *recreational activities* actually available at Camp Wildwood had little resemblance to those listed in the brochure.

10 Almost every day *small animals* would come around our cabin, looking for *food.*

Exercise 13 Be ready (1) to identify the person or thing (from the Bible, history, literature, or mythology) to which each of the following italicized allusions refers and (2) to explain how each adds to the meaning of the sentence in which it appears. Look up in a dictionary any allusion that is not familiar to you.

1 Often as not, a counselor who dared to argue with the camp director would suddenly find himself in charge of Cabin Ten, Camp Obigchee's *Botany Bay.*

2 Al and Louie were no *Damon and Pythias*; they stuck together because it was profitable.

3 We spent hours at the dump, gleefully sorting out the town's rejections—until our parents found out and declared our *Golconda* off limits.

4 The Pyms always scurried in and out of Dodge as though they were afraid of being caught in this *Gomorrah* on the day it got its just deserts.

5 To reduce the rat population in the barn, Dad brought home a huge gray tomcat named *Jack Ketch.* But it soon became apparent that Jack had no intention of living up to his name.

6 Pete marched up to the front gate bravely enough. But when he saw Ellie's brawny brothers and his rival practicing judo in the side yard, her *Lochinvar* turned pale and fled.

7 It would have amazed Harlan Clive to learn that most of Clivesdale considered him an officious, overeducated snob. He saw himself as another *Lorenzo de' Medici.*

8 To all who invited him to join a society of descendants of Mayflower voyagers, Mr. Apsley gave one answer: he did not practice *Shinto.*

9 The tattered almanacs and one-volume encyclopedias were Mr. Ruck's *Sibylline Books,* and he handled them with the proper reverence.

10 Having heard the students call Dean Prior's wife *Xanthippe,* I understood why he worried about being late for dinner.

Exercise 14 During the next week or so, you are to watch in your reading and conversation for allusions to contemporary people and things, such as a current sports favorite, a new fad, a recent political campaign. Note two allusions that you think especially effective. On a sheet of paper, (1) write the sentence in which each allusion was used, (2) give its source, and (3) identify the person or thing referred to.

On a day assigned, members of the class will be asked to read their examples. The class will then discuss the effectiveness of each allusion in conveying meaning clearly, concisely, and interestingly.

USING FIGURATIVE LANGUAGE

Although you may seldom be conscious of it, you use figurative language often in your conversation and writing. At school, for example, you sympathize with a friend who is having "tough sledding" in math. You "burn" because another friend is unjustly criticized. In a letter you tell a cousin about Uncle Ed, in your opinion the "mainspring" of the local Junior Chamber of Commerce. And while studying for a test, you might advise a pesty young brother to "blast off."

In other words, you do not need to be urged to make use of figurative language; you already use a great many figures of speech, naturally and easily. What you do need is to become more adept at using *new* figures—figures of your own making.

Using a fresh, apt figure of speech is an excellent way to make writing more clear, more exact, more vivid. Notice, for instance, how much the italicized figures of speech add to these passages from a report of Scott Carpenter's on his orbital flight:

281

> I had looked out the window once briefly when the escape tower was jettisoned, and I caught a glimpse of it right on the horizon, *streaking away like a scalded cat.*
> Flying through space, I felt a curious compression of time. ...I seemed always to be in a tremendous hurry as event upon event *popped up like ducks in a shooting gallery.*[1]

Commander Carpenter could have told only that he saw the escape tower falling away. But without the figure, the first sentence would not have been half so meaningful. Most readers would have little idea of how an escape tower falls. By adding six words likening the movement of the falling tower to the streaking getaway of a scalded cat, the commander made his description not only more meaningful but more vivid.

And notice how much force and meaning the commander's figure of speech adds to the second passage. A reader, recalling the rapid, steady, seemingly endless march of targets across a shooting range, would know immediately that, during the flight, event followed

---

[1]"I Got Let In on the Great Secret," *Life,* June 8, 1962.

event so swiftly that almost before one had ended the next had begun. And since at one time or another probably everyone has had the experience of too many things happening too fast, the reader could well understand—even share—the astronaut's feeling of being in a continual rush.

Simile and Metaphor

The two most common and probably most useful figures of speech are simile and metaphor. Both make comparisons that point out a striking likeness between two otherwise dissimilar things.

In a **simile** the likeness is explicitly stated. The figure is introduced by the word *like* or *as*:

> The yellow cabs *dozed* in formation *like enormous wasps....* —Alistair Cooke, *One Man's America.*
> ... weather *as fickle as the vows of diplomats.*—Gene Fowler, *Timber Line.*

In a **metaphor** the resemblance is implied rather than directly stated. The comparison is not introduced by *like* or *as*. For example, consider this metaphor:

> Over on the island, *a worm of yellow convicts* came from the shadow of a gray ominous building and *crawled* slowly along the river's bank.—Stephen Crane, *Maggie.*

In this sentence the writer does not say in so many words "The line of convicts looked like a worm" or even "The line of convicts reminded me of a worm." But by referring to it as "a worm of yellow convicts," he clearly implies a resemblance between the two: the convict line weaving in and out along the river's bank resembled a worm crawling along the ground.

In the following metaphor, the comparison is expressed in a slightly different way. The writer states that the sun "was" a branding iron. But it is clear he means only to suggest that the two were alike in one particular respect:

> The sun was a branding iron on the back of my neck....—Conrad Richter, *The Sea of Grass.*

Using Figures Effectively

Use appropriate figures. To do an effective job, a figure of speech should, first of all, be appropriate to the subject matter and to the style of writing. A formal, literary figure would certainly be inappropriate in an informal narrative. And if you use a slangy, conversational figure in a serious piece of writing, a reader will very likely take more notice of the figure itself than of the meaning it is intended to convey. For instance, look at the italicized figures in these passages:

> The Curies received little encouragement and even less help. Their facilities were inadequate, their apparatus primitive. Yet, *as a bulldog clings to its favorite bone,* Marie Curie held fast to her belief that they could and would isolate radium.

> Bryce possessed great ability, charm, and, even more important, the single-minded drive and determination so necessary for success in politics. A hard-working opportunist, he was *a big wheel* in the city machine by the time he was thirty.

To compare the holding on to a belief in an important scientific theory to a bulldog's holding on to a bone would certainly set many readers' teeth on edge. The passage about the Curies would be improved by omitting the simile.

The metaphor in the second passage is also inappropriate. Although the trite and slangy expression "big wheel" might be used in an informal, conversational piece, a phrase like "an important member of the city machine" or "a powerful influence in city politics" would better fit the serious, thoughtful tone of this passage.

Avoid mixed figures. When you carry a figure through two or more phrases, make sure it remains consistent. Otherwise, you might produce figures as incongruous as these:

> Armed with the sword of righteousness, he blasted away at the enemies of reform.

> Unless we stamp out the rising tide of crime, it will eventually throttle our society.

An alert reader would be quick to point out that it is difficult to do much blasting with a sword. He would probably also suggest that stamping out a tide would be a remarkable feat, especially a tide so unusual as to have hands to throttle with.

It is not inconsistent to compare one object to two different ones in separate figures. In order to bring out two different aspects of someone's home, for example, you might compare the home to a zoo in one sentence and to a ship two sentences later. The thing to avoid is making both comparisons at once, so that the home turns into a floating zoo.

Use natural figures. Finally, to be effective, a figure need not be fancy or "bookish." In fact, unless a fresh, natural-sounding figure comes to mind, it is better to stick to clear, precise, matter-of-fact language. A figure that sounds manufactured or is so involved the reader must stop reading to puzzle it out will make a poor impression and may very well obscure meaning.

The most effective figures will come from taking advantage of similarities that occur to you as you mull over a subject, trying to see it clearly yourself. The figures in the following passages, for example, sound as though they came to mind quite naturally as the writers considered their subjects:

> Somehow the war business kept creeping in. It was like a cloud shutting out the sun a little at a time until the light was gone.—Tommy Wadleton, "They Also Serve," *American Magazine*, December 1941.
>
> To ambitious journalists, the assignment was a stale loaf of beginner's bread....—Gene Fowler, *Timber Line*.
>
> The girls arrived and settled like flocks of garrulous starlings, perpetual chatter and perpetual motion.—May Sarton, *The Small Room*.

The most successful figures, like the ones shown here, have a personal quality: they sound as if the writer had actually thought them—and not made them up to impress.

***Exercise* 15** Be ready to (1) point out the similes and metaphors in the following numbered passages, (2) tell what two things are being compared, and (3) explain how you think each figure adds to the sense—by making it clearer, more vivid, more meaningful, more forceful, more exact.

1 An hour after midnight a flotilla of British destroyers came out of the dark. They circled the *Bismarck* like a pack of dogs around a wounded bear, darting in now and then to discharge torpedoes.—Edwin Muller, "The Last Days of the *Bismarck.*"

2 The flowers burned on their stalks like yellow tongues of flame. —Dorothy Canfield, "Flint and Fire," *A Harvest of Stories*.

3 As you look away from the sun, the sea is dark cobalt; looking into it, it is crinkled metal foil.—Wallace Stegner, "Corsica Out of Season," *Harper's,* October 1961.

4 A crashing chord caused the majority of the class to stand still. The glare of Miss Hobbs' eye, which swiveled over the top of the piano like a searchlight, stilled the rest within a minute.— Dora Jessie Saint, *Fresh from the Country.*

5 A whole tree of lightning stood in the sky.—Eudora Welty, "A Piece of News," *Selected Stories*.

6 Bernard had a mind that shot to and fro like a water bug.... —Robert Henderson, "A House on a Quiet Street," *The New Yorker,* April 15, 1961.

7 She felt herself curl up like a little autumn leaf and, with a dry rattle, blow about the rooms before the chill admonitory breath of Grandmother Purdon and Aunt Maria.—Dorothy Canfield, "Scylla and Charybdis," *Raw Material.*

8 [In August 1914] Europe was a heap of swords piled as delicately as jackstraws; one could not be pulled out without moving the others.—Barbara W. Tuchman, *The Guns of August.*

9 ... the Transcontinental Limited is stroking eighty miles an hour across the continent and the small dark towns whip by like bullets.... —Thomas Wolfe, *Of Time and the River*.

10 Records fell like ripe apples on a windy day.—E. B. White, *The Second Tree from the Corner*.

11 Memory is the diary that we all carry about with us.—Oscar Wilde, *The Importance of Being Earnest*.

12 The children fixed their eyes unwinkingly upon Anna. Anna gazed back warily, feeling as helpless as a jellyfish exposed to the proddings of innumerable sharp sticks.—Dora Jessie Saint, *Fresh from the Country*.

Exercise **16** During the next few days, watch in your reading for especially effective similes and metaphors. Bring three to class for discussion. Be ready to explain what is being compared in each figure and to tell why you think the figures are effective. To explain this last point fully, you may need to sketch in the background—or context—in which the figure appeared.

Exercise **17** In this chapter we have discussed only simile and metaphor, but there are a number of other kinds of figures of speech. Look up the Index articles on these five: **Hyperbole, Metonymy, Personification, Synecdoche**, and **Understatement**. Be ready to explain and give one example of each kind of figure. The examples may be from your reading or they may be ones you write yourself. **285**

Exercise **18** Write a sentence or two describing five of the following items, using at least one figure of speech in each description. Underline each figure. Be ready to read your descriptions to your classmates, who are to point out the figures, tell what kind they are, and comment on their effectiveness. You may, if you wish, substitute two items of your own.

1 A very old tree that has been struck by lightning
2 A littered farmyard
3 A city street late at night
4 A sudden breeze on a sticky summer day
5 Your street early on a foggy morning
6 An elderly man taking a walk
7 A float in a parade
8 The view from the top of a ski run
9 A group of people touring a museum, historic site, or _____
10 A puppy or lamb or _____ investigating its surroundings
11 A picnic table after the lunch has been eaten
12 A jet plane taking off (or landing)
13 A policeman directing traffic on a busy corner
14 A classroom before the beginning bell
15 A joke that didn't go over

13 *Special Writing Problems*

Throughout this year your thoughts will naturally turn to what you will be doing after high-school graduation. Some of you will end your formal schooling then and start full-time jobs. Others will plan to work during the day but take extension courses at night or correspondence courses. Many of you will have to decide which college or university you want to attend. You may also be considering the possibility of summer work, to earn part of your college expenses.

Whatever your plans for next year may be, they will probably involve some writing. Many of you will write business letters, especially those in which you apply for jobs, ask permission to use someone's name as a reference, or request catalogues and college-entrance forms. Most of you will fill out application forms, some of them simple but others more complex. This chapter will give you practice in such writing.

WRITING LETTERS OF APPLICATION

Even before you have a chance to meet a prospective employer, you can call his attention to your qualifications for a certain job by writing him a letter of application. Since your purpose in writing is to persuade him to consider you for the job, you should give information about yourself that will be helpful to him in arriving at a decision. In presenting this information, you will find it a good idea to follow this plan:

1) A sentence or two telling what job you are applying for and how you learned of the opening (Or, if you are looking for a

particular kind of job but are not sure whether there is an opening, explain that you are writing to inquire, and make clear what sort of job you are interested in.)

2) One or more paragraphs giving details about your qualifications —age, education, experience, and any special abilities that might prove useful in the work

3) A paragraph giving the names, positions, and addresses of several people (usually three) to whom the employer can refer for statements about your qualifications

4) A sentence or two asking for an interview at the employer's convenience and stating where and when you can be reached

Keep in mind that from your letter an employer can learn much about you in addition to the information you actually give. From the appearance of the letter and from your spelling and punctuation, he can get a fair idea of your neatness and accuracy. From the tone of your letter and from its organization and sentence structure, he can judge your ability to express yourself courteously and intelligently. Since the letter represents you—it is your sales letter, offering your services—make a special effort to let it represent you at your best. (For a review of the parts of a business letter, turn to the Index article *Business letters.*)

Here is a sample letter of application:

```
                               248 Walnut Street
                               Knoxton, Texas  79105
                               October 4, 19--


Mr. W. R. Haskins
Haskins and Baker, Inc.
489 West Appleton Street
Knoxton, Texas  79109

Dear Mr. Haskins:

     Miss Martha Elston, the placement counselor
at Knoxton West High School, has told me that you
have an opening in your office for a stenographer.
I should like to be considered an applicant for
this position.

     I am eighteen years old and am a graduate of
West High School, where I recently completed the
four-year commercial course.  My best grades (A's)
were in shorthand, typing, and office practice.
On standardized tests at school I took dictation
at one hundred words a minute and typed sixty
words a minute.

     During the past two Christmas vacations I
have been a salesgirl in the notions department of
```

the Webb Department Store, where I learned the importance of courtesy and attention to detail in business. Typing copy for the high-school annual during my senior year helped me gain both speed and accuracy in typing. This past summer I worked for three months as a vacation-replacement secretary in the sales department of Burns and Company.

The following people have given me permission to use their names as references:

Miss Annette Purcell, Head of the Commercial Department, West High School, 384 Oak Street, Knoxton, Texas 79105

Mr. John H. Webb, Webb Department Store, 1586 Ogden Avenue, Knoxton, Texas 79109

Mr. Arnold Baker, Sales Manager, Burns and Company, 638 West Owens Street, Knoxton, Texas 79111

May I have an interview, at a time convenient for you? My home telephone number is 582-8140. If I should be out when you call, someone will take a message for me.

Sincerely yours,

Eleanore P. Marston

The Personal Record Sheet

Many placement-bureau directors stress the value of preparing a personal record sheet, which presents in outline form many details about an applicant's training, education, and experience. Such a sheet is helpful to you when you apply for a job, because in it you can group many details that are difficult to incorporate in a letter of application and yet are significant enough to include. The sheet is also helpful to the employer, because it enables him to find at a glance the information he wants. The details included are usually grouped under headings like *Personal Data, Education, Experience,* and *References.*

If you plan to send a personal record sheet with your application, you will probably want to cut down on the details you include in the letter. For example, if you have listed two or three special skills on the record sheet, there would be no need to mention them in your letter unless they had an important bearing on the particular job you were applying for. Nor would you have to include a paragraph giving references, since they will be listed on the record sheet. After presenting the most pertinent of your qualifications, simply call attention to the data on the record sheet by including some such statement as this:

> The enclosed personal record sheet gives additional details about my education and experience, as well as the names and addresses of several people who have given me permission to use their names as references.

The personal record sheet shown here can serve you as a guide:

```
                    PERSONAL RECORD SHEET
                            of
                      John P. Carlson
                   819 West Grand Avenue
                   Lawson, Idaho  83702
                   Telephone:  361-8970

PERSONAL DATA

  Age:  18       Date of birth:  July 2, 1945
  Place of birth:  Varda, Ohio
  Height:  5'10"     Weight:  158 lbs.
  Health:  Excellent
  Social security number:  336-15-5895

EDUCATION

  Lincoln High School, Varda, Ohio:  Sept. 1959--June 1960
  Central High School, Lawson, Idaho:  Sept. 1960--June 1963
    Date of graduation:  June 4, 1963
    Course:  Academic, with electives in photography and
                mechanical drawing
    Average grade:  B (in upper third of class)
    School activities:  Trombone player in band
                        Treasurer, Spanish Club, 1962-1963
                        Stage carpenter and painter for
                          senior play

  Special skills:  Can develop and enlarge films
                   Can drive a car (have state license)

EXPERIENCE

  Office boy at Ames and Company, Lawson, Idaho:  summers of
    1961 and 1962

REFERENCES

  Mr. Andrew Frazer, Head of the Science Department, Lincoln
  High School, Varda, Ohio  45890

  Mrs. Ruth Petry, Personnel Manager, Ames and Company, 632
  North Avenue, Lawson, Idaho  83705  Telephone: 369-5687,
  extension 145

  The Reverend Thomas Milroy, 3524 Colfax Avenue, Lawson,
  Idaho  83702  Telephone:  361-6491
```

Asking Permission of References

The people you choose to serve as references should be people who can give reliable information about your ability, work habits, and character—all matters of importance to the prospective employer. Among those best qualified to give such information are former employers, clergymen who know you and your family well, scout leaders, camp directors, and teachers (especially those from whom you have taken courses that are related to the job). If your only former employer is a relative and you suggest his name as a reference, be sure to identify him as a relative.

Before giving anyone's name as a reference, you should, of course, get his permission, either by asking him directly or, if he lives in another town, by writing him a letter. Remember that if the person you want as a reference has not seen you for several years and his work brings him into contact with many new people each year, he may not easily remember you and will therefore appreciate your giving him clues to help in identifying you. For example:

819 West Grand Avenue
Lawson, Idaho 83702
June 19, 19--

Mr. Andrew Frazer
Head of the Science Department
Lincoln High School
Varda, Ohio 45890

Dear Mr. Frazer:

May I use your name as a reference when I apply for a job as a photographer's assistant at several advertising firms in Lawson?

Because you work with so many new students each year, both as head of the Science Department and as faculty adviser of several clubs, you may not be able to remember offhand who I am. Four years ago, when I was a freshman at Lincoln High, I was a member of the Camera Club. I am still grateful to you for all the help you gave me then, when I was learning to develop and enlarge films. In fact, my interest in photography as a career is in great part due to your encouragement.

I am enclosing a self-addressed, stamped envelope for your reply.

Sincerely yours,

John Carlson

Exercise 1 Write a letter applying for a part-time, summer, or full-time job for which you feel you have the necessary qualifications. For suggestions about the kinds of jobs available to you, you might read the advertisements in the Help-Wanted sections of several newspapers. If you decide to answer one of these advertisements, clip it from the paper and attach it to your letter.

After the letters have been read and discussed in class, a committee of three may be appointed to choose for a bulletin-board display the most effective letters, each applying for a different kind of work. If the letters are kept on file in the classroom, students interested in applying for similar work may use them as models.

Exercise 2 Prepare your own personal record sheet, using the one shown on page 290 as a model. After you have made any revisions that may be necessary, prepare several copies—typewritten, if possible—for future use.

Exercise 3 Write a letter to a former teacher (or a former employer, scout leader, neighbor, clergyman, etc.), asking permission to use his name as a reference in applying for the job you chose for Exercise 1.

SENDING FOR COLLEGE CATALOGUES

AND APPLICATION FORMS

Those of you who are going on to school have no doubt already examined the college catalogues available to you, generally in the high-school library or in the office of the guidance counselor, in order to make a preliminary selection of schools. But after you have limited your choice of schools (preferably to not more than three), you will probably want to send for catalogues of your own, to study more carefully at home. Address your letters either to the Director of Admissions or to the Registrar of each college. In writing to a large university, you will need to specify in the letter which catalogue you want—that for the College of Liberal Arts, for example, or the one for the School of Nursing or the College of Engineering.

After you have received a catalogue and have decided that you are seriously interested in attending the college, write a letter asking for an application form. (The catalogue will specify to whom you should address the letter.) State in your letter when you expect to graduate from high school, when you intend to enter the freshman class, and—if you know this already—what you plan to major in. This is also the time to request information and application forms for a college scholarship, a part-time job, or a student loan, if you are intending to ask for one.

Here is an example of such a letter:

819 Ocean Avenue
Carda, Alaska 99728
October 15, 19--

Director of Admissions
Arcton College
Arcton, California 95113

Dear Sir:

Please send me an application form for
admission to Arcton College. After graduating
from Carda High School next June, I would like to
enter the freshman class at Arcton in September
and to register for a liberal-arts course.
I intend to major in history.

I would also appreciate any information you
can send me about financial aid available to
freshmen. If application forms are required for
scholarships and student loans, will you please
send me these.

Sincerely yours,

William Broday   **293**

Do not send the original letter to one college and carbon copies
to others, with only the inside address and the name of the college
changed. In the first place, sending such a carbon copy is discourteous. In the second place, the Director of Admissions who receives
a carbon copy may assume that you are not seriously interested in
the college and so may not give your letter the serious consideration
it would otherwise get.

Exercise **4** (For those who are going on to school.) Write a letter to a
college or university of your choice, asking for an application form
for admission. Some of you may want to ask for information about
scholarships, student loans available to freshmen, and/or part-time
jobs.

FILLING OUT APPLICATION FORMS

There is something about an application form that tempts most
people to start writing immediately—with careless disregard for an
age-old, but sound, bit of advice: Read the directions first. The
result? Almost inevitably, errors.

When you are faced with an application form from a college, a business firm, or an employment agency, resist this temptation to start writing immediately. Before you fill in any of the blanks, read through the whole form carefully, to note what is expected of you. For instance, are you to print or write your name, and in what order—the last name first or the given one? Are you to list all your extracurricular activities, not more than five, or only those in which you have been active during the last two years of high school? In another spot, are you to write out an answer or simply underline, circle, or check one or more of the items that are listed below a question?

To fill in some of the blanks, you will need to have on hand such specific information as your social security number, your height and weight, details about school attendance, your scholastic standing, dates of previous employment and the salary earned, and names and addresses of references and of former employers. Since you may be filling out the forms right in business offices or employment agencies, it is a good idea to prepare ahead of time a list of such items. Referring to this list (or to a personal record sheet, if you have prepared one) will help you to spell names correctly and to give accurate addresses, dates, and figures.

To do a good job with some parts of an application form, you must exercise judgment in choosing the information to be supplied. For example, if a college application asks for a list of five books you have read recently and you have read ten, choose those that give some indication of your range of interests or your preferences, rather than list the first five that come to mind. If a job application provides a line or two for you to give information about your "physical defects" and you are so near-sighted that you once hailed a police car, mistaking it for a taxi, do not go into an explanation of how things look to you without your glasses; simply write "near-sighted" and move on to the next blank.

Sometimes the answer space on an application form is small, though the question itself seems to cover a great deal of territory. On a business application, for instance, only two lines may be provided for you to state why you think you are "especially well qualified for the position." Or on a college-entrance form, there may be just one line in which you are to explain "your present vocational interests." To use the limited space to best advantage, you will need to think through what you want to say and to write it out on scratch paper first. Your answer should be complete, yet fit into the space allowed.

It is usually a good policy to answer the questions in order, completing each one before moving on to the next. But sometimes, especially in filling out a college-application form, you might want to skip a question and come back to it later. It may be a question about what academic area you wish to specialize in, a matter that you may first want to talk over with one of your teachers. It may be a question about finances, which you will have to discuss with your father. Or it may be a question that you will have to postpone answering until you have had time enough to consider carefully what you want to say. When you do skip over a question, mark the spot, perhaps with a paper clip, to remind yourself to come back to it later. And if certain questions do not apply to you (those about military service, for instance), draw lines through the answer spaces or write *No* or *None,* to indicate that you have not neglected to consider the question.

The Written Composition

Just as you want to learn as much as possible about the school of your choice, so a college admissions committee wants to learn many things about you—what sort of person you are, how well you will fit into the college community, and what you are likely to contribute to it. A written composition, an important part of most college-application forms, is one means of getting information of this kind.

Because the composition is expected to give some indication of your ability to organize your thoughts and express them clearly in standard written English, you are to receive no help in the writing or revising of the essay. To emphasize this point, many colleges require the composition to be in your own handwriting. Some want it signed, as well.

For the composition, most colleges require an autobiographical essay, to be of a specified length, ranging from about one hundred to five hundred words. The directions for writing this essay vary greatly from college to college. On some forms, for example, these directions may be merely "Write a brief story of your life" or "Use this space (one page) to supply information about yourself that you think will be useful to the Admissions Committee."

The directions on most of the forms, however, are more specific, thus serving to indicate what sort of information an admissions committee would find useful. The applicant may be asked to discuss in his essay such topics as his hobbies, ambitions, ideals, special talents, and part-time jobs. He may be instructed to include paragraphs telling of his high school and his community and their influence on his interests and activities. Or he may be asked to write about a recent action of his and its consequences, unique aspects of his home life, obstacles he has overcome, a book that has increased his understanding of the society in which he lives, or (more difficult) his strengths and weaknesses as a person.

On some forms, such topics are to be covered by brief answers to several specific questions. On most of *these* forms, then, the "writing sample" assignment has to do with the applicant's educational and vocational plans. Specifically, he may be asked to discuss such topics as why he wants to attend a particular college, what he expects to make his main interest while there, and how college will help him realize his lifetime goals.

Writing the composition. You will find that writing the composition, no matter what the particular subject matter is, will not be easy; it will take time and thought—and plenty of scratch paper —to do a good job. The effectiveness of the composition will depend in great part on what ideas and details you have decided to include and on how well you have organized and then presented these ideas in unified, coherent paragraphs. You cannot simply start writing down the first words that occur to you and expect to turn out a good composition. For "writing" is just one part of the composition process—the last and easiest part. The most challenging part is the "composing": *first* thinking through ideas until they are clear in your own mind, and *then* figuring out how to put these ideas into an interesting, meaningful whole. Only after you have found something specific to say can you express yourself clearly and write to the point.

How do you go about getting ideas for such an essay? A good way to begin is to spend two or three hours (perhaps only ten or fifteen minutes at a stretch, over a period of several days) just mulling over what you *might* say about a subject. Taking this much time is important, for the first ideas that come to mind may not be the best ideas for your purpose.

By way of example, let us suppose that, from several suggested topics, you have chosen this one: "Discuss, in about 300 words, unusual educational experiences which have influenced you most." Let us suppose, further, that after you have cast about in your memory for noteworthy experiences to discuss, a number of possibilities have occurred to you, which you note down on a sheet of scratch paper:

1. Taking field trips—to an automobile plant, a school for retarded children, the art museum, a local hospital, the state capitol, etc.
2. Working as a camp counselor one summer
3. Being a member of the varsity debating team for two years
4. Being a sports reporter for the school newspaper during junior year
5. Taking an experimental course in world literature
6. Building a hot rod from parts bought at junkyards
7. Reading Charles Beard's *The Rise of American Civilization*
8. Growing up in a bilingual home

Though each of these experiences did have educational value for you, you soon realize that if you tried to cover all eight of them in just three hundred words, your essay would be far from effective. You would have to skimp on explanatory details to such an extent that no reader could possibly get a clear picture of the significance

of each experience. You therefore decide to limit your discussion to three experiences only. Which three will it be? To decide, you review your list, carefully assessing each item, thoughtfully weighing one against another.

Almost immediately you see that the first two experiences can readily be dropped—the field trips and the camp counseling. Compared with other items on the list, they do not seem particularly unusual or significant. The field trips, interesting as they were, did not really have much influence on your attitudes or your special interests. Though the camp counseling did give you valuable practice in dealing with people, its main importance, it seems to you, was simply that it gave you an opportunity to spend the summer out of doors.

The third experience on the list—the debating—is one you certainly want to include. More than any part of the formal curriculum, it encouraged you to keep up with current events. Moreover, you are convinced that it brought about a slow but steady improvement in your ability to think logically (which comes in handy every day of your life), to investigate a topic thoroughly (which comes in handy in several of your courses), and to speak more fluently under pressure (which had always been hard for you). In fact, you have enjoyed debate so much that you are thinking of going into law or politics or both.

In considering whether to include your experience as a sportswriter for the school paper, you remember your initial enthusiasm and your dreams of one day becoming a famous journalist. But, for you, journalistic writing turned out to be just plain hard work, work that you no longer intend to pursue as a career, since it gave you little personal satisfaction. You decide to omit this experience; after all, it had a negative influence only.

On the other hand, the fifth item on the list, taking the experimental course in world literature, has been of positive educational value. In the first place, it forced you to acquire study skills that are sure to prove useful in college: you learned to take effective lecture notes, to plan your study time around monthly rather than daily homework assignments, and to dig out for yourself the meaning of one difficult classic after another. In the second place, the reading assignments for the course gave you important insights into human nature. You began to see for yourself that the concerns and aspirations of civilized human beings do not change much over the centuries, that people the world over have always been interested in such things as freedom, justice, survival, love and friendship, the arts, nature, and religion. You feel that you must include this experience in the essay.

There are now three items left on your list—and room in your essay for only one more. You are reluctant to drop any of them; all seem highly significant. Building the hot rod gave you a sense of accomplishment you had seldom experienced in your life; reading

The Rise of American Civilization had a profound effect on your attitudes and thinking; growing up in a bilingual home has been a major factor in your development. But, while assessing the relative value of the three items, you remind yourself that you have already mentioned the first two on other parts of the form (the hot rod under "Hobbies and special interests" and the book under "Books that have influenced your life"). On this basis, then, you decide to drop these two items.

The more you think about the bilingual-home experience, the more important it seems. You have just recently come to realize that this background, far from being the disadvantage you had thought it in your childhood, has actually proved itself an advantage. Though you are not yet certain whether the experience will directly influence your choice of a vocation, it has already given you a firm grasp of a second language. Moreover, it has made you less opinionated, less provincial than you might otherwise have been; you have a deep interest in and a fairly clear understanding of the problems and policies of a country other than your own, and you know two cultures well enough to view both of them objectively and to appreciate more fully what is best in each. Everything considered, you are sure that this experience, more than any other one thing, has made you the sort of person you are.

Now that you have decided which three experiences will be the main topics in your essay, and have clearly in mind specific details to use in developing each of them, there is one more matter to settle before you begin the actual writing—the order in which to present the topics. After thinking it over, you decide that an order of climax would be best. You will start with the least important of the three topics, the world-literature course; move next to the debating; and end with the most interesting and most significant experience, growing up in a bilingual home.

Because you have taken the time to do the necessary thinking and planning, you find that the next step, writing the first draft, is comparatively easy. The sentences come fast; transitions seem almost to write themselves; even the number of words turns out about right. As you read through what you have written, you feel that you have done a fairly good job. Even so, you set the essay aside for a day or two, knowing that when you come back to it, you will be able to view it objectively and thus be more likely to detect spots that need revising.

Rereading the essay does reveal a number of flaws—among them, a misspelled word, several rough spots that need to be smoothed out, and two sentences which, though perfectly clear to you, might be confusing to others. You keep working at the revision until you are sure that your writing is as good as you can make it. Then you copy the essay on the application form. After proofreading to catch any mistakes made in copying, you prepare the form for mailing, send it off—and hope for the best.

Exercise 5 The following topics, all expressed as topic sentences, are auto-biographical (like those on college-application forms). Choose one of the sentences and develop it in a paragraph or two.

1 If I could relive my high-school years, I would _____. [Participate more in extracurricular activities? Follow a different course of study? Study more? Get to know a wider variety of people?]
2 I would like (or not like) to follow my father's (or mother's) occupation or profession.
3 _____ is one person (or place) that I do not want to see again.
4 My own experience has convinced me that it is impossible (or possible) for a senior in high school to hold down a part-time job and still do his best work in school.
5 I have found that having an active imagination is not always the blessing that many people think it is.
6 The writer (or statesman, scientist, etc.) I most admire is

_____.

Exercise 6 The following items suggest possible subjects for an essay based on your own observation, experience, and opinions. Write an essay of 300 to 500 words on one of these subjects (or, if you prefer, on a similar subject of your own).

1 A person (or book) that has changed your life [By opening up a whole new area of interest? By changing your attitudes or behavior in a significant way? By inspiring in you the faith and courage you know you will need if you are to achieve desired goals (learning to live with a handicap, for example; doing well in your school work; finding a way to help finance a college education)?]
2 How your reading tastes have changed within the last two years [What are your reading tastes? What were they? What factors have caused them to change? Is the change for the better or the worse? Why?]
3 The one thing that you consider most important to your long-range happiness [Success in your work? Faith in God? Friendship? Freedom? Education?]
4 The time and place you would live in, if you had the choice [Ancient Greece? Renaissance Italy? Elizabethan England? New England during or shortly after the Revolutionary War? California during the gold rush? Hawaii, now?]
5 What your political convictions are, and how you have arrived at them [Through TV programs on current issues? Through reading—newspapers, magazines, books? Through one of your courses at school? Through discussion with friends and relatives?]
6 Growing up in a bilingual home [What is it like? In what ways is it an advantage? A disadvantage?]

English on the Campus

"So you're going to college!" How many books and magazine articles have you read in the last few months with that title or on that theme? And all of them offered you advice—advice on study habits, on money management, on clothes, and on dozens of other aspects of college life. These pages will give you no such advice. Rather, they will serve to emphasize for the future what you have already realized about the present: that "English" is not just a subject you study in one class each day; it is, instead, something you use all the time. In your college courses (no matter what the field), in the job experience that may be a part of your curriculum, in the activities you elect, and in the friendships you form, your skill in English will be a vital factor in your success. It is *how well* you use everything you have been learning in these high-school classes called "English" —how well you read and write, speak and listen, think and study— that is and will continue to be important, both during your years at college and throughout your life.

Even before your freshman year begins, you will have to demonstrate your language proficiency. You will probably find it necessary to ask about courses offered, about dormitory facilities, or about part-time jobs available to students; and the letters you write will telegraph ahead a good impression of you or a poor one, depending on how you use written English.

301

Soon after you arrive at college, you will find yourself involved in the exacting process of registration. Ability to read and follow directions accurately—a basic language skill—is essential to successful completion of this important activity.

You will meet other students as you stand in the registration lines, too; and your conversational ability— another kind of language skill—will help you make new friends.

College also has a less serious side: the proms and football games, the float parades and campus elections, the activities that can best be described as just plain fun. Though you may not be aware of it at the time, language is important on these occasions too. The use of an appropriate and fresh vocabulary, a suitable standard of usage, clear thinking, and accurate expression will make such events more meaningful and even more enjoyable.

DRAMATIC ARTS

Geology

FINE ARTS

BANKING

Physics

AGRICULTURE

civil engineering

LAW

POLITICS

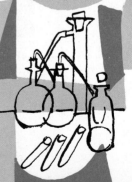

14 *Taking Tests*

Few of the people who complete a high-school education escape the necessity of taking standardized examinations of one kind or another. Most of these tests deal wholly or in part with the ability to use English accurately and effectively. It doesn't much matter whether you plan to enter college, a technical school, civil service, or the armed services—the tests that stand between you and these avenues to adult success are fairly similar. These tests are of two kinds: (1) *aptitude tests,* designed to determine the probability of your success in a particular activity or field; and (2) *achievement tests,* designed to measure what you have already learned.

These tests, for the most part, will be longer and more difficult than any you have been used to in school. On the other hand, you will not be expected to know all of the answers. Instead of being measured against an absolute grade of 100 per cent, your score on a particular test will be compared with the scores of all other people taking *that* test only. Thus, it is possible that you might answer as few as half the questions correctly, yet receive a high rating because the majority of those taking the test did no better.

Customarily, standardized tests are scored in terms of percentiles. This means that if you achieve a percentile score of 50 (or 500 on some tests), half of the people taking the test did better than you and half of them did worse. If your percentile score is 70, then you did better than 70 per cent of the people taking the test, while only 30 per cent did better than you. This, as you can see, is a fair way of grading, since you are compared only with people taking the same test, not with people taking other—easier or harder—tests.

Although standardized tests vary in the specific information or skill they are designed to measure, they are likely to use similar

forms of questions. This is especially true of vocabulary and reading questions. No one, not even your teacher, knows in advance what specific items of information such tests will ask for. You cannot prepare for them, therefore, by panicky, last-minute cramming. The best immediate preparation is a relaxing night's rest.

While there is little point in trying to anticipate what information the questions on such tests will ask for, you can and should become familiar in advance with the forms of the questions and the best way of dealing with each. Most standardized tests have a time limit; therefore, your familiarity with the form of each question and the principle underlying it may enable you to work faster and more confidently and thus perhaps add points to your score.

This chapter will show you some of the more common types of questions used in the verbal-aptitude and composition sections of such examinations as the College Entrance Board, National Merit Scholarship, State Regents, and other tests. [Besides discussing the form and testing principle involved in each kind of question, the chapter will refer you to specific parts of this book. Mastery of these sections will help you in preparing for the various question types.]

Whatever the actual form of the questions you must answer, your method of attack should be much the same. Before starting a test, be sure that you know how it is to be scored. On most tests your score will be computed from a count of the total number of right answers you have. (Items you answer incorrectly and items you fail to answer at all will not be counted.) On such tests, you should go straight through the items, answering all questions you are sure of. When you have completed these, turn back to the more difficult, and therefore more time-consuming, items. It is a good idea to try to answer every question, even if you have to guess. Ordinarily a test of this kind starts with the easiest items and ends with the most difficult.

On other tests, where a deduction is made for each wrong answer, you are usually advised in the directions to "guess intelligently," but to avoid "wild guesses." A "wild guess" would be one made when you have no idea at all about the correct answer, and you mentally toss a coin. An "intelligent guess" occurs when you can eliminate some of the choices, thus increasing your chance of selecting the right answer out of only two or three possibilities.

TIPS FOR TAKING TESTS

Read the directions carefully. The first and most important step in taking any examination is to be sure you clearly understand all the directions given. The directions usually include general instructions about entering your name and other personal data that may be required, about marking the answers when special answer sheets are provided, about guessing, and so on. They also include instructions on answering specific questions or sections of the test. Your failure to read and understand all the directions may easily cause you to answer incorrectly whole sections of the test.

Never start to answer any question until you have carefully read the directions. If you are not entirely clear as to what they require, *reread* them.

When a test is to be scored by electronic machine, a special separate answer sheet and a special pencil will be provided. You must be very careful on such a test to use *only* the pencil provided and to blacken neatly but completely each answer space you use. Any stray pencil marks on your paper may cause the machine to miscalculate. Also, you must take care to place each answer in the space on the answer sheet that corresponds in number exactly to the number of the question. A careless error here may trigger a whole column of "wrong" answers—wrong, because not indicated in the proper spaces.

Budget your time. Most standardized tests have some kind of time limit. You should not let a time limit cause you to panic. Work steadily along at your normal rate, but do not waste time. Never let yourself puzzle for too long over a question you are unsure of; instead, answer first the items you know. Then, if you have time, consider the ones that stump you.

Reread your work. If you have time, reread what you have written before you hand in your paper. Elimination of careless errors caught in this way can add points to your score.

TESTS OF WORD POWER

The extent and accuracy of your vocabulary, plus your ability to detect the relationships between words and ideas, pretty much determine your ability to think. This is the reason standardized tests place such emphasis on knowledge of words. While the forms of questions may differ slightly on different tests, all are trying to measure the same thing—your verbal aptitude; therefore, the questions do resemble one another in many ways.

Synonyms and Antonyms

Recognizing synonyms. Perhaps of all questions used, the most common type is that which asks you to identify a *synonym* of a given word. The best preparation for this, as for all vocabulary tests, is wide general reading and an interest in words. [You may find it helpful to review the discussion of synonyms in Chapter 12, pages 270-271, and the Index entry **Synonym**.] Directions and examples for a typical question about synonyms follow:

Directions: Each of the words printed below in capital letters is followed by five words lettered A through E. Choose the lettered word which is most nearly *similar* in meaning to the word in capital letters. Write the letter of that word after the appropriate number on your paper.

1 PERTINENT: A. saucy   B. relevant   C. nearby   D. panicky
   E. stubborn
2 LETHARGIC: A. drowsy   B. deadly   C. lively   D. corpulent
   E. round

Note that the directions ask you to indicate the word most similar in meaning to that in capital letters. In attacking vocabulary tests of this kind, you will find it a good idea to consider all the choices before selecting your answer. In Example 1, if you were not too sure of the meaning of PERTINENT, you might make the mistake of selecting *saucy* as the correct answer because it is similar in meaning to *pert* or *impertinent*. *Stubborn* means *persistent,* and you might choose it as the synonym for PERTINENT if you had confused PERTINENT with *persistent*. The word meaning most nearly the same as PERTINENT is, of course, *relevant*. None of the other words in any way suggests the meaning "related to the matter in hand."

In the same way, the word nearest in meaning to LETHARGIC is *drowsy. Deadly* is a synonym for *lethal,* while *lively* has a meaning more nearly opposite to that of LETHARGIC. The wider your own vocabulary, the more sure you are of the meanings of words you meet in your reading and conversation, the less likely it is that you will fall into traps of this kind when tackling a question of synonym recognition.

Exercise 1   Follow the directions for synonym recognition given above. (The answers to the following and all the exercise items in this chapter will be found on page 337.)

1 HOLOCAUST: A. saint   B. shipwreck   C. carnival
   D. conflagration   E. document
2 INCHOATE: A. angry   B. incomplete   C. stuffed
   D. wordless   E. chaotic
3 VERBOSE: A. wordy   B. active   C. large   D. green
   E. inarticulate
4 TORPID: A. explosive   B. birdlike   C. dormant   D. covered
   E. lukewarm
5 RAVAGE: A. enchant   B. wear out   C. rant   D. plunder
   E. score on
6 LUGUBRIOUS: A. humorous   B. greasy   C. lethal   D. heavy
   E. doleful

Recognizing antonyms.   A variation of the vocabulary test has the same form as the synonym test but asks you to identify *antonyms*—words of opposite meaning. A sample follows:

Directions: Each of the words printed below in capital letters is followed by five words lettered A through E. Choose the lettered word that is most nearly *opposite* in meaning to the word in capital letters. Write the letter of that word after the appropriate number on your paper.

1 AMIABLE: A. friendly B. accurate C. hostile D. neutral
   E. peaceable
2 CAPACIOUS: A. crowded B. roomy C. high D. topped
   E. hesitant

Often this kind of test item contains one or more words of meaning similar to that of the key word in capital letters. Remember that you have been asked to select the word which means the *opposite*. In Example 1, since AMIABLE means *friendly,* do not be misled into selecting A as your answer; you are looking for an antonym. The only word of opposite meaning among the choices is *hostile,* meaning "unfriendly."

Similarly, in Example 2, CAPACIOUS means *roomy;* but since you are looking for an antonym, B is not the correct choice. Neither is *topped;* for despite its seeming relation to the "cap" in *capacious,* it has nothing to do with the meaning you are seeking. The only one among the five choices that is opposite in meaning to CAPACIOUS is *crowded.*

Exercise 2 Follow the directions for antonym recognition given above.

1 FLACCID: A. flabby B. watery C. firm D. weak
   E. ended
2 INGENUOUS: A. clever B. naïve C. inventive D. new
   E. sophisticated
3 MARTIAL: A. musical B. peaceful C. nuptial
   D. indignant E. antagonistic
4 DIFFIDENCE: A. self-assurance B. sameness C. shyness
   D. coldness E. variety
5 PROFUNDITY: A. loss B. swearing C. depth
   D. replacement E. shallowness
6 COSMOPOLITAN: A. rural B. spiritual C. citified
   D. narrow E. readable

Recognizing synonyms and antonyms. Still another variation of the vocabulary test is more complicated, asking you to select the word that means either the *same as* or the *opposite of* the given word. In this kind of test, only one antonym or one synonym of the key word is given. All other words following the key word have neither the same meaning as the word in capitals nor an opposite meaning.

Exercise 3 Each of the words printed below in capital letters is followed by five words lettered A through E. Choose the lettered word that means either the *same as* or the *opposite of* the word printed in capital letters.

1 EMACIATED: A. sad B. discouraged C. plump D. free
   E. chewed
2 DETER: A. broil B. fail C. replace D. hinder E. return
3 SIMULATE: A. design B. imitate C. reckon D. incite
   E. arbitrate
4 DEROGATE: A. detract B. strain C. despise D. inquire
   E. halt
5 MUTABLE: A. silent B. edible C. unsung
   D. handicapped E. unchanging
6 INCREDULOUS: A. accredited B. animated C. content
   D. believing E. insolvent

Word Analogies

Increasingly, tests of verbal aptitude are using items designed to measure your ability to see a particular relationship between the objects or ideas for which words stand. This type of item tests not only your ability to recognize the meanings of the words themselves, but also your ability to sense their relationships to other words. Directions and sample test items may read as follows:

316

Directions: Each question below consists of two words which have a certain relationship to each other, followed by four lettered pairs of related words. Choose the lettered pair related to each other in the *same* way the words in the original pair are related. Write the letter of the pair you select after the appropriate number.

1 GRAVE:CEMETERY:: A. feather:bird B. death:birth
   C. building:city D. army:soldier
2 BEE:HONEY:: A. bread:butter B. legislator:law
   C. mechanic:car D. soup:cook

In these samples, two of the many possible relationships are shown. GRAVE is to CEMETERY, for instance, as a part is to the whole. Since a *building* is a part of a *city* as a GRAVE is a part of a CEMETERY, C expresses the correct relationship. *Feather:bird* is not as good a choice, because feathers are not part of a bird in the same sense that a grave is part of a cemetery. The relationship in *death: birth* is one of opposites. In *army:soldier,* the relationship is reversed—the army is not a part of the soldier—and so this pair too is wrong.

The relationship between BEE and HONEY is that of producer to product. The only parallel among the choices is *legislator:law.* That is, a legislator helps to make and pass laws. *Bread* does not produce *butter;* nor does *soup* produce *cooks,* though the opposite is true. *Mechanics* normally repair *cars,* rather than produce them.

Notice that the form of these items is like that used to express proportional relationships in mathematics: 2:6::4:X. That is, two is to six as four is to the answer. By determining that 6 is three times 2, you can then determine X as three times 4, or 12. Reading the word-analogy questions in the same way should help you to see the relationships more clearly. For example, the two samples on page 316 may be read, correctly, "Grave is to cemetery as building is to city" and "Bee is to honey as legislator is to law."

A variation of this type of question asks only for the X item in the relationship, as in the following:

1   WALL:HUNTER::TARIFF: A. senator   B. cargo ship
    C. teacher   D. importer   E. product
2   FIRE:DESTRUCTION::WORK: A. hate   B. jealousy
    C. admiration   D. marriage   E. accomplishment

In the first sample, WALL is an obstacle to a HUNTER, and TARIFF is an obstacle only to an *importer*. In the second sample, FIRE often leads to or results in DESTRUCTION, just as WORK generally leads to *accomplishment*.

Besides the relationships already shown in these samples, there are many others on which word analogies can be based. Here are some of the more common ones:

Word:Synonym   LIE:PREVARICATE::tempt:lure;
    famous:renowned; penetrate:pierce
Word:Antonym   GENIAL:DOUR::prodigal:parsimonious;
    eternal:ephemeral; plentiful:scanty
Cause:Effect   MOSQUITO:MALARIA::explosion:destruction;
    unemployment:poverty; bathing:cleanliness
Abstract:Concrete   REMEDY:ASPIRIN::vehicle:Cadillac;
    water:Lake Michigan; jewelry:engagement ring
Type:Characteristic   DOG:BARK::cow:low; wolf:howl; loon:cry
Action:Instrument   GLIDE:SKATE::sail:boat; bore:auger; raise:jack
Symbol:Abstract Idea   FLAG:PATRIOTISM::red light:danger;
    mace:sovereignty; scales:justice
Degree of Relationship   SERGEANT:MAJOR::apprentice:master;
    teacher:superintendent; instructor:professor
Degree of Intensity   ACHE:THROB::shower:thunderstorm;
    cologne:perfume; sadness:despair
Time Sequence   MORNING:EVENING::youth:age;
    January:December; kindergarten:college

These are only a few of the many possible relationships between words and ideas. Since the relationship is always expressed in parallel form, you must watch out for a switch in order. For instance, in the analogy "glide:skate::boat:sail," the relationship expressed seems so clear that you might overlook the inaccuracy of the change in order. To be accurate, the analogy must read "glide:skate::sail:boat."

Exercise 4   On your paper, after the appropriate number, write the letter of the pair of words (in Part I) or of the single word (in Part II) that best expresses the same relationship as that suggested by the words in capital letters.

Part I

1   DETECTIVE:QUARRY::   A. broom:dirt   B. rabbit:hound
    C. scientist:truth   D. persistence:achievement
    E. judge:prisoner

2   ACCELERATOR:AUTOMOBILE::   A. reins:horse
    B. anger:temper   C. motive:crime   D. kerosene:fire
    E. doorbell:housewife

3   SCOWL:ANGER::   A. dive:exercise
    B. blush:embarrassment   C. sound:music
    D. delay:postponement   E. amusement:laugh

4   ATYPICAL:NORMAL::   A. irrational:crazy   B. side:front
    C. noisy:incoherent   D. unusual:usual   E. crowd:individual

5   CAVIAR:GOURMET::   A. delicacy:beast   B. stew:starvation
    C. fish:worm   D. nature:man   E. masterpiece:connoisseur

Part II

6   CLOWN:CIRCUS::TEACHER: A. school   B. pupils   C. books
    D. principal   E. glee club

7   MARTINET:DISCIPLINE::SERGEANT-AT-ARMS: A. meeting
    B. chairman   C. minutes   D. reports   E. order

8   BEAST:JUNGLE::MOLLUSK: A. marsh   B. tank   C. ocean
    D. slum   E. insanity

9   KNIFE:METAL::SUIT: A. cloth   B. flannel   C. slacks
    D. tuxedo   E. tailor

10 FOOD:CAKE::BOOK: A. contents   B. atlas   C. binding
    D. library   E. volume

Word Meaning in Context

Still another kind of test used to measure the extent of your vocabulary is the completion test. In this test you are faced with a series of statements, each with one or more important words omitted. Following each statement are a number of words, one of which, or one set of which, will correctly complete the meaning of the statement. This is a test both of your knowledge of word meanings and of your ability to infer particular meanings of words from context. [See pages 263-266 for a discussion of the importance of context in determining the meanings of words.] Sample directions and items follow:

Directions: Following are a number of sentences, each containing one or more blank spaces where words have been omitted. Beneath each sentence are five lettered words or sets of words. Choose the word or set of words which, when used in the sentence,

A. B. C. D.

best completes the meaning of the sentence. Write the correct letter after the sentence number on your paper.

1 Though they had lost several players because of injuries and ineligibility, the _____ of the team was excellent.
A. temper B. prosperity C. morale D. plans E. roster

2 The response of the freedom-loving Colonists was _____; they had no need of goading, for they were _____ patriots.
A. immediate ... cruel B. spontaneous ... ardent
C. inestimable ... reluctant D. laggard ... independent
E. assured ... notorious

The word that belongs in the blank in Sentence 1 is C, *morale*. None of the other word choices offered makes proper sense in relation to the other words and ideas of the sentence. While several of the individual words might make sense in the second sentence, only the insertion of Pair B, *spontaneous ... ardent*, makes the whole sentence meaningful.

Exercise 5 Follow the directions beginning on page 318, for supplying words in context.

1 That he could be angry and yet laugh was a _____ which his children found difficult to understand.
A. reversal B. problem C. misunderstanding D. refusal
E. paradox

2 In the jungle, arrows painted with a bark poison that destroys the red corpuscles of a victim are used as a _____ weapon.
A. playful B. handsome C. humane D. lethal E. ticklish

3 His strongly expressed views led many citizens to regard him as a _____, but those who knew him well realized how _____ was his appraisal of the situation.
A. fanatic ... objective B. champion ... loyal
C. moron ... inconclusive D. revolutionary ... rebellious
E. scholar ... learned

4 No individual can be universally competent. Many who shout for reform illustrate this; their _____ outside their special interests is _____ revealed.
A. knowledge ... clearly B. ignorance ... starkly
C. skill ... poorly D. bent ... openly
E. prejudices ... enthusiastically

5 How can the jurors be certain of the degree of his guilt unless they are given more _____ information about the crime?
A. vivid B. enervating C. perverted D. explicit E. trivial

6 The speaker offered a great many points that were _____ to the subject; but the audience could not support his candidacy, for basically his ideas were _____ to their beliefs.
A. pertinent ... related B. relevant ... alien
C. antithetical ... attractive D. opposed ... negative
E. appropriate ... malnutritious

319

Some tests check spelling ability as a part of the mechanics of writing. In other tests, where it is checked as a separate item, you may be asked merely to identify the misspelled words in several groups of words, or you may be asked not only to identify them but also to respell them correctly. Directions for the latter kind of test item might be these:

Directions: Each of the lines below contains one misspelled word. Rewrite the word, correctly spelled, after the item number on your paper.

1 niece consent ache studying colision
2 shining indulgance readiness summons acknowledge

Careful scrutiny here will show you that *collision* and *indulgence* are the two misspelled words.

Ordinarily, the errors on such tests involve a single letter. They may be based on such troublesome matters as *ie-ei,* dropping final *e*'s before suffixes, and doubled consonants. Often when you are dealing with this kind of exercise, your first impression may well be the right one. Many people "think" too much on this test, and change from a right to a wrong answer. [Although accurate spelling is the result of many years of care and observation in writing and reading, if you are weak in this area, you may find it helpful to review the Index entry **Spelling**.]

320

Exercise 6   Follow the directions on this page for identification and correction of misspelled words.

1	volunteer	antique	deniel	busier	foretell
2	disquieting	acceptence	suspense	invisible	coerce
3	processes	settee	carress	attest	technician
4	manicure	tolerance	chimny	hydraulic	flagon
5	seperate	potatoes	gradual	justifiable	dining
6	gondola	democracy	agitate	goverment	siege
7	victuals	melodrama	booty	larceny	aparatus
8	previous	evadence	remedy	category	forty-four
9	supersede	finally	surely	begining	foreign
10	picniker	ceiling	burying	excellent	sincerely

READING COMPREHENSION

Most reliable tests of verbal skill or aptitude devote a major part of their attention to reading comprehension. Since reading techniques vary with the type of material to be read, these tests ordinarily include selections from a variety of fields, such as history, literature, science, and philosophy.

The questions based on the selections also vary in difficulty. Some of the questions merely require an understanding of the factual meaning of a selection. Others, more difficult, may require you to interpret and analyze what you have read. Still others check your ability to apply and test principles discussed by the author. And some questions may even ask you to express your judgment of the author's treatment of his material or his ability to use evidence in support of his statements.

Directions for a typical exercise dealing with reading comprehension might be the following:

Directions: Read each of the following passages and then answer the questions that follow it, by choosing the best among the five suggested answers. Write the letter of your choice after the appropriate number on your paper. Answer questions only on the basis of what is stated or implied in the passage to which each refers.

A sample passage and the questions based on it follow:

Julius Caesar, hunting Pompey over land and sea, arrived on the Rhoetian promontory and wandered about the ruins of the city burned forty years before by a Roman expeditionary force. All he found was the enveloping forest, rotting oak thickets growing over the palaces of kings and the temples of gods. He was crossing a stream which meandered through the sand when someone said: "This is the famous river Xanthus!" He stepped on a patch of grass, and someone cried: "This is where they brought Hector's body! Be careful not to offend his ghost!" And when he came to a pile of loose stones, someone plucked his sleeve and said: "Do you not see the altar of Hercaean Jupiter?"

Caesar had seen nothing, only ruins and the surrounding darkness, but he knew he had come to a sacred place, and feared the ghosts. So he hastily erected an altar of turf, burned incense on it, and prayed to the gods who guarded these sacred ashes, asking prosperity for himself and vowing to rebuild the shattered walls until they gleamed and sparkled as before. And then remembering Pompey he hurried off to Egypt, so impatient to kill his enemy that he sailed past all the wealthy cities of Asia and did not pause until he reached Alexandria.—Robert Payne, *The Gold of Troy.* Copyright © 1958 by Funk & Wagnalls, New York.

321

1) According to the passage, Caesar came to the Rhoetian promontory
    A. while seeking the treasures of old palaces and temples
    B. to search for the body of the Trojan hero Hector
    C. in the course of an expedition in pursuit of Pompey
    D. to make plans for rebuilding the ruined city
    E. in search of the altar of Hercaean Jupiter
2) On the promontory, Caesar's dominant mood seemed to be
    A. despair at his own helplessness

B. great reverence for the sacredness of the place

C. disgust at the pointless destruction of the city by an earlier Roman force

D. impatience to get on with his search for his enemy

E. greed at the thought of wealthy cities to plunder

3) From the information presented in the passage, one might gather that Caesar

A. was excessively superstitious

B. was a weak and careless military leader

C. was basically single-minded in his actions

D. was deeply interested in history

E. was intensely religious

In answering the questions about the preceding passage, notice that at first glance several of the choices offered seem possible. On close examination, you will find the reason for this is that certain conspicuous words from the passage are used in the questions. If you do not consider carefully the *meaning* behind the words, you may easily fall into the traps prepared for you and select the wrong answer. Take Question 1), for example. Palaces and temples are mentioned in the passage, and so are Hector's body, the altar of Jupiter, and Caesar's vow to rebuild the city destroyed by a Roman army. But none of these things has any bearing on Caesar's purpose in coming to the promontory. His purpose, as is stated in the first sentence of the passage, was to hunt down Pompey. The answer to this question, obviously, is C.

By elimination, the answer to 2) is D: dominating each of Caesar's actions is his impatience to find and kill his enemy.

Question 3) calls for an inference to be drawn from details given in the passage. The passage states that Caesar feared ghosts. But the fear of ghosts, which today would be considered superstitious, was not so considered in Caesar's time. Though Caesar erected an altar, prayed to the gods, and made a vow, he did so hastily and only after others had called to his attention the sacredness of the place. He cannot, therefore, be considered intensely religious. His indifference toward the sacred ruins, to the "famous" river Xanthus, and to Hector's burial place suggests that he had little interest in history. There is nothing in the passage which indicates that he was a weak military leader, but the whole passage does point up his relentless, single-minded pursuit of Pompey. Answer C is right.

Exercise 7 Follow the directions on page 321 for a test of reading comprehension.

1 In a Chicago laboratory a radiochemist stood before an oscilloscope connected to a Geiger counter. Across the oscilloscope screen, very much like the screen in a small television set, jumped a never-ending ribbon of green zigzags. The zigzags were made by the impulses coming from disintegrating atoms of radioactive

carbon within the counter. The carbon had been extracted from a piece of wood, but the wood was by no means ordinary. In fact, it was a piece of very old wood, part of a spruce tree that grew in a Wisconsin forest so long ago that when the tree was alive the Ice Age still had northern United States in its chill grip--so long ago that mastodons and mammoths still inhabited the country in force. Indeed, it is quite possible that a mastodon, crashing through the spruce forest in the chill glacial air, brushed against this very tree.

The wood had been sent to the laboratory for an exact determination of age—not the age of the living tree, which can easily be learned by counting its growth rings, but the time elapsed since the tree was alive. When a police surgeon examines a dead body, his medical skill tells him *about* how much time has elapsed since death occurred. But only *about*. He has no means of fixing the time exactly, even though the guilt or innocence of a person accused of murder may depend upon it. The surgeon can only look for certain signs and use his professional judgment.

Like the surgeon, geologists and archaeologists, trying to date the events of prehistoric periods, have only been able to look for signs and on the basis of them to make estimates which, although far better than nothing at all, are certainly not accurate. Some geologists, for example, had estimated the age of this particular spruce forest in Wisconsin at about 25,000 years, although they could not be sure.—Richard Foster Flint, "Pin-pointing the Past with the Cosmic Clock," in *A Treasury of Science*. Copyright © 1958 by Harper & Row, New York.

323

1) In the laboratory test described, a radiochemist
   A. is searching for data on mastodons and mammoths
   B. is attempting to determine the length of the Ice Age
   C. is measuring the age of a piece of spruce wood
   D. is determining the age of a murder victim for the police
   E. is searching for a new source of radioactive carbon
2) An oscilloscope is
   A. a form of Geiger counter with a screen like that of a TV
   B. a technical name for a television set
   C. a never-ending ribbon of green zigzags
   D. a device that may be used to record impulses from disintegrating atoms
   E. a device that may be used to compute age by counting the growth rings in trees
3) The discovery of radioactive carbon
   A. has revolutionized methods of crime detection
   B. explains the petrification of forests in prehistoric times
   C. helps make possible a more accurate dating of prehistoric events
   D. was the result of uncovering animal remains in Wisconsin
   E. took place 25,000 years ago

2　When I open my desk drawer I always see a number of things which shouldn't be there, but which have by long usage established a kind of right to rattle around where they don't really belong. There is a small screwdriver, the shell of a marine snail from the Mediterranean, a lump of Wood's metal which will melt in hot water, and a bead of amber.

The last is, as one should expect of a piece of jewelry, a very pretty bead. Its color is a nice full-bodied yellow clouded with white. It has a smooth and pleasant feel, and I know that it is hard enough to resist successfully any attempt to scratch it with a fingernail but that a knife would produce a deep scratch easily. I also know that its specific gravity is such that it would sink in quiet water but be tossed around in agitated water, most especially by agitated salt water. I know that it would turn a darker color if left for a month or so in a box with a radioactive substance. I know that it would radiate with a deeply beautiful blue luminescence if placed under an ultraviolet lamp—a test for genuineness. I know that chemical analysis would show it to contain at least 3 per cent— more likely 5 to 8 per cent—of something called succinic acid—a test for its place of origin. I know that it could be ignited with a match and that it would burn with a smoky flame and a pleasant smell, just like a piece of pine wood that is not pale in color, but reddish-brown because of the rosin it contains. My amber bead would do that for the simple reason that it is itself rosin, the fossil rosin of an extinct relative of our pine trees of today.—Willy Ley, *Dragons in Amber.* Copyright 1951 by The Viking Press, New York.

1) The author's amber bead came originally from
   A. the Mediterranean
   B. his desk drawer
   C. an ancient type of pine tree
   D. the ocean bottom
   E. a center of radioactivity
2) A test of the genuineness of amber is that it
   A. will emit a blue light under an ultraviolet lamp
   B. will float in a deep pan of water
   C. will turn a darker color if left in a box
   D. cannot be scratched with a knife
   E. will survive being tossed in a fire
3) The author's attitude toward the bead is mainly one of
   A. distaste
   B. delight in its beauty
   C. absolute objectivity
   D. possessive pride
   E. scientific interest

3　It is so difficult a task to form any correct estimate of one's own surroundings, largely on account of our very familiarity with them, that historical students have generally evaded this responsi-

bility. They have often declared that it was impossible to do so satisfactorily. And yet no one will ever know more than we about what is going on now. Some secrets may be revealed to coming generations, but plenty of our circumstances will be obscure to them. And it certainly seems pusillanimous, if not hazardous, to depute to those yet unborn the task of comprehending the conditions under which we must live and strive. I have long believed that the only unmistakable contribution that the historical student can make to the progress of intelligence is to study the past with an eye constantly on the present. For history not only furnishes us with the key to the present by showing how our situation came about, but at the same time supplies a basis of comparison and a point of vantage by virtue of which the salient contrasts between our days and those of old can be detected. Without history the essential differences are sure to escape us. Our generation, like all preceding generations of mankind, inevitably takes what it finds largely for granted, and the great mass of men who argue about existing conditions assume a fundamental likeness to past conditions as the basis of their conclusions in regard to the present and the still unrolled future.—James Harvey Robinson, *The Mind in the Making.* Copyright 1950 by Harper & Row, New York.

1) According to this writer, the main purpose of history is to
   A. enable us to contrast the present with the past
   B. tell us exactly what happened in the past
   C. prophesy the future
   D. show us that fundamentally life does not change
   E. increase our intelligence
2) People of this generation tend to regard history as
   A. a useful key to the future
   B. merely a record of the past
   C. a fascinating revelation of secrets of the past
   D. basically similar to the present
   E. misleading information about a no longer existent world

325

CORRECTNESS AND EFFECTIVENESS

OF EXPRESSION

In some examinations, your writing ability will be evaluated from a composition you write or from your response to certain questions requiring lengthy and carefully composed answers. Many tests do not include this kind of exercise, however. Instead, in these tests, your knowledge of the principles of good writing—from acceptable grammar, punctuation, and usage to use of a variety of sentence types, use of parallel structure, ability to avoid unnecessary words, and so on—is determined from your answers to several different kinds of sentence items containing problems in composition. [Your long-range preparation for the composition items in the tests you will take should include systematic review of the various entries in the Index section of this book dealing with matters of grammar, usage, and composition, with special attention to those items that you recognize as problems in your own writing. Careful rereading of Chapters 2, 9, 10, and 11, which deal with paragraphing, usage, and sentence structure, as well as of Chapter 15 on punctuation, may also help you to achieve a better score.]

Error recognition.   In one type of composition question, you are given sentences in each of which a number of parts are underlined and numbered. In some of these sentences one, and only one, of the underlined parts is "incorrect" and needs changing. In other sentences, none of the parts needs changing. You are asked to indicate which one, if any, of the underlined parts you think should be changed. When separate printed answer sheets are provided, a space is included in which to indicate that no change is needed.

Some examples of this type of item are the following:

1 Between the northern limits of New York City and the Croton
   (1)
   River lays a section of country that in the American Revolution
   (2)   (3)
   was known as the "neutral ground."
   (4)

2 My history teacher and me are taking a trip next spring to study
   (1)   (2)   (3)
   at first hand the Gettysburg battlefield.
   (4)

3 Not one of us were qualified for the skating race, but we
   (1)   (2)   race, but we
                                                      (3)
   decided among ourselves to enter it anyway.
           (4)

In this kind of test you will usually be asked to point out "errors" or examples of "incorrect" case, number, tense, punctuation, capitalization, or agreement, lack of parallel structure, excess verbiage, faulty word placement, poor word choice, and the like. Such tests actually are designed to test your knowledge of standard, *formal* usages. Many words widely used in informal English will be considered "incorrect" in these tests, and should be indicated as such.

In the first example sentence on this page, the verb form *lays* should, of course, be *lies,* and you should indicate (2) on your paper as the error. In the second sentence, the pronoun *me* should be the nominative case form *I,* since it is part of the compound subject. In the third sentence, the subject, *one,* is singular and in formal usage requires a singular verb, *was qualified.*

Exercise 8   Each of the following sentences contains four underlined parts, one of which *may* be incorrect. On your paper, after the number of the sentence, write the number of the underlined part you consider incorrect. If none is incorrect, write X on your paper.

1 A gun sounded <u>far off</u> in the <u>marsh; and</u> the next thing we
               (1)   (2)
knew, a mallard <u>drops</u> into our boat.
<u>(3)</u>   (4)

2 The <u>authors theirselves</u> <u>were not aware</u> that the book <u>was</u>
         (1)   (2)   (3)
filled with errors in punctuation, spelling, and <u>grammar.</u>
<u>(3)</u>   (4)

3 The class <u>valedictorian,</u> together with her <u>parents,</u> <u>has been</u>
         (1)   (2)
<u>asked</u> to attend the <u>faculty reception.</u>
<u>(3)</u>   (4)

4 I think you <u>should address</u> older people <u>respectfully,</u> <u>irregard-</u>
           (1)   (2)   (3)
<u>less</u> of whether you know them or not.
                          (4)

5 Everyone stood in line for <u>hours,</u> but scarcely <u>nobody</u> there
                    (1)   (2)
<u>was able</u> to <u>buy</u> tickets for good seats.
<u>(3)</u>   (4)

Correction choice.   Similar to the items in Exercise 8, but somewhat more difficult, is the type of exercise item in which you are 327 required to choose from among a number of possibilities the one best correction or improvement of an underlined word or phrase in the sentence opposite. Here too some of the underlined items are correct as they stand, so that one of the possibilities offered is "NO CHANGE." In this kind of exercise, the number of choices offered varies with the type of error. Here are two samples:

1 Don't Tim <u>live in</u> Putnam   A. NO CHANGE B. Do
   Valley any more?   C. Doesn't D. Doesnt

2 Each person should have   A. NO CHANGE B. supplies. A
   these <u>supplies,</u> a hammer,   C. supplies: D. supplies;
   tacks, and a yardstick.

To agree with the singular subject *Tim* in the first sentence, the verb should be *Doesn't,* choice C. Before an appositive list, as in the second sentence, the punctuation should be a colon, choice C.

Exercise 9   Select the best correction for the underlined word or words in each of the following sentences. On your paper, after the sentence number, write the letter of the correction of your choice. If the underlined word or words are correct, write on your paper the letter that indicates NO CHANGE.

1 <u>Us girls</u> would like to have   A. NO CHANGE B. We
   more intramural sports.   C. All us

2 You can do anything you want to, I am going home.
A. NO CHANGE B. omit comma C. to: D. to;

3 The Dramatics Club presented its play last night.
A. NO CHANGE B. it's C. its' D. their

4 I certainly wish you would have told me sooner about this complication.
A. NO CHANGE B. told C. had told D. might have told

5 What do you think of them having the school locked up?
A. NO CHANGE B. their C. they're

6 Several students chose to read *Dance to the piper.*
A. NO CHANGE B. *Dance To the Piper* C. *Dance to the Piper* D. *Dance To The Piper*

7 They invited us to their picnic and we were fed charcoal-broiled chops.
A. NO CHANGE B. we was fed C. omit *we* D. fed us

8 As a rule we usually meet on Monday nights.
A. NO CHANGE B. , usually, C. omit *usually*

Selecting acceptable sentences. Still another variation of the kind of exercise designed to test your knowledge of acceptable English forms presents sentences in groups of three or four. In some of the groups all but one of the sentences contain "errors" in grammar or usage. In other groups, the "errors" are points of style—lack of parallel structure, redundancy, faulty word placement, or awkward expression. In these groups you are expected to pick out the best sentence according to the standards of formal English. Here are some sample items from this kind of test:

1 A. She must feel strangely wearing one brown and one blue shoe.
   B. Dave is a poor bridge partner, but he plays Scrabble very good.
   C. Margaret annoys people because she always acts so wise.
2 A. Driving through Ames, many fine homes can be seen.
   B. Built in 1960, the house is completely modern, both inside and out.
   C. Standing on his feet all day, calluses soon developed.

In the first sentence group, in Sentence A, the adjective *strange*, not the adverb *strangely*, should be used after the linking verb *must feel* to describe the subject; and in Sentence B, the transitive verb *plays* should be modified by an adverb, *well*. In the third sentence, *wise* is correct after *acts* because *acts* is used in the sense of "pretends to be." Only Sentence C, therefore, is acceptable. Example 2 contains two dangling introductory phrases. Only in Sentence B does the participial phrase refer logically to the subject it modifies.

***Exercise* 10**   On your paper, after the number of the sentence group, write the letter of the best sentence in that group.

1   A. Without raising her voice, she managed to quiet the children.
    B. She did not raise her voice, managing nevertheless to quiet the children.
    C. Without raising her voice, the children were quieted.

2   A. Joan is not only pretty and full of fun, but also a very intelligent girl.
    B. Joan is not only pretty, but full of fun and a very intelligent girl.
    C. Joan is not only pretty and full of fun, but also very intelligent.

3   A. Because they left without permission, they have been suspended.
    B. On account of leaving without permission, they have been suspended.
    C. Being that they left without permission, they have been suspended.

4   A. You whistle almost as good as he does.
    B. Do you feel as bad as you look?
    C. He sure did good in the track meet.

5   A. You were the most unpredictable of the two contestants.
    B. She was more attractive and more friendlier then Ellen.
    C. The puppy is noisier than the cat when they are playing.

6   A. The farm machinery, including a tractor and a plow, have been sold.
    B. The farm machinery, including a tractor and a plow, has been sold.
    C. The farm machinery, including a tractor and a plow has been sold.

7   A. We were tired and we were hungry and we decided to pitch camp immediately and prepare our evening meal.
    B. We were tired and we were hungry. So we decided to pitch camp immediately and prepare our evening meal.
    C. Because we were tired and hungry, we decided to pitch camp immediately and prepare our evening meal.

8   A. We saw a large snake as we walked through the woods that had green and yellow stripes.
    B. Walking through the woods, we saw a large snake with green and yellow stripes.
    C. Walking through the woods, a large snake was seen that had green and yellow stripes.

329

Scrambled Paragraphs

A test of your ability to organize ideas in a logical order consists of paragraphs in which the sentences have been scrambled.

By noting the natural relationship between certain ideas, the connecting words in the sentences, and other clues, you should be able to rearrange the sentences in their original logical order.

Such a test requires that you recognize coherence in writing and that you understand the principles of good paragraph construction. [In preparing for this type of exercise, you will do well to review carefully Chapter 2 in this book, dealing with the writing of paragraphs. You will find that Exercise 9 on page 53 is like the type of question frequently used on standardized examinations.]

For this kind of question, a rather complicated answer form is used to ensure your getting full credit for every relationship that you indicate correctly, even though your answer as a whole is not perfect. Directions may be similar to this:

Directions: The sentences that follow are not in their proper order. Read them and decide how they should be arranged to make a well-organized paragraph. Do not leave out any sentence. Jot down (on scratch paper) the correct order of the sentences, and then answer the questions that follow.

In answering the questions, use X to mean that no sentence follows. If you have arranged the sentences in a group to read in the order B C A D, you will answer the question "Which sentence did you put after D?" by writing X.

Here is a sample of such a question:

A. A year ago the downtown section of Kalamazoo, Michigan, was typical of this old-fashioned urban confusion.
B. Today the same blocks have been transformed into a quiet, carless mall decorated with shrubbery and pools, with ample parking a few blocks away.
C. The noisy jumble of creeping cars, dodging pedestrians, and nonexistent parking space that most U.S. city-dwellers know as "downtown" can be untangled, as a few cities have strikingly demonstrated.
D. The area was decaying, no new buildings had been put up there in 25 years, and shoppers were deserting it in favor of suburban shopping centers.—"Downtown Gets Uplift," *Life,* October 29, 1959.

1) Which sentence did you put first?
2) Which sentence did you put after A?
3) Which sentence did you put after B?
4) Which sentence did you put after C?
5) Which sentence did you put after D?

The most logical order for these sentences is C A D B, so that the paragraph would read as follows:

The noisy jumble of creeping cars, dodging pedestrians, and nonexistent parking space that most U.S. city-dwellers know as "downtown" can be untangled, as a few cities have strikingly demonstrated. A year ago the downtown section of Kalamazoo, Michigan, was typical of this old-fashioned urban confusion. The area was decaying, no new buildings had been put up there in 25 years, and shoppers were deserting it in favor of suburban shopping centers. Today the same blocks have been transformed into a quiet, carless mall decorated with shrubbery and pools, with ample parking space a few blocks away.

Once you have established the logical order of the sentences, you can answer the questions that follow. For this example, your answers will read C D X A B. Note that in these answers, the order in which the letters are listed is not the same as the order of the sentences in the unscrambled paragraph.

The first step in handling this type of exercise item is to read through all the sentences and to find the one that logically will stand first. From this, the pattern of the other sentences can be worked out by recognizing the various connecting words and other sentence links. [See Chapter 2.]

***Exercise* 11**   Follow the directions on page 330 for arranging in logical order the sentences in the following paragraphs.

1   A. At first she was chairman of the House Committee on the District of Columbia for five years, the first woman to head a Congressional committee.
   B. She held this important chairmanship until 1947, when she became a member of the House Administration Committee.
   C. Mrs. Norton was the first woman elected to Congress by the Democratic party.
   D. Then she was named to the House Labor Committee and in 1937 became its chairman.

   1) Which sentence did you put first?
   2) Which sentence did you put after A?
   3) Which sentence did you put after B?
   4) Which sentence did you put after C?
   5) Which sentence did you put after D?

2   A. Like the old proverb about the weather, everyone talks about the poor quality of television entertainment, but most of us do little to effect a desirable change.
   B. But how many complainers take the positive step of praising the station, the sponsor, and the producer that provide good entertainment and public service?
   C. After all, a station director reading a letter of criticism merely knows what the writer doesn't like; only if we make it a point to commend the programming we approve will there be more hours of that kind of viewing to enjoy.

D. Some of us, true, do make an effort of sorts; that is, we send off a letter of protest when something on the screen particularly annoys us.

1) Which sentence did you put first?
2) Which sentence did you put after A?
3) Which sentence did you put after B?
4) Which sentence did you put after C?
5) Which sentence did you put after D?

3 A. For this reason, you should join only those organizations for which you have sufficient time and enthusiasm to be an active member.
   B. One important aspect of college life is, of course, participation in extracurricular activities.
   C. You do neither yourself nor the organization you join any good if you can make no real contribution to the group's success.
   D. In your eagerness to enjoy this kind of college fun, however, beware of spreading your energies too thin.

1) Which sentence did you put first?
2) Which sentence did you put after A?
3) Which sentence did you put after B?
4) Which sentence did you put after C?
5) Which sentence did you put after D?

4 A. If, on the other hand, he reads the questions carefully, makes sure he understands what is expected of him on a particular test, and works thoughtfully and cautiously, the test will inevitably reveal a true picture of his actual ability.
   B. All he has to do is permit himself to panic and to start marking up the answer sheet without taking time to think.
   C. The proper attitude is almost as important a factor for success in writing achievement tests as is the information a student possesses.
   D. A well-informed and able student can easily make a poor showing on such a test.

1) Which sentence did you put first?
2) Which sentence did you put after A?
3) Which sentence did you put after B?
4) Which sentence did you put after C?
5) Which sentence did you put after D?

Interlinear Tests

A kind of composition test frequently used consists of a piece of prose that is in need of revision. The passage used for such a test is printed with wide spaces between the lines so that you have room to make whatever corrections or improvements you think are desirable. You may wish, for example, to cross out unnecessary words, change the position of misplaced words, or cross out and rephrase more effectively parts of sentences or whole sentences. You are not expected to rewrite the entire passage.

Here is the kind of passage you might be expected to revise:

> The tornado is the most violent of storms. It is a whirlpool of winds. These winds spin around a center of low pressure at speeds up to 500 m.p.h. Tornadoes may strike anywhere in the world, including the United States, and they may strike at any time. In the United States most frequently they occur in the plains states in the late Spring and early Summer.
>
> As a general rule, a tornado usually developes at a time when a mass of cold dry air colliding with hot moist air causes the warm air to rise up rapidly. Which, in turn, sets off a revolving motion. As the air whirls moisture is condensed to form a greenish-black cloud sheet. The tornado cloud itself is the familiar twisting black funnel-shaped mass. It drops down from this cloud sheet.
>
> A tornado creates great destruction generally. Weaving along the ground like a giant vacuum cleaner, everything in its path is sucked up. The great differences in air pressure that it generates also causes windows to shatter, roofs to cave in, and buildings often collapse.

You can see that to improve this theme, you would have to make changes of various kinds. Errors in punctuation, incorrect verb forms, and other departures from acceptable grammar and usage you could probably correct without difficulty. Less easy to deal with, however, are sentence fragments, dangling modifiers, non-parallel constructions, and other faults which interfere with the composition's effectiveness. [You will find help in handling problems of this kind in Chapter 10, "Improving Sentence Structure," and in Chapter 11, "Writing Effective Sentences."] There is usually not just one right way to make the needed changes. Read through the composition again and decide what improvements you would make. Then look at the possible revision that follows:

> The tornado, is the most violent of storms, It is a whirlpool
>
> of winds/ These winds *that* spin around a center of low pressure at
>
> speeds up to 500 m.p.h. *miles an hour.* Tornadoes may strike anywhere in the
>
> world/ including the United States, and they may strike *and* at any
>
> time. In the United States (most frequently) they occur, in the
>
> plains states in the late Spring and early Summer.

~~As a general rule, a~~ A tornado usually ~~developes~~ develops ~~at a time~~ when a mass of cold dry air ~~colliding~~ collides with hot moist air, ~~causes~~ causing the warm air to rise ~~up~~ rapidly. ~~Which,~~ This, in turn, sets off a revolving motion. As the air whirls, moisture is condensed to form a greenish-black cloud sheet. The tornado cloud itself ~~is~~ the familiar twisting, black funnel-shaped, mass, ~~It~~ drops ~~down~~ from this cloud sheet.

A tornado creates great destruction generally. Weaving along the ground like a giant vacuum cleaner, it sucks up everything in its path ~~is sucked up~~. The great differences in air pressure that it generates also ~~causes~~ cause windows to shatter, roofs to cave in, and buildings ~~often~~ to collapse.

Taste and Sensitivity

A student's ability to recognize elements of style, such as tone, effective figurative language, rhythm, and the like, may be tested in several ways, using prose or poetry.

Prose passages. One type of examination includes several passages of prose with a phrase or clause omitted from each. Following each passage are a number of items from which you are asked to choose the one that you consider most appropriate in style and meaning to complete the passage. This is a typical example:

How strange a checkerboard of Providence is the life of man! and by what secret different springs are the affections hurried about, _______!—Daniel Defoe, *Robinson Crusoe.*

A. as different circumstances present
B. as we proceed to shuffle off this mortal coil
C. as we wend our weary way down life's highway
D. as fate kicks us around

In this passage, A is the expected answer. The idea of B makes no sense whatsoever; C is a cliché and not in keeping with the writer's style; and D, of course, is completely wrong in tone for the rest of the passage.

***Exercise* 12**   On your paper, after the appropriate number, write the letter of the item that best completes each prose passage below.

1 Satire is merely a literary way of raising a laugh at the expense of some person or thing. The writer can deliberate as long as he wishes in picking out the weakest points _____.—Dudley Miles and Robert C. Pooley, *Literature and Life in England.*
   A. in the subject that he holds up to derision
   B. in his adversary
   C. that it is his good fortune to apprehend
   D. of the poor bloke he wants to make a laughingstock of

2 He maintained a belligerent attitude toward all well-dressed men. To him fine raiment was allied to weakness, and _____.
   —Stephen Crane, *Maggie.*
   A. so he never wore clean clothes
   B. he wasn't afraid of anything
   C. he went out of his way to pick fights with dudes
   D. all good coats covered faint hearts

3 In the course of time, we grow to love things we hated and hate things we loved. Milton is not so dull as he once was, nor perhaps Ainsworth so amusing. It is decidedly harder to climb trees, _____.—R. L. Stevenson, "Crabbed Age and Youth."
   A. and much easier to sit around and talk
   B. not to mention running up hill
   C. and not nearly so hard to sit still
   D. an occupation best left to youth

4 At the voting-place they told him a clerk was wanted and asked if he could write. Of course, he might have answered that where he came from in Indiana he used to write letters for the whole township; instead he answered with an up-and-down of careless inflections, "_____"—Carl Sandburg, *The Prairie Years.*
   A. I'd be delighted to help you out.
   B. Oh, I guess I can make a few rabbit tracks.
   C. How much are clerks paid?
   D. Certainly I can write.

Poetry excerpts.   Another test of your taste and sensitivity to language uses stanzas of poems with a single line omitted. You are given directions very much like the following:

Directions: The dots in each of the following stanzas indicate that a line has been omitted. Following each stanza are four suggested lines which you might insert. However, only one of the lines is appropriate to the stanza; the others are unsuitable in various ways. On your paper, after the number of each line, indicate whether that line is or is not appropriate by writing:

A. if the line is appropriate
B. if the line is inappropriate in rhythm or meter

C. if the line is inappropriate in style or tone
D. if the line is inappropriate in meaning

Following is a sample item from this kind of exercise:

I know not whether Laws be right,
    Or whether Laws be wrong;
All that we know who lie in gaol
    Is that each wall is strong;
And that each day is like a year,

. . . .

           —Oscar Wilde, "The Ballad of Reading Gaol."

1) And year by year the days keep marching on.
2) A year whose days are long.
3) What's left is but a song.
4) And a ten-year stretch too long.

In this sample, the appropriate line (to be marked *A* on your paper) is Line 2). Line 1) is inappropriate in rhythm (and you should mark it *B*). Line 3) does not fit the rest of the stanza in meaning (to be marked *D*), and Line 4) does not fit the style or tone of the verse (to be marked *C*).

Exercise **13** Follow the directions on page 335 for completing poetry excerpts.

1 There's tempest in yon hornèd moon
    And lightning in yon cloud
But hark the music, mariners!
    The wind is piping loud;
The wind is piping loud, my boys,
    The lightning flashes free—
While the hollow oak our palace is,

. . . .

    —Allan Cunningham, "A Wet Sheet and a Flowing Sea."

  1) Our heritage the sea.
  2) Its moat the deep blue sea.
  3) It's tough to be at sea.
  4) Our domain the sea will ever be.

2 We have short time to stay, as you
    We have as short a spring;

. . . .

    As you, or anything.
           —Robert Herrick, "To Daffodils."

  1) We see our winter come just as swiftly
  2) As quick a growth to meet decay
  3) As many tasks to do each day
  4) As brief a time to live it up

3   He that roars for liberty
        Faster binds a tyrant's power;
    And the tyrant's cruel glee

    .   .   .   .

                    —Alfred, Lord Tennyson, "The Vision of Sin."

    1) Foretells, alas, the children's hour.
    2) Makes a must the freer hour.
    3) Calls forth eventually the freer hour.
    4) Forces on the freer hour.

4   The southern wind
    Doth play the trumpet to his purposes,
    And by his hollow whistling in the leaves

    .   .   .   .

                    —William Shakespeare, *King Henry IV, Part I.*

    1) Would call to mind my lady far away.
    2) Foretells a tempest and a blustering day.
    3) Predicts a rainstorm and a windy day.
    4) Plays an eerie note that rouses all the drowsing trees.

K E Y

Exercise 1:   1 D, 2 B, 3 A, 4 C, 5 D, 6 E
Exercise 2:   1 C, 2 E, 3 B, 4 A, 5 E, 6 D
Exercise 3:   1 C, 2 D, 3 B, 4 A, 5 E, 6 D
Exercise 4:   1 C, 2 D, 3 B, 4 D, 5 E, 6 A, 7 E, 8 C, 9 A, 10 B
Exercise 5:   1 E, 2 D, 3 A, 4 B, 5 D, 6 B
Exercise 6:   1 denial, 2 acceptance, 3 caress, 4 chimney, 5 separate,
    6 government, 7 apparatus, 8 evidence, 9 beginning, 10 pic-
    nicker
Exercise 7:   1–1) C, 2) D, 3) C; 2–1) C, 2) A, 3) E; 3–1) A,
    2) D
Exercise 8:   1 (4), 2 (1), 3 X, 4 (3), 5 (2)
Exercise 9:   1 B, 2 D, 3 A, 4 C, 5 B, 6 C, 7 D, 8 C
Exercise 10:   1 A, 2 C, 3 A, 4 B, 5 C, 6 B, 7 C, 8 B
Exercise 11:   1–1) C, 2) D, 3) X, 4) A, 5) B; 2–1) A, 2) D, 3) C,
    4) X, 5) B; 3–1) B, 2) X, 3) D, 4) A, 5) C; 4–1) C, 2) X,
    3) A, 4) D, 5) B
Exercise 12:   1 A, 2 D, 3 C, 4 B
Exercise 13:   1–1) A, 2) D, 3) C, 4) B; 2–1) B, 2) A, 3) D, 4) C;
    3–1) D, 2) C, 3) B, 4) A; 4–1) D, 2) A, 3) C, 4) B

BY
"LORD" TIMOTHY DEXTER

15 *Punctuation*

SOYOUHATETOBOTHERWITHPUNCTUATIONDOYOUWELLJUSTRUN
YOUREYEOVERTHISTHISISSOMETHINGLIKETHEWAYTHEEARLIEST
MANUSCRIPTSUSEDTOLOOKEXCEPTTHATTHEIRLETTERSWEREHARDER
TOREADWOULDNTYOUSAYTHATWEHADMADEALITTLEPROGRESS

How would *you* have liked to read the earliest manuscripts—written without punctuation marks and with the words all run together? Even with the words separated, the job is none too easy when there is no punctuation:

> So you hate to bother with punctuation do you well just run your eye over this this is something like the way the earliest manuscripts used to look except that their letters were harder to read wouldnt you say that we had made a little progress

At the beginning of the nineteenth century a man who called himself "Lord" Timothy Dexter actually wrote a pamphlet in this way—and then added a page of miscellaneous punctuation marks with which he invited his readers to "peper and solt" the pamphlet "as they plese." We can certainly be glad that other authors have not followed his example.

Punctuating for Meaning

As readers, we all depend greatly upon punctuation to help us interpret the meaning of what we read. As writers, we, in turn, have a responsibility to *our* readers—to make *our* intended meaning as clear as possible. Punctuation plays a great part in our achieving this objective. Punctuation marks (like the pauses and the changes in inflection that we use in speech) help others to understand more readily the meaning we intend our words to convey. Through our use of punctuation marks we can separate ideas that do not belong together. We can group and keep together ideas that we feel are related. We can give emphasis to ideas we want emphasized, so that their importance can be easily seen.

Punctuation marks are as important to readers as the symbols on a composer's score telling how to play or interpret the music. If we use too few punctuation marks, our readers will probably have to read many of our sentences twice in order to grasp our meaning. If we use too many marks, our readers may be slowed down in their reading and become annoyed at such needless interruptions. But if we use punctuation marks appropriately, our sentences (if phrased effectively) will be pleasant and easy to read.

PRACTICE IN PUNCTUATION

In the Index, for convenient reference, you will find a summary of the uses of each mark of punctuation, with illustrations. At the head of each of the exercises in this chapter, you will be referred to particular Index articles which explain and illustrate the marks to be used in punctuating the sentences in the exercise. You will find that gaining familiarity with these Index articles will be time well spent, partly because you will be reviewing punctuation practices and partly because you will be gaining facility in using the Index as a reference tool, so that you can easily refer to these articles (or sections of them) whenever questions of punctuation arise in your own work throughout the year.

Ending Sentences

Before doing Exercise 1, read these articles in the Index: *Period* (section 1), *Question mark* (sections 1 and 3), *Exclamation mark, Dash* (section 6), *Ellipsis* (section 2).

Exercise 1 Decide which punctuation mark should be used at the end of each of the following sentences. On a sheet of paper, write the number of each sentence, the last word, and then the appropriate mark —period, question mark, exclamation mark, dash, or ellipsis. If you think a sentence could end with either of two marks, write both and be ready to explain when you would use the first and when the second.

1 Watch out   Don't you see that car coming
2 Will you please confirm the order
3 Was the order ever confirmed

4   The nurse asked if Bob wanted anything before she left
5   Ouch   My toe   Why don't you look where you're going
6   We wondered why Uncle Paul never talked about his war experiences in Korea
7   The mail hasn't come yet, has it
8   Never had he been so insulted before
9   What does Ted mean by coming in at three in the morning
10   Dad asked Mom what she would like for her birthday
11   Phil worried about how he could pay the bill
12   Then it's agreeable to all that we sponsor the carnival
13   The new baby sitter should be satisfactory, and yet
14   You saw Jean at the supermarket yesterday   You couldn't have Jean is sick in bed with the mumps
15   Did you know that Catherine the Great wrote stories for her grandchildren
16   But why shouldn't she study Russian if she wants to
17   What you don't know may hurt you
18   Am I ever tired
19   What possible excuse can she come with this time
20   You're Bill's cousin from Montana, aren't you
21   So you've been raiding the refrigerator every night
22   Mr. Mearles wasn't really a grouch, but

Commas in Compound Sentences

Before doing Exercise 2, read this article in the Index: **Comma** (section 1).

Exercise **2**   All but two of the following are compound sentences in which the independent clauses are to be separated by commas. On a sheet of paper, write the number of each sentence. After it, write the word that should be followed by a comma, the comma itself, and the conjunction following. If no comma is needed, write "None."

1   Ted opened his mouth to speak but only a croak came out.
2   In the last sentence a comma is essential for the meaning isn't clear without it.
3   The TV repairman didn't show up in time so we missed our usual programs.
4   Alice opened the windows and the door slammed shut.
5   We didn't get a letter from Aunt Ella or Ken would have been at the station to meet her.
6   On the way back to school they met Sharon and Cathy and David gave her their tickets.
7   Everyone in the office came on time but the boss was still grumpy.
8   Mr. Mills chose the diamond-studded watch and asked to have it charged to his account.

9   Marie must have been tired or sick for she left an hour early.
10 Ben had already eaten his breakfast and fed the horse and the cow but Andy had not yet stirred.
11 Larry was willing to wait for Mrs. Ellis had always been kind to him.
12 They didn't know a word of French yet they could follow the movie from the English subtitles at the bottom of the screen.
13 Outside the post office the three old men sat in their customary chairs and entertained a new group of youngsters with stories about the Spanish-American War.
14 I stayed home to help Mom and Dad went to the garage with Phil.
15 Ruth wouldn't admit the mistake nor would she take any advice.

Setting Off Introductory Clauses and Phrases

Before doing Exercise 3, read this article in the Index: *Comma* (section 4).

Exercise 3   Read the following sentences and decide where commas are needed to set off introductory clauses and verbal phrases. On a sheet of paper, write the number of each sentence. After it, write the last word of the clause or phrase and the comma that should follow it. Some sentences do not require a comma. Write "None" after the numbers of these sentences.

1   When Marge telephoned Kathleen had already left for school.
2   Hearing sounds in the apartment above Eileen went up to deliver the package.
3   After promising to pay Nat forgot to mail the check.
4   To keep their hands from getting cold women used to put hot potatoes in their muffs.
5   While tourists gathered to watch the troop of dragoons went through the time-honored formalities of changing the guard.
6   Not wanting to complain about the late hours Sue kept silent.
7   To take pictures under water requires a quick eye and a steady hand.
8   Before leaving Carolyn straightened up the apartment and washed the breakfast dishes.
9   To impress Alice George would have stopped at nothing.
10 When the time came for Mr. Wilson to leave the company presented him with a gold watch.
11 While Paul and I were watching a deer came to drink.
12 Wanting to help Joyce tried to change the subject.
13 If you can be at the auditorium an hour before curtain time.
14 But when Kay came there were no more red suits in her size.
15 Making frequent trips to the pawnbroker seemed inevitable to Mr. Micawber.

Comma for Clearness

Before doing Exercise 4, read this article in the Index: **Comma** (section 8).

Exercise 4 Read the following sentences and decide where commas are needed to separate words that might be mistakenly run together when read for the first time. On a sheet of paper, write the number of each sentence. After it, write the word that should be followed by a comma. After each of these words, place the comma. Be ready to explain why you have punctuated as you have.

1 During the spring vacation plans are a frequent topic of conversation.
2 Why don't you think it over now and then write me your decision?
3 Ever since Mike has kept away from hornets' nests.
4 Tell those who want to come to come quietly and to shut the door after them.
5 With these students will be admitted at half price.
6 Next May Pat and Ann will both have worked here one year.
7 To the great obstacles are challenges to be faced.
8 Just the week before Don had accepted the job in Quincy.
9 Without her sister Carol seemed more vivacious.
10 Even one hour before the miners might have been saved.
11 Because of her safety regulations are now strictly enforced.
12 Most of the people who came came out of curiosity.
13 Imagine her surprise when instead of twenty nine showed up.
14 I say that what he does does make a great deal of difference.
15 Outside the house looked spacious and inviting.

Setting Off Elements Within the Sentence

Before doing Exercise 5, read this article in the Index: **Comma** (sections 2, 6, 7b, and 9).

Exercise 5 Read the following sentences and decide where commas are needed (to set off interrupting elements, appositives, contrasting expressions, etc.). On a sheet of paper, write the number of each sentence. After it, write any word or words that should be followed by a comma. After each of these words, place the comma. Be ready to explain why you have punctuated as you have.

1 The car stalled near Masset a small fishing village on the north coast of Graham Island.
2 Well he surely didn't cut much of a figure did he?
3 Strange as it seems Pat moved from Northfield Massachusetts to Northfield Minnesota.

4 That point to be sure might well have been made earlier.
5 Sometimes however the customer may be wrong.
6 But the next time Phil took Judy not Barbara to the dance.
7 On June 14 1919 John Alcock and Arthur Brown made the first nonstop Atlantic flight from St. John's Newfoundland to Clifden Ireland.
8 After all Dad did promise to meet us here at five o'clock didn't he Mary?
9 A Swedish chemist Nils Sefström discovered vanadium in 1831.
10 No Dr. Brown this time it's not Ted but Peggy who needs you.
11 From the top of Aloha Tower the tallest building in Honolulu we had a marvelous view of the city and its environs.
12 By the way where were you that evening Dave?
13 At the last moment of course Uncle Will couldn't find his favorite hat a battered brown fedora.
14 In 1959 at Iron Mountain Michigan Jim Brennan equaled the U.S. ski-jumping record set on February 18 1951 at Steamboat Springs Colorado by Ansten Samuelstuen of Norway.
15 Miss Allen it seems thought yours were better written than mine.
16 Mike Murphy Jr. was the next person to be interviewed.
17 Peter's new address is 1001 Cottonwood Street Grand Forks 3 North Dakota.
18 Ivan III became known as Ivan the Great; Ivan IV as Ivan the Terrible.
19 Oh the book you want is probably on the reserve shelf Pat.

Separating Items in Series

Before doing Exercise 6, read these articles in the Index: **Comma** (sections 3, 10e, and 10f), **Semicolon** (section 3).

Exercise 6   Read the sentences and decide where punctuation marks—commas or semicolons—are needed to separate items in a series. On a sheet of paper, write the number of each sentence. After it, write any word or words that should be followed by a punctuation mark. After each of these words, place the appropriate mark. Three of the sentences also need marks to set off various sentence elements. Be sure to include these marks in your answers. If no punctuation is needed, write "None."

1 As a young boy Frederick the Great liked to study French play the flute and write poetry.
2 On a cold blustery day in Chicago Sally's hat blew off zoomed ten feet up glided slowly down and landed right in front of a speeding car.
3 Mrs. Williams was too busy that morning to care who the salesman was whom he represented or what he wanted to sell.

4   The gnarled stunted weather-beaten trees were the one landmark Mr. Barnes could recognize after all these years.

5   Shrilly piercingly insistently the alarm rang out through the quiet village streets.

6   The company has subsidiaries in Caracas Venezuela Bogotá Colombia Lima Peru and La Paz Bolivia.

7   We looked for Mary Lou's pearl in the chair under the sofa and all around the baseboard.

8   The Dutch flag has horizontal red white and blue stripes.

9   Citrons bergamots tangelos and kumquats are all citrus fruits.

10   Frank Adams our former director of research made many enemies because he was impetuous outspoken and vain.

11   Last week the seniors elected Victor Swanson president Maureen Evans vice-president Geraldine Smith secretary and Virginia O'Keefe treasurer.

12   Little Maisie cried loudly angrily and persistently.

13   The restaurant was popular because it was near the highway there was ample parking space provided the waitresses were young and attractive and the food was excellent.

14   Developing sorting and mounting the color prints took hours.

15   Bibba's friends during her student days in Vienna were Hedwig an Austrian Augusta a German and Sonia a Norwegian.

16   The house was cold and dark and dreary.

17   For their camping trip Rob and Fred loaded their car with cans of peas pork and beans stewed tomatoes and sliced peaches.   345

18   The battered dog-eared book was still Fran's favorite.

19   Samuel Butler tried to prove that an unknown woman wrote the *Odyssey* that Lamarck's theory of evolution was superior to Darwin's and that Handel was a greater musician than Beethoven.

20   Betty's French improved when she had to use it to talk with her landlady to buy groceries in the local market and to find her way around in Paris.

Setting Off Nonrestrictive Modifiers

Before doing Exercises 7 through 11, read these articles in the Index: *Comma* (sections 5 and 6), *Restrictive and nonrestrictive.*

Exercise 7   Decide which of the modifying phrases in the sentences are nonrestrictive and should be set off by commas. On a sheet of paper, write the number of each sentence. After it, write any word or words that should be followed by a comma. After each of these words, place the comma. Write "None" after the number of any sentence in which commas are not needed.

1   George Washington's dental plates carved from rhinoceros ivory were heavy and uncomfortable.

2 Marjory galloped past her pigtails flying behind her.
3 At the bottom of the carton Geneva found a still smaller box also beautifully wrapped.
4 The next witness obviously hostile glowered at the prosecutor.
5 Every woman coming into the store on the opening day received a red rose.
6 Ted Evans ponderous in his diving equipment was hoisted over the side of the tugboat by a small crane.
7 Didn't the man wearing a Santa Claus costume look vaguely familiar?
8 The new hat limp and wet after the rain had been carelessly tossed on the hall table.
9 The main lodge was crowded and noisy with suitcases piled high inside the door and people clamoring for attention.
10 Whistler's mother dressed in black sits on a straight-backed chair her hands resting in her lap.
11 We thought that the hall poorly lighted and shabby was a fitting introduction to the rest of the house.
12 The night-blooming cereus was obviously thriving with new shoots jutting out like spears.
13 Mr. Kane wearing a Santa Claus costume led the folk dancing perspiration dripping down his face.
14 A Swedish engineer and a Brazilian diplomat assigned to the United Nations were the first to disembark from the *Queen Mary.* The diplomat greeted by a bevy of photographers and reporters smiled at everyone and answered questions briefly.
15 Uncle Paul stretched out on the sofa started to snore the *Evening Post* rising and falling with each breath.

Exercise 8 Decide which of the adverb clauses in the sentences are non-restrictive and should be set off by commas. On a sheet of paper, write the number of each sentence. After it, write any word or words that should be followed by a comma. After each of these words, place the comma. Write "None" after the number of any sentence in which commas are not needed.

1 The strange little man looked furtively around almost as if he feared pursuit.
2 Only then after the forest fire was well under control did the men realize how weary and muscle-sore they were.
3 The small pepper berries are picked as soon as they begin to turn red.
4 You will have to admit that Irene's views are vividly and forcefully expressed whether you agree with them or not.
5 Two weeks later when Mr. Clancy's offer finally came Art was in an army training camp in Texas.
6 Don merely shook his head in amazement probably because he did not know what to say.

7 Meanwhile just as we had suspected Mrs. Olson's pain increased though she did her best to hide it.

8 Maureen sat so far back in the auditorium that she couldn't hear the speaker no matter how hard she tried.

9 But at that very moment before anyone even suspected what he was up to Barclay jumped through the window and escaped.

10 Mr. Barnes however much you dislike him is an excellent actor.

Exercise 9 Decide which of the adjective clauses in the sentences are nonrestrictive and should be set off by commas. On a sheet of paper, write the number of each sentence. After it, write any word or words that should be followed by a comma. After each of these words, place the comma. Write "None" after the number of any sentence in which commas are not needed.

1 Marguerite who was surer of her French than the others spoke to the waiter first.

2 During the French attack on Lisbon the Portuguese royal family fled to Brazil where they remained for fourteen years.

3 The nominating committee finally chose Alvin Cobbs whom few in the party had ever heard of before.

4 Cyrano de Bergerac who was unduly sensitive about the size of his nose fought duels with anyone who taunted him about it.

5 The telephone call was from Jean who sounded really worried.

6 The letter that Don had been expecting came the day after he had left for Miami.

7 Ruth Peers whom I despise was wearing a green satin dress and a floppy straw hat. The hat which was a bilious green made her look like a frump.

8 Francisco de Goya whose oils now grace many museums began his artistic career by painting models for tapestry weavers to copy.

9 During the arctic blizzard Mary and Ted were saved by their sleds which they turned over to provide a windbreak and by their dogs whose thick fur kept them warm.

10 Sue came home from the market with a dozen peaches and two pears. The peaches she put in the refrigerator at once. But the pears which were not ripe yet she left out for a few days.

Exercise 10 The italicized modifiers in these sentences could be punctuated as either restrictive or nonrestrictive, depending on the meaning the writer intended in a particular context. Be ready to explain the difference in meaning when the modifiers are not set off and when they are.

1 The restaurant *recommended by the Fabers* proved to be expensive.

2 The boys *who had volunteered to help decorate the gym* came early.

347

3 Several months after Christmas Helen found more pine needles *under the sofa.*

4 At the bake sale many asked for the mince pie *which Mrs. McMasters had made.*

5 The next day Kay discovered another cigarette burn *on the table.*

6 The two teen-agers *absorbed in the latest hi-fi record* did not see the back door open.

7 Many people praised the costumes *which the art class had designed.*

8 The guards *posted at the west gate* could not hear his shouts for help.

9 George made out the receipt for the rent *as his dad had told him to do.*

10 By five o'clock the three new salesgirls *who were not used to being on their feet all day* were ready to quit.

Exercise **11**   Copy the following sentences, adding modifiers and appositives according to the instructions given before each sentence. Be sure to put in your sentences any punctuation marks needed after the additions are made.

1 Add an appositive to explain that Hannibal was a Carthaginian general:
Hannibal...................used armored elephants in battles against the Romans.

2 Add an adverb clause to indicate that the guest speaker had completed his talk just before Phil's leaving:
Phil left the meeting promptly at 8:15....................

3 Add a participial phrase identifying the girl by the white horse she is riding:
The girl....................will lead the parade.

4 Add an absolute phrase to tell that Timmy's eyes shone with excitement:
Timmy lit the festive candles....................

5 Add an adjective clause to explain that Dodgson is better known as Lewis Carroll:
Charles Lutwidge Dodgson....................wrote *Alice in Wonderland* for a young friend.

6 Add an appositive to explain that Noka was the tracker on the safari:
Noka....................spotted the lions first.

7 Add a participial phrase explaining that the diamond had been stolen from the forehead of a Hindu idol:
A diamond....................brought misfortune to John Herncastle and his niece.

8 Add an adverb clause explaining that Kathy's reason for having friends was probably her being friendly herself:
Kathy soon had friends at the new school....................

9 The first robin was in the elm tree; the second, on the fence. Add a prepositional phrase to make clear that the third robin seen by Ellen was near the bird bath:
Then Ellen saw a third robin...................

10 Add adjectives describing Mrs. Proudie as arrogant and sharp of tongue:
Mrs. Proudie..................is a character in several of Anthony Trollope's Barsetshire novels.

Using Dashes and Parentheses

Before doing Exercise 12, read these articles in the Index: **Dash, Parentheses.**

Exercise **12** Copy the sentences, adding whatever punctuation marks are needed—to set off nonrestrictive, parenthetical, or introductory elements, for example; to mark an abrupt break in the thought; to separate items in series; to enclose letters or figures. If you think a sentence could be punctuated in more than one way, put the alternative marks in brackets [ ] above the first marks. For these sentences, be ready to explain when one set of marks would be better than the other.

1 A shovel a pick a tin pan these were the favorite tools of the miners during the California gold rush.
2 When King Saul sank into one of his black moods only one person could help him David.
3 Then Betty or was it Alice moved that the meeting be adjourned.
4 Pete Williams you remember him don't you had the lead in the senior play.
5 Jean could think of only three things to do with the oversize lamp given her by her in-laws 1 to store it in the attic 2 to donate it to a white-elephant sale or 3 to give it to a neighbor.
6 When Arnie caught the ball but I don't need to tell you what happened then.
7 In September of 1922 Libya had the highest temperature ever recorded anywhere 136 degrees.
8 Soon other members of the family arrived first the twins and then our host himself.
9 The London publishers were surprised to learn that Currer Ellis and Acton Bell were really three young women Charlotte Emily and Anne Brontë.
10 We had trouble understanding our British cousin when he spoke about opening the bonnet the hood of his car to look at the dynamo the generator.
11 There is one woman I'll never forget Miss Murdock my first-grade teacher.

12 In the seventeenth century Salé pronounced sä lä′ was one of the active pirate centers in North Africa.
13 Many exiled kings and pretenders to thrones Umberto of Italy for example and Don Juan of Spain have chosen to live in Portugal.
14 The Japanese are so particular about their *tatami* their floor mats that they remove their shoes before going through the front door.
15 Mrs. Bennet's main concern in life seemed to be to marry off her five daughters Jane Elizabeth Mary Lydia and Kitty.

Using Semicolons to Separate Main Clauses

Before doing Exercise 13, read this article in the Index: **Semicolon.**

Exercise 13 Read the sentences and decide (1) where semicolons should be used to separate main clauses and (2) what other punctuation marks are needed. On a sheet of paper, write the number of each sentence. After it, write any words that should be followed by a punctuation mark. After each of these words, place the appropriate mark.

1 Phil is absolutely tone-deaf still he insists on singing in the barbershop quartet.
2 Now the trip takes three hours then it took three months.
3 After defeating Maxentius in the battle at the Milvian Bridge Constantine the Great became sole emperor of the West after defeating Licinius he became sole emperor of the Roman world.
4 The mountain climbers were tired hungry and discouraged nevertheless they struggled up the slope.
5 If you agree to all our terms however we will sign the contract.
6 George had made no reservations nor did he much care there were plenty of motels available.
7 Stephen Crane the author of *The Red Badge of Courage* wanted to be a soldier in the Spanish-American War however when he failed to pass the physical examination he became a war correspondent instead.
8 Inspired by Voltaire with whom she kept up a voluminous correspondence Catherine the Great tried to bring French culture to Russia but she did little to improve the lot of the serfs.
9 Jim could not eat the curry it was too highly spiced.
10 We had visited the Tower of Belem the Convent of Jeronimos and the Popular Art Museum and the Museum of Coaches was next on our sightseeing schedule.
11 First Roger made black-and-white enlargements of his butterfly prints then he tinted them by hand.

12 With a whir of wings the pigeons rose into the air and circled above the passers-by then they alighted again and resumed their pecking at the bread crumbs.

13 Distracted by a sound she could not identify Maureen looked up from her reading however though the door had opened a crack she noticed nothing at all suspicious.

14 The chairs were intended for children adults were uncomfortable in them.

15 The fan bought at the International Trade Fair however was made of buffalo hide and decorated with Indonesian figures.

16 To impress Faye Clifford bragged about having been in the movies but one thing he neglected to add that he had been an extra for only one day.

17 The form of Thomas Gray's *The Bard* is classical the subject and the setting of the poem however are romantic.

18 The old couple watched the swollen river creeping up the embankment still they refused to leave their home.

19 Mrs. Otis summoned her lawyers to her bedside she wanted to make another will.

20 Although most of the villagers thought the maid had stolen the ring Inspector Evans did not believe her guilty the circumstantial evidence against her seemed too pat.

Using Colons

Before doing Exercise 14, read this article in the Index: **Colon.**

Exercise 14 Read the following sentences and decide where punctuation marks are needed to introduce appositives or quotations, to call attention to a clause that explains a preceding one, to separate items in a series, and to set off nonrestrictive or parenthetical elements. On a sheet of paper, write the number of each sentence. After it, write any word or words that should be followed by a punctuation mark (colon, comma, or semicolon). After each of these words, place the appropriate mark.

1 At the base of the marble statue of John Hancock the first signer of the Declaration of Independence the following inscription is carved "He wrote his name where all nations should behold it and all time should not efface it."

2 Mr. Crane had to fire his new secretary every one of her letters had erasures or misspellings.

3 Six American authors have won the Nobel prize for literature Sinclair Lewis Eugene O'Neill Pearl Buck William Faulkner Ernest Hemingway and John Steinbeck.

4 Of all the inscriptions in the Library of Congress Marilyn remembered only this quotation from Carlyle "The history of the world is the biography of great men."

5 Dickens has given us many memorable characters Scrooge Mr. Micawber David Copperfield Uriah Heep to mention only a few.

6 Harvey Cheyne's enforced work on a Gloucester fishing schooner at ten dollars a month proved invaluable to him for the first time he learned the value of hard work obedience and good will.

7 From the fishermen's large net tumbled a colorful stream of parrot fish sea horses angelfish sea toads sponges crabs and shrimp.

8 Four friends shared the bleak attic room in the Latin Quarter of Paris Rudolph a poet Marcel a painter Schaunard a musician and Colline a philosopher.

9 Ed began his talk with the following quotation from Sir Arthur Conan Doyle "It is a great thing to start life with a small number of really good books which are your very own."

10 Pointers setters retrievers and most spaniels make excellent hunting dogs they are easily trained to find hold and retrieve game they have a keen scent and they are coöperative and gentle.

Using Quotation Marks

Before doing Exercise 15, read this article in the Index: **Quotation marks.**

352

Exercise 15 Copy the sentences, adding quotation marks, capital letters, and all other punctuation that is needed.

1 If you can wait five minutes Kay said to him my vases will be baked and you can use the kiln

2 I'm taking Sue to the dance Phil said who are you taking Jim

3 Just look at this the sales manager said caustically as he pointed to the next item on the expense account

4 Do you see those four dark shapes to your left the whaler asked they're blue whales the biggest of all

5 The opera singer said I have no comment to make then she turned on her heel and left

6 What's wrong with him is he sick the policeman asked

7 In a commencement address Nicholas Murray Butler gave this definition of an expert an expert is one who knows more and more about less and less

8 What a strange excuse Bob exclaimed are you sure that's what he said

9 If you are studying French you will probably enjoy French and English Spoken an essay by Theodore Pratt

10 How proud Mom looked when she said Allan bought me this with the first money he earned

11 I heard someone shout watch out don't you see that car Bill said after that I remember nothing

12 The manager told me he wants you to come in right away Walt told Sally you'd better hurry too he sounds cross

13 In his address to the United States Senate on January 22 1917 Woodrow Wilson stated I am seeking only to face realities and to face them without soft concealments

14 How would you Ruth asked like working for a boss who dictates long letters after four o'clock and then has the nerve to say please get these in the mail before you leave

15 After completing their unit on short stories the class decided to dramatize O. Henry's The Gift of the Magi

Underlining

Before doing Exercise 16, read these articles in the Index: **Underlining, Italics, Titles of books, articles, etc., Ships' names.**

Exercise **16** Copy each of the following sentences, underlining any titles, words, letters, and figures that should be italicized. Supply any other punctuation marks needed in the sentences.

1 Above Paul's desk hung a framed reproduction of Rembrandt's The Night Watch.

2 The foreign students in the class asked why there were so many prefixes with the same meaning un- ir- il- in- dis- and a-.

3 Sidney Allan R.N. the initials stand for Royal Navy not registered nurse was the next person interviewed.

4 In the Vatican Museum Erik saw Praxiteles' Hermes and other outstanding works of classical sculpture.

5 Sohrab and Rustum Matthew Arnold's finest poem is based on an incident in Firdawsi's Book of Kings.

6 Mr. Dawes had mistakenly read a 9 in one column as a 4 naturally he had trouble balancing his books.

7 As the matador extended and swirled his muleta the bull rushed at the red cloth but missed it.

8 Have you read Glenway Wescott's Isak Dinesen Tells a Tale in Harper's Magazine for March 1960?

9 Ingrid Bergman won the Motion Picture Academy Award as the best actress of 1956 for her work in Anastasia.

10 Is perceive spelled with ie or ei?

11 The Dynasts Thomas Hardy's monumental drama about the Napoleonic Wars has 19 acts and 130 scenes.

12 While waiting for her dental appointment Kathy read the latest issues of Holiday The Saturday Evening Post and Life.

13 The New York Times has unusually complete and accurate foreign coverage.

14 The captain of the Queen Elizabeth is being interviewed on Face the Nation this week.
15 Smiles is a long word there is a mile between the two s's.

Avoiding Unnecessary Punctuation

Before doing Exercise 17, read these articles in the Index: **Comma** (section 10), **Question mark** (section 3), **Quotation marks** (section 6). You may also have to refer again to other articles you have already studied, if you have doubts about whether some of the marks in the sentences are needed or not.

Exercise 17 Each of the sentences contains one or more unnecessary punctuation marks. Be ready to tell what these marks are and to explain why they should be omitted.

1 Ann was so tired last night, that she completely forgot, that she was supposed to leave an order for the milkman.
2 Lars did his best, but, not even he could move the heavy log.
3 Coleridge never did finish the poem, "Kubla Khan," which he had begun writing after awakening from a dream.
4 When Peggy flashed her diamond ring,—but you can probably guess the excitement at the office then!!!!
5 Students, who are that much overweight, should not eat double-fudge sundaes, for lunch.
6 Soon the fiddlers were playing, "Turkey in the Straw."
7 The man sitting in front of us on the crowded, subway train, was trying to read his newspaper.
8 Suddenly he put down his paper, and glared at his seatmate, who was also trying to read it.
9 The strangers asked, "why he was in such a hurry, and where he was going."?
10 Did you know that Robert Browning began and ended, one of his poems with the word, *Gr-r-r-*?
11 "Where Mr. Andros goes, what he does, and when he will be back, are no concern of mine as long as he pays his rent," the landlady said.
12 Brocades, silks, linens, pearls, jade, ivory,—these and many other items, make Hong Kong a shopper's paradise.
13 Mrs. Ames answered that "Marie had left over an hour ago."
14 Once more the lights, the crowds, the noise of the city, exhilarated him.
15 The only hope of the men on the deserted island was, that a tramp steamer might veer off its course, and see their improvised, distress signal.
16 The jonquils in the glass bowl on the table, and the roses in the pottery pitcher on the desk came from the Wrights.

354

17 She patiently, and accurately transferred the pattern to the white, linen, cloth.

18 The woman who claimed to be her best (?) friend, was the very one, who had spread all the rumors.

Hyphens

Before doing Exercise 18, read these articles in the Index: **Hyphen, Compound words, Fractions.**

Exercise **18** Decide which words in each of the following sentences should be hyphened. After the number of the sentence, write these words, supplying the hyphens. If no hyphens are needed, write "None."

1 The glib tongued Ulysses resorted to a stratagem to get past the one eyed giant.

2 After counting the one hundred thirty dollars, the cashier put the thirty one dollar bills for Mr. Lee in one pile and the twenty five dollar bills for Mr. Price in another.

3 Jack forgot to enclose a self addressed, stamped envelope.

4 Three fourths of the new houses in the development have been rented.

5 The carved figure is typical of a pre Columbian Aztec culture.

6 The six foot six basketball player was a distinct asset to the team.

7 Because of illness the celebration of their twenty fifth wedding anniversary had been long postponed.

8 He was proud of being a small town sheriff.

9 Are the leaders of the new nation pro American?

10 One fourth of the seniors got ptomaine poisoning at the picnic, probably from the mayonnaise in the potato salad.

11 Our Italian speaking friend got off the bus at Fifty first Street.

12 It was hardly worth while renting the auditorium; it was only two thirds full, probably because of the twenty inch snowfall.

13 Did you think that the speaker was anti intellectual?

14 Guarani, widely spoken in Paraguay, is a South American Indian language.

15 But *self conscious* and *self centered* are not synonyms.

16 Are Benjamin Franklin and Independence Hall on the fifty dollar bill or the one hundred dollar bill?

17 Can't you find a more worth while project?

18 The well to do middle aged woman and her conservatively dressed companion attracted little attention.

19 She said nothing, but her I told you so look was enough.

20 Use your dictionary to check the spelling of *great aunt, half sister, brother in law, fire escape, bird of paradise, olive oil,* and *mother of pearl.*

Capitalization

Before doing Exercise 19, read this article in the Index: *Capital letters.*

Exercise **19** Decide which words in each of the following sentences should be capitalized. After the number of the sentence, write these words, supplying the necessary capital letters.

1 in andrew jackson's time alabama, kentucky, tennessee, and mississippi were considered part of the west, not the south.
2 yesterday professor olson and his wife left for england on the *queen elizabeth.*
3 no, uncle mike, walnut street is one block south of lincoln avenue.
4 during the summer don wears only arrow drip-dry shirts.
5 in 1955 a bust of wilbur wright was added to the hall of fame on the campus of new york university.
6 the buckingham memorial fountain in chicago's grant park is made of georgia marble.
7 at rockefeller center the french tourists especially enjoyed radio city music hall and the studios of the national broadcasting company.
8 before labor day the board of education hired a young man from michigan to teach biology 2, english, and social studies.
9 in 1836 the democrats nominated martin van buren; the whigs, william henry harrison.
10 but oh, how i dreaded giving that five-minute talk in spanish!
11 on june 15, 1215, english noblemen at runnymede forced king john to sign the magna charta, guaranteeing civil and political rights to the people of england.
12 the new york drama critics' circle voted *a man for all seasons* by british playwright robert bolt the best foreign play of the 1961-62 season.
13 yes, thanksgiving always comes on a thursday; easter, on a sunday.
14 tom kent is president of the senior class and vice-president of the latin club at our high school.
15 the campers from stonegate lodge walked indian file through the woods.
16 the story about david and goliath is in the old testament, maurice, not the new testament.
17 you haven't met bill's mother yet, have you, mom?
18 every sunday arlene, a roman catholic, goes to st. patrick's cathedral; peggy, a methodist, to kelvyn park community church.
19 "when the mayor arrives—oh, there you are, mayor!"
20 dad turned first to the article entitled "why the cost of living keeps creeping up."

A

B

C

D

EF

GH

IJK

LMN

By lining up the guides at the edge of this divider page with the marks opposite them on the front edge of the book, you can quickly turn to the section containing the material you want.

OP

QR

S

TUV

WXYZ

INDEX

In the second part of this book, the INDEX, you will find an alphabetically arranged list of entries that fall roughly into four groups:

1) Particular words and constructions (like *sit, set; boughten; irregardless; this here, that there; due to; like, as; reason is because*) that you may have questions about. The Index describes their standing in actual usage today, so that you can decide for yourself whether or not a particular word or construction is appropriate for you to use in a given situation.

2) Grammatical items like *Preposition, Appositives, Relative pronouns, Objective complement, Antecedent, Dangling modifiers, Active and passive voice, Complex sentence.* The Index defines these and gives examples of them.

3) Topics of general interest to speakers and writers of English, such as *Familiar English, Blend, Anglicizing, Divided usage, Colloquial, Imagery, Jargon, Reference books, Readers' Guide.* In discussing these, the Index emphasizes what is likely to be most interesting and most helpful to high-school students.

4) Entries that have to do with the mechanics of writing—for example, *Spelling, Capital letters, Abbreviations, Division of words, Indention, Underlining, Footnotes, Plurals of nouns, Bibliography,* and the various punctuation marks (*Comma, Colon, Exclamation mark, Quotation marks, Parentheses, Dash,* etc.).

Throughout, the Index gives the pronunciation of any words that may be unfamiliar or difficult to pronounce, using the *Thorndike-Barnhart High School Dictionary* symbols. A key to these symbols is given in the article *Pronunciation.*

Subjects that are not discussed in the first part of the book are treated fully in the Index. (Examples are *American and British usage, Homonyms, Analogy, It's me, Double negative, Malapropism.*) Other topics, because they are given a rather full treatment in the chapters, are just briefly summarized in the Index. (See *Reference of pronouns* or *Redundancy* for an example.) Some few, covered in great detail in the first part of the book, are merely listed in the Index with a cross reference to the complete treatment in the chapters. (See *Allusion, Slang, Note taking.*) In general you will find that if you have a specific question (what verb form to use, whether to say *I* or *me*, whether or not to use commas in a certain sentence) the Index will give you the answer. When you want a discussion of a larger subject (the importance of details in paragraph development, beginning a theme effectively) the Index will refer you to the chapters.

To appreciate fully the value of the Index, you should be familiar with Chapter 8, "The Levels of Usage." This chapter not only gives you the background you will need for understanding the book's realistic approach to English usage, but also explains in detail how the Index should be used.

To do some of the exercises in the book, you will have to use the Index. In going over your themes, your teacher may use the marks listed in the entry *Correction marks,* and so refer you to the Index for help in correcting and revising your papers. But as Chapter 8 explains, the Index is meant primarily to be your private reference book—outside, as well as inside, of school. You should get help from it when writing letters or papers, or preparing talks. You should use it to check on new words and constructions that you read or hear, and want to use. Perhaps most important of all, you should browse through this part of the book, reading any articles that arouse your curiosity. By getting well acquainted with the Index, you will become much more confident in your use of current English.

A

a, an A and *an* are called "indefinite articles."

1 The choice between *a* and *an* depends on the beginning *sound*, not the beginning letter, of the word that follows. *A* is used before a consonant sound:

a theme	a *D*	a European capital
a university	a hand-me-down	a one-sided game

An is used before a vowel sound:

an apple pie	an *S*	an encyclopedia
an umbrella	an heirloom	an opening

2 Repeating *a* or *an* before each item of a series helps make the items more distinct. "A peach, a pear, and an apple were left on the plate" is more emphatic than "A peach, pear, and apple were left on the plate."

Abbreviations Abbreviations are appropriately used in lists, footnotes, and technical writing. With certain exceptions, discussed below, they are not appropriate in ordinary writing.

1 *Mr., Mrs., Messrs.,* and *Dr.* are always abbreviated when used as titles before names; *St.* (Saint) often is. *Esq., Jr., Sr.* are usually abbreviated when they follow a name, as are *A.B., B.S., Ph.D.,* and other academic degrees:

Mr. David Bryce, Jr.	Curtis F. Preston, A.M., Ph.D.
Mr. Martin Colfax, Sr.	Messrs. Benton and Drake
St. George	Carl J. Stern, M.D.

WRONG: The Sr. partner called on the Dr. that very day.
RIGHT: The senior partner called on the doctor that very day.
RIGHT: Mr. Fred Jordan, Sr., conferred with Dr. Dun.

2 In formal writing, titles such as *Senator, Reverend, Professor, Governor, Superintendent, Colonel,* and *Honorable* are not abbreviated. In

informal writing, they often are—but only when they precede initials or a given name:

FORMAL	INFORMAL
Senator Bradford Pendleton	Sen. Bradford Pendleton
Reverend James D. Morris	Rev. James D. Morris
Professor D. S. Robinson	Prof. D. S. Robinson

(See **Reverend.**)

3 Certain indications of time—A.D., B.C., *a.m.*, *p.m.*—are always abbreviated when used with figures:

1066 A.D.   399 B.C.   9:45 a.m.   3:15 p.m.

4 A few rather formal Latin expressions are almost always abbreviated:

cf.	confer	compare, see
etc.	et cetera	and so forth
e.g.	exempli gratia	for example
i.e.	id est	that is
et al.	et alii	and others
viz.	videlicet	namely

In informal writing the English equivalents of these Latin phrases are usually more appropriate.

5 Periods are used after abbreviations, except in certain cases:

a) Periods are seldom used with abbreviations of names of government agencies and organizations commonly referred to by their initials: *FHA, FBI, UN, NATO.*

b) Periods are not generally used with scientific and technical abbreviations, regarded more as symbols than as abbreviations: *WCAL* (in radio); *TNT, Rn, H_2O* (in chemistry); *cos, cosec* (in mathematics); *mph, cgs, cps* (used after figures).

c) When an abbreviation comes at the end of a sentence that is punctuated with a period, only one mark is used:

The next bus to Atlanta leaves at 2:15 p.m.
But: What famous conqueror died in 323 B.C.?

ability   After *ability* use *to* and an infinitive:

Miss Tracey has the ability *to* make poetry come alive.   [Not: the ability *of* making.]

Often the idea can be more simply expressed by using *can*:

Miss Tracey can make poetry come alive.

A noun following *ability* is preceded by *in*:

Betty was proud of her remarkable ability *in* design.   [Not: ability *for* design.]

able Using *able* and a passive infinitive instead of *can* results in awkward sentences:

AWKWARD: He is sure that his candidate is able to be elected.
BETTER: He is sure that his candidate can be elected.

above The use of *above* as a noun or adjective to refer to preceding material is appropriate in legal or business writing and in reference works:

The above is a true account of the voyage.
The above prices are subject to change without notice.

In other writing this use of *above* is avoided by many people, and the material identified in some other way: "The account you have just read...," "The prices quoted in the preceding paragraph...," and so on.

Absolute phrases Phrases that have no *grammatical* connection with any part of a sentence, though they are, of course, related in meaning:

Its hull battered and decks awash, the ship could not last much longer.
Horace the cat, *tail twitching ominously,* scowled at the puppy.
Lloyd was sitting in the front seat, *a smug look on his face.*

Absolute phrases offer a writer an effective means of adding details in a minimum number of words. Such phrases are set off from the rest of the sentence by commas.

(For further examples, see Chapter 7, "Participial Phrases," last paragraph, page 153. For suggestions concerning the use of absolute phrases in your own writing, see Chapter 11, "Showing the Comparative Importance of Details," pages 244-245.)

absolutely In informal speech, *absolutely* is used to mean "positively" or "quite":

Bert had absolutely the friendliest grin in town.

In conversation it is used as an emphatic "yes"; in this use, it is regarded as slang.

"Can you be here by 8:30?" "Absolutely."

In most writing (except for written conversation) *absolutely* should be used only in its original meaning, "completely":

Power tends to corrupt; absolute power corrupts absolutely.—Lord Acton
We were absolutely dumfounded at the crowd's enthusiasm.

Abstract and concrete words Concrete words are words that name persons, places, and things that we can see or touch: *actor, Spencer Tracy, Utah, river, mouse, airplane, trousers.* Abstract words are words that name feelings, ideas, and actions—things that we cannot see or touch: *jealousy, liberty, wisdom, honor, selfishness, cheating.*

Accent   In the pronunciation of words of more than a single syllable, one syllable is accented—or stressed—harder than the others. This increased emphasis is called the *primary* or main accent and is generally indicated in dictionaries and word lists by **'**: *be gin', sa lute', the'a ter.*

Words of two or more syllables sometimes also have another syllable stressed, but with less force than is given to the primary accent. This lighter stress is called the *secondary* accent and is indicated by **'**: *meal'time', like'wise', de nom'i na'tion, rep'ar tee'.*

Accent marks   French words that have been added to English sometimes keep the accent marks with which they are spelled in French. Three kinds of accent marks are used:

ACUTE ACCENT: attaché   blasé   fiancée   résumé
CIRCUMFLEX ACCENT: crêpe   tête-à-tête   rôle   fête   château
GRAVE ACCENT: suède   à la mode   à la carte

In informal English these borrowed words are often written without their accent marks, except when the marks are needed to show the pronunciation. In *blasé* and *attaché*, for example, the accents make the pronunciation clear, while *crepe* and *fete* and *role* can easily be pronounced without the help of the marks.

In formal writing, especially in print, the original accent marks are more often used.

361

accompany   When *accompanied* means "escorted" or "attended," the preposition *by* is used:

The contestants were accompanied by their parents.

When it means "supplemented," *with* is used:

Benson accompanied his handshake with a pat on the shoulder.

Remember to keep the *y* when you add the ending *-ing*: *accompany, accompanying.*

Accusative case   See **Objective case.**

acoustics   When *acoustics* means "the qualities of a room or hall that determine how well sounds can be heard in it," it is considered plural and takes a plural verb:

The fine acoustics in the opera house *are appreciated* by music lovers.

When its meaning is "the science of sound," it takes a singular verb (like the science of *physics*):

Acoustics *is* an essential study for an architect.

act When *act* means "seem or pretend to be," or "behave as though one were," it is a linking verb and is followed by an adjective, not an adverb:

> The bears act frantic when they scent the honey. [Not: *frantically.*]
> The boxer acted groggy to trick his opponent.

Active and passive voice A verb is said to be in the active voice when its subject is the doer of the action, and in the passive voice when its subject receives the action. A passive verb is a past participle with some form of the verb *be: is protected, was protected, had been protected,* etc. (Other verb forms are active.)

> ACTIVE: Sturdy sea walls protect the harbor.
> PASSIVE: The harbor is protected by sturdy sea walls.

(For a discussion of the effective use of active and passive verbs, see Chapter 11, "Emphasis Through Forceful Verbs," page 259.)

ad *Ad* is the short, or clipped, form of *advertisement.* Since it is not an abbreviation, it is not followed by a period. The abbreviation is *advt.* or *adv.*

> *Ad* is not usually appropriate in formal style but is used elsewhere. (See **Clipped words.**)

Adage See **Epigram.**

adapt When *adapt* means "adjust" or "make suitable," it is followed by *to:*

> They quickly adapted themselves to the desert.

When it means "modify or alter for a different use," it is followed by *for* or *from:*

> Heggens was able to adapt his novel for the theater.
> The theme song was adapted from a melody by Schubert.

Addresses When an address appears on a list or in a sentence, the second and all following parts are set off by commas:

> William Ford, 2419 N. Broadway Ave., Springfield 3, Mo.
> First prize in the contest went to Mrs. Arnold Foster, 19 Cliff Drive, Helena, Montana.

(For the forms of addresses in letters and on envelopes, see **Business letters.**)

Adjective An adjective modifies a noun or pronoun; that is, it makes the meaning of the noun or pronoun more exact by describing or limiting it: a *tall* building, *many* horses, *Sioux* warriors, a *sitting* duck, *few useful* suggestions.

1 Types. There are two general types of adjectives:

a) *Descriptive adjectives* modify nouns by naming a quality, characteristic, or condition: a *blue* sky, *loud* noises, a *toy* train, a *singing* waiter, a *baked* potato. (Notice that *toy*, often used as a noun, is here used like an adjective; and that *singing* and *baked*, parts of verbs, are here used like adjectives.)

b) *Limiting adjectives* point out in some way the object named or indicate its quantity or number: *this* door, *those* questions, *our eldest* brother, *many* people, *six* weeks, the *second* chapter, *no* money.

Proper adjectives are derived from proper nouns. Sometimes they are used as limiting adjectives: *American* states, *Canadian* provinces; sometimes as descriptive adjectives: *American* culture, *Canadian* education, *African* music. A number of proper adjectives have been used so frequently in a descriptive sense that they have become simple descriptive adjectives, written without a capital: *utopian* schemes, *turkish* towel, *quixotic* behavior.

2 Position of adjectives. (a) Adjectives ordinarily stand immediately before the word they modify:

a *pretty* face   *curly brown* hair   *frequent* trips

Sometimes, though, they are placed after their nouns:

Last of all came Ted, *footsore* and *weary*. [For greater emphasis.]
The castle, *high* above the valley, dominated the countryside. [Adjective is modified by other words.]
Their second child, a son, is heir *apparent* to the throne. [Adjective is part of special compound word.]

b) *Predicate adjectives* follow some form of the verb *be* or some other linking verb (*smell, feel, appear, become*, etc.):

The path is *narrow*.   I felt *sleepy*.   The choir sounds *splendid*.

(See **Linking verb** and "Adjective After Linking Verb," page 212.)

3 Effective use of adjectives. "Think twice before you use an adjective," Carl Sandburg is said to have advised a writer. In following his advice, keep three points in mind. First, the adjectives you use should add to the meaning of your statements, should make your word pictures more exact. Unless they do, they are excess baggage and are better omitted. For example, in the sentence "Before he was twenty, he was the author of a successful best seller," the adjective *successful* adds nothing to the meaning; all best sellers are by definition "successful."

Second, vague, general adjectives like *good, bad, awful,* and *nice* should be avoided, especially in writing. Such adjectives seldom convey exact meanings; they merely express approval or disapproval. Describing a person as *nice,* for example, tells only that you like him, but not why he is likable. Is it because he is *friendly, generous, amusing, honest, impartial, courteous, candid,* or *thoughtful?* Adjectives like these are needed to make descriptions meaningful and exact.

363

Third, avoid overloading your writing with useless, repetitious modifiers, as in "He had great big enormous hands." Using three adjectives here merely clutters up the picture; *great* and *big* add nothing once you have said *enormous*. Remember that it is not the number of adjectives you use, but their exactness, that makes writing effective.

4 Comparison. See Chapter 9, "Comparison," page 214. For the comparison of adjectives like *unique, perfect, round, square, impossible,* see ***Comparison of adjectives and adverbs,*** section 2.

Adjective clause A group of words containing a subject and verb that does the work of an adjective—that is, it modifies a noun or pronoun in the sentence. An adjective clause is usually introduced by a relative pronoun (*who, which, that*) or a relative adverb (*when, where, why, after*):

> The man *who solved the riddle* won the kingdom.   [Modifies *man,* the antecedent of *who.*]
> The climbers needed shoes *that were rugged and warm.*   [Modifies *shoes,* the antecedent of *that.*]
> Williamsburg, Virginia, is a place *where colonial life can be seen at first hand.*   [Modifies *place,* the antecedent of *where.*]

Often no introductory word is used:

> The girl *I met* had striking blue eyes.   [Instead of: *that I met* or *whom ·I met.*]

(For further discussion and examples, see Chapter 7, "Adjective Clauses," page 156. For the effective use of adjective clauses in your own writing, see Chapter 11, "Presenting Effective Word Pictures," page 244. For help with punctuation, see ***Comma,*** section 5.)

Adjective phrases Prepositional, participial, and infinitive phrases are often used as adjectives, modifying a noun or pronoun in their sentences:

PREPOSITIONAL: Plump Mr. Jarvis thought himself a man *of importance.*   [Modifies *man.*]
PARTICIPIAL: *Snapping his fingers,* Smedley beckoned to the waitress. [Modifies *Smedley.*]
PARTICIPIAL: The prize bull, *stung by a wasp,* charged into the crowd. [Modifies *bull.*]
INFINITIVE: The Arab bazaar had many exotic shops *to explore at our leisure.*   [Modifies *shops.*]

ad lib (or ad-lib) From the Latin *ad libitum,* meaning "without restriction." Informal English uses *ad lib* as a verb meaning "to make up as one goes along" or "to depart from a written or memorized speech," and as a noun meaning "a departure from a written or memorized speech":

> Great jazz musicians can ad lib in a style all their own.
> The senator's ad libs were not published with his speech.

adult Pronounced either ə dult′ or ad′ult.

Adverb   **1 Uses.**   (a) Most adverbs are used to modify a verb, an adjective, an adverb, or a whole clause or sentence:

VERB MODIFIERS: I watched *closely.*
They visit us *often.*   [Or: They *often* visit us.]

ADJECTIVE MODIFIERS: Her answer was *rather* sarcastic.
Honest criticism is *completely* welcome.

ADVERB MODIFIERS: The deer approached *quite* cautiously.
He paints *unusually* well.

SENTENCE MODIFIERS: *Unfortunately,* the package arrived late.
Truly, a man's word is his bond.

b) Conjunctive adverbs serve a double purpose—to modify a clause and also to connect it with another clause.

Mr. Hawkins had little faith in Dr. Fulton's ability; *however,* he kept his doubts to himself.

(See ***Conjunctive adverbs.***)

c) Interrogative adverbs are used to introduce questions:

Where does the dawn come up like thunder?
How can we get to the stadium in half an hour?

2 Types.   Adverbs can be conveniently grouped by meaning:

a) Adverbs of manner—tell how:

cleverly   peacefully   better   awkwardly   well   openly

b) Adverbs of time—tell when:

soon   eventually   previously   weekly   now   oftener

c) Adverbs of place and direction—tell where:

here   south   forward   beyond   around   there

d) Adverbs of degree and measure—tell how much or to what extent:

nearly   almost   entirely   much   very
more   somewhat   certainly   quite   less

3 Forms.   Though many adverbs are adjectives or participles plus the ending *-ly* (*neatly, wisely, smilingly, repeatedly*), the *-ly* ending is not a sure sign that a word is an adverb. Some common adjectives have an *-ly* ending: *saintly, costly, manly, stately.* And some adverbs have come down to us from Old English with no special ending to distinguish them: *now, quite, since, then, there, where.*

A number of adverbs have two forms, one ending in *-ly* and one that is the same as the adjective form:

brightly—bright   deeply—deep   highly—high
cheaply—cheap   fairly—fair   lately—late
closely—close   hardly—hard   loudly—loud

nearly—near	secondly—second	smoothly—smooth
quickly—quick	sharply—sharp	tightly—tight
rightly—right	slowly—slow	wrongly—wrong

Some of these pairs are used interchangeably: *Go slowly* or *Go slow*, *Sing loudly* or *Sing loud*. (Formal English is likely to use the *-ly* form of such words; informal English is likely to use the shorter form.) But others cannot be used interchangeably, since the two forms have quite different meanings:

Zero hour drew *near*. But: The work is *nearly* done.
I arrived *late*. But: I haven't seen him *lately*.
Don't rub so *hard*. But: He *hardly* dared to move.

4 Position. For the position of adverbs like *only, just, almost, even, hardly, nearly, scarcely* (in sentences like "He nearly ate all the cookies") see **only.**

5 Effective use. Adverbs, like adjectives, should be used for a definite purpose—to make the meaning more exact, to give the reader a more vivid picture. Adverbs, like all words you use, should also be appropriate to the tone of your writing as a whole. For a specific suggestion concerning appropriateness, see **Conjunctive adverbs,** section 2.

6 Comparison. See Chapter 9, "Comparison," page 214; Chapter 10, "Faulty Comparisons," page 231; and **Comparison of adjectives and adverbs.**

366

Adverb clause A group of words containing a subject and verb that does the work of an adverb—that is, it serves as a modifier answering such questions as How? When? Why? Where? An adverb clause is introduced by one of the subordinating conjunctions: *when, as, as soon as, if, because, although,* etc.

As soon as you went away, the telephone rang. [Tells when.]
If Napoleon had been satisfied, France might never have lost the war. [Tells under what condition.]
Jim was able to finish the test quickly *because he knew the subject well.* [Tells why.]
I want to go *where you go.* [Tells where.]

An adverb clause at the beginning of a sentence is usually set off by a comma unless it is very short and there is no danger of misreading the sentence.

(For further discussion and examples, see Chapter 7, "Adverb Clauses," page 157. For the effective use of adverb clauses in your own writing, see Chapter 11, page 247. For further help with punctuation, see **Comma,** sections 4a and 5.)

Adverb phrases Prepositional phrases and infinitive phrases are often used as adverb modifiers, answering such questions as How? When? Why? Where?

PREPOSITIONAL: He sat *in the first row.* [Tells where.]
The horse walked *with a limp.* [Tells how.]
The holiday begins *at sundown.* [Tells when.]
INFINITIVE: Keller wrote *to express his sympathy.* [Tells why.]

Adverbial nouns Nouns may serve as adverbs, telling when, where, how much, how far, and so on. But even though they do the work of adverbs, they are still considered nouns because they can be modified by adjectives.

The suit cost fifty *dollars.* [Tells how much; is modified by the adjective *fifty.*]
The composition is due the last *week* in May. [Tells when; is modified by the adjective *last* and by the adjective phrase *in May.*]

advertisement Pronounced ad vėr′tiz mənt or ad′vər tīz′mənt.

adviser, advisor *Adviser* has been the more common spelling, but the -*or* form, because of its similarity to *advisory,* is being increasingly used.

ae, oe The digraphs *ae* and *oe,* found in words that come from Greek and Latin, are both pronounced as if they were written *e* (long or short). Today the tendency is to simplify the spelling of such words to match their pronunciation:

367

ORIGINAL	SIMPLIFIED
aesthete	esthete
amoeba	ameba
archaeology	archeology
encyclopaedia	encyclopedia
mediaeval	medieval
phoenix	phenix
subpoena	subpena

Very formal and technical writings generally keep the digraphs. And the digraph is always kept in Latin and Greek proper names (*Caesar, Oedipus*) and in Latin plurals (*alumnae, larvae*).

Dictionaries frequently give both spellings. To find which is preferred for a particular word, consult a dictionary.

affect, effect The similarity in sound causes these words to be confused in spelling. *Affect* is always a verb; it is most frequently used to mean either "influence" or "pretend to have or feel":

Poor nutrition can affect physical growth.
Despite his fear, Caxton affected indifference to the snarling dog.

Effect is used chiefly as a noun, meaning "result":

The approach of Christmas had a marked effect on his behavior.

In formal English *effect* is also used as a verb, meaning "bring about or make happen":

> Learning to dance effected a change in Ted's attitude toward girls.

afflicted Followed by *with,* not *by:*

> Before every test Beth was afflicted with nausea.

again, against Usually pronounced ə gen′ and ə genst′ by Americans. In British usage, ə gān′ and ə gānst′ are more common.

aggravate In formal English *aggravate* means "increase or make worse":

> New snowstorms aggravated the already poor road conditions.

In informal speech it is used to mean "annoy" or "irritate":

> Chester's sarcasm aggravated his sister.

agree The preposition to be used with *agree* depends on the meaning intended:

> Preston always agrees *with* the coach—or pretends to. [Has the same opinion as.]
> Reluctantly Mason agreed *to* their proposal. [Consented to it.]
> Ellen and Jack agreed *on* a present for their aunt. [Came to a common decision about.]
> He seldom orders lobster, because it does not agree *with* him. [Have a good effect on.]

Agreement In grammar, when we say that two words *agree,* we mean that they are the same in person, number, case, or gender. In the sentence "Have either of the boys reported yet?" the subject and the verb do not agree. The subject *either* is singular, and the verb *Have reported* is plural. If the verb is changed to *Has reported,* the two words agree.

  1 A verb agrees with its subject in person and number:

> The first row of seats *is reserved* for them. [Singular verb *is reserved* agrees with singular subject *row.*]
> All the seats in the first row *are reserved* for them. [Plural verb *are reserved* agrees with plural subject *seats.*]

(See Chapter 9, "Agreement with the Subject," page 198.)

  2 A pronoun agrees with its antecedent in person, number, and gender:

> As Glen stopped to tie *his* shoe, *he* heard the tardy bell. [*His* and *he* agree with antecedent *Glen*—3rd person singular, masculine.]
> Each of the girls turned *her* head to the right. [*Her* agrees with antecedent *Each*—3rd person singular, feminine.]

(See Chapter 9, "Agreement with Indefinites," page 210; and Chapter 10, "Careless Use of Pronouns," page 228.)

3 A demonstrative adjective agrees with its noun in number:

> *This* kind of book is popular with teen-agers. [*This* is singular, to agree with the singular noun *kind.*]
> *Those* kinds of books are more suitable for other age groups. [*Those* is plural, to agree with the plural noun *kinds.*]

(See **Demonstratives; kind, sort.**)

ain't Used in nonstandard English as a contraction for *am not, is not, are not, has not, have not.*

Some authorities feel that *ain't* would be a useful addition to informal English, particularly as a contraction for *am I not,* for which there is no established contraction. They defend *ain't I* as an appropriate colloquial expression in questions: "I am taller than Jim, ain't I?" (For some reason *aren't I,* which is certainly no more "correct" grammatically than *ain't I,* is more readily accepted: "I am taller than Jim, aren't I?") But because of the strong social and educational pressure against *ain't,* most users of standard English avoid it, even as a contraction for *am I not.*

The problem does not arise in formal English, which avoids contractions.

a la, à la Originally French, but now generally accepted as an English preposition meaning "in the manner of":

369

> jazz a la New Orleans   adventure a la *Treasure Island*

In formal writing and most fashion advertising the accent mark is kept: *à la.* Informal writing usually omits it.

à la mode This French phrase meaning "according to the fashion" has become part of the English language. It is most frequently used to describe two American dishes: pie à la mode (pie with ice cream) and beef à la mode (beef with vegetables cooked in the gravy).

In informal usage it is usually written without the accent mark—*a la mode*—or as one word, without the accent mark—*alamode.* In formal usage the accent is generally kept.

alibi In formal and legal usage *alibi* means "the plea or the fact that a person accused of a crime was in another place when it was committed":

> The bank robber's alibi baffled the police.

In informal usage the meaning of *alibi* is much broader. It is used to refer to any kind of excuse for any offense, important or unimportant:

> Dr. Kent wondered what new alibi Ted could come up with for missing another dental appointment.

all and its compounds **1 All right** is used both as an adjective and as an adverb:

> Though too rusty for use, the old cannon was all right as a showpiece. [Modifies the noun *cannon*.]
> Oh, Benton returned Simpson's serves all right—until his arm tired. [Modifies the verb *returned*.]
> "May I sharpen my pencil?" "All right." [Adverb meaning "yes."]

The spelling *alright* is occasionally found in comic strips, advertisements, and familiar writing, but it is not yet generally accepted in either formal or informal writing. Always write the two words—*all right*.

2 All ready. When in doubt about writing *all ready* or *already*, use this test: If you could use the word *ready* alone, without changing the meaning of the sentence, *all ready* is the one to use:

> Ten minutes later Sam was all ready to leave. [Meaning is "completely ready."]

Already is an adverb of time:

> Before he was five, Mozart had already composed several short pieces.

3 All together. The same test applies to choosing between *all together* and *altogether*. If the word *together* could be used alone, without changing the meaning, write *all together*:

> We found the puppies huddled all together under the porch.

Altogether is a rather formal adverb meaning "completely":

> Our guide was altogether disgusted with the poor catch.

4 All-around is a compound meaning "having many abilities" or "not specialized":

> At Crawford you will get an all-around education.

In informal English the form *all-round* is often used.

all-around See **all and its compounds,** section 4.

all of The preposition *of* is usual with *all* before pronouns:

> The compliment was meant for all of us.
> He read all of it aloud to the class.

All of is often used before nouns, also, though the *of* is not necessary and would probably be omitted in formal writing:

GENERAL USAGE: You cannot fool all of the people all of the time.
FORMAL WRITING: You cannot fool all the people all the time.

all right See **all and its compounds,** section 1.

all the farther, all the faster, etc. Localisms for *as far as, as fast as,* etc.

> LOCALISM: Long's Peak was all the farther they could hike that day.
> STANDARD: Long's Peak was as far as they could hike that day.

Alliteration Repeating the same initial sound several times in rather close succession. Writers of poetry and literary prose often make use of alliteration to gain attention, to bind phrases together, or to create a musical effect:

> The *f*air *b*reeze *b*lew, the white *f*oam *f*lew,
> The *f*urrow *f*ollowed *f*ree. . . .
> —Samuel Taylor Coleridge, "The Rime of the Ancient Mariner."

Alliteration gives many advertising and political slogans their catchy quality:

> Better Buy Buttercrust Bread
> Win with Willkie

Inexperienced writers should be careful in their use of conspicuous alliteration. While it can be effective for special purposes, it is usually out of place in everyday factual writing. There it tends to attract attention to the words themselves and away from the ideas.

allow In some local dialects, used to mean "say" or "think":

> LOCALISM: I allow he'd make a good sheriff.
> STANDARD: I think he'd make a good sheriff.

allude Means "to call attention indirectly," in contrast to *refer,* meaning "to mention specifically":

> Though Major Hinkefeffer did not refer to Davison and Parkins by name, we knew he was alluding to them when he spoke of "the disastrous consequences of the incompetence of certain officers."

Allusion See Chapter 12, "Use Allusions," page 278.

allusion See ***illusion, allusion.***

alma mater This expression from the Latin, meaning "bountiful mother," is used to mean a person's school or college. It is pronounced al′mə mä′tər, al′mə mä′tər, or äl′mə mä′tər.

almost See ***most, almost.***

Alphabetizing Although business firms and publishers have their own rules to cover special situations, alphabetizing generally follows a few common conventions:

1 Names are listed with the surname first. When the surnames are the same, the order is decided by the first names or initials. If necessary, the second names or initials are then considered:

Robins, D. R.
Robins, Daniel
Robins, Daniel J.
Robinson, Arnold

Surnames with prefixes are usually alphabetized under the prefix, not under the main part of the name:

De La Roche, Mazo
Delavigne, Jean
Descartes, René
De Voto, Bernard

Surnames beginning with *Mc* and *Mac* are generally listed under *Mac,* but some files have them grouped separately, ahead of the rest of the *M's.* Surnames with *St.* (St. John) are sometimes filed with the *Sa's* (for *Saint*), sometimes with the *St's.*

2 A title or a name of an organization is usually listed according to the first word that is not an article:

Aladdin and the Wonderful Lamp
The American Heritage
An American in Paris
The Anglo-Saxon Chronicle
Anthony and Cleopatra

Sometimes the article is placed at the end of the title: *American Heritage, The; American in Paris, An;* etc.

3 An item in a book index is usually listed according to its important word—the one users of the index would probably look for first:

Rainfall, distribution of, 247

Different phases of a topic may be listed alphabetically after an entry item:

Massachusetts, 89-114; as Revolutionary battleground, 110; colonization, 90; government, 97; Indian Wars, 95

Sometimes the unimportant words are disregarded in alphabetizing an index. For example, you might find "as Revolutionary battleground" listed last instead of first in the entry above.

already   See *all and its compounds,* section 2.

also   Sometimes ineffectively used as a connective instead of *and. And* is preferred, either in the middle of a sentence or at the beginning:

POOR: She reached for her winter coat, also her mittens.
BETTER: She reached for her winter coat and her mittens.

although, though   Both of these subordinating conjunctions have the same meaning. *Although* is usually used when the adverb clause it introduces comes before the main clause. *Though* is more common when the adverb clause follows the main clause:

> Although the rain was pouring down, the umpire refused to call the game.
> The umpire refused to call the game, though the rain was pouring down.

The spelling *altho* is often used in familiar writing—letters, advertising, etc.—and is becoming increasingly common in informal writing. But it should be spelled out in full in formal writing.

altogether   See **all and its compounds,** section 3.

alumnus   *Alumnus* retains its original Latin forms in English:

One male graduate:	alumnus
Two or more male graduates:	alumni (ə lum′nī)
One female graduate:	alumna
Two or more female graduates:	alumnae (ə lum′nē)

Alumni is commonly used to refer to both men and women graduates of a coeducational school.

To avoid the confusion that may arise in pronouncing the plural endings of these words, many people prefer to use the word *graduates* (and, informally, the shortened form *alums*).

a.m., p.m.   Abbreviations for *ante meridiem,* "before noon," and *post meridiem,* "after noon": from 2:30 a.m. to 7:00 p.m.

These abbreviations are used only when the time is given in figures and are not ordinarily capitalized except in headlines and tables. In printed matter, small capitals are often used: 4:45 A.M. (See **Hours.**)

M. is the abbreviation for *noon: 12:00 m.* There is no corresponding abbreviation for *midnight; 12:00 p.m.* is used.

Ambiguity   An ambiguous construction is one that has two or more possible meanings. The most common causes of ambiguity are:
1 Unclear reference of pronouns.

AMBIGUOUS: Because the concert was presented on the same night as the senior play, Keith missed it.   [The concert or the play?]

If this sentence appeared in context, the meaning would probably be clear. But to avoid any confusion, it would be better to make unmistakably clear which of the two nouns the pronoun *it* refers to:

CLEAR: Keith missed the concert because it was presented on the same night as the senior play.   [Or: Keith missed the senior play because it was presented on the same night as the concert.]

(For further examples of unclear reference of pronouns, see Chapter 10, "Careless Use of Pronouns," page 228.)

2 Squinting and misplaced modifiers. A squinting modifier is ambiguous because it might refer to either the preceding or the following construction:

AMBIGUOUS: I told George at a quarter to five to report to Mrs. Allen.
CLEAR: At a quarter to five I told George to report to Mrs. Allen.
CLEAR: I told George to report to Mrs. Allen at a quarter to five.

Misplaced modifiers, because of their position in the sentence, do not clearly modify the word they are intended to modify. (They are also frequently a source of humor that the writer does not intend.)

MISPLACED: McGraw figured out that it was the butler who had been blackmailing Mr. Schwartz by a process of elimination.
CLEAR: By a process of elimination McGraw figured out that it was the butler who had been blackmailing Mr. Schwartz.

(For further discussion, see Chapter 10, "Squinting Modifiers," page 221, and "Misplaced Modifiers," page 220.)

3 Incomplete expressions, especially in comparisons:

AMBIGUOUS: Ed dislikes Bob as much as Melvin.
CLEAR: Ed dislikes Bob as much as Melvin does.
CLEAR: Ed dislikes Bob as much as he dislikes Melvin.
CLEAR: Ed dislikes both Bob and Melvin.

374

American   Since no convenient adjective or noun can be formed from the name of our country, the United States, we use *American*, from the name of the continent. This is an obviously inexact term, for citizens of other North American countries and of Central and South America are as "American" as we are. Our use of the word for people and products of our country has been resented by other Americans. Despite inexactness and complaints, long-standing habit encourages our continuing to use *American*. But where the usage may be offensive, other words should be substituted: "a citizen of the United States" instead of "an American"; "a product of the United States" instead of "an American product."

American and British usage   Both Americans and Englishmen speak English, but they do not speak exactly the same kind of English. The most extreme language differences are found in regional or provincial dialects. You would have a great deal of trouble understanding a Yorkshireman, for instance, or a London cockney. The contrast between the standard language (the language of the majority of educated people) in the two countries is less striking. But there still are differences to be noted.

There are, to begin with, a few variations in spelling. The English prefer the *-re* ending for words like *saber, luster, somber*. They still keep the -*our* ending in words like *humor* and *rigor*. They use *x* in words like *inflexion* and *connexion* (which we spell *inflection* and *connection*). And they double more consonants than we do (*kidnapper, signalling, focussed*).

There are a number of differences in vocabulary. For example:

AMERICAN	BRITISH
billboard	hoarding
candy	sweets
clipping (newspaper)	cutting
doctor's office	surgery
gym teacher (female)	games mistress
head nurse	sister
hood (automobile)	bonnet
line up	queue up
napkin	serviette
overpass (highway)	flyover
phonograph	gramophone
radio	wireless
rummage sale	jumble sale
schoolteacher (male)	master
sidewalk	pavement
spool (thread)	reel
subway	underground *or* tube
taxpayer	ratepayer
trunk (automobile)	boot

Words and phrases belonging peculiarly to the English, we call *Briticisms;* those that belong peculiarly to us (*windshield, bowling alley, movies, ragtime, lifeguard, electioneering, to pull up stakes, to monkey with*) we, and especially the English, call *Americanisms.* Such words and phrases are a frequent source of amusement in the two countries—and sometimes also a source of confusion. For instance, by taking words like *sister* and *tube* in their American sense, you might completely mistake the meaning intended by an English speaker.

You will notice only a few differences in grammar if you compare the standard spoken and written English of the two countries. For instance, collective nouns are more likely to be plural in British usage— *the government have agreed.* And where Americans say *different from* or *different than,* Englishmen are likely to say *different to.*

There are enough differences in pronunciation to make an "English accent" and an "American accent" clearly recognizable. The English have different values for the vowels, different stresses, and in general a more rapid speech and a tendency to slur syllables (like the *ar* in *secretary* or *necessary*). American pronunciations are slower and fuller.

But as time goes on, the differences between the two branches of the English language will probably tend to diminish. Modern developments in transportation and communication will bring the two nations closer together through a steady exchange of books, periodicals, movies, teachers, students, entertainers. As a result, Americans and Englishmen will find it increasingly easier to understand each other.

among, between   See **between, among.**

amount, number   *Amount* is used of things that can be measured or weighed; *number* is used of things that can be counted:

a small *amount* of change	a *number* of coins
a large *amount* of butter	a *number* of cakes

(See also **number.**)

Ampersand   The name for the sign &, which means "and." This sign is often used as a space saver in business writing and in charts and tables. The ampersand is not appropriate as a substitute for the word *and* in general writing.

In addressing or referring to a business firm, you should use the form the firm uses:

Little, Brown & Company   Murphy and Son, Inc.

an   See **a, an.**

376   **Analogy**   A figure of speech in which a comparison is rather fully developed, suggesting several points of similarity:

Grammar is somewhat like a freshly caught fish. Take it in your hand to wash it in the stream; two wriggles, and it is gone. So with grammar, and I speak as one who has gone through the chastening experience of asking himself quite soberly what our grammar is. I have tried to divest myself of old grammatical prejudices beaten into me at an early age, and acquired later with the profligate expenditure of midnight electricity. I have at times thought I had drawn from the deceptive grammatical waters a fine, trim, grammatical fact. I grasped him firmly by the tail, and meant only to clean him up a bit. Two flips, and he was gone.—Charlton Laird, *The Miracle of Language.* Published by Fawcett Publications, Inc., Greenwich, Conn. Copyright © 1953 by Charlton Laird.

and   1 *And* is a coördinating conjunction that connects elements of equal grammatical value:

NOUNS: dogs and cats; pencils, rulers, and notebooks
VERBS: Jack fell down and broke his crown.
ADJECTIVES: a black and tan cap; a green, brown, and orange quilt
ADVERBS: The leopard leaped quickly and quietly.
PHRASES: into the house and up the stairs; after eating supper and washing the dishes

SUBORDINATE CLAUSES: After the cat had scratched the thief and [after] the dog had bitten him, the donkey kicked him out through the door.

COÖRDINATE CLAUSES: Jansen threw the pass, and I caught it.

2 Inexperienced speakers and writers often use too many *and*'s, with resulting monotony. In some sentences a subordinating conjunction would express the idea more exactly than *and*:

INEXACT: Our train had been delayed half an hour by the snow, and we arrived in plenty of time to see the opening play.

BETTER: Though our train had been delayed half an hour by the snow, we arrived in plenty of time to see the opening play.

In other sentences, *and* is used when no connective is needed:

Sergeant Ritter charged boldly up the fire escape, and calling on the fugitive to surrender.

The participial phrase *calling on the fugitive to surrender* modifies *Sergeant Ritter*. It should not be joined to the main verb *charged* by *and*:

Sergeant Ritter charged boldly up the fire escape, calling on the fugitive to surrender.

A monotonous succession of *and*'s, as in the following sentence, can easily be avoided by writing the clauses as separate sentences or by using semicolons:

MONOTONOUS: A hundred yards from the finish line Stevens still lagged behind Trent and Barry, and we gave up hope of his winning, and then he suddenly burst past them in the final sprint for the ribbon.

BETTER: A hundred yards from the finish line Stevens still lagged behind Trent and Barry; we gave up hope of his winning. Then he suddenly burst past them in the final sprint for the ribbon.

There is no need for using *and* before *so,* since *and* adds nothing to the meaning:

I knew Miss Gates wanted us to prepare an outline, so I brought paper. [Not: *and so* I brought paper.]

3 *And* is sometimes effectively used at the beginning of a sentence, to place special emphasis on the idea in the clause that follows.

USUAL: The wicked fairy, filled with hatred, swore to revenge herself on the king and queen; and before the day was over, she succeeded in her evil purpose.

MORE EMPHATIC: The wicked fairy, filled with hatred, swore to revenge herself on the king and queen. And before the day was over, she succeeded in her evil purpose.

(For punctuation of compound sentences with *and* and of a series with *and,* see **Comma,** sections 1 and 3a.)

and etc. Since *etc.* is an abbreviation for the Latin *et cetera,* which means "*and* others" or "*and* so forth," the *and* should not be used with it. (See ***etc.***)

and/or A business and legal expression that serves as a brief way of indicating three choices—one item or another item or both items:

> The merchandise will be sent by truck and/or train.

Because many people dislike its business connotation, *and/or* is infrequently used in general writing.

and which, and who *And which* or *and who* is appropriate only when joining a second relative clause to the first:

> Edison's greatest invention was probably the incandescent lamp, which won him great acclaim during his lifetime and which today is the best-known reminder of him.

Using *and which* or *and who* (or *but which, but who*) when there is no preceding *who* or *which* clause is often a sign of careless writing:

CARELESS: Mrs. Betz is looking for a dining-room table, no more than thirty inches wide, and which can be extended to seat twelve people.

ACCURATE: Mrs. Betz is looking for a dining-room table, no more than thirty inches wide, which can be extended to seat twelve people.

CARELESS: Mrs. Olson liked Mr. Teague, the butcher, a sour-faced and short-tempered man, but who always saved the choicest cuts for her.

ACCURATE: Mrs. Olson liked Mr. Teague, the butcher, who was sour-faced and short-tempered, but who always saved the choicest cuts for her.

angle Guard against overusing *angle* (meaning "aspect" or "point of view"), especially in sentences where it is merely deadwood:

POOR: Mr. Hart, who was familiar with all angles of the problem, approached it from a different angle.

BETTER: Mr. Hart, who was familiar with all the aspects of the problem, approached it differently.

Anglicizing English has borrowed and is still borrowing many words from other languages. We keep the foreign pronunciation and form of some of these words—*gauche, tortilla, ersatz, slalom.* But many borrowed words—especially the ones that prove very useful but are hard for us to pronounce or spell—we *Anglicize.* That is, we bring them into line with English usage by giving them an English pronunciation or form.

The Spanish word *mantilla* (män tē′yä) is generally given the pronunciation of man til′ə in our country. The French *hors d'oeuvres* (ôr dœ'vrə) we usually pronounce ôr'dĕrvz', transposing the *v* and the *r* and sounding the *s* at the end. The German *sauerbraten* (zou'ər brä'tən) we pronounce with an initial *s* sound. And the words *fête, crêpe,* and *naïve,* borrowed from French, are most commonly spelled without the circumflex accents and the dieresis: *fete, crepe, naive.* (See **Borrowed words.**)

angry *Angry at* and *angry about* are used in referring to things:

> He finally grew angry at their stubbornness.
> Alice was angry about having to wait an hour for Jack.

In referring to persons, *angry with* is general:

> My sister is angry with me because I won't lend her my scarf.

But when the angry feeling is to be stressed, *at* is used:

> Mr. Tuttle was extremely angry at his son for lying.

(See **mad.**)

annoyed We are annoyed *at* things and *with* people:

> The teacher was annoyed at Henry's constant interruptions.
> The comedian was annoyed with the talkative audience.

By is used when the meaning is "molested" or "bothered":

> The campers were annoyed by swarms of mosquitoes.
> All day long we were annoyed by peddlers selling balloons and souvenirs.

Antecedent The word, phrase, or clause to which a pronoun (or a relative adverb) refers. A pronoun agrees in person, number, and gender with its antecedent, which may precede or follow it:

> Pat's *cousin,* who had mislaid her *purse,* spent an hour looking for it. [*Cousin* is the antecedent of the relative pronoun *who* and the possessive *her; purse* is the antecedent of *it.*]
> Because of their long friendship with him, *Mrs. Surratt* and her *son* helped *Booth* in the plot. [Here both antecedents follow the pronouns that refer to them: *their—Mrs. Surratt* and her *son; him—Booth.*]

anti- A prefix meaning "against; opposed to; the opposite of." It usually is hyphened only before root words beginning with *i* and before proper nouns and adjectives:

antibiotic	anti-intellectual
antifreeze	anti-Nazi
antiaristocrat	anti-European

Anti- is pronounced an'ti, an'tī, or an'tē.

Anticipatory subjects See *Expletives.*

Anticlimax In writing, *climax* means the arrangement of a series of items in the order of importance—from the least important to the most important. *Anticlimax* means an abrupt departure from this order. In other words, the writer unexpectedly ends his series not with the most important item, but with a trivial or commonplace one. Anticlimax is sometimes used intentionally—and effectively—as a device for humor:

> For ours is the age of the four "A's": anxiety, apprehension, agonizing, and aspirin.—James Thurber, *Lanterns and Lances.*

Used unintentionally, anticlimax can make a piece of writing seem ridiculous:

POOR: The new secretary was worse than the two he had fired: she pilfered office supplies, filed letters inaccurately, misspelled even simple words, and chewed gum as she typed.

BETTER: The new secretary was worse than the two he had fired: she chewed gum as she typed, misspelled even simple words, filed letters inaccurately, and pilfered office supplies.

(See Chapter 11, "Using the Order of Climax," page 258.)

Antonym A word meaning the opposite of another word: *rough* and *smooth* are antonyms, as are *fast* and *slow, high* and *low, sick* and *healthy, thin* and *thick, expand* and *contract, acquit* and *condemn, above* and *below, concave* and *convex.*

anxious When *anxious* means "eagerly desiring," it is followed by an infinitive or by *for*:

> The naturalist was anxious to photograph the carnivorous plant.
> The hot-blooded braves were anxious for war.

When *anxious* means "worried," it is followed by *about* or *at*:

> Mrs. Stevens was anxious about Tom, who was more than an hour late.
> She became anxious at the delay.

any and its compounds 1 *Any* is used as an adjective, as a pronoun, and as an adverb:

ADJECTIVE: He will take any work he can find.
PRONOUN: There aren't any left in the room.
ADVERB: She could not finish any faster.

2 As a pronoun, *any* may be either singular or plural (and may take either a singular or a plural verb), depending on the meaning intended:

> *Isn't* any of the boys going to learn to dance? [Singular; speaker means "Isn't there even one who is going to learn to dance?"]

As the cars drive past, policemen follow any that *are* speeding. [Plural; speaker has in mind more than one speeding car.]

3 *Anyone* and *anybody* always take singular verbs. They are referred to by singular pronouns in formal English and in most writing:

Anyone who *wears* bright green polish on *her* nails *wants* to be noticed.
Anybody can enter if *he says*, "Open sesame!"
Has anyone forgotten *his* or *her* report?

In colloquial usage, though, plural pronouns are frequently used:

Anybody can enter if *they* say, "Open sesame!"
Has anyone forgotten *their* report?

4 *Anybody, anyhow, anything,* and *anywhere* are always written as single words. *Anyone* and *anyway* usually are, but when each part has a separate meaning, they are written as two words. (*Any* is then used as an adjective.) The pronunciation gives a clue to the spelling. If *any* is stressed, the single word should probably be used:

STRESS ON *any*:   They'll take anyone they can get.
STRESS ON *one*:   Any one of them would be able to do the work.
STRESS ON *any*:   Benton won the balloon-blowing contest anyway.
STRESS ABOUT EQUAL: You may write the report any way you wish.

5 Informal usage sometimes substitutes *any place* for *anywhere*. **381** Nonstandard English includes *anywheres* and *anyways*.

Aphorism   See **Epigram.**

Apostrophe (') **1** The most common use of the apostrophe is to form the possessive (also called "genitive") case of nouns and indefinite pronouns:

a man's name   the four players' helmets
one's pocket change   his brother-in-law's job
anybody's book   a good night's sleep

The apostrophe is not used to form the possessive of the personal pronouns (*hers, its, ours, yours, theirs*) or of *who* (*whose*).
(For further examples, see **Possessive case.**)

2 The apostrophe is used to indicate the omission of one or more letters in contractions:

he'll   didn't   it's (it is)   you're

It also shows the omission of letters representing sounds not pronounced in conversation:

"We were doin' jus' what you told us to do," Pete drawled.

(See **Conversation.**)

3 An apostrophe is generally used to form the plural of figures, symbols, letters of the alphabet, and words being discussed as words:

> Many great American novels were written in the 1920's and 1930's.
> He likes to add a flourish to his *h*'s and *y*'s.
> Dave mistook my *7*'s for *9*'s.
> "Don't use so many *if*'s and *but*'s," snapped the sales manager.

(For further examples, see **Plurals of nouns.**)

Apostrophe   A figure of speech in which a speaker or writer addresses an absent person as if he were present, or a thing or idea as if it could understand. Here are two examples:

> Oh little town of Bethlehem, how still we see thee lie. . . .
> Break, break, break, / On thy cold grey stones, O Sea!

Appendix   An addition at the end of a book or document. It may contain lists of definitions, biographical sketches, maps, charts, or other supplementary material like long tables and documents.

The plural of *appendix* is now generally written *appendixes* except in formal usage, which retains the Latin plural *appendices* (ə pen'-də sēz').

Appositives   **1** *Apposition* means, literally, "putting beside." An appositive is a second noun, or the equivalent of a noun, that is placed beside a first noun to explain it more fully:

> Roger, *my eldest brother,* has a habit of ordering people around.
> The cheetah, *one of the fastest mammals,* can be trained to hunt deer.
> The fact *that he had cheated* made us angry.

Occasionally an appositive comes before the noun it explains:

> A sturdy *individualist,* Grandma Wilson scorned such modern conveniences as electric can openers, rotisseries, and driers.

An appositive is sometimes separated from its headword by other parts of the sentence:

> The coral reef lay a few feet under the waters—a beautiful, hidden, navigator's *nightmare.*

An appositive does not always explain a single headword. It might sum up the idea expressed in a preceding group of words:

> Fleming noticed that the mold had destroyed the bacteria around it—an *observation* which led to the discovery of penicillin.

An appositive might sum up a preceding series of nouns:

> Physics, biology, chemistry, astronomy, geology—these *studies* are all explored in the course known as general science.

Or a series of appositives might be used to explain a single noun:

> In the historic southern Appalachians—the *Great Smokies,* the *Black Mountains,* the *Cumberlands,* the *Blue Ridge Mountains* —we get glimpses of the isolated life the early settlers must have lived.

2 Appositives agree with their headwords in case:

> The debating team—*Herb, Milly,* and *I*—had to ride a hundred miles to the Culver City contest. [Pronoun in nominative case to agree with the subject *team.*]
> The audience politely applauded the string trio—*Jean, David,* and *me.* [Pronoun in objective case to agree with the object *trio.*]

3 For the punctuation of appositives, see **Comma,** section 6.

Appropriateness   Good English must be not only clear and lively, but *appropriate.* For a discussion of appropriateness in language, see Chapter 8, "The Levels of Usage."

apt   See **likely, liable, apt.**

Archaic   A term applied to words and expressions that once were common in the language but are no longer in general use. Such expressions are now found only in books of an earlier period or in books that imitate the style of an earlier period: *prithee, saith, peradventure, eftsoons, zounds, fardel, burthen.* Student writers would be wise to avoid these expressions.

arise   Situations *arise,* but people *rise* (rather formal) or *get up:*

> Most of his problems arise from his own stupidity.
> He rose (*or* got up) from his chair and walked slowly to the safe.

In formal writing and in poetry, *arise* is sometimes used in referring to people.

around, round   In informal English *around* and *round* are used interchangeably. The tendency is to use *round* (or to clip the *a* of *around* so that it sounds like *round*).

> The children danced round the Maypole.
> The children danced around the Maypole.

Formal English generally uses *around* to mean "here and there" or "in every direction," and *round* to mean "in a circular or a reverse motion":

> Dennis searched all around his room for the cuff links.
> The satellite travels round (*or* around) the world in a polar orbit.
> Antony turned round (*or* around) to see who had made the remark.

Articles   *A, an,* and *the* are known as *articles. A* and *an* are *indefinite* articles; they refer to any one of a group (*A* leaf quivered. He bought *an* automobile). *The* is the *definite* article; it points out a certain one of a group (*The* leaf fell. He drove *the* automobile). (See *a, an* and *the.*)

as   One of the most versatile words in our language, *as* has several uses:

1 The conjunction *as* introduces several kinds of adverbial clauses:

I tried to pronounce the word *as Mr. Lee did.*   [Shows manner.]
Anson hit the ball as hard *as he could.*   [Shows degree.]
As he raised his spear to hurl it at his enemy, a gnat settled on the end of his nose.   [Means "when."]
He must have lost the keys *as he was running through the alley.* [Means "while."]
As there was nothing more for Charlotte to say, she ended the letter.   [Means "since" or "because."]
Lovely *as it is,* mistletoe is actually a parasite.   [Means "though."]

The conjunction *as* is a problem in writing. Because of the very variety of its meanings, it is overused. Often a more exact conjunction would make the intended meaning clearer:

WEAK: As the Warfields' house was being redecorated, the whole family stayed in a hotel.
BETTER: While the Warfields' house was being redecorated. . . .
BETTER: Since (*or* Because) the Warfields' house was being redecorated. . . .

2 As an adverb, *as* shows degree:

Lambert parked *as* close to the curb as he could.

3 Used as a relative pronoun, *as* usually follows *the same* or *such:*

He is *the same* troublemaker *as* he was in his freshman year.
Make only *such* revisions *as* you think are necessary.

In nonstandard English, *as* is sometimes used for *who* or *that:*

NONSTANDARD: People as live in glass houses shouldn't throw stones.
STANDARD: People who live in glass houses shouldn't throw stones.

4 As a preposition, *as* means "in the role of" or "in the capacity of":

In his dreams, Ichabod saw himself as master of Van Tassel's farm.
She volunteered to serve as interpreter for the group.

(See also *as . . . as; like, as.*)

as . . . as   **1** When making a double comparison (like "as much as, if not more than") in informal speech, we often drop the second *as:*

Cats are as clever if not cleverer than dogs.
His acting is as bad or worse than his singing.

But in writing, the *as* should be included:

> Cats are as clever as, if not cleverer than, dogs.
> His acting is as bad as or worse than his singing.

Many people, feeling that this construction is rather stilted, avoid the problem by stating the comparison in this way:

> Cats are as clever as dogs, if not cleverer.
> His acting is as bad as his singing, or worse.

2 Guard against carelessly using *than* for the second *as* in a comparison like this:

> The juniors spent twice *as* much money on decorations *as* the seniors did. [Not: twice as much money on decorations *than* the seniors did.]

3 In negative comparisons some formal writers use *not so . . . as* (or *neither so, never so . . . as*), but *not as . . . as* is the more common idiom in all styles.

> FORMAL: French fairy tales are not *so* grim *as* German fairy tales.
> GENERAL: French fairy tales are not *as* grim *as* German fairy tales.

as, like   For a discussion of the choice between *as* and *like* (They don't behave *as* we do. They don't behave *like* we do), see **like, as.**

as if, as though   Formal English uses the subjunctive after *as if* or *as though*. Informal English does not always do so.

> FORMAL: He acted as if (as though) he *were* the owner of the clock.
> INFORMAL: He acted as if (as though) he *was* the owner of the clock.

(See Chapter 9, "Subjunctives," page 197.)

as to   Often used as a clumsy substitute for a single preposition—usually *about, on,* or *of*:

> POOR: The post-office clerk promised a full report as to the missing letters.
> BETTER: The post-office clerk promised a full report on the missing letters. [Or: *about* the missing letters.]

Sometimes *as to* is simply deadwood and should be omitted in writing:

> Mrs. Pickens was not sure [as to] how much money she had spent at the supermarket.

at   Nonstandard English often adds an unnecessary *at* to questions beginning with *where*:

> NONSTANDARD: Where did you get it at?   Where is she working at?
> STANDARD: Where did you get it?   Where is she working?

athletics Pronounced ath let′iks (three syllables, not four). When *athletics* refers to physical sports, games, and exercises, it generally takes a plural verb:

> In ancient Rome, athletics *were* popular—especially boxing and wrestling.

When it refers to the principles of athletic training, it usually takes a singular verb:

> Athletics *was* one of his chief interests.

Author card See **Card catalogue.**

Auxiliary verb A verb used with another verb to form a verb phrase. An auxiliary verb helps show the tense, voice, and mood of the main verb. Forms of *be, have,* and *do* are the most common auxiliaries (*was* taking, *had been* found, *did* use). Others frequently used are *can, could, may, might, shall, should, will, would, ought, must.*

awful The original meaning of *awful* is "inspiring with awe" (the *awful* grandeur of the heavens). But informal usage has weakened the meaning of *awful,* making it a general word of disapproval (an *awful* pun, an *awful* smell). As a result, the word is seldom used in its original sense; *awe-inspiring* is used instead. And as a result of the overuse of *awful* as a term of disapproval, it is rarely used in writing.

awhile, a while One word when an adverb; two words when *while* is a noun in a prepositional phrase:

> Carol read awhile; then she grew sleepy and turned off the bed lamp.   [Adverb modifying *read.*]
> Old Curly prospected for quite a while in the Sierra Nevada before striking gold.   [*While* is object of preposition *for.*]

Awkward writing Awkwardness in writing may be the result of any one of a number of faults in construction—vague pronoun reference, awkward interruptions, shifted constructions, and so on. For a discussion of these faults and how to avoid them, see Chapter 10, "Improving Awkward Sentences," page 220.

B

back of, in back of Both of these phrases are now established as standard usages in the United States, though many people consider the preposition *behind* more appropriate in writing, especially formal writing:

> The garage is back of the house.   [Or: in back of the house, behind the house.]

backward, backwards   Used interchangeably as adverbs:

> Move the car backward by shifting to the reverse gear.
> Move the car backwards by shifting to the reverse gear.

Only *backward* is used as an adjective:

> Disobeying the order, Orpheus cast a backward look at Eurydice.

bad, badly   *Bad* is generally used as an adjective, *badly* as an adverb:

I have a bad headache.	He plays tennis badly.
He made a bad guess.	The article was badly written.

In formal English and in informal writing, *bad*—not *badly*—is used as a predicate adjective following a linking verb:

> He feels bad about losing the match.
> The eggs smelled bad.

In informal speech *badly* is sometimes used as a predicate adjective, and *bad* as an adverb:

> Gladys must have felt badly about the results.   [Formal: felt bad.]
> I hope I won't do so bad in the next test.   [Formal: so badly.]

But these forms are not appropriate in writing.
Informal English uses *badly* to mean "very much":

> The old man needed a friend badly.
> Jarvis wanted the extra money badly.

387

Bad and *badly* are both compared irregularly:

bad	worse	worst
badly	worse	worst

Bad grammar   A term of disapproval applied to all sorts of expressions ranging from "I ain't seen nothing" to "We wondered if he would come" (instead of "We wondered whether he would come") and "Who did he appoint?" (instead of "Whom did he appoint?"). People who use this term to condemn *all* such expressions believe that there is only one kind of English that is "good," and that any departure from this one kind is "bad." They do not take into account that there are several kinds of English—each one "good" or appropriate for certain occasions, social groups, or geographical sections.

There is nothing wrong with these expressions in themselves. What makes them wrong is using them in situations where they are not appropriate. And then the objection to them is not that they are sins against grammar, but that they are sins against usage. For example, in informal speech "*Who* did she call?" and "I can't help but feel sorry for him" are appropriate. In formal English they are not. "*Whom* did she call?" and "I can't help feeling sorry for him" are the appropriate forms there.

Your goal should be to learn enough about the various kinds of English so that you can recognize and use the forms and constructions that are appropriate at different times. (See Chapter 8, "The Levels of Usage.")

balance   Often used in informal English to mean "part that is left over" (in reference to things other than money):

> She gave me ten of the books and sent the balance to Mrs. Hill.

Balanced sentences   Sentences in which two or more parts are noticeably similar in length and form. Using balanced sentences is an effective way to emphasize important ideas, especially ideas expressing comparisons and contrasts:

> Sighting a bighorn is not unusual; catching one is rare.

(See Chapter 11, "Emphasis Through Balanced Sentences," page 259.)

Barbarism   A term applied to a word or expression that is not in good (standard) use: *hisself, we'uns* (for *we*), *that there* (for *that*), *had ought* (for *ought*), *drownded* (for *drowned*), etc.

barefoot   *Barefoot* is used as an adjective or adverb; *barefooted* is used as an adjective:

388

ADJECTIVE: A barefoot child ran down the dirt road.
ADVERB: Big Oley liked to wrestle barefoot.
ADJECTIVE: The Andean Indians were barefooted despite the cold.

be   **1 Forms.**   *Be* is a highly irregular verb, but because it is used so often, its forms are rarely troublesome:

INFINITIVE: (to) be
PRESENT PARTICIPLE: being
PAST PARTICIPLE: been
PRESENT: I am, you are, he is; we, you, they are
PAST: I was, you were, he was; we, you, they were
SUBJUNCTIVE: be, were

2 As linking verb.   *Be* is the most common linking verb, a verb that links a subject with a predicate complement (noun, pronoun, or adjective):

> Patricia's father is a *lawyer.* [Predicate noun.]
> The overcoat was dark *brown.* [Predicate adjective.]

Pronoun complements after the verb *be* are in the nominative case in written English:

> It must have been *she* who called. [Not *her.*]
> He is positive that it was *we.* [Not *us.*]

In informal speech and writing "It's me" has practically replaced the formal "It is I." But other objective-case pronouns (*him, her, us, them*) are not as yet acceptable—even in informal speech. (See ***It's me.***)

3 As auxiliary verb. Forms of *be* are used with the present participles of other verbs to form the progressive tense forms:

I am coming.	We were watching.
You have been loafing.	He had been studying.
He has been typing.	They will be working.

Forms of *be* are used with the past participles of other verbs to form the passive voice forms:

Next it is dyed.	They will be sent.
They were fined.	She had been warned.
It has been mailed.	He will have been fired.

In informal speech one form of *be* is often used to serve both as a linking verb and as an auxiliary:

The pilots *were* ready and waiting for further instructions.

In formal usage the form of *be* is repeated:

The pilots *were* ready and *were* waiting for further instructions.

beau The plural is either *beaus* or *beaux* (formal), both pronounced bōz.

because A subordinating conjunction used to introduce a clause that gives the reason for the statement in the main clause:

Because I am his brother, I understand his attitude.

The conjunction *as* is often used in place of *because* in such clauses. But since *because* is more definite and emphatic than *as, because* is preferred in written English:

AMBIGUOUS: *As* they were watching the game, I decided to come back later. [Seems at first to mean "while."]

DEFINITE: *Because* they were watching the game, I decided to come back later.

In formal English the coördinating conjunction *for* is often used instead of *because*, especially when the clause gives evidence for or states an explanation of the main clause:

INFORMAL: I was sure he was honest, because I had worked with him for years.

FORMAL: I was sure that he was honest, for I had worked with him for years.

(See ***reason is because*** and ***as.***)

Beginning paragraphs For discussion and examples, see Chapter 1, "The Opening Paragraph," page 15.

being as, being that Certain dialects use *being as* and *being that* in place of the conjunctions *since* and *because,* which are used in standard English:

DIALECT: Being as we have the money, let's go skating.
STANDARD: Since we have the money, let's go skating.

DIALECT: Being that Clay refused to help, we didn't finish till noon.
STANDARD: Because Clay refused to help, we didn't finish till noon.

beside, besides *Beside* is most commonly used as a preposition meaning "by the side of":

A tiny jade vase stood beside the old clock on the mantelpiece.

It is also used in certain rather formal idioms:

Jerry's remarks were completely beside the point.
Longfellow was beside himself with worry about his wife's illness.

Besides is used both as an adverb and as a preposition meaning "in addition (to)" or "except":

Rain helps the crops, replenishes the ground water, and cleans the air besides.   [Adverb—"in addition."]
Besides watering the garden, Ted pulled weeds for an hour.   [Preposition—"in addition to."]
The nurse admitted no visitors besides his parents.   [Preposition—"except."]

Besides is also used as a conjunctive adverb meaning "moreover":

Willy thought it might be fun to walk all the way to Lincoln Park; besides, he had not a penny in his pockets for fare.

between, among *Among* implies more than two persons, places, or things:

There was a strong feeling of loyalty among the club members.

Between is generally used to refer to only two:

In 1846 the Oregon region was divided between England and the United States.

When used to refer to more than two, *between* suggests that the persons, places, or things are being considered two at a time:

The conferences ended in a treaty between the three nations.
Blake could see no difference between an exaggeration, a fib, and a lie.

Between is followed either by a plural (*between acts, between them*) or by two expressions joined by *and*—not by *or* or *to*:

ILLOGICAL: Lathrop lay in bed trying to decide between going back to sleep *or* facing the cold, confusing world.

LOGICAL: Lathrop lay in bed trying to decide between going back to sleep *and* facing the cold, confusing world.

ILLOGICAL: Rapid physical growth usually takes place between the ages of twelve *to* sixteen.

LOGICAL: Rapid physical growth usually takes place between the ages of twelve *and* sixteen.

Although we commonly hear such expressions as "between each store" and "between every class," it would be more logical to say:

There is a parking lot between each store and the next.
We have a five-minute recess after each class.
We have a five-minute recess between classes.

between you and me In standard English the objective-case pronouns are used as objects of prepositions: *between you and me, between you and her, between you and him, between you and us, between you and them.*

Because so much emphasis is placed on the use of the nominative pronouns in sentences like "You and he will win," "Dick and I left," "It is they," some people have the mistaken idea that "you and him" and "Dick and me" are always incorrect. In an effort to speak correctly, they say "between you and he" and "between Dick and I," not realizing that in these phrases the objective forms, not the nominative, are called for: "between you and him," "between Dick and me."

Bible, bible *Bible* is capitalized but not italicized when it refers to the **391** Holy Scriptures:

Most of his quotations were taken from the Bible.

Bible is neither capitalized nor italicized when it refers to a book that is regarded as an authority:

Roget's Thesaurus is the professional writer's bible.

Forms used in referring to parts of the Bible are:

the Old Testament   the New Testament
I Kings 10:6-12 [The 6th to the 12th verses in the 10th chapter of First Book of Kings.]
The Last Supper is described in Matthew 26:20-29 and in John 13-17. [The 20th to the 29th verses in the 26th chapter of the Gospel of Matthew and the 13th to the 17th chapters of the Gospel of John.]

The adjective *Biblical* is often not capitalized: *biblical.*

Bibliography Most research papers have at the end a *bibliography*—a list of the books and other published material actually used in writing the paper. (Sources in the working bibliography that were consulted but not referred to in the paper are not listed.) The bibliography serves two purposes: First, it shows what research was done for the paper.

Second, it suggests to readers who are especially interested in a subject various sources that they may find useful.

Although the form of bibliography entries has been pretty well standardized, there are slight differences in the forms used by various writers, as you can see by comparing bibliographies in different books. But these are minor matters; the important thing is to see that the entries include the necessary information and are consistent in form.

In your bibliographies, use the following forms:

1 For a book—one author:

Ewen, David, The World of Jerome Kern, New York, Henry Holt & Company, 1960

2 For a book—more than one author:

Nephew, William, and Michael Chester, Beyond Mars, New York, G. P. Putnam's Sons, 1960

3 For a book—compiled by an editor:

Mannheim, Hermann, ed., Pioneers in Criminology, Chicago, Quadrangle Books, 1960

4 For a book—only one chapter used:

Franck, Frederick, "Life in Lambaréné" in Days with Albert Schweitzer, New York, Henry Holt & Company, 1959, pp. 20-36

5 For a magazine article—author given:

Kantor, MacKinlay, "If the South Had Won the Civil War," Look, vol. 24, November 22, 1960, pp. 29-42

6 For a magazine article—no author given:

"Gentlewoman from Maine: Margaret Chase Smith," Ladies' Home Journal, vol. LXXVIII, January 1961, pp. 65 ff.

7 For a pamphlet—no author given:

Official Baseball Annual, Wichita, National Baseball Congress, 1960

8 For an encyclopedia article—author given:

Eaton, Vincent L., "District of Columbia," Encyclopedia Americana, 1956 edition, vol. 9, pp. 193b-194b

9 For an encyclopedia article—no author given:

"Stocks and Bonds," Compton's Pictured Encyclopedia, 1954 edition, vol. 13, pp. 398-406

All the items in the bibliography are put in one list, arranged alphabetically by the last name of the author. If no author is given, the first word of the title (not counting A or The) determines the order.

Big words "Big words" are not necessarily long words. Instead they are uncommon, formal words that seem out of place in ordinary writing: *repast* (for *meal*), *masticate* (for *chew*), *elucidate* (for *explain*), *celerity* (for *speed*), *edifice* (for *building*), *cogitate* (for *think over*), *salubrious* (for *healthful*). Big words tend to weaken the effectiveness of your writing by calling attention to themselves and away from what you are saying. (For a full discussion, see Chapter 12, "Avoid Big Words," page 275.)

blame Both *blame . . . for* and *blame . . . on* are standard English idioms. Notice the difference in meaning:

> They *blamed* Paul *for* the delay. [They held him responsible, accused him of being at fault in this instance.]
> They *blamed* the delay *on* Paul. [They claimed that he was responsible, ascribed the responsibility for the delay to him.]

Blend A coined word made by telescoping two words into one:

> Cinerama (from *cinema* and *panorama*)
> betatron (from *beta rays* and *electron*)
> slanguage (from *slang* and *language*)
> fantabulous (from *fantastic* and *fabulous*)
> humiture (from *humidity* and *temperature*)

Until a blend has become accepted as part of the general vocabulary, as *gerrymander* (from *Gerry* and *salamander*), *camporee* (from *camp* and *jamboree*), and *Amerind* (from *American* and *Indian*) have, it is appropriate only in informal English—not in formal.

393

blond, blonde As a noun, *blond* is a man; *blonde,* a woman:

> The blond with him is his brother.
> We need a blonde to play the heroine.

Although the adjective is spelled with or without the final *e, blond* is the more common spelling:

> He rented a costume and a blond wig.

Boners Blunders that result from confusing two similar words or from combining ideas that do not belong together. Boners are often quite funny—though not in a way intended by the writer. Here are some examples from student papers:

> Everyone at the ball was formerly dressed.
> Bob, Dan, and Oscar were aged ten, twelve, and fourteen respectfully.
> Brady, however, was too ambitious to rest on his morals.
> My favorite is Schubert's *Unfinished Sympathy.*
> If a person faints, stretch him out on his back and keep his feet elevated until he becomes conscientious again.

Watch for amusing boners in the books and magazines you read, and share the fun with your friends. But unless you do not mind a laugh at your expense, scan your own writing carefully to catch any boners before they are found by others.

bore   Followed by *with* when it means "make someone weary":

Steve bored his sister with his constant bragging.

born, borne   1 The past participle of *bear* in most of its meanings is *borne:*

Sturdy columns have borne the weight of the temple for many years.   ["Supported."]
He has never borne a grudge against us.   ["Held."]
Mrs. Betts had borne six boys.   ["Given birth to."]

But *born* is the usual spelling in such sentences as:

Lincoln was born in Kentucky.
Kitty was a born actress.
Franklin, though born in Boston, is usually identified with Philadelphia.

2 Students asked to write their autobiographies often become self-conscious and coy or else they attempt humor in giving the facts of their birth: "I first put in my appearance in this vale of tears on May 14, 1946" or "Early one lovely morning in August—August 21, 1944, to be exact—I entered this confused and confusing world." A simple and natural statement like "I was born May 14, 1946" is usually much better.

borrow   Usually followed by *from*, sometimes by *of:*

Don't try to borrow any money from him.
Why not borrow it of the bank?

Borrow . . . off and *borrow . . . off of* are nonstandard:

NONSTANDARD: Last week he borrowed another dollar off of me.
STANDARD: Last week he borrowed another dollar from me.   [Or: of me.]

In certain regional dialects *borrow* is sometimes used to mean "lend":

DIALECT: Will you borrow me your ruler?
STANDARD: Will you lend me your ruler?

Borrowed words   In the course of its history, English has borrowed words from many other languages. Some of these borrowings have been deliberate: scientists and scholars have often gone to foreign languages for names for new discoveries, ideas, or situations. Others have been brought in by groups of immigrants, introduced through commerce and trade, or picked up by large groups of our citizens (such as soldiers) who have visited foreign lands. Some of these borrowed words retain their original forms and pronunciations (*terrazzo, précis, soufflé, laissez faire*). But many of them—generally the most useful ones—are gradually Anglicized to bring their pronunciation (and sometimes their spelling) in line with English usage. (See **Anglicizing.**)

1 Use. The reason for the common use of many borrowed words is that they supply a real need in our language. Many times they say in one word what it would take several English words to say—for example, *entrepreneur*, "a person who organizes and manages a business enterprise, taking the risk of not making a profit and getting the profit when there is one." Many times they are the only names we have for certain objects or ideas: *pizza, glockenspiel, habeas corpus*. In other cases they carry with them strong connotations that are extremely important in certain contexts: *coup de grâce, ersatz, émigré*. Borrowed words for which there are adequate English equivalents are not so likely to become common or Anglicized, retaining always a foreign flavor: *mal de mer, sotto voce, milieu*. For these we can say *seasickness, in an undertone, environment*.

Borrowed words have greatly enriched our language; it would be difficult to communicate without them. Here is a list of some that are in common use:

adobe (Spanish)	emphatic (Greek)
alumni (Latin)	filibuster (Spanish)
bazaar (Persian)	ghoul (Arabic)
boomerang (Australian)	ketchup (Malay)
casserole (French)	kibitzer (Yiddish)
chaise longue (French)	rendezvous (French)
criterion (Greek)	smorgasbord (Swedish)
decoy (Dutch)	toupee (French)
do, re, mi, etc. (Italian)	veranda (Hindustani)

2 Italics. Borrowed words so commonly used that they have become part of the general vocabulary are written without italics. Those that have not been Anglicized and are not thought of as English words are usually italicized in print (underlined in writing):

ad nauseam	*hasta mañana*
de rigueur	*Realpolitik*
fait accompli	*sine qua non*

When in doubt about whether to italicize a certain word or phrase, consult a dictionary. In some dictionaries borrowed words that are not part of the general English vocabulary are indicated by a double dagger (‡), in others by two parallel bars (||), in others by a label (*Italian, French,* etc.) preceding the definitions.

both *Both* is used to emphasize twoness:

The pitcher and the catcher both struck out.
The leading actor and his understudy were both sick.

In speech *both* is sometimes used in sentences like these:

> The novel and the movie were both alike.
> Both the west face and the south face of the mountain were equally challenging to the climbers.

But since *alike* in the first example and *equally* in the second one express the intended meaning clearly, the word *both* is unnecessary. In writing, it should be omitted as a bit of deadwood.

In some regional dialects *both* is used in place of *two*:

> DIALECT: The both boys wanted to join the navy.
> STANDARD: The two boys wanted to join the navy.

both ... and Used as correlative conjunctions (conjunctions that work in pairs):

> Both the headache and the dizziness were caused by lack of sleep.

(See **Correlative conjunctions.**)

boughten Used only in certain regional dialects to distinguish articles bought at a store from those that are homemade:

> DIALECT: Mrs. Tyler thought it disgraceful to serve boughten pie.
> STANDARD: Mrs. Tyler thought it disgraceful to serve pie that was not homemade. [Or: bakery pie.]

Brackets [ ] Used mainly to enclose an explanation, comment, or correction that has been inserted into quoted material:

> "The populations of the two playground states [California and Florida] have increased enormously in recent years."

Brackets are sometimes used as parentheses within parentheses:

> Mencken's chapter on slang (see his *American Language* [fourth edition], pages 555-589) is amusing as well as informative.

breath, breathe *Breath,* pronounced breth, is a noun; *breathe,* pronounced brēTH, is a verb:

> NOUN: He took a deep breath and jumped.
> VERB: The explorers found it difficult to breathe at the high altitude.

British usage See **American and British usage.**

Broad reference When a pronoun refers to a preceding idea (expressed in a group of words) rather than to a specific, one-word antecedent, it is said to have broad reference:

> The snow covered everything to a depth of two feet, *which* pleased the small boys but dismayed their fathers. [*Which* refers to the whole idea stated in the main clause.]

(For further discussion and examples, see Chapter 10, "Vague Reference," page 228.)

Bromide   A figurative term for a commonplace idea or a trite remark:

> Beauty is only skin deep.
> You can't teach an old dog new tricks.
> It never rains but it pours.

Since the literal meaning of *bromide* is "a medicine used to calm nervousness and cause sleep," the term is an effective—though harsh—name for such expressions. (See **Cliché.**)

brunet, brunette   As a noun, *brunet* is a man; *brunette,* a woman:

> Isn't his twin brother a brunet?
> The new model was a tall brunette.

As an adjective, either *brunet* or *brunette* is used.

bunch   Formal English limits the use of *bunch* to things that grow together or can be fastened together:

> a bunch of grapes   a bunch of weeds   a bunch of tags

Informal English uses *bunch* to refer to a small group of anything—including people:

> Another bunch of girls were practicing cheers.

397

burned, burnt   The past tense and the past participle of *burn* are either *burned* or *burnt:*

> One of the firemen was badly burned (*or* burnt) in the blaze.
> Agents burned (*or* burnt) all secret papers before they fled.

Burned is the more common form, except when the participle is used as an adjective:

> Even the burnt marshmallows tasted delicious.

burst   The principal parts are *burst, burst, burst:*

> Closed windows sometimes burst when a tornado strikes.
> Mr. Stubbs burst into a sprint when he saw the bus.
> At the mere mention of Bob's name she had burst into tears.

(See **bust.**)

bus   The plural is either *buses* or *busses.* The first is more common.

Business letters   **1 Stationery.**   Standard business stationery comes in two sizes. For most letters, a sheet 8½ by 11 inches is used; for shorter letters, a sheet about 7½ by 10½ inches.

2 Parts of the letter. A business letter usually has six parts:

HEADING	63 Center Street Elm, Ohio 45892 June 6, 19--
INSIDE ADDRESS	Atlas Office Service 12 North Dearborn Street Chicago, Illinois 60602
SALUTATION	Gentlemen:
BODY	. . . .
CLOSING	Sincerely yours,
SIGNATURE	*Gerald Price* Gerald Price

a) *The Heading.* The writer's complete address (street, city, state, and ZIP Code) and the date (month, day, and year) are placed near the top of the sheet, slightly to the right of the center of the page:

> 625 Myrtle Street
> Barton, Florida 33830
> November 3, 19--

If stationery with a printed letterhead is used, only the date is added, two or three spaces below.

b) *The Inside Address.* The name and address of the person or firm written to is begun at the left margin, from two to four spaces below the heading:

Mr. Henry Rakove   Walsh and Berry, Inc.
Rural Route 3, Box 6   438 Colfax Avenue
Westport, Arkansas 72118   Kiowa, Colorado 80117

A letter may be directed to a particular member of a firm by putting his name (with his title, if he has one) either at the head or at the end of the inside address:

```
Mr. Mark Clow, President      Metal Products Company
Atlas Stamp Company           593 Morgan Street
425 Liberty Avenue            Webster, Ohio  45175
Canby, New York  13743
                              Attention: Mr. Roy Smith
```

If the business title is long, it is usually placed on a separate line, directly below the name:

```
Mr. Earl Lanham
Director of Admissions
Abbott College
Abbott, Vermont  05201
```

Abbreviations are usually avoided in the heading and inside address. However, if the name of a firm (as it appears in advertisements) contains an abbreviation, that abbreviation is used: *Allen & Miller, Inc.; Wm. F. Carsello and Bros.* And some addresses require an abbreviation designating a particular section of the city: *358 H Street, S.E.* But all other words are generally written out, including street names that are numbers below ten: *Third Avenue and 75th Street.*

No punctuation is used at the ends of the lines in the heading and inside address. Inside the lines, a comma is used between the city and the state, the rural route and the box number, the day of the month and the year. No comma is used between the state and the ZIP Code.

c) *The Salutation.* The salutation, a conventional greeting, is placed two spaces below the inside address and flush with the left margin. A colon (:) is the usual mark of punctuation after the salutation.

The following are common salutations:

```
If the name is unknown:  Dear Sir:      Dear Madam:
If the name is known:  Dear Mr. Polk:   Dear Miss Ames:
More formal:  My dear Mr. Lee:          My dear Miss Cox:
To a business firm:  Gentlemen:         Ladies:
```

A letter addressed to a firm or organization generally has the salutation *Gentlemen:*, even though an attention line may direct the letter to a particular person.

d) *The Body.* The body of the letter is begun two spaces below the salutation. The message should be stated clearly and concisely, preferably in simple, direct words. All relevant information should be included, with a separate paragraph for each main thought. Although generally impersonal in tone, the letter should always be courteous.

(See also "Writing Letters of Application," page 287; "Asking Permission of References," page 291; and "Sending for College Catalogues and Application Forms," page 292.)

e) *The Closing.* The closing is aligned with the first word of the heading or started to the right of the center of the page, two lines below the body of the letter. Only the first word of the closing is capitalized. A comma follows the last word.

The closing should match the salutation and the body of the letter in degree of formality or informality:

Very truly yours,   (formal)
Yours very truly,   (formal)
Sincerely yours,   (more personal)
Cordially yours,   (more friendly)
Respectfully yours,   (to a church or government official)

f) The Signature. The writer's first and last names (and his middle name or initial if desired) should be handwritten, in ink, below the closing.

In typewritten letters the name and title (if one is writing as a representative of an organization or firm) are usually typed below the signature. The name of the organization or firm is sometimes typed before the signature.

Very truly yours,
George Collins
George Collins
Vice President

Sincerely yours,
THE LATIN CLUB
Marjory A. Balke
Marjory A. Balke
Secretary

A man does not use the title *Mr.* before his signature, but a woman may write *Miss* in parentheses before her name or add her married name below her signature to indicate how she wishes to be addressed in the reply:

Sincerely yours,
(Miss) Norma White

Cordially yours,
Frances Long
(Mrs. John S. Long)

3 Appearance and styles. The letter should be centered neatly on the page, with from one-inch to two-inch margins at right and left. Unless the letter is short, it is usually single spaced, with double spacing between the paragraphs. If the letter is handwritten, there is no extra space between paragraphs.

The most common letter styles are the block, the semiblock, and the indented. In the block style there are no indentions in the heading, inside address, salutation, or paragraphs. In the semiblock style, indentions are used only for paragraphs, which are indented five to ten spaces. In the indented style, which is now seldom used except in handwritten letters, the second and third lines of the heading and the inside address and the first line of each paragraph are indented (usually three to five spaces) to the right of the word above. Which style to use for a particular letter is a matter of personal preference.

4 The envelope. The style used for the addresses on the envelope —block, semiblock, or indented—should match that used for the heading and the inside address of the letter. The envelope address (or outside address), which gives the name and address of the person or firm written to, is centered slightly below the middle of the envelope. The return address is placed in the upper left-hand corner.

```
Ralph Schneider
680 Center Street
Orton, Utah   84056




            Central Film Company
            1065 Morton Street
            Winchester, Michigan   49349
```

5 Folding the letter.   When a short envelope is used, the letter is folded up to within a quarter of an inch of the top of the sheet. The right-hand third of the doubled sheet is next folded to the left and creased. Then the left-hand third is folded over to within a quarter of an inch of the crease made at the right. Finally, the letter, held by the right-hand crease, is inserted into the envelope.

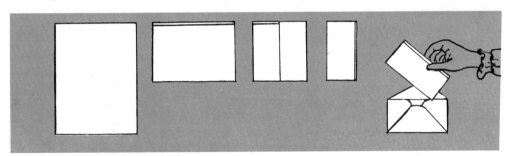

When a long envelope is used, the bottom third of the letter is brought up and creased. Then the top of the sheet is brought down to within a half inch of the bottom crease. Finally, the letter, held by the top fold, is inserted into the envelope.

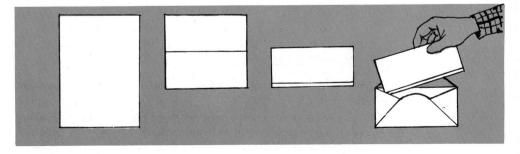

business world   A pretentious term for *business* or *businessmen*:

PRETENTIOUS: My uncle urged me to enter the business world.
BETTER: My uncle urged me to go into business.

bust   Used in nonstandard English for *burst* or *break*:

NONSTANDARD: The thug busted a window to get inside the store.
STANDARD: The thug broke a window to get inside the store.

The expressions *bust a bronco, bust a trust, bust an officer* (reduce in rank) are labeled *Slang* in some dictionaries. But they are so generally used in informal English that they may be considered standard.

but   1 *But* is a coördinating conjunction used to connect two contrasting expressions. The words, phrases, or clauses joined by *but* should be of the same grammatical form:

ADJECTIVES: The new chair was handsome but uncomfortable.
ADVERBS: The glacier advanced slowly but inexorably.
PHRASES: He will help out on Saturday, but not on Sunday.
SUBORDINATE CLAUSES: Some people go to the opera not because they enjoy the music, but because they want to be seen.
MAIN CLAUSES: George tried to memorize the poem, but his mind was elsewhere.

The parts joined by *but* should actually be contrasting or opposite in thought. If they are not, *but* should not be used to join them:

CONTRASTING IDEAS: Mrs. Evans is strict, but she is never sarcastic.
NOT CONTRASTING: The directions were printed in small type, *and* he couldn't read them without his glasses. [Not: *but* he couldn't read them.]

But should not be doubled by a word like *however*, which adds nothing to its meaning:

The gale had abated, but the waves were still high. [Not: but however the waves were still high.]

(For the punctuation of compound sentences with *but,* see **Comma,** section 1.)

2 *But* is sometimes used at the beginning of a sentence to emphasize the contrast between ideas:

The desperate effort to save the trapped miners began soon after the explosion occurred. Rescue teams, working through the night, finally succeeded in reaching the group entombed in the tunnel. But they were too late.

Used too often, however, this introductory *But* becomes tiresome and loses its effectiveness.

3 *But* is also used as a preposition meaning "except" and as a rather formal adverb meaning "only" or "no more than":

402

PREPOSITION: No one had the right answer but Joan.
ADVERB: If someone had but warned him, he might have been saved.
ADVERB: When she was but a child, her family moved to Canada.

Using *not* with *but* (in the sense of "no more than") makes a double negative:

When she wasn't but a child, her family moved to Canada.

Though this double negative with *but* is found in informal speech, it is not appropriate in writing. There the *not* should be dropped. If the sentence then seems too formal in tone, the *but* can be changed to *only*:

When she was only a child, her family moved to Canada.

but that, but what   In informal written English *but that* is the usual conjunction in sentences like these:

He doesn't doubt but that they will hire more men.
She has no doubt but that the gift will be delivered tomorrow.

In informal speech, *but what* (or *but* alone) is common:

She has no doubt but what the gift will be delivered tomorrow.
I don't doubt but he will complain to the manager.

In formal English, *that* alone is preferred:

I do not doubt that he will complain to the manager.

but which, but who   See **and which, and who.**

buy   Used with *from*, not with *off* or *off of*:

NONSTANDARD: We bought the souvenirs off of (*or* off) a peddler.
STANDARD: We bought the souvenirs from a peddler.

Buy off is an idiomatic phrase meaning "bribe":

The outlaws tried to buy off the Wells Fargo agent.

can, may   1 In informal English (both spoken and written) *can* is used to express permission as well as ability:

PERMISSION: Can I come in?
                     Patients can't have more than two visitors at a time.
ABILITY: Anyone can learn to drive.
                Yes, but can he wiggle his ears?

May is rarely used except to express possibility:

I may be late.   She may want to ask a few questions.

2 In formal English *can* is used only to express ability:

> She can drive a golf ball three hundred yards.
> Can you translate this letter into German?

To express permission, *may* is used:

> May I stay at Ann's house tonight?
> You may go if you can find your way in this fog.

cannot, can not   Both are used, but *cannot* is more common.

can't help but   A colloquial expression, common in everyday speech. It is not appropriate in writing or in formal speech.

> COLLOQUIAL: I can't help but wish I had gone to the dance.
> WRITTEN: I can't help wishing I had gone to the dance.

Capital letters   **1 Sentence capitals.**   (a) The first word of a sentence is always capitalized.

b) In quotations, the first word of a quoted sentence is capitalized; but if the quoted sentence is interrupted by explanatory words, the first word of its second part is not capitalized:

> Then, pointing to the bulky volume, Ben said, "It took me two hours to read just the first chapter."
> "At that rate," remarked Sam, "you'll never finish your report by Friday. Why don't you help him, Joan?"
> She answered quickly, "Because he hasn't asked me to."

c) A sentence enclosed in parentheses is capitalized when it stands *between* other sentences:

> *The Red Badge of Courage* was one of the first American novels to portray realistically the feelings of soldiers caught up in the fury of war. (The hero is a young Union recruit who learns, in battle, to face his fear and cowardice with courage.) Stephen Crane, the author, wrote convincingly of fighting men, though he had had no first-hand experience of war at the time he wrote.

But a sentence enclosed in parentheses is not usually capitalized when it comes *within* another sentence:

> The women looked silly and self-conscious in their costumes (this was one of those come-dressed-as-your-favorite-character parties), and I heard several men muttering that this was the first and last time they'd submit to such nonsense.

2 Proper names and abbreviations of proper names are capitalized:

PEOPLE: John L. Sullivan, Captain John Paul Jones
PLACES: The Hague, Hot Springs, Lookout Mountain, York Road
RACES, LANGUAGES, POLITICAL PARTIES: Caucasian, Arabic, the Republican candidate

CHURCHES AND THEIR MEMBERS: the Episcopal Church, Beth-El Temple, Baptist, Seventh Day Adventists, Catholics

DAYS, MONTHS, HOLIDAYS, HOLY DAYS: Friday, May, Labor Day, Lent, Yom Kippur

COMPANIES: General Foods Corporation, Ohio Edison Company

INSTITUTIONS: Grinnell College, the Applied Physics Laboratory

ORGANIZATIONS: the American Automobile Association, the National Honor Society, the League of Women Voters

SHIPS, TRAINS, PLANES: S.S. *Constitution,* the *Twentieth-Century Limited,* the *Constellation*

HISTORICAL EVENTS, PERIODS, AND DOCUMENTS: the Thirty Years' War, the Stone Age, the Atlantic Charter

BUILDINGS: the Merchandise Mart, the White House

TRADE NAMES: Kodak, Pepsodent, Stetson

SACRED FIGURES, BIBLE, PARTS OF THE BIBLE: God, our Father, in His service, the New Testament (See **Bible, bible.**)

3 Adjectives formed from proper nouns are generally capitalized, but the words that they modify are not, unless they themselves are proper nouns:

Spanish literature	Heinz pickles
a British colony	Irish Renaissance

4 The names of the seasons are not capitalized:

A bird's plumage is bright in the *spring* and dull in the *fall*.

5 The points of the compass (north, east, southwest, etc.) are not capitalized when they show direction:

The cold front moved *south* and then turned *east* into Ohio.

They are capitalized when used as the names of geographical regions:

The population of the *West* is growing faster than that of the *South*.

6 School subjects are not capitalized unless they are names of languages or of specific numbered courses:

Lydia does best in *French* and *history*; Maude, in *German* and *biology*.
Mr. Tatfield is teaching *Biology 1* this semester.

7 Words like *street, avenue, highway, river, tunnel, park, bridge, high school, university,* and *senior* are not capitalized unless they are used as part of a proper name:

There is an excellent view of the *river* from the *highway*.
You can use either the *bridge* or the new *tunnel* to cross the bay.
The *seniors* at our *high school* have many electives to choose from.

But:	the Potomac River	Brooklyn Bridge	the Senior Prom
	the Dixie Highway	the Holland Tunnel	Cook High School

Note: Many newspapers and magazines do not capitalize words like *street, avenue, river,* and *park* when they follow a proper name: *Adams street, the Merrimac river, Yellowstone park.* But in your school writing you will probably be expected to follow the more conservative practice of capitalizing the words.

8 Personal titles. Nouns showing office, rank, or profession (*congressman, colonel, governor, judge,* etc.) are always capitalized when used with the name of a person and are usually capitalized when used alone in place of the person's name:

> As *Governor Hibbs* waved to the crowd, he looked up.
> "What do you see up there, *Governor?*" asked a reporter.
> The *governor* made no reply.

President referring to the President of the United States is generally capitalized.

9 Nouns showing relationship. Capitalize *mother, father, sister, brother, aunt, uncle,* etc., only when they are used as part of a person's name or as a substitute for a person's name:

> My *father* and *mother* both like to visit *Aunt Helen.*
> "Seriously, *Grandma,* was your *grandmother* a pioneer?"

10 Titles of articles, books, etc. The usual practice is to capitalize the first and last words of the title, all important words (nouns, pronouns, verbs, adjectives, adverbs), and all prepositions of more than four letters:

> "How to Choose the Right College"   *Of Mice and Men*
> "In the Valley of the Kings"   *The Fleet's In*

11 Lines of poetry. In most poetry each line begins with a capital letter. But in much modern poetry this is not true. Remember that poetry must always be copied exactly as it originally appeared—with or without capitals, however the poet wrote it.

12 O and oh. The formal and rather rare interjection *O,* used in direct address, is always capitalized. The interjection *oh* is not capitalized unless it begins a sentence:

> Hear me, *O* king, before you judge them.
> He fell asleep immediately, and *oh,* how he snored!

Card catalogue An alphabetical list of all the books in a library, arranged on cards in a series of drawers. In the catalogue you can find (1) whether the library has a book of a certain title, (2) what books it has by a certain author, (3) what books it has on a given subject, and (4) where you will find a book on the library shelves.

The catalogue usually contains at least three cards for every book: an *author* card, a *title* card, and a *subject* card. When you know who wrote the book, you generally look for the author card. This is filed alphabetically by the author's last name, which is the first item at the top of the card. When you know the title but not the author of a book, you look for the title card. It is filed alphabetically according to the first important word of the title.

Often you may want to find books on a certain subject, but you have no particular authors or titles in mind. Then you look in the catalogue for subject cards, filed alphabetically according to the subject. Under every subject heading there are cards for the books in the library that deal with that subject. And a book may be listed under several subject headings. (A study of American Indian crafts and dress, for example, might be listed under INDIANS OF NORTH AMERICA, HANDICRAFTS, and COSTUME AND ADORNMENT.) If you do not find the first subject heading you look for, try related subjects. (MORSE CODE may not be listed, but books treating the subject may be found under CIPHER AND TELEGRAPH CODES, COMMERCE, or TELEGRAPH.)

Here are three catalogue cards for Ralph E. Lapp's *Man and Space*:

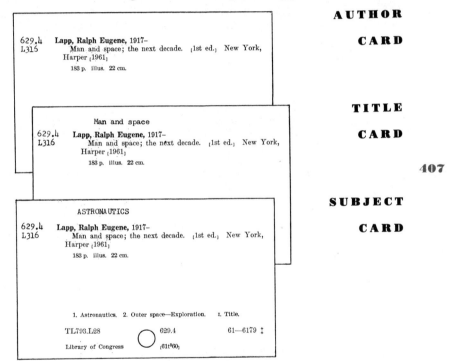

AUTHOR CARD

TITLE CARD

SUBJECT CARD

The top lines differ, but otherwise the cards are exactly the same. The *call number* in the upper left-hand corner of each tells where you will find the book in the library. The top line, **629.4**, is the Dewey classification number. (See *Dewey Decimal System*.) The second line, **L316**, is the author's initial and number. Since this call number is also printed on the spine of the book, it makes it easy for you to find the book on the shelves.

Catalogue cards tell you other things that you may want to know about a book: the place and date it was published; the name of the publisher; the number of pages; whether it has illustrations, maps, appendixes; and all the subject headings it is listed under.

Caret (∧)   A mark put in a line of manuscript to show that something should be inserted at that point:

> south
> The cafeteria is just past the ∧ entrance.

> although
> No one seemed to recognize him, ∧ he had been away for only a year.

You will seldom need to use carets in your themes if you take time to revise your first drafts carefully before making final copies. But in general (on exam papers, official forms, committee reports) there is no objection to your using carets to make corrections, if you do it neatly and not too frequently.

Case   Pronouns change in form depending on how they are used in a sentence (*He* wanted *his* brother to listen to *him*). This change of form to show the function of a word is called *case*.

Personal pronouns (except *you* and *it*) and the pronoun *who* have three case forms:

NOMINATIVE CASE: I, you, he, she, it, we, you, they; who
    Peter and *I* did most of the work.   [Used as subject.]
    Who is he?   [Used as subject and as complement.]

OBJECTIVE CASE: me, you, him, her, it, us, you, them; whom
    Mr. Vale saw Peter and *me*.   [Used as direct object.]
    The librarian handed *me* a book.   [Used as indirect object.]
    With *whom* did you go?   [Used as object of preposition.]

POSSESSIVE CASE: mine, yours, his, hers, its, ours, yours, theirs; whose
    That pencil is *mine*.   [Shows possession.]
    Whose is this green one?   [Shows possession.]

Nouns have only two case forms—a possessive, and an ordinary form that is used for all other functions: *driver's, driver; Mary's, Mary.*

Since nouns and pronouns in present-day English have so few special case forms, we have few problems concerning case. The chief ones are discussed in Chapter 9, "Pronouns," page 205. (See also **Nominative case, Possessive case, Objective case.**)

case   Expressions with *case* are often merely deadwood that could easily be pruned away in revision:

> Although John Gunther has written many books about foreign countries, in not one [case] has he relied on someone else's observations.
> The logical, moral approach of the eighteenth-century thinkers can be seen in [the case of] Thomas Jefferson's writings.
> [In] several [cases] sophomores were permitted to sign up for the course.

Cause and effect   For a discussion of this method of developing paragraphs, see Chapter 2, "Details Giving Causes and Effects," page 37. For a discussion of the cause-effect relationship in logical reasoning, see Chapter 4, "The *Post Hoc* Fallacy," page 95.

center around (or about)   *Center around* and *center about* are informal idioms:

> Usually the publicity centers around the stars of the movie.

In formal English *center on* or *center in* is used:

> Usually the publicity centers on the stars of the movie.
> All his hopes were centered in his two sons.

Centuries   A simple rule for naming a century correctly is to add one to the number of its hundred. The present century, the nineteen hundreds, is called the twentieth century. The sixteen hundreds are called the seventeenth century, and so on.

Dates before Christ are figured in the same way as those after: The first century B.C. runs back from the birth of Christ through the year 100; the second century, from 101 through 200; and so on.

cf.   An abbreviation for the Latin *confer*. It is used in footnotes to mean "compare" or "see" a given reference for further information.

Chinese   Because the words *Chinaman* and *Chinamen* have developed belittling connotations, *Chinese* is preferable:

> A Chinese, Dr. Chen Ning Yang, won the Nobel prize for physics in 1957.
> Many Chinese were brought to America to work on the railroads.

Circumlocution   The use of several words for an idea that might be conveyed by fewer words: he took his departure = he left; filled with disillusionment = disillusioned. (See Chapter 11, "Roundabout Expressions," page 255.)

Cities   In expository writing the name of the country or state need not be given with the names of well-known cities: *Paris, Boston, Miami, Berlin, Tokyo, Detroit, Rome.* But cities or towns that are not well known or have the same names as other cities should be fully identified if there is a possibility that readers may be puzzled or misled: *Paris, Tennessee; Rome, Georgia; London, Ontario; Sheldon, Iowa.*

Clause   A group of words that has a subject and a verb and is used as *part* of a sentence. (A simple sentence like "He borrowed two books" has a subject and a verb, but we do not call it a clause, because it is a whole sentence, not part of a sentence.) There are two kinds of clauses—*main* and *subordinate*:

1 Main clause (also called independent or principal clause). A main clause is one that, though part of a sentence, is grammatically independent; that is, it could stand alone as a sentence. The main clauses are italicized in the examples:

He borrowed two books, and *I returned them.*
The report that the commission released *was very interesting.*
While he was at the library, *he borrowed two books for me.*
I had a suspicion that Campbell had written the article, but *I hesitated to say so without proof.*

2 Subordinate clause. A subordinate clause cannot stand alone as a sentence; it depends on the rest of the sentence to complete its meaning:

The clerk *who had waited on us* had left. [Adjective clause.]
While I was waiting, I read a magazine. [Adverb clause.]
I had a suspicion *that Campbell himself had written the article.* [Noun clause used as appositive.]

Subordinate clauses, as the examples show, are always used in sentences as single words might be used—as adjectives, adverbs, or nouns.
(For further examples and discussion, see **Adjective clause, Adverb clause, Noun clause, Compound sentence, Complex sentence.** See also Chapter 11, "Presenting Effective Word Pictures," page 244.)

410 *Cliché* An expression that has been used so often that it has become commonplace and stale: *green with envy, to the bitter end, as brave as a lion.* (See Chapter 12, "Avoid Trite Words," page 276; and **Bromide.**)

Climax Climax is the arrangement of a series of words, phrases, clauses, or sentences in an ascending order—that is, each item in the series is longer, more striking, more forceful, or more important in some way than the preceding item:

The prisoners spoke guardedly of home, of the possibility of escape, and of the ceaseless struggle to stay alive. [Order based on length of phrases.]
As soon as he saw the barracuda, he became aware of a sudden stillness in the air, a sensation of cold in his fingertips, and a wild rush of fear that left him powerless to move. [Order based on forcefulness of ideas and striking way in which they are phrased.]
Napoleon's life is a study in adventure, in calm mastery of the situation, in short-lived glory, in heartless indifference to the desires of millions of people, and in monstrous greed for total power over the world. [Order based on importance of ideas and amount of emotion they will arouse.]

Climax is the natural order for arranging the items of a series unless there is some special reason for another order. Failure to use climactic order usually results in a weak sentence or, if the last member of the series is conspicuously less important than the preceding ones, in anticlimax. (For a discussion of this point, see **Anticlimax.**)

Clipped words   Words made by dropping a syllable or more from another word are called *clipped words* or sometimes *clips*. They are used in informal speech and writing: *lab, tux, pre-med, grad, sub, el.* (Some clips are shoptalk or slang: *hypo, doc.*) Since these words are not abbreviations, they are not followed by periods.

Coherence   When we say that a piece of writing has coherence (or is coherent), we mean that the ideas move in a smooth, straight, uninterrupted line from beginning to end. In this book the word *continuity* is used instead of the word *coherence*. This important quality of good writing is discussed in Chapter 2, "Continuity in Paragraphs," page 49.

Coining words   Making up a new word for a particular occasion (like *golfomaniac* or *know-it-allitis*) or for general use (*nylon, Kleenex, radar*) is called *coining*. The made-up word is called a *coinage*, or, if it is never used again, a *nonce word*.

Collective nouns   A *collective noun* is one that though singular in form names a group of objects or persons:

crowd	squad	cast	club	family
flock	jury	mob	panel	orchestra

411

   1 Agreement.   When the writer intends the collective noun to mean the group taken as a whole, he uses a singular verb and pronoun:

The clean-up squad *was finishing its* work.

When the writer intends the collective noun to mean the individual members of a group, he uses a plural verb and pronoun:

The squad *were putting* away *their* brooms when we arrived.

   2 Consistency.   In speech we often use a collective noun with a singular verb and then inconsistently shift to a plural pronoun. But in writing, a collective noun should be treated consistently as either singular or plural:

The committee *is meeting* at ten o'clock and will let us know *its* decision by noon. [Not: *their* decision.]

Sometimes you will find that the meaning of a collective actually changes from singular to plural within a sentence. Then, rather than be inconsistent, substitute a regular plural noun for the collective:

INCONSISTENT: The panel *has chosen* a subject but *haven't* yet *prepared their* talks.
CONSISTENT: The panelists (*or* The members of the panel) *have chosen* a subject but *haven't* yet *prepared their* talks.

Colloquial *Colloquial* means "characteristic of conversation." When words and constructions are labeled *colloquial* in this book, it means that they are found chiefly in informal speech but are also generally considered appropriate in informal writing. (There are some colloquialisms that are not considered appropriate in writing; that point is always made clear when such an expression is discussed in this Index.)

Dictionaries also use *Colloquial* (usually abbreviating it to *Colloq.*) to label words and phrases like *pal, bamboozle, take it easy,* and *pick on,* which are used more often in speech than in writing. Remember when you see this label that, contrary to what many people think, the dictionary makers are not frowning on the use of the labeled word. They are indicating that the word is inappropriate in formal situations, but acceptable in most informal writing and completely appropriate in informal speech.

Colon **(:)** The colon is a rather formal and emphatic mark that directs attention to what follows. As a "go ahead" signal it has three common uses:

1 A colon is used to introduce a list of appositives (at the end of a sentence) that the writer wants to emphasize:

> Each student is to bring with him the following items: a slide rule, two pencils, a drawing compass, and a pad of scratch paper. [The four nouns are in apposition with *items.*]

> Whenever Cliff thought of his approaching date with Gloria, the same problems troubled him: what to wear, how to act, and what to talk about. [The three phrases are in apposition with *problems.*]

Note: The colon is not used before a list unless the items are appositives. When they are simply objects or predicate complements, no mark of punctuation should be used before them:

> Each student was asked to bring [ ] a slide rule, two pencils, a drawing compass, and a pad of scratch paper. [The four nouns are objects of *to bring.*]
> Now Cliff's only problems are [ ] what to wear, how to act, and what to talk about. [The three phrases are predicate complements.]

2 A colon is used to introduce a long or formal quotation in factual writing:

> In discussing the task of the historian, Macaulay says: "The perfect historian is he in whose work the character and spirit of an age is exhibited in miniature. He relates no fact, he attributes no expression to his characters which is not authenticated by sufficient testimony. But by judicious selection, rejection, and arrangement, he gives to truth those attractions which have been usurped by fiction."

3 A colon may be used between the clauses of a compound sentence when the second clause explains or illustrates the first:

> Earl was dissatisfied with the pictures he had taken: all but two of them were out of focus.
> The charge of plagiarism was, in fact, quite fair: Martin had taken his plot from a play he had read years before.

4 The colon has several conventional uses:
a) After the salutation in a business letter:

> Dear Mr. Hinchley: Dear Sir:

b) Between hours and minutes expressed in figures:

> 10:48 a.m.   9:05 p.m.   at 10:30 tomorrow morning

c) Between volume and page numbers of a magazine:

> *Consumer Reports,* 25:580-583

d) Between Biblical chapter and verse:

> Exodus 24:3   II Kings 17:19-23

Comma   The purpose of the comma is to help make what you write clear. You will find it useful to think of the comma as making a slight separation—just enough to keep words or phrases distinct. It represents the slight pause that we use automatically in speech to help get across our meaning.

413

Today the tendency in writing is to use as few commas as possible and still make the meaning clear. Narrative writing generally uses fewer commas than expository writing; formal writing generally uses more than informal.

The following sections point out places where commas are very likely to be needed, to make reading easier or to prevent misreading.

1 In a compound sentence.   A comma is generally used before the coördinating conjunction (*and, but, for, or, nor, yet, so*) that joins the two independent clauses of a compound sentence:

> Anthony wanted very much to go to college, but his parents could not afford to send him.

When the clauses are short and easily distinguishable, the comma is often omitted. This is especially true in informal narrative:

> Mrs. Hale must have suspected Ted or she wouldn't have had the sheriff question him.
> But: Mrs. Hale must have suspected Ted, or the sheriff wouldn't have questioned him. [Without the comma the sentence might first be read "Mrs. Hale must have suspected Ted or the sheriff. . . ."]

(For punctuating compound sentences when the clauses themselves contain commas, see **Semicolon,** section 2.)

2 To set off interrupting elements. Parenthetical expressions like *for example, I believe, it seems, in fact*; nouns of address; words like *yes, no, oh, well*; and constructions repeated to ask questions ("You agree, *don't you?*") are all set off by commas:

> Bill, I believe, would make a fine class president.
> The guest of honor, it seems, had forgotten all about the party.
> His carelessness, in fact, is the real reason for his failure.
> Your face, young lady, is quite dirty.   [Noun of address.]
> Gentlemen of the jury, your duty is clear.   [Noun of address.]
> No, ignorance of the law is no excuse.
> Well, the weather bureau did predict rain.
> Oh, you mean St. Louis, Minnesota.
> Jackson Pollock's paintings are strange, aren't they?

Remember that expressions like *I believe* and *it seems* are set off only when they are used parenthetically. When they are closely connected in meaning with other words in a sentence, they are not set off: "I can explain why I believe this." "It seems to be the right answer."

Conjunctive adverbs coming in the middle of a sentence or clause are considered parenthetical and are set off by commas:

> The evidence, moreover, is purely circumstantial.

Many writers also set off conjunctive adverbs at the beginning of a sentence or clause, as parenthetical expressions or for emphasis:

414

> The high Andes force moisture-laden air to drop rain and snow on their eastern slopes; consequently, the coast of Chile has some of the driest deserts on earth.

3 Between items in a series.   (a) Words, phrases, and clauses in a series are separated by commas:

> The manager, his assistant, and a bellboy were in the elevator when it stalled.
> We took off our shoes and tiptoed through the hall, up the stairs, and into the storeroom.
> She likes blue and green, blue and pink, but not blue and orange.
> They argued for hours about where the dance should be held, which orchestra would attract the biggest crowd, and how much they should charge for the tickets.

Commas are generally not used when the items in the series are joined by conjunctions:

> He was fascinated by the sights and sounds and smells of Haiti.

In formal English a comma is always used before the last member of the series; in informal English it is often omitted, especially in newspaper and business writing:

FORMAL: Bring canteens, flashlights, matches, and hunting knives.
INFORMAL: Bring canteens, flashlights, matches and hunting knives.

Choose whichever style you prefer. But remember always to use the comma before the last item if there is any possibility of confusion, as in this sentence:

> The funniest skit was the one put on by the two exchange students from Florida, Bill Bowers, and Marie Calvetti.

Without the comma before *and* it would seem that *Bill Bowers* and *Marie Calvetti* were appositives explaining the word *students*. But the meaning intended in the sentence is that the skit was put on by four people—not two.

(For punctuating a series of items that contain commas themselves, see **Semicolon,** section 3.)

b) Commas are used between two or more adjectives in a series:

> Maurice reported that Senator Platty made a long, dull, pointless speech.

Since the three adjectives in this sentence are equal modifiers of *speech,* each should have equal emphasis. Separating the three with commas shows that they are equal modifiers. At each comma the reader pauses slightly and then gives the next adjective as much emphasis as the one before.

When the last adjective in a series is thought of as part of the noun, no comma is used before it:

> Grandpa Peters was a crotchety old man.
> According to Mr. Bane, the sheriff was an imposing, impatient, imperious old man.

415

In these sentences the adjective *old* is so closely connected in meaning with *man* that the writer thinks of the two words together as one noun (like *short cut, white lie, iron lung*). The other adjectives in the sentences modify the word group *old man*—not *man* alone.

4 After introductory clauses and verbal phrases. (a) An adverb clause that precedes the main clause is generally followed by a comma:

> Though many young people like poetry, they are often unwilling to say that they do.

When the adverb clause is short and closely related to the main clause, and the two clauses are easily distinguishable, the comma may be omitted:

> When they met they shook hands.
> But: When they met, Phyllis greeted him first. [Without the comma the clauses are not easily distinguishable. The sentence might first be read "When they met Phyllis...."]

> If Henry leaves we'll get Mason to pitch.
> But: If Henry leaves, the team hasn't a chance to win. [Without the comma the sentence might first be read "If Henry leaves the team...."]

b) A modifying verbal phrase at the beginning of a sentence is usually followed by a comma:

> Confused by these contradictory orders, Jim went to the section boss. [Participial phrase.]
>
> To learn a foreign language well, the student must practice it constantly. [Infinitive phrase.]
>
> In reading the description of the war between Athens and Sparta, Richard was reminded of present-day world tensions. [Gerund phrase.]

5 To set off nonrestrictive modifiers. *Restrictive modifiers*—those that are needed to get across the basic meaning of a sentence—are not set off by commas:

> Jim hated to play chess with anyone who was a better player than he. [The adjective clause *who was a better player than he* is necessary if the reader is to understand the intended meaning.]

Nonrestrictive modifiers are not essential in getting across the basic meaning. They add details, helping to explain, illustrate, or describe; but the sentence would be clear without them. They are always set off:

> Kathryn, who was a better player than he, easily won the game. [Basic meaning: Kathryn won the game. The adjective clause *who was a better player than he* adds an explanatory detail, but is not essential in getting across the intended meaning of the sentence.]
>
> The streets were clear and ice-free, though it had snowed recently. [Nonrestrictive adverb clause.]
>
> Mrs. Limpkin, comfortable in her easy chair, began the crossword puzzle. [Nonrestrictive adjective phrase.]
>
> The bear, driven to the edge of the river, turned and faced the hounds. [Nonrestrictive participial phrase.]
>
> The old elm plunged to the ground, its branches clawing at the surrounding trees. [Absolute participial phrase; this construction is always nonrestrictive.]
>
> The 78th Division, under this great enemy pressure, slowly gave ground. [Nonrestrictive prepositional phrase.]

Remember that a modifier may be either restrictive or nonrestrictive, depending on the meaning intended by the writer. Both of the following sentences are punctuated appropriately, each one for a different meaning:

> The song taken from *Showboat* won loud applause. [There was more than one song; *taken from Showboat* is necessary to indicate which one is meant.]
>
> The song, taken from *Showboat*, won loud applause. [The reader knows from the context that there was only one song. The phrase *taken from Showboat* is not needed; it is just a descriptive detail.]

6 To set off appositives. Appositives are set off by commas when they are nonrestrictive—that is, when they are added not to identify but to give additional information about the preceding noun:

John Turpin, a sophomore, won the high hurdles.
The oldest lion, Tuffy, was suffering from a toothache.

When the appositive is needed to identify the noun, to distinguish it from others of its kind, it is restrictive and is not set off:

my cousin Al [There are other cousins.]	the composer Brahms
the word *effect*	the play *Medea*
John the Baptist	William the Conqueror

7 For emphasis and contrast. (a) Since a comma tends to make the reader pause, it is sometimes used before an expression that the writer wants to emphasize:

More delays in the work on the canal seemed inevitable. The yellow fever had been spreading daily, and now had reached epidemic proportions. [Ordinarily a comma would not be put between the parts of a compound predicate; here it is used to call special attention to the second part.]

b) This use of the comma is especially common before contrasting expressions introduced by *but* or *not*:

It was not the faculty, but the students, who made the suggestion.
The birthday present was meant for my brother, not for me.

417

c) With certain idioms like *the more...the greater, the fewer... the better* formal writing uses a comma for emphasis; informal writing does not:

FORMAL: The more water he drank, the thirstier he became.
INFORMAL: The more she practices shorthand the easier she finds it.

8 For clearness. Often a comma is used to prevent reading together two parts of a sentence that do not belong together:

At our school, dances are always held in the boys' gymnasium. [To prevent: At our school dances.]
In heavy traffic, signs along the side of the road are not always visible. [To prevent: In heavy traffic signs.]
For Roger, Longfellow was too sentimental a poet. [To prevent: For Roger Longfellow.]
Of the first twenty, eight housewives refused even to answer the door. [To prevent: Of the first twenty eight housewives.]
The nurse ordered him to sit up, and down the medicine at one swallow. [To prevent: The nurse ordered him to sit up and down.]
Who he was, was of no interest to her. [To prevent the reader from tripping over the repeated word.]

9 Routine uses of the comma. (a) To set off the second and all following items in addresses and dates:

Boise, Idaho   Hammond, Lake County, Indiana
Victoria, B.C.   Dresden, Germany
The Dunns moved to 14 Ashley Drive, Clinton, Iowa, last month.

June 9, 1964   [When the day of the month is not given, usage is
   divided—either June, 1964 or June 1964.]
On June 9, 1964, the orchestra will begin its summer concert series.

b) After the salutation in personal letters and the complimentary close in all letters:

Dear Skip,   Dear Mr. Clay,   Yours truly,   Sincerely yours,

c) In figures, to separate thousands, millions, etc.:

$8,213,604   40,000 Indians

d) To set off degrees and titles:

Cyrus Meade Lindsay, M.S.   Claude Ford, Sr.
Horace Knox, Litt.D., Ph.D., edited the dictionary.

e) To show omission of a word required to fill out a grammatical construction, if confusion would result without the comma; if the meaning is clear, the comma may be omitted:

Lee's strategy was delay; Grant's, attack. [Sentence would be
   hard to understand without the comma.]
Perkins was a captain and Hilton a major. [Meaning is clear without the comma.]

10 Unnecessary commas. A comma should not be used:
a) Between the parts of a compound subject:

Across the English Channel winged the bomber squadron [ ] and
   its fighter escort.

b) Between a subject and its verb:

Whether he succeeds or not [ ] will depend on his ability.

c) Between a verb and its object or complement:

After a long period of observation the doctors declared [ ] that he
   was completely cured.
His real reason for resigning was [ ] his unwillingness to compromise.

d) Between the parts of a compound predicate—unless the comma is necessary for clearness or is wanted for emphasis (as in section 7):

The hawk glided in a circle [ ] and scanned the ground below.
Jim hung the coffee pot over the campfire [ ] and waited for the
   other boys to wake up.

e) At the end of a series of words, phrases, or clauses unless the series is part of a construction that requires a comma:

> Smoothly, cleverly, persuasively [ ] he presented his case to the jury.
> Carolyn kept insisting that confetti, serpentines, noisemakers, and paper hats [ ] would be out of place at a spring formal.
> But: When Ned saw the uprooted trees, smashed houses, and overturned cars, he realized the ruinous force of the storm. [To set off adverb clause.]

f) Between an adjective and the noun (or word group) it modifies:

> Then a pompous, overbearing, disdainful [ ] waiter led us to a table.
> This was the heyday of the incredibly dull, trashy [ ] soap operas.

g) Between a coördinating conjunction and the words that follow it —unless it is followed by an interrupting expression:

> The food at Henri's is unusual, delicious, and [ ] expensive.
> He never says much, but [ ]what he says always makes sense.
> But: The criticisms were harsh but, in my opinion, fully deserved.

h) Before an indirect question or an indirect quotation:

> Mr. Falls asked [ ] when the doctor could come.
> The nurse said [ ] that Dr. Hilton was out of town.

419

i) Before directly quoted words and phrases that are built right into the construction of a sentence:

> Aunt Lorna greeted them with a warm [ ] "Hello."
> He soon learned the wisdom of saying [ ] "I don't know."

j) Before a title, unless the title is being used as a nonrestrictive appositive:

> The words of the song [ ] "Yankee Doodle" were supposedly written by a British army surgeon in derision of the American army.
> But: The longest story in the book, "Heart of Darkness," is probably Conrad's most famous.

k) Before *that* in a *so ... that* construction:

> Moriarity was so confident he would win [ ] that he didn't bother to train for the fight.

Comma fault   When you put two independent statements into one sentence, you ordinarily join them with a conjunction and a comma, or separate them with a semicolon. If you use a comma alone between the clauses, you have a comma fault—or, as it is called in this book, a *run-together sentence*: Redding knew the route, he had studied the map carefully. (Correctly punctuated: Redding knew the route; he had studied the map carefully. Or: Redding knew the route. He had studied the map carefully.) For a full discussion of this writing fault and how to avoid it, see Chapter 10, "Revising Run-together Sentences," page 238.

Commands and requests 1 Direct commands are expressed by the simple form of the verb (the infinitive form). The subject is not usually expressed unless special emphasis is wanted:

Halt!	Get me another nail.
Come here.	Nick, you be here five minutes early.

The helping verb *do* is used in negative commands:

Don't say anything.	Do not lean on the guardrail.

Commands are usually punctuated with periods, unless the writer wants to suggest strong feeling by using an exclamation mark.

2 Softened commands or polite requests may be expressed in several different ways:

Let's move to the next item on the agenda.
Please make an effort to keep your room neat.
Do phone me the next time you're in town.
Pass the asparagus, please.
Suppose you pay me that two dollars now.
You are to outline only the first two sections.

Often polite requests have the word order of questions—but these are generally punctuated with periods:

Will you please sign both copies and return one to me.
Would you please forward my mail to my new address.

committee   See **Collective nouns.**

common, mutual   See **mutual, common.**

Common noun   A noun used as the name of any one of a class or group of persons, places, or things: *geologist, village, tiger, chair, explosion, university, planet.* (See **Proper noun.**)

compare   Differs from *contrast*, which always points out differences. *Compare* has two meanings: (1) Used with *to*, it means "point out similarities between":

The old prospector compared his burro to a child.   [Said his burro was like a child.]
The easiest way to understand the function of the eye is to compare it to a camera.   [To show in what ways the eye is like a camera.]

2) Used with *with,* it means "point out similarities and differences between":

> The scientist compared Mars with Venus as possible dwelling places for man.
> The assignment was to compare the new African governments with our own government in its early days.

Comparison and contrast   One interesting and emphatic way of presenting material to a reader is to set two or more people, things, situations, or ideas side by side and point out their likenesses (comparison) and their differences (contrast). For examples, see Chapter 2, "Details Giving Similarities and/or Differences," page 36.

Comparison of adjectives and adverbs   1 To show a greater degree of the quality or characteristic named by an adjective or adverb, *-er* or *-est* is added to the word or *more* or *most* is put before it:

ADJECTIVE:

POSITIVE:	Fred is *tall.*
COMPARATIVE:	Fred is *taller* than Harvey.
SUPERLATIVE:	Fred is the *tallest* boy on the team.
POSITIVE:	Dairy products are *nutritious.*
COMPARATIVE:	Dairy products are *more nutritious* than candy.
SUPERLATIVE:	Dairy products are the *most nutritious* foods of all.

ADVERB:

POSITIVE:	Glen was standing *close* to the edge.
COMPARATIVE:	He was standing *closer* to the edge than I.
SUPERLATIVE:	Frank insisted on standing *closest* to the edge.
POSITIVE:	Walter was *bitterly* opposed to the idea.
COMPARATIVE:	Shirley was even *more bitterly* opposed than he.
SUPERLATIVE:	Of all of us, Eve was the *most bitterly* opposed.

(For further details, see Chapter 9, "Comparison," page 214, and Chapter 10, "Faulty Comparisons," page 231.)

2 In formal English, adjectives and adverbs like *perfect, perfectly, unique, round, dead, impossible* are generally used only in their exact, literal meanings—that is, to name qualities that do not vary in degree. A thing is either perfect or not perfect, unique or not unique, dead or not dead. If it is perfect or unique or dead, something else cannot logically be *more* perfect, *more* unique, or *more* dead; it can only be *more nearly* perfect, *more nearly* unique, *more nearly* dead.

But in informal English these words are not always used in their exact, literal sense. *Dead,* for instance, is used to mean not only "without life" but also "dull; quiet." *Unique* is used not only to mean "the only one of its kind" but also "rare; unusual." *Impossible* is used not only to mean "not possible" but also "not easily possible." When the words are used in these broader meanings, they are often compared, as in these sentences:

'In the case were some of the most unique coins I have ever seen.
If anything, Oakville was even deader than Gale's Corners.

Complement of a verb See **Predicate complement.**

Complex sentence A sentence made up of one independent clause and one or more subordinate clauses (italicized in these examples):

Mrs. Higby has a parrot *that speaks German.*
When the reporters arrived, Mrs. Higby explained *that the parrot never spoke before strangers.*

(See **Clause** and Chapter 11, "Presenting Effective Word Pictures," page 244.)

complexioned, complected In such phrases as "a light-complected girl," *complected* is colloquial or dialectal for "a light-complexioned girl."

Compound-complex sentence A sentence that contains two or more main clauses and one or more subordinate clauses:

Clancy tried to call the Andersons as soon as he got word of the washed-out bridge, but the telephone lines were down.

The two main clauses *Clancy tried to call the Andersons* and *the telephone lines were down* make the sentence compound. The subordinate clause *as soon as he got word of the washed-out bridge* makes it compound-complex.

Compound predicate Two or more verbs having the same subject:

Now he *washes* and *irons* his own shirts.
A wolverine *had sneaked* into the cabin, *eaten* the trapper's bacon, and *carried* away most of his belongings.

Compound sentence A sentence made up of two or more independent clauses (each could stand alone as a sentence). The clauses are joined either by a comma and a coördinating conjunction or by a semicolon:

He submitted his photographs, but they were not accepted.
We slept on the ground; Dad had forgotten to pack the bedrolls.

(See **Clause** and Chapter 11, "Avoiding Faulty Coördination," page 250.)

Compound subject Two or more nouns (or noun-equivalents) used as the subject of one verb:

Both *Florence* and *Jeanne* learned to dance the Jarabe in Mexico.
His *sarcasm, impatience,* and *arrogance* had cost him many friends.

(For the agreement of verbs with compound subjects, see Chapter 9, "Compound Subjects," page 201.)

Compound words Combinations of two or more words, some of which are written as one word (*teaspoon, schoolboy, fireman, fingerprint, lifeboat, sawdust*); some as hyphenated words (*father-in-law, good-for-nothing, go-between, self-defense, jack-in-the-box, double-dealer*); and some as separate words (*fishing rod, plaster of Paris, truck farm, cottage cheese, hair trigger, field house*). Regardless of how it is written, a compound word is thought of as a single word.

If you are not sure how to write a given compound, look it up in a dictionary. (See also **Hyphen** and **Plurals of nouns,** section 8.)

conclude Used with *by* before a gerund:

The mayor concluded his plea by quoting from the Bible.

Used with *with* before a noun:

The mayor concluded his plea with a quotation from the Bible.

Used with *from* when it means "infer":

I concluded from her evasive answers that she had wrecked the car.

Concluding paragraphs For discussion and examples of concluding paragraphs, see Chapter 1, "The Final Paragraph," page 17.

423

Concrete words Concrete words name persons, places, and things that can be seen and touched: *lawyer, farm, prairie, radio, pepper, mosquito.* They contrast with abstract words, which name ideas, qualities, and relationships: *justice, evil, beauty, bravery, trustworthiness, depth.*

Conditions In simple, straightforward conditions—those that state a condition that is likely or possible—indicative verb forms are used:

If the paint *gets* too thick to spread easily, thin it with turpentine.
If you *will call* at ten o'clock, you will find Dr. Travis in.
If he *approves* our applications, we can start working tomorrow.

When a condition is less likely or possible, the helping verb *should* or *would* or the past tense is used:

If I *should* ever *drive* that fast, he would fire me.
If I ever *drove* that fast, he would fire me.

In conditions that are contrary to fact—those that cannot be met—the subjunctive is often used in formal English, but rarely in informal:

If I *were* the coach, I would let Ted pitch. [Informal: If I *was* the coach.]
If Nils Larsen *were* governor, our taxes would be just as high. [Informal: If Nils Larsen *was* governor.]

Had with the past participle (not *would have*) is used if the condition refers to past time:

> If you *had been watching,* you would have seen Les steal second base. [Not: If you *would have been watching.*]
> *Had* he *notified* me earlier, I would have compiled the necessary statistics. [Informal: If he *had notified* me earlier.]

Conjugation A verb has various forms to show person, number, voice, mood, and tense. An orderly arrangement of these various forms of a particular verb is called a *conjugation.* For a typical conjugation, see **Tenses of verbs.**

Conjunctions Connecting words; used to join words, phrases, clauses, and sentences. For discussion of specific conjunctions, see the following Index items: **Coördinating conjunctions** (*and, but, for, yet, or, nor, so*), **Conjunctive adverbs** (*therefore, thus, moreover, consequently, etc.*), **Correlative conjunctions** (*both . . . and, either . . . or, neither . . . nor, not only . . . but also, whether . . . or*), **Subordinating conjunctions** (*after, although, while, etc.*).

Conjunctive adverbs 1 Adverbs used as connectives to join two independent clauses (or sentences) by showing the relationship in meaning between them are called *conjunctive adverbs*:

424

> Engineers aimed the space vehicle accurately; however, a failure in the guidance mechanism threw it off course. [*However* shows a contrast between the two clauses.]
> Next week their production schedule will be cut from three shifts to two; consequently, a thousand more men will be out of work. [*Consequently* shows that the second clause is the result of the first.]

2 The most common conjunctive adverbs are:

accordingly	furthermore	otherwise
anyhow	however	nevertheless
anyway (colloquial)	indeed	still
besides	likewise	then
consequently	moreover	therefore

Some of these—*consequently, furthermore, however, moreover, nevertheless, therefore*—are "heavy" connectives, rather stiff and formal. Simpler conjunctions are generally more appropriate in informal writing:

INAPPROPRIATE: Frank, who is near-sighted, wanted us to get main-floor seats. I, however, had only two dollars left. Therefore I persuaded him to sit in the balcony with me.

IMPROVED: Frank, who is near-sighted, wanted us to get main-floor seats. But I had only two dollars left, so I persuaded him to sit in the balcony with me.

3 When the clauses of a compound sentence are joined by a conjunctive adverb, a semicolon (not a comma) is used between them—whether the adverb begins the second clause or comes within it:

> Being a bellboy, I told myself, would be fun; besides, I did need the money.
>
> I felt a yank on the line; then I saw the marlin break the surface.
>
> Mr. Styles, unlike his sons, was always pleasant; his pleasantness, moreover, was never tinged with condescension.

When the adverb comes within the clause, as in the third example, it is generally set off by commas. When it comes first in the clause, as in the first example, it may or may not be followed by a comma. If the writer intends it to be parenthetical, he uses a comma; otherwise he does not.

connected with, in connection with   Wordy phrases that often can be effectively replaced by a simple *in, with,* or *about*:

> WORDY: Mr. Metz said nothing in connection with the National Merit Awards.
>
> BETTER: Mr. Metz said nothing about the National Merit Awards.

Connotation   Besides its recognized dictionary meaning (its denotation), a word may suggest an additional shade of meaning—its connotation. *Candid* and *outspoken,* for instance, both have the denotation "frank; open," but their connotations are different. The first word suggests or connotes approval; the second connotes disapproval.

For a discussion of connotation, see Chapter 3, "Be Wary of Loaded Words," page 64.

425

considerable   Although in speech a clear distinction is not always made between the adverb *considerably* and the adjective *considerable,* in both formal English and informal writing it is:

> We were helped considerably by his encouragement. [Adverb modifying the verb *were helped.*]
>
> His encouragement was of considerable help to us. [Adjective modifying the noun *help.*]

In informal speech *considerable* is sometimes used as a noun:

> SPOKEN: The new tenants found considerable to complain about.
>
> WRITTEN: The new tenants found a great deal to complain about.

Context   Used to mean (1) "the parts that come before or after a word or sentence," (2) "the whole passage, speech, or situation in which a word or sentence comes." To understand words and ideas completely, you must see or hear them in context. For a discussion of learning word meanings through context clues, see Chapter 12, "Increasing and Using Your Vocabulary," pages 263-266.

Contractions *Contractions* are words from which an unstressed syllable is dropped in speaking; in writing, the omitted letter or letters are indicated by an apostrophe:

it is—it's	where is—where's	they are—they're
he has—he's	you are—you're	must have—must've
she will—she'll	I would—I'd	shall not—shan't
does not—doesn't	we had—we'd	we are—we're
will not—won't	who is—who's	they have—they've

Contractions are ordinarily out of place in formal writing. Because they are typical of spoken English, they are often found in informal writing—especially, of course, in the conversation and dialogue of plays and stories.

Conversation A great deal of writing—exposition as well as narrative—can be made more interesting and vivid by the use of direct quotation and conversation. Notice how quotation enlivens this passage:

> Across the aisle by the door a tiny red light glowed; simultaneously the strident voice of Lt. Toland, the jump master and platoon leader, cracked out, "Stand up and hook up!" Reeling under the weight of two parachutes and heavy battle equipment, we hooked our anchor-line snap fastener to the cable and waited. Again cracked that strident voice, "Check your equipment!" Each man checked his own chute and his buddy's chute in front of him. The last man turned his back so that the man in front of him could check his back chute. A third time the voice cracked out, "Sound off for equipment check!" The last man, who was to the front of the plane and farthest from the exit, yelled out, "Fourteen okay." The next man yelled, "Thirteen okay," and so on toward the door. Toland was to jump first and I after him. When I yelled, "Two okay," he nodded and yelled in that unforgettable gritty voice, "Okay, we jump when the green light comes on. Make it good!"
> —Ross S. Carter, "We Jumped into Sicily," from *Battle Stations; True Stories of Men in War,* ed. by Margaret C. Scroggin. Copyright © 1955 by Alfred A. Knopf, Inc., New York.

426

Quoted speech is effective, of course, only if it sounds real. If you are interested in learning to write good conversation, start by observing carefully how you talk, and how people around you talk. You will find that contractions, clipped expressions, and informal words and idioms are typical of everyday speech, and that the use of them will help make your written conversations sound natural. But don't overdo them. Though written conversation is based on real speech, it should not be a word-for-word reproduction. If you wrote down conversations as they were actually spoken, you would often end with a hodgepodge of apostrophes, distorted spellings (*comin', s'pose, kinda, childern, purty, skeered, figger, acrost*), and coarse expressions. This would be confusing, distracting, and possibly offensive to your readers. In reproducing speech on paper, it is better to use just enough such spellings and expressions to *suggest* the way speech is supposed to sound. Take the following passage, for example:

> He began again. "It's a funny story," he said. "Get ready to laugh. Get ready to bust your sides, for it is sure a funny story. It's about a hick. It's about a red-neck, like you all, if you please. Yeah, like you. He grew up like any other mother's son on the dirt roads and gully washes of a north-state farm. He knew all about being a hick...."—Robert Penn Warren, *All the King's Men*. Copyright 1946 by Harcourt, Brace & World, Inc., New York.

It is quite likely that the speaker would actually say *git* for *get*, *t'* for *to*, *an'* for *and*, *bein'* for *being*, and so on. But these complicated spellings are not needed; for the use of expressions and words like *bust your sides*, *hick*, *red-neck*, and *Yeah* and the general rhythm and tone of the sentences strongly suggest the man's speech pattern, personality, and background.

A few words about the speaker, coming before or after his quoted words, sometimes help tell the story:

> "Let's leave this swamp to the alligators," Meyer growled, vainly slapping at the cloud of gnats and mosquitoes that enveloped them.

> Captain Kozak patted the barrel of his carbine, smiled faintly at Sergeant Hill, and said softly, "I know one answer to their ultimatum."

But this kind of description or explanation should not be overdone. For instance, it isn't always necessary when labeling speeches to use a picturesque synonym for *said* (*yelled, stammered, whispered, bellowed, blurted*). In fact, unless there is a good reason for using one of these more specific terms, the word *said* is preferable because it is less conspicuous.

And you need not even indicate who is speaking if the conversation leaves no question in the reader's mind:

> An hour later George dragged into the room, looking utterly miserable. "Hullo, Pete."
> "I guess you lost the race, huh, George?"
> "Yup."
> "Did you place at all?"
> "Third."
> "Well, that's something, anyway!"

Some of the conventions of paragraphing and punctuating conversation are illustrated in the examples you have just read. More details can be found in **Quotation marks.**

Coördinating conjunctions 1 The coördinating conjunctions—*and, but, for, or, nor, yet, so*—are used to connect words, phrases, subordinate clauses, independent clauses, and sentences (parts of equal value):

WORDS: cowboys and Indians; Monday, Tuesday, and Wednesday; black or white; gruff but kind

PHRASES: after school but before supper; pacing the floor and muttering to himself

SUBORDINATE CLAUSES: The pupils acted like angels only when the principal was in sight or when there were visitors in the classroom.

INDEPENDENT CLAUSES: Snowflakes seem to be identical, yet under a microscope they show an infinite variety.

SENTENCES: The meal she prepared was a masterpiece. But I simply was not hungry.

2 For a discussion of the use of coördinating conjunctions to connect independent clauses, see Chapter 11, "Avoiding Faulty Coördination," page 250.

3 The conjunction *and* is badly overworked. Sometimes it is used where there is no need for it; sometimes it is used where another conjunction would express more exactly the relationship between two parts. For a discussion of this point, see the Index item *and*, section 2; and Chapter 11, "Too Many *And's*," page 251.

4 There is a special group of coördinating conjunctions that are used in pairs—*both . . . and, either . . . or, neither . . . nor, whether . . . or, not only . . . but also.* These are called *correlative conjunctions* and are discussed under that heading in the Index.

428

Correction marks In correcting your themes, your teacher may indicate the revisions that are needed by using certain abbreviations or symbols. The following list gives some of the most common correction marks. Each one is followed by a reference either to an Index article or to pages in the first part of the book where you will find help in making the appropriate revisions.

Ab	*Abbreviations*	Local	*Localism, Dialect*
Agr	*Agreement*	Mis	*Misplaced modifiers*
Amb	*Ambiguity*	Prep	*Preposition*
Apos	*Apostrophe*	Pn	Punctuation mark
Awk	*Awkward writing*		misused. See Index article on appropriate mark.
Big W	*Big words*		
Cap	*Capital letters*		
CF	*Comma fault*	Ref	"Careless Use of Pronouns," page 228
Dang	"Dangling Modifiers," page 222		
		Shift	"Shifted Constructions," page 225
Dead	*Deadwood*		
Div	*Division of words*	Sp	*Spelling*
Frag	"Revising Sentence Fragments," page 232	Tense	*Tenses of verbs*
		Wordy	*Wordiness*

¶ This symbol means a new paragraph is needed. If you have trouble paragraphing your themes effectively, you will find it helpful to read Chapter 2, "Writing Paragraphs."

Correlative conjunctions Coördinating conjunctions used in pairs:

not only . . . but also	either . . . or
not only . . . but	neither . . . nor
both . . . and	whether . . . or

Correlative conjunctions should be used to connect parts that are parallel in form. If the first conjunction is followed by a prepositional phrase, the second should be followed by a prepositional phrase; if the first is followed by a verb, the second should be followed by a verb; and so on.

NOT PARALLEL: I knew I'd find Tony either *tinkering* with his car or *he would be playing* tennis at the park.

PARALLEL: I knew I'd find Tony either *tinkering* with his car or *playing* tennis at the park.

NOT PARALLEL: The Minellis did not know whether *to keep* their city apartment or *if they should buy* a house in the suburbs.

PARALLEL: The Minellis did not know whether *to keep* their city apartment or *(to) buy* a house in the suburbs.

NOT PARALLEL: He not only *criticized* the plot but also the *actors*.

PARALLEL: He criticized not only the *plot* but also the *actors*.

PARALLEL: He not only *criticized* the plot but also *panned* the actors.

429

Counter words Vague, general adjectives (like *nice, wonderful, fabulous, grand, lovely, awful, lousy* [slang], *dull*) that are used not for their exact meanings but only to express approval or disapproval. Counter words are common—and useful—in conversation, but they are not appropriate in writing. There it is important to use words that express exact meaning, words that help give the reader a specific picture.

couple Strictly, the noun *couple* means "two persons or things that are associated in some way":

The Lathrops were the most highly respected couple on the block.

In informal speech and writing, *couple of* is used to mean "two or three; a few; several":

Wait for me a couple of minutes, if I'm not right on time.
Chip walked east a couple of blocks and then turned north.

In informal speech the *of* is often omitted:

Jed's gone skiing only a couple times, but he thinks he's an expert.

But this usage is not considered appropriate in writing.

credible, credulous *Credible* means "believable"; *credulous* means "too ready to believe":

> An old letter and an authentic map made the treasure story credible.
> Sly Mr. Herz got rich selling watered stock to credulous store-keepers.

creek Pronounced krēk or krik.

Dangling modifiers A modifier that has no word in the sentence which it can sensibly modify is said to be *dangling*:

> DANGLING: *Turning to face his opponent,* his chin caught the full force of the punch. [The participial phrase seems to modify *chin*.]
> REVISED: Turning to face his opponent, *he* caught the full force of the punch on his chin. [Now the phrase has a word—*he*—for it to modify.]

(For further examples and discussion, see Chapter 10, "Dangling Modifiers," page 222.)

Dash Since dashes are conspicuous and emphatic marks of punctuation, they should be used sparingly—only when they serve a specific purpose, when no other marks will carry the intended meaning as well. They should not be used as substitutes for all other marks, as some writers use them.

1 A common use of the dash is to mark an abrupt change in the thought of a sentence:

> At this point Howard came and—no, that happened later.
> Please pass the—never mind; it's right in front of me.

2 Dashes are used to set off parenthetical expressions—explanatory comments or side remarks—that make an abrupt interruption in the thought or structure of a sentence:

> We soon discovered that O'Reilly Owens—his mother's maiden name was O'Reilly—was a better quarterback than Ted Loomis.
> Fred believed his story—what gullibility!—and gave him two dollars for the tickets.
> In spite of the weather—do you remember how it snowed that day? —Ernest hunted all afternoon until he found the kitten hiding under a car.

Notice that the first word of the interrupting expression begins with a small letter, even when the interrupter is a sentence. A period is not used after an interrupter, but a question mark or an exclamation mark is—right before the second dash.

Parentheses, which are more formal than dashes, are sometimes used to set off interrupting expressions. Parentheses tend to lessen the emphasis, to make the interrupter seem less conspicuous. Dashes make the interrupters stand out more than parentheses would. In informal writing—unless it is serious expository writing—dashes are more common than parentheses, though both should be used sparingly.

3 Nonrestrictive modifiers are usually set off by commas. But when special emphasis is wanted, dashes are used. And dashes are usual if the modifiers themselves have commas.

> He is very kind and considerate—when he wants to borrow money.
> Swimming across the lagoon is easy—if you don't mind the sharks.
> Ordinary pork—which Hindus relish, but Moslems detest—was one cause of friction in nineteenth-century India.

4 Nonrestrictive appositives are usually set off by commas; but when the writer wants to call special attention to an appositive or when the appositive phrase itself has commas, dashes are better:

> High in the tree sat the object of months of hard work and a great deal of expense—a bored gorilla.
> The mistral—a cold, dry, northerly wind that blows from the Alps across southeastern France—often put Van Gogh in a melancholy frame of mind.
> Ambassador Wilson was a good choice for the post in India because he knew three Indian languages—Hindustani, Bengali, and Tamil.

431

If a comma were used instead of a dash in the third example sentence, a reader might think that Ambassador Wilson knew six languages. The dash shows clearly that the three names are appositives explaining *Indian languages.*

5 A dash is used before a word or phrase (like *these* or *all these*) that sums up a preceding list of items, to clearly mark the division between the list and the statement that follows:

> Distrust, misguided loyalties, greed, unwillingness to negotiate differences peaceably—all helped cause World War I.

6 A double-length dash is used at the end of a sentence to show that the sentence is left unfinished or that a speaker is interrupted. No period is used after the dash:

> A way must be found for converting sea water to fresh water or else——

> "But Officer," she began, "I only——"
> "You only ran three red lights and hit a squad car," he interrupted.

7 In handwriting, distinguish between a dash and a hyphen by making the dash twice as long. On the typewriter, you will have to use two

hyphens (not spaced away from the words before and after), since the standard keyboard has no dash.

data Pronounced dā′tə, dat′ə, or dä′tə. *Data* (from Latin) is the plural of the singular *datum,* which is rarely used. Since to most people its meaning is singular—"a group of facts" or "a mass of information"—*data* is commonly used with a singular verb in informal English:

> Data on earthquakes *is recorded* by the seismograph.
> This data *was taken* from the census report.

In formal English *data* is usually regarded as plural:

> The data that Mendel collected *were disregarded* for many years, despite *their* revolutionary importance.

Dates The usual form for writing dates is:

> April 9, 1865   September 19, 1964

The form *19 September 1964* is becoming popular, partly as a result of its use by the armed services.

In personal letters and in business memos and forms, figures are often used:

> 5/18/63   10/3/63

The month is put first, then the day of the month, then the year.

The *st, nd, rd, th* are now generally omitted from the day of the month when the day is given as a figure:

> May 15   Not: May 15th
> November 2   Not: November 2nd

In very formal style the day of the month is often written out in full when the year is not given:

> July fifteenth   April third

But the year is not written out in words except in formal social announcements or invitations, which are usually engraved or printed.

If it is necessary to save space in letter headings, the names of months with more than four letters may be abbreviated:

Jan.   Feb.   Mar.   Apr.   Aug.   Sept.   Oct.   Nov.   Dec.

Dative case Nouns or pronouns used as indirect objects of verbs are sometimes said to be in the *dative case.* Actually English (unlike Latin and German) has no distinctive form for the dative case. A noun used as an indirect object is in the ordinary case form and a pronoun is in the objective case form:

> The clerk gave the *customer* a receipt.
> My aunt sends *me* a fruitcake every Christmas.

Deadwood   A term used to describe a word or phrase that adds nothing to the meaning of a sentence:

> [The way] I arrived at the right answer to the multiple-choice question [was] by [using] a process of elimination [to rule out the unlikely choices].
>
> Several pages in her autobiography [of her life] are devoted to her great interest in [the subject of] hypnosis.

Omitting the deadwood in sentences like these makes for clearer, crisper writing.

(For further examples and discussion, see Chapter 11, "Deadwood," page 254.)

deaf   Pronounced def, and in certain dialects dēf. Formerly the pronunciation dēf was in good usage, and it is still used by many older people.

decided, decisive   Good English makes a distinction between *decided,* meaning "definite" or "unmistakable," and *decisive,* meaning "having or giving a clear result" or "showing determination or firmness":

> After her illness, there was a decided change in her attitude.
>
> The guard's testimony provided decisive proof of Maxwell's guilt.

Declarative sentences   Sentences that make statements:

> A copperhead was sunning itself on the roadway.
>
> I wondered what we should do.
>
> I tapped Pete's elbow and whispered, "What do we do now?"
>
> "Hey, you fat old copperhead, get out of the way!" Pete yelled.
>
> "Shut up!" I said, before remembering that snakes can't hear.

433

Declension   The change in the form of nouns, pronouns, and adjectives to show case (*who—whose—whom, I—me*); number (*pen—pens, mouse —mice*); or gender (*blond—blonde*). In a highly inflected language like Latin or German, declension plays an important part in grammar. But in English, where so few words change in form to show case or gender, declension plays a relatively small part.

Defining words   Many times in your writing you use words or phrases whose meaning your readers may not know. To make your ideas clear, you should find some way to explain what the words mean. If the word is abstract like *equality, courage, loyalty,* the best way to explain it is to give concrete examples of what it means to you. If the word is concrete, you can often make its meaning clear by tucking in a synonym that you think your readers will know. For example:

> Uncle Pat enjoyed telling us stories of his days on the Burlington line as a gandy dancer—or section hand, to use a more familiar term.

By adding the synonym *section hand,* you explain what the job was and still keep the word *gandy dancer* with its picturesque connotation that helps readers get a vivid picture of the uncle.

There are two other common ways of pinning down the meaning of words for your readers—one formal and direct, the other informal and indirect:

> My first assignment was to collate the new books—a job far less impressive than it sounds. *To collate* is a librarian's term meaning to examine a book page by page to see that none is missing.
>
> My first assignment was to check each new book page by page to make sure none was missing—a rather boring job which the librarian dignified by the high-sounding term "collate."

In the first example *collate* is defined directly; in the second its meaning is made clear indirectly. This indirect way of explaining is preferable in narrative writing, since it does not interrupt the story with a formal definition.

In expository writing a formal definition is often best—especially to define a term for which there is no well-known synonym that will explain its meaning fully. In defining a word, give (1) its general class and (2) the characteristics that make it different from other things in that class:

> The *bubonic plague* [the word being defined] is a contagious disease [the class it belongs to] that is accompanied by inflamed swelling of the lymph glands, chills, fever, exhaustion, and delirium, and is usually fatal [characteristics that distinguish it from other contagious diseases].
>
> A *caucus* is a meeting of leaders or members of a political party or faction to decide questions of policy, candidates, campaign strategy, etc.

The number of distinguishing details you should use depends on how much information you think your readers need to understand fully the point you are making.

In your written work avoid using *when* and *where* in defining words. Definitions like "Reclamation is where you bring into cultivation land that was formerly swamp, desert, or otherwise unproductive" and "A boom is when there is a sudden growth in business prosperity, prices, or property values" make the meaning clear enough, but they sound amateurish. They are better stated in a less childish way—by giving the general class first and then the distinguishing characteristics: "Reclamation is the process of bringing into cultivation...." "A boom is a period of business prosperity...."

Definite article   The adjective *the.* (See *the; a, an.*)

Degree (of adjectives and adverbs)   One of three stages in the comparison of adjectives and adverbs:

POSITIVE DEGREE:	hot	bravely
COMPARATIVE DEGREE:	hotter	more bravely
SUPERLATIVE DEGREE:	hottest	most bravely

(See also *Comparison of adjectives and adverbs.*)

Degrees Academic degrees (titles given by a college or university to show the completion of a required course of study or as an honor) are not ordinarily given with a person's name except in college publications or in reference works. When used, they are set off by commas:

> The encyclopedia article on Roman engineering was written by Mitchell Du Boise, B.E., and Claire Hostetter, A.M.

Demonstratives *This, that, these,* and *those*—used to specify or point out —are called demonstrative adjectives or demonstrative pronouns, depending on how they are used in a sentence:

ADJECTIVES:	That stamp belongs to this set.
	Load those crates into these trucks.
PRONOUNS:	Wasn't this next to that in the jewelry case?
	These will last longer than those.

(See *kind, sort.*)

Denotation The *denotation* of a word is its exact, literal meaning as contrasted with its *connotation,* the added meaning the word suggests or implies. The adjectives *assertive* and *pushy* have the same denotation ("conspicuously or obtrusively energetic or active"), but their connotations differ. *Assertive* suggests desirable characteristics like determination and self-confidence; *pushy* implies such undesirable qualities as officiousness, rudeness, and offensive forwardness.

435

Dependent clause See *Clause,* section 2.

Descriptive writing See Chapter 1, "Special Types of Writing: Description," page 28.

Details For a discussion of the importance of details in writing good paragraphs, see Chapter 2, "Adequate Development in Paragraphs," page 33.

Dewey Decimal System To make it easy to find available material on a particular subject, most high-school libraries classify and arrange their books according to the Dewey Decimal System, devised by a New York librarian, Melvil Dewey, in 1876. In this system all subject matter is divided into ten main classes and assigned certain numbers:

000-099	General works (encyclopedias, periodicals, etc.)
100-199	Philosophy (psychology, ethics, logic, etc.)
200-299	Religion (Bible, churches, church history, etc.)
300-399	Social sciences (economics, law, education, etc.)

400-499	Language (grammar, derivations, etc., of various languages)
500-599	Pure science (mathematics, chemistry, astronomy, etc.)
600-699	Technology (agriculture, medical sciences, business, etc.)
700-799	The arts (recreation, music, sports, etc.)
800-899	Literature (novels, plays, essays, poetry, etc.)
900-999	History (geography, travel, collective biography, etc.)

Each of these ten classes is subdivided into ten more specific groups. For example:

500	Pure science	550	Earth sciences
510	Mathematics	560	Paleontology
520	Astronomy and allied sciences	570	Anthropology and biology
530	Physics	580	Botanical sciences
540	Chemistry	590	Zoological sciences

Each of the ten groups is in turn subdivided into ten smaller fields:

530	Physics	535	Optics
531	Mechanics of solids	536	Heat
532	Mechanics of fluids	537	Electricity and electronics
533	Mechanics of gases	538	Magnetism
534	Sound	539	Modern physics

Still smaller subdivisions are made by using decimals. For example, books dealing with radioactivity are classified under the number 539.752; those dealing with thermonuclear fission, under 539.764.

In most small libraries books of fiction are not given a classification number; instead they are marked with an **F** and are arranged on the shelves alphabetically by the last name of the author.

Individual biographies are marked **B** in some libraries; in others they are given number 92 or 920. The biographies are arranged alphabetically by the last name of the person the book is about.

The Dewey classification number, which is part of the *call number,* is placed on the spine of the book. The call number is put in the upper left corner of the author, subject, and title cards in the card catalogue. Once you know the call number of a certain book, you can easily find it on the shelves. (See also *Card catalogue.*)

Dialect The speech of people in one section of a country that has characteristics making it different from the speech of people in other parts of the same country. Dialects differ in vocabulary: in one section, for example, *faucet* is common; in others, *tap* or *spigot*. (Do people in your locality say *pancake, flapjack, hot cake,* or *griddlecake? snap beans, green beans,* or *string beans? kinfolk* or *relatives? clothes press, clothes closet,* or *wardrobe?*) They differ in idioms (*a quarter of four, a quarter to four,* or *a quarter till four*), and particularly in pronunciations. In some New England regions, for example, a broad *a* is used in words like *mask, graft, wrath*—which people of other regions pronounce with a short *a.* Easterners and Southerners slight the *r* in words like *farm, chair, heard,* yet sound an *r* where there is none in the spelling (as in "idear of" and "the lawr of the land"). Westerners sound their *r*'s more strongly than other people, and use an "ah" sound for the *o* in words like *pond* and *hot.*

Dialects exist because groups of speakers are now—or once were—separated from each other. They are not limited to users of nonstandard English, as many people mistakenly think. Educated, as well as uneducated, people of the South speak somewhat differently from educated Westerners or New Englanders. The speech of Boston is just as much a dialect as is Brooklynese or the speech of the Scandinavian sections in the Midwest. All of us speak a dialect (or several dialects), though we may not realize that we do, since our neighbors for miles around speak the same way we do. Only when we visit other sections of the country or listen to the speech of a visitor from far away do we realize that there are regional differences in our language. A dialect is, after all, speech that does not attract attention to itself among the people of a region.

Linguistic scholars now believe that there are three major dialect regions in our country: the *Northern,* the *Midland,* and the *Southern.* Within these three main areas there are minor dialects, as in the Ozarks, in New York City, in New Orleans.

The differences between the dialects of our country are fewer than those between the dialects of other countries—England, for example, or France or Italy. This is due in part to travel, but even more to movies, radio, and television, and to the nationwide circulation of books and magazines. Because of these, people in all parts of the country become familiar with and tend to use the same language forms.

Dialectal words, phrases, and pronunciations are sometimes called *localisms* or *provincialisms.* In dictionaries they are usually labeled *Dial.* (for *Dialect*). In speaking to or with people of your section, it is appropriate for you to use localisms, avoiding of course those not in good standing among the educated people of your community. In speaking with others or to a general audience, it is best to avoid words, phrases, or pronunciations that might seem overly conspicuous or might be confusing or distracting.

In informal writing, localisms are often appropriate—in stories or personal narratives especially, where they help make the setting seem real and the conversation of people seem natural. In formal writing, localisms are generally avoided; the rare ones used for special effect are usually put in quotation marks.

See also "American English Dialects," page 180.

Dialogue   For the use and punctuation of dialogue in writing, see **Conversation** and **Quotation marks.**

die   Generally used with *of*—not *from* or *with*—before the name of an illness: Napoleon died *of* cancer. But we say *died by violence, died in an accident, died from lack of care.*

differ Followed by *from* when the meaning is "be unlike or dissimilar":

> The French spoken in Paris differs from that spoken in Quebec.

When the meaning is "disagree in opinion or belief," *differ* is followed by *with* or *from:*

> We expected Mr. Pine to differ with us on the matter.
> Sylvia differs from (*or* with) me on political questions.

different In formal English and in informal writing, *different* is generally followed by *from:*

> But *decry* is different in meaning from *descry.*
> The cottage was quite different from what we had imagined it.

Colloquial usage is divided; occasionally *from* is used, sometimes *to* (very common in England), and more often *than:*

> Jim's answer was entirely different than mine.

In both speech and writing, *different than* is becoming more common before a clause:

> The cottage was quite different than we had imagined it.
> Actual road conditions were different than the map described them.

Direct address The name or descriptive term by which persons are addressed:

> *Ladies and gentlemen,* we welcome you to Thornton Hall.
> Wait for me, *Uncle Earl.*
> Will you explain, *Mr. Bentley,* why you voted against the bill?

Words in direct address are set off by commas—one comma if they come at the beginning or the end of a sentence, and two commas if they are in the middle of a sentence.

Direct object A noun or pronoun (or phrase or clause used as a noun) that tells who or what receives the action expressed by the verb is called a *direct object.* The direct object usually follows the verb:

> Harry put the *film* into the camera.
> She thanked *me* and went to the vacant seat.
> They enjoyed *hiking in northern Maine.* [Gerund phrase.]
> We wondered *why he looked so gloomy.* [Noun clause.]

Occasionally, for emphasis, the object comes before both the subject and the verb:

> *Patience* [object] a chess player [subject] must have.

Direct quotation The actual words used by a speaker, as contrasted with indirect quotation, in which the sense rather than the actual words is given:

DIRECT: "There once was an Indian village here," the guide said.
INDIRECT: The guide told us there had once been an Indian village here.

(For punctuation, see *Quotation marks.*)

discover, invent These verbs are not interchangeable. *To discover* is "to see or learn of for the first time something already existing"; *to invent* is "to make or work out something that did not exist before":

> In 1958 Van Allen discovered two belts of radiation around the earth.
>
> Whitcomb Judson, a Chicagoan, invented the first slide fastener in 1893.

disinterested, uninterested A distinction is generally made between these two words. *Disinterested* is used to mean "free from selfish motives; impartial"; *uninterested,* to mean "not interested":

> For disinterested advice, go to someone who won't profit from the sale.
>
> Many people love kittens but are quite uninterested in cats.

In colloquial usage, *disinterested* is sometimes used as a synonym for *uninterested.*

Ditto marks (") Ditto marks are used in accounts, lists, and tables to avoid repeating words that appear directly above: **439**

> *Cooking Magic,* 13 days overdue
> *The New Africa,* 8 ''   ''

Ditto marks are not appropriate in most of your written work (themes, tests, reports, letters) nor in footnotes or bibliographies.

dived, dove Formal English prefers *dived* for the past tense of *dive;* informal English often uses *dove.*

Divided usage The spellings, pronunciations, and constructions used by speakers and writers of the same education often differ. Whenever there are—in the same level of language—two or more forms that are equally acceptable, usage is said to be divided. There are many more of these divided usages than most people realize. Here are just a few examples:

IN SPELLING:
ax—axe	gray—grey
calcimine—kalsomine	inquiry—enquiry
caliber—calibre	licorice—liquorice
dialogue—dialog	poky—pokey
employee—employe	pygmy—pigmy
gauge—gage	sulfur—sulphur

IN PRONUNCIATION: abdomen: ab′də mən—ab dō′mən
almond: ä′mənd—am′ənd
Caribbean: kar′ə bē′ən—kə rib′i ən
exquisite: eks′kwi zit—eks kwiz′it
juvenile: jü′və nəl—jü′və nīl
palm: päm—pälm
roof: rüf—rüf
route: rüt—rout

IN VERB FORMS: Past tense: waked—woke, sped—speeded
Past participle: swelled—swollen, woven—wove

Remember that in all such instances of divided usage either of the forms is acceptable. Use whichever seems to you the most appropriate in a particular situation. You may choose the one that you think is preferred by the audience you want to reach or, better still, the one that comes most naturally to your own speech.

Division of words Though the right-hand margin of your papers does not have to be absolutely even (as the margin at the left should be), your papers will look better if you keep a fairly straight right margin. To do so, you may occasionally have to divide words at the end of lines. Whenever it is necessary to divide a word, break it between syllables. The following rules will help you determine in general where the divisions should be made. If you are in doubt about a particular word, consult your dictionary.

440

1 Both parts of a divided word should be pronounceable; words of one syllable—like *switched, thought, scheme, preach, masque, tired, patched*—should never be divided.

2 Words should not be divided so that a single letter stands by itself. For example, do not divide a word like *again* (which would leave a lone *a* at the end of a line) or *many* (which would put a lone *y* at the beginning of a line).

3 As a rule, divide a word after a prefix or before a suffix:

super-sonic	amaze-ment
bi-cycle	perfect-ible
inter-view	astute-ness

4 As a rule, divide between double consonants:

bat-tle	com-mis-sioned
tomor-row	bag-gage
snap-ping	fol-low
tis-sue	muz-zle

But if the double consonants are part of the root word, they are not split; the division is made after the double consonants, before such endings as *-ing, -er,* and *-able*:

spell-ing	putt-ing
guess-er	till-able

5 Two consonants that come between two vowels may be divided if the consonants are pronounced separately:

chap-ter	mag-netic
com-pare	pros-perous
elas-tic	elec-torate

6 Two vowels may be divided if they are pronounced separately:

sci-ence	vi-olin
cre-ation	tru-ancy
zo-ology	pedi-atrics

7 If two consonants or two vowels are pronounced as one sound, do not divide them:

gath-ering	bea-ver
bish-op	nau-tical
sema-phore	pneu-matic

8 As a rule, divide between parts of a compound word:

hand-writing	store-keeper
here-after	over-flow
break-water	under-current
any-body	rattle-trap

If the compound word itself is actually spelled with a hyphen, divide at the hyphen to avoid the awkwardness of two hyphens in one word:

441

vice-president	make-believe
moth-eaten	open-minded

9 If a single consonant comes between two sounded vowels, the consonant generally is put at the beginning of a syllable with the second of the vowels:

de-le-tion	chi-na-ware
sa-li-va	fa-ce-tious

But if the preceding vowel is *short* and *accented*, the consonant is kept with that vowel:

cit′-adel	clam′-orous
div′-idend	pan′-el

10 Do not divide words in a way that will at first glance cause readers to be confused about the meaning or pronunciation:

Not:	mean-der	But:	me-ander
	die-tary		di-etary
	leg-islator		legis-lator

do **1** Besides its use as a predicate verb meaning "perform; make; accomplish; bring about; etc.," *do* has five uses (as a helping verb) where it has no definite meaning of its own:

a) For emphasis, especially in an answer to a question or in a statement contradicting a preceding statement:

> Though seldom right, they *do* have the correct answer this time.
> I *did* pay $2.98; I have the receipt to prove it.

b) In asking questions:

> *Do* they always make so much noise when they have a party?
> *Does* this train leave at 9:15 p.m.?

c) With negative verbs:

> "*Don't* fire until you see the whites of their eyes."
> The trouble was that Mike *did* not want to be a doctor.

d) As a substitute for a verb that has just been used, to avoid repeating it:

> People eat more when they go out to dinner than they *do* at home.
> They had long planned to visit Alaska, and last summer they finally *did*.

e) In inverted sentences, after such adverbs as *seldom, rarely, hardly:*

> Seldom *do* people foresee the full horrors of war.
> Only rarely *does* she write to her aunt.

2 *Do* has many idiomatic meanings and is part of many idiomatic phrases: hard work *does* people good; housewives *do* the dishes; some people have *nothing to do with* their relatives; one *does away with* old newspapers; gifts are *done up* in fancy wrappings; everyone has to *make do* with what is available; an ambushed cowboy is *done for*.

442

doff, don Rather formal words for *take off* and *put on*, which most people prefer because *doff* and *don* sound affected or old-fashioned in everyday speech and writing. (See **Big words.**)

don't, doesn't These contractions are universally used in conversation and often in informal writing, especially in sentences where *do not* or *does not* would seem too emphatic or where the rhythm seems smoother with the contraction.

In nonstandard English *don't* is used with a singular subject ("She don't speak German," "He don't care"). Educated speakers and writers avoid this usage, using *doesn't* with a singular subject and *don't* only with a plural:

> She doesn't speak German.   We don't speak German.
> He doesn't care.   The members don't care.

Double negative In formal and informal English two negative words are not used together to express one negative meaning. In nonstandard English the double negative is often used, especially when the negative meaning is to be emphasized:

NONSTANDARD: They didn't give her nothing.
STANDARD: They didn't give her anything.
STANDARD: They gave her nothing.

NONSTANDARD: I'm afraid they won't never invite us again.
STANDARD: I'm afraid they'll never invite us again.
STANDARD: I'm afraid they won't ever invite us again.

The objection to the double negative is not, as many people like to explain, that "two negatives make an affirmative." No one (unless he is being stubbornly contrary) ever mistakes the intended meaning of "He hasn't told nobody"—the double negative makes it only too clear. The real objection is that double negatives are just not used by educated people, except in a joking mood. Centuries ago double negatives were common in all levels of English; you have probably seen examples in Chaucer and in Shakespeare. But they are out of fashion now in the standard language.

Obvious double negatives like those in the examples above are easy to spot. Somewhat more tricky are those made with the adverbs *hardly*, *scarcely*, *barely*, which have a negative meaning and should therefore not be combined with other negative words:

NONSTANDARD: The baby can't hardly walk yet.
STANDARD: The baby can hardly walk yet.

NONSTANDARD: Dean is scarcely never at home before six.
STANDARD: Dean is scarcely ever at home before six.   **443**

Double prepositions   In colloquial usage double prepositions like *off of* (for *off*), *inside of* (for *inside*), *outside of* (for *outside*) are common. In informal writing all of these but *off of* are acceptable, though the *of* is unnecessary and could neatly be dropped, since it adds nothing to the meaning. In formal English these double prepositions are avoided.

Doubling final consonants   See **Spelling,** section 1a.

doubt   In negative statements (where there is no real doubt) *doubt that* is used in formal English, *doubt but that* in informal writing, and *doubt but what* or *doubt but* in informal speech:

FORMAL: I do not doubt that he intended to pay.
INFORMAL WRITING: I don't doubt but that he intended to pay.
INFORMAL SPEECH: I don't doubt but what he intended to pay.

In positive statements (where doubt really exists) *doubt whether* is used in formal English and *doubt if* in informal English:

FORMAL: He doubts whether the watch can be repaired.
INFORMAL: He doubts if the watch can be repaired.

When unbelief rather than doubt is indicated, *doubt that* is used:

He doubts that the watch can be repaired.

draft, draught   Both are pronounced the same: draft or dräft. Since the simpler spelling represents the pronunciation, it is more common than the spelling *draught*. *Draft* is always the spelling for a *bank draft*, the *military draft*, a *draft of a composition*, the *draft of a furnace*, a *draft of air*. *Draught* is more common for a *draught of fish*, a *ship's draught*, a *draught of ale*—though there is a growing tendency to use *draft*.

Usage is divided on the word meaning "a person who makes plans or sketches": either *draftsman* or *draughtsman*, the first more common.

drought, drouth   Both forms are in good use; *drought* (drout) is more common in formal English and *drouth* (drouth) in informal.

drowned   Pronounced as one syllable ("drownd"), not two ("drown-ded") in standard English.

drunk   Since one meaning of *drunk* is "intoxicated," some people shy away from using it as the past participle of *drink*, saying "We have drank all the lemonade" to avoid saying *drunk*. But *drunk* is the form to use: "We have drunk all the lemonade."

The past tense form is *drank:* "We drank all the lemonade."

due to   Originally *due* was used only as an adjective, and in formal English it is still restricted to this use:

444

> The accident was due to faulty brakes.   [*Due* modifies *accident;* *due to* means "caused by."]

In informal English *due to* is commonly used as a preposition meaning "because of":

> Due to Brian's hard work, the campsite was ready in an hour.
> Schools were closed, due to the heavy snows.

Since in spite of its commonness there is some prejudice against using *due to* as a preposition, it would be wise to avoid this use when writing for readers who you know are rather formal in language. You can easily substitute *because of* or *owing to:*

> Schools were closed because of the heavy snows.

each   1 *Each,* used as an adjective or pronoun, is singular; it takes a singular verb and is referred to by singular pronouns:

> Each senior *was* to have *his* picture taken for the yearbook.
> Each of the eighty seniors *has had his* picture taken.
> Each of the interns *checks his* patients before *he leaves.*
> Each of the nurses *turns* in *her* report before *she leaves.*

In colloquial usage, the pronoun *each* is sometimes regarded as a plural and is referred to by a plural pronoun:

> If *each* of the men had done *their* best, we would have won.

But in formal writing, either singular or plural forms should be used together:

> If *each* of the men had done *his* best, we would have won.
> If *all* the men had done *their* best, we would have won.

2 *Each* is sometimes used as a pronoun in apposition with a plural subject:

> The Mississippi-Missouri, the Nile, and the Amazon *each* are about 4000 miles long.
> They *each* have entered their best drawings in the contest.

Notice that in these sentences the pronoun *each* does not affect the number of the verb. Since the subjects are plural, the verbs (and the pronoun referring to the subject of the second sentence) are plural. (See Chapter 9, "Agreement with Indefinites," page 210.)

each other, one another Formal English makes a distinction between these pronouns, using *each other* with two, *one another* with more than two:

> Byrd and Bennett congratulated each other on their success.
> All the men congratulated one another on their success.

Informal English does not make this distinction, often using *each other* to refer to two or to more than two:

> All the men congratulated each other on their success.

economic, economical *Economic* means "having to do with business or economics"; *economical* usually means "avoiding waste; thrifty":

> The stock-market crash of 1929 was an economic disaster.
> Pierce's economical use of his earnings left him with enough money for a vacation.

Economy in writing Getting your meaning across to the reader as clearly and as directly as possible. For specific suggestions, see Chapter 11, "Avoiding Wordiness," page 254.

Editorial An article in a newspaper or magazine written by the editor or under his direction, stating opinions and attitudes on a subject of current interest. Editorials are generally printed on a special page, called the "editorial page," to set them apart from other material. The timely problems or events discussed in newspaper editorials are usually covered in news stories in the same issue. The news stories are supposed to give just the facts, which the editorials interpret according to the political or social theories that the paper represents. Although most editorials are intended to influence opinion, they are sometimes written to inform or merely to entertain.

Editorial we   See *we*, section 2.

effect, affect   See *affect, effect.*

e.g.   Abbreviation of Latin *exempli gratia,* which means "for example." Usually not italicized, *e.g.* is a formal abbreviation appropriate in documents, legal statements, and academic writing:

> Some of these Indians, e.g., the Seminoles and the Cherokees, have managed to preserve their tribal customs.

In informal writing the expressions *for example* and *for instance* are more appropriate.

ei, ie   For the spelling of words with *ei* and *ie,* see **Spelling,** section 1f.

either, neither   1 The usual meaning of *either* is "one or the other of two":

ADJECTIVE: Mark and Ronald are both fine students. *Either* boy could win the scholarship award.
PRONOUN: I would have liked *either* of the two rings in the window.

When referring to more than two, *any one* is generally preferable:

> Raymond applied for admission to Cornell, Antioch, and Iowa. *Any one* of them would be a good place to get an education. [Not: *Either* of them.]

The same distinction applies to the negative *neither. None* is used for more than two:

> *Neither* of Clifford's two radios worked.
> Dogs, cats, and chimpanzees can make meaningful sounds, but *none* of them can truly speak.   [Not: *neither* of them.]

2 *Either* and *neither* are usually regarded as singular, although informal English sometimes uses plural verbs with them:

> Neither *is* tall enough for the basketball team.
> *Is* (or *Are*) either of the two men really qualified?

3 *Either* meaning "each" is formal English and is seldom used now:

RARE: The high bluffs on either side of the Rhine made it a formidable barrier.
USUAL: The high bluffs on each side (*or* both sides) of the Rhine made it a formidable barrier.

4 In all but a few sections of the United States, the pronunciations ē′THər and nē′THər are generally heard; ī′THər and nī′THər are re-

garded as affectations except in some New England communities or among families or groups in which they are naturally used.

either . . . or, neither . . . nor   Used as correlative conjunctions (conjunctions that work in pairs):

> Either a moving shadow or a noise must have made Cass look up.
> Caesar was neither frightened nor angered by these threats.

(See **Correlative conjunctions.**)

Ellipsis   A punctuation mark of three spaced dots (. . .) used to show an omission in writing or printing. (Plural: *ellipses.*)

1 An ellipsis is used chiefly to show where one or more words that are not essential to the meaning have been omitted from a quoted passage:

> Few will ever write with real ease . . . unless they listen and read a good deal.

Note that when an ellipsis comes at the end of a quotation a fourth mark is needed for the period:

> The assault troops were, moreover, insufficiently trained. . . .

2 An ellipsis is sometimes used to show that a statement is left unfinished:

> The moth balls looked like candy and Billy was hungry, so . . .

447

(See also **Dash,** section 6.)

3 An ellipsis is sometimes used instead of *etc.* to show that a series could be continued:

> The French impressionists (Renoir, Manet, Degas . . .) decidedly changed our ideas about painting.

Elliptical clauses   Clauses in which a word or words necessary for complete construction but not for meaning are not used. The meaning of elliptical clauses is clear from words borrowed from the rest of the sentence or from the context:

> She arrived even later *than I* [arrived].
> Grace tried a little harder *than Shirley* [tried].
> *While at work,* Mr. Grundy developed pains in his stomach.   [The meaning is obviously "While he was at work."]

(See Chapter 10, "Dangling Modifiers," page 222.)

else   **1** Since *else* follows the word it modifies, the sign of the possessive is added to *else* rather than to the modified word:

> It wasn't my idea; it was someone else's. [Not: someone's else.]
> Nobody else's act drew as much applause as theirs.

2 In everyday speech *else* is sometimes used for emphasis in sentences where it actually adds nothing to the meaning. This use is not appropriate in writing. You can check your use of *else* in this way: if it is followed by *but, except,* or *besides* and an object, *else* is deadwood:

> There was nothing but some old newspapers in the abandoned mine shaft. [Not: nothing *else* but.]
> After an hour, I began to wish he would talk about something besides electronics. [Not: something *else* besides.]
> But: Interested as I was in electronics, I did wish he would talk about *something else* for a change.

Emphasis   Emphasis in writing means giving prominence to the ideas that are important. For ways of gaining emphasis, see Chapter 11, "Gaining Emphasis," page 257.

empty out   *Out* is not necessary since it adds nothing to the meaning:

> Empty [out] the radiator before pouring in the antifreeze.

Encyclopedias   Books or sets of books giving information, usually arranged alphabetically, on various branches of knowledge. Encyclopedias give authoritative general articles on persons, places, things, and events. Lists of books for further reading and cross references to other related subjects in the various volumes will often be found at the end of important articles. The information is kept up to date by frequent revisions or by annual supplements. Among the best-known general encyclopedias are:

> *Collier's Encyclopedia*
> *Columbia Encyclopedia* (one volume)
> *Encyclopaedia Britannica*
> *Encyclopedia Americana*
> *Lincoln Library of Essential Information* (one volume)
> *New International Encyclopedia*

And, planned especially for high-school use:

> *Compton's Pictured Encyclopedia*
> *World Book Encyclopedia*

Compton's Pictured Encyclopedia consists of fifteen volumes, each of which has at the back an "Easy Reference Fact-Index." This gives useful definitions, facts, statistics, dates, and pronunciations, as well as volume and page references to related material in the various volumes. Such an index will often help you find quickly and effortlessly the exact information you want.

Volume 20 of *World Book Encyclopedia* is a "Reading and Study Guide," with well-organized study outlines for the major fields of knowledge such as history, literature, medicine, music. The outlines give volume and page references to material in the various volumes.

In many of these encyclopedias important articles are signed. The full names of the authors may be given, or only their initials, with an index to the initials at the beginning of each volume (or in the first volume of the set).

End-stop A mark of punctuation, usually a period, question mark, or exclamation mark, used at the end of a sentence. (See **Period, Question mark, Exclamation mark, Ellipsis, Dash,** section 6.)

ensure, insure *Ensure* is preferred when the meaning is "make sure or certain": This scrupulous attention to details *ensures* the quality of their products. *Insure* is used to mean "arrange for money payment in case of loss, accident, or death." Remember *insure* in connection with *insurance:* Lloyd's of London *insures* everything from steamships to postage stamps.

enthuse A verb formed from the noun *enthusiasm.* Although many people object to *enthuse,* it has gained wide acceptance as the colloquial expression for the more formal *be enthusiastic about* or *over.*

COLLOQUIAL: Nat enthused about the car he had bought.
WRITTEN: Nat was enthusiastic about the car he had bought.

Epigram A short, pointed, often witty statement of a fact or opinion, either in verse or prose. Such statements are useful for focusing attention on a particular idea, making it easy to remember and to quote:

Elbow grease gives the best polish.—Robert Forby

Aphorisms are similar to epigrams, but are more likely to be abstract and are not necessarily witty:

Nothing prevents our being natural so much as the desire to appear so.—La Rochefoucauld

Proverbs are short, wise sayings, generally about character or conduct, that have been used for a long time by many people. Most proverbs have no known author. The terms *adage* and *maxim* are also used to identify such sayings:

A watched pot never boils.
You cannot have your cake and eat it too.
Birds of a feather flock together.

A special type of epigram is the *paradox,* which presents an idea in seemingly contradictory words:

Women are wiser than men because they know less and understand more.—James Stephens

err Generally pronounced ėr (as in *her*), but the pronunciation er is becoming more common because of the similarity of *err* to *error* (er′ər).

449

Esq. (Esquire)   A formal title of respect written after a man's name in the inside and outside addresses of a letter. *Esq.* is frequently used in England, where it signifies a definite social position. Its use in the United States—chiefly with names of professional men—has become rare, though it is used occasionally, particularly with lawyers' names.

Preceding titles (Mr., Dr., Hon.) are not used when *Esq.* follows a name: Robert W. Fairfax, Esq.

etc.   1 *Etc.*, the abbreviation for the Latin *et cetera,* is usually read *and so forth* in English. It is appropriate in reference and business usage:

> The zodiac is divided into twelve equal parts, each named after a different constellation—Leo, Cancer, Libra, etc.
> The inventory of small items—screws, tacks, nails, etc.—took much longer than Mr. Fisk had expected.

As you can see from the examples given above, only one period is necessary when *etc.* comes at the end of a sentence, but other punctuation marks are used after *etc.* according to the needs of the sentence. When *etc.* comes inside a sentence it is set off by commas:

> Screws, tacks, nails, etc., took much longer to inventory than Mr. Fisk had expected.

450

2 *Etc.* is out of place in both formal and informal writing, which avoid abbreviations in general. If you want to write out the term, the English *and so forth* is less conspicuous—and better—than *et cetera.* But the best advice is to avoid all such terms. An *and so forth* weakens your writing by giving the impression that either you are too lazy to complete a list or you are bluffing to indicate that you know more than you do. One solution is to rephrase the sentence, using *such as* or some other expression to show that the list is not intended to be complete:

WEAK: While in New York, we visited the standard tourist attractions —the Empire State Building, Rockefeller Center, etc.
BETTER: While in New York, we visited such standard tourist attractions as the Empire State Building, Rockefeller Center, and Coney Island.

And etc. should never be used, since the *et* of *et cetera* means "and." Remember *et* also to fix the correct spelling of the abbreviation in your mind: *etc.*—not *ect.*

Euphemism   A mild, indirect word or phrase used instead of one that is more direct or harsh or that may have unpleasant connotations for some people: *perspire* for *sweat, passed on* for *died, underprivileged* for *poor, senior citizens* for *old people,* and so on. (For a discussion, see Chapter 12, "Avoid Euphemisms," page 276.)

ever   In colloquial usage, *ever* is sometimes added to the interrogatives—*what, where, how, when*—for emphasis: "Whatever made him take up the tuba?" "Wherever did I put my pen?" "However did he get the money to buy a car?" "Whenever did you leave Texas?"

every and its compounds 1 The adjective *every* and the pronouns *everybody* and *everyone* are grammatically singular; they take singular verbs and are usually referred to by singular pronouns:

Every qualified voter *has cast his* ballot.
Has everyone *asked himself* why *he* chose to take this course?
Everyone decides for *herself* what career *she wants* to follow.

In colloquial usage, plural pronouns are sometimes used to refer to *everybody* and *everyone*, especially when they are thought of as plural in meaning:

Everybody in the club *brings their* own binoculars.
After everyone in the band had reached the field, *they* began forming ranks. [Not: *he* began. A plural meaning is clearly intended.]

In formal English, singular pronouns would be used or—if the meaning is clearly plural—the sentence would be rephrased:

Everybody in the club *brings his* own binoculars.
After all the bandsmen had reached the field, *they* began forming ranks.

(For further examples, see Chapter 9, "Agreement with Indefinites," page 210.)

451

2 *Everybody, everything,* and *everywhere* are written as one word. *Everyone* may be written as one word or two, depending on the meaning intended. The pronunciation can help you decide which form to use. If *every* is stressed, use the one-word form. If *one* receives an equal amount of emphasis or more, use two words:

Everyone agreed that Friday would be the best night for the dance.
Every one of the kittens was given away.

When used as an adjective, *everyday* is one word. When *day* is a noun modified by *every*, two words are used:

Chris packed his jeans and a pair of everyday slacks.
Every day seemed a week long.
A train leaves for Chicago at 9:35 a.m. every day.

3 Informal usage sometimes substitutes *every place* for *everywhere*. There are several other useful informal idioms formed with *every*, but like *every place*, they should be avoided in formal speech and writing:

INFORMAL: Every place we stopped, we found the motels full.
FORMAL: Everywhere we stopped, we found the motels full.

INFORMAL: Every so often we have a guest speaker in assembly.
FORMAL: Now and then we have a guest speaker in assembly.

INFORMAL: Crates were piled ceiling high, every which way we looked.

FORMAL: Crates were piled ceiling high in whatever direction we looked.

ex-   A hyphen is used when *ex-*, meaning "former," is prefixed to words showing position, rank, occupation, profession:

ex-governor   ex-coach   ex-king   ex-judge

Exaggeration   See **Hyperbole.**

Exclamation mark (**!**)   A mark or point used after a word, phrase, or sentence that the writer intends to be very emphatic. Such a word, phrase, or sentence is called an *exclamation:*

Hey! Down there! A truck's rolling backwards!
Why can't you keep quiet!
What a mess he's made of things!

Exclamation marks are used more frequently in narrative writing than in other types. They should always be used thoughtfully and sparingly (and only one at a time!) because too many exclamation points weaken the emphasis they are intended to provide:

OVERDONE: There was no Spanish treasure! ! ! The map was a forgery! The old sailor was a fraud! Clemson had been tricked out of all his money and had very nearly lost his life!

BETTER: There was no Spanish treasure! The map was a forgery. The old sailor was a fraud. Clemson had been tricked out of all his money and had very nearly lost his life.

excuse, pardon   Minor faults are *excused;* more serious faults and crimes are *pardoned:*

We excused Steven's interruptions because they were so witty.
Excuse me; I didn't mean to step on your toes.
The governor pardoned one member of the gang years later.

But in some circles "Pardon me" is considered more elegant than "Excuse me," and would be used in a sentence like the second.

Excuse is also used to mean "ask or give permission to leave": Please excuse me; I must see who is in the kitchen.

"I beg your pardon" is often used with the meaning "I don't agree with you" or "I didn't hear what you said."

Expletives   *It* and *there* are called *expletives* when they begin sentences in which the real subject follows the verb:

It was difficult *to follow the path in the darkness.*
It is too bad *that you must leave so early.*
There were only three *weeks* remaining before graduation.

Since the only function of *it* and *there* in sentences like these is to point ahead to (or "anticipate") the subjects, they are sometimes called "anticipatory subjects."

Expository writing Writing intended primarily to inform others by explaining a process or idea, presenting and interpreting facts, and explaining reasons. (See Chapter 1, "Writing Your Compositions," pages 1-19.)

extracurricular Written as one word, without a hyphen. *Extracurricular* means "outside the regular course of study":

Don't let extracurricular activities interfere with your studies.

fact (the fact that) Often used as a roundabout expression for *that,* which would express the same meaning more concisely:

He was finally informed [of the fact] that he could enter Yale.

(See also Chapter 11, "Roundabout Expressions," page 255.)

falls Although plural in form, *falls* takes a singular verb when preceded by *a,* and usually when a particular falls is named:

There is a falls to the east, just above the campground.
Yosemite Falls is in the eastern part of California.

When preceded by *the, falls* usually takes a plural verb:

The falls near Blakeville are becoming a tourist attraction.

Familiar English Familiar English is a casual sort of English, the kind of language you use in talking to members of the family or intimate friends, and in writing friendly letters, personal notes, diaries, or journals. Familiar English is not necessarily slovenly or slipshod; it is simply more free and easy than the English used in situations requiring greater formality. Since familiar English is based on everyday speech, it shows all the traits common to informal conversation: contractions, abbreviations, clipped words, nicknames, shortened constructions, localisms, shoptalk, and slang. The use of some or all of these is entirely appropriate in any writing intended only for the eyes of close friends. In fact, avoiding these traits will generally result in writing that lacks the warmth and intimacy your friends and family will expect from you.

famous *Famous* should not be used to label people who are obviously well known to everyone:

Pygmalion was written by [the famous] George Bernard Shaw.

If you were writing about someone whose fame was limited to a certain period of time or to a certain field that your readers might not be familiar with, *famous* would be appropriate:

> Bob Fitzsimmons, famous master of the solar-plexus punch, was thirty-four years old when he won the world heavyweight title.

farther, further   In formal English some people distinguish between these words, using *farther* to refer to physical distance and *further* to refer to time, degree, or addition:

> Each day the boys swam out farther from shore.
> If I were Phil, I would inquire further into the matter.

In informal English the distinction is not kept and there seems to be a definite tendency for *further* to be used in all senses. (See also **all the farther.**)

faze   An informal verb meaning "disturb; worry; bother." *Faze* is usually used negatively:

> This heckling from the grandstand didn't faze the pitcher.
> The bus driver's grumpiness had never fazed Mrs. Netherby.

Faze is also less commonly spelled *feaze* and *feeze* (both pronounced fēz or fāz).

Do not confuse the verb *faze* with the noun *phase*, meaning "aspect": Seth was most interested in the naval *phase* of World War II.

Feature   A *feature* is a special story, article, column, comic strip, or cartoon in a newspaper or magazine. The feature, often prominently displayed, attracts attention because of its subject matter or because of the reputation of the writer.

A *feature story* is an unusual article or story whose appeal lies in some factor other than its news value. It holds attention by dramatizing the human-interest element contained in everyday incidents. Such unimportant but interest-arousing incidents as the arrival in town of a coast-to-coast bicyclist; the adopting of a litter of orphaned skunks by a mother cat; and the display of unusual bravery, courtesy, or discourtesy are the kinds of subjects on which the feature writer thrives.

feel   For the use of *feel* as a linking verb, see **bad, badly.**

fewer, less   See **less, fewer.**

fiancé, fiancée   *Fiancé* refers to the man, *fiancée* to the woman. Both are pronounced the same: fē'än sā' or fē'än sā. The plurals are *fiancés* and *fiancées*.

Fiction   Prose writings, particularly novels and short stories, that tell about imaginary people or events.

field (in the field of)   Often used unnecessarily in sentences like the following:

> In [the field of] the theater, the trend has been away from his-torical settings and toward the contemporary scene.
> Leo would like to get a job in [the field of] advertising.

Figurative and literal use of words   Words can be used in one of two ways, either literally or figuratively. In a literal sense we use them for their ordinary meanings:

> The stage manager has misplaced the box of *blank cartridges*. [That is, powder-filled cartridges without bullets.]

Words can also be used figuratively—that is, for meanings that are suggested by their literal meanings:

> In commenting on the intellectual poverty of these business "geniuses," Mencken says: "... in a man's world they were successful men, but intellectually they were all *blank cartridges*." [That is, intellectually they were like blank cartridges.]

(See Chapter 12, "Using Figurative Language," page 281.)

Figures (3, 58, 241 ...)   See *Numbers* for the use of figures and the choice between figures and words in writing.

Figures of speech   Figures of speech are expressions in which words are used in an unusual sense or out of their literal meaning to add beauty or force. The most common figures are *simile* (Swift, who felt that Ireland was like a rathole, resented having to spend the rest of his life there), *metaphor* (Swift, who felt that Ireland was a rathole, resented having to spend the rest of his life there), and *personification* (The engine coughed, spat, and finally sprang into action). For a discussion of figures of speech, see Chapter 12, "Using Figurative Language," page 281.

455

fine   In "ground into a fine powder," "a pen with a fine point," "sheets made of fine linen," "fine gold," the adjective *fine* has a specific, exact meaning and is a useful and effective modifier. But *fine* (like *nice, grand, cute*) is often used as a counter word—a vague modifier that expresses only general approval. As a counter word, it has little value in writing and is usually better omitted:

> Lund proved to be a [fine,] courageous mountaineer.

first   See *former, latter; first, last.*

First draft   The preliminary version of a paper. For a discussion, see Chapter 1, "Writing the First Draft," page 14; and Chapter 6, "Step Five: Writing the First Draft," page 136.

fish The plural is also *fish,* unless different kinds or species are being discussed:

> After three whole days, Brad had caught only two small fish.
> The two fishes most commonly found along the shore of Hourglass Lake are smelt and perch.

fix In general usage *fix* has several meanings: "fasten securely" (fix a post in the ground), "set" (fixed the rent at ninety dollars), "direct" (fix your eyes on the flag), "put definitely" (fix the blame on careless drivers), "repair" (fix the broken watch).

In informal English *fix* is used to mean "punish" or "get revenge" (He'll fix Fred!) and "a predicament" (I'm in a bad fix). Both *fix* and *fix up* are used informally to mean "put in order" (fix your tie, fix up the guest room). And although *fix* is in general usage to mean "repair," *fix up* used in the same way is considered informal English.

folk, folks The plural of *folk,* meaning "people; persons," is *folk* or *folks:*

> Farm folk and town folk alike fled the rising river.
> Some folks waited in line for six hours or more to buy tickets for the play-off.

In informal usage *folks* is used to mean "parents; relatives":

> His folks are planning a trip to Mexico next summer.

456

Folk is used as an adjective and in some compounds: *folk ballads, folk art, folk tale, folklore, folkway.*

Footnotes In papers based on the writings of others, common .courtesy demands that you give credit for their ideas and words that you use in your own work. Such acknowledgments, usually made in *footnotes,* tell your reader where you got your facts, so that he can judge for himself the sources your material is based on and can turn directly to them for further information. Footnotes are used in scholarly articles and books. You will need to know how to use them in your research paper.

1 Footnotes are used:
a) To give the source of a direct quotation
b) To give credit for other people's ideas even though you write them in your own words
c) To give the source of diagrams, tables, statistics, and figures
d) To give additional information that may be of interest to the reader but not important enough to be given in the text

2 For your research paper, number your footnotes consecutively (1, 2, 3) throughout the paper. Place the number slightly above the line at the end of the sentence to be footnoted. Type or write the footnotes at the bottom of each page, below a short line to separate text from notes. Be sure to allow room enough for footnotes at the bottom of each page.

The first time reference is made to a book, give the author's name, the title of the book (underlined to represent italics), and the page or pages:

¹Gene Fowler, Good Night, Sweet Prince, p. 210.
²William Allen Neilson and Ashley Horace Thorndike, Facts About Shakespeare, p. 100.

To refer to a magazine article, give the author's name, the title of the article (in quotation marks), the name of the magazine (underlined to represent italics), the date of issue, and the page or pages:

³Stark Young, "Hamlet," New Republic, December 6, 1922, pp. 45-46.

If the author's name is not given, use this form:

⁴"Olivier's Hamlet," Time, June 28, 1948, pp. 54-55.

If the reference is to an article in an encyclopedia, give the author's name, the title of the article, the name of the encyclopedia (underlined), volume, and page:

⁵Thomas Marc Parrott, "Hamlet," Collier's Encyclopedia, vol. 9, pp. 501-502.

If the author's name is not given, use this form:

⁶"Shakespeare," Compton's Pictured Encyclopedia, vol. 13, p. 130.

If you have a number of references to the same source, use a shortened form for the footnotes after the first. To refer to a source mentioned in the immediately preceding footnote, use *ibid.* (Latin *ibidem*, meaning "in the same place"). If the page number differs from that given above, place a comma after *ibid.* and write the page number:

⁷Bernard Sobel, ed., The New Theatre Handbook, p. 343.
⁸Ibid.
⁹Ibid., p. 312.

When you refer to a work quoted earlier but not in the immediately preceding footnote, you may write the author's last name alone if no more than one source by the same person is used:

¹⁰Fowler, p. 213.

If there is more than one source by the same person, write the author's last name and one or two key words from the title:

¹¹Fowler, Sweet Prince, p. 219.

In print each footnote is indented like a paragraph, but there is no objection to beginning each one flush with the left margin of the paper.

for   A comma is usually needed between two coördinate clauses joined by *for*, to prevent misreading *for* as a preposition:

> I had to pay the deliveryman, for Mr. Karns was busy with a customer. [To prevent: I had to pay the deliveryman for Mr. Karns.]

(For the distinction between *because* and *for*, see **because.**)

for example   The abbreviation used for *for example* is *e.g.* (from the Latin *exempli gratia*). *E.g.* is not commonly used in informal writing, but is appropriate in scholarly papers, definitions, scientific writing, and legal documents. (For punctuation, see **namely and other introductory words.**)

Foreign words in English   See **Borrowed words** and **Anglicizing.**

Formal English   Formal English is the English used by educated people on formal occasions. For a discussion of the characteristics and uses of formal English, see Chapter 8, "Formal English," page 168.

former, latter; first, last   *Former* and *latter* are used to refer to a group of two only:

458

> Chicago and Rome are in the same latitude, yet the former has much colder winters than the latter.

First and *last* are used with three or more in a series:

> Although *stiff, excessive,* and *steep* are synonyms meaning "too much," the first and the last are appropriate only in informal writing.   [Not: the former ... and the latter....]

When used with a number, *first* precedes the number:

> The first three members that Bill asked refused to help.

Though *first* and *firstly* are both used as adverbs meaning "in the first place," *first* is generally preferred. Say *first, second, third, last:*

> First, the summers in Maine are generally cool. Second, inexpensive living quarters are not hard to find. Third, the....

(See **last, latest.**)

Fractions   Fractions are written in figures when they are attached to other figures (54⅓), when they are in a series that is being written in figures (6, ½, 12, ¼, 18), and when they are in tables or reference material. Usually in ordinary writing they are written in words.

Fractions used as adjectives or adverbs are hyphenated:

> A two-thirds majority is needed to pass a bill after a veto.
> The fuel gauge showed that the tank was three-fourths full.

Fractions used as nouns are not hyphenated:

Nine tenths of the delegates voted in favor of the motion.
Gene spent four fifths of his savings on an outboard motor.

But if the fraction contains a compound number from twenty-one to ninety-nine, that number is usually hyphenated:

Six twenty-fourths equals one fourth.
Next subtract fifteen thirty-sixths of the amount.

Decimals are increasingly used in place of fractions in expository writing. They are always written in figures:

.0025   .6   .87   3.14159

(See **Numbers.**)

Fragmentary sentence   For an explanation of fragmentary sentences, see Chapter 10, "Revising Sentence Fragments," page 232.

freshman, freshmen   Because they are pronounced alike (fresh'mən), these words are sometimes misspelled (one freshman, ten freshmen). The adjective is *freshman* (freshman Spanish, freshman classes). *Freshmen* should not be used to modify a noun.

You need not capitalize *freshman* (or *sophomore, junior, senior*) unless courtesy or emphasis makes a capital appropriate, as when you refer to the Freshman Class (the Junior Class, the Senior Orchestra) as a definite organization.

-ful, full   The adjective has two *l*'s: a *full* pail, in *full* bloom. The suffix has only one *l*: *pailful, handful, hateful, playful.*

The standard plural of nouns ending in *-ful* is made by adding *s*: *pailfuls, handfuls, armfuls, tablespoonfuls, pocketfuls.* Colloquially *tablespoonsful, pocketsful,* etc., are sometimes heard.

funny   In formal English *funny* means "amusing or comical"; in informal English it also means "strange; queer; odd":

INFORMAL: It's funny that so many people drown in shallow water.
FORMAL: It is strange that so many people drown in shallow water.

Future tense, future perfect tense   See **shall, will** and **Tenses of verbs.**

G

Gender   Gender is a classification of words to show whether they are masculine, feminine, or neuter.

1 In many languages nouns and the adjectives modifying them have special endings to show gender, but except for a few pronouns (*he, she,*

it) and nouns (such as *waiter, waitress; executor, executrix; tragedian, tragedienne; marquis, marquise; widow, widower*), gender in English is indicated simply by the meaning of the word: *brother—sister, bachelor—spinster, uncle—aunt, ram—ewe,* and so on. Nouns referring to inanimate objects are neuter: *window, sky, pin.*

2 Many English nouns can be either masculine or feminine. Their gender is shown only by the pronouns used with them:

> The doctor canceled all *her* appointments because of an emergency operation *she* had to perform.   [The doctor here is feminine.]
> Though the baby looks like *his* mother, *he* has *his* father's appetite. [The baby here is masculine.]

3 Compounds, partly to show gender, partly for emphasis, are common in English: *schoolboy, schoolgirl, woman driver, manservant.*

4 Neuter nouns are frequently given gender through a sort of personification:

> *Her* defeat in World War I cost Germany all *her* colonies.

In informal usage such personification is frequent, especially where intimacy or affection is felt:

> I was sure the *Elvira* could sail us to Tahiti if we gave *her* half a chance.

(See **he or she, his or her.**)

460

General usage   Words, forms, and constructions that are used in all kinds of English—formal, informal, and nonstandard. For a discussion, see Chapter 8, "General Usage," page 176.

Generalizations   A *generalization* is a general statement, principle, or rule inferred from particular facts or instances. When the generalization is based on enough facts or on enough particular instances, it is sound: "Energy can be transformed, but it cannot be created or destroyed," "All objects have inertia." Generalizations like these, which check with the facts, are sound and valuable.

Generalizations, though they sound impressive, must be viewed with caution, for many of them are false (or at least partially false) and could be dangerous. Propagandists, unscrupulous politicians, and many advertisers use them as their chief tool for influencing public opinion, for making unthinking people do as they want them to.

The majority of unsound generalizations are the product of well-meaning, but careless, writers and speakers. In conversation and in some kinds of informal writing, generalizations are common—in fact, seem almost unavoidable. And ordinary conversational generalizations, such as "All blondes are conceited" or "All bricklayers (or carpenters or plasterers) are overpaid" or "Every politician is an opportunist," usually cause no particular harm: both the speaker and his hearers recognize them as just a "manner of speaking."

But in serious expository speaking and writing, where every statement should come as near to truth as possible, you must guard against using hasty or unsound generalizations. This is especially true of statements designed to influence others. To say "Without a college degree, no one can get a good job or win promotions" or "All teen-agers are reckless drivers" or "Teaching machines will rapidly make textbooks obsolete" is to make statements that are hardly warranted by the facts, yet these statements may be believed by many readers.

It would be more accurate and less misleading to qualify such statements in some way—"Not having a college degree limits a person's chances of getting a good job or winning promotions," "Some teenagers are reckless drivers," "In a number of schools where teaching machines have been tried, they have proved valuable teaching aids"—and then back up the qualified statement with evidence.

While you must guard against making inaccurate generalizations in your own writing and speech, you must be equally careful not to accept as true all of the generalizations that are hurled at you daily in books, in newspapers, over the radio, and on television. Challenge the generalizations you run across. Ask yourself such questions as: Is this statement always true? What evidence is given to prove it is sound? Is it only partially true? Is it just one man's opinion? Why is the statement made? Is it intended to give me important information? Or is it used to persuade me to feel as the writer does so that I will think or do as he wants?

(For a more complete discussion of generalizations, see Chapter 4, "Inductive Reasoning," page 82.)

461

Genitive case   See **Possessive case.**

gentleman   See **man, woman.**

Gerund   1 A gerund is a verb form ending in *-ing* that is used as a noun. It should be distinguished from the present participle, which has the same form but which is used as an adjective:

GERUND: *Boiling* eggs is Harry's idea of cooking.   [*Boiling* names an action.]

PRESENT PARTICIPLE: *Boiling* with anger, the chairman called for a standing vote.   [*Boiling* modifies *chairman.*]

The gerund has the same uses as a noun:

SUBJECT: *Interfering* would merely make matters worse.
DIRECT OBJECT: He had considered *patenting* his invention.
PREDICATE COMPLEMENT: My first mistake was *contradicting* the coach.
APPOSITIVE: Vince's hobby, *designing* cars, won him a scholarship.
OBJECT OF PREPOSITION: Ten senators voted against *raising* the tax.

Nouns are often used as modifiers: *salt* shaker—"a shaker for salt." Gerunds, too, may be used as modifiers: *diving* board—"a board for diving," *bowling* alley—"an alley for bowling."

2 The possessive form is usual before gerunds in sentences like these:

Ted's resigning from the club was the start of our troubles.
Then his son learned about *his* willing his fortune to his dogs.

(For exceptions to this usage, see Chapter 9, "Using Pronouns and Nouns with Gerunds," page 209.)

3 A gerund phrase used as the object of a preposition should be related to the subject of the sentence. Otherwise the phrase will dangle:

DANGLING: By shading his eyes, the tower could be clearly seen.
CORRECTED: By shading his eyes, he could clearly see the tower.

(For further examples and discussion, see Chapter 10, "Dangling Modifiers," page 222.)

get   **1** The principal parts are *get, got, got* or *gotten*:

I get sporting goods from a mail-order house in Maine.
He got a ride to the lake from a passing truck driver.
We had already got (*or* gotten) Mr. Hanson's permission.

In England the past participle *gotten*—once the usual form—has been replaced by *got*. But in America both forms are common and in good use; the choice between them depends partly on which form a person is most used to saying and partly on the emphasis or the rhythm of a particular sentence.

462   **2** In informal usage *get* is often used as an emphatic helping verb in passive forms:

I don't think he is getting paid enough.   [Less emphatic: he is being paid enough.]
Mr. Dever got hit by a car last night.   [Less emphatic: Mr. Dever was hit.]

3 In colloquial usage *have got* (never *have gotten*) is sometimes used instead of *have* alone as an emphatic way of expressing obligation or possession:

I have got to turn in that money; you've got to pay it back now.
Have you got another pencil? I haven't got time to sharpen mine.

In these sentences the *have* alone would carry the meaning, but many speakers feel it is not emphatic enough and so expand the verb to *have got*. This usage, though common in informal speech, is avoided in formal English.

Given names   Given names are usually spelled out in full, or initials are used. Abbreviations such as *Geo., Jas.,* and *Robt.* are no longer considered appropriate.

George L. Mancuso	G. L. Mancuso
James Walsek	J. Walsek
W. Robert Bolden	W. R. Bolden

The second and other given names are not usually written out unless specifically called for (as in legal documents, wills, diplomas) to make identification more certain.

go In colloquial usage *go and*—used when no actual movement is meant—is a common form of emphasis:

> As soon as he sees her, he'll *go and* complain about what I said.
> When they asked Sue where we had been, she *went and* told them we had been at the beach.

This usage is appropriate in informal narrative writing, but not in exposition or in formal writing. In these, the *go and* would be omitted: "he'll complain about what I said," "she told them we had been at the beach."

Going on is a common colloquial idiom in stating ages (She's seventeen, going on eighteen) or time (It was going on ten o'clock). The more formal—and less emphatic—expressions are "nearing eighteen," "almost ten o'clock," "nearly ten."

Gobbledygook A word coined by former Congressman Maury Maverick for speech or writing that is hard to understand because technical terms, involved sentences, and "big words" have been used too much. *Gobbledygook,* so called after the sound made by a turkey (a gobble followed by a gook), applies especially to government and business writing that sounds like this: **463**

> Extra supplies may be requisitioned in accordance with procedures outlined in the revised operational manual by entering on the appropriate form the source of the extraordinary requisition request, the amount in which said extraordinary request exceeds the annual budgetary allotment designated for that supply category, and a written statement of permission for filing said request from the highest-ranking operational authority available.

(See also Chapter 12, "Avoid Big Words," page 275.)

Good English Good English is language that most effectively serves the user's purpose. To be good, language must be clear, lively, and appropriate—to the subject and the situation, to the listener or the reader, to the speaker or the writer. For discussion and examples, see Chapter 8, "The Levels of Usage."

good, well *Good* is used as an adjective, *well* as either an adjective or an adverb:

ADJECTIVE: Her flattery made me feel *good.* ["Pleasant."]
ADJECTIVE: Once the fever left, she felt *well.* ["Not ill."]
ADVERB: In spite of his nervousness, he spoke *well.* ["In a satisfactory way."]

Nonstandard English almost always uses *good* in place of *well*:

NONSTANDARD: Can she skate *good* enough to be his partner?
STANDARD: Can she skate *well* enough to be his partner?

Avoid this nonstandard usage in your own speech and writing.

graduate from   *Graduate from* has generally replaced the formal and somewhat archaic idiom *to be graduated from*:

RARE: He was graduated from Princeton in 1962.
USUAL: He graduated from Princeton in 1962.

In nonstandard English the *from* is omitted:

NONSTANDARD: He graduated college in 1962.

Habitual action   *Would* is commonly used as a helping verb to express habitual action in the past:

He would practice on those drums for hours every evening.

Habitual action is also shown by *used to* or by the past tense and an adverb:

He used to practice on those drums for hours every evening.
He constantly practiced on those drums.

had   Used (now rather rarely) in formal writing to introduce a subordinate clause of condition:

RARE: Had she known that Don Waitko was going to drive the car, she would have taken the bus.
USUAL: If she had known that Don Waitko was going to drive the car, she would have taken the bus.

had better, had best   Usual idioms for giving advice or making indirect commands:

You had better leave now, before the rush hour starts.
He'd better not interfere, or he will get hurt.
They had best turn the matter over to a lawyer.

In informal speech the *had* is sometimes dropped:

You better leave now, before the rush hour starts.
They best turn the matter over to a lawyer.

In formal English and in most writing (unless you are reporting directly what a person said) the *had* should be used.

had ought   *Had ought* and *hadn't ought* are nonstandard forms of the standard *ought* and *ought not*:

NONSTANDARD: He had ought to call a committee meeting soon.
STANDARD: He ought to call a committee meeting soon.

NONSTANDARD: Paul hadn't ought to jump to conclusions so fast.
STANDARD: Paul ought not to jump to conclusions so fast.

had rather, would rather   Both are used to express preference; the second is more emphatic and perhaps more common:

> He had rather face a hungry lion than apologize to her.
> I would rather read a book than spend an evening with them.

In speech the *had* or *would* is often slurred or contracted (He'd rather face a hungry lion....) so that it is impossible to tell which is being used.

half   The generally used idiom is *half a*; the more formal is *a half*:

GENERAL: It took us half an hour to go half a mile.
FORMAL: It took us a half hour to go a half mile.

The article *a* (or *an*) may come before or after *half*, but two articles are not needed. Expressions like *a half a mile* and *a half a ton*, used in nonstandard English, are generally avoided in standard usage.

465

hanged, hung   In formal English the principal parts of *hang* when referring to execution or suicide are *hang, hanged, hanged*; in other senses they are *hang, hung, hung*:

> Despite the sheriff's order, the posse hanged the two rustlers.
> Dad hung the moose head in the dining room.

In informal usage there is a tendency to use *hang, hung, hung* in all senses.

hardly   Since *hardly* has a negative meaning ("not easily; not quite"), it should not be combined with another negative word:

NONSTANDARD: We couldn't hardly see the pitcher from where we sat.
STANDARD: We could hardly see the pitcher from where we sat.

NONSTANDARD: There wasn't hardly enough room for our own gear.
STANDARD: There was hardly enough room for our own gear.

(See also **Double negative.**)

have got   See **get,** section 3.

he or she, his or her   Since English has no third person singular pronoun to refer to antecedents that mean either or both men and women, the language has developed three different ways of referring to such words:

1 Generally *he* and *his* are used, even when some of the persons meant are women:

> Every doctor and nurse in the area can be proud of the unstinting help *he* has given during this emergency.
> Mr. Wilkins and Mrs. Russo sat in the front row, pretending indifference but each hoping *his* team would win.

When the majority of the group referred to are women, *she* and *her* are used:

> Each committee member is to interview as many parents as *she* can before making *her* report to the chairman.

2 Sometimes the phrase *he or she* (or *his or her*) is used, but it is generally clumsy and usually sounds pedantic:

> If a person is sincerely interested in increasing *his or her* vocabulary, there are several ways in which *he or she* can do so.

The single pronouns *his* and *he* would be less awkward in this sentence, and the meaning would be just as clear.

3 People who avoid *he or she* (and *his or her*) as unnecessarily awkward, and dislike using *he* (and *his*) alone when women as well as men are meant, solve the problem by using a plural pronoun:

> Every senior had to have *their* picture taken for the yearbook.
> Ed and Sue were present, but neither expressed *their* views.

The plural pronoun is becoming more and more common and is appropriate in all but formal usage.

healthful, healthy Formal English distinguishes between these words, using *healthful* to mean "giving health" or "good for the health," and *healthy* to mean "having or showing good health":

> Dr. Barnes recommended the healthful climate of Cedarville.
> How can anyone be healthy if he does not eat healthful foods?

In informal English *healthy* is often used to mean "healthful":

> The doctor told him to move to a more healthy climate.

height In nonstandard English often pronounced hīth; in standard English pronounced hīt.

here, there Nonstandard English often adds an unnecessary *here* to *this* (and *there* to *that*):

NONSTANDARD: I like this here car; that there one is too fancy.
STANDARD: I like this car; that one is too fancy.

high school Capitalized only when used as part of a proper name:

> Wilson High School was then the only high school in our town.

When used as an adjective, *high school* is often hyphenated:

Most of the passengers were high-school students.

himself, herself See ***Reflexive pronouns.***

Historical present For the sake of vividness or liveliness the present tense is sometimes used in narratives about the past:

A few minutes later, just when I think everything is fine, pandemonium breaks loose again. The twins start pummeling each other and wake the baby, who starts screaming....

As a rule you will find it easier and more effective to stick to the past tense in narratives. Used throughout a story, the "historical present" becomes quite monotonous. And unless careful, you may find yourself shifting without reason from present to past and then back—to the confusion of your reader.

home Nonstandard English uses *to home* for the generally used *at home* or *home*:

NONSTANDARD: He said that Chris wasn't to home.
STANDARD: He said that Chris wasn't at home. [Or: wasn't home.]

homely In formal English *homely* means "simple; unassuming; suited to home life": *homely pleasures, homely food*. But in general usage it is most frequently used to mean "not good-looking; ugly; plain": Brigid O'Meara, once the *homeliest* girl in our town, had become a great beauty.

467

Homographs Words that have the same spelling but a different origin and meaning: *pile* ("to heap up"), *pile* ("a heavy beam driven into the earth to serve as a support"), *pile* ("a soft, thick nap, as on velvet").

In most dictionaries homographs are entered separately; the one that is likely to be used most is generally put first. The Thorndike-Barnhart dictionaries put a small number after each homograph (pile¹, pile², pile³) as a signal that there are other entries (or another entry) which may have the definition a person needs.

Homonyms Words that have the same pronunciation but different meanings: *straight—strait, road—rode—rowed, pore—pour*.

The meaning of such words is usually made clear by the context, but their spelling is likely to cause trouble. Keeping the words separated in your mind by visualizing them in phrases that give a clue to their meaning will help you spell them correctly:

a ten-minute *break* for coffee	stepped on the *brake*
the objective *complement*	flattered by his *compliment*
coarse cloth and *coarse* manners	for a first *course*, of *course*
soldiers who *desert* their posts	strawberry sodas for *dessert*

a plane with *dual* controls	fought a *duel* over her
always *fair* and honest	ten cents for bus *fare*
hit·a *foul* ball	hunting *fowl* for food
the *heir* to millions	the birds of the *air*
idle men and *idle* machines	worshiping an *idol*
the *key* to the puzzle	ships loading at the *quay*
led the men to safety	pipes made of *lead*
a *metal* like tin or aluminum	a true test of *mettle*
a *missile* on the launching pad	the prayers in the *missal*
a *piece* of pie	smoking a *peace* pipe
based on a moral *principle*	the *principal* and faculty
the *rain* in Spain	during Napoleon's *reign*
threw the ball to first	tunnel *through* the mountain
Who's there?	*Whose* is it?

Honorable   When used as a title of respect for persons in high political offices (congressmen, judges, governors, mayors), *honorable* is capitalized, is usually preceded by *the*, and is followed by the first name or initials as well as the surname:

> The guest speaker will be the Honorable Eldon G. Crane.

Honorable is generally not abbreviated except in addresses, and then only if *The* is not used:

Hon. Aldo Fermi	The Honorable Aldo Fermi
Hon. A. P. Fermi	The Honorable A. P. Fermi

Hours   Hours are usually written in words:

> The second feature starts at eight o'clock and ends at nine.
> The debate team is to meet at two-fifteen Friday afternoon.
> The meeting was adjourned at four-thirty.

With the abbreviations *a.m.* and *p.m.*, figures are used:

> His plane leaves at 9:40 a.m. and arrives at 1:27 p.m.
> The photographer will be in the library at 10:15 a.m.

Notice that a colon is used between hours and minutes written as figures and that the phrase *o'clock* is not added after *a.m.* or *p.m.*

how?   A colloquialism often used instead of *What?* or *What did you say?* in asking a speaker to repeat something he said. Many people avoid both *How?* and *What?*, feeling that the single words are not as polite as using the full sentence "What did you say?" Formal English generally uses the conventional formula *I beg your pardon?*

how come?   A colloquial shortening of "How does (did) it come that?": *How come* Jerry didn't have to pay a fine?

however   See **Conjunctive adverbs.**

Hyperbole (Pronounced hī pėr'bə li.) Exaggeration for the sake of effect and not meant to be taken literally:

> Big? He weighs just a pound or two less than a whale!
> I warned them ten thousand times not to leave the yard.

Hyphen   **1 With compound modifiers.**   A compound modifier (two or more words used as a single adjective) preceding a noun is generally hyphened:

an up-to-date report	his I-do-as-I-please attitude
this so-called expert	a take-it-or-leave-it offer
a big-city slicker	well-balanced meals

If the compound modifier comes after the noun or if the first part is an adverb ending in *-ly*, no hyphen is used:

> The meals, though filling, were seldom *well balanced*.
> His *badly bruised* ego showed through the *beautifully phrased* sentences.

Compound proper adjectives or compound proper nouns used as adjectives are not hyphened:

Little League teams	West Indian problems
North American peoples	New Deal advocates

2 With numbers and fractions.   Hyphens are used in compound numbers from twenty-one to ninety-nine:

seventy-six trombones	two hundred fifty-four

> Under the mattress they found forty-five dollar bills.   [Compare with "forty five-dollar bills ($200)"—in which the hyphen is used for a compound modifier.]

Fractions are not hyphened unless they are used as modifiers:

> *Three fourths* of the votes have been tallied.   [Noun.]
> He left *one half* of his savings to his cats.   [Noun.]
> When we left, the tank was *two-thirds* full.   [Adverb modifier.]
> A *two-thirds* vote will override the veto.   [Adjective modifier.]

3 With prefixes.   A hyphen is used (a) between a prefix and a proper noun or adjective:

anti-Fascist	pro-Irish
pre-Marxian	un-American

b) Between a prefix ending in a vowel and a root word beginning with the same vowel (to prevent pronouncing the two vowels as one sound):

re-entered	pre-establish
anti-icer	co-ordinal

469

(Note: Words with *re-* and *pre-* are also spelled with a dieresis: *reëntered, preëstablish.* Common words with *co-* are also written as solid words, with or without a dieresis: *coördinate, coordinate; coöperative, cooperative.*)

c) To avoid confusion with another word that has the same spelling but a different pronunciation and meaning:

Again I *recounted* the strange events of the day.   [ri kount′id]
We *re-counted* the votes and again made a mistake.   [rē kount′id]
He promised to *relay* the message to Harris.   [rē′lā or ri lā′]
The men will *re-lay* the tiles tomorrow.   [rē lā′]

d) After the prefixes *self-* and *ex-* (when *ex-* means "former" or "formerly"):

self-government   ex-senator
self-assured   ex-treasurer

4 With compound words.   There is no simple rule for hyphenating ordinary compound words, since usage varies so widely. For example, though the compounds *hair-raising, blue-black,* and *short-tempered* are hyphened, *hair trigger, blue book,* and *short circuit* are written as two words. And related compounds—*hairspring, bluejacket,* and *shortstop*—are written as one word. In one newspaper or magazine, you may see *super market,* in another *super-market,* and in a third *supermarket.*

Many compound words go through three steps before they are written as one word. For example, in an article (published in 1891) in which James Naismith described a game he had invented, he wrote its name as two separate words—*basket ball.* Then for many years a hyphen was used—*basket-ball.* Finally the two words became fused into one—*basketball.*

Since there is no simple rule to guide you in spelling compounds, the safest practice is to consult a dictionary for words you are in doubt about. If the dictionary does not list the compound you are looking for (either as one word or with a hyphen), write it as two words, without a hyphen.

5 For dividing words.   A hyphen is used to mark the division of a word at the end of a line of writing. The problem here is to divide the word between syllables. For a list of rules to guide you, see *Division of words.*

I   *I* is written with a capital simply because in the old handwritten manuscripts a small *i* was likely to be lost or joined to a neighboring word. Contrary to a widespread belief, using *I* as the first word in a letter (or as the first word in a series of sentences in a paragraph) is not a sign of conceit. *I* can be used wherever it is needed to express ideas simply and clearly. People who use roundabout expressions to avoid using *I* usually turn out awkward, unnatural sentences that are far less effective than sentences with *I*:

AWKWARD: It is my sincere opinion that my training and experience provide the background required for this position.

BETTER: I believe that I have had the necessary training and experience to do the work efficiently.

If every sentence in a paragraph you have written begins with *I*, you may feel that the pronoun is too conspicuous, that so many *I*'s will be annoying to your reader. By shifting a modifying phrase or clause to the beginning of two or three of the sentences, you can take the emphasis away from the *I* and make it seem less conspicuous:

> Knowing how busy Miss Bruno was, I retyped the two letters myself. [Instead of: I retyped the two letters myself, knowing how busy Miss Bruno was.]

Ibid.   An abbreviation of the Latin *ibidem,* meaning "in the same place." It is used in a footnote to refer to the work mentioned in the immediately preceding footnote. (See **Footnotes.**)

Idiom   An idiom is a combination of words that seems perfectly natural to the native speakers of a language but seems odd or peculiar to other people (usually because it has a meaning different from the literal meaning of the words):

walked on air	hauled them over the coals
pull yourself together	ran across an old friend
be on pins and needles	blow hot and cold
set her cap for him	has a bee in his bonnet

(For further discussion and examples, see Chapter 9, "Idiomatic Prepositions," page 216, and **Preposition,** section 3.)

ie, ei   For the spelling of words with *ie* and *ei,* see **Spelling,** section 1f.

i.e.   An abbreviation of the Latin *id est,* meaning "that is." It is now seldom used except in reference works; *that is* is used instead. (For punctuation, see **namely and other introductory words.**)

if, whether   **1** *If* is used to introduce a clause of condition; *whether* (with *or*) is used to introduce alternatives:

> If it rains, there will be a buffet supper instead of a picnic.
> What should we do if he refuses to leave?
> Whether he pays the bill or sends it to Dad, I'm in trouble.
> Whether he had a ghost writer or not is his secret.

2 In formal usage *whether* (usually with *or*) is used to introduce indirect questions and expressions of doubt:

INDIRECT QUESTION: He wants to know whether or not we approve.

INDIRECT QUESTION: The officer asked whether we had seen any strangers in the area.

DOUBT: We could not be sure whether he suspected us or the Fagins.

DOUBT: Frank wondered whether or not she had even read the play.

In informal usage *if* rather than *whether* is generally used in such sentences:

> He wants to know if we approve.
> The officer asked if we had seen any strangers in the area.
> We couldn't be sure if he suspected us or the Fagins.
> Frank wondered if she had even read the play.

illusion, allusion   *Illusion* means "a false impression" or "a deceptive appearance":

> By using polysyllabic words and quotations from Emerson, he managed to create an illusion of profundity.

Illusion is sometimes confused with *allusion*, meaning "an indirect reference to something or someone generally familiar":

> In his articles he made no allusion to his recent defeat at the polls.

(See also Chapter 12, "Use Allusions," page 278.)

Imagery   Imagery in writing is the use of words that appeal to one of the senses: sight, hearing, taste, smell, touch, and the muscular tension known as the kinesthetic sense. Some words may appeal to more than one sense (*firecracker* to sight and hearing, *rancid* to smell and taste), but one of the sense appeals would ordinarily be dominant, as in the following:

SIGHT: burnished copper, jagged scar, fluffy baby chicks
HEARING: grinding brakes, rattle of empty bottles, squeaky shoes
TASTE: lukewarm cocoa, lemony flavor, spiced with cinnamon
SMELL: musty cellar, acrid fumes, grass freshly mown
TOUCH: scratchy tweed, cobblestone path, stubby mustache
KINESTHETIC: skin-tight gloves, cramping pains, sudden chills

Imagery is an important part of all writing, except very abstract discussions of ideas. Try to use images frequently in your own writing, but remember that they are most likely to be effective when they come directly from your own experience. The things you are interested in—dogs, football, clothes, food, camping, anything—should be the source of many images, not only in writing in which they are the main subject but in other writing too.

Imitative words (Onomatopoeia)   A number of words imitate or suggest the sound associated with a certain thing or action: *buzz, clash, sizzle, ack-ack, squawk, plop, whiz, clang, squeal, chickadee, twang.*

The use of imitative words to gain a special effect in writing is called *onomatopoeia* (on′ə mat′ə pē′ə):

> The blade whizzed past his head and hit the target with a twang.

Imperative mood   A verb in the imperative mood is used to give commands or to make requests:

> *Keep* this under your hat.

(See also **Commands and requests, Mood.**)

Imperative sentences   Sentences that give commands or make requests:

> Drive carefully.   Don't be a road hog.

(See also **Commands and requests.**)

Impersonal it   In talking about weather and time, *it* is used as an impersonal subject in sentences like these:

> It was raining, unfortunately.
> It was long after midnight.

It is called impersonal because it does not refer to a definite person or thing.

Impersonal style   Writing in which the author carefully avoids the personal pronoun *I* or any other direct reference to himself is said to be in the impersonal style. The types of writing that are usually impersonal include editorials, most serious discussions of situations and ideas, academic and professional writing, compilations of facts, and term papers.

Impersonal writing makes use of such devices as the editorial "we," "the writer believes," and "in the opinion of the writer." Used too often, such expressions become tiresome and detract rather than add to the effectiveness of the writing. Yet they are better than such meaningless phrases as "many believe," "it has been said," "it seems," and the colorless impersonal pronoun "one."

For most student purposes, an informal personal style is more appropriate than a formal impersonal style, with the possible exception of the formal research paper.

imply, infer   Careful speakers and writers distinguish between these two words, using *imply* to mean "indicate without saying outright," and *infer* to mean "draw a conclusion by reasoning":

> His shrug implied that he no longer cared who won.
> I inferred from his closing words that he would not let the matter drop.

However, *infer* has so often been used in the sense of "imply" that many dictionaries record "imply" as a secondary meaning of *infer*.

in, into, in to *In* generally shows location (in a literal or figurative sense); *into* generally shows direction:

They are in the office.   They came into the office.
He was in the foxhole.   He dived into his foxhole.
She is still in a coma.   She fell into a deep sleep.

Colloquially *in* is often used for *into*:

Don't fall in the creek.   He jumped in the creek.

Do not confuse the preposition *into* with the adverb *in* followed by the preposition *to*:

Bates went into the locker room to question his manager.
Before going in to dinner, Bates made a phone call.

Incoherence Lack of connection between ideas in speech or writing. For ways of gaining coherence—or continuity, as it is called in this book—see Chapter 2, "Continuity in Paragraphs," page 49, and Chapter 1, "The Body of the Paper," page 16.

Incomplete sentences See Chapter 10, "Revising Sentence Fragments," page 232.

Indefinite articles The words *a* and *an,* used to refer to any one of a group of persons, places, or things: *a* chemist, *an* observatory, *a* horse, *an* animal. (See *a, an; the.*)

474

Indefinite it Formal English and careful informal writing avoid the use of the indefinite *it*:

INDEFINITE: In the first chapter *it* merely sets the stage for the complications to come.
REVISED: The first chapter merely sets the stage for the complications to come.

(See also Chapter 10, "Indefinite Reference," page 229.)

Indefinite pronouns Pronouns used to refer to any one or more of a number of persons or things:

all	either	none
another	everybody	nothing
any	everyone	one, oneself
anybody	everything	other
anyone	few	several
anything	many	some
both	neither	someone
each	nobody	such

(Some of the specific usage problems concerning these are discussed under the separate words. See also Chapter 9, "Indefinites," page 200;

"Words of Measure," page 200; and "Agreement with Indefinites," page 210.)

Indention Beginning a line in from the left-hand margin. Since an uneven margin makes a page look unsightly, take pains to keep the margin straight and the indentions consistent.

In longhand copy, paragraphs are indented about an inch; in typewritten copy, from five to ten spaces. These measurements may vary according to the writer's taste or special need.

Hanging indention is the setting in of lines below the first line, as in outlines, newspaper headlines, and headings and addresses of letters (in slant style). If a line of verse is too long for one line, indent the part brought over to the second line:

> True ease in writing comes from art,
>   not chance,
> As those move easiest who have learn'd
>   to dance.
>   —Alexander Pope, *An Essay on Criticism.*

Independent clause   (Also called *main* clause.) See **Clause,** section 1.

Indicative mood The mood of the verb in statements of fact or questions about a fact:

> We *decided* to walk, even though it *was* late.
> We *took* a cab because Nora *insisted.*
> He *was fired* two days later.
> *Did* anyone *complain* about the noise?

(See **Mood.**)

Indirect object A noun or pronoun (or phrase or clause used as a noun) that shows, without the use of a preposition, to whom or for whom an action is done:

> He left the *waitress* a five-dollar tip.
> Who told *her* my phone number?
> They asked *Joe* and *me* the same question.   [Compound.]
> I wouldn't give *his winning the first round* a second thought.   [Gerund phrase.]
> Tell *whoever calls* that he is out of town.   [Noun clause.]

Notice that the indirect object precedes the direct object.

Indirect question A question that is reworded in the speaker's or writer's own words instead of being quoted as first heard or read. A period, not a question mark, is used after an indirect question:

INDIRECT: The waiter asked who had ordered the spinach.
DIRECT: The waiter asked, "Who ordered the spinach?"

Indirect quotation   A quotation that is reworded in the speaker's or writer's own words instead of being quoted as first heard or read. Quotation marks are not used to enclose an indirect quotation:

INDIRECT: Dan said he didn't know how much it would cost.
DIRECT: Dan said, "I don't know how much it will cost."

individual   See **person.**

infer, imply   See **imply, infer.**

Infinitive   1 The infinitive is the simple form of the verb, usually preceded by *to: to groan, to hesitate, to interfere, to watch* him *play.* Infinitives, alone or in phrases, are used as nouns (subjects, objects, complements), as adjectives, and as adverbs:

SUBJECT: *To criticize* is easy.
OBJECT: He is planning *to resign,* in fact.
COMPLEMENT: My first thought was *to sneak* out.
ADJECTIVE: Bruno is not in a position *to quibble.*
ADVERB: She stayed *to help* Clifford with his report.

(See also Chapter 7, "Infinitive Phrases," page 154.)
   2 Objective-case pronouns are used for predicate complements of infinitives that have subjects:

Many people took Laura to be *me.*   [*Laura* is the subject of the infinitive; *me* is the predicate complement.]

The predicate complement of an infinitive that has no expressed subject may have either the nominative or the objective form. The nominative is generally used in formal English; the objective, in informal English:

FORMAL: I surely would not like to be *he.*
INFORMAL: I surely wouldn't like to be *him.*

(See also Chapter 9, "Tenses of Verbals," page 196, and **Split infinitive.**)

Inflection   In grammar *inflection* means a change in form of a word to show case (*they—them*), number (*dollar—dollars; is—are*), gender (*actor—actress*), person (*I think—he thinks*), tense (*hate—hated*), or comparison (*prettier—prettiest*).

Informal English   The language that educated people ordinarily use in speech and writing in all but formal situations. For discussion and examples, see Chapter 8, "Informal English," page 166.

inside of   In informal English *inside of* is used in expressions of time:

INFORMAL: The bill will be ready inside of a week.   [Or: in a week.]
FORMAL: The bill will be ready within a week.

The *of* is not necessary in sentences such as:

He was standing just inside [of] the gate.

Intensive pronouns   Personal pronouns plus the suffix *-self* or *-selves,* used after a noun or pronoun to add emphasis:

The mayor himself gave the order.
He gave the order himself.
They themselves couldn't agree on a fair price.

(See **myself.**)

Interjection   An exclamatory word or phrase: *oh, ouch, my goodness, horrors.* An emphatic interjection is followed by an exclamation point; a mild or weak interjection is followed by a comma:

Pooh! He doesn't scare me.
Oh! You startled me. [Or: Oh! you startled me.]
Oh, what difference does it make?

Interrogative adjectives   Words that introduce questions as well as modify nouns:

Which twin was it?   [Modifies *twin.*]
What supplies will be needed?   [Modifies *supplies.*]
Whose place did he take?   [Modifies *place.*]

Interrogative pronouns   Pronouns used in asking questions: *who, whose, whom, which, what,* and sometimes *whoever, whatever.*

Interrogative sentences   Sentences that ask for information:

Who made the touchdown?
How does she hide her freckles?
Has everyone sent in his registration form?

When a sentence is phrased as a statement but is meant as a question, it is followed by a question mark:

Tom Koscko made the touchdown?

A polite request phrased as a question for the sake of courtesy is generally followed by a period rather than a question mark:

Will you please express my thanks to the members of the club.

Intransitive verbs   Verbs whose meanings are complete without a direct object:

Even Uncle Frank *slept* until noon.
He *fumbled* in his pocket for the key.
At a signal from the firemen, the woman *jumped.*

Linking verbs are always intransitive, merely connecting a predicate noun or adjective with the subject:

> His sister Laura *became* a Broadway actress.
> The toast *was* black, and the eggs *were* raw.

(See *Transitive and intransitive verbs.*)

Inverted sentences   The usual order in sentences is subject–verb, subject–verb–object, or subject–verb–complement. Sentences in which this order is changed are called *inverted sentences*:

> There goes the last of my hard-earned money.   [Verb before subject.]
> And very grateful he was for my help.   [Complement first.]

(See also Chapter 11, "Varying the Sentence Order," page 257.)

Irony   A form of expression implying something different, even opposite, from what is actually said:

> *His memory is remarkable,* all right; before he reaches the end of a sentence, he can't quite remember what its subject is.

irregardless   See *regardless.*

it   Informal English often uses *it* to refer to the idea of a preceding statement; formal English rarely does so:

> INFORMAL: Paul could usually get out of doing his share of the chores by pretending to be sick. But *it* didn't work when his father was there.
> FORMAL: Paul could usually get out of doing his share of the chores by pretending to be sick—a ruse that did not work when his father was there.

(See also Chapter 10, "Indefinite Reference," page 229.)

Italics   In type, letters that slant to the right. (*This sentence is in italic type.*) In longhand and typewritten manuscript, italics are shown by underlining. (For specific uses of italics, see *Underlining.*)

its   The possessive adjective does not have an apostrophe:

> The dog hurt *its* paw.   Nobody doubts *its* authenticity.

To avoid misspelling, associate *its* with *his* and *hers.*

it's   The contraction of *it is* or *it has*:

> *It's* on the top shelf.   *It's* been there for weeks.

As a contraction, *it's* is always spelled with an apostrophe.

It's me Formal grammarians explain that the verb *be* should always be followed by the nominative case: *It is I.* But in actual practice *It's me* is so generally used by educated people that it is now accepted standard usage (even though some users of formal English still prefer *It is I*).

Though *It's me* is fully acceptable, *It's him, It's her, It's us, It's them* are not.

J

Jargon Most commonly used in one of these two senses: "confused, meaningless talk or writing" or "the language of a special group, profession, or class":

> His latest directive—more pompous, wordy, and involved than usual —was simply jargon; none of us could understand it.
> If Pierce would avoid all that legal jargon and talk in everyday terms, he'd have more clients.

Linguists use *jargon* to mean "a dialect composed of a mixture of two or more languages." Many non-English-speaking people, in doing business with us, use jargons made up partly of English and partly of their native language. In the Pacific Northwest, for example, the Chinook jargon (a mixture of Chinook, French, and English) was used by Indians in their dealings with American fur traders. In some islands of the Pacific the Beach-la-Mar jargon (a mixture of English and Malay) is used as a trade language. The Chinese-English jargon, commonly called "pidgin English," is used by Orientals and South Pacific natives in carrying on trade.

479

job, position *Job* is the informal word for the formal *position*:

INFORMAL: I would like a job at an advertising agency.
FORMAL: I would like a position at an advertising agency.

The two words have different connotations. Though *job* is used informally to apply to any kind of employment, it usually suggests the idea of work to be done for hourly wages. *Position* usually suggests white-collar or professional employment with a fixed salary.

join together The *together* is unnecessary, since *join* means "bring, come, or put together":

> The two roads join [together] about a mile from here.
> Joining the six pieces [together] will give us the length we need.

Journalese A style of writing found in some newspapers and magazines. Its chief characteristics (generally considered faults) are the overuse of "big words," roundabout expressions, and trite phrases.

just In informal English *just* is often used to mean "very; positively":

> The steaks were just delicious.

Guard against overusing *just* in this sense in your written work. (For the position of *just,* see **only.**)

K

kid Used as a noun meaning "child" or "young person," *kid* is colloquial. Used as a verb meaning "tease playfully" or "deceive; fool," *kid* is slang.

kind, sort In formal English the singular adjectives *this* and *that* are used to modify the singular *kind* or *sort*:

> This kind of shrub seldom needs pruning.
> That sort of person makes trouble for everyone.

The plural adjectives *these* and *those* are used only when *kind* and *sort* are plural:

> These kinds of errors are inexcusable.
> Those sorts of jobs require special training.

In colloquial usage the plural adjectives are often used with *kind* and *sort*:

> But these kind of programs were not popular.
> Those sort of games are for children.

In spite of the fact that this usage is common in the speech of educated people, it still has only colloquial standing. You will be wise to avoid it in writing, especially formal writing.

In both speech and writing, avoid the nonstandard *them kind*:

NONSTANDARD: No one wears them kind any more.
STANDARD: No one wears that kind any more.

kind of, sort of In informal speech *kind of* and *sort of* are often used as adverbs meaning "rather; somewhat; almost; nearly":

> She kind of expected Paul to win first prize.
> Now that I think of it, his question was sort of strange.

In written English the appropriate forms would be:

> She rather expected Paul to win first prize.
> Now that I think of it, his question was somewhat strange.

kind of a, sort of a Formal English omits the *a*:

> That kind of driver ought to lose his license.
> The showcase was filled with every sort of toy one could imagine.

480

But in informal English, especially in speech, *kind of a* and *sort of a* are common:

> That kind of a driver ought to lose his license.
> The showcase was filled with every sort of a toy you could imagine.

lady   See **man, woman.**

last, latest   Formal English makes a distinction between these two words—using *last* to refer to the final item of a series, and *latest* to refer to the most recent of a series that may or may not continue:

> *The Big Money*, the last novel of the trilogy *U.S.A.*, was completed in 1936.
> Both these films are reviewed in the latest issue of *Time*.
> *Googolplex Squared* is the cryptic title of Jerrit's latest play.

In informal English *last* is commonly used in place of *latest*:

> Both these films are reviewed in the last issue of *Time*.

But this usage should be avoided wherever it might be ambiguous:

> AMBIGUOUS: *Googolplex Squared* is the cryptic title of Jerrit's last play.   [This could mean that Jerrit will write no more plays.]

latter, last   See **former, latter; first, last.**

lay   See **lie, lay.**

Lead   The introductory section of a news story, which tells the reader important facts, such as *who* is concerned, *what* happened, *when, where,* and perhaps *how* or *why.* The lead (pronounced lēd) may vary in length from one sentence to several paragraphs.

lead, led   The present tense is spelled *lead* and pronounced lēd. The past tense (and past participle) is spelled *led* and pronounced led:

> Now they lead a miserable, cat-and-dog life.
> His second cable merely led to more confusion.
> This clue, in turn, had led him to Mr. Myer's shop.

Leading question   A question worded in such a way that it suggests the answer wanted:

> Mr. Jonas was annoyed at your complaints, wasn't he?   [Contrast with: What was Mr. Jonas's reaction to your complaints?]

Leading questions are not permitted in a law court.

learn, teach Nonstandard English often uses *learn* in the sense of *teach*. Standard English (formal and informal) does not:

NONSTANDARD: That experience learned me not to believe all I read.
STANDARD: That experience taught me not to believe all I read.
STANDARD: I learned from that experience not to believe all I read.

leave, let A common nonstandard idiom is the use of the verb *leave* (*left*, *left*) where formal and informal English would use the verb *let* (*let*, *let*). Remember that when you mean "permit" or "allow to pass, go, or come" *let* is the verb to use:

Let me help you. [Not: *Leave* me help you.]
Why won't he *let* you drive? [Not: *leave* you drive.]
Before *letting* us in, he asked to see our passes. [Not: Before *leaving* us in.]
Let go of that end of the wire! [Not: *Leave* go.]

With *alone*, however, either word is standard usage: "Leave me alone" or "Let me alone."

leisure In America usually pronounced lē′zhər, less often lezh′ər.

lengthways, lengthwise Mean the same and are used interchangeably.

482

less, fewer Formal English makes a distinction between these two words, using *fewer* to refer to number (to things that are counted) and *less* to refer to amount or quantity (to things that are measured):

He could have said the same thing in fewer words.
There are fewer accidents now that the street has been widened.
We planted less corn this year than last.
Dave requires much less sleep than the rest of us.

In informal English *less* is commonly used in place of *fewer*:

He could have said the same thing in less words.
There are less accidents now that the street has been widened.

less, lesser Both are comparatives of *little*, but they are not used interchangeably. *Less* refers to amount or quantity; *lesser*—a formal word—refers to value or importance:

I eat less food than he and weigh forty pounds more.
Taking the blame myself seemed to me the lesser of two evils.

let's us, let's don't Since *let's* is a contraction of *let us*, another *us* should not be added to it. "Let's us hide" is repetitive—the same as saying "Let us us hide." Say "Let's hide," "Let's warn them."

In the negative, either *let's not* or *let's don't* is used: "Let's not eat there again." "Let's don't tease him." Though *do* (in the second example) is not necessary to the meaning, the expression *let's don't* is a common and well-established idiom.

Letters   For a discussion of the form of business letters, see **Business letters.**

Letters of the alphabet   The plural of letters of the alphabet is usually formed by adding *'s*:

Let "strawberry soda" remind you of the two *s*'s in *dessert*.
Sam did better than I; he got two A's and two B's.

Notice that a letter used only as a letter (see the first sentence) is italicized—underlined in handwriting and typing.

Levels of English usage   There are two main levels of English—the standard level, which is made up of formal and informal English, and the nonstandard level. We classify as standard the kind of English used by the majority of educated people. We classify as nonstandard the kind of English that educated people tend to avoid.

(For a description of standard and nonstandard English, see Chapter 8, "Nonstandard English," page 165; "Informal English," page 166; and "Formal English," page 168.)

liable   See **likely, liable, apt.**

Library   See Chapter 6, "Step Two: Gathering Information," page 125; **Card catalogue; Dewey Decimal System; Encyclopedias; Readers' Guide; Reference books.**

lie, lay   Notice the distinctions between these verbs:

lie, lay, lain—"to recline," intransitive (no object)
lay, laid, laid—"to place," transitive (takes an object)

You *lie* down to rest. He *is lying* on the floor. Mexico *lies* to the south of us. You *lay* bricks, *lay* money aside, *lay* your coat on a chair, *lay* a trap. Yesterday you *lay* down on the job, but you *laid* your rake down. Terry *has lain* there long enough. They *have laid* the rough flooring.

Nonstandard English tends to use only the verb *lay* (*laid, laid*)—making it do the work of both these verbs. And sometimes in casual informal speech we use *lay* instead of *lie* in such an expression as "Lay down, Spotty!" But this usage is inappropriate in careful speech and in writing.

lighted, lit   Both of these forms are used as the past tense and past participle of *light*:

He lit a match.   Who lighted the fire?
Has anyone lit the fire?   She had lighted the candles.

When the past participle is used as an adjective preceding a noun, *lighted* is more common:

> I told her to leave a lighted lamp in the window.

In general, use whichever form seems to fit the rhythm of your sentence best.

like, as 1 In writing and in formal speech *as, as if,* and *as though* are used as conjunctions—to introduce clauses:

> We all tried to pronounce the words as Mlle. Benet did.
> Stop shying away from them as if they were poison.
> For a while it looked as though we would win.

In informal speech, *like* is commonly used as a conjunction in such sentences:

> We all tried to pronounce the words like Mlle. Benet did.
> Stop shying away from them like they were poison.
> For a while it looked like we'd win.

But this usage is considered inappropriate in writing, except in the South, where it is standard in formal as well as in informal usage.

2 In both formal and informal English *like*—not *as*—is used as a preposition in phrases of comparison:

> He waddles like a duck.   They screamed like banshees.
> Don't act like a prude.   I, like him, objected.

likely, liable, apt All three words may be used to suggest that something is probable. Formal English keeps the three distinct, using them with the following shades of meaning: *Likely* is used to mean simply "reasonably to be expected":

> The plumber is likely to arrive the minute we leave.

Liable is used to mean "in danger of something disagreeable":

> Anyone who contradicted him was liable to be fired.

Apt is used to mean "fitted by nature; habitually inclined":

> Private detectives are apt to be cynical.

Colloquially, however, *liable* and *apt* are often used in the ordinary sense of *likely*:

> The plumber is *liable* (or *apt*) to arrive the minute we leave.

line Expressions with *line* are often clumsy and roundabout, and should be replaced by simpler, more direct wording:

ROUNDABOUT: Dean Harold's advice was along much the same lines as Professor Kahane's.
BETTER: Dean Harold's advice was much like Professor Kahane's.

Linking verb   A verb used chiefly to connect a subject with an adjective or noun or pronoun that describes or means the same as the subject:

> That boy *is* a real troublemaker.   [Connects subject *boy* with predicate noun *troublemaker.*]
> His attitude *was* unreasonable.   [Connects subject *attitude* with predicate adjective *unreasonable.*]
> The next victim *may be* you.   [Connects subject *victim* with predicate pronoun *you.*]

Be is the most common linking verb. Other verbs frequently used as linking verbs are *act, appear, become, feel, go, grow, look, run, seem, smell, taste, turn.* Remember that when they are used as linking verbs (rather than as action verbs), they are followed by adjectives, not adverbs:

> None of us felt *sad* about his leaving.   [Not: *sadly.*]
> Miss Blake looked quite *skeptical* when I told her that Mother was ill.   [Not: *skeptically.*]
> Bobby and Ruth both insisted that the shrimp tasted *peculiar.* [Not: *peculiarly.*]

Litotes (lī′tə tēz′)   A form of understatement in which the writer or speaker says in negative form the opposite of what he actually means:

> And Arnold Palmer, after all, is no amateur at golf.   [Meaning: Palmer is an expert at golf.]
> Our property taxes went up to six hundred dollars this year, and that is no small sum.   [Meaning: that is a large sum.]

485

loan   Used both as a noun and as a verb. As a verb it is interchangeable with *lend.*

NOUN: The interest on the *loan* is due Friday.
VERB: I wouldn't *loan* (or *lend*) him fifty cents.

Localism   A word or expression used regularly in one section of a country, but not in other sections. Localisms are also called *provincialisms* or *dialectal expressions.* (See **Dialect,** and "American English Dialects," page 180.)

locate   Used colloquially to mean "settle." This use should be avoided in writing that is at all formal:

COLLOQUIAL: The Hills decided to locate in Quincy.
FORMAL WRITING: The Hills decided to settle in Quincy.

Long variants   Needlessly long forms of words. Amateur writers sometimes add an extra prefix or suffix to a word that already carries the meaning they intend. They write *irrigational systems,* though *irrigation systems* would be clear and acceptable. They write *irregardless,* though *regard-*

less already means "without regard to." Some other common long variants to be avoided are:

preventative for *preventive*
intermeddle for *meddle*
remorsefulness for *remorse*
reassemble when simple *assemble* is meant
insertion for *insert*
discolorization for *discoloration*
radicalistic for *radical*
wastage for *waste*

Loose sentence   A sentence in which the grammatical form and the essential meaning are complete before the end:

Jim Taft made the winning run in Friday's game, belting a beautiful homer that brought Panther fans to their feet in a wild burst of applause.

This sentence could be stopped after "run," "game," "homer," or "feet" without destroying the sense of the main statement.

Loose sentences are typical of conversation. Used too consistently in writing, without an occasional *periodic sentence* for variety, they are likely to produce an unemphatic style. (See *Periodic sentence.*)

lose, loose   These two words are frequently confused. Try to associate the spelling of each with its pronunciation and meaning:

lose (lüz)—lose a key, lose track of time, lose a bet
loose (lüs)—a loose bolt, break loose, at loose ends

lot of, lots of   Informal expressions meaning "a great number or amount":

INFORMAL: Because of this skillful advertising, lots of people buy a lot of things they do not need.
FORMAL: Because of this skillful advertising, many people buy a great many things that they do not need.

mad   Used in informal English to mean "angry":

INFORMAL: The coach was mad at Powers for breaking training.
FORMAL: The coach was angry with Powers for breaking training.

madam   *Madam,* a polite title used in speaking to a married or unmarried woman, is often shortened to *ma'am:*

"Take the elevator to your left, madam."
"Yes, ma'am, you may go right in."

Dear Madam: is the usual salutation in a business letter to a woman whose name is not known to the writer. If the letter is to a group of women, either *Mesdames:* or *Ladies:* is used.

majority, plurality   When referring to a total divided into two parts, *majority* means "more than half." If, of 82 votes cast, 49 are for a motion and 33 against, the motion is passed by a majority of 8.

When referring to a total divided into three or more parts, *majority* usually means "an excess of votes over all others cast"; *plurality* means "the difference between the largest number of votes and the next largest." If 9000 votes are cast, and A gets 4800, B gets 2700, and C gets 1500, candidate A has a majority of 600 and a plurality of 2100.

Majority applies only to numbers; it should not be used to mean "the greater part" of a *thing*:

> A *majority* of the jury favored his acquittal.
> *Most* (or *The greater part*) of the book is pure fiction.   [Not: The *majority* of the book.]

Malapropism   A ridiculous misuse of words, caused by confusing two words that are similar in sound but different in meaning:

> take it for granite (take it for granted)
> to give a facetious name (to give a fictitious name)
> a congenial disease (a congenital disease)
> with incredulous bravery (with incredible bravery)
> the shirts on the closed horse (the shirts on the clotheshorse)
> a heart-rendering drama (a heart-rending drama)

Malapropisms are named after Mrs. Malaprop, a character in Sheridan's comedy *The Rivals,* whose amusing misuse of words has made her one of the best-known comic characters in literature.

Malapropisms are sometimes used intentionally—for humorous effect. But used unintentionally, because of not knowing the meaning of the words, they make the user seem ridiculous. Guard against them in your speech and writing by checking unfamiliar words in a dictionary to make sure of their meanings. And listen carefully to expressions you pick up from others, to make sure of the words. *Cycle* may sound like *circle,* but the expression is "a vicious circle"—not "a vicious cycle."

man, woman   Now generally preferred to the more pretentious *gentleman* and *lady,* unless a note of special courtesy or respect is wanted. The original social distinctions between *man* and *gentleman, woman* and *lady* have practically disappeared in general American usage. At times, in fact, it seems that the distinctions have been reversed; statements like "The lady that cleans for the woman next door had parked her car in our driveway" and "Will one of you gentlemen show this man to his table" are quite common.

Ladies and gentlemen is the customary formal expression in addressing an audience.

487

math A colloquial clip for *mathematics.* Like other clipped words (*gym* for *gymnasium, phone* for *telephone, dorm* for *dormitory, grad* for *graduate*), *math* is written without an apostrophe or period. In formal English the full form *mathematics* should be used.

may, can See **can, may.**

may be, maybe *May be* is a verb form; *maybe* (a shortening of *it may be*) is an adverb meaning "possibly; perhaps":

VERB: The experts may be wrong this time.
ADVERB: Maybe he is the one who reported us.

may of In speech the words *may have* are often spoken so rapidly that they sound like *may of.* In writing, they should be spelled correctly: *may have* or *may've*—never *may of.*

    The same is true of all other verb phrases with *have.* Write *could have* or *could've* (not *could of*), *might have* or *might've, should have* or *should've, would have* or *would've.*

me See **It's me** and **between you and me.**

measles Plural in form, but generally used with a singular verb:

Is measles *caused* by a virus?

Mechanics of writing The technical part of writing, including such things as spelling, punctuation, forms of words, order of words, and sentence structure (as distinguished from the style, content, and organization).

Messrs. The abbreviation of the French *messieurs* (meaning "men; gentlemen") is generally pronounced as English, mes'ərz. It is now used chiefly as the plural of *Mr.*:

All entries should be sent to Messrs. Davies and Bonner.

Metaphor A figure of speech in which a comparison is implied rather than explicitly stated:

To our right lay the pond, *a swatch of shimmering green satin.* [The writer means that the pond resembled a small piece of smooth, shiny, green satin cloth.]

(For further examples and discussion, see Chapter 12, "Simile and Metaphor," page 282.)

Metonymy (mə ton'ə mi) A figure of speech in which the name of something closely associated with a thing is substituted for its name:

The *White House* refused to comment further. [That is, the President refused.]

Cousin Will's great fondness for the *bottle* again cost him his job. [That is, his fondness for liquor.]

(Compare **Synecdoche.**)

Misplaced modifiers   In revising your papers, watch out for sentences with misplaced modifiers. Sometimes these modifiers are so placed that the intended meaning is not clear. For example, in "Mike suddenly remembered his promise to help Jerry with his algebra at noon the next day," *at noon the next day* seems to modify *to help*—that is, Mike was to help Jerry at this time. But the meaning the writer intended was that Mike remembered his promise too late—at noon of the day after he should have helped. To make this meaning clear, the writer should move the modifying phrase away from the wrong word and closer to the right word: "At noon the next day, Mike suddenly remembered his promise to help Jerry with his algebra."

Sometimes modifiers seem to modify words they could not sensibly modify:

> Hanging from the handle of the trunk, Corey noticed a small metal tag.

At first glance most readers would find this sentence amusing; they would smile at the thought of Corey "hanging from the handle of the trunk." Though the intended meaning is obvious even with the misplaced modifier, the sentence could easily be improved by moving the phrase closer to the word it clearly is intended to modify:

> Corey noticed a small metal tag hanging from the handle of the trunk.

(For further examples, see Chapter 10, "Misplaced Modifiers," page 220. See also "Squinting Modifiers," page 221, and "Dangling Modifiers," page 222.)

miss, misses   The title *Miss* (with a capital *M*) is always used with a name: *Miss Rubin, Miss Elvira Pankhurst*. The noun *miss* (spelled with a small *m*) is used without a name as a term of address: "You'll have to endorse this check, miss."

Misses is the plural title: *the Misses Ruiz and Quinn*. When the misses are from the same family, formal English uses *the Misses Daly;* informal English often uses *the Miss Dalys*.

Mixed figure of speech   Combining two figures of speech that are inconsistent or incongruous produces a "mixed figure." Such a figure ruins the effect of what otherwise might be an excellent bit of writing:

> I tried to get Nan to leave, but her thirst for gossip made her blind to reason.   [Thirst does not make a person blind.]

(For further examples and discussion, see Chapter 12, "Avoid Mixed Figures," page 283.)

Modifiers Words or groups of words that restrict, limit, or make more exact the meaning of other words. In the following examples the italicized words modify the words in small capitals:

> *a long, sharp* KNIFE   *greenish* BLUE
> *the* ONE *at the top*   *unusually* HARD
> MONEY *to burn*   *boiling* HOT
> We *often* SWIM *in the creek.*
> *Stammering an apology,* GEORGE *left.*
> *Any* STUDENT *who is caught cheating* will fail.
> LOOK *before you leap.*

The modifiers of nouns and pronouns are usually adjectives, participles, adjective phrases, and adjective clauses. The modifiers of verbs, adjectives, and adverbs are adverbs, adverb phrases, and adverb clauses. (For discussion of the different kinds of modifiers, see the various Index items.)

Money 1 In ordinary writing (especially in a formal style) sums of money that can be expressed in two words are usually spelled out; others are put in figures:

> Ernie lent me thirty cents for a hamburger.
> He paid fifty-six dollars for it and sold it for seventy-five.
> After paying the bills, we had $11.42 left in the treasury.
> The cost, he estimated, would be $75,800.

If two or more sums are used in a sentence and only one can be expressed in two words, all are written in figures:

> The Drama Club netted $83 last fall and $136 this spring.

In technical, statistical, or business writing exact sums are written in figures (even if they could be expressed in one or two words):

> 64 cents   64¢ $.64
> After July 1 the wholesale price will be $8 a dozen.
> All silk suits are reduced to $29.95 and all spring hats to $8.98.

Round sums (approximate sums in even units of hundreds or thousands) are usually spelled out:

> He was awarded some fifteen hundred dollars for damages.
> Even a small lot in Hillview costs about three thousand dollars.
> At least two and a half million dollars will be raised.

2 When the sum is used as an adjective modifier, it is generally spelled out (with a hyphen):

> Imagine the taxes on a million-dollar inheritance!
> She always wears that two-dollar locket Jim gave her.
> Tom's favorite gift was a twenty-cent pen from the supermarket.

(See **Numbers.**)

Months   Except in reference books (where saving space is important) and in the headings of letters (where abbreviations may be used), the preferred usage is to write out in full the names of months:

> In a test flight on December 4, 1959, a Mercury capsule and its monkey passenger were successfully recovered.
> Dan had planned to take his vacation from June 15 to July 1.
> Dave enlisted in April, 1963.   [Or: in April 1963.]

(See **Dates.**)

Mood   The form of a verb that indicates the way in which the speaker or writer regards the sentence. A verb in the *indicative* mood shows that the sentence is regarded as a statement of fact: "The twins *are* out on the porch." A verb in the *imperative* mood shows that the sentence is regarded as a command: "*Be* quiet, you two." A verb in the *subjunctive* mood shows that the statement (or clause) is regarded as doubtful, improbable, or contrary to fact: "If I *were* Kay, I'd send the twins home." (See also **Indicative mood, Imperative mood, Commands and requests, Subjunctive.**)

most, almost   In colloquial English *most* is commonly used as a clipped form of *almost*:

> Most all of them were flawed.
> The happy ending will please most everyone but the critics.
> She told me he most always walked to the office.

491

Though common in speech, this usage is inappropriate in writing, except in reporting conversation. Otherwise, use *almost: almost all, almost everyone, almost always, almost anybody.*

mostly   An adverb meaning "for the most part; mainly; chiefly":

> The contributions, mostly dimes, barely paid for the decorations.

It is not appropriate as a substitute for *most* meaning "in or to the highest degree":

> However, the men *most* interested in his invention did not have money to invest in it.   [Not: the men *mostly* interested.]

Mr., mister   The title *Mr.* (generally abbreviated) is always used with a man's name or the name of his office: *Mr. Wentink, Mr. Frank C. Pace, Mr. Chairman, Mr. Mayor.* The noun *mister*, meaning "sir," is a colloquial form of address. It is written out in full and not capitalized: "Here's your change, mister." In formal English *sir* would be used instead. (See **Messrs.**)

Mrs., missis   The title *Mrs.* is always used with a name: *Mrs. Bennewitz, Mrs. David Olson, Mrs. Martha King.* The noun *missis* (or *missus*), meaning "wife" or "woman in charge of a household," is not appropriate in writing except to represent dialectal usage: "I'll have to check with the missis." "What did the missis say?"

The title *Mrs.* should not be combined with a husband's title. Good usage calls for *Mrs. Rubin,* not *Mrs. Professor Rubin* or *Mrs. Dr. Rubin.*

MS. MS. (usually in capital letters, though *Ms.* and *ms.* are also used) is the conventional abbreviation for *manuscript*—an author's copy of his work in handwriting or typewriting. The plural is *MSS.* (or *Mss., mss.*).

must Ordinarily used as an auxiliary verb (I must leave soon), *must* is also used as a noun meaning "something necessary or vital" and as an adjective meaning "demanding attention or doing; necessary":

NOUN: For anyone interested in politics, Drury's book is a must.
ADJECTIVE: Everything on this list is a must item.

mutual, common Many careful speakers and writers distinguish between these two words, using *mutual* to mean "each to the other; done, said, or felt by each toward the other" and *common* to mean "shared equally by each or all of a group":

> After two weeks of sharing the same tent, the boys' *mutual* admiration changed to *mutual* dislike. [Each admired the other; then each disliked the other.]
> Though we disliked each other, we had a *common* interest in mathematics that threw us together quite often. [Each found mathematics interesting; it was an interest they shared in common.]

But in general usage *mutual* is used not only to mean "each to the other" but also "shared in common":

> A mutual interest in mathematics brought us together.
> We got news of Jerry through a mutual friend of ours.

myself 1 As a reflexive pronoun, *myself* is used as the object of the verb or a preposition in a sentence whose subject is *I*:

> I outsmarted myself. [Direct object.]
> I gave myself a pat on the back. [Indirect object.]
> I thought it up by myself. [Object of preposition.]

2 As an intensive pronoun, *myself* is used for emphasis:

> I myself was to blame.   I thought it up myself.

3 In nonstandard and some colloquial English *myself* is used instead of *I* as the second part of a compound subject, but not in good written style:

NONSTANDARD AND COLLOQUIAL: Two sailors and *myself* were the only ones in the coach.
WRITTEN: Two sailors and *I* were the only ones in the coach.

In informal English *myself* is sometimes used instead of *me* as the second part of a compound object:

> She tricked my brother and *myself* into doing all the work.
> But Tom wouldn't dare complain to Clifford or *myself*.

Though this usage is common in both speech and writing, many people avoid it and use *me* instead:

> She tricked my brother and *me* into doing all the work.
> But Tom wouldn't dare complain to Clifford or *me*.

Note: Although this article covers only the first person pronoun *myself*, the usage facts apply as well to other reflexive pronouns—*yourself, himself, herself,* etc.

namely and other introductory words   1 Introductory expressions like *namely, viz., i.e., e.g.* are found chiefly in reference books and in rather formal expository writing. They are out of place in other kinds of writing, where less formal expressions—*for example, for instance, that is,* and *such as*—would be more appropriate. Often in informal writing it is most effective to omit a specific introductory word and simply give the examples, setting them off with a colon or a dash:

> Miss Vandervort fussed and fumed about little things: [such as] erasures or blots on our papers, uneven margins, *t*'s carelessly crossed, and our using *can* instead of *may*.
> There was only one way for him to avoid the lawsuit—[namely,] to publish a retraction.

2 In formal style, the introductory words *namely, for instance, for example,* etc., are usually preceded by a semicolon and followed by a comma:

> Three of the witnesses were later indicted for perjury; namely, Seaborg, Harmon, and Rossini.
> There is a wheel-and-axle machine in many household objects; e.g., meat grinders, egg beaters, screwdrivers, and doorknobs.

In informal writing, usage varies. When the introductory word is followed by a clause, a semicolon or a colon is used:

> Once in a great while he was given an assignment he felt was worthy of his talents; for example, he was sent to Washington to cover a Presidential press conference.
> Andy kept forgetting one important question: namely, how many students could afford to spend thirty dollars for an evening's entertainment?

When the introductory word is not followed by a clause, either a dash or a comma is used:

> A number of adjectives with the negative prefix *un-* have no affirmative counterparts in current usage—for example, *uncouth, unkempt, unscathed,* and *unspeakable.*
> He advised us to delay selling the shares until the market was bullish, that is, rising in price.

The introductory expression *such as* is not followed by a comma:

> Many of their daily necessities, such as [ ] flour and rice, had to be imported.

Names In factual writing—for example, in news items for the school paper —you should be careful to have the right names for people, places, and titles. Common courtesy demands that you spell the names correctly.

But in imaginative writing, such as short stories, you will probably want to make up names rather than use the names of real people. Here care must be taken to choose names to fit the characters. The names chosen should suggest real names of people, but should not be those of actual people (except by accident). The names should be interesting, but not conspicuously queer. If you have trouble thinking of names, look through newspapers and books and study the names of people around you. Keep a list of likely names that you come across.

494 *Narrative writing* See Chapter 1, "Special Types of Writing: Personal Narrative," page 25.

nature Often deadwood that could be omitted with no loss in meaning:

> Being shy [by nature], she found it hard to make new friends.
> Most of the soil in these parts is [of a] quite sandy [nature].

(See also Chapter 11, "Deadwood," page 254.)

necessary Verbs like *must* and *have to* are often more direct and emphatic (though sometimes less courteous) than a construction with *necessary*:

> INDIRECT: It is necessary that every member of the club sell at least three boxes of the cards.
> DIRECT: Every member of the club *must* (or *has to*) sell at least three boxes of the cards.

necessity The idiom is *necessity of doing* (or *for doing*) something—not *necessity to do* something:

> Frankly, I can't see the necessity *of* (or *for*) making out all the reports in triplicate.

Need is more concise than *necessity*:

> I can't see the need of making out all the reports in triplicate.

need, needs   Although these are both third person singular forms of the verb *need,* they are used in different ways. *Needs* is the form in affirmative statements:

> She needs to hurry if she is to get there on time.

Need not and *does not need* are used in negative statements:

FORMAL: She need not hurry.
INFORMAL: She does not need to hurry.

In questions *need* or *does . . . need* is used:

FORMAL: Need she hurry so?
INFORMAL: Does she need to hurry so?

negotiate   Generally used to mean "arrange terms for":

> Colonel Masterson had been sent to negotiate a treaty with the Senecas.

Colloquially *negotiate* is used to mean "get past or over":

> At that speed, not even Barney Oldfield could have negotiated the curves safely.

neither   See **either, neither** and **Correlative conjunctions.**

never   *Never* means "not ever; at no time." It should not be used when you mean simply *not*:

> But I didn't compare notes with Mark this noon.   [Not: But I never compared notes with Mark this noon.]

(See also **Double negative.**)

Newspaper English   Good newspaper English is simply informal English applied to the recording and interpreting of events. It places a premium on accuracy and directness in telling a story, and is written to be read easily and quickly. The essential information—who, what, when, where, why—is therefore usually given first, with details coming later. (See **Lead.**)

"Big words" and trite expressions are the two common faults of a careless style of newswriting called *journalese.* (See Chapter 12, "Avoid Big Words," page 275, and "Avoid Trite Words," page 276.)

nice   In formal English *nice* means "exact; discriminating":

> This young Chicago artist displays a nice sense of color.

Nice is also used as a counter word showing approval, with such a wide range of possible meanings that it is of little use in writing. In your written work substitute a more exact modifier wherever you can. (See **Adjective,** section 3.)

Nicknames Nicknames are generally out of place in formal writing. In informal writing—where they are appropriate, especially in narratives—they should be used naturally, without quotation marks or other sign of apology.

no-account Colloquially used as a compound adjective: a *no-account* nephew. In formal English, *worthless* or *shiftless* would be used.

nohow Used as an adverb in nonstandard English:

NONSTANDARD: We just couldn't convince him nohow.
STANDARD: We just couldn't convince him at all.

Nominative absolute See **Absolute phrases.**

Nominative case A noun or pronoun that is used as the subject or predicate complement of a verb is said to be in the nominative case:

Larry and *I* worked out the negative brief together.
Mr. Creel, who judged the entries, is her *uncle.*

I, you, he, she, it, we, you, they are the nominative forms of the personal pronouns; *who, which,* and *that,* of the relative pronouns.

Nonce word A word that is made up for a particular occasion and is not used again. If, in talking of an acquaintance who had too high an opinion of himself, you said that he "had a bad case of conceititis," *conceititis* would be a nonce word.

none, no one *None* may be either singular or plural, depending on the meaning intended:

None of the money *was spent* foolishly. [No part of it.]
Ernie suggested five other synonyms, but none of them *was* just right in the context. [Not a single one was just right.]
There were twenty questions, none of which *were* easy. [No questions in the group were easy.]

When *none* tells how many (as in the third example), a plural verb is generally used unless the idea of "not a single one" is to be emphasized (as in the second example).

No one is singular. It is often used instead of *none,* for emphasis:

No one of them really *understands* the problems.

Nonrestrictive modifiers Modifiers that are used not to identify the word they modify but merely to add a descriptive detail. Nonrestrictive modifiers are set off from the words they modify:

Ed's nose, *swollen to twice its normal size,* was a sight to behold.
Mrs. Timmons, *who has a voice like a bassoon,* led the singing.

(For discussion, see **Restrictive and nonrestrictive.**)

Nonstandard English The kind of English used by people who do not have much formal education or have not been much affected by the schooling they did have. For examples and an explanation of why this kind of English is not appropriate for general use, see Chapter 8, "Nonstandard English," page 165.

no place Colloquially used for *nowhere*:

COLLOQUIAL: No place in his report did he mention the failures.
WRITTEN: Nowhere in his report did he mention the failures.

not hardly, not scarcely See **Double negative.**

not only . . . but also See **Correlative conjunctions.**

Note taking See Chapter 6, "Step Three: Reading and Taking Notes," page 128, and Chapter 5, "Précis Writing," page 109.

notorious, famous *Notorious* means "widely known, but in an unfavorable way" (this notorious spy); *famous* means "widely known for accomplishment or excellence" (a famous surgeon). *Infamous* is sometimes used as a synonym of *notorious.*

Noun A word used as the name of a person, place, thing, quality, action, or idea:

497

COMMON NOUNS: lawyer, park, capsule, strength, invasion, justice
PROPER NOUNS: John Glenn, the Yukon, Ohio, the Renaissance

Noun clause A group of words with a subject and verb that is used in a sentence as a noun is used:

SUBJECT: *Whether it was a wise move* is another matter.
PREDICATE COMPLEMENT: That is not *what I meant.*
DIRECT OBJECT: He asked *why she hadn't reported her suspicions.*
INDIRECT OBJECT: Al told *whoever came in* the same hard-luck story.
OBJECT OF PREPOSITION: We paid no attention to *what he said.*
APPOSITIVE: His first assumption, *that Marlowe himself had stolen the formula,* was ridiculous.

(See also Chapter 7, "Noun Clauses," page 157.)

no use An informal idiom for *of no use*:

INFORMAL: The visa is no use to him now; it has expired.
FORMAL: The visa is of no use to him now; it has expired.

nowheres A nonstandard form of *nowhere.*

Number The form of a noun, pronoun, or verb that shows it to be singular or plural in meaning. (See **Plurals of nouns.**)

number   A *number,* meaning "several" or "many," takes a plural verb; *the number* takes a singular verb:

> As a result, a number of people *have canceled* their orders.
> The number of fan letters a star receives *is* important to him.

(See also **amount, number.**)

Numbers   1 In ordinary writing, numbers that can be expressed in one or two words are generally spelled out; other numbers are usually written in figures:

> There were only four people in the cast.
> Within an hour we had eighty-seven signatures.
> Tiny Forbes weighed 676 pounds—or so his press agent said.
> Andy himself must have sold at least 175 tickets.

The form in which numbers are written should be consistent. If one of two or more numbers in a sentence cannot be expressed in two words or less, figures are used for all:

> After I had painfully memorized 125 idioms, 40 irregular verbs, and 15 irregular adjectives, the French test was called off.

2 In statistical, technical, or business writing, figures are generally used, since expressing dimensions, weights, totals, distances, sums, and measures in figures makes it easier for the reader to work with the numbers:

22 centimeters	15 tons	68 miles
3 per cent	32 quarts	12 knots
130 cubic feet	74 pounds	4500 r.p.m.
90 barrels	125 acres	8 ounces
7 by 13 inches	40 rods	10 bushels

3 A number at the beginning of a sentence should be written out:

> One hundred seven voted against the motion.
> Forty per cent of the crop was damaged.

If writing out the number is awkward, rephrase the sentence so as to change the position of the number:

AWKWARD: Two thousand four hundred and sixty of the tickets had been sold a week before the game.
IMPROVED: A week before the game 2460 of the tickets had been sold.

4 The plural of figures is usually made by adding an apostrophe and *s,* though the *s* alone is sometimes used:

> He remembered only that the first two numbers were 6's. [Or, less common: 6s.]
> She asked them to count off by 3's. [But: by threes.]

(See also **Dates, Fractions, Money.**)

O

O, oh   *O* is ordinarily used with a noun in direct address or in such exclamatory phrases as *O dear!* It is always capitalized; but since it is so closely related to the words used with it, it is not followed by a mark of punctuation:

> Help us, O Lord.
> O dear, I wonder what's wrong now!

Oh is an independent exclamation that may be followed by a comma or an exclamation mark, depending on the stress wanted. It is capitalized at the beginning of a sentence, but not within the sentence:

> Oh, what difference does it make?
> Oh! Watch out!
> I managed to hold my temper but, oh, how I wanted to hit him.

Object   See *Direct object, Indirect object.*

Object of preposition   A noun or pronoun (or a phrase or clause used as a noun) whose relationship to some other word in the sentence is shown by the preposition:

> The quarter rolled under the *truck.* [Noun—object of *under.*]
> Now he's thinking seriously of *prospecting for uranium.* [Gerund phrase—object of *of.*]
> They even quarreled about *where they should spend their honeymoon.* [Noun clause—object of *about.*]

499

Objective and subjective writing   A writer whose purpose is mainly to present facts about a topic and who does not let emotion or personal prejudice influence his statements is said to have an *objective* point of view and to be writing *objectively.* Good scientific and technical writing —most serious exposition, in fact—is objective.

If the writer's purpose is to present the topic from a personal point of view, and he emphasizes his feelings and opinions instead of presenting only the plain facts, he is said to have a *subjective* point of view and to be writing *subjectively.* Lyric poetry, informal essays, and autobiographies are almost always subjective.

Objective case   A noun (or its equivalent) that is used as the direct or indirect object of a verb, as the object of a preposition, or as an objective complement is said to be in the objective case:

DIRECT OBJECT: Daly caught the *ball* and threw *it* to first base.
INDIRECT OBJECT: "I'll give *you* just two minutes," he yelled.
OBJECT OF PREPOSITION: The man in the *middle* glared at *us.*
OBJECTIVE COMPLEMENT: I call it *treason.*

Nouns do not have a special form for the objective case; the same form is used for both the nominative and the objective cases. The personal pronouns (*I, he, she, we, they*) and the relative and interrogative pronoun *who* have separate forms for the objective case: *me, him, her, us, them,* and *whom.*

Objective complement A noun or adjective following the direct object that completes the meaning of the verb and explains or describes the object:

> He used to consider all girls *nuisances*. [Tells what he considered all girls to be.]
> From then on, just the sight of a lobster made Neil *sick*. [Tells what the sight caused Neil to be.]

Obsolete Dictionaries use the label *Obsolete* (often abbreviated *Obs.*) for a word or a particular meaning of a word that is no longer used in ordinary speech or writing, but exists in earlier writings: *aroint thee* meaning "go away," *nim* meaning "to steal," *naughty* in the sense of "evil," *pose* in the sense of "to question."

o'clock Usually added only to the actual hour: *eight o'clock*, but *five-twenty, a quarter to six, half past four*. Do not forget the apostrophe in spelling *o'clock*.

500

of 1 *Of* is often used to show possession: the estate *of* his cousin (his *cousin's* estate), the assets *of* the firm (the *firm's* assets). (See **Possessive case**.)

2 In colloquial English *of* is often used in the unnecessary doubling of prepositions: *inside of, outside of, off of. Inside of* and *outside of* are also used in informal writing, but not *off of*:

> He got off [of] that ladder in a hurry!

(See also **inside of**, for its use as applied to time.)

3 The colloquial contraction *'ve* (for *have*) is sometimes carelessly written *of*:

> Leo *should've* warned the rest of us. [Not: *should of*.]
> I *must've* added instead of subtracted. [Not: *must of*.]

off of Nonstandard for *from*:

NONSTANDARD: Mr. Wiley bought his parrot *off of* a sailor.
STANDARD: Mr. Wiley bought his parrot *from* a sailor.

oh See **O, oh.**

OK, O.K. Used in business and informal English for "all right; approved; approval":

The second draft was OK. [Used as adjective.]
The manager put his OK on the bill. [Used as noun.]

The verb forms are *OK, OK'd, OK'ing* (or *O.K.'d*, etc.):

Unfortunately, he OK'd the letter without reading it.

OK is also spelled *okay. Oke* and *okeydoke* are slang.

Omission in a quotation Indicated by marks of ellipsis (...). (See **Ellipsis**, section 1.)

one   1 In formal speech and writing the pronoun *one* is used to refer to the indefinite pronoun *one*:

There are times when *one* should keep *one's* opinion to *oneself.*

But to avoid a displeasing repetition of *one* within a sentence, *he, his, him* (or *she, her*) are commonly used:

There are times when one should keep *his* opinion to *himself.*

2 General usage prefers *you* to the impersonal and more formal *one*:

There are times when *you* should keep *your* opinion to *yourself.*

3 *One* and *ones* are often used to avoid repeating a preceding noun:

They ordered three large pizzas and a small one.
Put the green apples in the box and the ripe ones in the basket.   **501**

4 In many sentences *one* is deadwood, taking attention away from the important word, and should be omitted in writing:

Tony's idea was [an] especially ingenious [one].

(See also **every and its compounds**, section 2.)

one of those who   The verb in the relative clause following *one of those who* (and similar expressions) agrees in number with the antecedent of the pronoun *who*:

Tom is the only one of those debaters who *argues* logically. [Singular verb; the antecedent of *who* is *one.*]
He is one of those people who *use* big words to conceal their ignorance. [Plural verb; the antecedent of *who* is *people.*]

(For further examples, see Chapter 9, "Relative Pronouns," page 202.)

only   In formal English *only* (like *almost, even, hardly, nearly, just, scarcely*) usually comes right before the word or words it modifies:

I saw only one of the test questions.

In informal usage *only* is often placed before the verb:

I only saw one of the test questions.

Whenever the intended meaning of a written sentence might not be clear because of the position of the adverb, be sure to put it before the word or words it modifies:

AMBIGUOUS: He almost convinced all the board members.
CLEAR: He convinced almost all the board members.

Onomatopoeia   See **Imitative words.**

onto, on to   *Onto,* written solid, is a preposition:

> The cat jumped onto the ledge, out of my reach.
> Phil tried to throw the rope onto the roof.

When *on* is an adverb and *to* a preposition, they are written as two words:

> She just told me to go on to the next question.
> Few stayed on to the end of the demonstration.

or   A coördinating conjunction that connects words, phrases, or clauses of equal grammatical value:

WORDS: Dad wouldn't say *yes* or *no.*
PHRASES: They're going to go with her permission or without it.
CLAUSES: Should I call him, or will you send him another bill?

502

Two subjects joined by *or* take a singular verb when each is singular, a plural verb when both are plural:

> An evasion or a lie *is* all you'll get from him.
> Evasions or lies *are* to be expected from him.

When one subject is plural and the other singular, the verb agrees with the one standing nearer:

> The sheriff or the reporters *are* not *telling* all the facts.
> The reporters or the sheriff *is* not *telling* all the facts.

-or, -our   American spelling prefers *-or* in words like *humor* and *honor;* British spelling, *-our* (*humour, honour*). In your writing, use the American spelling except when quoting from British writings or referring to British institutions like the Ministry of Labour. (See also **American and British usage.**)

oral, verbal   Strictly, *oral* means "spoken," and *verbal* means "in words, spoken or written." But *verbal* has been used so often in the limited sense of "spoken words" that dictionaries list "oral" as one meaning of *verbal: an oral request* and *a verbal request* mean the same.
The opposite of both *oral* and *verbal* is *written:*

> Raymond accepted an oral promise; Kenneth insisted on a written one.

Originality Originality in writing means saying something new or saying something old in a new way.

Since you are an individual and differ in your thinking and observations, even if slightly, from all other people, saying something new is merely a matter of presenting your own ideas, rather than someone else's. If you say or write what you yourself believe, have observed, or think, instead of copying what other people before you have reported, you are bound to obtain a degree of originality.

Saying something in a new way is difficult: it may often seem to you that every possible effective expression has already been used numberless times by others. It is perhaps best not to try too hard to be original, for doing so generally results in strained, affected language. Concentrate instead on an accurate choice of words and the use of figures of speech based on your own observation, and you will find that originality often appears as a by-product. (See also Chapter 12, "Using Figurative Language," page 281.)

In general, do not let the feeling that you should be original worry you unduly in your writing. Let originality come naturally, as the result of clear thinking and accurate observation, rather than dragging it in by force.

other *Other* is used in a comparison of things in the same class, but not in a comparison of things of different classes:

> That highly praised pitcher of theirs made more errors *than any other* player on their team. [Same class.]
> Al is a better cook *than* any of the girls. [Different classes.]

If *other* were omitted in the first sentence, the statement would be illogical, since "any player on their team" would include the pitcher himself. *Other* is not used with a superlative:

> One thing we did agree on: Nero Wolfe is the *fattest* of all the fictional detectives. [Not: of *any other* detective; of *all the other* detectives.]

(See also Chapter 9, "Comparison," page 214, and Chapter 10, "Faulty Comparisons," page 231.)

ought See **had ought.**

out loud Informal expression for the formal *aloud*:

> The man behind me kept on counting out loud. [Formal: aloud.]

out of date Expressions like *out of date, out of doors, out of town* are generally hyphenated when they are used as compound adjectives preceding the noun they modify:

> His out-of-date ideas would go well with a frock coat.
> The play had an out-of-town tryout.

Outline form   An outline is a general plan of the material that has been or is to be presented in a speech or paper. The outline shows the order of the various topics, the relative importance of each, and the relationship between the various parts. Outlines are useful in studying material assigned for reading, since in an outline you can give in a clear, concise form an overall view of the subject. But the chief value of outlines is to help you in planning talks or papers of your own. (For help in organizing material for outlining, see Chapter 1, "Gathering and Organizing Your Material," page 7, and Chapter 6, "Step Four: Sorting the Notes and Outlining the Paper," page 133.)

There are four main types of outlines that you will find useful in preparing papers of various kinds:

1 Work outline.   For most of the papers you write or talks you give, an elaborate outline with parallel heads and subheads is not necessary. An informal plan—just a simple listing of the topics and subtopics arranged in a way that shows the order in which they are to be discussed—is enough. The form of the topics is unimportant: some may be expressed in single words, others in phrases or clauses—whichever is most convenient. Since a work outline of this sort is not a showpiece, but merely a rough map to guide you in speaking or writing, any form you work out is acceptable, as long as the ideas are clearly organized.

2 Paragraph outline.   Outlines for short papers can be made by listing the main topics to be discussed in each paragraph. This type of outline would not do for long papers because it does not indicate subheads (which might be forgotten at the time of actual writing). A paragraph outline is the only outline in which the headings correspond exactly to the paragraphs of the paper.

3 Topic outline.   For some papers, you may have to submit a formal outline as part of your work. The most common type of formal outline required is the topic outline. The headings are given in brief phrases, clauses, or single words, and are numbered and lettered consistently, as in this example:

The St. Lawrence Seaway—A Canadian-American Achievement (Title)

    I. History of Seaway idea (Main head)
       A. Early indifference (Subhead)
       B. Later struggle
          1. Opponents of Seaway (Sub-subhead)
             a. Gulf of Mexico shipping interests
             b. Great Lakes shipowners
             c. Eastern shipping interests
             d. Eastern railroad interests
          2. Supporters of Seaway
             a. Eastern power users
             b. Midwestern business interests
             c. Midwestern farm interests
             d. Canadian government
       C. Final agreement between United States and Canada

II. Construction of Seaway
    A. Erecting power dams
    B. Enlarging old locks
    C. Dredging river channels
    D. Building new locks
    E. Digging new canals
III. Present uses of Seaway
    A. As power source
       1. For residential use
       2. For industrial use
    B. As waterway
       1. For domestic shipping
       2. For international shipping
    C. As tourist attraction
IV. Future plans for Seaway
    A. To enlarge and extend power facilities
    B. To deepen locks
       1. At Welland
       2. At Massena
    C. To operate during winter freeze-up
       1. By using icebreakers in open water
       2. By using compression method in locks and canals
    D. To eliminate bottlenecks by "twinning" the locks

Notice the system used in a formal topic outline, the way numbers and letters are alternated—and indented—to show which items are of equal importance and how the various items are related. All items labeled with Roman numerals are main heads, giving the main divisions of the subject. All items marked by capital letters are equally important divisions of a main head, and so on.

Notice, too, that items in the different groups are parallel in form. In the outline shown, all the main heads are nouns modified by phrases. The five subheads under II, for example, are all gerund phrases. The two numbered items under IV C are prepositional phrases. The first item in any group determines the form; all following items in that group should be phrased the same way.

4 Sentence outline. A sentence outline is like a formal topic outline except that each head and subhead is expanded into a complete sentence. A sentence outline takes more effort than the topic outline because it requires that you thoroughly think through the ideas and then put them into specific, rather detailed statements. But for those very reasons it will be more valuable to you than the sketchier topic outline. (For an example of a sentence outline, see Chapter 6, "The Research Paper," page 135.)

over with   Used colloquially to mean "over" or "finished":

COLLOQUIAL: They wouldn't leave until *Eyewitness* was over with.
WRITTEN: They wouldn't leave until *Eyewitness* was over.

P

paid, payed *Paid* is the spelling of the past tense and the past participle of *pay* in all its senses except "to let out (a line, rope, etc.)." In that sense, the form is *payed*.

> I paid for my stupidity.   Has he paid his bill yet?
> They payed out the rope, and we swung clear of the dock.

pair The usual plural of *pair* is *pairs*:

> How many pairs of galoshes did he buy?

In business usage and in some informal speech the plural is often *pair* when it follows a number:

> Bill Mrs. Frenz for six pair of white gloves.

pants, trousers *Pants* is the informal word, *trousers* the formal.

Paradox See **Epigram.**

Paragraphs For help in writing paragraphs, see Chapter 2, "Writing Paragraphs."

Parallel constructions Ideas in a sentence that are of equal importance should be expressed in parallel (or similar) forms:

NOT PARALLEL: The room was *cold, with unattractive furniture,* and *it had little light.*

PARALLEL: The room was *cold, unattractively furnished,* and *poorly lighted.*

NOT PARALLEL: *Filing* the orders myself took less time than *when I tried* to get Dora to do it right.

PARALLEL: *Filing* the orders myself took less time than *trying* to get Dora to do it right.

(For other examples of shifted—or unparallel—constructions and suggestions for correcting them, see Chapter 10, "Shifted Constructions," page 225.)

Paraphrase A restatement—in one's own words—of the ideas in a passage (written or spoken). (See Chapter 5, "Paraphrasing," page 101.)

Parentheses ( ) 1 Parentheses are used to enclose added explanations or comments that the writer does not want to stand out conspicuously in a sentence. When the material in parentheses comes within a sentence, it is not begun with a capital letter or followed by a period, even if it is a sentence itself. But commas and semicolons are used, just as they would be in any sentence:

> The following year he moved to Quincy (in Illinois, not Massachusetts) and opened his own law office.
> The Mays were wealthy (he owned a chain of motels; she earned thousands in royalties) but lived very simply.

If the material enclosed in parentheses is a question or an exclamation, a question mark or an exclamation mark is used within the parentheses:

> Mr. Greatleach (have you ever heard of a name more apt?) sponged on them for six months.
> He had decided to ask Mr. Fry for a raise (what a mistake that turned out to be!) and was thinking up arguments to use.

Punctuation marks (commas, periods, semicolons, etc.) that belong to the sentence come after the parentheses, not before:

> Although Sam doesn't usually have a vote (he is president of the council), he did vote in this instance—to break the tie.
> Moreover, Ambassador Dunlap could speak Urdu (the language used by Moslems in India).
> Kay tipped the cab driver a thousand lire (about $1.50); she never was good at arithmetic.

2 Parenthetical material that is not in the body of a sentence begins with a capital letter and ends with a period (or question mark or exclamation mark):

> Tom scoffed at my last statement. (Since reading *The Hidden Persuaders,* he scoffs at many of my ideas.) "It's Madison Avenue that determines how you spend your money," he began.

3 Parentheses are often used to enclose letters or figures that mark items in a series:

> In order to continue publishing the school paper, we must do one of three things: (a) raise the subscription rate, (b) sell more advertising space, or (c) reduce the size to four pages.

4 Parentheses, dashes, and commas are all used to set off explanatory comments. In the sentence "Mrs. Frankel (who had not read the book) was the most vociferous in condemning it" the parentheses show that the writer wants to play down the comment, considering it unimportant in this particular context. Dashes would emphasize the explanatory comment, while commas would show that the writer wanted it to be considered more closely related to other words in the sentence.

Parentheses are effective when they are used only occasionally. Used too often, they become tiresome and may distract attention.

5 Parentheses should not be used to enclose words that you want omitted from a sentence. Draw a straight line through such words.

part   Used with *from* when it means "go away from; leave" and with *with* when it means "give up; let go":

> Though sorry to part from us, he looked forward to his new job.
> Nothing would persuade Dad to part with that old leather chair.

part (on the part of)   Often a clumsy substitute for *by, among, for,* and the like:

> CLUMSY: At Morton High the honor system resulted in less cheating *on the part of* the older students.
> BETTER: At Morton High the honor system resulted in less cheating *by* the older students.

partake of   A pretentious expression for *eat*:

> AFFECTED: Never before had he partaken of such exotic foods.
> NATURAL: Never before had he eaten such exotic foods.

Participial phrase   A modifying phrase made up of a participle and its objects (or complements) and modifiers:

> *Holding his breath,* Oscar handed his report card to his father. [Modifies the noun *Oscar.*]
> All cars *parked on the east side of the street* will be ticketed. [Modifies the noun *cars.*]

(See Chapter 7, "Participial Phrases," page 153.)

508

Participle   **1 Forms.**   The present participle ends in *-ing: skating, skiing, aquaplaning.* The past participle usually ends in *-ed, -t, -d, -en,* or *-n: defeated, burnt, heard, stolen, thrown.*

2 Uses.   (a) Participles are used in forming various tenses of verbs:

> They are hiding.   Tom was fired.
> She had been crying.   It must be shortened.

b) When not part of a verb form, participles are used (alone or in phrases) as verbal adjectives modifying nouns or pronouns:

> the *blinding* snow   the *melted* ice
> a *nagging* woman   a *bent* nail
> The dog *tagging at his heels* was twice his size. [Modifies *dog.*]
> *Hoping for a miracle,* he waited for the winning number to be called.   [Modifies *he.*]
> He found a diamond ring *buried in the sand.*   [Modifies *ring.*]

c) Though generally used to modify a particular noun or pronoun, participles are sometimes used in phrases that relate to the whole sentence (to the situation) rather than to a particular word. For example:

> *Considering his lack of experience,* Roy did a fine job.
> *Speaking objectively,* our punishment was well deserved.

Phrases like these are equivalent to subordinate clauses ("If you consider his lack of experience, Roy did a fine job"). Since they are not intended as modifiers of a particular word, they are not considered "dangling" modifiers of the type discussed in Chapter 10.

(For further examples and discussion, see Chapter 7, "Participial Phrases," page 153, and Chapter 10, "Dangling Modifiers," page 222.)

party   See *person.*

Passive voice   See *Active and passive voice.*

Past tense, past perfect tense   See *Tenses of verbs.*

peeve   Informal for *annoy* or *annoyance*:

> He seemed peeved at my asking about it.
> Luckily, he soon forgot his peeve.

per   *Per* (Latin, "through; by; by means of") is used chiefly in business and technical English: *$9000 per annum, $1.25 per hour, 35 hours per week, 39¢ per gallon, $7 per diem, $8 per capita.*

In general usage an equivalent English expression is usually more appropriate: *$9000 a year, $1.25 an hour, 35 hours a week, 39¢ a gallon, $7 a day, $8 for each person.*

per cent, percent   Written as either two words or one and not followed by a period: *a gain of 13 per cent, a 6 per cent profit.*

Colloquially *per cent* is used in place of *percentage*:

COLLOQUIAL: Only a small per cent of the juniors signed up.
WRITTEN: Only a small percentage of the juniors signed up.

Perfect tenses   The *present perfect tense* shows action completed at the present time: The rescue squad *has arrived.*

The *past perfect tense* shows that the action had been completed before a specific time or happening in the past: The rescue squad *had arrived* shortly before the reporters reached the mine.

The *future perfect tense* shows that the action will have been completed at some time in the future: We hope that by midnight more help *will have arrived.* (See *Tenses of verbs.*)

Period   1 The chief function of a period is to mark the end of a sentence that is not regarded as a question or an exclamation:

> I wonder why the verb *drowned* is so often mispronounced.
> Save first and buy later.
> Will you please give Tom and Helene my best wishes. [In the interrogative form but intended as a polite request, not as a question.]

2 Periods have several conventional uses:

a) After abbreviations and initials:

N.Y.C.   etc.   Penn.   Mr. A. L. Wilson, Sr.

b) Between dollars and cents when the dollar sign is used:

$14.95 $189.98 $.75 [But: 75 cents or 75¢]

c) Before decimals or between the whole number and the decimal:

.8   2.024   13.5%

3 Three spaced periods (...) are used to show the omission of words in a quotation. (See *Ellipsis.*)

4 A period coming at the end of a quotation is generally placed inside the quotation marks:

> "I told only one person," Christopher said, "but he told everyone else."

(For the use of periods with parentheses, see *Parentheses,* sections 1 and 2.)

Periodic sentence   A sentence in which the main thought is not complete until the end:

> In his second year at Cambridge, when he joined "The Apostles," a debating society, Alfred Tennyson began to make friends.

Because the reader has to wait for the main idea until after he has read all the minor details upon which it is based, the effect of a periodic sentence is one of suspense.

Used occasionally, periodic sentences add a pleasant variety and emphasis to writing. Used too often, though, they give an unnatural, stilted tone. (See also *Loose sentence.*)

Person   Personal pronouns change form to indicate person:

FIRST PERSON, THE ONE SPEAKING: I, me, mine; we, us, ours
SECOND PERSON, THE ONE SPOKEN TO: you, yours
THIRD PERSON, THE ONE SPOKEN OF: he, him, his; she, her, hers; they, them, theirs

In English the only change in the form of verbs to indicate person occurs in the third person singular: I come, you come, he *comes*; we, you, they come.

The verb *be* is exceptional: I *am*, you *are*, he *is*; we, you, they *are*.

person   *Person* is the word generally used to refer to a human being. Many people use *individual* interchangeably with *person*; but *individual* is a rather heavy and pretentious word to use unless the person referred to is being contrasted with others, or his distinctiveness is being emphasized:

PRETENTIOUS: He is a rather secretive individual.
BETTER: He is a rather secretive person.

Though *party* is used colloquially to mean "person" (What did the *party* who called me want?), this use is not generally considered acceptable. *Party,* used in legal English, means "each of the persons or sides in a contract or lawsuit."

Personal pronouns   Pronouns whose forms show person; that is, the forms show whether the speaker (first person), the one spoken to (second person), or the one spoken of (third person) is meant: *I, we; you; he, she, it, they.* (See also Chapter 9, "Nominative and Objective Forms," page 205, and "Using Pronouns and Nouns with Gerunds," page 209.)

Personification   A figure of speech in which a lifeless thing or quality is spoken of as if alive:

> The mother, father, and two sons had scurried into a cellar while the twister tucked their shanty under its arm and raced like a monstrous halfback over a gigantic field.—Gene Fowler, *Timber Line.*

perspire, sweat   The once-popular distinction between these words— "Horses sweat; men perspire"—is not now generally observed. In fact, many people prefer the simpler, more direct word *sweat* to its polite substitutes *perspire* and *perspiration,* and always use *sweat* except in situations where it might offend more sensitive people.

511

phenomenon   The usual meaning is "an observable fact, event, or circumstance": The erosion of metal by rust is an only too common phenomenon. The plural is *phenomena*: Among other phenomena revealed by the telescope was the revolution of satellites about other planets.
Phenomenon is also used to mean "something or someone extraordinary." Used in this sense, the plural is generally *phenomenons.*

phone   Informal for *telephone.* No apostrophe is needed: I will *phone* him today. Use the *phone* in the hall.

photo   An informal clipped word for *photograph,* similar to *phone* but not so widely used, since *picture* is a handy substitute.

Phrases   A *phrase* is a group of words without a subject and verb, used as a single word in a sentence:

PREPOSITIONAL PHRASE: Martha opened the lock *with a bobby pin.*
[Used as an adverb to modify the verb *opened.*]
PARTICIPIAL PHRASE: He tripped over an umbrella *propped against the counter.*   [Used as an adjective to modify the noun *umbrella.*]
GERUND PHRASE: She enjoys *spying on her neighbors.*   [Used as a noun, as direct object of *enjoys.*]

INFINITIVE PHRASE: *To appeal to his pride* was a waste of time. [Used as a noun, as subject of *was*.]

(For further discussion, see Chapter 7, "Phrases," page 152.)

Plagiarism   A person who knowingly takes the ideas, expressions, or writings of others and passes them off as his own is just as dishonest as if he took money, clothing, or anything else belonging to another. A writer's ideas and his way of expressing them are his own property, and using them without permission is called *plagiarism* (plā′jə riz əm).

When a writer has established a thought as his own in writing, common honesty requires all others to respect his ownership rights. This does not mean that you are not to use his material. It simply means that you must not use his words, facts, or ideas without giving him credit (see **Footnotes**), and in writing intended for publication you should not use more than a sentence or two of his without getting his permission.

plenty   As an adverb *plenty* is colloquial:

They were *plenty* worried, nevertheless.
Even the smallest piece was *plenty* big enough.

This adverbial use is avoided in formal English.

Plurals of nouns   **1** Most nouns are regular, forming their plurals with *s*:

paper—papers	sundae—sundaes	ray—rays
Mr. Lane—the Lanes	grudge—grudges	donkey—donkeys

2 Nouns ending in *sh, s, x, z,* or *ch* (when pronounced as *ch* and not as *k*) add *es*:

wish—wishes	hoax—hoaxes	birch—birches
genius—geniuses	topaz—topazes	Rogers—Rogerses
moss—mosses	bench—benches	quiz—quizzes

3 Nouns ending in *y* preceded by a consonant change the *y* to *i* and add *es*:

berry—berries	caddy—caddies	century—centuries
army—armies	salary—salaries	vacancy—vacancies

Names of people are exceptions to this rule:

There are two *Bettys* in our class. [Not: *Betties*.]
The *Murphys* live next door. [Not: *Murphies*.]

4 Nouns ending in *o* preceded by a vowel add *s*:

cameo—cameos	ratio—ratios	shampoo—shampoos
rodeo—rodeos	folio—folios	tattoo—tattoos

But nouns ending in *o* preceded by a consonant vary. Some add *s*, others *es*, and still others either *s* or *es*:

WITH *s*:   auto—autos   silo—silos   alto—altos

WITH *es*:   veto—vetoes   potato—potatoes   torpedo—torpedoes

WITH *s* OR *es*:   lasso—lassos or lassoes   tornado—tornadoes or tornados   zero—zeros or zeroes

5 Nouns ending in *f* and *fe* also vary:

WITH *s*:   proof—proofs   belief—beliefs   safe—safes

WITH *ves*:   loaf—loaves   shelf—shelves   wife—wives

WITH *s* OR *ves*:   hoof—hoofs or hooves   wharf—wharves or wharfs

6 A few nouns form their plural by a change in spelling:

foot—feet   child—children   die—dice
goose—geese   seaman—seamen   ox—oxen

7 Some nouns borrowed from foreign languages have English endings, others foreign endings, and still others have both:

ENGLISH PLURALS: circus—circuses   prima donna—prima donnas   arena—arenas   asylum—asylums   pizza—pizzas

FOREIGN PLURALS: alumnus—alumni   alumna—alumnae   datum—data   diagnosis—diagnoses   monsieur—messieurs   château—châteaux

BOTH: curriculum—curriculums or curricula   nebula—nebulae or nebulas   appendix—appendixes or appendices   Nisei—Nisei or Niseis   dilettante—dilettantes or dilettanti

In scientific and formal writing, the foreign plurals of words that have both forms are more likely to be used. But in other situations the English plurals are more common and are the appropriate forms to use.

8 Compound words vary. When they are written as one word, the plural is usually formed by adding *s* or *es* to the end:

teaspoonful—teaspoonfuls   workbench—workbenches

When the parts are separate or hyphenated, the principal part is usually made plural:

board of trade—boards of trade   looker-on—lookers-on
sister-in-law—sisters-in-law   vice-consul—vice-consuls
bill of lading—bills of lading   stop watch—stop watches

But in these compound words the principal parts are not made plural:

smash-up—smash-ups   get-together—get-togethers
tie-in—tie-ins   one-year-old—one-year-olds

9 Letters, numbers, signs, and words discussed as words usually add *'s*:

+'s and —'s
Aren't there four *s*'s in *Mississippi?*
His *3*'s and *5*'s look much alike.
Why do you use so many *if*'s?

10 A few nouns have the same form for both singular and plural:

> one Iroquois and one Lebanese—two Iroquois and five Lebanese
> a précis [prā′sē]—several précis [prā′sēz]
> One *moose* was caught.   Five *moose* got away.

p.m.   Abbreviation for the Latin *post meridiem,* "after noon." (See ***a.m.***, ***p.m.***)

Poetry (quoted)   When quoting poetry in your writing, copy it exactly as originally written, keeping each line, capital letter, and punctuation mark. If the quotation consists of only one line or part of a line, it is put in quotation marks and written into the text. If two lines or more are quoted, they are usually set below the text and indented from each margin. When they are set off in this way, no quotation marks are needed.

When possible, a line of poetry should be written complete on one line of your paper. If it is necessary to carry a long line over, it should be indented deeper than the other lines.

politics   Usually singular, but plural when it means "political principles or opinions":

> Politics *makes* strange bedfellows.
> His politics *were* of great concern to his employers.

Possessive adjectives   *My, your, his, her, its, our, your,* and *their,* the possessive forms of the personal pronouns, are called *possessive adjectives* when they modify a noun:

> my opinion   your mistake   her next move   its tail

Possessive case   **1 Forms.**   The possessive case (sometimes called the genitive case) is formed in various ways:

a) Singular nouns and indefinite pronouns add an apostrophe and *s*:

lady's	the Shah of Iran's	everybody's
Margie's	his mother-in-law's	someone's

If the singular noun ends in *s*, usage is divided:

Mr. Bates's schedule	Mr. Bates' schedule
Croesus's wealth	Croesus' wealth

b) Plural nouns ending in *s* add only the apostrophe:

the ladies' coats	the Bateses' car	ostriches' plumes
the armies' matériel	the donkeys' brays	nurses' uniforms

But plural nouns not ending in *s* add both the apostrophe and *s*:

the men's hats	the dormice's tails	the women's rights
the oxen's yokes	the alumnae's rooms	his sons-in-law's cars

c) To show joint ownership, the last noun is made possessive:

> Betty and Ann's apartment [They share it.]
> Uncle Roy and Aunt Emma's farm [They own it together.]
> nieces and nephews' visits [They come together.]

But to show separate ownership, each noun is made possessive:

> Betty's and Ann's withholding taxes
> Uncle Roy's and Aunt Emma's toothbrushes
> nieces' and nephews' coats

d) The personal pronouns and the relative and interrogative *who* have special possessive forms, spelled without the apostrophe:

USED BEFORE NOUNS: my, your, his, her, its, our, their; whose
USED ALONE: mine, yours, his, hers, ours, theirs; whose

e) The possessive may also be formed by using a phrase with *of*:

> the heat of the engine (the engine's heat)
> the humor of Mort Sahl (Mort Sahl's humor)

The *of*-possessive is more common with names of inanimate objects than the *'s*-form, but both are used. The *'s*-form is more common with names of people, although both are used:

> the speed of the computer   the computer's speed
> Mrs. Martin's complaints   the complaints of Mrs. Martin

515

In general, choose the form that sounds best in the sentence.

f) The *'s*-form and the *of*-form are often combined, especially with *that* or *this*:

> that young brother of Ben's   those stupid remarks of Al's
> these cronies of Dad's   this brilliant idea of Eve's

2 Uses.   Although the principal use of the possessive case is to show ownership (*the umpire's mask, my shirt, Tom's golf clubs*), it is also used to show a number of other relationships:

DESCRIPTION: a man's responsibility, the softness of fur
DOER OF AN ACT: the manager's disappearance, the ocean's roar, the roar of the ocean
RECIPIENT OF AN ACT: Foley's betrayers, the city's capture
AUTHORSHIP: Shelley's poems, the poetry of Shelley
MEASURE: a boat's length, ten dollars' worth

Possessive pronouns   The possessive forms of the personal pronouns and of *who* are *mine, yours, his, hers, ours, theirs; whose.* (Compare **Possessive adjectives** and **Pronominal adjectives.**)

pre-   Prefix meaning "before in place, time, or rank." Most words with *pre-* are written without a hyphen: *preatomic, precool, prefabricated, prejudge, prerequisite, presuppose.* But a hyphen is generally used (1) when the part following *pre-* is a proper name: *pre-Restoration, pre-Shakespearean;* and (2) when the part following *pre-* begins with an *e*: *pre-existent, pre-establish* (or *preëxistent, preëstablish*).

precede, proceed   *Precede,* meaning "to go or come before," is often confused in spelling with *proceed,* meaning "to go on after having stopped" or "to move forward":

> Trygve Lie preceded Dag Hammarskjöld as Secretary-General.
> He then turned back to me and asked me to proceed with my story.

Précis   A brief summary of the essential thought of a passage, article, or other piece of writing. (See Chapter 5, "Précis Writing," page 109.)

Predicate   The verb and the words used with it to make a statement about the subject of a sentence or clause:

> The audience *booed.*
> The umpire *quickly ducked behind the pitcher.*
> Al *carefully counted the change before putting it in his pocket.*
> *The following year* he *became president of the firm.*

Two or more verbs used with one subject are known as a *compound predicate*:

> Mr. Hill *checked* the figures again, *found* another error, and *yelled* for the manager.

Predicate complement   A word that completes the meaning of a linking verb or of a transitive verb in the passive voice is called a *predicate complement*. The predicate complement is usually a noun or pronoun that means the same person or thing as the subject, or an adjective that modifies the subject:

PREDICATE NOUN: Someday a woman will be *President.*
PREDICATE NOUN: He was considered an *expert.*
PREDICATE PRONOUN: The one in the back seat must have been *he.*
PREDICATE ADJECTIVE: No one felt *bad* about her dismissal.

(For further examples, see Chapter 7, "Predicate Complements," page 149.)

prefer   The better idiom is *prefer ... to:*

> Everyone there preferred dancing *to* playing bridge.   [Not: Everyone there preferred dancing *more than* playing bridge.]
> But Dad preferred a fedora *to* a homburg.

With infinitives, in order to avoid a repetition of *to, rather than* is used:

> He preferred to go to jail *rather than* [to] pay that bill.

Prefix A syllable, syllables, or word put at the beginning of a word to change its meaning or to form a new word. For example, adding *semi-* (meaning "half") to *tropical* makes *semitropical,* meaning "halfway between tropical and temperate."

Knowing the meanings of the common prefixes is often a help in figuring out the meanings of new words you run across in your reading. The following list gives just a few of the more common prefixes and illustrates one of their meanings:

a- (not; without): agnostic, asymetrical, atonal
ante- (before): antenatal, antepenult, antediluvian
anti- (against): antitank, antiseptic, antifreeze
bi- (two): bicameral, biangular, bilingual, biweekly
contra- (against): contradistinction, contrastimulant
dis- (not): discourteous, dishonest, dissatisfied
ex- (former): ex-actor, ex-convict, ex-chancellor
in- (in): inbreed, incoming, indraft
in- (not): inarticulate, inattentive, incautious
inter- (between; among): interspace, international, interclass
mis- (wrong): misapply, misspell, misgovern, misdirected
non- (not): nonporous, nonrestricted, nonconformist
pre- (before): predestined, prepaid, preview
pro- (in favor of): prolabor, promanagement, pro-German
re- (again): reassess, reënlist, reinoculate, re-pose
super- (over; above): superabundant, superhuman
trans- (across): transatlantic, transmigration, transpolar
un- (not): unalterable, unarmed, unhackneyed, unscrupulous

517

Preposition **1** A preposition is a word used to show the relation between a noun or its equivalent (called the *object of the preposition*) and some other word in the sentence:

The dust *behind* the couch was as thick as ever. [Shows the relationship between *couch* and the noun *dust.*]
Si climbed *over* the fence. [Shows the relationship between *fence* and the verb *climbed.*]

2 Among the most common prepositions are:

above	before	except	of	since
across	behind	for	on	to
against	below	from	on account of	under
at	by	in	out of	until
because of	down	in spite of	past	with

But remember that it is the use of a word, not its form, that determines what part of speech it is. *After,* for example, is often a preposition (Meet us *after* dinner); but it may also be a subordinating conjunction (*After* he left, we had some peace and quiet) or an adverb (And Tommy, as usual, came following *after*).

3 The right preposition to use after certain words depends sometimes on the meaning intended. We say, for example, "go *over* the hill," "go *without* food," "go *against* his wishes," "go *around* the class." At other times the right preposition is a matter of idiom. We say "skeptical *of* his claims"—not "skeptical *about*" or "skeptical *toward*." We say "dissent *from* the decision"—not "dissent *with*" or "dissent *in*."

Ordinarily you learn the idiomatic prepositions to use with common words by hearing or seeing them in phrases. Words not in your everyday vocabulary may raise questions. Here is a list of such words and the idiomatic prepositions to use with them. (For words not in this list or not covered in separate Index items, consult a dictionary.)

an *abhorrence of* violence
acquiesced in the plan
quite *adequate to* our needs
the supplement *appended to* it
an *authority on* birds
views that *coincide with* mine
complied with her request
concern for her health
conducive to clear thinking
ideas that *conformed to* mine
demur at his plan
disconcerted by this heckling
dispossessed of their land
eligible for the office
encumbered with debts
engrossed in their game

enveloped in clouds
his *familiarity with* Latin
her great *fear of* spiders
hankered after the sea
kept *harping on* the cost
a *hindrance to* us
identical with his
intolerant of any delay
irrelevant to the matter
irrespective of their ages
mindful of his warning
a *partiality for* sweets
proficient in typing
to *requite* evil *with* good
one *similar to* this
tolerant of his opinion

(See also Chapter 9, "Idiomatic Prepositions," page 216.)

4 It was once a general practice for textbooks to warn against ending a sentence with a preposition—and many writers, as a result, wrote quite awkward and unnatural sentences in an effort to avoid doing so. The taboo against the final preposition holds only in certain cases: (1) in sentences like "No one knew where he was at" and "Where could he have gone to?"—in which the prepositions are not needed; (2) in sentences like "There sat the clerk to whom I had given the bill to"—in which either the second *to* or the first should be dropped; (3) in sentences like "What heading should I list the topics he talked about under?"—in which the two prepositions at the end sound awkward.

Except for cases like these three, there is no reason for hesitating to end sentences with prepositions. "Where in the world did it come from?" is far more natural and less awkward than "From where in the world did it come?" Except in very formal writing, a sentence like "There was no one he could turn to" is generally preferable to "There was no one to whom he could turn." And in a sentence like "The place and the date had already been agreed on," the preposition not only fits smoothly and naturally at the end, but would be impossible to shift from that position without rewording the sentence.

Prepositional phrase A preposition and its object, which together serve as a modifier—either adjective or adverb:

> The car *with the Wisconsin license* passed us again. [Used as an adjective modifying the noun *car*; tells which car.]
> Tom was standing *behind the post*. [Used as an adverb modifying the verb *was standing*; tells where.]

Present tense See **Tenses of verbs.**

Principal parts of verbs Chapter 9, "Tense Forms," page 192, gives lists of many of the more common troublesome verbs with their principal parts. Here is a list of other troublesome verbs:

INFINITIVE	PAST TENSE	PAST PARTICIPLE
arise	arose	arisen
awake	awoke, awaked	awaked, awoke
be	was	been
bear	bore	borne, born (as in "was born in 1816")
beat	beat	beaten, beat
become	became	become
begin	began	begun
bid ("offer")	bid	bid
bid ("order")	bade, bid	bidden, bid
bind	bound	bound
bite	bit	bitten, bit
blow	blew	blown
break	broke	broken
bring	brought	brought
broadcast	broadcast, broadcasted	broadcast, broadcasted
build	built	built
burn	burned, burnt	burned, burnt
catch	caught	caught
choose	chose	chosen
cling	clung	clung
creep	crept	crept
deal	dealt	dealt
dive	dived (informal: dove)	dived
draw	drew	drawn
dream	dreamed, dreamt	dreamed, dreamt
eat	ate	eaten
fight	fought	fought
flee	fled	fled
fling	flung	flung
forbid	forbade, forbad	forbidden

519

forget	forgot	forgotten, forgot
freeze	froze	frozen
get	got	got, gotten
grow	grew	grown
hang ("put to death")	hanged	hanged
hang ("suspend")	hung	hung
kneel	knelt, kneeled	knelt, kneeled
knit	knitted, knit	knitted, knit
lead	led	led
lean	leaned, leant	leaned, leant
leap	leaped, leapt	leaped, leapt
leave	left	left
lend	lent	lent
light	lighted, lit	lighted, lit
lose	lost	lost
mean	meant	meant
pay	paid (of ropes: payed)	paid (payed)
prove	proved	proved, proven
put	put	put
read	read	read
rise	rose	risen
say	said	said
sew	sewed	sewed, sewn
shine	shone, shined	shone, shined
show	showed	shown, showed
shrink	shrank, shrunk	shrunk, shrunken
sing	sang, sung	sung
sink	sank, sunk	sunk
slay	slew	slain
slide	slid	slid, slidden
slink	slunk	slunk
sow	sowed	sown, sowed
speak	spoke	spoken
speed	sped, speeded	sped, speeded
spell	spelled, spelt	spelled, spelt
spit	spat, spit	spat, spit
spring	sprang, sprung	sprung
stand	stood	stood
steal	stole	stolen
stick	stuck	stuck
sting	stung	stung
stink	stank, stunk	stunk
stride	strode	stridden
strike	struck	struck, stricken
string	strung	strung
strive	strove, strived	striven, strived

swear	swore	sworn
sweat	sweat, sweated	sweat, sweated
swim	swam	swum
swing	swung	swung
take	took	taken
tear	tore	torn
tread	trod	trodden, trod
understand	understood	understood
wake	waked, woke	waked
weave	weaved	weaved
weave (cloth)	wove	woven, wove
weep	wept	wept
wind	wound	wound
wring	wrung	wrung
write	wrote	written

principal, principle   Let the *a* in *principal* remind you that the adjective *principal* (meaning "chief") ends in *al*: France's *principal exports,* the *principal parts* of verbs. Then if you remember that the *principal* of a school is the "principal person," that the *principal* in your bank is the "principal sum," and that the *principals* in a play or movie are the "principal actors," you will spell all these nouns correctly with an *a.*
  To spell the noun *principle* right, remember that it means "a rule of conduct" and, like *rule,* ends in *le.*

521

prior to   Sometimes used when the simpler word *before* would be better:

HEAVY: Prior to his promotion, he was Mr. Crouse's assistant.
BETTER: Before his promotion, he was Mr. Crouse's assistant.

Progressive verb forms   See **Tenses of verbs,** section 2g.

prohibited   Followed by *from,* not *against*:

No visitors are prohibited from picnicking in the park.

The noun *prohibition* is followed by *against*:

The prohibition against parking in the alley incensed Uncle Irv.

Pronominal adjectives   In the sentence "Before the twins left, Ted gave them ten tickets to sell," *them* is a pronoun—used as the indirect object of the verb *gave.* In the sentence "The twins paid their dues," *their* has two uses—as a pronoun referring to the twins and as an adjective modifier of *dues.* Pronouns that are used also as adjectives are sometimes called *pronominal adjectives.*

Pronouns   Words that represent persons, places, or things without naming them. For a discussion of the kinds and uses of pronouns and special problems in connection with them, see Chapter 7, "Words That Name," page 143, and Chapter 9, "Pronouns," page 205. For more detailed information, see also the special Index items: **Reflexive pronouns, Personal pronouns,** etc., and the individual pronouns (for example, *every and its compounds; who, whom, whose*).

Pronunciation   Wherever pronunciations have been given in this book, the Thorndike-Barnhart dictionary symbols have been used. The key to those symbols is given below:

a hat, cap	o hot, rock	ə represents:
ā age, face	ō open, go	a in about
ã care, air	ô order, all	e in taken
ä father, far	oi oil, voice	i in pencil
	ou house, out	o in lemon
b bad, rob		u in circus
ch child, much		
d did, red	p paper, cup	
	r run, try	
e let, best	s say, yes	FOREIGN SOUNDS
ē equal, see	sh she, rush	Y as in French *du*. Pro-
ėr term, learn	t tell, it	nounce ē with the lips
	th thin, both	rounded as for English
f fat, if	TH then, smooth	ü in *rule*.
g go, bag		
h he, how		œ as in French *peu*. Pro-
	u cup, butter	nounce ā with the lips
	u̇ full, put	rounded as for ō.
i it, pin	ü rule, move	
ī ice, five	ū use, music	N as in French *bon*. The
		N is not pronounced,
j jam, enjoy		but shows that the vow-
k kind, seek	v very, save	el before it is nasal.
l land, coal	w will, woman	
m me, am	y young, yet	H as in German *ach*. Pro-
n no, in	z zero, breeze	nounce k without clos-
ng long, bring	zh measure, seizure	ing the breath passage.

522

Propaganda   Propaganda is the systematic attempt of a person or a group to lead others to accept certain opinions, principles, or beliefs. Since words are the chief medium of propaganda, readers (and listeners) must be constantly alert. Facts and even statistics can be presented in such ways that they lose their true significance and seem to prove what the propagandist wants them to prove—unless readers can see through any attempts to mislead and can think clearly for themselves.

Propaganda may be present in any form of writing—in novels, adver- tising, and poetry—and in various kinds of oral expression—radio and TV addresses, political speeches, drama, motion pictures. It may be used to advance a good cause by truthful and legitimate means, but in general the term is applied to writing or speaking that resorts to deceit and distorting facts to achieve its purpose.

Some of the more common methods used by propagandists which you should learn to detect are:

a) *Emotionalizing,* appealing to such emotions in the reader or hearer as hate, fear, greed, jealousy, etc.

b) *Generalizing,* making broad statements that permit a wide variety of interpretations or that are true in only a few exceptional instances: "These bureaucrats in office don't understand our problems," "Our party keeps in mind the interests of the whole country," "Doctors everywhere say Prestpills are better," "Great beauties are not born; they are made by Elegantissimo cosmetics," and so on. (See also **Generalizations.**)

c) *Name-calling,* labeling a person or idea with a term of unfair or unpleasant connotation: "radical," "reactionary," "tyrant," "the great spender," and the like.

d) *Distorting facts,* giving only one side of a picture or so confusing an issue that the average person will get only the meaning the propagandist wants.

As a good reader or listener you must try to separate facts and honest opinion from propaganda and to arrive at your own opinions uninfluenced by the deceptions that are hidden in many of the words that you read and hear. As an intelligent person you will want to arrive at convictions through your own reasoning power.

(See also Chapter 3, "Language and Thinking," and Chapter 4, "On Thinking Logically.")

523

Proper adjectives   Adjectives that are formed from proper nouns and proper nouns that are used as adjectives are capitalized:

Irish linen	Elizabethan drama
Laotian troops	New England granite
Falstaffian swagger	a Chicago newspaper

When a proper adjective no longer suggests its origin, it is treated as a simple adjective and is not capitalized:

oxford cloth	raglan sleeves
italic type	pasteurized milk
guinea pig	voltaic battery

Proper noun   The name of a particular person, place, or thing. Proper nouns are always capitalized: *Joan, Robert E. Lee, Afghanistan, the Pacific Ocean, the Bridge of Sighs.* (See **Common noun.**)

prophecy, prophesy   *Prophecy,* pronounced prof′ə si, is the noun; *prophesy,* prof′ə sī, is the verb:

NOUN: Apollo gave Cassandra the gift of prophecy.
VERB: But later he decreed that no one should believe what she prophesied.

proved, proven *Proved* is the usual past participle of *prove*, but *proven* is also used, especially as a predicate adjective:

> He has proved his loyalty.
> Its validity is not yet proven.

Proverb See **Epigram.**

provided, providing Both are used (often with *that*) as conjunctions meaning "on the condition that":

> Mr. Lepp will contribute a thousand dollars provided the city council will match his contribution. [Or: provided that, providing (that).]

Provincialism See **Localism.**

Pun A figure of speech in which a word is used humorously in two senses at the same time:

> On hearing about the pilot who had fallen into the farmer's well, Stu remarked, "That's really having an ace in the hole."

The best puns play on both sound and meaning. A reasonable amount of punning adds variety to writing. Overdone, puns lose their effectiveness.

Punctuation See the Index articles on the various marks of punctuation: **Colon, Comma, Dash, Ellipsis, Exclamation mark, Parentheses, Period, Question mark, Quotation marks, Semicolon.** For exercises covering the main uses of these marks, see Chapter 15, "Punctuation."

quay Place where ships load and unload. Pronounced kē.

Question See **Interrogative sentences, Question mark.**

Question mark (?) 1 Uses. (a) A question mark is used at the end of a sentence that the writer intends as a question:

> Was he telling the truth?   Why does the metal expand?
> Larry made the touchdown?   It isn't legal, is it?

b) A question mark may be used after each item in a series of interrogative expressions, for emphasis:

> But can we count on this coöperation from the Science Club? from the Student Council? from the Masquers?

c) A question mark, generally in parentheses, may be used as an editorial mark to show that a statement of fact is questionable or a date is only approximate:

> According to the preface, Karl Eck is really one Elmo Rotterman, the son of a German baron (?) who had incurred the Kaiser's displeasure.

2 With other punctuation. (a) When a question mark and a quotation mark fall together, the question mark is placed inside the closing quotation mark if it applies to the quoted sentence, and outside if it applies to the complete sentence:

> He looked up finally and growled, "Well, what do *you* want?"
> What did he do when you said, "I'd like a bit of courtesy"?

When both the complete sentence and the quoted sentence are questions, only one question mark is used—inside the closing quotation mark:

> Why shouldn't he deny that he actually said, "Whom is calling?"
> Would anyone else have dared ask him, "Have *you* read the book?"

b) When a parenthetical question within a sentence is set off by dashes or enclosed in parentheses, the question mark is put before the second dash or inside the parentheses:

> But Mrs. Peyton persisted—could even a mule have been as obstinate?—and, as usual, got what she wanted.
> He told me I should write more convincingly (just how does one do that?) if I hoped to sell the stories.

c) When a question mark and parentheses fall together at the end of a sentence, the question mark goes inside the parentheses if it applies only to the parenthetical material, outside if it applies only to the rest of the sentence:

> Frankly, many students are bored by this overemphasis on teenage problems (could anyone blame them?). [Notice that another punctuation mark must be used to end the complete sentence.]
> Why isn't there a comparable student interest in qualifying for membership in Excelsior (the all-school honorary society)?

When both the complete sentence and the parenthetical material are questions, only one mark is used—outside the parentheses:

> How many of you students would actually volunteer for such service (in other words, how many would practice what you preach)?

3 Unnecessary question marks. (a) A question mark is not used after indirect questions or after polite requests phrased as questions:

> I asked him how much a new tire would cost.
> Would you please send me ten copies of the report.

b) A question mark in parentheses used to indicate sarcasm or irony is a weak, amateurish device and is better omitted:

> Mr. Eddy, who admitted to forty of his sixty-five years, prided himself on his youthful appearance. [Not: his youthful (?) appearance.]

Quotation marks (" ") **1** Quotation marks are used to enclose the exact words of a speaker:

> "I've searched every inch of this house," I said, "but I couldn't find my report card."
> Mother said, "That's because you're not using your head."
> "What do you mean by that crack?" I asked, bristling.
> "I simply mean that you'd get better results if you'd think instead of going off half-cocked," she explained. "It wouldn't take much mental effort to remember that you were reading that novel for English when I handed the card back to you. So I'm quite sure you'll find it between the pages of *Pride and Prejudice.*"

a) Notice that introductory and explanatory expressions (*I said, she explained*) are set off by a comma or, if they interrupt the quoted sentence, by two commas. If a quoted sentence ends with a question mark or an exclamation point, though, that mark serves; no comma is added.

b) All sentences belonging to one uninterrupted quotation are put in one set of quotation marks. (See the last two sentences in the example conversation.)

c) Periods and commas are put inside the closing quotation marks:

> After thinking a moment, he replied, "I can't make exceptions."
> I said, "That isn't fair," but I didn't say it with conviction.

d) Semicolons are always put outside the closing quotation marks:

> Dr. Barnes said flatly, "He can't play"; and this, of course, put an end to the matter.

e) A question mark or an exclamation point is put inside the quotation mark if it applies only to the quoted matter, outside if it applies to the complete sentence that contains the quotation:

> Startled by the noise, I yelled, "How do I turn this off?"
> The machinist shouted, "Take your foot off that pedal!"
> Why did none of us realize what he really meant when he said, "Unless you read, you can't write"?
> How ridiculous Bill was to keep repeating, "Prove it"!

When both the sentence and the quotation ending the sentence are questions or exclamations, only one mark is used—inside the closing quotation mark:

> Why didn't they speak up when I asked, "Does everyone agree?"
> What a shock it was to hear this tiny woman yell, "Get out!"

f) A new paragraph is generally used for each change of speaker, as in the example conversation at the beginning of this article. But when short bits of conversation are given to illustrate a point, rather than for their own sake, they may be put together in one paragraph:

> The best stories told about Calvin Coolidge illustrate not only his laconic speech but also his ready wit. One evening at a dinner in Washington a matron boasted to a group of friends, "I'll bet *I* can get him to talk." With this, she went up to Coolidge and said, "Mr. President, I've just bet that I can make you say at least three words." "You lose," he replied.

When a quoted passage is made up of more than one paragraph, an opening quotation mark is put at the beginning of each paragraph, but a closing quotation mark is put only at the end of the last paragraph.

2 Quotation marks are used to enclose any direct quotation from another writer. Before such quotations, which are not part of a conversation, a colon rather than a comma is generally used, especially if the quotation is more than one sentence:

> These critics should take to heart Cardinal Newman's words on this matter: "If . . . a practical end must be assigned to a University course, I say it is that of training good members of society. Its art is the art of social life, and its end is fitness for the world. It neither confines its views to particular professions on the one hand, nor creates heroes or inspires genius on the other."

On the plaque was inscribed this motto: "Think; then act."

A very long quoted passage is often presented without quotation marks, especially in typed and printed material. Then the whole passage is indented, and in typed matter single-spaced, in printed matter often set in smaller type than the rest of the text.

3 Quotation marks are generally used to enclose titles of chapters of books, magazine articles, essays, short stories, short poems, and songs:

> "Mutiny in the Offing" is the first poem in *Out of My Head.*
> The song "Barney Google" was anything but highbrow.

(See *Titles of books, articles, etc.*)

4 Quotation marks may be used to call the reader's attention to words that the writer is defining or explaining, and to special or technical terms that may be new to the reader:

> A "chauvinist" is an unreasoning and fanatical patriot.
> In his report, "sophisticated" is used to mean "very complex."
> The author is at his caustic best in his stories about the intellectual pretensions of Mrs. Smythe, a modern counterpart of Mrs. Montague, the first of the "bluestockings."

(Many writers prefer to italicize such words. See *Underlining.*)

5 A quotation within a quotation is enclosed in single quotation marks:

> "I couldn't even remember who said, 'All the world's a stage,' " complained George.
> Then the coach asked, "Which of you said, 'Coach Evans doesn't know the score'?"
> "And," added Lil, "Dad kept screaming, 'You get off that ledge!' "

6 Unnecessary quotation marks. (a) Quotation marks are not used to enclose *indirect* quotations:

> Mrs. Huston told me that Frank had gone to the library. [Not: Mrs. Huston told me that "Frank had gone to the library."]

However, even when you are reporting someone's speech indirectly, you may want to emphasize the fact that certain of the words you use are the exact words spoken; then you may put those words in quotation marks. If you have no particular reason for emphasizing that they are the exact words, there is no need to use quotation marks.

> Mr. Ruby made it clear that thinking was something more than just "sitting and staring at facts."
> Ten minutes of the clerk's "dearie" and "darling" was all Mary could take. [If the quotation marks were omitted here, the words would be italicized. See **Underlining**, section 3.]

528 b) It is rarely a good idea to enclose in quotation marks words or phrases that seem a little informal or slangy for the context. If a word is appropriate, using it requires no apology; if it isn't appropriate, it should not be used at all:

> But when we were late again the next day, Mr. Bly really "raised the roof." [The quotation marks should be omitted; the phrase is perfectly appropriate in this informal context.]
> Boswell gives a fascinating view not only of Dr. Johnson but also of Johnson's famous "side-kicks"—Sir Joshua Reynolds, Oliver Goldsmith, and David Garrick. [*Side-kicks* is clearly inappropriate in this formal context. Either substitute a word like *friends* or *associates,* or rephrase the sentence.]

c) The use of quotation marks to indicate sarcasm or irony is a weak and amateurish device and should be avoided:

> Uncle Pat, with his customary tact, guffawed at Mrs. Rizzo's pronunciation of *heir.* [Not: with his customary "tact."]

radio The verb and noun forms are regular: *radioed, radioing; radios, radio's.*

raise, rear *Raise* is good informal usage in the sense of "bring up"; *rear* is formal:

INFORMAL: Art, who had been raised on a farm, knew how to ride.
FORMAL: Like his famous cousin, he had been reared in Vienna.
GENERAL: I reminded him that I had not been brought up in a barn.

re- Words made with the prefix *re-*, meaning "again," are usually written as solid—or single—words: *reappear, reheat, reorganize, reinstall.* But the prefix is hyphened: (1) When joined to a root word beginning with *e*:

re-entry (*or* reëntry)   re-establish (*or* reëstablish)

2) When the form without the hyphen has a different meaning:

resort to violence   re-sort the cards
redressed these wrongs   re-dressed the children

3) When the prefix is to be especially emphasized:

The letter, now re-typed for the tenth time, still had mistakes.

Readers' Guide One of the best sources of information on subjects of current interest is magazine articles. A valuable help in finding the articles quickly and easily is the *Readers' Guide to Periodical Literature.* The *Guide* is an index of all articles, stories, and poems that have appeared in over a hundred magazines. The articles are listed alphabetically, both by subject and by author. Here is a typical subject entry:

> **COMMUTERS**
> Can the commuter survive? J. A. Morris. il
>   Sat Eve Post 234:32-3+ My 6 '61
> Cost of getting to work. il Changing T 15:
>   7-11 My '61
> How to unchoke our cities. G. Burck. il
>   Fortune 63:118-23+ My '61

A key at the front of the *Guide* explains the abbreviations and symbols that are used. The first item shown under the subject "Commuters," for example, means that an illustrated article "Can the Commuter Survive?" by J. A. Morris appears in volume 234 of the May 6, 1961, issue of *The Saturday Evening Post,* on pages 32 and 33. The + sign after the page number means that the article is continued on later pages not immediately following page 33.

The first article, listed under the full name of the author, Joe Alex Morris, looks like this:

> **MORRIS, JOE ALEX**
> Can the commuter survive? Sat Eve Post
>   234:32-3+ My 6 '61
> Venice. Nat Geog Mag 117:542-69 Ap '61
>   (ed) See Hanes, R. P. jr. We're cultured
>   too

Readers' Guide is always up to date, since it is issued not only in hard-bound volumes covering a two-year period, but also in paperbound supplements indexing articles in the latest magazines. If the article you want or need is a recent one, look in the latest supplement. If you need other material, look in the hard-bound cumulative volume.

real, really In formal English and informal writing *real* is used only as an adjective, and *really* as an adverb:

> The jeweler said it was a real diamond. [Adjective.]
> It is going to be a really close game. [Adverb.]
> He really appreciated our help. [Adverb.]

In colloquial usage *real* is often used as an adverb meaning "very," but this use is not appropriate in writing:

COLLOQUIAL: The first act went off real well.
WRITTEN: The first act went off very well. [Or: The first act really went off well.]

reason is because In formal English the expression "the reason is" is followed by a noun or by a noun clause beginning with *that*:

> The main reason for firing him was his *insolence*.
> The main reason for firing him was *that he was insolent*.

In informal speech and frequently in informal writing many people use the more natural connective *because*, which more obviously stresses the idea of reason:

> The main reason for firing him was *because of his insolence*.
> The main reason for firing him was *because he was insolent*.

530 ***receipt, recipe*** Both mean "a set of directions for preparing something." In a certain locality one or the other may be preferred by cooks, but they are interchangeable in this meaning. *Receipt* (ri sēt′) also means "a written statement that something has been received."

reckon A localism for *think* or *suppose*:

LOCALISM: How long do you reckon he'll be gone?
GENERAL: How long do you think (*or* suppose) he'll be gone?

Redundancy The use of unnecessary words, especially of words that repeat an idea expressed elsewhere in the sentence:

> But the woman at the counter [she] didn't notice us.
> The table at which we usually sit [at] was taken.
> Mr. Potter kept making irrelevant comments [that had nothing to do with the subject].

(For further examples and discussion, see Chapter 11, "Deadwood," page 254.)

refer back Though *refer back* is commonly used, the *back* is unnecessary in most sentences:

> In the last paragraph, he once again refers [back] to his opening sentence.

Reference books   Besides the encyclopedias, which supply background information on almost any subject, libraries have a number of other reference books that are useful for different purposes.

To find facts about important people, consult the following:

Who's Who (mainly living Englishmen)
Who's Who in America
Current Biography (annual volumes and monthly supplements)
New Century Cyclopedia of Names
American Authors 1600-1900 (by Kunitz and Haycraft)
Twentieth Century Authors (by Kunitz and Haycraft)

To find miscellaneous information, statistics, dates, records, etc., look through one of these:

The World Almanac and Book of Facts
Information Please Almanac

To find maps, statistics, and other geographical information, see:

Goode's World Atlas
Rand McNally-Cosmopolitan World Atlas
Hammond's Library World Atlas

Reference of pronouns   A pronoun has little specific meaning of its own; it gets its exact meaning from the word or words to which it refers (its antecedent). Therefore if you are to make your intended meaning clear, the reference of the pronouns you use must be clear. For a discussion of ways to make pronoun reference clear, see Chapter 10, "Careless Use of Pronouns," page 228.

531

Referent   The meaning of any word lies in what the word stands for—or "refers" to. Whatever person or thing the word refers to is called its *referent* (ref′ər ənt).

Reflexive pronouns   Pronouns with the ending *-self* or *-selves*: *myself, yourself, himself, herself, ourselves, yourselves, themselves*. They are called *reflexive* because the action of the verb is turned back on the subject:

She outsmarted *herself*.   [Direct object.]
He did *himself* an injustice.   [Indirect object.]
Grandfather was mumbling to *himself*.   [Object of preposition.]

(For a discussion of usage, see **myself.**)

regard, regards   The standard idioms are *in regard to* and *with regard to* ("In regard to his complaint, I have nothing to say"). In nonstandard English *in regards to* and *with regards to* are often used ("In regards to his complaint").

regardless   The ending *-less* gives *regardless* a negative meaning: "without regard to." Adding the prefix *ir—irregardless*—makes a double negative.

Though *irregardless* is often heard, it is not considered good usage and should be avoided:

STANDARD: He will resign regardless of the consequences.

In colloquial usage *regardless* is used as an adverb meaning "anyway": She'll make the trip, *regardless*.

Relative adverb   When an adverb like *where, when, why, since, before,* or *after* is used to introduce an adjective clause, it is called a *relative adverb*:

A plaque now marks the spot *where* the treaty was signed.
An hour *before* he was to sign the contract, he changed his mind.

Relative clause   Since adjective clauses are usually introduced by a relative pronoun (*who, which, that*) or a relative adverb (*where, when, why, after*) that refers, or "relates," to an antecedent, they are often called *relative clauses*:

Phil blurted out the first answer *that popped into his head.*   [Modifies the antecedent *answer.*]
The climax came the day *when the water main broke.*   [Modifies the antecedent *day.*]

A succession of relative clauses in one sentence is likely to be awkward. In revising first drafts, watch out for sentences that follow a "house that Jack built" pattern.

AWKWARD: The guards that are posted at the entrance that leads to the laboratory that is devoted to the research projects will let no one enter that doesn't have a special permit.
BETTER: The guards posted at the entrance leading to the laboratory devoted to the research projects will let no one enter without a special permit.

(For punctuation of relative clauses, see **Comma**, section 5.)

Relative pronouns   The pronouns *who, whose, whom, which,* and *that*— used to introduce adjective clauses. Ordinarily *who* is used to refer to persons, *which* to refer to things, and *that* to refer to either persons or things:

Many people *who* (or *that*) extoll the classics never read them.
Ideas *that* (or *which*) startled us then seem commonplace now.

(For a discussion of particular points in the use of relatives, see **that, which; which; who, whom, whose.**)

remember   Standard English does not use *of* after the verb *remember*:

NONSTANDARD: I don't remember of meeting him.
STANDARD: I don't remember meeting him.

Repetition   Intentionally repeating a word, a thought, or a sound is often an effective way to gain emphasis in speech or writing. But repetition that serves no purpose, that occurs mainly because of carelessness or haste, is likely to be distracting and annoying to readers. Make it a point to remove unpleasant repetitions while revising your papers.

(For discussion and examples of effective repetition, see Chapter 11, "Emphasis Through Repetition," page 260.)

Research paper   See Chapter 6, "The Research Paper," for a detailed discussion of the steps in preparing a paper based on research.

resign   Usually followed by *from*, though sometimes immediately by the object:

> He decided to resign from the editorship.   [Or: to resign the editorship.]

Resolution   A formal statement of opinion adopted by a committee, club, or other organization. It is used typically for group expressions of sympathy, thanks, and so on, and for recommendations of action. The style is formal and impersonal, and the wording is standardized:

> WHEREAS, The Student Council of Lucas High School has received many inquiries about the possibility of a trip to Washington for the seniors; and
> WHEREAS, This Council feels that such a trip would be a worthwhile educational experience; therefore be it
> Resolved, That a special student committee be formed to draw up feasible plans for such a trip; and be it further
> Resolved, That a formal request for permission and copy of the plans be presented to the Faculty Executive Committee for consideration.
>
> Paul Harper, Secretary

Restrictive and nonrestrictive   A *restrictive* modifier—one that is used to tell which particular person or thing is meant—is not set off by commas from the word it modifies:

> Frank was curious about the letter *on Larry's desk.*
> A man *wearing a bright pink jacket* got on at the next corner.
> The boy *seated next to me* kept eating popcorn from a noisy bag.
> The woman *who was in the accident* sued the bus company.
> A roof *that leaked* was just one of the hazards at our cottage.
> Those were the days *when children were to be seen but not heard.*

But a *nonrestrictive* modifier—which is used merely to add a descriptive or explanatory detail—is set off from the word it modifies:

> The letter was right where he had left it, *on Larry's desk.*
> Sue's date, *wearing a borrowed coat a bit too small for him,* was with them.

Alderman Thomas, *seated beside the governor*, fairly bristled with self-importance.

The owner of the newsstand, *who had witnessed the accident*, gave the officer his name.

The money was needed to replace our old roof, *which leaked in a dozen places*.

Such a scene could have occurred only at the turn of the century, *when Victorianism was a way of life*.

Adverb clauses that tell the particular time, place, reason, purpose, manner, condition, etc., are *restrictive* and are not set off:

He sat on the bench *before the paint was dry*.
Miss Finney had always let us sit *where we pleased*.
She had been fired *because she couldn't spell*.
He pulled up his sleeve *so that we could see the scar*.
And he said it *as if he meant it*.
The contract is not binding *unless Mr. Otis signs it*.
The test was so hard *that only three students passed*.

Those that merely add explanatory details or comments (which could be omitted without changing the basic meaning of the sentence) are *nonrestrictive* and should be set off from the rest of the sentence:

Dr. Porter left early, *before the last act was over*.
He pushed me forward, *where I could see better*.
No one would be there on Friday, *because it was a legal holiday*.
The note was written in code, *so that it was meaningless to me*.
He merely shrugged his shoulders, *as though he no longer cared*.
She was given a raise, *though it came too late to do any good*.
The report had to be finished, *no matter how tired he was*.

(For further discussion and examples, see **Comma,** section 5; **Dash,** section 3; and **Parentheses,** sections 1 and 4.)

Reverend A term of respect for clergymen, not to be used without the first name, initials, or title of the person. The abbreviation *Rev.* is used only in newspaper and rather informal writing.

Reverend James Allen	Reverend Mr. Allen
Reverend J. P. Allen	Reverend Dr. Allen
Rev. James Allen (informal)	Reverend James Allen, D.D.

Putting *the* before *Reverend* is more formal:

Next week he will interview the Reverend Father Paul J. Lisco.

Using *reverend* as a noun meaning "clergyman" (One of the delegates was a reverend) is increasingly found in informal English.

Revision See Chapter 10, "Improving Sentence Structure"; Chapter 11, "Writing Effective Sentences"; and Chapter 1, "Revising Your Paper," page 18.

Rhetorical question Question asked only for effect—usually to emphasize a point, to suggest an opinion, or to introduce a topic. No direct answer is expected (though it is, of course, obvious).

> Authorities agree that safety belts, properly installed and of adequate strength, would lessen the risk of serious injury and death. Yet in spite of their demonstrable value, safety belts are not being widely used. Is this entirely the fault of the car manufacturers? Or is it we—the owners and drivers of the cars —who are to blame?

rise, arise In referring to people, *arise* is formal and poetic; *rise* is rather formal; *get up* is general.

rise, raise *Rise* (*rose, risen*) is intransitive and does not take an object; *raise* (*raised, raised*) is transitive and takes an object:

> At noon the next day the flood waters *were* still *rising*.
> They *raised* the bar another two inches.

rôle, role In formal writing the circumflex accent is sometimes kept; in informal, it is usually dropped.

Root A word or part of a word that is used as a base for forming other words, as *civil* is the root of *civilize, civilly, civilian, civilization, uncivil*; *voc* is the root of *vocal, vocation, vocalist, provocation, avocation*. 535

round See **around, round.**

route The pronunciation rüt (rhymes with *suit*) is general, but rout (rhymes with *trout*) is used in the Army and informally, for newspaper and delivery routes.

Run-together sentence When you put two independent statements into one sentence, you ordinarily join them with a conjunction and a comma or separate them with a semicolon. If you use a comma alone between the clauses or no punctuation at all, you have a run-together sentence (sometimes called a *comma fault*). For a full discussion of this writing fault and how to avoid it, see Chapter 10, "Revising Run-together Sentences," page 238.

S

saint *Saint* is abbreviated with proper names (*St. Lawrence, St. Joseph*). The plural *Saints* is abbreviated SS. or Sts. (*SS. Cyril and Methodius, Sts. Andrew and Thomas*). Sometimes the French feminine form *Sainte* is used (*Sainte Genevieve*) with the abbreviation *Ste.*

salary, wages   *Salary* is used to refer to a fixed compensation paid at regular intervals (often monthly or semimonthly) for clerical or professional work. *Wages* is used for money paid an employee at relatively short intervals, often daily or weekly, especially for manual or mechanical work.

same   *Same* as a pronoun is no longer used in such business expressions as "Enclosed is a money order for same." Current usage prefers *it* or *them*:

> The seniors who want extra pictures may call for them at the office. [Not: may call for same.]

Sarcasm   A remark made with the intention of hurting someone's feelings by taunting, ridiculing, mocking at, or sneering at him. Sarcastic remarks are often ironical (saying one thing but meaning another):

> When we realized that Ed's directions had led us ten miles past the camp, I groaned, "You certainly are a fine navigator!"

But sarcasm may also be direct:

> "I think it's the biggest disaster since the *Titanic*," declared my younger brother sarcastically when I asked him how he liked my new hairdo.

Since sarcasm is often indicated by the tone of the voice, it sometimes passes unnoticed in writing. In dialogue, if it is not unmistakably indicated by the context, writers often label it, as in the second example. But usually the sarcasm is obvious. (See also **Irony**.)

Satire   The use of ridicule, irony, or sarcasm to make fun of a person, a custom, an idea, or an institution. This "fun-making" may be harmless, intended only to amuse the reader or listener, or it may be a bitter attack intended to discredit by ridicule the person or thing at which it is aimed. It may be concerned with a trivial and laughter-provoking subject, such as women's hats; or it may expose the weaknesses of the social and political customs and policies of a nation.

say, state, talk   *Say* is a general word for speaking: Pat *said* he didn't believe a word of her story. *State* implies a more formal, orderly communication: He *will state* his position on this question at the next press conference. *Talk* implies conversation, especially of an informal kind: The men sat around the fire and *talked* until midnight. (For the use of *say* in reporting conversation, see **Conversation**.)

scarcely   See **Double negative**.

scarcely ... when   The idiom is *scarcely ... when*, not *scarcely ... than*:

> I had *scarcely* read the first paragraph *when* she grabbed the note out of my hand.

School subjects The name of a school or college course is not capitalized unless it is the name of a language or of a specific numbered course:

> Dorothy is taking English literature, Spanish, and biology.
> Since he plans to major in science, he signed up for both chemistry and Physics 2.

Schwa (ə) The *schwa* (pronounced shwä) is the symbol used in this book and in many recent dictionaries to simplify the system of showing pronunciation: *havoc—*hav'ək, *stalactite—*stə lak'tīt. The schwa represents the neutral vowel sound of many unstressed syllables:

a as in *abode*	*i* as in *tonsil*	*u* as in *focus*
e as in *bitten*	*o* as in *salmon*	*y* as in *satyr*

Seasons *Spring, summer, autumn, winter, midwinter,* and so on, are not capitalized except in some poetry or nature essays, for emphasis.

secretive Generally pronounced si krē'tiv, though sē'krə tiv is usually heard in the sense of "not frank or open."

seem *Can't seem* is a useful informal idiom for the more formal and logical *seem unable:*

INFORMAL: I can't seem to make her understand.
FORMAL: I seem unable to make her understand.

self As a prefix *self-* is usually hyphened to the root word:

> self-esteem   self-confident   self-regulating

But there is no hyphen in words like *selfish* and *selfless,* in which *self* is the root word to which the endings *-ish* and *-less* have been added.

For the use of pronouns ending in *self* (*myself, yourself, himself,* etc.), see **Intensive pronouns** and **Reflexive pronouns.**

Semantics The scientific study of the meanings of words and the relationship between language and thinking. Chapter 3, "Language and Thinking," is a chapter on semantics.

semi- Prefix meaning "half" (*semielliptical*), "occurring twice within a certain period" (*semiweekly*), or "partially" (*semiautomatic*). Before proper nouns or words beginning with *i* a hyphen is used: *semi-Norman, semi-idleness.*

Semicolon (;) 1 A semicolon is used to separate the clauses of a compound sentence when they are not joined by a coördinating conjunction (*and, but, for, or, nor, yet*):

> I had suspected the bookkeeper all along; he had both motive and opportunity.

Remember that connectives like *then, still, however, moreover, never-theless, consequently* are not coördinating conjunctions but conjunctive adverbs. Main clauses joined by these adverbs are separated by a semi-colon:

> Mrs. Todd listened patiently to Jim's account of what had hap-pened; then she turned to me for my side of the story.
> The men knew there was little hope of reaching the boy in time; nevertheless, they would not give up.

2 A semicolon is generally used (instead of a comma) between main clauses joined by *and, but, for,* etc., if either of the clauses contains a comma:

> Her uncle had been a prospector, a lumberjack, and a sandhog; and the tales he told made life on the farm seem even more drab.
> His campaign manager, who knew the political situation in Oakton, suggested several changes in the speech for the rally; but Len, stubborn as usual, refused to alter a single word.

3 A semicolon is used (instead of a comma) between items of a series if the items contain commas:

> In an hour Frank had sold advertising space to Haley's, a depart-ment store; McLaughlin's, a pet shop; and Peterson Brothers, an employment agency.
> Miss Doty's substitute assigned *Vanity Fair* to Ron Phillips, who hates novels; *For Whom the Bell Tolls* to Laura Karnes, who shudders at the mere thought of violence; and *Othello* to Pete Frenz, who has a hard time reading very simple prose.

Sentences   Chapter 10, "Improving Sentence Structure," explains the most common sentence errors and tells you how to avoid or correct them. Chapter 11, "Writing Effective Sentences," shows you several ways of making your sentences more effective and forceful.

Sequence of tenses   See **Tenses of verbs,** section 3.

Series   For the punctuation of items in a series, see **Comma,** section 3, and **Semicolon,** section 3.

shall, will   **1** In informal English *will* or its contraction *'ll* is generally used in all persons to show simple future:

> I will write the thank-you notes next week.   [Or: I'll write.]
> They will pay us a dollar an hour.   [Or: They'll pay.]

To give emphasis or to show determination, informal English gen-erally uses *shall* in all persons:

> I shall keep complaining until something is done.
> Nothing shall stop us.

Less often *will* is used, and emphasis is shown by stressing the word in speech or underlining it in writing:

> I will' make the trip, even if I have to walk.
> He will regret this; I'm sure of it.

In questions, informal English generally uses *shall* with *I* and *we*, *will* with other subjects:

> Shall I tell you the answer? Shall we meet again tomorrow?
> How will you pay for them? When will they get here?

In negative questions, *won't* is generally used:

> Won't he be disappointed? Why won't they come?

2 In formal English *shall* is used with *I* and *we*, *will* with other subjects:

> I shall have the book read by next week.
> You will be tired of that job within a month.
> Ned will be on the varsity if he keeps his grades up.

To give emphasis or to show determination, formal English reverses the words, using *will* with *I* and *we*, *shall* with other subjects:

> We will not give up, no matter what happens.
> Dave shall apologize, I promise.

In questions, formal English uses the form expected in the answer:

> Shall you be a delegate again? (Yes, I shall.)
> Will you ask for a refund? (I certainly will.)

539

Shifted constructions   For a discussion and examples of shifted (or non-parallel) constructions and for help in avoiding them, see Chapter 10, "Shifted Constructions," page 225.

Ships' names   In most books and generally in formal writing, the names of ships (and aircraft, submarines, trains) are capitalized and italicized (underlined in handwriting): the *Ivernia* (ship), the *Caroline* (airplane), the *James Whitcomb Riley* (train), the *Skate* (submarine), the *Aurora 7* (spaceship). Use this style in your written work.

In some informal writing, especially in newspapers, such names are treated simply as proper names, capitalized but not italicized (or underlined): the Rotterdam (ship), the Spirit of St. Louis (airplane).

Shoptalk   The informal language of people used in, or in talking about, their particular occupations. For a discussion, see Chapter 8, "Shoptalk," page 174.

sic   *Sic* (Latin for *thus, so*; pronounced sik) is used to show that a mistake has been copied exactly as it appeared in the original: The leading article was titled "A Freind [*sic*] in Need."

similar to   A wordy way of saying *like*:

> WORDY: I hope I never have an experience similar to it again.
> BETTER: I hope I never have an experience like it again.

Simile   A figure of speech in which a comparison between two unlike things is introduced by *like* or *as*:

> The seven children descended upon them like a horde of locusts.

(For further examples and discussion, see Chapter 12, "Simile and Metaphor," page 282.)

Simple sentence   A sentence that has only one subject and one verb, either or both of which may be compound, is called a *simple sentence*:

> Ben had left the key in the ignition.
> Every night the cat and the dog took their posts in the alley and disturbed our sleep with their discordant yawps.

sit, set   *Sit* (*sat, sat*) is generally intransitive and does not take an object; *set* (*set, set*) is generally transitive and takes an object:

> *Sit* there.   *Set* the plant there.
> He *sat* there last night.   Who *set* it there?
> I *have* often *sat* here.   I *had set* the plant down.

540   But in certain phrases and constructions, *sit* takes an object and *set* does not:

> *Sit* the baby up straight!
> The sun *will set* at six o'clock tonight.
> Most of his hens *are setting*.

situated   Often deadwood that should be pruned away in writing:

> Dr. Kent's office was [situated] directly under a dance studio.
> I was sent to live with relatives in Pickford, a pleasant town [situated] in the eastern part of the Upper Peninsula.

(See **Deadwood.**)

size, sized   In advertising matter, the form *size* is commonly used: a small-size package, a king-*size* box. In general writing, the more formal form *sized* is usual: two middle-*sized* boys, a fair-*sized* portion, a large-*sized* cap. Often the word is better omitted altogether: a small package, a large cap.

ski   Plural *skis*, sometimes *ski*. As a verb the parts are *ski, skied, skiing*. *Ski* is pronounced skē or sometimes, following the Norwegian, shē.

Slang   For a discussion of slang and its appropriateness, see Chapter 8, "Slang," page 173.

slow, slowly Both *slow* and *slowly* are used as adverbs. Use whichever sounds better in the sentence:

> Let's go slow; we have time.
> The tug with its string of barges moved slowly up the river.

so   1 In speech *so* is often used to introduce clauses of purpose:

COLLOQUIAL: We moved to the front row so we could hear better.
WRITTEN: We moved to the front row so that we could hear better.
   [Or: to hear better; in order to hear better.]

So is common in clauses of result, which written English would usually introduce by *so that* or change to a *since* (or *because*) construction:

COLLOQUIAL: Paul had lost his bus fare to Memphis, so he had to hitchhike to get there.
WRITTEN: Paul had lost his bus fare to Memphis, so that he had to hitchhike to get there.
WRITTEN: Since Paul had lost his bus fare to Memphis, he had to hitchhike to get there.

2 The overuse of *so* to connect sentences is sometimes referred to as the "so-habit." It is common in speech, particularly in narratives:

> Mrs. Monsen's two daughters were married last month, as you know, so she wanted something to do to occupy her time, so she wondered about taking some adult-education courses. So she went over to the University Extension Office so she could find out what was being taught this semester. Two of the classes sounded interesting, so she signed up for both of them.

541

Sentences like these should be revised in order to avoid the overuse of *so*. (See Chapter 11, "Too Many So's," page 252.)

3 The use of *so* as an intensive is mainly colloquial; in written English it is usually avoided or the comparison completed:

COLLOQUIAL: His speech was so boring!
WRITTEN: His speech was so boring that I caught myself nodding.

so-called   When *so-called* is used, quotation marks are not needed, because they would duplicate the idea: *a so-called intellectual*—not *a so-called "intellectual."*

So-called is usually hyphened when it comes before the word it modifies but not when it follows: His altruism, *so called*, is just a mask for his egoism.

so . . . that   Even though several words come between *so* and *that*, no comma should precede *that*:

> Laura was so intent on catching Mr. Blumberg in a grammatical error [ ] that she missed the point he was making.

some   Used colloquially as an adverb meaning "somewhat" or "a little."

> COLLOQUIAL: He seemed some worse today.
> WRITTEN: He seemed somewhat worse today.   [Or: a little worse.]

sooner . . . than   *Than,* not *when,* is used as a connective after *no sooner*:

> The nurse had *no sooner* reached her desk *than* his light flashed on again.   [Not: *no sooner* reached her desk *when*.]

sort   See **kind, sort; kind of, sort of; kind of a, sort of a.**

Species   Has the same form in both singular and plural: one *species,* several *species.* It is pronounced spē'shiz or, especially in the plural, spē'shēz.

Specie (spē'shi), meaning "money in the form of coins," is a different word, a collective noun without a plural form.

Spelling   The argument that many of our celebrated writers and great men have been notably bad spellers does not alter the fact that accurate spelling has become a generally applied test of literacy—one of the minimum requirements of an educated person. Not only your future employers, but any person or friend who reads your writing, will expect you to be able to spell. It would be foolish to disregard this universal respect for accurate spelling, when with a bit of work and practice you could learn to spell well enough to escape unfavorable notice.

To be a good speller does not mean you have to be a perfect speller, one who without help can spell correctly every word he uses. It does mean that you should master the spelling of simple, everyday words (*it's, business, meant, writing, choose, quiet, across*) and should form the habit of referring to a good dictionary for less common words whose spelling you may be unsure of (*inoculate, Fahrenheit, desiccated*).

1 One of the best ways to improve your spelling is to master a few general rules that apply to large groups of common words:

a) **Doubling final consonants.**   Words of one syllable ending in a single consonant preceded by a single vowel double the consonant before a suffix beginning with a vowel:

cut + er = cutter	fad + ist = faddist
pin + ed = pinned	prig + ish = priggish
hop + ing = hopping	snob + ery = snobbery

If the word has more than one syllable, the final consonant is doubled only if the accent is on the last syllable:

re bel' + ed = rebelled	con cur' + ence = concurrence
be gin' + er = beginner	re mit' + ance = remittance
pre fer' + ing = preferring	re gret' + able = regrettable

(But: en vel'op + ed = enveloped; pro'fit + ing = profiting.)

b) **Final silent e.** Words ending in a final unpronounced *e* drop the *e* before a suffix beginning with a vowel:

pine + ed = pined	force + ible = forcible
narrate + or = narrator	argue + able = arguable
change + ing = changing	guide + ance = guidance

There are a few exceptions: the *e* is kept in words like *dyeing* and *singeing* (to keep them distinct from *dying* and *singing*) and in words like *peaceable* and *outrageous* (to keep the *s* sound of the *c* and the *j* sound of the *g*).

Before a suffix beginning with a consonant, the final *e* is usually kept:

care + ful = careful	immediate + ly = immediately
spine + less = spineless	advance + ment = advancement
rude + ness = rudeness	safe + ty = safety

A number of common words are exceptions: *ninth, truly, duly, argument, wholly.*

c) **Words with y.** Words ending in *y* preceded by a consonant change the *y* to *i* before a suffix beginning with a consonant:

sleepy + ly = sleepily	embody + ment = embodiment
ready + ness = readiness	mercy + less = merciless
fancy + ful = fanciful	glory + fy = glorify

The same change is made before the suffixes -*ed*, -*er*, -*es*, -*est*:

rectify + ed = rectified	whinny + es = whinnies
easy + er = easier	silly + est = silliest

But before the suffix -*ing*, the *y* is kept:

marrying	scurrying	worrying	pitying

d) **Adding prefixes.** The prefixes *dis-*, *mis-*, and *un-* end with a single consonant. When they are attached to a base word beginning with the same letter, there will be two *s*'s or two *n*'s. Otherwise there will be only one:

dis + satisfy = dissatisfy	dis + agreement = disagreement
dis + soluble = dissoluble	dis + approve = disapprove
mis + spelling = misspelling	mis + arranged = misarranged
mis + spent = misspent	mis + inform = misinform
un + noticed = unnoticed	un + certain = uncertain
un + named = unnamed	un + interesting = uninteresting

e) **Adding suffixes.** No letter is dropped from a base word ending in a consonant when the suffix -*ness* or -*ly* is added:

thin + ness = thinness	liberal + ly = liberally
open + ness = openness	practical + ly = practically

But remember that if the base word ends in *y* preceded by a consonant, the *y* is changed to *i*: *friendliness, cheerily.*

543

f) Ei and ie.   Use *ie* when the sound is long *e* (as in *fee*):

achieve	belief	piece	grievance
yield	shield	shriek	besiege

A few common exceptions are: *either, neither, leisure, seize, weird.*
Use *ei* after *c*, or when the sound is not long *e*:

deceiver	ceiling	eighth	weighed
conceited	heifer	reign	counterfeit
received	veil	heirloom	freight

The most common exceptions are *friend, mischief, handkerchief, sieve, view, fiery, financier.*

2 Often pronouncing words correctly will help with the spelling. For example, if you pronounce *lightning* and *hindrance* as they should be —two syllables rather than three—you will not be tempted to write "lightening" and "hinderance." If you pronounce *athletic* and *disastrous* correctly as three syllables, you will not put an extra vowel in the words ("athaletic" and "disasterous").

If you remember that *tian* (as in *Christian*) spells a "chən" sound, you will not use *tian* in spelling words like *fountain, certain, Britain,* and *chieftain*—which end with a "tən" sound (not "chən"). If you remember that the "shən" sound in words like *admission, concession, discussion* is spelled with *ssion,* you will use two *s*'s in these words. But you will use only one *s* in words like *decision, collision, confusion*—since they end with the sound "zhən." Make it a practice to compare the way words sound with the way they are spelled. The pronunciations are not always foolproof clues, but they help with many groups of words of similar sound.

3 For single words whose spelling is hard or seems unreasonable or illogical, try to figure out some formula to fix the spelling in your mind. Notice, for example, the "arc" in *arctic* and the "nun" in *pronunciation* (the trouble spots in those words). Keep *stationery* (paper for letters) distinct from *stationary* (having a fixed place) by letting the *e* in *paper* remind you of the *e* in *stationery.* Remember that *restaurant* (some of the best of which are owned by Greeks) has *tau,* a letter of the Greek alphabet, as its second syllable. Any device, however nonsensical it may seem, that helps you with the spelling of difficult words is valuable.

4 Finally, since many misspellings are due to carelessness or haste rather than ignorance, make it a point to proofread all your written work carefully before handing it in. Keep a list of all words that you habitually misspell and check your papers especially for those. Wanting to be a good speller is half the battle.

5 Following is a list of words frequently misspelled in high-school papers. (The words are divided into syllables so that you can more easily visualize their spelling.) Look over the list carefully, making sure you know the meaning and pronunciation of each. Check the particular words that cause you trouble and review them from time to time. Refer to the list when you proofread your papers.

ac cel er a tor
ac cu rate
ac quaint ance
ac quit tal
al lege
al ly, al lies
a lu mi num
am bas sa dor
a nal o gy
a nal y sis
an a lyze
an ni hi late
a non y mous
ant arc tic
anx i e ty
a pol o gize
ap pro pri ate
as cend ed
as cent
as cer tain
as sent ed
as so ci a tion
at tacked
at tend ance
at tor ney
au thor i ty
aux il ia ry
aw ful
bach e lor
bal ance
bar gain
bat tal ion
beg gar
bis cuits
bound a ries
bril liant
Brit ish
bul le tin
buoy
bu reau
cam paign
car bu re tor
car i ca ture
ca tas tro phe
cel lo phane
char ac ter is tic
co er cion
col le giate

co los sal
com e dy
com pet i tive
com plaint
com ple ment
com pro mise
con cede
con nois seur
con sen sus
con sist ent
con ven ience
corps
cor rob o rate
crit i cize
cru el ty
cur ric u lum
dair y
dealt
debt or
de ceased
de ci sion
de fense
def i ni tion
de scend ants
des per ate
de spise
di a ry
di lap i dat ed
diph the ri a
dis ci pline
dis cre tion
dis eased
dis si pate
di vis i ble
does n't
dom i nant
du al
ef fi cien cy
el i gi ble
em bar rassed
em i nent
en deav or
e quip ment
et i quette
eu lo gy
ex ceed
ex haust ed
ex hil a rat ing

ex ist ence
ex traor di nar y
ex u ber ant
fa cil i ty
fal la cy
fas ci nate
fa tigued
fem i nine
for eign er
fran ti cal ly
fu tile
gauge
gen u ine
gov ern ment
gran deur
guard i an
guessed
guid ance
gym na si um
hap pened
har assed
Ha wai ian
hei nous
hel i cop ter
his to ry
hoarse
hun dredths
hy giene
hyp no tize
hy poc ri sy
il lit er ate
im mi grant
im ple ment
in ci dent
in cred i ble
in dict ment
in dis pen sa ble
in ev i ta ble
in fi nite
in gen u ous
i ni ti at ed
in nu en do
in quir y
in stance
in stead
in tel li gent
in ter pret ed
in ter rup tion

ir rel e vant
ir re sist i ble
ir rev er ent
is land
it self
ja lop y
jew el ry
judg ing
khak i
kin dle
knuck les
lau rels
law yer
le git i mate
li brar i an
li cense
lieu ten ant
liv a ble
loy al ty
lux u ry
ly ing
man u al
mar i time
med i cine
me di e val
met tle
min i a ture
mir a cle
mis cel la ne ous
mis sile
mo rale
mus cles
mus tache
na ïve
nau se ate
ne ces si ty
ne go ti ate
nine teenth
nour ish
now a days
nui sance
o be di ence
o bliged
ob sta cle
oc cur rence
oil y
op po nent
op po site

op ti mism
os tra cize
o ver whelm
pag eant
pan to mime
par a lyzed
pa ren the ses
pa tience
pen i cil lin
per ma nent
per mis si ble
per spi ra tion
phase
phe nom e non
Phil ip pines
phy si cian
pic nick ing
play wright
pleas ant
pneu mat ic
prec e dence
pre mier
pres ence
prim i tive
pri or i ty
pro ce dure
pro ceed
prod i gy
pro tein
pub lic ly
qual i fied
quar ter
ques tion naire
qui et ly
quit ting
quix ot ic
quiz zes
re cip i ent
ref er ences
rel a tive
rem i nisce
ren dez vous
re pel lent
res er voir
rhe tor i cal
rhyme
ri dic u lous
ri fle

route
sac ri le gious
sce nar i o
scen er y
scis sors
sol dier
sol emn
so phis ti cat ed
sou ve nir
spec i men
speech
spon sor
stac ca to
sta tis tics
strat e gy
stretched
sub si dize
sub tle
sug ar y
sul fa
sum ma rize
su per sede
sus cep ti ble
syl la ble
sym met ri cal
sym pho ny
syr up y
tech nique
tem per a ture
tend en cy
thou sandths
to mor row
tour na ment
traf fick ing
trai tor
treas ur er
ty ing
tyr an ny
un con scious
un doubt ed ly
un prec e dent ed
va can cies
vac u um
va ri e ty
vi cin i ty
vig i lant
vil i fy
vil lag ers

546

vi o lence	war rant	wool en
vis i bil i ty	wel come	wrought
vis i tors	whoop ing	yacht
war fare	will ful	zo ol o gy

Split infinitive Putting an adverb modifier between *to* and the infinitive form of the verb results in what is called a "split infinitive":

> Paul advised Jerry *to simply forget* what he had heard.
> He was too angry *to fully appreciate* the humor of the situation.

Split infinitives that sound awkward are to be avoided in writing:

AWKWARD: I expected him to at least once in a while help us out.
BETTER: I expected him to help us out at least once in a while.

But otherwise there is no point in revising a sentence just to avoid splitting an infinitive. Good writers, in fact, prefer using split infinitives in sentences where not doing so would result in ambiguity or awkwardness:

CLEAR: He was too ill to really understand the danger he was in.
UNCLEAR: He was too ill really to understand the danger he was in.
AWKWARD: He was too ill to understand really the danger he was in.

Squinting modifier A modifier that is ambiguous because it could refer to a preceding or to a following construction:

SQUINTING: He vowed before he left Paris he would be a success.
CLEAR: He vowed he would be a success before he left Paris.
CLEAR: Before he left Paris, he vowed he would be a success.

(See also Chapter 10, "Squinting Modifiers," page 221.)

Standard English The language used by educated people. For a discussion, see Chapter 8, "The Levels of Usage."

state See ***say, state, talk.***

Story The word *story* is most commonly applied to a narrative of imaginary happenings—to a short story or a novel. It is also used to refer to a narrative of actual events—to a newspaper story, for example.

Articles, editorials, reviews, essays, treatises, and so on, are not narratives, but pieces of expository writing—writing that discusses ideas or explains processes. The word *story* should not be applied to them.

street In many newspapers *street* is not capitalized as part of an address: *4803 Edmund street.* In other forms of writing it is generally capitalized: *4803 Edmund Street.*

The abbreviation *St.* or *st.* is not much used except to save space in lists or reference works and occasionally in letter headings.

Subject and verb   The *subject* names the person or thing about which the *verb* makes a statement or asks a question (My **head** *was throbbing.* **Who** *will pay* the bill?).

For a complete discussion, see Chapter 7, "Subjects and Verbs," page 147; and Chapter 9, "Agreement with the Subject," page 198.

Subjunctive   The italicized words in the following sentences are examples of verbs in the subjunctive mood:

I move that debate *be closed*.	If he *were* chairman, I'd join.
I wish I *were* a movie star.	Dr. Neal insists that Ed *diet*.

The subjunctive is far less common in English than it once was. (See Chapter 9, "Subjunctives," page 197.)

Subordinating conjunctions   Subordinating conjunctions connect dependent, or subordinate, clauses with main clauses:

I laughed *because* he did.   We wondered *why* he had resigned.

Among the most common subordinating conjunctions are:

after	because	since	unless
although	before	so that	when
as	how	that	where
as if	if	though	while
as long as	in order that	till	why

The relative pronouns (*who, which, that*) and the interrogative pronouns (*who, which, what*) serve as subordinating conjunctions:

RELATIVE: The clerk *who* had waited on me had left.
INTERROGATIVE: I asked him *which* was the real diamond.

such   Colloquially, *such* is used as an intensive:

He had such a pleasant manner.

In writing that is at all formal this use is avoided or the comparison is completed:

He had a most pleasant manner.
He had such a pleasant manner that we felt completely at ease.

such as   When used to introduce examples, *such as* is not followed by a comma:

Subjects such as [ ] millinery, typing, and judo are more popular than the academic subjects taught at the night school.
He also had a number of unlovely habits, such as [ ] procrastinating and lying, which tempered our admiration for him.

Suffix   An addition made at the end of a word to form another word of different meaning or function:

-able: peaceable, curable	*-ize*: idolize, revolutionize
-en: darken, weaken	*-less*: valueless, pitiless
-er: fighter, diner	*-ly*: fatherly, ghostly
-ful: sorrowful, plentiful	*-ment*: improvement, adornment
-fy: falsify, solidify	*-ship*: hardship, dictatorship

Sunday school   Capitalize only the *Sunday* except in names of particular Sunday schools:

> He missed Sunday school three weeks in a row.
> Toby, I believe, goes to the Park Church Sunday School.

sure   *Sure* is used primarily as an adjective:

> This is a sure way to ruin your health.   He is sure to lose.

Sure used as an adverb meaning "yes" or "certainly" is a colloquialism. It is frequently heard in conversation, but is inappropriate in writing (except in dialogue).

> "Do you really know Robert Kennedy?"   "Sure."
> "That sure was a waste of time!"

suspicion   Used as a verb, *suspicion* is nonstandard:

> NONSTANDARD: He spoke as if he suspicioned me.
> STANDARD: He spoke as if he suspected me.

549

swell   As an adjective meaning "excellent" or "first-rate," *swell* is generally inappropriate in serious writing and in careful speech. Like *nice* and *fine, swell* is a counter word—used not to express a specific meaning but merely to convey general approval (a swell girl, a swell vacation, a swell picnic). It has been so badly overworked in conversation that many people find it objectionable.

swim   The principal parts are *swim, swam, swum.* The past tense form *swum* is archaic or dialectal.

Synecdoche   (si nek′də ki) A figure of speech in which the writer names (1) a part when he means the whole, or (2) the whole when he means only a part:

> He ordered all *hands* on deck. [That is, the members of the crew.]
> *Washington* vigorously denied the rumors. [That is, the Administration in Washington.]

(Compare **Metonymy.**)

Synonym   Synonyms are words that have the same basic meaning, but suggest slightly different things. That is, they have much the same denotation but different connotations. For example:

anger—enrage—infuriate—madden—incense—inflame
gaudy—showy—flashy—tawdry—garish
predicament—quandary—dilemma—plight—fix—jam

(For a discussion of synonyms, see Chapter 12, page 270.)

The best way to build up your fund of synonyms is to observe and use the new words that you come across in reading and conversation. But when in your writing you need a synonym for a specific word, it may be necessary to use a special reference book. Four good ones are:

Webster's Dictionary of Synonyms (Springfield, Mass., 1951)
Funk and Wagnalls Standard Handbook of Synonyms, Antonyms, and Prepositions (New York, 1947)
Roget's International Thesaurus (New York, 1962)
The New Roget's Thesaurus of the English Language in Dictionary Form (New York, 1961)

The first two not only list synonyms but make clear what their different connotations are. Both editions of the *Thesaurus* simply list the words without giving the distinctions between them. Remember too that most standard dictionaries give special help with synonyms.

T

talk   See *say, state, talk.*

Tautology   The needless repetition of an idea:

Ancient architecture [of long ago] is still copied today.
Rob's suggestion was unanimously approved [by everyone there].

(See also Chapter 11, "Deadwood," page 254.)

taxi   The plural of the noun is *taxis*. The principal parts of the verb are *taxi, taxied, taxiing* or *taxying.*

teach   See *learn, teach.*

telephone, phone   In informal usage *telephone* is commonly shortened to *phone*. Since *phone* is a clipped word, not an abbreviation, it does not have a period.

Tenses of verbs   **1 Forms.**   The form of a verb helps to show the time of the action. Though there are only three divisions of time—present, past, and future—English has six tenses to show various distinctions within these divisions. The simple present tense and past tense forms are single words: he *pays*, she *paid*. All other tense forms are phrases in which helping verbs are combined with a part of the main verb. The following table shows the forms most commonly used to show time distinctions:

		Active	Passive
PRESENT TENSE		he pays he is paying he does pay	he is paid he is being paid
PAST TENSES	Past	he paid he was paying he did pay	he was paid he was being paid
	Present perfect	he has paid he has been paying	he has been paid
	Past perfect	he had paid he had been paying	he had been paid
FUTURE TENSES	Future	he will pay he will be paying	he will be paid
	Future perfect	he will have paid he will have been paying	he will have been paid

2 Uses. (a) The *present* tense is used not only to show that the action takes place at the present time, but also to make a statement that is generally true, regardless of time:

Brazilians *speak* Portuguese, not Spanish.
Dr. Moss reminded the officers that ether *is* highly inflammable.
Rough plaster, he explained, *absorbs* sound waves.

Occasionally the present tense is used to tell of things that happened in the past, especially when the speaker or writer wants to make the past events seem more vivid. This use of the present tense is called the *historical present*.

In an instant a curious crowd *gathers* in the street, and all *stare* up at the man on the ledge.

b) The simple *past* tense form is used for action completed in the past:

The glare temporarily *blinded* the driver.
Everyone *laughed* but me.

To show customary or repeated action in the past, a form with *used to* or *would* is used:

Her column *used to appear* in all the leading newspapers.
Every day he *would sit* there for hours, watching the waves.

c) The *future* tense, which shows that the action will occur in the future, is usually formed with the helping verb *shall* or *will*. But it can be formed in other ways. The present tense form, used in combination with an adverb of time, is common:

> *Next Monday* they *land* in Madrid.
> The Cubs *are playing* in Milwaukee *tomorrow*.

Phrases with *be* or *go* and an infinitive are also often used to refer to future time:

> I *am to introduce* the speaker.
> There *is to be* a dance after the game.
> He *is going to ask* for his money back.

d) The *present perfect* tense indicates an action begun in the past and extending to the time the statement is made:

> They *have rehearsed* the last scene at least a dozen times.
> Earl *has called* twice already.

e) The *past perfect* tense indicates an action completed earlier than some other past action:

> Before I could get my camera focused, the bear *had ambled* off.
> I suspected that Nancy *had hidden* the key.

f) The *future perfect* tense indicates an action to be completed at some definite time in the future:

> By the time he makes up his mind, both cars *will have been sold*.
> She *will have forgotten* her promise before the end of the week.

g) The *progressive* tense forms (made with the helping verb *be* and the present participle) are used to show continuing action:

> I *am rowing* as fast as I can.
> She *has been saying* that for years.
> Jake *was washing* the car when I saw him last.
> Mr. Sawyer *will be watching* the football game on TV.

h) The *emphatic* tense forms (made with the helping verb *do* and the infinitive) are used for emphasis and in negative statements and questions:

> She's wrong; I *do want* tickets for the game.
> He *did not feel* like working just then.   [Not: He *felt not*.]
> *Did* they *realize* its value?   [Not: *Realized they* its value?]

3 Sequence of tenses.   When the verb in the main clause is in the present tense, the verb in the subordinate clause is in whatever tense expresses the meaning intended:

> Nora *thinks* that he *is* a reporter.
> I *don't know* where he *went*.
> The landlady *doubts* that they *will* ever *return*.
> The Chapmans *say* they *may move* before June.

552

When the verb in the main clause is in a past tense, the verb in the subordinate clause is also in a past tense form, except in a sentence like the last in the following group:

> Nora *thought* that he *was* a reporter.
> I *didn't know* where he *had gone*.
> The landlady *doubted* that they *would* ever *return*.
> The Chapmans *said* they *might move* before June.
> He *told* us that the human brain *weighs* about three pounds. [The subordinate clause states a fact that is generally true.]

(See also Chapter 9, "Special Problems in Sequence," page 195.)

terrible   Colloquial in the sense of "bad; unpleasant; annoying": a *terrible* commercial, a *terrible* shirt. Avoid this use in writing.

than   1 In formal English the case of the pronoun after *than* in elliptical clauses of comparison depends on the use of the pronoun in the clause. The nominative form is used if the pronoun is the subject; the objective form is used if the pronoun is the object:

> After all, you are taller than *he* [is].
> My brother stayed up later than *I* [did].
> We don't like him any better than [we like] *her*.

In colloquial usage the objective form is often used in sentences like the first two (You are taller than *him*. My brother stayed up later than *me*). But this usage is not considered appropriate in writing or in formal speech.

Using the right form of the pronoun is often important in avoiding ambiguity. A sentence like "She trusts Clyde more than me," for example, might mean "She trusts Clyde more than I do" or "She trusts Clyde more than she trusts me." If in your writing you consistently use *I* when you mean the first, and *me* when you mean the second, you will make your intended meaning clear.

2 *Than* is the idiomatic conjunction after *no sooner*:

> He had *no sooner* left his office *than* the telegram arrived. [Not: *when* the telegram arrived.]

But *when*—not *than*—is used after *barely*, *hardly*, or *scarcely*:

> He had *scarcely* left the office *when* the telegram arrived.

than, then   Since, when spoken rapidly and without stress, *than* is pronounced ᴛʜən, careless writers tend to spell it *then*. Remember that *then* is an adverb of time (*Then* she turned), and *than* a conjunction (She was more confused *than* we).

than whom   In the phrase *than whom* (meaning "compared to whom"), *than* is a preposition and *whom* the object of the preposition. The

553

phrase is formal and old-fashioned, and many people avoid it as rather awkward.

AWKWARD: My cousin Oscar, than whom there is no greater bore, is Jane's idea of a brilliant conversationalist.
BETTER: My cousin Oscar, the greatest bore I know, is Jane's idea of a brilliant conversationalist.

that **1 Conjunction.**   *That* should usually be repeated with each of a series of parallel subordinate clauses:

> He replied *that* he had not ordered the ring, *that* he would not be pressured into paying for it, and *that* one more word from them would result in his reporting the matter to his lawyer.

But *that* should not be repeated within a single clause:

> She thinks *that* unless a man makes a lot of money [that] he is a failure.

2 Adverb.   In general usage *that* (or *this*) is commonly used as an adverb modifying adjectives and adverbs of quantity and extent:

> Only a family like his would have *that* many pets.
> No human being had ever flown *that* high before.

In colloquial usage *that* is also used to modify other adjectives and adverbs:

> Why should a grade-school auditorium be *that elaborate?* [Formal: *so elaborate.*]
> We had not realized the spider was *that dangerous.* [Formal: *so dangerous* or *as dangerous as that.*]

In the speech of some localities *that* is used instead of *so . . . that*:

LOCAL: We were that crowded we could barely move.
GENERAL: We were so crowded [that] we could barely move.

(For pronoun use, see **this, that,** section 1.)

that, which   *That* is usually preferred as a relative pronoun in restrictive clauses, and *which* in nonrestrictive:

> Ronald couldn't think of an excuse *that sounded plausible.*
> Frank Bergen's excuse, *which sounded quite plausible to me,* didn't fool Mr. Farley.

that is   A connective used to introduce examples or explanations. When it introduces a clause, it is usually preceded by a semicolon (sometimes a dash) and followed by a comma:

> The Book Fair was really Dave Brodda's brain child; that is, it was Dave who thought up the idea and sold it to the faculty.

554

When it introduces words or phrases, commas are usual:

> In the last round, the contestants had to speak extempore, that is, without preparation.

In informal writing the *that is* would often be omitted before a short construction:

> Mr. Rosen had one important quality his predecessor lacked, [that is,] a sense of humor.

the 1 When spoken without stress, *the* is pronounced THə before consonants and THĬ before vowels. When stressed, as in "He was *the* Beau Brummell of his day," it is pronounced THĒ.

2 Repeating *the* before the various nouns in a series emphasizes their distinctness:

> The former tenants had painted the floors, the stairs, and the doors a brilliant pink. [Compare: had painted the floors, stairs, and doors....]

3 *The* should always be used before the name of our country: *the* United States.

4 *The* is used as an adverb in expressions like "the bigger the better." In formal writing, a comma is used in such expressions: "According to him, the bigger the lie, the greater its effectiveness." In informal writing, the comma is generally omitted. (See also **Articles.**)

theater, theatre *Theater* is now the more common American spelling except in proper names of long standing: the Group Theatre of New York, the Abbey Theatre, *Theatre Arts Anthology.*

The standard pronunciation is thē′ə tər; the nonstandard, thē ā′tər.

their, theirs Both are possessive forms of *they. Their* is used before nouns; *theirs* (no apostrophe) is used alone:

> It was not *their* car; Al had parked *theirs* in the alley.

The form *theirn* (for *theirs*) is nonstandard English.

theirself, theirselves Nonstandard for *themselves.*

them Used only in nonstandard English as a demonstrative adjective and a demonstrative pronoun:

NONSTANDARD: *Them* men had no right to interfere.
STANDARD: *Those* men had no right to interfere.

NONSTANDARD: *Them* on the table were his.
STANDARD: *Those* on the table were his.

themselves See **Reflexive pronouns** and **Intensive pronouns.**

then   When used as a conjunctive adverb, joining the two clauses of a compound sentence, *then* should be preceded by a semicolon:

> Jean waited for the signal; then she plunged into the pool.
> Dr. Rauen thought for a minute; then he nodded his approval.

If *and then* is used, a comma separates the clauses:

> He warned me not to answer, and then he himself blurted out the two names.

there is, there are   1 When the subject following the introductory word *there* is singular, a singular verb is used; when the subject is plural, a plural verb is generally used:

> There *is* always a long line of fans backstage.
> There *were* no new reports from the flood area.

(See also Chapter 9, "Verb Before Subject," page 202.)

2 Though the occasional use of sentences beginning with *there is* adds variety, an overuse tends to make writing unemphatic:

UNEMPHATIC: There was a dilapidated laundry truck parked on the side street.
DIRECT: A dilapidated laundry truck was parked on the side street.

UNEMPHATIC: There were many articles in the magazine that were inaccurate and poorly written.
DIRECT: Many articles in the magazine were inaccurate and poorly written.

therefore   See **Conjunctive adverbs.**

they   In speech often used as an indefinite pronoun (one without a specific antecedent), but this use is not considered appropriate in writing:

COLLOQUIAL: They buy and sell scrap iron at the Hobart Company.
WRITTEN: The Hobart Company buys and sells scrap iron.

COLLOQUIAL: They have discontinued foreign aid to these countries.
WRITTEN: Foreign aid to these countries has been discontinued.
WRITTEN: The government has discontinued foreign aid to these countries.

thing   Often deadwood that should be pruned away in revision:

WORDY: Our missing the train turned out to be a fortunate thing.
IMPROVED: Our missing the train turned out to be fortunate.

WORDY: The first thing he must have is a passport.
IMPROVED: First he must have a passport.

this, that   1 The pronouns *this* and *that* are often used to refer to the whole idea of a preceding group of words:

Charlie had two flat tires on his way to work, and *that* made him grumpy the rest of the day.

But this use should be avoided if there is any danger that the reader may think the pronoun refers to a particular noun in the group:

AMBIGUOUS: Ellen's next assignment was to type a twenty-page scientific monograph. *This,* she found, was quite boring. [The monograph? Or typing it?]

CLEAR: Ellen's next assignment was to type a twenty-page scientific monograph—a job she found quite boring.

2 In everyday speech *this* is sometimes used as an emphatic definite article (instead of the usual *the*):

Then she saw *this* guard at the entrance run after *this* man and search him.

This use is out of place in writing except in quoting conversation.

this here, that there Used only in nonstandard English for *this* and *that*:

NONSTANDARD: Why is this here painting better than that there one?
STANDARD: Why is this painting better than that one [there]?

till, until Both have the same meaning; choose whichever best fits the rhythm of the sentence. *Until* is more usual at the beginning of sentences:

557

Until he gave the all-clear signal, nobody dared move.
Nobody dared move *till* (or *until*) he gave the all-clear signal.

Titles of books, articles, etc. **1 Formal usage.** (a) In most books, in some magazines, and in most school writing, the titles of books, pamphlets, movies, radio and television programs, plays and poems published as separate volumes, and the names of newspapers and magazines are put in italics—underlined in writing:

Book: *The Miracle of Language*   Newspaper: the Toledo *Blade*
Pamphlet: *Politics and Ethics*   Magazine: *Harper's*
Movie: *Ben Hur*   Long play: *Margin for Error*
TV program: *Meet the Press*   Long poem: *Odyssey*

b) The titles of artistic works (paintings, statues, concertos, operas, ballets, musical comedies) are also put in italics:

Painting: Rousseau's *The Waterfall*   Opera: *The Magic Flute*
Statue: Brancusi's *Bird in Space*   Ballet: *Union Pacific*

c) Titles of short stories, articles, essays, short poems, and songs are enclosed in quotation marks:

Story: "A Lucky Burglar"   Poem: "Young Grimes"
Article: "The Fearless Frogman"   Song: "Summertime"

2 Informal usage. In some magazines and newspapers the titles of books, movies, magazines, etc., are treated as proper names—capitalized but not italicized or enclosed in quotation marks. In other periodicals the titles are capitalized and put in quotation marks. For your school writing, follow the formal style of italicizing such titles.

together with   A phrase beginning with *together with* (or *along with, as well as, with*) is sometimes added to a singular subject. When the phrase is used in a clearly parenthetical way, it does not affect the number of the verb:

> A color wheel, together with suggestions for its use, *comes* with the kit. [Not: *come.*]

When the phrase is not intended as a parenthetical addition, usage varies. In informal English, a plural verb is often used, since the singular subject and the phrase are felt to be the same as a compound subject:

> His first draft together with his notes for a new chapter *were destroyed* in the fire.

Formal English sticks to the singular verb or changes the *together with* to *and* and then uses a plural verb:

> His first draft *and* his notes for a new chapter *were destroyed* in the fire.

too   See *very, too.*

Topic outline   See **Outline form,** section 3.

Topic sentence   See Chapter 2, "Topic Sentences," page 42.

Transitions   For a discussion of transitions, see Chapter 2, "Continuity Through Sentence Links," page 51, and Chapter 1, "The Body of the Paper," page 16.

Transitive and intransitive verbs   A verb is called *transitive* when it is used with an object to complete its meaning:

> Hal *swallowed* his gum.   The magician *sawed* the lady in half.

A verb is called *intransitive* when it does not need an object to complete its meaning or when the receiver of the action is not named:

> We *lay* on the beach all day.   He *has been practicing* for a week.

Linking verbs (those that merely link a predicate adjective or noun to the subject) are regarded as intransitive:

> Soon after, Sarah *became* less finicky.
> The violets *were* so large that they *looked* artificial.

Many verbs are used either transitively or intransitively, usually with different meanings:

TRANSITIVE: Gus *fished* an olive out of the jar.
INTRANSITIVE: Gus usually *fished* in Beagle Lake.

Trite expressions   Usually figures of speech that through constant overuse have lost their original effectiveness: *slick as a whistle, the spice of life, by the sweat of his brow.* The overuse of such expressions marks writing as amateurish. (See Chapter 12, "Avoid Trite Words," page 276.)

try and, try to   Although the formal idiom is *try to,* informal English has long used *try and:*

FORMAL: We are going to try to get Mr. Dale's permission.
INFORMAL: We are going to try and get Mr. Dale's permission.

Underlining   Underlining in longhand and typewritten copy corresponds to the use of italic type in printed matter.

    1 Titles of books and magazines are underlined:

       Who but Dr. Seuss would write books entitled Green Eggs and
          Ham and How the Grinch Stole Christmas?
       His aunts never miss an issue of Coming Events in Britain.

(For more details about this use, see **Titles of books, articles, etc.**)

    2 Any word that a writer wishes to emphasize may be underlined (italicized in print), but this kind of emphasis loses its force if used too frequently:

       Mark Harris was the man to see if one wanted a political favor.
       He always had an opinion, but never an unbiased one.

    3 Letters, figures, and words used not for their meaning but as words are generally underlined, especially in books and articles on language:

       The sign painter forgot to put the u in restaurant.
       The bank teller had written 6 instead of 16.

    4 Foreign words are underlined:

       Evidently the Fräulein of Cologne had impressed him more than
          the jeunes filles of Paris.

Understatement   A figure of speech in which words less strong than expected are used in order to impress the reader or hearer:

       O. Henry did have something of a knack for surprise endings.

(See also **Litotes.**)

unique   In strict formal usage *unique* means "the only one of its kind" and therefore cannot be compared. In informal usage it has become generalized to mean "rare or unusual," and is compared with *more* or *most* or modified by *very* or *rather*:

> Harold won the prize for the most unique costume.
> I had to admit that his plan was rather unique.

(See also **Comparison of adjectives and adverbs,** section 2.)

United States   As the name of a country *United States* is singular and is preceded by the article *the*:

> The United States belongs to an international atomic pool.

For lack of a better word, *United States* is also used as an adjective, as in *the United States policy,* although *the policy of the United States* is preferred as less awkward. (See also **American.**)

Unity   Writing is said to have unity when it gives a oneness of effect. Unity results from (1) selecting material that is pertinent to the subject and (2) presenting it so that it produces a single effect or impression. (For a discussion of paragraph unity, see Chapter 2, "Unity in Paragraphs," page 41.)

until   See **till, until.**

560

up   Colloquial English often uses *up* after certain verbs though it adds no new element of meaning:

> We quickly finished [up] the work and then went swimming.
> They planned to meet later and divide [up] the loot.

In formal writing this use of *up* would be avoided.

Usage   Usage—the ways in which words are actually used—determines whether the words are appropriate or inappropriate English. The three main kinds of English usage (formal, informal, and nonstandard) are described in Chapter 8, "The Levels of Usage." Most of the entries in the Index also discuss usage.

used to   Though the *d* is not pronounced, it should not be omitted in writing:

> He *used to* be quite an athlete in his day.   [Not: He *use to*.]

But the negative and interrogative forms are usually made with *did* and *use* (without the *d*):

> I *did not use* (or *didn't use*) to like murder mysteries.   [More formal: I *used not* to like.]
> *Did* you *use* to have spelling bees in the fourth grade?

Used to could is a nonstandard idiom:

NONSTANDARD: Tom can't ski as well as he used to could.
STANDARD: Tom can't ski as well as he once could. [Or: as well as he used to be able to.]

Variant   A different form or spelling of a word. Spellings such as *catalogue* —*catalog, gaily—gayly;* pronunciations such as jü′və nəl—jü′və nĭl, dī′- mənd—dī′ə mənd; and constructions such as *the roof of which—whose roof, strictest—most strict, were sewed—were sewn* are variants.

Though most variant forms are equally good, there may be slight differences in the shade of meaning expressed or in the degree of formality that makes one or another more appropriate. The form *appendices,* for example, is preferred in formal English, *appendixes* in informal.

Variety   Variety, which is necessary for interesting writing, can be gained by varying sentence length, sentence order, and sentence types. (See Chapter 11, "Varying the Sentence Order," page 257.)

Verb   A word or group of words used to "assert" or express action or being:

ACTION: Just as he *was tiptoeing* past Danny's room, Tom *sneezed.*
BEING: The plant *is* a rare hybrid.

561

For a discussion and examples, see Chapter 7, "Words That Assert," page 144; Chapter 9, "Verbs," page 192; ***Tenses of verbs;*** and ***Principal parts of verbs.***

Verb-adverb combinations   In the sentence "Hearing a noise in the basement, I ran down to investigate," *down* is an adverb. It has the usual adverb use—it modifies the verb *ran.* But in "During the night the clock ran down," *down* (although technically an adverb) is actually a part of the verb. *Run* means "move swiftly," but *run down* means "stop operating"; it has nothing to do with "moving swiftly."

English has many such verb-adverb combinations, two-part verbs that have a meaning different from the literal meaning of their parts:

VERB AND MODIFIER	TWO-PART VERB
He ran across to the bus.	I *ran across* an old friend there.
Break a piece off for me.	He and she *broke off* last week.
They called up to us.	I *called up* George.

Sometimes the two-part verb is separated, as in "I *called* him *up* twice." But the verb in this example is still *called up* ("telephoned") rather than *called* (modified by *up*), as in "They called up to us."

The examples cited and hundreds of other verb-adverb combinations are in common use, especially in informal and colloquial English. Formal English is likely to prefer instead single words: *investigate* for *look into, yield* for *give in, discuss* for *talk over,* etc. Informal English prefers the emphatic rhythm of the verb-adverb combinations.

Verb phrases   Verbs that consist of more than one word:

am leaving	should have known	is being built
had learned	have been studying	must have been seen

Verb phrases are also called *phrasal verbs.*

verbal   See **oral, verbal.**

Verbals   Verb forms that are used as nouns (*Wishing* isn't *doing*), adjectives (the *squirming* children), or adverbs (They are here *to interview* him). For further information, see **Gerund, Participle,** and **Infinitive.**

very, too   1 *Very* and *too* are adverbs of degree used to modify adjectives (*very old, too young*) or adverbs (*very often, too seldom*). In formal English *very* and *too* are not used to modify a past participle directly unless the participle is clearly being used as an adjective rather than as part of a verb phrase (as in "He was a *very distinguished* writer" and "The answers were *too varied* to classify easily"). Otherwise, formal English uses *very much* or *too much* before participles:

> Paul was *very much* discouraged by this second failure.
> She was *too much* engrossed in the book to hear us.

Informal English usually makes no such distinctions, and uses *very* and *too* to modify all participles:

> Paul was *very discouraged* by this second failure.
> She was *too engrossed* in the book to hear us.

2 *Very* has been so commonly overused that it really has little value as an intensive. Avoid using it unless you are sure that it really adds meaning to your statement:

WEAK: Knowing that the course was very difficult, Sam and I worked very hard. Though we enjoyed the classes, we were very glad when the semester ended.

IMPROVED: Knowing that the course was difficult, Sam and I worked hard. Though we enjoyed the classes, we were glad when the semester ended.

viewpoint   *Viewpoint* is an economical substitute for *point of view* (though some purists object to its use as unidiomatic). In sentences in which *point of view* would be followed by another *of* (I agreed with the point of view of the editor), *viewpoint* would perhaps be less clumsy (with the editor's viewpoint, with the viewpoint of the editor).

viz. Abbreviation of the Latin *videlicet* (vi del'ə sit), meaning "that is to say" or "namely." *Viz.* is used only in rather formal documents or reference works. It is usually read "namely."

Voice A form of the verb that shows whether the subject is the doer of the action named by the verb (active voice: The sheriff *warned* the boys) or is the receiver of the action (passive voice: The boys *were warned* again). For a discussion of the use of active and passive verbs, see Chapter 11, "Emphasis Through Forceful Verbs," page 259.

wages See **salary, wages.**

wait on, wait for *Wait on* used in the sense of "wait for" is dialectal:

DIALECT: I waited on him in the station at least an hour.
STANDARD: I waited for him in the station at least an hour.
STANDARD: The clerk who waited on me knew nothing about the stock.

want The standard idiom with *want* has an infinitive phrase (not preceded by *for*):

STANDARD: He wanted me to sign the petition.
LOCAL: He wanted for me to sign the petition.
NONSTANDARD: He wanted I should sign the petition.

563

Want is colloquial for *should, ought,* or *had better*:

You want to make sure of the facts before you accuse anyone.
You want to be there early if you expect to get a good seat.

Want meaning "lack" or "need" is formal, and chiefly British usage:

The shed wants paint and a new roof.

want in, off, out, up, etc. Localisms (common in the Middle West and the South) for *want to come in, want to get off, want to go out,* etc.

LOCAL: Ask him if he wants in.
GENERAL: Ask him if he wants to come in.

LOCAL: I wanted off at the next stop.
GENERAL: I wanted to get off at the next stop.

way, ways Colloquially, *ways* is often used instead of *way* in a sense of "distance":

COLLOQUIAL: The drugstore was only a little ways up the street.
WRITTEN: The drugstore was only a little way up the street. [More formal: a short distance.]

Way is informal in the sense of "condition" or "state":

> I would say that his business was in a fair way.

we 1 *We* is sometimes used as an indefinite pronoun referring to people in general:

> We must not think that the world owes us a living.
> We seldom appreciate good health until we no longer have it.

2 In editorials and other featured columns of newspapers and magazines the writer often refers to himself as *we*, thus suggesting that he speaks also for his newspaper or editorial staff (though he may be speaking for himself alone).

This editorial *we* is sometimes used in familiar and informal writing, especially of a light tone. But used only to avoid using *I*, *we* is conspicuous and is better avoided.

we boys, us boys, etc. Whether to use the nominative form *we* or the objective form *us* in such expressions depends on the function of the pronoun in the sentence:

> *We* boys objected to the plan. [Subject of the verb.]
> But it was *we* boys who did the work. [Predicate complement.]
> Why did he choose *us* two? [Direct object.]
> Give *us* girls the credit we deserve. [Indirect object.]
> Leave it to *us* men. [Object of preposition.]

564

well See **good, well.**

whatever, wherever, whyever See **ever.**

when, where, in definitions See **Defining words,** last paragraph.

where Although in informal speech *where* is sometimes used in place of *that,* it is not appropriate in writing:

> I read in the sports page yesterday that the Sox have hired a new manager. [Not: I read . . . *where* the Sox have hired.]

where . . . at, where . . . to Though used in certain dialects, the *at* and *to* are generally omitted in standard English:

> Where are they? [Not: Where are they *at*?]
> No one knew where he had gone. [Not: where he had gone *to*.]

whether See **if, whether.**

which 1 As a relative pronoun, *which* is used for things and for collective nouns referring to people (*team, regiment, board, crew, committee*) when the group, not the individuals, is meant:

Professor Arnett's analogy, which seems valid on first reading, has several weaknesses.

The St. Olaf team, which debated here last week, won the trophy.

When the individual members of the group are meant, *who* is used:

The affirmative team, who were the most experienced debaters, must have been overconfident.

(See also **that, which.**)

Which is used to refer to the whole idea expressed in a preceding group of words:

The deadline was getting uncomfortably close, which made Foley even more snappish than usual.

But this use should be avoided if there is any danger that the reference of *which* will not be clear; that is, if *which* may seem to refer to a particular noun in the group instead of to the group as a whole.

NOT CLEAR: Mr. Carter insisted on taking full responsibility for the decision, which proved to be a costly mistake.

CLEAR: Mr. Carter's insistence on taking full responsibility for the decision proved to be a costly mistake.

(See also Chapter 10, "Vague Reference," page 228.)

Whose is often used as the possessive of *which,* instead of the more awkward *of which*:

The only other newspaper in town was the *Blade, whose* owners violently opposed his candidacy.

2 *Which*-clauses are subordinate clauses and should not be carelessly joined to a main statement by *and* or *but*:

CARELESS: It is an exciting and informative novel, and which fully deserves its place among the best sellers.

BETTER: It is an exciting and informative novel, which fully deserves its place among the best sellers.

CARELESS: The racer's bicycle was made of Duralumin, a lightweight alloy of aluminum, but which is very strong and hard.

BETTER: The racer's bicycle was made of Duralumin, a lightweight alloy of aluminum which is very strong and hard.

while 1 *While* is used mainly as a subordinating conjunction introducing adverbial clauses of time:

While the guard was answering the phone, Ness darted past the open door.

2 *While* is also used, rather weakly, in the sense of "though" or "but":

While we criticized everything he wrote, we envied his talent.
Guitars have six strings, while banjos usually have only four.

3 *While* is used colloquially and in journalese for *and*, a construction avoided in careful writing:

> The first was a triangle, the second was a rhombus, *while* the third was a rhomboid. [Better: *and* the third was a rhomboid.]

who, whom, whose **1** The pronoun *who*—used both as a relative and as an interrogative—refers to people and sometimes to animals:

> The starlet who played the lead has much to learn about acting.
> Blackie, who mistrusts all deliverymen, began to growl.

2 When the relative or interrogative pronoun is the subject of the verb, the nominative form *who* is used, even when the subject is separated from its verb by other words:

> We were to vote for the three students *who* we thought had done the most for the school. [Subject of *had done*.]
> Then *who* would you say was really at fault? [Subject of *was*.]

When the interrogative pronoun used as the object of a verb or preposition comes at the beginning of a sentence or clause, informal English generally uses *who*, while formal English uses the objective form *whom*:

FORMAL: *Whom* can we trust?
INFORMAL: *Who* can we trust?

FORMAL: For *whom* should we vote?
INFORMAL: *Who* should we vote for? [Or: For *whom* should we vote?]

FORMAL: Mr. Hines refused to tell them *whom* he suspected.
INFORMAL: Mr. Hines refused to tell them *who* he suspected.

When the relative pronoun is the object of a verb or preposition, formal English uses the objective form *whom*. In informal English the pronoun object is often omitted or *that* is used:

FORMAL: Most of the workers *whom* he supervised admired him.
INFORMAL: Most of the workers [that] he supervised admired him.

FORMAL: The writer with *whom* she collaborated used a pseudonym.
INFORMAL: The writer [that] she collaborated with used a pseudonym.

The form you should use in a particular context depends, of course, on the situation. On formal occasions—during an interview, in giving an address or report before a group, in a research paper or other serious expository writing—you should use the forms preferred in formal English. In informal situations—in conversations with friends, in personal letters, in informal narratives—the forms used in informal English are appropriate.

(For further discussion, see Chapter 9, "*Who* and *whom*," page 207.)

The possessive form *whose* shows ownership:

> Whose is the coat hung over mine?
> Anyone whose handwriting is so illegible should type his letters.

(For *whose* as the possessive of *which,* see **which,** section 1.)

3 When *who* is the subject of a relative clause, its verb agrees in number with its antecedent:

> He was the only one of these men who *was taken* in by Foley's promises. [Antecedent is *one.*]
> Jamison is one of those people who never *read* the fine print. [Antecedent is *people.*]

will   See **shall, will.**

woman, lady   See **man, woman.**

wonderful   Used exactly, *wonderful* means "causing wonder; marvelous; remarkable": the northern lights, a truly *wonderful* sight. *Wonderful* is also used informally as a counter word of approval: *wonderful* steak. (See **Counter words.**)

woods   Although plural in form, *woods* takes a singular verb when preceded by *a,* and usually when a particular woods is named:

> A woods *is* a source of fascination for Andrew.
> Beecham Woods *was* much smaller than I remembered.

567

When preceded by *the, woods* usually takes a plural verb:

> The woods *were* then a part of the Wilson estate.

Word order   For a discussion of ways to gain variety and emphasis through word order, see Chapter 11, "Emphasis Through Word Order," page 257.
   For a discussion of the importance of word order to meaning, see Chapter 10, "Improving Awkward Sentences," pages 220-224.

Wordiness   The use of more words than are needed to express ideas clearly and accurately results in weak, often vague, writing. The commonest types of wordiness are:
   1 Circumlocution—a roundabout way of speaking: (a) Saying in an indirect way what might be put directly:

WORDY: Mrs. Macomber insisted on consulting several members of the medical profession.
BETTER: Mrs. Macomber insisted on consulting several doctors.

b) Using several words instead of one exact word:

WORDY: He had to be inoculated with a cowpox vaccine.
BETTER: He had to be vaccinated.

c) Using many words instead of a few:

WORDY: It was often the case that his decisions proved to be wrong.
BETTER: Often his decisions proved [to be] wrong.

    2 Deadwood—words that add nothing to the meaning:

Paul, his older brother, was aggressive [by nature].
These statistics, though [of an] interesting [character], are hardly
reliable.

(See Chapter 11, "Avoiding Wordiness," page 254.)

world   Deadwood in such expressions as "in the industrial world," "in the
world of politics." "In industry" or "in politics" is enough.

worth while   Written as two words when it is a predicate complement and
hyphened or written as one word when it precedes the noun:

Listening to John Ciardi discuss poetry is always worth while.
Why don't they present worth-while (*or* worthwhile) plays?

would of   A misspelling of *would've* (*would have*).

would rather   See **had rather, would rather.**

Xmas   The preferred pronunciation is kris′məs, not eks′məs. This form is
sometimes used in advertising and in headlines. In other writing,
Christmas is generally spelled out because the shortened form is objectionable to so many people.

X-ray, X ray   Usually written with a capital *x*. When used as a verb or an
adjective it is hyphened; when used as a noun it is not: to *X-ray* the
fracture, an *X-ray* treatment, a stomach *X ray*.

Y

ye, the   The *ye* in such names as *Ye Olde Curiosity Shoppe* is simply the
archaic form of *the*. It is correctly pronounced THē, not yē. (In Old
English the sound of *th* was represented by a single symbol, the letter
thorn: *þ*. Early printers who did not have this symbol substituted the
letter *y*, which somewhat resembled the letter thorn.)

yes, no   These adverbs may modify sentences (*Yes*, he's the man) or may
stand by themselves as complete sentences ("Didn't Harvey feed the

dog?" "*No*."). Remember that when *yes* or *no* modifies a sentence it is always set off by a comma.

yet *Yet* is used chiefly as an adverb:

He has not decided yet.   They had a yet more difficult job.

It is also used as a coördinating conjunction, equivalent to *but*. Then it is preceded by a comma:

She saw the accident, yet she refused to testify.

you In informal speech and writing *you* is commonly used as an indefinite pronoun, referring to people in general:

You can spend quite a bit on groceries these days.
First you must remove the old varnish.

In formal English *one* is preferred, or else a different construction:

One can spend quite a bit on groceries these days.
First the old varnish must be removed.

The indefinite *you* should be avoided whenever it might be misunderstood as personal rather than impersonal—especially if the misunderstanding would turn a generalization into an insult, as in the sentence "You ought to watch your weight."

you all In Southern American speech *you all* (often contracted to *y'all*) is widely used as the plural of *you*:

Seab smiled sleepily and made no answer, but instead bowed elaborately to the ladies. "I hope you all weren't disappointed," he said.—Allen Drury, *Advise and Consent*.

Educated Southerners avoid its use as a singular.

your, you're Do not confuse the possessive form *your* (your mistake) with the contraction *you're* (you are). Remember that an apostrophe is never used in forming the possessives of the personal pronouns.

yourself, yourselves The reflexive forms of *you*. (See **Reflexive pronouns** and **myself**.)

Z

zh The phonetic symbol representing the sound in *vision* (vizh'ən), *abrasion* (ə brā'zhən), *seizure* (sē'zhər), and so on.

zoology Pronounced zō ol'ə ji, not zü ol'ə ji. People who mispronounce it may be confused by the word *zoo* (a clipped form of *zoological gardens*).

General Subject Index

[Grammar and usage items on particular words that are given in the reference section of the book, the "Index" (for example, entries on *ain't, between you and me, get, mutual* and *common*), are not listed in this general subject index. Since such items are given in alphabetical order in the reference Index, you can readily find them by turning directly to that section.]

Abbreviations, 358-359

Absolute phrases, 153, 360; for combining ideas, 245; punctuation of, 360, 416

Abstract words, 360-361

Academic degrees, 358, 435

Accent marks, 361

Accents, 361

Achievement tests, 311

Active verbs, 362, 551; effective use of, 259-260; shift from active to passive, 227

Addresses, 362, 398-399, 400-401, 418

Adjective clauses, 156-157, 364, 532; for combining ideas, 245, 246-247; punctuation of, 416, 533-534

570 Adjective phrases, 152, 364, 519

Adjectives, 145, 362-364; after linking verbs, 212-213, 363, 485; as "counter" words, 363, 429; as objective complements, 149, 500; as predicate complements, 149, 213, 363, 388, 485, 516; comparison of, 214-215, 421-422; demonstrative, 435; descriptive, 363; effective use of, 363-364, 429; in series, 415; indefinite, 200; limiting, 363; position of, 258, 363; possessive, 514; pronominal, 521; proper, 363, 405, 523; verbals as, 153, 154

Adverb clauses, 157-158, 366; for combining ideas, 247-248; punctuation of, 415, 416, 533-534

Adverb phrases, 152, 366-367, 519

Adverbial nouns, 367

Adverbs, 145, 212, 365-366, 501-502; and adjectives, 212; comparison of, 214-215, 421-422; conjunctive, 145, 365, 424-425; forms of, 365-366; position of, 501-502; relative, 156-157, 532; types of, 365; uses of, 365

ae, oe, 367

Agreement: of appositive and headword, 206, 383; of demonstrative adjective and noun, 369, 480; of pronoun and antecedent, 210-211, 368, 379; of subject and verb, 198-202, 368; of subject and verb in adjective clauses, 202, 501

Alliteration, 371

Allusions, 278

Alphabetizing, 371-372

Ambiguous reference of pronouns, 229-230, 373

American and British usage, 374-376

"American English Dialects" (picture story), 180-189

Ampersand, 376

Analogy, 376

And: effectively and ineffectively used, 250-252; for emphasis, 377; overuse of, 251-252, 377; use of *and which, and who,* 378

Anglicizing, 378-379

Antecedents, 156-157, 379; faulty reference, 228-230

Anticipatory subjects, *see* Expletives

Anticlimax, 380

Antonyms, 380; in tests, 314-316

Any and its compounds, 200, 210-211, 380-381

Aphorisms, 449

Apostrophe (figure of speech), 382

Apostrophes: in contractions, 381, 426; to form plurals, 382, 513; to show possession, 381, 514-515

Appendix, 141, 382

Application forms: filling out, 293-295; writing sample in, 295-298

Application, letters of, 287-289, 289-290

Appositives, 149-150, 382-383; for

574

575

Nominative case, 408, 496; forms of pronouns, 205-208

Nonce words, 496

None, no one, number of, 200, 496

Nonrestrictive modifiers, 496; commas with, 416, 533-534; dashes with, 431; parentheses with, 506-507; *exercises on,* 345-350

Nonstandard English, 164-166, 170, 497

Note cards: preparing, 130-132; sorting, 133-134

Notes, taking, 109-110, 128-132

Noun clauses, 157, 497

Nouns: adverbial, 367; capitalization of, 404-406; collective, 200, 411; common, 420, 497; defined, 143, 497; of direct address, 438; plurals of, 512-514; possessives, 514-515; proper, 497, 523; with gerunds, 209-210

Number, 497; *see also* Agreement

Numbers, 498; comma with, 418; hyphen with, 469; plurals of, 513

Object of verb, *see* Direct objects, Indirect objects

Objective and subjective writing, 499

Objective case, 408, 499-500; pronoun forms, 205-208, 500

Objective complements, 149, 500

Objects: direct, 148, 438; indirect, 148-149, 475; of prepositions, 145, 499; pronouns as, 205-208

Obsolete, as dictionary label, 500

Omission in quotations, ellipsis to show, 447

Omitted words: comma to show, 418; ellipsis to show, 447

Onomatopoeia, 472-473

Opinion: evaluating, 72-73; statements of, 72

-or, -our, 502

Order of details in writing: chronological order, 8, 26, 50; logical order, 9-12, 50-51; spatial order, 29, 50

Organizing materials for writing, 8-12, 133-136

Originality, 503

Other and *else,* in comparisons, 231, 503

Outlines, 504-505; paragraph, 504; sentence, 135-136, 505; topic, 11-12, 134-135, 504-505; work, 504

Paradox, 449

Paragraph outlines, 504

Paragraphs: adequate development of, 33-38; beginning, 15-16; continuity in, 49-53; final, 17-18; for dialogue, 527; importance of planning, 31-33; linking together, 17; methods of developing expository paragraphs, 34-38; number needed in paper, 16, 32; scrambled, in standardized tests, 329-332; super-, 44-45; topic sentences in, 42-45; unity in, 41-45; writing expository paragraphs, 31-53

Parallel constructions, 225-227, 506; with correlatives, 226, 429

Paraphrasing, 101-105; poetry, 103-104; prose, 102-103

Parentheses, 506-507; *exercise on,* 349-350

Parenthetical expressions, commas to set off, 414; *exercise on,* 343-344; *see also* Dashes, Parentheses

Participial phrases, 153, 508; dangling, 222-223; for combining ideas, 244-245, 246; introductory, 416; misplaced, 221; restrictive and nonrestrictive, 416, 533-534

Participles, 153, 508-509; tenses, 196

Parts of speech, 143-146

Passive voice: defined, 259, 362; effective use, 259-260; forms, 551

Past perfect tense, 192, 509, 551, 552

Past tense, 192, 550-551

Perfect tenses, 192, 509, 551, 552

Periodic sentences, 510

Periods, 509-510; *exercise on,* 340

Person, 510; avoiding shifts in, 227

Personal pronouns: defined, 511; forms indicating person, 510; list of, 144; nominative and objective forms of, 205-208, 496, 499-500; possessive forms of, 144; with gerunds, 209-210

577

579

456789 10 11 12 13 14 15 16 17 18 19 20 21 22 23 24 25 V 70 69 68 67 66